KU-128-217

Contents

Preface

This volume had its origins in a seminar held in Cambridge in March 2007. The papers of the speakers at that conference have been swelled by invitations to other colleagues to provide a geographical and regional balance. The editing was undertaken by Simon Stoddart, Skylar Neil and Gabriele Cifani.

Contributors

(in alphabetical order)

JOHN BINTLIFF studied Archaeology and Anthropology at Cambridge, where he also completed his PhD on landscape and settlement in prehistoric Greece. After teaching at Bradford University and then Durham, he moved to Leiden University in 1999 to the Chair in Classical and Mediterranean Archaeology. His research interests include Greek and Mediterranean Archaeology from prehistory to post-medieval times, landscape archaeology, regional survey methodologies, and archaeological theory. His published work to 2007 can be accessed in PDF form by personal request to j.l.bintliff@arch.leidenuniv.nl.

GERT-JAN BURGERS received a degree in Ancient History and in Archaeology in 1989, moving on to a doctoral thesis on settlement dynamics, social organization and culture contact in the margins of Graeco-Roman Italy. In 1998, he published a monograph on this subject, for which he received a PhD degree in Mediterranean Archaeology at the Amsterdam Vrije Universiteit. Since 1994 he has been a lecturer in Mediterranean Archaeology at the same university. In 2006 he was appointed Director of Ancient Studies at the Royal Netherlands Institute in Rome. His research focuses on long term settlement and landscape history, in particular that of Italy. Major issues of interest include first millennium BC urbanization processes and related town-countryside relations, Greek colonization and Romanization. To investigate these he has been directing a series of excavations and field surveys in the Salento peninsula.

ANDREA CARANDINI is professor of Classical Archaeology at the University of Rome "La Sapienza". His recent research focuses mainly on the landscape archaeology of Rome and Italy. He has carried out fieldwork in Italy (Ostia, Settefinestre, Volterra, Rome, Veii), Tunisia (Carthago) and Algeria (Castellum Nador). Since 1985, he has been the director of the excavation project of the northern slopes of the Palatine in Rome. His recent books include: *La nascita di Roma: dei, lari, eroi e uomini all'alba di una civiltà* (Torino, 1997); *Archeologia del mito: emozione e ragione fra primitivi e moderni* (Torino, 2002); *Remo e Romolo: dai rioni dei quiriti alla città dei romani (775/750–700/675 a.C. circa)* (Torino, 2006); *Archeologia classica* (Torino, 2008).

GABRIELE CIFANI is a researcher of Classical Archaeology at the University of Rome "Tor Vergata"; he was previously Marie Curie Research Fellow of the Department of Archaeology at Cambridge University (2005–2007), Alexander von Humboldt fellow at Freie Universität Berlin (2005), fellow of the Italian Academy at Columbia University (2004), and research fellow of the Scuola Normale Superiore di Pisa (2001). He carried out survey and excavations in Italy and Libya; his main interests are the landscapes of pre-Roman Italy and Tripolitania, and early Roman architecture. His publications include: *Storia di una frontiera* (Roma 2003); *L'architettura Romana arcaica* (Roma, 2008).

LETIZIA CECCARELLI is currently studying for her doctorate at the University of Cambridge, researching Archaic and Republican temples in *Latium vetus*. She graduated from the University of Florence and studied for a Masters at the University of Southampton. Since 2003, she has been regularly collaborating with the Soprintendenza per I beni Archeologici del Lazio studying the architectural decorations and structures excavated at the site of Ardea (Rome). She also supervises the processing and the study of material from international excavations such as the University of Texas, Austin at Ostia and for the British School at Rome at the excavations of Falacrinae (RI).

TIM CORNELL is Professor of Ancient History at the University of Manchester.
His publications include: *Atlas of the Roman World* (with J. F. Matthews; (Oxford, 1982); *The Beginnings of Rome: Italy and Rome from the Bronze Age to the Punic Wars, c. 1000–264 BC* (London, 1995).

FRANCESCA FULMINANTE specialized in Classical Archaeology at the University of Rome 'La Sapienza' and in 2008 obtained her PhD from the University of Cambridge with a thesis on the political landscape of Early Rome and *Latium vetus* (Cambridge, forthcoming). She published a monograph on 'princely tombs in *Latium vetus* between the end of the Early Iron Age and the beginning of the Orientalizing Age' ('L'Erma' di Bretschneider, 2003) and a number of articles on the early history of Rome and the surrounding region, with a wider interest in urbanization and state formation in the Mediterranean during the first millennium BC.

ALFREDO GONZÁLEZ-RUIBAL is a Staff Scientist with the Heritage Laboratory of the Spanish National Research Council (CSIC). He has been an Assistant Professor at the Department of Prehistory of the Complutense University of Madrid and a postdoctoral fellow with the Archaeology Center of Stanford University. His research interests include Iron Age Europe, ancient and modern colonialism, cultural contact and trade, ethnoarchaeology, and the archaeology of the contemporary past. He has done fieldwork in Spain, Italy, Brazil, Sudan, Ethiopia and Equatorial Guinea. His publications have appeared in several international journals.

IGNACIO GRAU MIRA is a Lecturer in the Department of Archaeology of the University of Alicante, Spain. His research is focused on the study of the Iberian Iron Age and Early Roman Empire in Eastern Spain. He is also interested in methodological and theoretical approaches to the study of landscape archaeology in the context of the ancient Mediterranean, especially GIS in archaeology. He is running fieldwork projects in Alicante (Spain) and Perugia (Italy).

PROF. DR HANS LOHMANN, born in Berlin (West) in 1947, studied Classical Archaeology, Archaeology of the Roman Provinces, Ancient History, and Prehistory at the Universities of Berlin, Basle and Würzburg. His promotion dates to 1975 (*Grabmäler auf unteritalischen Vasen;* Berlin, 1979). In 1976 and 1978 he was excavation director at Augst and Kaiseraugst (Switzerland), in 1977 he had the scholarship of the Deutsches Archäologisches Institut and in 1979/1980 was Head of Division at the Rheinisches Landesmuseum Bonn. From 1981, he was Assistant Lecturer at the Ruhr-University Bochum, achieving his habilitation in 1990 (*Atene – Studien zur Siedlungs und Wirtschaftsstruktur des Klasischen Attika*; Köln, 1993). Since 1997, he has been Associate Professor at the Institut für Archäologische Wissenschaften, Ruhr-University Bochum. His fieldwork (surveys and excavations) has been in Germany, Switzerland, Attica, Miletus and Mycale.

Dr Kathryn Lomas is an honorary Senior Research Associate at the Institute of Archaeology, University College London. She is the author of *Rome and the Western Greeks* (London, 1993) and *Roman Italy, 338 BC–AD 200* (London, 1996), and has published numerous articles on Roman Italy, urbanism and colonization in the Greek and Roman world, and on ethnic and cultural identities. Her current research, funded by the AHRC, is on the development of literacy in early Italy.

Manuel Molinos is a Professor of Archeology at the University of Jaén and deputy director of the Centro Andaluz de Arqueología Ibérica (Andalusian Centre of Iberian Archaeology). He is coauthor of *The Archeology of the Iberians* (Cambridge, 1999) and *Íberos en Jaén.* (Jaén, 2008). He has directed archaeological projects in the oppidum of Puente Tablas, the sanctuary El Pajarillo and the hypogeum of Hornos. He has also developed projects about Iberians and Romans in Jaén. His research focuses primarily on the Iron Age, the archaeology of territory, social processes and aristocracy, and the distribution of archaeological heritage in the territory.

Alessandro Naso, born in Rome in 1960, went on to take his doctorate at University of Rome 'La Sapienza'. After initial fieldwork in Italy and abroad (England, France, Sri Lanka and Turkey), he spent annual visits in Germany, first at the Römisch-Germanisches Zentralmuseum of Mainz and then at the University of Tübingen with a Humboldt Fellowship. He has successively been a researcher in archaeology at the Universities of Udine (1998–2003) and Molise (2003–2008), until his more recent appointment as Professor of Pre- and Proto- history at the Leopold-Franzens University of Innsbruck. From 1999, he has taken part in the Miletus excavation to study Etruscan imports. He has published *Architetture dipinte* (Rome, 1996), *I Piceni* (Milan, 2000), and *I bronzi etruschi e italici del Römisch-Germanisches Zentralmuseum* (Bonn, 2003) as well as many articles on pre-Roman Italy. His current research is on Etruscan and Italic imports found in the Aegean and the Levant.

Robin Osborne is Professor of Ancient History in the University of Cambridge and a Fellow of King's College. His recent works include *Greek History* (London, 2004); *Greek Historical Inscriptions 404–323 BC* (ed. with P. J. Rhodes; Oxford, 2003); *Mediterranean Urbanization 800–600 BC* (ed. with B. Cunliffe; Oxford 2005); *Rethinking Revolutions through Classical Greece* (ed. with S. D. Goldhill; Cambridge, 2006), *Art's Agency and Art History* (ed. with J. J. Tanner; Oxford, 2007); *Classical Archaeology* (ed. with S. Alcock; Oxford, 2007).

Ulla Rajala is a postdoctoral researcher affiliated with the University of Cambridge. She was recently granted an honorary docentship at the University of Oulu, Finland, after holding a three-year postdoctoral research post funded by the Academy of Finland. As part of her PhD (graduated in 2003) she supervised the *Nepi Survey Project* and later managed the *Romanisation of a Faliscan Town* project funded by the British Academy. She ran the *Remembering the Dead* excavation project between 2004 and 2008. She is currently working towards publishing the results of her field projects.

ARTURO RUIZ is a Professor of Prehistory at the University of Jaén and currently runs the Centro Andaluz de Arqueología Ibérica (Andalusian Centre of Iberian Archaeology). He is coauthor of *The Archeology of the Iberians* (Cambridge 1999), and *Íberos en Jaén*. (Jaén, 2008) and has conducted archaeological work on emblematic sites such as the sanctuary El Pajarillo, the hypogeum of Hornos, the battle of Baecula and the *oppidum* of Puente Tablas. His main research interests include: historiography, the Iron Age, the archaeology of territory, social processes and aristocracy, and the distribution of archaeological heritage in the territory.

CHRISTOPHER SMITH is Director of the British School at Rome. His publications include: *Early Rome and Latium: Economy and Society* c. *1000 to 500 BC* (Oxford, 1996); *The Roman Clan: The Gens from Ancient Ideology to Modern Anthropology* (Cambridge, 2006).

ANTHONY SNODGRASS is emeritus Professor of Classical Archaeology at the University of Cambridge. His publications include: *Archaic Greece*, (London, 1980); *Homer and the Artists: Text and Picture in Early Greek Art* (Cambridge, 1998); *Archaeology and the Emergence of Greece* (Ithaca (NY), 2006).

SIMON STODDART is a Senior Lecturer at the University of Cambridge and a Fellow of Magdalene College, Cambridge. He undertook postgraduate work at the British School at Rome (Rome Scholar) and the University of Michigan (MA Anthropology), before completing his PhD at Cambridge on Etruscan settlement organization in 1987. He has held posts in Cambridge (Junior Research Fellow, Magdalene College; University Lecturer and University Senior Lecturer), Oxford (Charter Fellow, Wolfson College), Bristol (Lecturer and Senior Lecturer) and York (Lecturer) and was until 2002 editor of *Antiquity*. He has directed several fieldwork projects in Central Italy (Casentino, Grotte di Castro, Montelabate, Gubbio and Nepi) and has written/edited books on Etruscan Italy, the Mediterranean Bronze Age, Maltese mortuary customs, the Gubbio fieldwork, landscapes and the Celts.

JAIME VIVES-FERRÁNDIZ holds a PhD degree in Archaeology from University of Valencia (Spain), and he is Curator of the Museum of Prehistory of Valencia since 2004. His principal field of research focuses on East Iberia during the first millennium BC. He is especially interested in colonial situations and exchange relations from postcolonial approaches, about which he has published his book *Negociando encuentros* (2005). Currently he is field co-director of the research project in the Iberian settlement of Bastida de les Alcusses (Valencia, Spain), and he is a member of the research and excavation project in Lixus (Larache, Morocco).

Introduction: Contextualizing ethnicity

Simon Stoddart and Gabriele Cifani

The concept of ethnicity can lack focus. For this reason, the contributors to this volume were set some very clear areas of concern. Firstly, they were asked to examine and contextualize contrasting definitions of ethnicity and identity as implicit in two perspectives, one from the classical tradition (Ruby 2006) and another from the prehistoric and anthropological tradition (Jones 1997). Both these traditions converge on an emphasis of the multi-layered, slippery, negotiable characteristics of ethnicity. Secondly, they were asked to take a view on the role of textual sources in reconstructing ethnicity. Thirdly, they were invited not just to present a theoretical argument, but to introduce fresh and innovative archaeological data in reconstructing ethnicity, be it from fieldwork or from new combinations of old data. Finally, in contrast to many traditional approaches to ethnicity they were asked to examine the relative and interacting role of natural and cultural features in the landscape in the construction of ethnicity.

The papers collected here address these themes with different emphases on the relative impact of theorization and data. Similarly different strands of ethnicity are stressed by different authors, partly through their theoretical background and partly through the nature of their material. There are some papers which emphasize the importance of text (Carandini, Cifani) and others which subordinate it to archaeological material (Stoddart, Lomas). For some landscape is relatively central (Cifani, Stoddart). For some ethnicity is elusive for the society under consideration (Greek contributions). For many, ethnicity is but a scale of identity that is perhaps less the principal focus of society and more fragile in its formation (Osborne, Fulminante, Rajala, Stoddart, Lomas) and, like other forms of identity subject to situational slippage. For these authors, ethnicity cannot be studied in isolation.

The volume is headed by the contribution of Andrea Carandini whose work challenges the conceptions of many in the combination of text and archaeology. He begins by examining the mythology surrounding the founding of Rome, taking into consideration the recent archaeological evidence from the Palatine and the Forum. Here primacy is given to construction of place and mythological descent. Several scholars comment on this take of the past.

After this challenging introduction, a geographical mosaic (Fig. 1.1) is presented from East to West (although it is tempting to go in the opposite direction: cf. Mathers and Stoddart 1994 to avoid perceptions of a matching trend of complexity). Within this structure there is helpful pairing of more theoretical papers (Osborne, Fulminante) and corresponding investigative examples (Lohmann, Rajala).

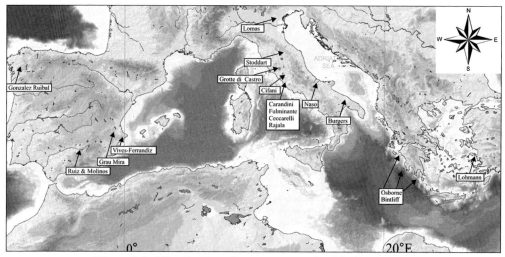

Figure 1.1. Distribution of papers across the Mediterranean.

Robin Osborne considers the evidence for the existence and expression of ethnic identity in Ancient Greece and questions the role of ethnicity in shaping the political and cultural identity of a *polis*. He emphasizes the primacy of politics over landscape, descent, ethnicity or any other factor. He gives a convincing account of how it is the *polis* community scale that is paramount over other scales of identity. Hans Lohmann presents evidence from the excavation of the Archaic Panionion in the Mycale and the implications of this find for the relationship between Greek colonists and the indigenous Carian population. This is dramatic evidence for the importance of new data as well as new theory. John Bintliff uses interdisciplinary case-studies, particularly an ethnographic study of early modern Boeotia, to refine the conception of ethnicity in Ancient Greece and challenge conclusions drawn solely from ancient authors. He unravels the diversity and complexity of the concept of ethnicity.

We re-enter the Italian peninsula at the interstices between ethnic groups. Gert-Jan Burgers explores the ritual landscape of the Salento isthmus in Apulia during the Hellenistic period and proposes a more refined methodology in the study of Mediterranean landscape, using concepts of hybridity and negotiation of political power. For him the use of the past in the form of cosmologies is crucial in the construction of identity. Moving north, Alessandro Naso utilizes an integrated spatial model and the archaeological evidence to elucidate further the current understanding of the Molise during the eighth and sixth centuries BC. He evokes ways in which landscape affects mountain material culture and attempts to use distributions of distinctive material culture against a landscape background. He also hypothesizes the expansionist politics of powerful coastal centres into more 'marginal' regions, recognized by the presence of distinctive grave-goods.

Six papers are located geographically in central Italy. Fulminante takes a more theoretical approach suggestive of new investigations of central Italian identity, drawing on recent work to show how a new understanding could be implemented. Ceccarelli investigates the materialization of myths in the construction of ethnic identities, concentrating on the exciting recent discoveries from Ardea. Rajala implements a related approach through fieldwork, emphasizing the landscape dimension of identity. Her examples are in crucial boundary areas (Nepi and *Crustumerium*) based on recent fieldwork in two different fields of settlement and burial, both situated in landscape. In the case of the Faliscan territory, the evidence of political independence and the causes of a florescence of identity are disputed, a theme also covered by Cifani in this volume. It is also suggested that landscape can be politically subverted to create identity. Cifani follows with a theoretical approach to ethnicity grounded in the classical tradition, showing that some of the classic divisions have a *longue durée* existence, proposing that many concepts from post-processualism to post-colonialism have not been uncovered *ex novo* by the Young Turks of the modern world. He also belongs to the school of thought, which considers material culture to be insufficient in defining identity and more than subliminally places literary, sources above non-documentary material sources as the foundation of understanding ethnicity. Since ethnicity often coincides with state formation and thus at least with restricted literacy this is less of a problem than it may seem. He combines this theoretical approach with a chronicle of the territorial changes over time, specifically focusing on the middle Tiber Valley during the ninth to the end of the fourth century BC. This is paired with fieldwork illustration of the workings of a version of this model in the Grotte di Castro area. Gabriele Cifani and colleagues review the evidence from a recent survey of the Civita di Grotte di Castro and its significance within Italian landscape and frontier studies. This central Italian section concludes with a radical and already controversial approach by Simon Stoddart who deconstructs a prominent textual approach to identity in the Gubbio Valley, suggesting that natural places may have been slightly altered to create a landscape of identity. Before moving to the western Mediterranean, Kathryn Lomas examines the expression of group identity on various levels – from descent groups to regional ethnic identities – within the context of ancient Veneto. She stresses the inter-relationship between identities and their hierarchical relationships, and notes, in common with previous work by Wilkins (1990), that many perceptions of ethnicity were external to the community itself. For her, writing may have had the power to alter natural places in the landscape.

Finally, within the context of the western Mediterranean, Arturo Ruiz and Manuel Molinos apply the theory of space delimitation to the study of ethnicity in the upper and middle Guadalquivir Valley during the sixth century BC, exploring an explicitly Marxist framework. These authors stress the value of the ancient textual sources in alluding to ancient ethnicity, provided this is addressed with an appropriate caution. The study of boundary formation gels nicely with studies of community boundaries in Italy and Greece. Ignacio Grau Mira addresses the interplay between the ethnic and political articulation of territory over time among the *Contestani* and *Edestani* peoples of the eastern Iberian peninsula, applying a more critical approach to the ancient texts. A comparison of these two papers shows the debate in understanding the sources of ethnicity. Alfredo González-Ruibal questions the previous methodological approach to ethnicity in Iberian archaeology and constructs a more diverse conception of ethnic delineation using northwestern Iron Age Iberia as an example. Jaime Vives-Ferrández explores the interaction and power dynamics between Phoenician colonists and indigenous peoples between the eighth and sixth centuries BC in southeastern Iberia as interpreted through post-colonial theory.

We hope that the landscape dimension of this volume, written substantially by archaeologists who practise as well as think archaeology adds to the contributions on similar themes that are emerging from the Mediterranean (e.g. most recently Hales and Hodos 2010; Derks and Roymans 2009; Pohl and Mehofer, 2010). The volume ends by placing these contributions in a broader, non Mediterranean, perspective.

The papers collected in this volume together emphasize the importance of the spatial dimension of ethnicity, the influence of such ideology in shaping a landscape or a place. Within this spatial framework, the complex debates over the definition of ethnicity reveal the importance of a positive dialogue between specialists of different areas and phases in the study of ancient identities. Anthropological comparison between different cultures is in a dialectic with the knowledge of the historical, social and political, more particularistic reasons behind the shaping of ethnicities.

This book focuses essentially on the central and western Mediterranean, but we should remember the debates over the not-so-geographically distant Near Eastern communities. Three sectors are most prominent: Hebrew (see the recent controversial work, Sand 2009), the Egyptian and other civilizations of the eastern Mediterranean area, and the multi-stratified identities of the Hellenistic kingdoms (e.g. Strobel 2009; van der Spek 2009). These are further examples of the dominance of a written tradition in shaping ethnicities and the tension implicit in the integration of material culture. Thus a modern interdisciplinary and international archaeology which combines material data and textual evidence – critically – can provide a powerful lesson for the full understanding of the ideologies of ancient and modern societies.

The editors hope that the papers collected in this volume will be a further step toward this intellectual challenge.

Acknowledgements

The volume is based on a Marie Curie funded seminar (MEIF-CT-2005–514523) held in Cambridge in March 2007, hosted by the McDonald Institute. In addition to those who presented in the original seminar, other papers were recruited from the Iberian peninsula. The main editing of the volume was undertaken by Simon Stoddart with invaluable assistance from Skylar Neil and Gabriele Cifani. Martin Randall Travel kindly provided a subvention for this volume. We are additionally grateful to a set of anonymous reviewers. Formatting was undertaken by Sam McLeod and the Oxbow production was overseen by Clare Litt. The index was constructed by Skylar Neil and Simon Stoddart.

2

Urban landscapes and ethnic identity of early Rome

Andrea Carandini

Key words: Rome; ethnicity; urban landscape; myths; Latins; foundation ritual

The ethnogenesis of the Romans can be traced through a series of legends that enshrouded a crucial event: the foundation of the city and the reorganization of its territory into an urban landscape. Roman identity itself was a hybrid phenomenon from the beginning; the *ethnos* of the Latins and *ethnos* of the Sabines were integrated. Additionally there are contributions from Etruscan culture: the rituals of *sulcus primigenius* and of the *murus sanctus* (Varr. *L.L.* V.143, Macrob. *Sat.* V.19.13).

The formation and the foundation of the city of Rome and of the *res publica*, the *regnum* and the Roman state are phenomena of the same period. One cannot state that the city was established first and then the politics – both coexisted simultaneously. It is a question of the identity and cultural memory of a people in relationship to their work and their production. One should imagine the agricultural production and the human life cycle, around which the early calendar was organized: time was organized in relation to labour and production; space was organized in relation to the rural and urban landscape; political actions, cults, ceremonies and the representations of this reality were organized through the framework of myth. The Romans adopted a constitution that shared freely the concept of ethnicity, whether in the army, the community or the tribes; foreigners could even occupy the highest office. Social mobility was already a well-known phenomenon in the Etruscan, Latin and Italic communities of the seventh century BC (Marchesini 2007), but mobility was especially evident in the myth of the two kings: Romulus and Titus Tatius, presented as *principes* who had left their respective ethnic capitals, *Alba Longa* and *Cures,* for Rome, and who had founded a city-state in a new ethnic context. Archaeological evidence contributes significantly to understanding the myths about the foundation and formation of Rome (my actual synthesis is always in progress; for the archaeological evidence: Carandini and Carafa 2000; Filippi 2004, 2005; historical interpretation: Carandini 1997, 2002, 2006a, 2010, 2011; Carandini and Cappelli 2000).

The majority of new archaeological evidence comes from stratigraphic excavations in the Roman Forum, which can be considered an historical archive of amazing potential:

the period from the first human act, in the sanctuary of Vesta, in the middle of the eighth century BC to 1602 AD (the date of the door of the church of S. Lorenzo in Miranda), is represented by 13 metres of stratigraphy (Fig. 2.1). Roman historians thought that the foundation of Rome took place between the second and third quarter of the eighth century, roughly between 758 and 728 BC. The archaeology of Rome supports a similar conclusion; as a matter of fact, there is a significant discontinuity around the second quarter of the eighth century, 775–750. In particular where there was a residential zone of huts, the huts were destroyed and a wall was built around the Palatine, at the foot of the hill. Legend tells of the enterprises of three kings, Romulus, Titus Tatius and Numa, who were considered the founders. Excavations have uncovered traces of these enterprises in public monuments evidently ordered by the central authority between 775 and 675.

However, understanding the period before the founding of Rome is a real problem. The legend says that Rome was established *ex novo*. Evidently the purpose was to stress the achievement of the founders; however, in doing so, two main realities were obscured. The first was the existence of the *populi albenses,* whose metropolis was Alba at the foot of the Mons Albanus (Chiarucci 2000). In particular, I think that three pre-urban districts were located on the site and in the *ager* of Rome, and probably served as the source for the three future tribes. According to my reconstruction, these districts date to the Final Bronze Age, around 900 BC, and are located near to where the Tiber meets with other streams (Fig. 2.2); after the occupation of these villages we have the placement of two groups: *Montes* and *Colles*. First, significantly, the *Septimontium* is on one side and the *Colles* on the other; I would place this phase around 900–850 BC. (Carandini 1997: 267–380). Then there were phases in which these two entities were unified under the hegemony of the *Septimontium* who swallowed up the *Colles*. Between 850 and 775 BC, this was probably the configuration of population immediately before the founding of Rome. Varro wrote about the second *Septimontium* (Varro *Lingua Latina* V.41); there were ceremonies at the *Argei* that seem to relate to this unified settlement, which Varro believed predated Romulus and were not, as has generally been stated, contemporary with the first monarchy.

From the middle of the ninth century BC, settlement became more concentrated in the valleys. Necropoleis were established outside the communities, a distinctive trait found in Villanovan centres, and this separation indicated significant cultural interactions between early Etruscans and Latins in the area of Rome – perhaps even an expression of Etruscan ethnicity. The site of Rome had become a significant proto-urban settlement; Renato Peroni estimates its size at 205 hectares, about 15 hectares more than *Veii* and Tarquinia (Müller Karpe 1959, 1962; Peroni 1988; Pacciarelli 2001).

By the time of Romulus, Rome was slightly larger, at 241 hectares, very close to the size of the most extensive urban centres in Greece. However, the importance of Romulean Rome is not in its extent, since a considerable settlement was already there by the Final Bronze Age. The innovative aspect of the Romulean city was qualitative – that is to say, related to sovereignty and government, and the organization of men, space and time. Moreover, equally ranked component parts of the settlement had been centralized into one entity. Nevertheless, Romulean Rome was a large settlement comprised of districts, perhaps already *Curiae*, although I am not so fond of that term. These were equals among equals, as can be seen in the ceremony of the *Septimontium*

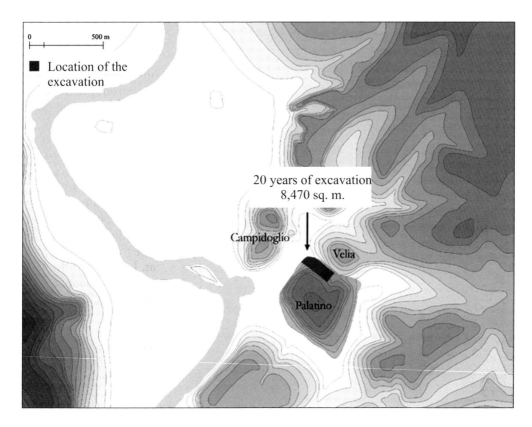

Figure 2.1. (A) Above: The northern slopes of the Palatine, showing the area of excavation. (B) Below: The vertical location of the excavation in relation to the Church of S. Lorenzo in Miranda.

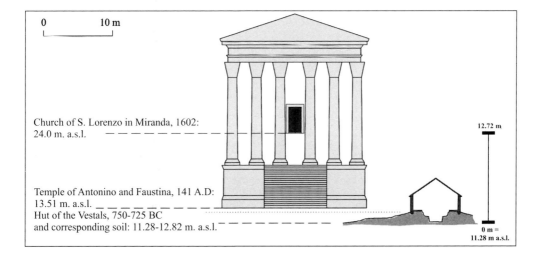

Andrea Carandini

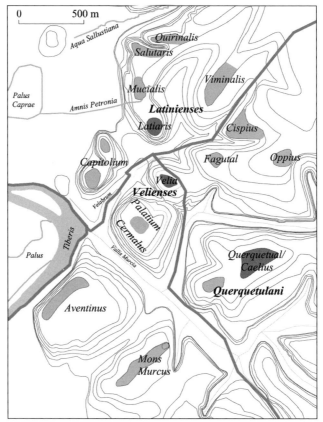

Figure 2.2. Rome in the Final Bronze Age.

and the ceremony of the *Argei*, both of which had no centrally coordinated ceremonial event. Other district feasts – *Fornacalia*, for instance – were celebrated centrally.

To transform this centralized settlement into a state, three necessary steps had to be undertaken. First the *auspicia* and the *auguria* had to be observed on the Aventine and the Palatine. The second task was the creation of a sacred and political centre: in the *Forum*, in the *Capitolium* and in the *Arx*. The third enterprise was the re-organization of the rest of the settlement that was not part of the original foundation, but articulated in districts. The legend informs us mainly of the first and second of these steps, while the third has to be understood through the archaeological evidence.

The foundation ritual

The traditions of the Latin kings, before the insertion of Aeneas and Ascanius into the mythical narrative, can be dated before the sixth century BC; additionally, this tradition is depicted in the famous bronze mirror from Bolsena of the fourth century BC, where

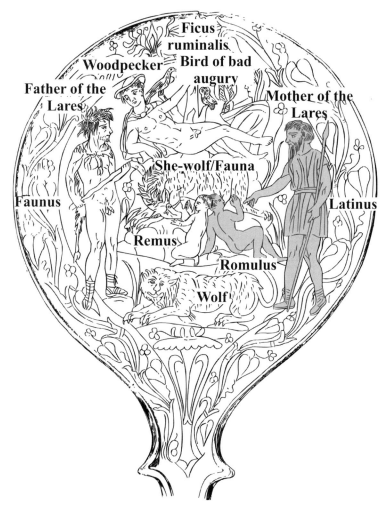

Figure 2.3. The Bolsena Mirror with identification of the represented figures.

there is a transition in images from the *Lares* who are always co-operating, to the twins who create conflict (Fig. 2.3). The second-born – the *Altellus*, as Romulus was called – is pointed out by a royal figure, which I consider to be the founder of the Latins. I think that a certain narrative logic existed between Romulus taking the *auspicia* on the Aventine and then, as we know from Servius, approaching the *Cermalus* and throwing the famous spear made out of European dogwood.

We can reconstruct the line of sight of such *auspicia*, thanks to the use of three-dimensional models. As a matter of fact, the best views of the Palatine hill are from the Aventine: the first one in the western area of the Aventine, near the church of Sant'Alessio where the temples of Minerva and Diana were built, and the second one

in the eastern area of the hill, near the church of Santa Balbina. The process involved
in building a *templum in aere* is described by the *Tabulae Iguvinae* (Sisani 2001; on the
templum: Nissen 1869; Catalano 1978; Linderski 1986). Two points are very important,
n. 1 and n. 5 (Fig. 2.4). N. 1 is the *angulus summus* and n. 5 is the *angulus infimus*, which
will correspond to the Latin city of Aricia on the Alban hills. This is a scheme – as you
see 1, 3, 4, and 8 make the circle around the Palatine of the *pomerium*; 8, 4, 5, 6, 7 is the
ager and also beyond the *ager* up to the horizon. This is the theoretical construction of
the view of what the augur would have seen from that position and, on the left, one can
see what could have happened on the Palatine. The endpoint of this view is the *Mons
Albanus* at *Alba Longa* and *Aricia*. On the Palatine, you can see that the scheme needs
four angles, which serve as the four limits of the *pomerium*. Therefore the augur first
had to place *lapides* to delimit the area into which the benediction had to fall; otherwise
it would have escaped the bounded area, like unregulated water. You cannot ask for
a benediction without the placement of the limits.

Archaeological documentation gives just some chronological data of interest. A Late
Bronze and Iron Age settlement is known on the *Cermalus*, within which a particular
hut was kept in good condition right up until the Imperial period; this is the so-called
casa Romuli, a place which has been always preserved, as distinct from other buildings.
Subsequently, the fortification walls, found at the northern slope of the Palatine, were
built around the middle of the eighth century BC (Fig. 2.5; Carandini and Carafa 2000).
The construction of this wall destroyed an old quarter of earlier proto-urban huts.
The foundations of this wall were marked by enormous stones set in clay of a type
unknown to the area. I have the distinct sense that these were markers of a wall linked
with a foundation ritual.

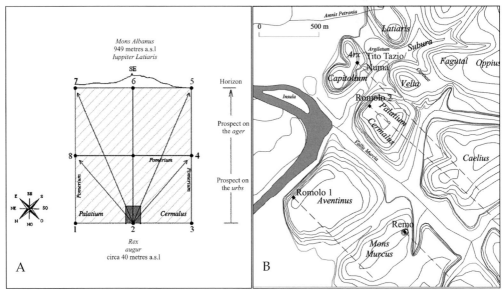

*Figure 2.4. Templum in aere. (A) Diagram to show the topology of the Templum. (B) The mapping
of the templum onto the Roman landscape.*

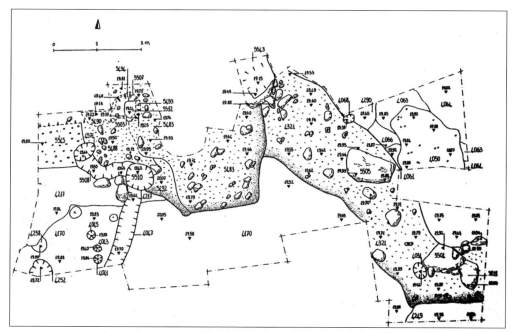

Figure 2.5. The fortification wall on the slopes of the Palatine.

Figure 2.6. Votive deposit found in the threshold of a gate of the fortification wall on the slopes of the Palatine.

In my publications, I have attempted to reconstruct this ritual: first a furrow had to be dug, with the earth thrown to one side; then stone had to be placed, so that rain could not obscure the furrow. After the transformation of the furrow into a foundation ditch, smaller stones were placed against the larger stones to form a wall. Those stones could have been sacred to *Terminus*, a *signum* to the divinity of boundaries, and given their sacred condition could not be violated (Piccaluga 1974). A foundation deposit was then laid under the threshold. This was a sort of a funerary deposition of a small girl, dated to the Latial period IIIB1, which, in my point of view, corresponds to the second quarter of the eighth century BC (Fig. 2.6).

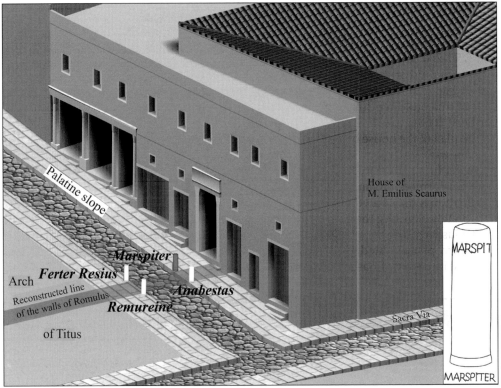

Figure 2.7. A Late Republican dedicatory inscription from the slope of the Palatine.

In this area in the Late Republican period there was still a memory of the foundation myth, giving respect to Remus, who according to the legend attacked the Palatine from the Velia. Four *cippi* were placed in the traditional position of the wall; the most interesting one was dedicated to *Marspiter* and *Anabesta*, the divinity of jumping (*CIL* I², 969–71; Tassini 1993; Fig. 2.7).

The sanctuary of Vesta

The second enterprise is related to the Forum. At the edges of this area the identity of the new Roman community was emphasized by the foundation of two new sanctuaries: the sanctuary of Volcanus at the foot of the *arx* and the sanctuary of Vesta at the foot of the Palatine, both built outside the walls. The literary tradition links the Sanctuary of Vesta to the early history of Rome, referring to the houses of the kings Numa and Ancus Marcius in the complex of Vesta, but until 2003 the archaeological evidence was very limited: we knew of just one pit, filled with Archaic and Orientalizing pottery. Consequently, the most common opinion of scholars was that the Forum was planned only after the middle of the seventh century (Colonna 1964). Now there is firstly evidence of a small rectangular hut, dated to around 750 BC just after the construction of the wall (Fig 2.8; Filippi 2004: 103–7, 2005: 199). Immediately afterwards, in phase II–1 (750–700 BC), excavations have revealed the plan of a huge *domus* with courtyard, built with mud and clay, which I would call a *domus regia* (Filippi 2004: 107–14, 2005: 200 1; Fig. 2.9). An inhumation tomb of a young girl was placed in the perimeter wall of this building during its construction (Filippi 2008; Filippi and Gusberti 2006; Gusberti 2008).

The plan of the house has been reconstructed as comprising a huge banquet hall, with two big wooden columns, a *pronaos*, an internal bench against the walls and external fireplace. In a second sub-phase (II–2), which can be dated to 725–700 BC, the building was transformed into an L-shape with a new porch sitting room, or *sacrarium*. Another inhumation tomb of a young girl was laid in the main wall of the last sub-phase (II–3), deliberately slighting the wall to mark its destruction (Filippi 2004: 107–14, 2005: 200–1, 2008; Gusberti 2008).

A third phase, dated to the first half of the seventh century BC, was followed by the very important Phase 4, 650 or 625–600, which had two big halls and a courtyard

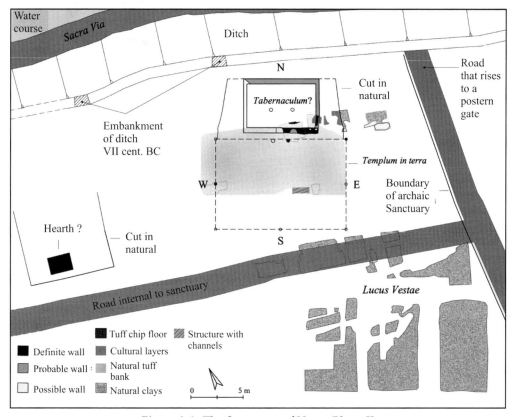

Figure 2.8. The Sanctuary of Vesta. Phase II.

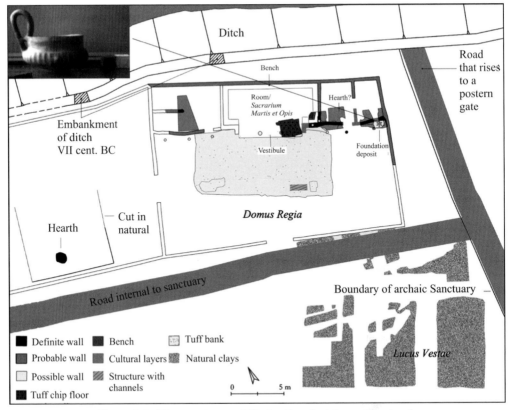

Figure 2.9. The sanctuary of Vesta. Female inhumation tomb.

(Filippi 2004: 116–21, 2005: 202), interpretations that are supported by the presence of tiles (Ammerman and Filippi 2004: 26, note 85; Fig. 2.10). This building with a tiled roof and stone foundations was destroyed around 600 BC as confirmed by a further inhumation tomb, which was dug inside the main wall of the building. So one can conclude that the tract of land to the east of the sanctuary of Vesta was occupied by a building of extraordinary importance, around the middle of the eighth century BC, just after the construction of the wall around the Palatine. This area was rebuilt in the sixth century BC as a huge house within the bounds of the Sanctuary of Vesta. One knows from the literary sources that the house of Tarquinius was near this sanctuary and one would be tempted to identify these remains with the royal quarter.

The house of the Vestals Virgins was almost completely unknown. In the Late Republican period it was an L-shaped building with the *aedes Vestae* in the courtyard (Arvanitis 2004). In this area, recent excavations have found remains of an archaic building which covered a rectangular hut, just partially excavated. It can be dated between 750 and 700 BC by the presence of Late Geometric pottery. The same area was not inhabited before the mid-eighth century, when the surface of this building plot was

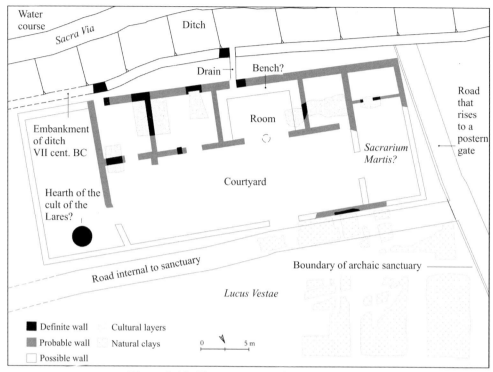

Figure 2.10. The sanctuary of Vesta. Phase IV.

Figure 2.11. The sanctuary of Vesta: traces of plough (end of the eighth century BC).

ploughed for the first time for the construction of the sanctuary (Fig. 2.11; Arvanitis 2010). This is probably the evidence of a purification ritual before the foundation of a civic cult. Then, between the end of the eighth and beginning of the seventh century this plot was enclosed by a wall, whose remains were found in 2006 to the north, facing the area of the *Regia*.

The Forum and Capitolium

A recent re-examination of the Forum stratigraphy revealed an initial layer of pavement in the Early Orientalizing phase (Filippi 2005); the main sources of documentation are the drawing of the section of the *equus Domitiani* made by Giacomo Boni (1900) and the materials taken from the strata, stored in the *Antiquarium Forense* (Fig. 2.12). Pebble pavement 2 is the Forum pavement, dated correctly by Giovanni Colonna to the middle of the seventh century (Colonna 1964). Until recently, this was considered to be the first pavement, but in the famous drawing of Giacomo Boni, when enlarged, we can see that there is another pavement underneath, shown by a layer of pebbles on top of a fill. Further underneath, there was the initial natural level, then a fill of the second half of the eighth century, in which three skeletons were found; then, sealing

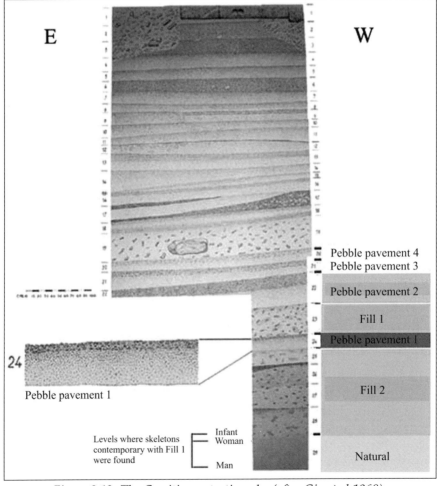

Figure 2.12. The Comitium, stratigraphy (after Gjerstad 1960).

this first fill, there was the first paving (Level 24: Filippi 2005; Gusberti 2005). Then there was another fill, probably dating to the beginning of the seventh century, whose top was paved during the first half of the seventh century – technically no later than 670 BC (Carafa 1998). The deposit of the *Doliola* dates to this period, 775–50 BC, and the wall found by Gjerstad is probably that of the Archaic *sacellum*, which of course had a preceding *sacellum* of the seventh century. The material from the *Doliola* certainly dates to this period and I think that, considering the skeletons in the fill and this deposit, it probably indicates a funerary context. All public buildings in Rome older than 600 BC generally have foundation or obliteration deposits which I consider to be ritual, because of the presence of infant remains; moveover, these are not *suggrundaria* (perinatal infants) that are part of standard mortuary practices (Modica 2007). The drainage of the Forum, together with the organization of a political centre inside the settlement, was evidently the biggest public work (Ammerman 1990, 1996). Although the finished work is all that remains, from a historical point of view, the process of this work is more important than the moment when the work was accomplished. As a matter of fact, according to literary sources, the *Volcanal* nearby was a meeting place of the *comitia*, which moderated the authority of the king. This is the politically charged spatial context in which materials from the end of the eighth century BC were found (Carafa 1998: 100–2).

On the *Capitolium*, a deposit has been found in the place where we could imagine the *aedes* of *Jupiter Fereretrius*, a civic cult preceding the well-known cult of *Jupiter Capitolinus* of the Tarquinii (Cifani 2007: 80–109); as the *meta* of *ovationes*, it had a triumphal character and the *ius iurandum*, the beginning of law (*iurare*, to swear, is the verb of *ius* (Calore 2000)), was permanently located here. The *lapis silex* was the *signum* of *Jupiter Feretrius* and it was with this tool that the priest hit and killed the sow to honour *Jupiter* (Paul. Diac. in Festus, 81 L). The votive deposit known under the *Protomoteca* could refer to the cult of *Jupiter Feretrius*; it has votive elements characteristic of the second half of the eighth century BC (Bartoloni 1990; Filippi 2000; Guidi 1980; Gusberti 2005; Fig. 2.13).

The ritual of the foundation of Rome is the definition of a religious landscape; the first ethnicity of Rome was shaped through a reorganization of cults and rituals around the middle of the eighth century; it was a reformation of the territory previously allocated to smaller Bronze and Early Iron Age settlements. The new urban landscape was the first step in a long-term process towards the formation of the Roman identity.

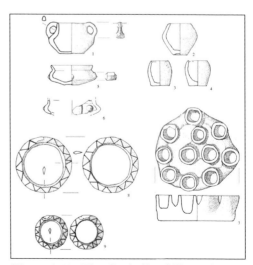

Figure 2.13. The Capitoline hill: Early Iron Age materials from the votive deposit of 'Protomoteca'.

Acknowledgments

The author is grateful to Gabriele Cifani and Simon Stoddart for the editing of this contribution.

Comments

ANTHONY SNODGRASS

I first of all acknowledge that this is a highly compressed version of Andrea Carandini's original presentation, and that we are not seeing anything like all of the supporting evidence, in the form of stratigraphy for instance, that he offered.

'Archaeological evidence contributes significantly to our understanding of the myths about the foundation and formation of Rome', he writes. But there must be readers whose first instinct is the same as mine: to stand this statement on its head and then turn it into a question: 'How much can the myths contribute to our understanding of the archaeological evidence?'. More specifically, I wonder how far we would have taken our interpretations of the archaeology, if the myths had not existed. The answer, I think, is that we are asked to accept early Rome as a special case: to treat the founding legends with a degree of respect that we should never dream of allowing in a parallel case. It certainly is special in the quantity of circumstantial detail preserved in these legends, but that is not in itself a guarantee of their reliability. Andrea Carandini himself concedes one substantial modification that has to be made to the legends, in the shape of their claim that Rome was founded *de novo* on a virgin site. This is quite a concession. If the very existence of the villages of the Final Bronze Age could be either forgotten or, as seems to be suggested here, air-brushed out of the tradition, then how much can we trust of the story that took their place?

The claim would be that the archaeology has itself redeemed that story. But first, there is a clear danger of circularity in any argument that has already used the myths to build a narrative out of the archaeology. Secondly, it is not possible for an excavation, even when of the quality of the work shown here, itself to supply names and identities for what is, at best, a proto-historical phase. It is, then, the names and identities that I would question but, even without them, we have here a very substantial advance in the understanding of early Rome. In one location after another, a case can be made for a major discontinuity at the middle of the eighth century, or shortly before or just after, whether based on stratigraphic or on typological evidence. For the general lines of the tradition, this is an important vindication, whether we put it down to luck, genuine memory, or well-informed invention.

ROBIN OSBORNE

Andrea Carandini's paper wonderfully reveals the extraordinary nature of the history of early Rome. In no other ancient city could one claim to uncover ethnic identity by tracing the myths by which the citizens defined themselves almost half a millennium later in the material remains of the earliest urban settlement. The ancient tombs which become the stuff of the mythical Greek landscape are very largely a feature of country, not town; and for all that Sparta heroised an Archaic Lycurgus, and Athens determinedly traced its laws to an early sixth-century Solon, neither of them were inscribed into the space of the Classical city. It is an overwhelmingly *Classical* past that determines the archaeology of Pausanias' Greece. Rome's obsession with foundation. and with the physical space in which founding events occurred, is the anxiety of a Jonny-come-lately, who has been none too particular about its alliances and intermarriages. Rome has to forge a tangible link to a local past if she is to claim any distinct ethnic identity.

There is something appropriate and charming about the uniqueness of Roman identity being sustained by the uniqueness of modern scholarship. But there are grave disadvantages. The longer that early settlement at Rome is described in the terms of her own fictions, the longer she remains incomparable. If we are to understand Rome's history or its archaeology we will only do so if we can compare that history and that archaeology to the history and archaeology of other Italian settlements and to settlement around the Mediterranean generally. For these, there is no Varro, Festus or Livy. Such settlements are understood from the ground up, through the changing nature and position of their cemeteries, the contacts and the engagement revealed in imported grave-goods and local responses, the development of communal resources in the form of temples and other group investments. Signs of planning, reservation of areas for communal use, density of habitations, frequency of rebuilding – all of these show something of the dynamics of a community. All offer themselves up for comparison with other places that faced similar conditions and responded in various ways that can be assessed by comparison of traits and by simple measurements.

The histories of Archaic Greece and of Archaic Rome alike have been plagued by the assumption that history begins as soon as ancient texts begin to tell a story. Scholars have attempted to treat Greek history as beginning in 776 BC. because it is from that moment on that we have a list of Olympic victors compiled in antiquity. They have similarly attempted to treat Roman history as beginning with the stories told in later texts to explain how Rome came to be founded. But in truth Greece remains 'prehistoric' until the fifth century and Rome until the third century BC. For oral history is always homeostatic, and until we have accounts from near-contemporaries, we cannot expect to do historical analysis. For archaic Rome as for archaic Greece, we must reconstruct the political and social order from a broad survey of archaeological remains, vigilant as much for preserved traces of changing flora and fauna as for the sight-lines of *auspicia*. Only then, do we give the long slow birth of local identities the lengthy gestation period they need. For to read later stories about foundation back into earlier remains is to condense a hard-won history, and to obscure the political manipulation of social memory.

No story is interesting for its own sake. Stories become interesting when they press against expectations, surprising the listener by revealing unexpected differences and unpredicted similarities. The historians of the third, second and first century BC played with their audiences' expectations as they developed the story of early Rome, and from their accounts a rich picture of Middle and Late Republican assumptions and priorities can be, but has yet to be, culled. If archaeologists are to reveal anything interesting about early Rome, beyond the fact that eighth-century buildings and other structures really do exist, it has got to be by the more or less surprising confirmation (or denial) that patterns of urbanization in Rome match those of other towns in Italy and more generally, and by the more or less surprising revelation that Roman difference had deep roots. To achieve that we need first an Archaeology that has the courage to dispense with the armature of resonant Latin names upon which scholars since the Late Republic have exercised an ingenuity that would solve the hardest of crossword puzzles, and to embrace close measurement and description of *all* the material remains.

TIM CORNELL

The recent discoveries by Professor Carandini and his team on the Palatine and in the Forum Romanum have an extremely important bearing on our understanding of the historical development of Rome. The wall at the foot of the Palatine, stratigraphic excavations at the temple of Vesta, and a new examination of the stratigraphy of the *Comitium* seem to show that a dramatic shift occurred in the nature and organization of the settlement in the second and third quarters of the eighth century BC. These discoveries provide evidence of political authority, communal cult activity, and the organization of public space – developments which had previously been dated no earlier than the third quarter of the seventh century. This was the date archaeologists had assigned to what was thought to be the first paving of the Forum Romanum, an event that many described as the foundation of the city. This opinion will now have to be revised if Paolo Carafa is right to identify an earlier paving dating to the eighth century.

None of these discoveries affect the wider point, which has long been recognized, that the settlement or settlements occupying the site of the later city of Rome go back to a much earlier date – and represent continuity of habitation going back at least to the Final Bronze Age. What historians and archaeologists have been trying to do ever since Einar Gjerstad opened the new phase of archaeological investigations after the Second World War is to define and characterize the relationship between the urban and the pre-urban phases of the settlement. While some have argued for a gradual transition over a long period (the so-called *Stadtwerdung* model, associated with H. Müller-Karpe), others prefer to see it as a decisive political moment, and to identify the beginning of the urban stage with the beginnings of the city-state. This was the view of Gjerstad, who regarded the 'foundation' as a largely political act, which was effected by the political unification of a number of pre-existing villages. It is my impression that the great majority of current experts would accept this broad notion in some form, and Carandini is no exception. In fact Carandini envisages a complex series of unifications during the proto-urban phase, culminating in the foundation under Romulus.

The novelty of Carandini's vision is twofold: first, his archaeological discoveries allow him to raise the date of the 'foundation' to the mid-eighth century, thus bringing it into line with the traditional chronology; secondly, and much more radically, he believes that the written sources contain reliable historical information preserved by oral tradition and amounting to a collective memory of real events. The two propositions are not linked directly by a naive argument that the latter follows from the former; if anything, Carandini's method suggests that the relationship is the other way around. But Carandini himself is prepared to concede that there is a contradiction between the archaeology and the foundation story in one particular: this is the fact that the legend presents the foundation as the creation of a new city *ex novo*, on an uninhabited site frequented by shepherds and menaced by wolves. He argues that this served to emphasize the achievement of the founders. Perhaps so, but the consequences are serious for his reconstruction.

In the first place the pre-urban settlement revealed by archaeology cannot easily be associated with anything in the literary sources. Carandini has recourse to antiquarian notices concerning early cult ceremonies, such as Pliny's list (*Natural History* 3.69) of thirty *populi* 'who used to take meat on the Alban Mount', and Festus' description (458, 475–6 L) of the *septimontium*. But the interpretation of these difficult texts is controversial; the festivals they describe are undated and cannot be matched to any archaeological reality. Carandini's attempts to map them on the ground at particular periods (in the decades before and after 900 BC, respectively) are based on nothing more than hypothetical conjecture.

Secondly, the clear implication of the literary accounts that Romulus' city arose on a previously uninhabited site is not a trivial or incidental detail, but rather represents a fundamental part of the story. For the ancients that is what the foundation of a city signified. The augural contest, the debate over the site of the city, the ritual ploughing of the *sulcus primigenius*, the quarrel between the brothers and the death of Remus, all presuppose the creation of a new settlement, rather than the reorganization of an existing one; so too does the idea that Rome was a colony of *Alba Longa*. This, together with two other central elements of the story, the *asylum* and the rape of the Sabine women, would make no sense if the site of Rome was already inhabited by an existing population. The point is important in the present context because it is precisely these elements that Carandini uses as evidence for the ethnic identity of 'Romulean' Rome. I think he is right to link these features with the ethnic diversity of Rome in the Archaic period and with the evidence for horizontal social mobility in Tyrrhenian central Italy; but as parts of the foundation story they are demonstrably mythical and have no bearing on real events in the middle of the eighth century.

These reflections prompt two observations: one specific, the other more general. First, the fact that a long-standing settlement on the site of Rome can be shown to have undergone significant changes in the eighth century cannot be regarded as a historical confirmation of the famous legend; on the contrary, it would be more correct to say that key elements of the foundation story have been disproved by archaeological evidence.

Secondly, I find it difficult to assess Carandini's theories and to engage in critical debate because of his habit of combining his evidence with his interpretation of what it means. What he offers is always an integrated reconstruction mixing archaeological data with passages from ancient literary texts, ethnographic comparisons, plausible hypotheses, imagination and guesswork. He invites us to take it or leave it, and I for one find it hard to do either.

CHRISTOPHER SMITH

The critical aspects of Carandini's account of recent archaeological work on the early settlement of Rome are to my mind threefold: the emphasis on the ninth and eighth century transformations; the suggested discontinuity around the second quarter of the eighth century; and the sophistication of the eighth to seventh century settlement.

In an important article, Paolo Carafa distinguished between a Romulean-Numan and a Tarquinian city, by that terminology, a kind of self-conscious shorthand, indicating that there was sufficient archaeological material from Rome to encourage attention away from the sixth century and back to the eighth century (Carafa 1996). Recent discoveries have increased our knowledge of the earlier phases, as Carandini here shows. The finds are of course exiguous, and therefore interpretation will always be controversial, but the very fact of the amount and complexity of development around the Forum, Palatine and Capitoline is itself important.

Inevitably, questions will focus on the extent to which one can move from the material evidence to the literary texts. There are well-known problems over the kings, and although they are here used as signifiers rather than as realities, there are still lingering concerns over the extent to which the historical record is being read back. For instance, only someone who was wedded to the historical reality of an eighth-century foundation moment would expect the archaeological record to show a sort of preceding void. In fact, Rome was clearly the site of important settlement from the tenth century, and whatever developments took place were not foundations from nothing. Furthermore, the accounts of the kings can only be used as evidence of social mobility with the greatest of caution; at best they are perhaps myths created at a time where social mobility was a feature of Roman life.

More problematic is the assumption of the great antiquity of the augural rite. Our textual evidence here is of course late, but it is also surely the product of invention, antiquarian research, elaborated rituals corresponding to new realities and so forth. It is not clear to me what we can do with the survival of augural rituals and information; that these had some topographical connections cannot prove either their antiquity, or the antiquity of the topography.

Yet change there was at Rome, and whether or not the discontinuity here identified is real or illusory, it was significant, and that change itself places Rome within the broader context of the transformations attendant on the wider consequences of colonization, trade and general mobility. The Mediterranean was in flux, and whilst it might have been reasonable in earlier times to regard Rome as something of a backwater whilst this change was taking place, it becomes harder to sustain that as the evidence builds up. I continue to think that the changes at Rome seem to follow more rapid transformations in Etruria, and that that is a consequence of different material conditions of life, but the reorganization of the settlement is a sign of economic and political change. I remain nervous of speculation based on comparisons of the size of settlements which are poorly understood and whose internal articulation is hard to fathom.

Yet, if one were to remove all reference to historical or mythological figures, and simply set the evidence from Rome against the evidence for other settlements in Italy, and in Greece, as Carandini here does, then one would surely deduce from the Roman evidence the existence of a sophisticated and politically complex settlement from the early eighth century, since it is not simply the size of Rome that would count, but the variety of types of evidence, the indications of reorganization of the Forum, the shifting necropoleis, suggesting changes in the attitudes towards the dead and towards space, and so forth.

This in itself is an important and crucial change in the way we think about early Rome, with consequences for Latin civilization more generally in the Archaic period, and it makes the emergence of Rome as a highly significant settlement in the later sixth century more explicable and comprehensible. (The problem of explaining the changes in the fifth century then remain). The recovery of Rome as the site of a significant and economically important settlement, or group of settlements, in the eighth century is both important and suggestive, and whilst the detailed reconstruction will always be fraught with difficulty, Carandini's work here gives further impetus to study, investigation and theoretical and comparative reflection.

3

Landscape, ethnicity and the *polis*

Robin Osborne

Keywords: *polis*, ancient Greece, alphabet, genealogy, pottery

Greeks would standardly identify other Greeks by their *polis*, that is, by the autonomous political unit to which they belonged (on the nature of the *polis*, see further Hansen 2006, Hansen and Nielsen 2004). However, in certain circumstances, a Greek would be identified as part of a larger group which might have, but would not necessarily have, a political identity. Thus a man might be identified as a Tegean or an Arcadian, a Theban or a Boiotian, a Samian or an Ionian. Those larger groups are known in Greek as *ethnê* (singular *ethnos*), and it is with what sort of identity a Greek had by virtue of belonging to an *ethnos* that I will be primarily concerned in discussing ethnicity in this paper. Ethnic identity, in that sense, was undoubtedly deployed to a variety of effects by Greeks both in their own interest and to promote or undermine the interests of others. I shall argue here, however, that the part ethnic identity played in determining cultural divisions was small. For the historical period, at least, it is the independence of cultural traits from ethnic or geographical constraints that is remarkable and that gives them their political power.

No one has any doubts that the Greek landscape shaped the Greek *polis*. Historical geographies have long maintained that the mountainous landscape of the Greek peninsula determined the division of the Greeks into a large number of more or less independent political units. Economic historians have held it as an item of faith that land transport was expensive, and anything that further increased the disincentive to land transport was bound to contribute to economic regionalism. The arrival of intensive survey in Greece in the late 1970s stimulated renewed thought about exactly how the landscape might relate to the history, with a focus both upon the factors common to almost all city states, in particular modes of agricultural exploitation, and upon factors localized within the landscape, above all mineral resources and their manner of exploitation (Osborne 1987). However, the prime concern during the 1980s in discussions of these archaeological data was with what might be generally true of the Greek landscape. Interest in regional difference has developed during the last fifteen years, both as a result of increasing awareness that survey archaeology was not finding the same pattern of settlement changes over time in all areas, and as a result of growing interest in cultural identity. The changing focus can be seen by comparison of Osborne (1987) and Osborne (2004), or by comparing van Andel and Runnels (1987) to McInerney (1999). What more natural than that the sort of separation between poleis manifest in economic and political terms should also result in marked cultural differentiation? Jonathan Hall's repeated insistence (1997, 2002) that Greek ethnic identity emerged only late – in the sixth and fifth centuries – would seem only further to confirm the expectation that the separateness of the different Greek *poleis* marked itself out culturally.

On the face of it, the cultural evidence would seem strongly to support this basic view. Take the case of the Greek alphabet. Even here, where we have strong reason to believe in a single founding model for a cultural form, what we find more or less immediately across the Greek world is marked differentiation. The idea of taking on the letters of the Phoenicians but charging them with different sounds in such a way as to transform their vocalization can only have been an idea that occurred to one individual and group and was disseminated from that group. However fast and furious as the adoption of this idea seems to have been, those who adopted the idea did not adopt all the original mechanics. Different local scripts use different letters as well as different forms of letter, and they translate different Greek sounds into different representations, taking the principle of 'one sound, one letter' rather less than literally in some cases – the Athenians write short and long o and the diphthong 'ou' all with the letter omicron. Scholars since the nineteenth century have divided the local scripts of Archaic Greece into groups, but within these groups there is considerable diversity, and although there is quite a high degree of coherence to the letter forms found within a single *polis*, the different letter forms of any particular *polis* may have their closest connections with, and their putative origins in, different *poleis* and different areas (Jeffery 1961/1990: esp. 40–2). Athens came to claim to be the mother city from which all Ionians came, but down to the end of the fifth century Athens employed an alphabet which was quite distinct from the Ionic alphabet: the Athenian adoption of the Ionian alphabet followed the political claim to kinship (d'Angour 1999).

Or take fine pottery (Coldstream 1968; Boardman 1998). Here too there are some moments where ideas from a single source seem to have been important catalysts for local production. That is true of the so-called Protogeometric, where ideas about shape and decoration initially stemming from Athens seem to have had a wide impact (Desborough 1952). Nevertheless what follows is the development of regional styles which may be more or less easily distinguished. Or again, at the end of the eighth century there seems to be a more or less correlated turning away from the geometric style, usually presumed to have occurred under the impact of decorative ideas from the east (Osborne 1998: chapter 3). Not only is this explanation itself at best partial – most of the eastern ideas have been available for imitation for some time, so why various Greek regions should feel their impact at this particular point requires some additional factors to be involved (Morris 1992) – but what different regions do with the oriental ideas is distinctly different, and the range of shape and decoration to be observed in archaic Greek pottery is extremely wide. While in some cases the 'orientalism' may be purely decorative, a matter of the application of new techniques or decorative forms to existing types of object (as with the change from 'geometric' to 'naturalistic' figures on

Attic gold bands; Osborne 2009: 78–82), in other cases issues of lifestyle are involved. So the enormous production of small perfume vessels in seventh-century Corinth made available a particular lifestyle, rather than just a new packaging. And in another way too, regional patterns of pottery production correlate with increasingly divergent regional patterns of behaviour: Corinth's 'orientalizing' perfume vessels are very widely distributed across the central Mediterranean; Attic 'orientalizing' amphoras and other large pots get no further than Aigina (Morris 1984).

On the face of it, too, description of the separation of Greek *poleis* in ethnic terms would seem to be well supported. If the key feature of identities which are properly ethnic is the tracing of distinct ancestry (as Hall 1997: 25 insists: 'Above all else, though, it must be the myth of shared descent which ranks paramount among the features that distinguish ethnic from other social groups'), Greek cities certainly were inclined to do that (Hall 1997: 40–51). The Athenians' claim to have been 'born from the earth' makes sense only in a world where origins are thought to matter, and provides the ultimate trump card in debates about ethnic identity (Hall 1997: 53–6). Scholars have been able to convince themselves that by the sixth century, at least, Greek cities were all busy trying to distinguish their ancestry by claiming different branches, at least, of a family tree, if not wholly separate trees, and the *Catalogue of Women*, attributed in antiquity to the Boiotian poet Hesiod but more or less universally thought to date to a hundred or more years after his time, has been seen as a poem attempting to link in the determined local traditions to create a claim to common origin (Fowler 1998; West 1985).

But there is the rub. What the *Catalogue of Women* seems to show quite as well as it shows determined local differentiation is a desire to be part of a whole. That desire, what is more, is to be found right back in the earliest of Greek literature, since it is the coming together of all Greeks to defend Menelaus' prior claim to Helen, the episode with was the climax of Hesiod's *Catalogue*, which provides the basis for the story of the *Iliad*, and it is the parade of *polis* contingents side by side that is so clearly flagged up by that other catalogue, the catalogue of ships in *Iliad'* Book Two. The motor for this desire to come together, however, is not common descent. That *Iliad* catalogue, and the *Iliad* in general, are not averse to observing genealogical relationships between individuals, but there is no sign of any concern to create any over-arching genealogy. Genealogy is used to explain relationships, or to justify the way in which one individual treats another, but it is not made the entry card for joining any club. The various contingents of people represented at Troy have been brought there because what their leading families have in common is that a member of them had been among the suitors of Helen whom Helen's father had made swear to defend the interests of whichever of them was successful in his bid for her hand. The common factor which brings all these Greeks together at Troy is not presented in ethnic terms of ancestry but by reference to common participation in an entirely artificially manufactured bond. It was a cultural, not a natural, event, contract not birth, which lay behind this extraordinary grouping.

So Early Iron Age Greece presents a situation where the divided landscape maps onto cultural and political division, and where those divisions can come to be thought of in terms of divided descent histories. However, there is some reason to think that the divided descent histories are secondary, not primary, that separate lines of descent from a common ancestry were wheeled in to explain political separation rather than themselves being primary. A closer look at the regional cultures and at the landscape arguably offers further support for this construction.

If we take the two Early Iron Age pottery cultures with which archaeologists are most familiar, Athenian and Corinthian, the temptation to map cultural boundaries onto political boundaries and political boundaries onto landscape division is strong. The territory of Attica is formed by the plains which surround the two great mountain ranges of Hymettos and Pendele, and is divided off from the northern land mass by the continuous chain of Parnes. Later myth history alleged that there had once been a number of separate political units in this geographical space, but archaeology has offered little support for those claims (cf. review in Hornblower 1991: 262–4). The strongest cultural indicators of separation within Attica come from the southern tip of the peninsula, and in particular from Thorikos, more or less cut off from the plains of Attica by mountains, and displaying distinct cultural choices well into the Archaic period – perhaps most markedly in pottery deposits which are dominated by Corinthian, rather than by Athenian, vessels (Devillers 1988). Some further support for such separation might be found in the curious phenomenon that the *genos* (priestly family) of the Salaminioi, plausibly a group which should be traced at least back into the Geometric period, has two branches, the Salaminioi of Sounion and the Salaminioi of the Seven Tribes. Those 'seven tribes' must be 'tribes' in the sense of the ten tribes created by Kleisthenes at the end of the sixth century, since the earlier Athenian division had been into four tribes, but the separateness of the Sounion branch of the *genos* must go back well before that date (Osborne 1994). Whether we can see separation of southern Attica in any further terms is uncertain; should we, in the early sixth century, see division and rivalry or close links when both at Sounion and in Athens over life-sized *kouroi* get erected? Does the use of *korai* as funerary markers in Attica only in southern Attica or its immediate northern fringe – the Berlin Standing Goddess, so called, and Phrasikleia from Merenda – mean this was a local southern Attic practice? If this meagre collection of pretty disputable cultural distinctions is the best we can do for cultural division within the Attic peninsula, the unity of landscape, politics and culture looks pretty strong.

So too for Corinth, a territory again in a sense united around a mountain, Acrocorinth, as well as separated by mountains from its neighbours. Here the distinctions between the assemblages found at different Corinthian sanctuaries seem to argue strongly in favour of, rather than against, unity of culture and politics (Osborne 2009: 89–92). That is, the sanctuary of Hera at Perachora and the sanctuary of Poseidon at Isthmia offer us assemblages with a very different range of votive objects, but the assemblages seem best interpreted as complementary, displaying the ways in which sanctuaries in different landscapes offered themselves to different ways of thinking about the world, rather than as rival complete takes on the world. Hera at Perachora is a good candidate for the sort of boundary marker which François de Polignac famously interpreted as both a sign of and a means of the establishment of political territories in the eighth century (de Polignac 1984, 1994). However, the relationship of the Perachora sanctuary with the Poseidon sanctuary at Isthmia suggests that to treat the political function of such sanctuaries as only boundary-marking would be to miss something much more important: these sanctuaries use the landscape to explore political and social relations, not least gender relations, within the political body (compare Morgan 1990: 230–2) on the sanctuaries at Emborio on Chios) – not, one suspects, according to some formally devised master plan, a sort of religious landscape gardening in which an eighth-century Capability Brown planted temples in places which enjoyed a particular social vista, but through processes of use, domination and differentiation which were themselves products of geographical position.

The unity of territory and cultural and political unit which can be constructed for Corinth and which is at best weakly challenged for Attica, however, fares distinctly less well when we look further afield. Take Boiotia. Boiotia is always a problem for classification. In various contexts the Boiotians acted together as early as the sixth century, but the different poleis were independent although from time to time they were formally confederated (Corsten 1999: 27–60). It is certainly possible to find features of the landscape which justify the division between poleis here, but only at the expense of having to admit that there are even more prominent landscape divisions which are invested with no political significance. Nor is this simply a way of explaining why it is that the Boiotians have a common identity, why they constitute an *ethnos*, despite political divisions whereas e.g. Corinth, Megara and Sicyon do not unite to form any larger group, despite much that is common to these neighbouring *poleis* culturally. For not only does geography not mark e.g. Thebes off from Haliartos by anything more than the slightest of physical impediments at the north end of the Taeneric plain, but nor is the impediment that separates e.g. Khaironeia from the cities of Phokis any more significant (McInerney 1999: 60–1). The investment of geography with political significance – or equally the deprivation of geography of political significance (e.g. in terms of the incorporation of the geographically markedly separate coastal plains on the Corinthian gulf into the territories of Boiotian *poleis*) looks close to being arbitrary. How far it was not arbitrary but cultural is hard to determine. Modern scholars are in the habit of simply talking about 'Boiotian' pottery, asking no further questions, but the extent to which there was a uniform ceramic culture to the whole of Boiotia remains in need of further investigation. Kilinski, in his standard study of the Archaic pottery both outlines the evidence for production centres near Koroneia, in the north, at Thebes, in the centre, and Tanagra in the south-east, and notes the absence of communication between those centres:

> The abrupt and staggered evolution of the painted style suggests that the vase painters were more often attuned to external influences from other vase painting schools than they were aware of – or at least interested in – each other's handiwork. This lack of uniformity and fluid development is symptomatic of contemporary workshops scattered over different Boiotian centres and responding to select imported stimuli. (Kilinski 1990: 59). Nor is that pattern of diversity limited to the archaic period: a similar pattern has been found in Boiotian tombstones (Fraser and Ronne 1957: 35).

That political boundaries do not always correspond to cultural boundaries can be demonstrated by taking one striking case: Sparta and Tegea. Sparta's material cultural history is in many ways strikingly separate from the material cultural history of other Greek cities and regions. I've commented in another place on the way in which Sparta bucks the trend elsewhere for the seventh century to be relatively materially impoverished, in quantitative if not qualitative terms, by comparison with the eighth.

The surprising presence in Sparta, alone of all places in the Aegean except Ionia, of an ivory carving 'industry' is one sign of this (Carter 1984). Another, on the face of it, is the extraordinary tradition of lead votives revealed by the Artemis Orthia excavations – more than 100,000 lead votives, the great bulk of them dating to between 700 and 500 BC (Dawkins 1929). However, it is precisely those votives which nicely show the failure of cultural traits neatly to follow political and what one might expect also to be ethnic boundaries. For the one other place which turns out to produce very significant numbers of lead figurines is the sanctuary of Athena Alea at Tegea (Voyatzis 1990). Not only is this a city separated from Sparta by marked landscape features, as cycling from Tegea to Sparta once demonstrated to me, but Tegea is an Arcadian city, belonging to an *ethnos* which will claim, like Athens, to be autochthonous.

It is not just this claim to autochthony that is important, but the actual facts about Arcadian descent. We do not know how the Arcadians came to be resident in the central Peloponnese, but their language notoriously displays peculiar linguistic forms which have links with Cyprus so close that scholars have termed the dialect 'Arcado-Cypriot'. There are dialect features which Arcadian of the Classical period does share with other Greek dialects, including Attic-Ionic, Lesbian, and West Greek (a family of dialects that includes the Doric dialects of which Laconian is one), but there is also a core of features shared only with Cypriot, including the spelling of such basic words as the words for 'in', 'towards' and 'and', and the case taken by nouns following the preposition 'from' (Buck 1955: 144–5). All these features shared by dialects found in two physically separated areas suggest that the Arcadians and Cypriots are likely to have shared ancestors. When the Tegeans adopt a cultural practice from Sparta, therefore, they are not only adopting a cultural practice from a city with which they did not claim to share descent, but from a city with which they in fact had no deep historic ties.

The existence of a common cultural feature in two *poleis* that are, after all, neighbours might, for all that, seem unsurprising and unable to bear much significance. After all, Arcadian inscriptions of the archaic period show script features which are in different cases identical to the script of Elis and of Sparta, as well as, in other cases, showing particular letter forms contaminated by contact with nearby non-Arcadian cities (Jeffery 1961/1990: 208). What makes it worth dwelling on the lead votives in this context is the tradition regarding the political relations between Sparta and Tegea handed down for us by Herodotos, writing in the last quarter of the fifth century BC. According to Herodotos (1.66–8) Sparta had made a number of attempts to conquer Tegea, with a view to political subordination and reducing the Tegeans to the position of slaves, that is making them like the Messenians. Those attempts were unsuccessful, and Sparta finally achieved some sort of political control over Tegea when she gave up attempts at conquest and instead came to stress what Sparta and Tegea had in common, expressing that claim in terms of common interest in the figure of Orestes, son of Agamemnon and therefore nephew of Sparta's Menelaus, whose bones were supposedly excavated at Tegea. What lies behind these stories interests paleontologists (Mayor 2000), but my interest is merely in the existence of this story. Whatever the instrumental role of identifying some particular old bones as those of Orestes had been in the formation of the political ties which made Tegea enter a diplomatic agreement with Sparta to have the same friends and enemies (on this, Osborne 2009: 271–4, with references), it was convenient to the Spartans, and probably to both sides, that they made their common link to Orestes the basis for a political relationship. However, this claim is not a claim about descent, but a claim about past politics. And it is unlikely in the extreme that it is because of this claim that Tegeans come to share the peculiar cultural practice of dedicating lead votives. Rather, the shared myth becomes the means by which sharing common cultural practice can be converted into a political bond.

What I want to draw out of these reflections on landscape, ethnicity and the *polis* is the degree to which both landscape and ethnicity can be means to achieve political ends which are otherwise desirable. That is, for all that mountains offer convenient divisions and plains convenient means of communication, that a particular mountain comes to be a political barrier or a particular valley or plain an undivided political unit is not in the end determined by the landscape. A landscape that produces clearly separate areas can be, as in Corinth, a way of thinking about the different parts of society rather than a way of ensuring that there are several politically separate societies. Common cultural features no doubt help to make a presumptive case for sharing other aspects of life also, but the culturally distinct practices of a Thorikos almost certainly were found despite political unity, and the culturally common practices of Tegea and Sparta almost certainly prevailed while the cities were politically opposed and did not have to await political accommodation.

Ethnicity plays a part that is at best secondary and in most cases completely negligible. Athenian claims to autochthony cannot be traced back beyond the fifth century BC. When in 451/450 the Athenians passed a law stipulating that in future no one should be an Athenian citizen who did not have both a father and a mother who were of Athenian descent, they were imposing, for reasons which scholars still debate, a requirement which had not previously prevailed (Osborne 1997). Intermarriage between men from different cities was common in the Archaic period: the Kleisthenes who moved the reforms that created the democratic constitution in late sixth-century Athens was named after a maternal grandfather who had been tyrant of Sikyon. In order to find a husband for his daughter, Kleisthenes of Sikyon had made an announcement at the Olympic games and attracted suitors from all over Greece, including the cities of Sybaris and Siris in Italy and Aetolia and Molossia in northwestern Greece (Herodotos 6.126–31). Athens had no distinct cultural links with Sikyon at the time of the marriage of Kleisthenes' daughter, but Herodotos can think it plausible that the Athenian Kleisthenes was influenced by his grandfather's politics. A family line formed in this way in no way compromised the Athenian Kleisthenes' 'Athenianness'. The restriction of citizenship in the fifth century to those with two Athenian parents was not about securing ethnic identity, but about maintaining an unbreachable political distinction from the members of the cities which the Athenians ruled in what has become known as the 'Athenian empire'.

Cities found all sorts of common interests that caused them, temporarily or over long periods, to co-operate, but city particularism was strong. Cities did join together permanently in acts of synoikism still in the classical period, but such synoikisms were generally local and in the face of powerful neighbours (Moggi 1976). They did not result in the formation of 'ethnic groups'. Indeed it is notable that none of the various 'ethnic' federations (Boiotian, Arcadian, Achaean) ever led to the formation of a single ethnic super-state, and most ended by breaking down into completely independent units, sometimes more than once. Stories of a common interest in a mythological personage were just one means of persuading a city into a temporary alliance; as in the case of Orestes at Sparta and Tegea, such links could serve quite as well to justify political alliance as did elaborate genealogical affiliation. Like genealogical affiliation, the links formed by these common interests lasted only as long as the common interest served a political purpose. That Khaironeia ends up as part of Boiotia rather than part of Phokis is arguably determined as much by politics as by geography, and determined least of all by ethnicity. Pausanias tells the story that the principal cult at Khaironeia was the cult of the staff of Agamemnon (Pausanias 9.40.5–6). This staff was said to have been found, along with some gold, exactly at the boundary between Khaironeia and its Phokian neighbour of Panopeus. The Panopeans took the gold, the Khaironeians the staff. Pausanias says he is sure that it was brought to Phokis by Agamemnon's daughter Elektra. More was clearly going on with regard to this relic and its history than Pausanias either discovered or is concerned to tell, with the Khaironeians characterizing their neighbours by the choice they claim them to have made. However, what is striking is that this relic is not an object that secures Khaironeia's *Boiotian* identity, but rather one that links it in to the figure who stands for the united Greek expedition against Troy. As with the bones of Orestes, it is figures who cannot be claimed easily by a particular *ethnos* that often proved politically the greatest use.

In the Hellenistic period, as recent work by Olivier Curty (1995) and Christopher Jones (1999) has served to stress, claims to ancestral kinship were repeatedly made the basis on which one city approached another to ask for political support or financial assistance. One way of interpreting this is that in the final analysis the ethnic identity based on common descent was basic to city identity in Greece. However, that seems to me to be precisely wrong. What a city that laid claim to a shared past was doing was not claiming that blood required a city to make common cause. Rather it was saying that it wanted to consider itself linked to that other city, conveying by its request a tacit recognition of that other city as powerful and at the same time offering to form a potentially reciprocal tie that would justify future exchange. Any excuse would do, and quite different excuses could be used in approaching different cities. The exercise had nothing to do with ethnicity – it worked as well to tie Aphrodisias to Rome as to tie one Greek city to another (Reynolds 1982). Just as landscape was a resource, which could be variously exploited or ignored, so too common descent was a resource, affirmed or ignored at will by communities who continually constructed and reconstructed their identity as local social and political needs required. Both the old fashioned primacy of geography in shaping the Greek political world and the more recent obsession with constructions of ethnicity (and indeed of social memory, but that's another argument) need to be resisted if we are properly to understand how communities determine, and continually redetermine, their cultural and political identities.

Ionians and Carians in the Mycale: the Discovery of Carian Melia and the Archaic Panionion

Hans Lohmann

Keywords: Mycale; survey; sanctuary; Greek; architecture

Up-to-date concepts of ethnicity and ethnogenesis increasingly gain in importance even in an historical discipline like archaeology. The recent discovery of the so-called Panionion, the central sanctuary of the age-old Ionian League, allegedly dating back to the time before the Trojan war, sheds new light on the ethnogenesis of the Ionian tribe and provides glimpses of evidence how the ethnic identity of the Ionians developed. In a famous passage concerning the Panionion, Herodotos (1. 143) mocks the 12 Ionian *poleis* united in the league. They denied other Ionians access to the cult at the Panionion by asserting, that only they are 'true' Ionians, whereas in the historian's opinion they were a mixed group of immigrants from different parts of Greece. This critique fits astonishingly with modern concepts of ethnogenesis and ethnicity as developed by social sciences. The case of the Panionion might, therefore, serve as a case study for ethnicity of a cultural self-construct by human groups. It is one of those cases in which the members of a an ethnic community claim to be 'a named human population with myths of common ancestry, shared historical memories, and one or more common elements of culture, including an association with a homeland, and some degree of solidarity, at least among the élites' (Smith 1999: 13). The relationship between the indigenous Carian population of western Asia Minor and the ethnically mixed immigrants who were named and later named themselves as 'Ionians' is characterized by a high degree of ethnocentrism on the side of the Ionians. Ethnocentrism implies the tendency to look at other ethnic groups from the perspective of one's own culture and to downgrade them. In the eyes of the Greeks, the Carians were simply 'barbarophones' – i.e. bafflegab speaking people. Carians and Greek immigrants were evidently competing for the common goals of power and territory. This competition was driven, as Bobo and Hutchings (1996) put it, by self-interest and hostility, and resulted in conflict – the *Meliakos Polemos*, which ended with the destruction of the Carian '*polis*' of Melia. The archaeological discoveries mentioned above make clear that this happened as late as the beginning of the sixth century BC. Carians and Ionians differed in terms of material culture, settlement patterns, and land use. While the

Carians willingly adopted Greek pottery, which they imported in large quantities and also tried to copy to some extant, Ionian settlements were situated exclusively on the coast, while the Carians preferred mountains and high places. It also seems, that the Ionians were to a greater extent engaged in agriculture and trade while the Carians, due to the potential of the landscape, were more engaged in breeding animals, mostly sheep and goat, but evidently also cattle. The discovery and excavation of Melia and the Archaic Panionion in the Mycale mountain range between 2005 and 2007, therefore, provides a factual background against which the identity endowing myth of the common ancestry of the Ionian tribe and its age-old devotion to the cult of Poseidon Helikonios can be tested.

North of the Milesian and Latmian gulf, Mount Mycale, the present Dilek Dağları in the province of Aydın, rises up to 1250 metres above sea level, in this way forming a natural boundary between the northern and southern territories of Ionia. Between the modern town of Söke and Cape Dip Burun (ancient Trogilion), the Mycale extends for more than 30 kilometres from east to west. Its ridge, 'Mycale's airy summit' in the words of Homer (*Iliad* 2.268), is slightly nearer to its southern foot, making the slopes less steep in the north, whereas those in the south are often extremely precipitous. In 2001, an extensive survey of ancient Mycale was started in the western half of the mountain range. In 2004, and with the kind permission of the General Directorate of Antiquities and Museums of Turkey, this work was continued in the eastern section which might be roughly described as situated between the town of Söke to the east and the villages of Güzelçamlı and Tuzburgazı to the northwest and southwest respectively (Lohmann 2003: 247–60, 2004: 251–64, 2006: 241–52; Lohmann *et al.* 2007: 59–178). The results of these surveys can be summarized as follows.

Apart from some level ground in Mycale's eastern region there is hardly any room for human settlement within the mountain range. The inhabitants have preferred instead the lower slopes and foothills. Little wonder, therefore, that in Byzantine times the Mycale, like the nearby Latmos (Beşparmak), served as a place of refuge. Several important Byzantine churches and monasteries have been known since the late nineteenth century: examples include Hagios Antonios on top of Dayıoğlou Tepe (900 metres above sea level; Wiegand and Schrader 1904: 487, fig. 603–5, Map II) and the famous Kurşunlu Manastır (Wiegand and Schrader 1904: 487; Wiegand 1970: 51) which was completely mapped for the first time during the current survey programme. Other complexes are less well preserved and in several instances no conclusion can be drawn as to whether a site should be interpreted as a large Byzantine farmstead or, because of their remote situation, whether some should be seen as monasteries.

The Byzantine period forms an important part of the cultural heritage of Mount Mycale because of the generally good state of preservation of its monuments. The Byzantine fortresses at Atburgazı (Müller-Wiener 1961: 44ff., fig. 9 left) and Akçakonak (Gümelez kale; Müller-Wiener 1961: 58, fig. 12 left) in the foothills of the southern slopes of the mountain range were mapped, and the large Byzantine fortress of Fındıklı Kale (Müller-Wiener 1961: 62, fig. 14), high above modern Davutlar, intensively surveyed. From the enormous amount of pottery visible in holes made by occasional illegal excavations, as well as from the huge cistern in the centre, it is obvious that Fındıklı Kale was more than simply a place of refuge. It might well have been the residence of the local dynast Sabas Asidénos, who established himself in the Mycale during the reign of the Latins (AD 1204–61; Orgels 1935: 72, note 1).

At the other extreme of the time scale, prehistoric sites are extremely rare. In 2002, numerous obsidian flakes and blades were observed together with a great number of Late Chalcolithic to Middle Bronze Age pottery sherds on the shore of the beautiful bay at the westernmost tip of Mycale (Classical Glauke limen: Thucydides 8.79.2; cf. Lohmann 2004: 251–64; for the Glauke limen, see Böhne 2005: 191–5). By far the largest prehistoric site was found in 2004 near the southeastern corner of Mycale at Yenidoğan, a few kilometres southwest of Söke. On top of the hill next to a water cistern, masses of Middle and Late Bronze Age pottery sherds were found mixed with shells of *cerastoderma edule* which seems to indicate that, during the second half of the second millennium BC, the shoreline was still not far away. The pottery had close relations with the pottery of the Arzawa people in the area north of the Latmian gulf. Surprisingly though, no Mycenaean imports have been found. Furthermore, since no Early Iron Age or Protogeometric pottery turned up in this location, the prehistoric settlement at Yenidoğan evidently must have been abandoned before the Greeks appeared. The site of Archaic Priene, which still has not been found, cannot be far away. However, it lies in the former foothills of Mycale, buried under the enormous mass of alluvium brought in by the river Menderes since ancient times.

This brings us to the problems of historical topography. From its very beginning the survey in the Mycale has contributed considerably to our knowledge of the historical landscape of southern Ionia (for full discussion, see Lohmann 2005b: 163–272). Many old questions have been answered, others have remained open, and, of course, new ones have come to light. During the Classical period, the only ancient town of some importance was Priene which was refounded on the southern slopes of the Mycale in the late Classical period at about 350 BC (for Priene, see Koenigs and Rumscheid 1998, with ample bibliography). The little *polis* of Thebai near the modern village of Doğanbey in the southwestern part of Mycale and its surroundings were surveyed and mapped during the first campaigns of the survey (Müller 1997: 618, fig. 16, 619, fig. 17, 623, 627; Lohmann 2002: 294, 2003: 247–60, 2004: 251–64, 2005b: 247, fig. 21, under the heading of Thebai). From the pottery collected on the surface and the abundant exposures made by illicit digging, it became obvious, that Thebai was founded in the late fifth century BC and was already abandoned by the second.

A well-preserved fortification of the early seventh century BC surrounds the top of Kale Tepe west of Güzelçamlı, measuring 205 metres from east to west and about 95 metres from north to south. Its date has been established by Subgeometric pottery found in a trial trench near the gate by Kleiner and Hommel (Kleiner *et al.* 1967: 133ff.; for the date, cf. also Cook 1969: 717). The site is today heavily overgrown and the trial trenches dug fifty years ago are difficult to discern. Nevertheless, there can be little uncertainty about this type of fortification: close parallels in building technique and plan are known in Caria, for instance on Zeytin Dağ close to the Carian town of Latmos (Peschlow-Bindokat 1989: 79–83, 1996a: 22s, fig. 19, 21, 1996b: 212, fig. 2), but also at Hydai near Mylasa, the modern town of Milas (Rumscheid 1998: 389), or on the Halikarnassos peninsula. Therefore the circuit wall on Kale Tepe is clear evidence of Carian presence in the Mycale. Since Protogeometric pottery was also found in sites that later never became an Ionian *polis*, it seems that, from the very beginning of the so-called Ionian migration, the indigenous Carian population established relations of trade and exchange with the immigrants and started to imitate their pottery. For example, the Protogeometric tombs (cf. Kleiner *et al.* 1967: 161ff., fig. 102–117, Pl. 7–9, IX) at the foot of the Kale Tepe, do not necessarily indicate an early Greek or 'Ionian' settlement. Indeed, Huxley (1966: 24) assumed that the people buried in these tombs might have been Carians.

Already at the beginning of the twentieth century the renowned philologist U. von Wilamowitz-Moellendorff (1906: 43) correctly identified the fortification on Kale Tepe with the *karion phrourion* (Carian fortress), mentioned no less than eighteen times in the inscription no. 37 from Priene (Hiller von Gaertringen 1906: 37ff., no. 37, lines 9, 23. 53, 66, 73, 75, 81, 98–99, 101, 103–5, 108–109, 123, 129, 133; Lohmann 2005a: 79s., 2005b: 202s., fig. 8–9 under the heading of Karion). The inscription, one of the most important documents as far as the historical topography and the history of Mount Mycale is concerned, was set up at the beginning of the second century BC to mark an end to the age-old conflict between Samos and Priene about the *chora* of Melia after the *Meliakos polemos* of the seventh century BC.

In 1967, G. Kleiner and P. Hommel abandoned this hypothesis, by calling the place Melie instead, following other inscriptional evidence, a spelling which developed from the original Melia (Μελία) as shown by Hekataios of Miletos. (Hiller von Gaertringen 1906: 37ff., no. 37.; for this inscription, cf. also Curty 1989: 21–35; Franco 1993: 75ff., 162ff., with bibliography). From the ancient written sources we learn, that Melia was an ancient town or settlement destroyed by the allied forces of the Ionians in the so-called Meliakos Polemos before the middle of the seventh century BC. The origin of this war is reported by Vitruvius (4.85), writing that the Ionians formed a coalition against Melia '*ob adrogantiam civium*'. The translation of the Latin term '*adrogantia*' by the English term 'arrogance' does not capture the correct meaning. As K. Tausend has pointed out, '*adrogantia*' is equivalent to the Greek term '*hybris*' which has always been the traditional accusation in religious wars (Tausend 1992: 73).

Exploratory trenches within the ring wall of Kale Tepe dug by Kleiner and Hommel in the 1950s produced no evidence of a settlement. Only a single apsidal house was found (Kleiner *et al.* 1967: 166, fig. 62), which did not in itself prove the existence of a town. A Greek dedicatory inscription (Hommel, in Kleiner *et al.* 1967: 127ff., fig. 68–70, first half of sixth century BC) at the main gate only shows that the Greeks were in possession of the site in the second half of the sixth century BC. This is neither surprising nor does it lend support to the identification of the site as Melia.

Since Melia was neither small nor insignificant, the ring wall on Kale Tepe could not, in any way, be taken to represent the important site of ancient Melia. Indeed, it took a whole coalition of several Ionian cities to overcome it. Its vast territory extended from the westernmost tip of Mycale as far as Marathesion (Lohmann 2005b: 214, fig. 10, 16–7, under the heading of Marathesion) south to modern Kuşadası. Even in Hellenistic times, the island of Samos and the city of Priene were still debating the division of the hinterland of Melia, as we learn from the Priene inscription no. 37 already mentioned. Immediately after the *Meliakos Polemos*, the chora of Melia was divided among the victorious parties of Samos, Miletus, Priene and Ephesos. The conclusion might be that these four *poleis* formed the original Ionian League, and that other *poleis* entered it later. The coast north of Mount Mycale was divided between Samos and Priene yet the issue still caused endless quarrels between the two cities into Hellenistic times. Samos held the western part of Mycale between Cape Dip Burnu (ancient Trogilion) to the west and modern Güzelçamlı to the east, but also the northernmost part of the former Karaova around Anaia (for details, see Lohmann 2005b: 174ff., under the heading of Anaeitis Chora and 176ff., under the heading of Anaia). A large piece of land held by Priene stretched north between these two parts of the Samian *peraia*. Was this persistent trouble the reason why during the survey, with one exception, no significant remains of Classical and Hellenistic farmhouses were found in the surroundings of Güzelçamlı and Davutlar? The one exceptional farmhouse is the so-called 'Kastell' (see Kleiner *et al.* 1967, 37ff. fig. 15–19, 63ff. fig. 26–33) which is clearly a Hellenistic farmhouse with a tower. Since the Early Classical period this type of farmhouse has been very common in Greece, especially in Attica and in the Megarid, and on the Greek islands. They spread into Caria during the fourth century BC, but so far the type seems to be rare in Ionia. Only a few examples are known. Another was found during the campaign on top of a hill some 500 metres west of Priene, thanks to a suggestion by W. Raeck.

The important role of the Ionian League for the ethnogenesis of the Ionian tribe and the ethnic identity of the Ionians was already noted by Herodotos (1.143), and was stressed by Wilamowitz-Moellendorff and others in the early twentieth century. However, the Ionian League has been largely neglected for some time, for reasons we will hope to explain below. The Panionion, a sanctuary of Poseidon Helikonios, was always considered the cult centre of the Ionian League (cf. Lohmann 2005b: 234., under the heading of Panionion). Already Homer (*Iliad* 20.403) alluded to the cult of Poseidon Helikonios, comparing the groaning of a hero killed by Achilles with the groaning of the bull killed as an offering to Poseidon Helikonios. As a point of difference from the typical Greek sacrifice, in which much care was taken that the animal willingly walked to the altar, bending its head to signal its submission, in the cult of Poseidon Helikonios young men dragged the bull to the altar forcibly; and the more the animal groaned and roared the better was considered the omen.

Homer, it has to be said, mentioned neither the Ionians nor the Panionion. This has in later times given support to the theory that the Ionian League was not founded prior to the seventh century BC, much less one year before the Trojan war, as asserted on the Marmor Parium (IG XII.5.444), the Early Hellenistic marble chronicle from the island of Paros (Meister 1999: 938).

Where did this sacrifice to Poseidon Helikonios take place? As early as 1673 AD Dr. Pickering and J. Saltier found an inscription (Hiller von Gaertringen 1906: 122, no. 139; for Dr. Pickering, i.e. Picretin, and J. Saltier, see Pontremoli and Haussoullier 1904: 18) concerning the Panionium at the Byzantine church of Panagia situated between the village of Güzelçamlı at the northern foot of Mount Mycale and a low hill to the east of that village traditionally called Prophitis Elias. In 1900, Th. Wiegand, the first excavator of Priene and Miletus, located the Panionion on that hill (Wiegand and Schrader 1904: 24ff.). On top of it remains of an altar are preserved and a semi-circular theatre cavea was visible in the western flank of the hill. No excavations were carried out until the late 1950s when G. Kleiner and P. Hommel took a fresh interest in the site, which had received the new name of Otomatik Tepe. Shortly after their excavation they published an extensive report giving full details (Kleiner *et al.* 1967: 18–37). Irrespective of the fact that they found no Archaic material neither on the spot itself nor within its surroundings they had no hesitation in identifying it as the original 'Panionion', the central cult place of the Ionian League.

J. M. Cook in his review of their publication summed up the disappointment with such meagre results in writing 'There was every reason to expect new light on early Ionic history' (Cook 1969: 717). But should we really discard an eminent ancient author of Herodotos' standing, simply because some archaeologists did not find what they had expected to find? Strangely enough, the results of that excavation of 1956 were never subjected to a comprehensive critique despite the fact that there was sufficient ground for concern.

First, the Archaic age of the altar on top of the Otomatik Tepe could well be called into question since no architectural fragments of the Archaic period were found. The dowels used for the construction of the altar are untypical of the Archaic period. Secondly, the half-circle cavea of the theatre is a construction which was first conceived for the theatre of Dionysus at Athens, built under the archonship of Lycourgos around the middle of the fourth century BC., and from there spread all over the Greek world (Junker 2004: 10ff., esp. 11, with bibliography). The theatre at Güzelçamlı cannot be supposed to be earlier. As W. Müller-Wiener has pointed out (Kleiner *et al.* 1967: 36), its measurements resemble closely the theatre at Priene which has been dated around 300 BC by A. von Gerkan (1921: 61ff., esp. 62 – about 300 BC at the latest; Rumscheid and Koenigs 1998: 161ff., esp. 173). More importantly, only a handful of Archaic sherds was found at Otomatik tepe; while elsewhere excavations of Archaic Greek sanctuaries have consistently yielded vast quantities of pottery. Moreover, also the surroundings of the Otomatik Tepe, which had been thoroughly cleared and investigated by large groups of Turkish workers, did not yield a single piece of Archaic pottery.

From the results of the survey of the site in 2004, I wish to offer another explanation of these finds: the so-called 'Panionion' in Güzelçamlı was never used and it was left unfinished. Looking more closely at the so-called *bouleuterion* it can quickly be discerned that the cutting of the rock within the *koilon* or cavea was never finished. In many places the underlying rocks are even today protruding into the seat rows (cf. esp. Kleiner *et al.* 1967: 28ff., fig. 11–4). Furthermore large gaps, clefts and fissures interrupt the rows and wait to be covered with nicely worked marble seats which were, however, never set up. It seems highly improbable that the ambassadors of the twelve Ionian cities were forced to sit on natural rock without any properly fashioned seats. Looking at the present state of the place it seems almost unbelievable that in the course of more than fifty years since Kleiner and Hommel's publication nobody has realized that the sanctuary at Güzelçamlı was still under construction when it was abandoned.

A second inscription of the second half of the fourth century BC found by Kleiner and Hommel in the former mosque of Güzelçamlı clearly speaks of a 'refoundation' of the Panionion and of the regulation of the financial contributions of the members of the Ionian League (Kleiner *et al.* 1967: 45ff.). The attempt to renew the cult of Poseidon Helikonios and the festival of the Panionia in the middle of the fourth century BC may well have been in connection with the re-foundation of the town of Priene. A couple of Hellenistic honorific decrees granting free meals to the recipients of the honour 'in the Prytaneion and the Panionion' were found exclusively in Priene itself. As far as the Panionion is concerned they belong to a type of unrealizable honour or the cult had already been transferred to Priene itself by that time. Diodorus (15.49) provided important evidence of the refoundation of the Panionion: 'Formerly the Panionion was in a lonesome place, later they re-founded it in the neighbourhood of Ephesus'. His mention of Ephesus as a point of reference for his Roman audience should not detract from the fact that he explicitly wrote of two Panionia, an older and a younger one. Herodotos (1.148) noted in a famous, frequently quoted, passage that the Panionion was a holy place in the Mycale, extending or protruding to the north, a formula which in no way could be applied to the topographical situation existing at Otomatik Tepe near Güzelçamlı.

In short, these critical assessments imply that the location of the site of Archaic Melia and of the Archaic Panionion were still in question. However, during the survey campaign of 2004, we found a site two kilometres east of the Byzantine fortification of Fındıklı Kale which, despite its enormous size and its marvellous state of preservation, had been completely unknown to archaeologists. This site not only fulfills all the requirements of a Carian site called Melia, but also exactly fits the wording of Herodotos (1.148) for the Archaic Panionion. The situation is as follows: on the southwestern slope of Çatallar Tepe, at 780 metres a.s.l., some walls of up to 3 metres wide form a huge triangle, orientated with its tip to the north and its base to the south, in total covering a space of more than 5 hectares.

The southern wall had almost completely collapsed. There were neither towers nor bastions. The main gate was difficult to make out among the huge mass of collapsed stones. But two wall-ends could be seen to overlap for a couple of metres, thereby forming a gate characteristic of fortifications of the seventh and sixth centuries BC. The southern wall connects to separately walled enclosures on higher elevations to the southwest and the northeast. The walls were built in the usual manner with two outer surfaces which contained a fill of rubble and mud in between, but the stones are unworked, as is the underlying rock; the stones are more thoroughly worked only in special places, like the small gate in the northeast circuit. The entire manner of construction suggests Carian rather than Greek workmanship. We are obviously dealing with another Carian fortification which, however, with exception of its northeastern acropolis remained unfinished. The discovery of this Carian site, formerly completely unknown, nicely fits with the lines in Homer (*Iliad* 2.867ff.), where, in enumerating the allies of the Trojans, he mentions the Carians holding the Phthiron Oros (Mount Grium), the Maiandros, Miletus and 'Mycale's airy summit'.

In 2005, an intensive survey of the area within the fortification produced numerous traces of poorly preserved houses as well as thousands of fragments of early Archaic pottery of the second half of seventh century BC, which, where datable, were, however, Greek. This clearly indicates that the area was densely occupied during that period. The situation, therefore, differs strongly from that on Kale Tepe where no traces of a settlement were ever observed. Obviously the former identification of the site by Wiegand and Wilamowitz-Moellendorff as 'Karion phrourion' indicated by the inscription Priene no. 37 is proven correct, although its identification with the Archaic town of Melia by Kleiner and Hommel has to be rejected (Kleiner *et al.* 1967: 78–124).

Moreover, there were even better discoveries. Within the fortification on the south-western slope of Mount Çatallar, the remains of an Archaic temple were discovered (Lohmann 2005a: 57–91, pl. 3–8, 2006: 241–52, fig. 1–10). Unfortunately illicit digging, partly by heavy earth-moving machinery, had already done extensive damage to the temple site in the 1980s. Nevertheless, in 2005, during the first phase of a rescue excavation, we managed to uncover more than 50 per cent of the temple ruin. Due to the impressive results of the first campaign, the General Directorate of Antiquities and Museums was convinced of the necessity of two more campaigns of rescue excavation of the Archaic temple in 2006 and 2007. During these campaigns we succeeded in excavating the other 50 per cent of the temple, that is its southern half.

The results of the three campaigns may be summarized as follows: The orientation of the temple is due east (Fig. 4.1). Its length – measured on the northern wall between the northwest corner and the anta in the northeast – was 28.8 metres which is close to 100 feet. The temple, therefore, is a true *hekatompedos*. It has three sections: the *pronaos*, of 8.65 metres with eight columns in two rows of four, an almost square *naos* or cella of 8.05 metres to 7.57 metres with two columns in the transverse axis of the room and a Westroom measuring 10.4 metres in length with three columns in the longitudinal axis. In this way, the temple had 13 interior columns, but neither a prostyle front nor a *peristasis*, nor even a continuous step in front of the *pronaos*. The span of the column axes in the *pronaos* was only 2.16 metres, and the alignment of the columns was, therefore, extremely narrow. All parts of the marble architectural elements were heavily affected by fire. The temple walls were made of pounded clay, rather than of adobe, over stone

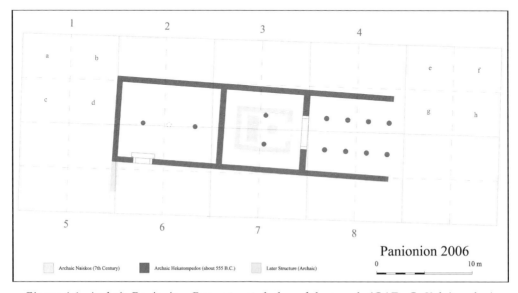

Figure 4.1. Archaic Panionion. Reconstructed plan of the temple (CAD: G. Kalaitzoglou).

foundations of approximately 1.5 metres height. In relation to the height of the entire building of 6 metres they seem rather weak, since their width measured no more than 0.59 metres. During the campaigns of 2005 and 2006, a total of 560 architectural fragments have been catalogued, drawn and photographed, particularly during the second campaign.

The walls of the pronaos ended with huge marble slabs, which resemble more a pilaster strip (German: *Lisene*) than a true anta, since they lack the typical characteristics of the fully developed anta, such as a capital above the anta and an anta foot.

The few fragments of the columns which were preserved were all unfinished (Fig. 4.2). The fragments of the columns display three different stages of treatment starting from completely smoothed drums, to a rather rough prepared surface, to those which are still bossed. Fragments of the latter were usually found in the western part of the temple. Several tools for working the marble were also identified in this location. Obviously the process of completion of the architectural elements started in the east and proceeded toward the west, but was not completed before the temple was destroyed by fire.

The lower edges of the drums were smoothed not fluted. This indicates that no fluting was intended. The lower diameter of the drums is approximately 0.54 metres, and the upper diameter 0.48 metres. It seems, therefore, that the columns became slightly narrower with increasing height. The height of the entire columns may have reached up to 6 metres. There were no dowels to fix the column drums to each other or to the marble slabs of the stylobates, which all differ in size and shape.

From the exact mapping of the find spots of all the architectural fragments, it became obvious that fragments of Ionic capitals were exclusively found in the eastern sector of the excavation. No complete capital has been reconstructed so far. But from the few fragments preserved, we realised, that the capitals were of the so-called *torus* type, well

Figure 4.2. Archaic Panionion. Fragment of unfinished column, no. PA-S150 (Photo: H. Lohmann).

known from two Archaic capitals found at Didyma (Tuchelt 1991: fig. 58, 1–2). These capitals were also part of an architectural monument and can be defined as votive columns, since they were similarly not dowelled to the column drums. However, the

Ionic capitals of the temple on Mount Çatallar differed from them in one major respect: the volutes had not been carved, but were simply incised (Fig. 4.3). There were no bases but the columns were erected directly over the stylobates. Fragments of *tori* were also found. Their base measures 0.48 metres across. Since the lower diameter of the columns is, as already stated, 0.54 metres, while their upper diameter was also 0.48 metres, it seems that the *tori* served as capitals in the *cella* and the Westroom, while the use of Ionic capitals was limited to the eight columns of the *pronaos*.

For the time being, no remains of architraves have been identified amongst the debris. They were presumably made of wood, like the architraves of the third Heraion at Samos, the so-called Rhoikos temple (Furtwängler 1984: 97–103) made convincingly clear that Rhoikos was the architect of the fourth Heraion, built by the tyrant Polykrates).

Figure 4.3. Archaic Panionion. Fragment of volute, no. PA-S182 (Photo: H. Büsing).

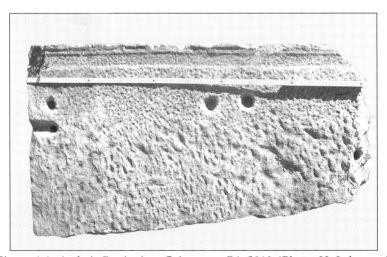

Figure 4.4. Archaic Panionion. Geison, no. PA-S012 (Photo: H. Lohmann).

The top layer of the pounded clay walls was formed by marble slabs, which protruded 0.3 metres from the wall (Fig. 4.4). Almost identical elements were found on the site of the Archaic temple of Dionysos of Yria at Naxos, where, however, the walls were seemingly made entirely of stone (Gruben 2001: 375–80, fig. 283; Ohnesorg 2005a: 135–52, with bibliography in note 1). These simple slabs are forerunners of the later *geison* and were fitted to each other by iron clamps, embedded in lead. Pairs of cylindrical holes every 0.6 metres served to fix the spars.

Generally speaking the overall appearance of the temple was extremely similar to that of the temple IV of Dionysos at Yria on Naxos dating to almost the same period. Like the temple at Yria the temple on Çatallar Tepe also had a wooden roof-truss, forming a ridged roof covered with roof tiles of the Corinthian type C2 according to the typology established by Wikander (Wikander 1988: 210s, fig. 4, 'C2'). The *stroteres* were 0.6 metres wide, which fits nicely with the distance of the spars. The length of the *stroteres* is unknown, since no complete *stroter* specimen was found, but it seems unlikely that it differed from the length of the *kalypteres* which is also 0.6 metres. The eaves were decorated with an interlace and the *kalypteres* at the edge of the roof with lionhead antefixes (Fig 4.5). The fixing of the

Figure 4.5. Archaic Panionion. Lionhead antefix, no. MYK 139-TK10 (Photo: H. Lohmann).

antefixes to the eaves is identical to Archaic roofs at Miletus (von Gerkan 1925: 23, fig. 16). However, ground-up mussel shells of the *cerastoderma edule* species which live in the Menderes delta were added to the clay of the rooftiles. This points strongly to the making of the roof in the Archaic town of Priene, which is today inaccessible under metres of alluvium in the Menderes plain south of the village of Akçakonak. An inscription, which might be interpreted as 'Prieneon', lends further support to this assumption (Fig. 4.6).

Unfortunately, some looted artefacts from the site have already found their way into the antiquities market. Three terracotta antefixes were donated in 1992 to the Metropolitan Museum of Art in New York by the widow of a Swiss dealer. The curator of the Metropolitan, Dr. Carlos Picón, is of the opinion that these pieces are of a mass-produced eastern Greek type and, in support of this abstruse assertion, points to antefixes from Kalabaktepe and from Didyma (Anon 2005: 10, fig. 13–4; for Milet, Kalabaktepe: von Gerkan 1925: 23ff., fig. 17, pl. IIA; Åkerström 1966: 103 pl., 53.1; for Didyma: Knackfuss 1941: pl. 223). However, as everybody will be immediately aware, these pieces are similar *to* but not identical *with* the antefixes in the Metropolitan Museum. By contrast it is indeed the case that the antefixes found at Çatallar Tepe *are* identical with those in the Metropolitan Museum and *are* made from the same moulds. A particular antefix design was always produced exclusively for a specific temple. To my knowledge, different Archaic buildings do not exist which are decorated with identical antefixes. Therefore, in accordance with the UNESCO-Convention of 14 November 1970 (Convention on the Means of Prohibiting and Preventing the Illicit Import, Export and Transfer of Ownership of Cultural Property), which has also been signed by the US government, the antefixes in the Metropolitan Museum can evidently be regarded as illegally exported cultural property of the Türkiye Cumhurriyet.

Let us now turn to the Westroom. The type of building with an eccentric door and a row of columns in the longitudinal axis of the room is well known as a *lesche*. The combination of a temple and a *lesche* in the same building is rare but not unique. The closest parallel is the late geometric temple of Apollo at Halieis in the Peloponnese (Mazarakis Ainian 1997: 162–4, fig. 243–5). The Westroom of the building was entered from the south through a huge marble doorframe. Not until the second campaign in 2006 was it evident that the door consisted of two elements: a lavishly marble doorframe integrated into the south wall of the Westroom and an inner threshold made from two marble blocks joined by two visible

PA 2c/d-42

0   5 cm

Figure 4.6. Archaic Panionion. Fragment of stroter with inscription ΠΡ]ΙΗΝΕ[ΩΝ.

iron cramps (Fig. 4.7). Visible cramps are but rarely used in Archaic architecture (cf. Ohnesorg 2005: 49, note 250). The outer threshold, which was reassembled from six fragments, lying scattered around on the surface, shows no signs of door hinges. The components of this doorframe are the most nicely worked architectural elements of the temple. With a length of 1.94 metres, a width of 0.6 metres and a height of 0.34 metres, it was the largest monolithic block discovered. Only the (not completely preserved) door lintel, which shows traces of intensive burning, equals it in size.

The door span measures 1.41 metres between the parastades (door jambs), although its height could not be ascertained. On the other hand, the centre distance between the two pans (horizontal beams) for the wooden wings of the inner threshold measures 2.21 metres. The wooden wings, therefore, when opened, displayed the full outer doorframe. This is not unusual in the Archaic architecture of the Cyclades.

It seems remarkable, however, also given the life span of the temple, that while on the one hand the interior threshold of the Westroom was not completely finished, on the other hand, the surface of the threshold displays different traces of use: The eastern block is more worn than the western. This points to the fact, that most of the time the eastern wing of the door was open, while the western wing was closed.

The find of one of the two upper door hinges is of special interest for everybody interested in Greek architecture. It consists of a thick cylindrical tube with an inner diameter of 12.5 centimetres and a long iron mandrel or spike protruding from the cylinder (Fig 4.8). The existence of such door hinges has always been proposed by architectural specialists, but this is the first ever found in the excavation of a Greek temple.

Figure 4.7. Archaic Panionion. Westroom. Interior door lintel with two visible cramps, no. PA-S520 and PA-S521 (Photo: H. Lohmann).

Within the Westroom the excavation produced clear evidence of the destruction of the building through fire (Fig. 4.9). The entire roof was laid out on the earthen floor, covered by the collapsed mud of the temple walls, partly burnt red by the fire. At an unknown interval after the fire, a severe earthquake shook the temple, which, by that time, was a mere heap of rubble. None of the columns were found lying on the temple floor which seems to indicate (combined with their damaged state) that they were exposed to the fire while still standing. This points to the fact, that the earthquake was not the cause of the fire.

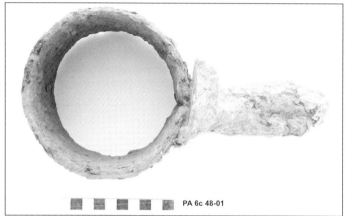

Figure 4.8. Archaic Panionion. Upper door hinge made from iron (inner diameter: 10.5 centimetres), no. PA 6c48-01 (Photo: K. Burgemeister).

Figure 4.9. Archaic Panionion. Westroom. Destruction level, quadrant PA 6b (Photo: H. Lohmann).

A poorly made wall was found in the last week of the second campaign. This wall was built against the southwestern corner of the temple and belongs to a room or small building which had been erected after the destruction of the temple, when parts of it still stood upright. It is the first architectural find within the temple area, which postdates its destruction. This discovery is of keen interest for the understanding the use of the structure after the fire, and merits thorough investigation.

Many symposium artefacts such as a wine sieve, drinking cups and ivory appliqués for beds, demonstrate the intended use of the Westroom as a lesche. Its walls were decorated with weapons. We found no less than seven spearheads, a *sauroter* and part of a bronze cuirass with little holes to fix it to a leather coat. It strongly resembles the cuirass worn by the Archaic statue of a warrior from Samos (with a later date of 520 BC, Boardman 1981: fig. 176). If the temple is, as I have argued elsewhere (Lohmann 2005a: 80ff.), the Archaic Panionion mentioned by Herodotos 1.148, we have here the assembly hall of the Ionian League.

The latest item found on the floor of the Westroom was a kylix, a drinking cup made by the well-known Attic potter and perhaps also vase painter Tleson dating to the middle of the sixth century BC (for Tleson, see Beazley 1956: 178ff., 688; Mommsen 2000: 777; Fig 4.10). This item dates the destruction of the temple. The roof of the temple was substantially finished shortly before its destruction, and the Westroom had evidently already been in use as a dining room and assembly hall. However, the final finish of the columns, as well as perhaps a floor made of stone slabs, was still missing. The construction of the temple was started in approximately 570/60 BC, which means that the temple, was in use for no more than 20 years or a generation at most.

If, as I uphold, the temple on Çatallar Tepe is indeed the Archaic Panionion, we should be able to find traces of an older cult, which became later the cult of the main god of the Ionian League and the Panionion. This is because the Greeks, after having attacked the Carian population of Melia and having defeated them in the *Meliakos Polemos*, continued the cult of Poseidon Helikonios in the Panionion, the central sanctuary of the twelve Ionian cities united in the Ionian League (for ample details, see Lohmann 2005a: 65ff.).

It was, therefore, not completely unexpected that we found the well preserved remains of an older *naiskos* of

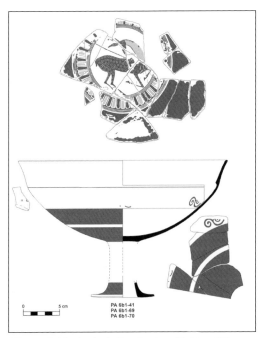

Figure 4.10. Archaic Panionion. Kylix of Tleson, c. 550 BC, from the destruction level of the Westroom (Drawing: G. Kalaitzoglou).

the seventh century BC underneath the cella of the Archaic temple, which – obviously for reasons of piety – had not been completely removed but was nicely preserved when the younger temple was built in 570/560 BC (Fig. 4.11). Blocks of yellow tuff which evidently belonged to the older phase had been re-used to some extent in the construction of the *hekatompedos*.

A fill below the floor of the cella consisted of red clay mixed with small stone chips produced when cutting the stones for the walls of the younger temple; it also contained many precious objects belonging to the older phase of the sanctuary. Some beautiful silver earrings are of a type which was also present in a late seventh century grave in the southeast necropolis on Samos, already excavated at the end of the nineteenth century and on the island of Chios (for Samos, Boehlau 1898: 46 pl. XV no. 13 (grave no. 45); Boehlau *et al.* 1996: 62, no. 45.8–12.; for Chios, Boardman 1967: 221s., no. 350, fig. 144 – from period IV of the harbour sanctuary, *c.* 630–600 BC). The statuette of a lion, carved from limestone, was also part of the votive offerings belonging to the *naiskos*. It was already damaged when it was buried beneath the threshold of the cella. A very similar lion was found at Salamis on Cyprus (Fourrier 2001: 43, pl. 3, no. 2 – inv. no. Sal. 1788) but was not necessarily made there. It should however, be pointed out that neither the offerings found in the *naiskos* nor in the younger *hekatompedos*, show any evidence of the strange sacrificial ritual mentioned in Homer's *Iliad* in which a bull

Figure 4.11. Archaic Panionion. Naiskos, seventh century BC, seen from north (Photo: H. Lohmann).

was dragged with brutal force to the altar by young men. However, votives found in Archaic sanctuaries rarely show any connection with the deities venerated in that particular sanctuary.

A group of two Siamese twin terracotta warriors (Fig 4.12) also belongs to the older phase. They were found at the foot of a *bathron* in the naiskos of the seventh century BC. They might represent a mythological group, in particular the siamese twins Aktorione-Molione, sons of Poseidon. They wear exactly the same type of helmet at Geryoneus fighting Herakles on a bronze plate from Samos dating to the second half of the seventh century BC (Pflug 1988: 37, fig. 12).

To sum up the rich finds of precious metal objects, as well as the pottery from the fill of the younger temple, allows a precise dating of the older *naiskos* to the period 650/600 BC. This fits exactly with the results of the intensive survey, which points to exactly the same time. The *hekatompedos* therefore, was erected within an older settlement which at the time was already lying in ruins.

Unfortunately, the temple has been seriously damaged by looting and illegal excavation. The southern wall of the *pronaos* have been completely bulldozed away. On the other hand, to my knowledge, there is no other temple of this period in the whole of Anatolia in a comparable state of preservation. In the strata untouched before excavation a number of precious objects were found, giving us a precise date for the construction both of the *naiskos* and of the later *hekatompedos* and for the destruction of the latter. This is of equally great relevance to the history of early Ionian architecture. The exact date of the temple gives us an important point of reference within the development of this architectural form. This is especially so since the temple combines monumental and pre-monumental elements in a highly unusual manner. Its walls of pounded clay which were erected over a solid base with two frontal faces made of stone, relate the edifice to older, pre-monumental buildings, while its size and representative appearance, as well as the use of large marble elements, link

Figure 4.12. Archaic Panionion. Group of two terracotta warriors, late seventh century BC, found at the foot of a bathron in the naiskos of the seventh century BC. (Photo: H. Lohmann).

it with the monumental architecture of Ionia. Only the columns and the *torus*-capitals are fully developed architectural elements while the antae are simple large stone slabs without any capitals or bases. The marble slabs on top of the walls are the precursors of the *geison* (cornice) of later temples; the architraves and the roof-trusses were made of wood, a fact which amply explains the serious damage done by the fire to the marble elements of the temple.

Given that the sanctuary at Emecik near Datça on the Knidian peninsula had erroneously been claimed as the Triopion by D. Berges (Berges and Tuna 1990: 19–35, 2001: 155–66; Berges 1995–6: 103–20; Berges and Attula 2000: 171–214; Bankel 2004: 100–13, esp. 109ff.), the central sanctuary of the Doric Pentapolis, the site at Çatallar tepe is the first Archaic sanctuary of an *amphictyonia* which has ever been excavated. The importance of the discovery of Melia and the Archaic Panionion as the central sanctuary of the Ionian League on Mount Çatallar for our understanding of the history of early Ionia and the Ionian League can, therefore, hardly be overestimated. In spite of the somewhat vague ancient traditions about the Meliakos Polemos it now seems clear that this war and the foundation of the Ionian League did not take place before the end of the seventh or the beginning of the sixth century BC. It is also evident at this time that Melia and the Panionion occupied the same topographical location as had been argued by U. von Wilamowitz-Moellendorff already in 1906. And the Austrian historian K. Tausend was right when he convincingly suggested that the *Meliakos Polemos* ought to be seen as a conflict between Greek colonists and the indigenous Carian population (Tausend 1992: 72; von Wilamowitz-Moellendorff 1906: 46, note 1 – 'Ein weiterer Schluss ist, dass das Panionion in oder bei Melia gelegen haben wird'). The Carians, who according to the already quoted passage in Homer (*Iliad* 2.868), were in the possession of Mount Mycale by the second millennium BC were expelled by that war. This might also explain why so far no typical Carian tombs and oval buildings have been found during the survey since these structures mostly belong to the sixth century BC when the Carian presence in the region had already come to an end.

To sum up in terms of the central theme of this volume, it becomes evident from the archaeological data, that the Ionian League was not founded before the Trojan war but at the end of the seventh or even in the beginnings of the sixth century BC. While Ionians and Carians clearly differed in terms of their material culture we might safely conclude that the fortified settlement at Çatallar Tepe was Carian, not Greek, while the temple erected one generation later within the ruins of Melia does not only represent an early stage of the Ionian architectural order, but should also be considered as a victory monument over the Carians and as such an important element of Ionic ethnocentrism towards them. The foundation of the Ionian League and the war, which led to the destruction of the only and largest Carian settlement within the Mycale mountain range, evidently played a major role for the ethnogenesis and the ethnic identity of the Ionians.

Acknowledgments

This contribution is an enlarged version of the paper I intended to give at the conference. I thank Dr G. Cifani and Dr S. Stoddart for inviting me to the conference and for their encouragement to publish it here. I also wish to express my warmest thanks to Dr. N. Kunisch (Oxford), J. Boswell (Llantwit Major) and the English editor (Simon Stoddart) for improving the English version of my text. The campaigns at the Panionion in 2005, 2006 and 2007 were carried out under the auspices of the Museum of Aydın and with funds provided by the Fritz Thyssen Foundation at Cologne. Participants were Prof. Dr H. Büsing (Bochum), Dipl. ing. K. Größchen (University of Applied Sciences, Wiesbaden), Dr. G. Kalaitzoglou (Essen), Dr. H. Marg (Mainz), Ö. Özgül, M.A, F. Hulek, and J. Hartung. The handling of the finds was done by Dr. G. Lüdorf, who was supported by the students A. Busching, K. Burgemeister, L. Kolla and J. Meyer. My colleagues Prof. Ing. H-S. Haase and Prof. Ing. A. Mischke, expert engineers of the University of Applied Sciences at Bochum, made a three dimensional scan of the temple and its predecessor by means of a RIEGL laser scanner. I am deeply indebted to D. Gansera (Cologne) for the marvellous aerial photos he took before, during and after the excavation of the temple by means of a kite. I wish to express my sincere thanks to all my German colleagues and collaborators and especially to Emin Yener, Director of the Museum of Aydın for all the magnificent help he gave us during the three campaigns, to Mehtap Ateş who acted as representative of the Ministry of Culture and Tourism and last not least to Handan Özkan, representative of the museum of Aydın, whose enormous help in all concerns should be acknowledged here.

5

Are there alternatives to 'Red-Figure Vase People'? Identity, multi-ethnicity and migration in Ancient Greece

John Bintliff

Keywords: Identity; ethnicity; Greece

Our image of the Ancient Greeks is formed by iconographic stereotypes – a white and beautiful Mediterranean race (Fig. 5.1). However our own experience of modern nations is rather one of considerable physical diversity and multiple ethnic origins. The third century BC traveller Herakleides Kritikos, journeying through parts of my own study region of Boeotia, central Greece, tells us that in Thebes he saw blonde people, and in Anthedon red-haired people. Pfister, who edited these fragments, argues that we should take this account as a genuine contemporary record of life in Boeotia, if spiced by citations from contemporary comedies and from folklore (Pfister 1951).

Figure 5.1. Characteristic physical types on a Classical Greek Red-Figure vase.

A mixing of ethnic groups has usually been assumed for Ancient Greece, as a result of Dark Age migrations, and earlier more controversial folk movements in prehistory (and reflected in the maps drawn by scholars for the dispersion of the major Greek dialects in early historic times). However the mythical and semi-mythical accounts of ethnic migrations and the heroes who founded cities or peoples, do not offer a coherent and plausible history of the peoples of Greece. Although modern scholars still attempt to separate out layers of Greek myth corresponding to prehistoric periods (for example, Decourt and Decourt (2001) provide a recent clever use of Thessalian myth to try and identify the major phases of settlement in the landscape), closer study shows how contradictory and often imaginary most other Greek origin legends seem to be.

Robert Buck has thus also much earlier (1979) attempted to find layers of myth, like archaeological layers, for Boeotia, but had to admit that the several versions of ethnic and city origins are generally incompatible (Fig. 5.2) and show strong evidence of Archaic era manipulation to suit contemporary political agendas.

Indeed the whole field of ethnicity studies in Ancient Greece has been revolutionized by the publication of Jonathan Hall's monograph on the subject (1997), using both literary theory and anthropological approaches to Greek ethnic accounts to recast the whole subject of study. Fast following have come edited volumes using the same approach (Malkin 2001), and an excellent study of ethnicity in ancient Phokis (McInerney 1999) which I recommend as the most accessible and up-to-date statement of the new thinking into ancient Greek ethnicity. Nino Luraghi (2002) has convinced me that the Messenians probably did not exist, or at least not until their Classical-era emergence in revolt against their Spartan overlords; but he also unintentionally persuaded me that the Laconians themselves also did not exist before early historic times.

These key revisionary studies of the last ten years have made a number of points very clear:

1. Ethnicity is generally seen to be in large part a cultural construct, aligning its study with the broader movement of 'social constructivism' in social studies
2. Anthropological insights include this from Frederick Barth: 'Ethnicity is the pursuit of political goals – the acquisition or maintenance of power, the mobilization of a following – through the creation of cultural commonness and difference';
3. The 'ethnos' is an open and changeable structure, and many *ethne* arose as consensual social groupings designed to unify the inhabitants of a region even when their origins were heterogeneous;
4. The profusion of heroic genealogies anchoring ethnic groups to a heroic past are not historical documents of the Bronze Age attesting the deep antiquity of related clans and tribes, each deriving from an eponymous ancestor, but cultural artefacts of the eighth century BC and later, manufactured to give legitimacy to the present;
5. Local application might run like this example: 'The emergence of the Phokian ethnos is from a highly variegated landscape in which dozens of small and medium communities remained physically autonomous – rather than see the ethnos as a relic of a tribal past, it is better to see it as a contemporary response to the dilemma of the Archaic period: the conflicting tendencies toward local separatism' (McInerney 1999: 41).

	Hecataeus	Hellanicus	Pherecydes
1.	?Leleges and Pelasgians?	Ogygus autochthonous	*Ogygus, s. of Boeotus, King of Boeotia
2.	Barbarian Aones, Temmikes and Hyantes from Attica	Founding of Thebes by Ogygus and Ektenes	Founding of Thebes by Amphion and Zethus
3.	Cadmus subdues above and founds Thebes, walling the Cadmea	Native Aones and Hyantes from elsewhere in Boeotia to Thebes. They attack Athens	Phlegyians destroy Thebes
4.	Amphion and Zethus found Eutresis. Possibly here a Thracian incursion	Cadmus subdues above; founds Cadmea	**Cadmus refounds Thebes
5.	Usual stemma Cadmus-Oedipus	Amphion and Zethus as usurpers in reign of Laius	Cadmus-Oedipus
6.	Oedipus	Oedipus and Jocasta	Oedipus and three wives
7.	Seven and Epigoni	Seven and Epigoni	Seven and Epigoni
8.	Expulsion of Cadmeans to Thessaly and Encheleis under Laodamas; returnees under Thersander	Expulsion of Cadmeans to Histiaea or Thessaly; Laodamas killed	Expulsion to Doris; return to Thebes under Creon
9.	Trojan War	Trojan War and friendly Phlegyians	Trojan War; Pelasgi expel Thebans
10.	Phlegyians expel Thebans and Minyans	Thracians expel Minyans	– – –
11.	Cadmeans return	Cadmeans return	Boeotians return

*Ogygus, s. of Boeotus in Corinna.

**Cadmus as son of Ogygus in Mythographer Phot. App. Nov. 5, 42.

Figure 5.2. Incompatible generations of Boeotian myth from various ancient authors (Buck 1979).

A very different but equally radical source of rethinking about ethnicity has come from physical anthropology, dealing with the difficult question of 'race' (cf. Ananthaswamy 2002). Modern genetic studies show that genetic variation is greater *within* 'nations' than between them. Of course in appearance, i.e. the phenotype rather than the genotype, one can often spot distinctions between people who come from different parts of the world – most strikingly through skin colour. But such differences

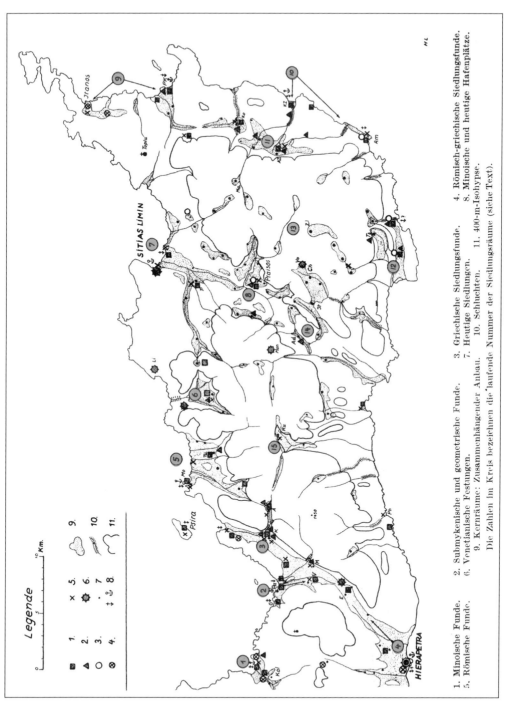

Figure 5.3. Eastern Crete and its Settlement Chambers (Siedlungskammer, highlighted), the focus of long-term horizontal displacement of nucleated settlements (Lehmann 1939).

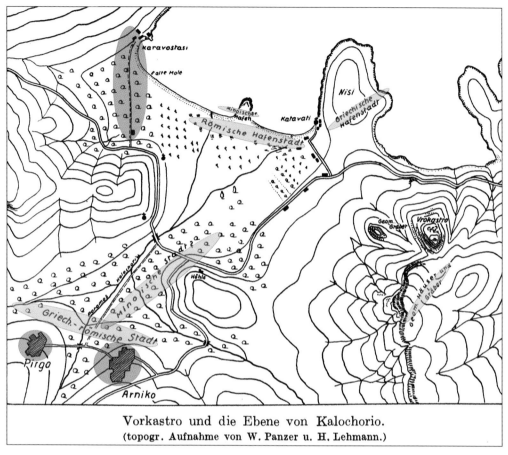

Vorkastro und die Ebene von Kalochorio.
(topogr. Aufnahme von W. Panzer u. H. Lehmann.)

Figure 5.4. A case-study settlement chamber with its main communities (highlighted) at different periods of time (Lehmann 1939).

are in any case not permanently locked into our DNA – they arose through population adaptation to different climates. In time, these outward differences will become blurred as people grow increasingly more mobile at the generational level around the world, not just by intermarriage, because the human genes contain the potential to create all human population types. After all, human origins research tells us that we must all descend from Black Africans. Furthermore, historic research allied with DNA analysis in the Oxford Ancestor Project (Sykes 2000), is now showing that our families can often stem from places we have never heard of in our official family histories!

What this implies perhaps for Ancient Greece, is that although many different peoples may have moved in and out of the region, reflecting sometimes earlier physical adaptations to variable geographies, over time we might also expect to see a tendency towards some physical homogeneity to suit the local environment as well. 'Red-Figure' people may have been very common, but unlikely to have been alone, with local communities retaining for a long time rather contrasted physical, and maybe linguistic varieties. In addition, the tendency for long periods of relative stability of residence to promote regional and even district in-breeding, will have emphasized a significant degree of not only genotypical but also probably phenotypical contrasts. Many city-states practised wide-ranging limitations on immigration even from neighbouring *poleis*, or confined it to females, and then often in ways to minimize its effects on the traditional citizen body. Moreover, if we add to this variety – hidden by stereotypical iconography of a desirable, idealized physique – the modern ancient historians' case that most ethnic and city origin stories are artificial constructs with only limited historical truth about them, where do we arrive at if we come now to study any region and people of Ancient Greece?

Surely the first thing we can say now is that the legends the Greeks told of local origins must be contextualized into the period when they are likely to have been 'constructed' or at the very least 'drastically reorganized', usually long after the times they claim to be describing. We must 'deconstruct' them since generally they are highly selective and often fabricated tales to suit later ideology and people's desire to assert a particular set of identities vis-à-vis other groups of people. Secondly, we can assume that the well-attested process of merging of diversity into larger political groupings – *poleis*, *ethne*, federations – the key units of mature Ancient Greece, conceals from us a great variety of sub-populations with their own history of settlement and perhaps migration, and maybe also physical contrasts.

Let me now illustrate these new insights with the help of some recent case-studies, beginning with Dark Age Knossos. Nicholas Coldstream (1998) and Mieke Prent (2007) have recently argued that although Post-Palatial sanctuary use near the Knossos palace reflects continuity of Minoan culture by local people living around the abandoned palace, the North Cemetery established in the eleventh century BC represents incoming Dorian peoples from the mainland. If the latter's initial culture is clearly alien, by Geometric times these new arrivals were actively establishing roots of local identity through recycling Minoan coffins and copying Minoan designs onto their cremation urns – is this a claim to an heroic past by an elite warrior caste with mythological aspirations? A new Rhea sanctuary on the Minoan palace is also suggested to symbolize a tangible claim to heroic connections.

Let us also in this context make a link to the German *Landeskunde* (Landscape History) tradition, and recall the precociously pioneering case-study of 1939 by Lehmann in East Crete: long-term occupance of natural settlement-chambers (*Siedlungskammer*; Fig. 5.3) was a kind of game, in which each period of human settlement shifted the main nucleated site around micro-locational possibilities *inside* settlement districts of small scale (Fig. 5.4), as a result of changing sociopolitical, economic and strategic factors. By implication, as far as settlement maps are concerned, the *longue durée* in the landscape could override changing or stable population composition in a biological sense. We already saw this with the convergence of Dorian immigrants and indigenous Minoan people at Knossos, both eventually identifying with Bronze Age traditions at the site.

The Dutch Aetolia Project, led by Sebastiaan Bommeljé and Peter Doorn, has given a powerful analysis (Bommeljé and Doorn 1984) to show that the formation of local tribal groups or subethne within the Aetolian 'tribal polity' (*ethnos*) was also centrally-conditioned by geographical factors shaping regional senses of identity: however varied the ethnic origins of the Aetolians in prehistoric and Dark Age times, in the longer-term their group identities converged into districts defined by physically-conditioned land-use regions and natural communications (*modes de vie*; Fig. 5.5–5.7).

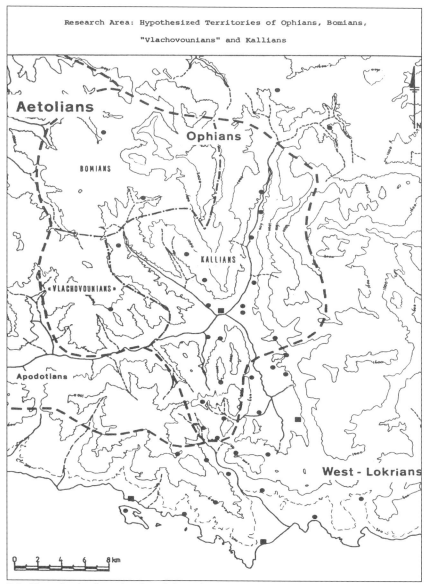

Figure 5.5. Hypothesized territories of the subgroups within the ancient ethnos ('tribal people') of the Aetolians, northwestern Greece (Bommeljé and Doorn 1984).

I would like to end this series of case-studies by turning back to my own study-region of Boeotia, where I wondered if Herakleides Kritikos really did see different ethnic communities hidden beneath the surface of the Boeotian ethnos. A case-study from more recent times in this province offers better-documented insights into the possible complexities of community origins and identity.

Our intensive archaeological survey in Boeotia has found numerous *Siedlungskammer* such as the Valley of the Muses, where, as in the *Landeskunde* model, since later prehistory a single farming village has migrated around a small landscape, always over limited distances (Bintliff 1996). The modern village of Askra, for example, could thus be traceable through short-distance site displacement via its Ottoman era and later Medieval predecessor at site VM4, to yet another site – ancient Askra – an earlier Greco-Roman village – where for sure the poet Hesiod must have lived around 700 BC. In reality though, as I have discussed in detail in a recent paper (Bintliff *et al.* 2000), although I think it reasonable to argue for some population continuity between Hesiod's Askra and the Medieval and then Modern village, the change of name from Askra to Zaratova in Byzantine times should indicate a significant-enough addition of Slav settlers in the sixth–seventh century AD to cause a complete renaming of the Greco-Slav peasant settlement at Askra. With the reincorporation of the Boeotian countryside into the Byzantine Empire in the eighth century AD, the Slav language, names of villages and persons were all increasingly Hellenized – so that by the fifteenth century AD the incoming Ottoman Turkish administrators classify the Zaratova (Askra) community, now displaced by a Crusader lord to a nearby site, VM 4, as 'Greek'. Incidentally Byzantine 'Hellenization' has also provided our settlement with a new but Orthodox name of Panayia. Were it not for rare archive references to Zaratova, the archaeology, settlement history, and earlier and later records of the village, would have been read as prime evidence for the ethnic continuity of ancient Greeks into the present day in this micro-landscape.

More dramatic is the situation in the rest of Boeotia. Today all the villages are Greek-speaking, Orthodox Christian, typical in all cultural forms for the homogenized world of Modern Greece: only social anthropologists, medieval historians and the linguistically sharp-eared know differently!

In the fourteenth century AD, most of the Greek, or maybe Slavo-Greek villages of Boeotia, were abandoned due to the Black Death and warfare. The Frankish Dukes of Athens and later the Ottomans encouraged Albanian immigrants – clans of 'Arvanites' – to recolonize the deserted village locations; most modern settlements are thus in origin entirely exotic to Greece (Bintliff 1995; Fig. 5.8). The same can be shown for Attica. Today in private many old Arvanites speak a mix of Greek and Albanian to each other. The longer survival of this tradition, compared to the fate of the Slav colonization, especially as regards the language, is due to the tolerant multiculturalism of the Ottoman Empire, in contrast to the Hellenocentric policy of Byzantium and then the Modern Greek state (Bintliff 2003). It is not too fanciful to see still some strong physical resemblances amongst many of the contemporary villagers to modern-day Albanians, but there are also many other physical types just as clearly represented – just as we might expect from our earlier discussions.

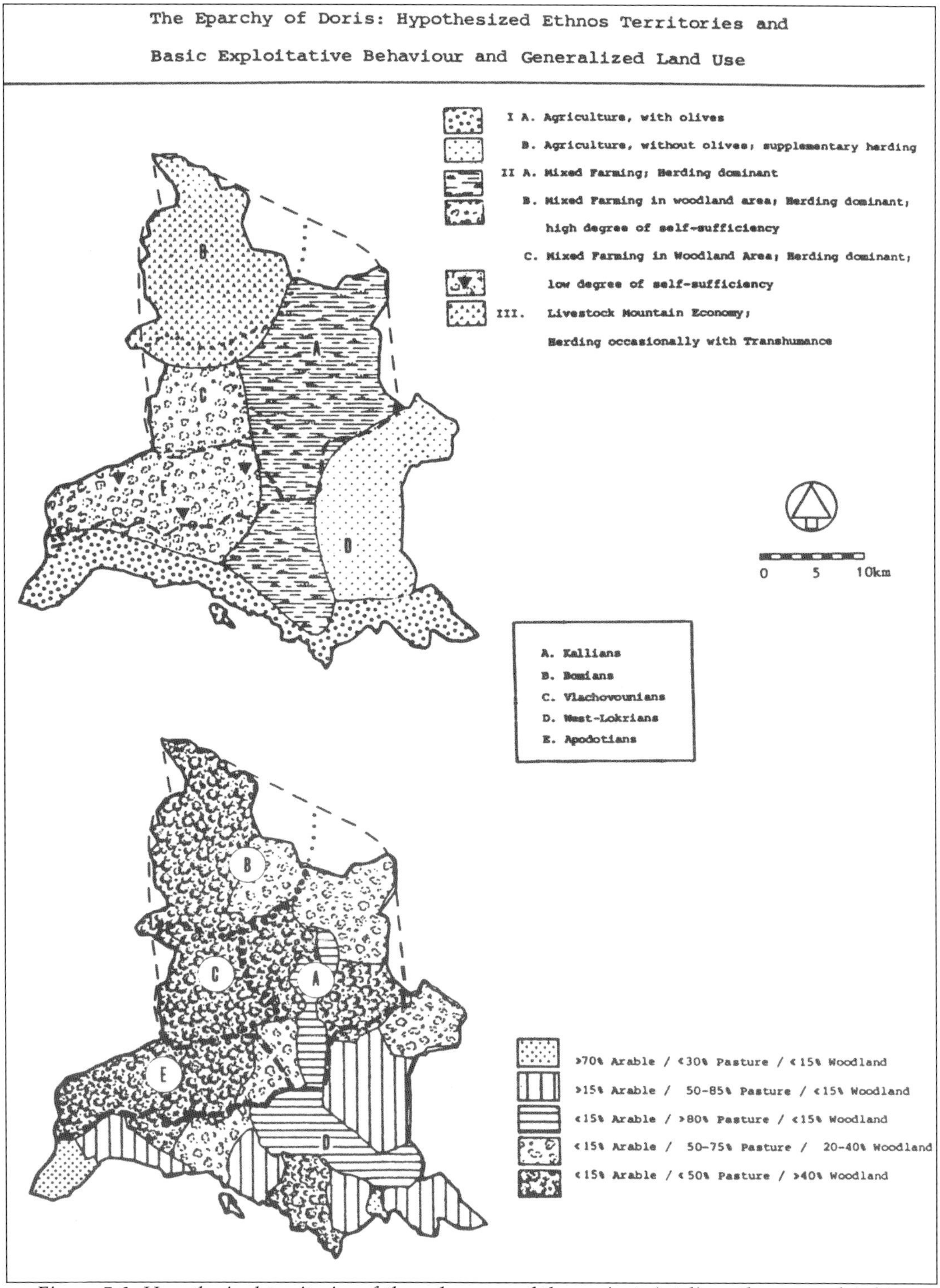

The Eparchy of Doris: Hypothesized Ethnos Territories and
Basic Exploitative Behaviour and Generalized Land Use

I A. Agriculture, with olives

B. Agriculture, without olives; supplementary herding

II A. Mixed Farming; Herding dominant

B. Mixed Farming in woodland area; Herding dominant;
high degree of self-sufficiency

C. Mixed Farming in Woodland Area; Herding dominant;
low degree of self-sufficiency

III. Livestock Mountain Economy;
Herding occasionally with Transhumance

0   5   10km

A. Kallians
B. Bomians
C. Vlachovounians
D. West-Lokrians
E. Apodotians

>70% Arable / <30% Pasture / <15% Woodland

>15% Arable / 50-85% Pasture / <15% Woodland

<15% Arable / >80% Pasture / <15% Woodland

<15% Arable / 50-75% Pasture / 20-40% Woodland

<15% Arable / <50% Pasture / >40% Woodland

Figure 5.6. Hypothesized territories of the subgroups of the ancient Aetolian ethnos correlated to natural geography and reconstructed ancient land use (modes de vie; Bommeljé and Doorn 1984).

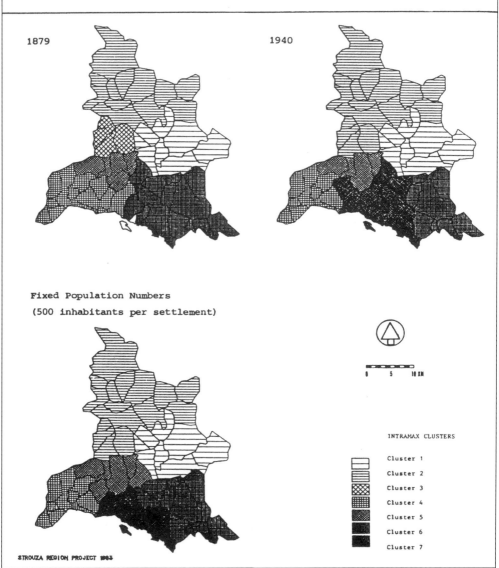

Figure 5.7. Population interaction dynamics in ancient Aetolia, based on the historical geography of AD *ninteenth–early twentieth centuries (Bommeljé and Doorn 1984).*

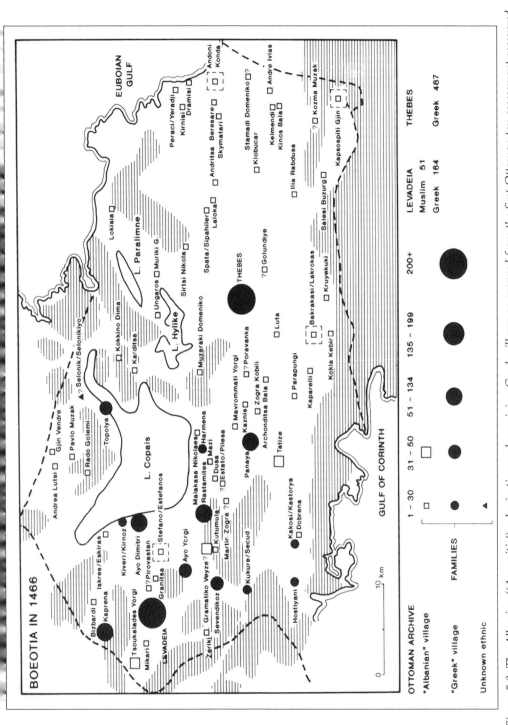

Figure 5.8. The Albanian ('Arvanitic') colonization and surviving Greek villages as mapped from the first Ottoman tax assessment recovered, from 1466 (Bintliff 1995; the tax records were located and translated by Machiel Kiel, the geographical mapping was by the author).

Figure 5.9. Peasant longhouse with typical material life for the Greek lowlands in the AD *seventeenth–nineteenth century (a painting from Megara by Stackelberg).*

Officially the Arvanitic component is suppressed in local and national education, and hardly any visitors to Greece, and many Athenians, are unaware of the long-settled district ethnic group in their midst – not only in Attica and central Greece but also many parts of the Peloponnese. In *Siedlungskammer* terms, the new AD fourteenth–fifteenth centuries colonizing villages are close to deserted 'Greek' sites, have the same house types and material culture as the surviving Greek villages (Fig. 5.9), and there is almost no written record of, or by, these people. In the early twentieth century especially, their villages have been renamed after local Classical toponyms, to elide the presence of 'The Other'– thus for example the modern village Leondarion was until recently Zogra Kobili! Without rare historical indications, how easy it would be to have missed the very different story lying behind the apparent continuity and cultural uniformity shown by the archaeological and settlement history of Boeotia, and by inference of the rest of Greece?

And yet the seeds of cultural diversity and ethnogenesis are always present, even amongst regional peasant societies living in similar 'modes de vie' and primarily interacting with each other on a local scale. Thus each small district of a few villages in Boeotia (and the rest of Greece) possessed during the last few centuries its own distinctive formal dress, male and female, used till recently in all kinds of festivities throughout the year (Fig. 5.10; Broufas 1993), marking its members as distinctive from other surrounding

Figure 5.10. The distinctive traditional formal dress of the women of the village of Tanagra and its nearest neighbouring villages, central Greece (Broufas 1993).

village clusters. Marriages also till recently were predominantly between such neighbours, hence the kinship related to dress codes. Ethnohistoric evidence suggests that Mediterranean societies have been exhibiting such forms of identity at least as far back as the eighteenth century, when the first scholarly records of variable peasant dress were made, in images and texts. I am sure they also characterised the dress codes of ancient Greece and prehistory.

Note

This article is a slightly extended version of a conference paper given at a conference in Stuttgart in 2002, with a different range of illustrations. The Stuttgart paper was published in the Conference Proceedings (2006) *'Troianer sind wir gewesen' – Migrationen in der antiken Welt*. Edited by E. Olshausen and H. Sonnabend. Stuttgart, Franz Steiner Verlag: 108–114.

6

Landscape and identity of Greek colonists and indigenous communities in southeast Italy

Gert-Jan Burgers

Keywords: landscape archaeology, community identity, Greek-native relations, sanctuaries, Salento

Modern landscape archaeology in the Mediterranean is a flourishing field of enquiry. Its success is reflected in the exponential increase in field survey projects in plains, valleys and mountains alike. Another index of its success is its increasingly interdisciplinary character. Field-walking nowadays is combined with geophysics, historical geography, palaeo-geographical reconstruction and other sophisticated analyses. Also from a theoretical perspective, significant advances have been made. As a matter of fact it has been notable in landscape archaeology that traditional cultural-historical paradigms have been replaced by approaches of a more processual nature. A current perspective in Mediterranean landscape studies has been inspired by Braudel's theory regarding time and change as being articulated in three different domains, that is landscape, social structure and events (e.g. Bintliff 1991; Knapp 1992). Whilst many advances have been made, it should also be observed that method and theory do not seem to have developed at an equal pace. The most progress has been made in methodology. With regard to theory, few Mediterranean landscape archaeologists have gone beyond Braudelian or processualist approaches. In this paper I wish to discuss how we could achieve this goal.

As a reference point, I will take the field project of the Vrije Universiteit of Amsterdam in the Italian region of Apulia, on the isthmus of the Salento peninsula (Fig. 6.1). Major syntheses of this work have already been published (Yntema 1993; Burgers 1998a; Burgers and Yntema 1999a. On the Valesio-project, see especially Boersma 1995; Boersma and Yntema 1987; Yntema 2001. On the Muro Tenente-project: Burgers 1998a, 1999b; Burgers *et al.* 1998; Burgers and Yntema 1999b. On the Li Castelli di S. Pancrazio Salentino-project: Maruggi and Burgers 2001. On the field surveys in general: Burgers 1998a, Burgers *et al.* 2003; Yntema 1993). The 'Salento Isthmus' is the common denomination for the stretch of land between Taranto and Brindisi, connecting the Salento peninsula to the rest of Italy. Apart from the limestone tableland of the Murge to the north, the major landscape units in the region are the Taranto plain in the southwest and the larger

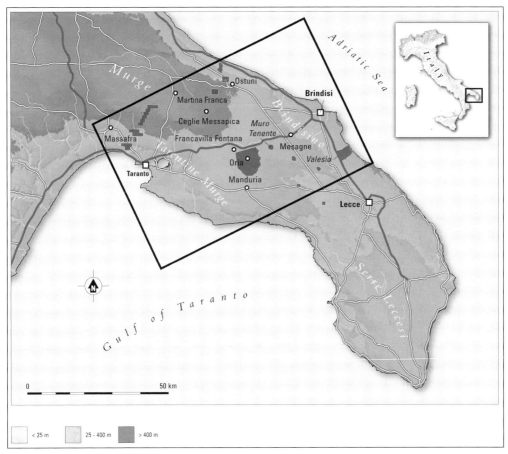

Figure 6.1. The Salento isthmus. Sample areas surveyed and sites excavated by the Vrije Universiteit of Amsterdam.

Brindisi plain, or *piana messapica*, to the southeast. Since 1981 the AIVU has carried out a series of excavations and surveys in various rural and urban units throughout this region. This fieldwork is aimed to define the occupational history of the region in the first millennium BC and to analyse it in the light of three major supra-regional processes:

1. Greek colonization (eighth–seventh century BC);
2. Urbanization, that in Salento is mainly detected during the late Archaic and early Hellenistic periods (550–250 BC);
3. Romanization of the early urban landscape, that took place after the Roman conquest of Salento in the first half of the third century BC.

Like most regional projects, at the basic level, the Salento Isthmus Project was started with a focus on specific landscape units, which were studied by surveying sample areas. Figure. 6.1 shows the major landscape units and sample areas surveyed so far. Initially,

UNIVERSITY OF WINCHESTER
LIBRARY

in the 1980s, the settlement patterns that emerged were interpreted mainly in Braudelian terms. However, we have gradually realised that such an approach ignores any dialectic relationship between the three domains identified by Braudel. As within functionalism, Braudel regards the history of human action as basically subordinate to and constrained by the landscape and by *conjunctures*. Later generations of Annales historians and post-processual archaeologists alike have criticized this structural determinism (for a general overview of this criticism see especially Knapp 1992; Moreland 1992). They have tried instead to restore a recursive relationship between the three Braudelian domains. Indeed, any fundamental dominance of landscape or social structures over human action can be questioned considering that the former are also created, reproduced and transformed by human action. From this perspective, the archaeologist's main fields of study, material culture and landscape cannot be investigated solely as the passive reflection of all determinant social structures. Instead, they should be investigated as active media through which people order social relations. Such a recursive relation certainly exists between people's actions and the landscape.

This approach is central to the latest research questions touched on by our Italian project. I would like to demonstrate this by referring to two major research issues. The first is that of the construction of identity in a Greek colonial context. The second issue explores the role of ritual in the formation of community identity.

Landscape and identity in a Greek colonial context

The western half of the Salento isthmus is dominated on one side by the tableland of the so-called Murge and on the other side by the coastal Taranto plain. It is in the Taranto plain that the city-state of *Taras* developed, which is generally considered to have been one of the most powerful Greek cities of Italy. Crucial to this status was its large territory, which is thought to have been created when the colony was reportedly founded during the late eighth century BC. Right from the beginning of colonization, one draws a clear distinction between a Greek colonial landscape on the one hand, and on the other hand a peripheral outlying territory. The identification of settlements in the Greek *chora* is based largely on finds indicating a Greek type of material culture. In contrast, the outlying landscape is generally considered to have been inhabited by indigenous communities. In these cases, indigenous material culture elements are more pronounced. This identification, of course, is not always clear cut. Thus, at the extremes of the Tarentine side of the border, Lo Porto has identified a series of Greek *phrouria*, most of which are in strategic locations on the ridges of the Murge plateau, overlooking the fertile coastal Taranto plain (Lo Porto 1990: 92–3; notably the sites of Monte Salete, Fullonese, Mass. Vicentino, S. Marzano and Li Castelli di Manduria). However, others consider these sites as native strongholds since, at least for some phases, native material culture is thought to be much more apparent (e.g. Alessio and Guzzo 1989–90). Whatever the identification, interpretation of the archaeological record often figures in terms of a rigid indigenous-Greek dichotomy.

Archaeological contexts are valued according to their adherence to sets of allegedly contrasting typologies that are interpreted in ethnic terms and corresponding political-territorial configurations, that is, they are projected on to the map as belonging either to Greek or to indigenous territory.

One also finds Greek objects in indigenous territories. However, these are commonly taken to confirm the widespread power of Hellenization, a concept denoting the dissemination of Greek culture amongst indigenous peoples. This diffusion, in turn, was interpreted to support the general belief in the political and technological superiority of Greek culture (e.g. in particular, Dunbabin 1948; Boardman 1964). This type of interpretation has recently been severely challenged. The concept of Hellenization in particular has been questioned more and more in terms of its usefulness in studying cultural change. Scholars have abandoned the notion that Greek culture spread in a unilinear and uniform process. Rather, they now emphasize the geographical, as well as diachronic, variability in Greek-indigenous contacts (e.g. Whitehouse and Wilkins 1989; Lombardo 1991; d'Andria 1991). A more fundamental criticism has also been advanced, namely that the concepts of Hellenism and Hellenization are rooted in an unquestioned belief that Greek culture was inherently superior and that, correspondingly, its diffusion was a natural and benevolent civilizing enterprise (e.g. Morris 1994; van Dommelen 1997; Lomas 1996; Whitehouse and Wilkins 1989).

In our project, we have particularly questioned the traditional belief that cultures can be readily identified from archaeological remains and associated with ethnic

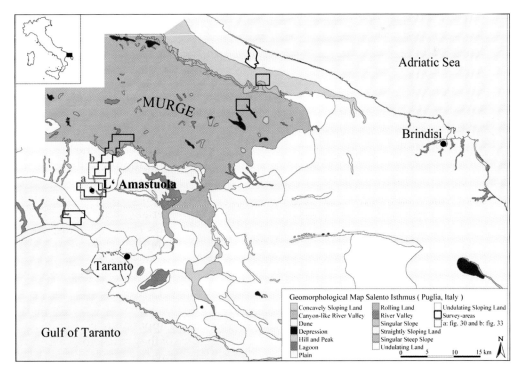

Figure 6.2. The Salento isthmus. Geomorphological map. Indicated are sample areas surveyed in the province of Taranto.

groups, either Greek or indigenous. Instead we have investigated the dynamic and situational nature of identity and ethnic identification. These issues are at the basis of our field surveys and excavations in the Taranto region (Burgers and Crielaard 2007). The surveys comprise a transect crosscutting all major landscape units (Fig. 6.2). This research has identified no surface remains in these landscapes that relate to the Iron Age and Archaic phases, with the exception of a site called L'Amastuola, some 14 kilometres northwest of Taranto (Figs 6.2–6.4). The site is located on one of the most visually dominant hilltops in the entire Taranto region, within easy reach of both the coastal plain and the valley immediately to the north-west. According to our field surveys, during the eighth century BC this hilltop was reclaimed for human occupation after a long phase of marginality; we conclude that sometime during the second half of that century, a local community founded a settlement *ex novo* on this spot. However, as stated, it is the only contemporary site identified in the sample areas. Our preliminary thesis is indeed that the settlement pattern in the Taranto region was of a nucleated type, focused on sites such as L'Amastuola. This is likely to have continued throughout much of the Classical period. Significant transformations occurred only towards the late fourth century BC, when a rural infill that had started in the late Classical phase, accelerated considerably.

In 2003, we started to excavate the site of L'Amastuola, in collaboration with the *Soprintendenza per I Beni Archeologici della Puglia*, who had been digging there as early

Figure 6.3. Oblique aerial photograph of the hilltop site of L'Amastuola (municipality of Crispiano). Published with the kind permission of the società Kikau.

as the 1980s. In those years, Grazia Angela Maruggi of the Apulian superintendency uncovered parts of an Iron Age/Archaic settlement, as well as of an adjacent necropolis (Fig. 6.4; Maruggi 1996). The earliest excavated traces of the settlement also date to around the middle of the eighth century BC; they comprise hut-structures common in the contemporary native world. That, indeed, the site was inhabited by native groups is inferred also from the ceramic repertoire used, which largely consists of characteristic native coarse *impasto* and fine matte-painted wares. Maruggi's stratigraphic analysis suggested that these huts were abandoned between 680/660 BC, to be overbuilt rather abruptly by dwellings, displaying a rectangular ground plan (little more than 10 square metres) and a more stable construction technique (mudbrick or stone superstructures and tile roofs, as compared with the wattle and daub of the earlier huts). The new houses were similar to those of contemporary Greek urban contexts. Also the ceramics associated with these dwellings differ from those of the preceding huts; they comprised mainly colonial and mainland Greek wares. Indeed, the observed settlement transformation at L'Amastuola could easily lead to the interpretation of an early, and rather sudden, Greek takeover of the site.

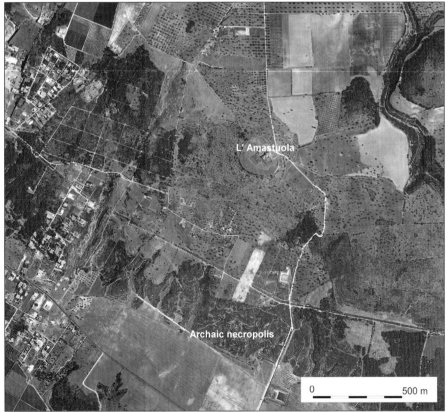

Figure 6.4. Vertical aerial photograph of the hilltop site of L'Amastuola and its adjacent necropolis.

Further evidence for this interpretation has been inferred from the provisional analysis of the excavation of the nearby necropolis (Fig. 6.4). According to Maruggi's estimate, the graveyard contains some 1000 tombs (Maruggi 1996). The date of the earliest of those excavated corresponds with that established for the settlement reorganisation. Moreover, the burials all closely adhere to Greek types common in Taranto, not only with regard to the type of deposition (inhumation in a supine position), but also to the type of tomb architecture, grave goods and related burial rites. No traditional native elements were found in this graveyard, which was in use until the fifth century BC. These data significantly add to the theory of a Greek community substituting the native.

In the Taranto plain, we have investigated other sites like L'Amastuola with our field surveys. These sites are generally also interpreted as Greek. We conclude, however, that the issue is not as clear-cut as it may seem. In concordance with what I have said in my introduction, we approach material culture and landscape as media through which people actively order social relations. From this perspective, it is imperative to emphasize that the apparent Greekness of the landscape hides a myriad of social strategies. Thus, elsewhere I have argued that leading members of indigenous communities appropriated Greek material culture, and possibly even concepts, in order to grasp and/or maintain a stable power basis in their own community (Burgers 1998a: 173–224). Indeed, this may be one explanation for the so-called Greekness of the landscape. In this light it must be recalled that there is evidence to suggest that, at the same time as the early Greek colonization in southern Italy, local indigenous communities were affected by social differentiation, population growth and increased competition for available resources and territorial expansion. Correspondingly, I have argued that groups of Greek migrants were allowed to exchange, settle and integrate amongst these indigenous communities, because association with them, or with the items they traded or produced, were useful in local or intra-tribal, competitive, social strategies (Burgers 2004). In my view, the Greek foreigners constituted one of the elements in the ferment of shifting power structures.

If the above holds true, coexistence and integration become major research issues. Drawing on the most recent studies of colonial encounters, it seems prudent to allow for the complexity of the communities involved and to identify mixed groups and hybrid identities within them (see for a detailed discussion in an archaeological context, van Dommelen 1997, 1998). It is in this light that we have executed new excavations at L'Amastuola and what has come up is indeed a much more nuanced, differentiated picture (Burgers and Crielaard 2007). The Archaic site and its surroundings appear to be characterized by a very heterogeneous material culture. What we have found is so-called 'Greek' items – such as house plans and burial customs, but these are not alone; they are fused with so-called 'indigenous' items, which are contemporary to the Greek examples. Thus, we have excavated a defensive system, hut plans and ceramic repertoires that are traditionally attributed to indigenous cultures. This also goes for a funerary stele that was found in the midst of the supposedly pure Greek necropolis (Fig. 6.5).

The find of the stele is a particularly significant piece of evidence in this context. The stele has its closest parallels in neighbouring indigenous Salento, amongst others at the sites of Cavallino, Mesagne and Muro Tenente. In the case of L'Amastuola, its presence in the midst of an extensive necropolis clearly relates it to funerary practices.

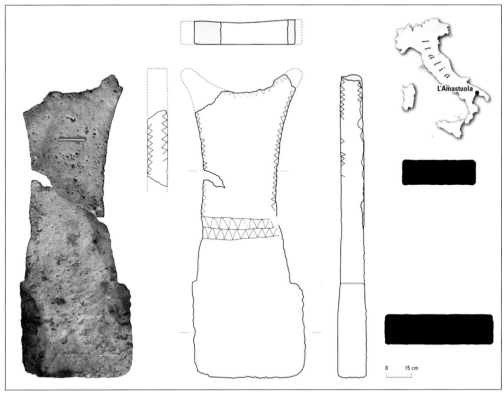

Figure 6.5. Stele found amidst the debris of the Archaic necropolis of L'Amastuola.

A similar conclusion is reached by d'Andria and Mastronuzzi (2008) with regard to the Salento stelae (Lombardo 1994). As to dating, the chronological limits of the L'Amastuola necropolis also fit in with d'Andria and Mastronuzzi's study (d'Andria 2005: 36). If this is accepted, it will be observed that the presence of a stele is at odds in an otherwise Greek-type funerary context, as stelae are commonly defined as indigenous. The context shows that some of the tombs must have belonged to indigenous occupants, amongst whom were individuals who enjoyed a high status – although the tombs generally seem to have been of Greek type and contained Greek pottery and other burial items. It will be difficult to identify such contexts as proof of the presence of an ethnically Greek settlement controlling an extensive Greek territory. In our view, the L'Amastuola community should be interpreted in terms of mixed groups and hybrid identities. It probably was composed of groups of various backgrounds, who redefined material culture and rearranged the local landscape in order to negotiate identity and socio-political status. Seen from this perspective, L'Amastuola may have much in common with other contemporary sites along the Ionian coast, such as Siris and L'Incoronata (cf. Yntema 2000). These are the issues we are currently investigating at L'Amastuola and in the Taranto *chora* in general.

Ritual landscapes and community identity

The undulating landscape of the Salento isthmus abounds with ancient strongholds boasting monumental stone fortifications. In many cases, these fortifications enclose settlement areas of over 50 hectares. It is only in the 1950s that archaeological interest in these sites has gradually awakened (for early excavations in southeast Italy, see Scarfi 1962 for Monte Sannace, and Pancrazzi 1979 for Cavallino). At some of them, excavations and other fieldwork revealed a range of features that were interpreted as having (proto-)urban characteristics. From this it was deduced that many indigenous regions of interior southern Italy were far less static than was presumed before. As a matter of fact, it appeared that, from the sixth century BC onwards, they were likewise marked by processes of urbanization. The second case study that I wish to discuss in the present paper relates to this phenomenon.

Mostly on the basis of incidental finds, it is generally believed that the extension of most fortified sites on the isthmus reached its maximum expansion during the early Hellenistic phase (late fourth to mid-third century BC). The excavations and field surveys of the Vrije Universiteit clearly confirm this trend. Thus, open area excavations at the site of Muro Tenente show that in this phase new stable dwellings were erected in large nucleated blocks that extend well within the previously uninhabited peripheries of the intra-mural area (Burgers and Yntema 1999b). Moreover, intensive surveys at several other fortified settlement areas indicate that at all of them intra-mural habitation expanded considerably in the late fourth century BC (Burgers 1998a).

The field surveys make it clear that the process of urbanization was not confined to these major sites but also involved the wider landscape. Archaeologically, one of the most remarkable features of this phenomenon is the spread of small concentrations of surface artefacts virtually all over the regional landscape, from the wet coastal zones to the sandy soils of the interior Brindisi plain and the hard limestone hills of the Murge. It was observed already in the 1980s, when we surveyed, amongst others, a transect cutting across the coastal plain along the Adriatic south of Brindisi (Fig. 6.6, Boersma, Burgers and Yntema 1991).

Here a fortified urban site was accompanied by dozens of small rural sites, that were found all over the landscape. Most of these early Hellenistic surface scatters were of minor extent; on average they measure a mere 500 square metres. These scatters invariably contained artefacts that had direct parallels in the larger settlement nuclei. Apart from tiles and fine and coarse kitchen wares, they generally also contained loomweights, *dolia* and amphorae. They have been commonly interpreted as isolated farmsteads. Occasionally, fragments of funerary wares have been found at, or in close proximity to, these sites, notably of Apulian red-figured, Gnathia and banded pottery. Such finds have also been recorded in reports about incidental discoveries of small isolated graveyards in the Brindisino. Apparently the farms were accompanied by small necropoleis, which suggests that they were inhabited not on a seasonal, but on a permanent basis. Occasionally, these farms can be shown to have clustered into small hamlets. The surveys have discovered such larger, open sites in various landscape units. The one in the periphery of present day Cellino S. Marco may serve as an example (Burgers 1998a: 161–9). Here, some ten concentrations of early Hellenistic dwellings have been found dispersed over an area of some six hectares.

The distance between the various concentrations is 100 metres on average. The differences in extent, density and content between them were small. They all measured about 2500 square metres and contained the same artefact categories as those found at the isolated farms.

Some of these new farms and hamlets were likely to have been constructed on land that was already cultivated in earlier times by peasants living in the larger settlements. However, the scale of the transformation suggests that previously untilled land was also increasingly brought under cultivation. Farms and villages were now found even on marginal soils and/or at large distance from the major settlements. To understand this phenomenon, it should be underlined that it was contemporary with the expansion of the major sites; there was nothing to suggest that subsequent shifts of nucleation or dispersion occurred. One may conclude that both phenomena were intimately related.

In the 1980s we considered this, i.e. the expansion of rural occupation accompanying urban development, as indicative of a process of expansion and intensification of agricultural production (cf. Halstead 1987: 83; Alcock 1993; Bintliff 1997). However, in

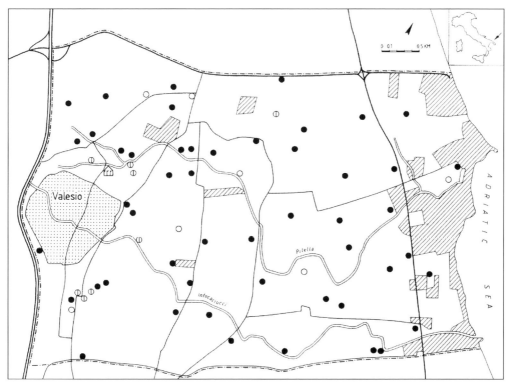

Figure 6.6. Transect of the Adriatic coast surveyed by the Vrije Universiteit of Amsterdam. Early Hellenistic phase. Valesio is the name of the dotted fortified site. Black dots: rural sites. Open dots: possible rural sites. House-symbol: sanctuary site.

line with the hypothesis that I have just set out, a different picture can be painted. In this case, there are even data available to study the role of ritual in the reorganization of the landscape. Following theoretical studies on this theme, we approach landscape not only as a physical and measurable geographical entity but also a mental construction (cf. Ingold 1993; Hirsch 1995; Derks 1997). The way people arrange their landscape is not only dictated by economic and socio-political reality, but also by their perception of the very same landscapes. Cosmologies often are at the basis of this perception. The physical, observable world is generally rooted in these cosmologies and it is recognized as originating from them and as a reflection of them. This goes for landscapes in general as well as for its constituent parts such as mountains and rivers, and also for such anthropogenic elements as settlements, graveyards and sanctuaries. It is in these phenomena that the world of the gods and ancestors was materialized. They functioned as anchors for the recognition of the supernatural and the afterlife and it is in this sense they were central to the way local communities defined themselves; it was notably by continuous interaction with landscape, whether through myths, monuments or ritualized contact with the sacred, that people established, transformed or reshaped their community relations.

From this cognitive perspective, evident sites to search for are cult places. They were pre-eminent spaces where cosmologies were materialized. Accordingly, our focus is currently on the role of a series of larger cave sanctuaries on the early Hellenistic Salento

Figure 6.7. Ostuni. Cave sanctuary of S. Maria d'Agnano (Photo: G.-J. Burgers)

isthmus. They were generally located in dominant positions in the rural territory or on the coast, at various distances from the major settlements. A good example in our Murge survey area is provided by the cave sanctuary of the Grotta di S. Maria d'Agnano, just a short distance uphill from one of our survey samples (Fig. 6.7, Coppola 1983: 249–52). The cave is located some four kilometres north of Ostuni. It opens out onto a natural terrace overlooking the coastal plain, just below a cliff top which harboured a major fortified Bronze Age site. Investigations carried out here have demonstrated that the cave became the scene of a formal cult dedicated to a female divinity from the sixth century onwards. It was reorganized in a more formal way in the early Hellenistic period.

The best-known cult place in this region is that at Oria, the major pre-Roman urban site on the isthmus. Here, in the course of the sixth century BC, a sanctuary was founded on a small natural terrace just outside the ancient town. The terrace is backed by a cave dug into the hill and opens up to face Oria's central hill, which lies some 300 metres away. It has been excavated with great care by the Archaeological Institute of the Università del Salento. These digs have demonstrated that the sanctuary reached its most prominent physical appearance in the early Hellenistic period (d'Andria 1990: 239–306). Then a complex structure was erected on the terrace. Votives suggest that the main cult here was dedicated to Demeter. This sanctuary, as most of the others known in the Salento peninsula, was in use at least from the Archaic period and must be considered part of the *longue durée* of the regional landscape. In the early Hellenistic period one witnesses a monumentalization and an intensification of cult activities, still at these very same places. My argument is that these phenomena were closely related to the urban growth and rural infill of the landscape that I have just discussed.

Central to this argument is the concept of community construction, as introduced recently into archaeology through anthropology (e.g. Canuto and Yaeger 2000; Cohen 2003; Gerritsen 2003; Knapp 2003); contrary to functionalist perspectives on communities as 'natural', closed and homogeneous social entities, recent approaches rather problematize the genesis of a community. In the most recent views, communities are socially constituted. They are being created and redefined through the construction of symbolic boundaries that stress differences with outsiders. Significantly, it is especially in phases of major social and spatial transformation that groups tend to create new symbolic community borders or to emphasize and enhance old ones (Cohen 2003). They do it in order to articulate group identity. Moreover, they often do so in a ritual context and by re-interpreting the past.

It is in this light that one must point to the apparent emphasis on traditional cult places in the early Hellenistic Salento region. These sanctuaries were likely to have been considered central elements in the cosmological ordering of the landscape. By reviving cult activities at these sacred places, it can be argued that the local communities either strengthened traditional group identities, or otherwise constructed new ones. What is also relevant is the location of the sanctuaries; they are often to be found at the interface between the expanding urban sites and the newly filled rural territories. This suggests that cults at these sanctuaries were revitalized in order to bind the urban and rural communities living in the area. In this light, both urban and rural dwellers experienced these ritual places as anchors of identity in a landscape that was continuously becoming more complex.

Clearly, this rationalization still has to be developed in more detail, as is the case with the first issue that I discussed above, that of the Greek colonial landscape at L'Amastuola. However, I believe the potential of such studies is great. In my view, it is one of the tasks of landscape archaeology in the Mediterranean to test and refine hypotheses like this by contextualizing our survey data.

Acknowledgements

The Salento Isthmus project of the Vrije Universiteit of Amsterdam is directed by the present author, together with Jan Paul Crielaard (responsible of excavations at the site of L'Amastuola) and Douwe Yntema (artefact studies). It is carried out in close collaboration with the *Scuola di Specializzazione in Archeologia Classica e Medievale* 'Dinu Adamesteanu' of the Università del Salento and the *Soprintendenza per I Beni Archeologici della Puglia*. The fieldwork is sponsored by the Faculty of Arts of the Vrije Universiteit Amsterdam, the NWO (Netherlands Organization for Scientific Research) and the Royal Netherlands Institute at Rome. Drawings and maps for this article are produced by Bert Brouwenstijn and Jaap Fokkema of the Vrije Universiteit. I would like to thank them for their outstanding work. I am also grateful to the various staff members and organizations for their contributions to the project and to the students and other volunteers for their invaluable help in the field.

Before the Samnites: Molise in the eighth and sixth century BC

Alessandro Naso

Keywords: Molise; central Italy; southern Italy; Samnites

Molise was recently defined by G. Brancaccio as a non-existent and artificially constructed region, because it was formed by putting together geographical and administrative spaces originally belonging to surrounding regions like Campania and Apulia (Fig. 7.1) (Brancaccio 2005). If this construction may be partially right for modern times, it is not correct for the past, when the present Molise was part of Samnium, comprising both the land settled by the Samnite tribes of the *Pentri* in the hinterland around Isernia and by the *Frentani* in the coastal region. In the division of the Italian peninsula undertaken in the first century BC under Augustus, these peoples were deliberately put together in the fourth region, called *Sabini et Samnium* (La Regina 1968: carta A; La Regina 1989). We cannot generally speak of a Samnite people before the end of the fifth century BC. Using literary sources, archaeological data, epigraphic texts and numismatic documentation, G. Tagliamonte was recently able to date to this time the ethnic self identification of the Samnites, whose origins are probably defined by contrast with surrounding populations (Tagliamonte 2005: 129–35). This hypothesis is supported by the evidence relating to other communities settled in central Italy, like the Sabines and Picenes; key monuments such as the inscribed stones from Penna Sant'Andrea near Teramo for the *Safinim*, or the cippus from Castignano near Ascoli Piceno for the *Pupun* – show that such ethnic processes also took place in Central Italy for the Sabines and the Picenes in the fifth century BC (Franchi dell'Orto 2001).

The increasing archaeological evidence coming from the regions settled by the future Sabines and Picenes documents the first existence of flourishing settlements and of complex societies from at least the seventh century BC in both regions, where we are able to identify typical local cultural attributes, as revealed many years ago by the necropolis of Campovalano near Teramo (Chiaramonte Treré and d'Ercole 2003). Cemeteries such as Fossa and Bazzano near L'Aquila, both recently explored under the direction of Vincenzo d'Ercole, gave a huge amount of information based on 170 graves from Fossa (Cosentino *et al.* 2001; d'Ercole and Benelli 2004) and the more than 600 graves from Bazzano, belonging to the seventh to sixth centuries BC. At Bazzano,

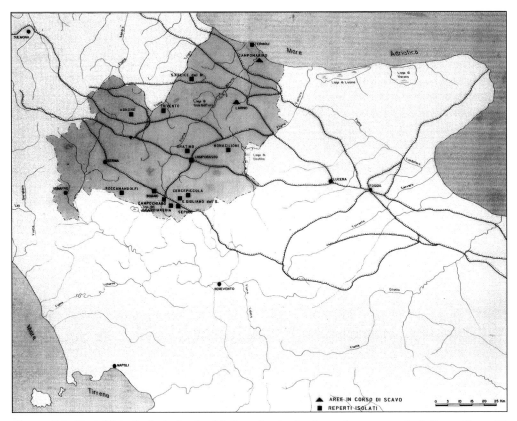

Figure 7.1. Protohistoric finds in the Molise: the tratturi can be seen as dark lines (from Di Niro 1991a: 32).

Fossa and other surrounding places like Caporciano (all in the province, L'Aquila) the seventh century BC male graves included some special material culture of a mountain landscape typified by the Gran Sasso area: leather boots with bronze hooks and wooden walking-sticks with an iron tip have been convincingly reconstructed by J. Weidig in his ongoing Marburg dissertation (Weidig 2005, 2007). It is hard not to judge this equipment and the better known contemporary bronze disc breastplates (Naso 2003; Tomedi 2000) as characteristic materializations of a particular area and people, namely the future Vestinians, and therefore to classify them as identity markers.

The knowledge of ancient peoples living in the modern day Marche and Abruzzo is enormously increased thanks to recent excavations, carried out particularly in cemeteries; the achieved and ongoing publication of these finds will permit us to challenge the old hypothesis of M. Suano of a 'princeless society in a princely neighbourhood (Suano 1991).' With regards to the settlement patterns, we can note that some fieldwork teams are investigating the landscape of Adriatic central Italy and have already produced many preliminary reports (Marche: Pearce *et al.* 2005, Vermeulen 2005; Abruzzo: Bell *et al.* 2002; Molise: Francis *et al.* 2002, Stek and Pelgrom 2005). However, at the present time a synthesis of the settlement patterns during the archaic period of the Marche and Abruzzo is still impossible.

The opposite situation applies to the Molise, where extensive cemetery explorations are still missing. In comparison with the archaeological evidence in central Italy as a whole, Molise is still quite a neglected and little known region. We know some bronze artefacts as scattered finds in the western Molise dating back to the ninth and eighth century BC, whose typology can give important indications of the connections between the find spots and production places of these artefacts; a few cemeteries have been explored, particularly in the coastal region, but they are not fully published. Thanks to the pioneering work directed by G. Barker in the 1970s and 1980s along the Biferno Valley, we are able to know the settlement patterns in the valley, cross-cutting the Molise region from east to west in a quite typical rural landscape of central Italy. According to Barker, 'The survey evidence demonstrates the development of a settlement hierarchy, at the top of which were large nucleated settlements of perhaps two or three dozen houses at least, substantial communities quite unlike the farms and hamlets of the Bronze Age'; (Barker 1995: 176). At the same time, two important cultural changes took place in the peninsula: the development of the Etruscan city-states in Etruria (Pacciarelli 2000) and the establishment of Greek *apoikiai* in the south (Settis and Parra 2005). According to the traditional view, these two changes led to the domination of two social models, lasting from the eighth century BC until the Roman conquest in the Italian peninsula, namely the protourban and urban communities of the Etruscan city-states and the chiefdoms of Abruzzo, Molise and elsewhere. I have spoken of a traditional view, because, thanks to the research of Alessandro Guidi and other scholars, we know that the distribution of the urban model was not limited to Etruria, but, from the eighth century BC, it was present in at least several places in Latium (Guidi and Santoro 2004), southern Apulia and the Veneto (De Min *et al.* 2005), perhaps even of the Marche (Naso 2007). The idea of a rural landscape based on the chiefdom is true for what we know about the Molise, where an important role was played by the routes used for long-distance transhumance (*tratturi*). In the rural economy of the Apennines, as elsewhere in the Mediterranean, long-distance transhumance was an enterprise of primary importance (Barker 1995).

Old and more recent finds show the importance of the *tratturi* already by the early first millennium BC, particularly in the heart of the Molise on the plateau of Bojano. These large plains, the only ones in all the mountain area of Molise, were crossed by the *tratturo* Pescasseroli-Candela, using the natural routeway from Aesernia to Saepinum along the Matese mountains. Near the modern day Bojano two Samnites hill-forts dating back to the fourth century BC are located on the Civita Superiore (756 metres) and on the top of the Monte Crocella (1040 metres; For Bojano: De Benedittis 1977, 1978, 1991: 233–7, 1995; La Regina 1989: 697; Oakley 1995: 107–8; for Monte Crocella: De Benedittis 1996: 74–7, fig. 3–5, 2004: 26–8; Caiazza 2003, with new information; for the land use in the Bojano area: Carta 1959, commented on by Ortolani 1964). Scattered finds, such as three bronze spear heads which have Bojano as generic findspot (Fig. 7.2), show an ancient usage of the plain: the three artefacts are of the Manduria type and their chronology may belong to the Final Bronze Age III in two cases and to Early Iron Age I for the decorated example (the three spearheads from Bojano are in Campobasso,

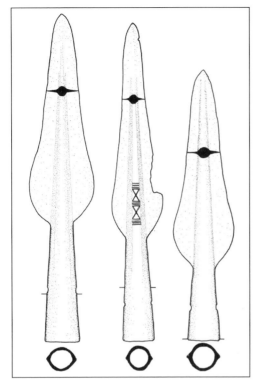

Figure 7.2. Spearheads from Bojano (from Gastaldi 1980: tav. 4).

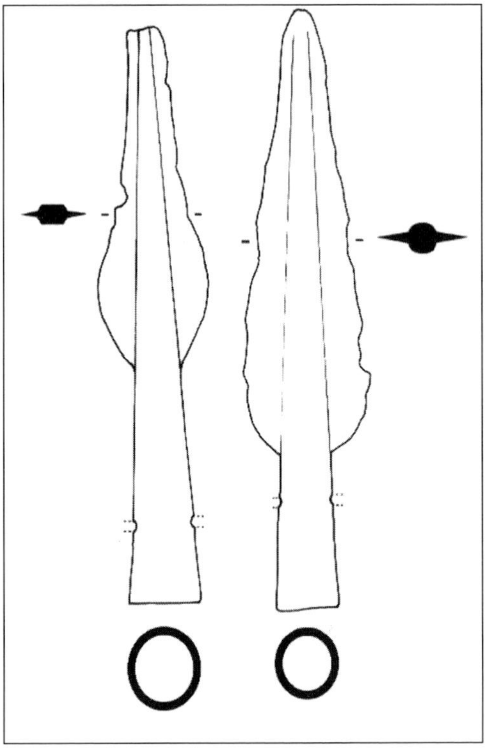

Figure 7.3. Spearheads from Campomarino (from De Benedittis et al. 2006: dis. 9).

Museo Provinciale Sannitico, inv. n°. 1257–8, 1260; Sogliano 1889: 154, nn. 1257–8, 1260; d'Agostino 1980: 22; Di Niro 1980: 47, nn. 10.1–3, tav. 4; Di Niro 1991a: 31; V. Ceglia, in De Benedittis 2005, 115–6, nn. 2–4. For the Manduria type: Bruno 2003–2004: L 39, 2007: 178–80; for the bronze hoard I in Manduria: Carancini and Peroni 1999: 68, n. 79; for the Bronze Age spearheads: Bruno 2006, 2007). A bronze spearhead of the Manduria type has been found in the necropolis near Campomarino (CB), loc. Difensola (De Benedittis *et al.* 2006: 126–7, b, fig. 9, dis. 9; Fig. 7.3). Another example from this necropolis near Campomarino loc. Difensola (De Benedittis *et al.* 2006: 126–7, a, fig. 9, dis. 9; Fig. 7.3), similar to spear heads from Trivento (d'Agostino 1980: 22, dated to the Early Iron Age; Di Niro 1980: 48, n. 12, tav. 4; Fig. 7.4) and Monacilioni (d'Agostino 1980: 22, dated to the Early Iron Age; Di Niro 1980, 48, n. 13, tav. 4; Fig. 7.4), seems to me to be slightly later.

Along the same *tratturo*, but from the *Saepinum* area are known a bronze eyelet axe of the Crichi type (Fig. 7.5) and a bronze scabbard of a Narce sword type. The typology of the artefacts from *Saepinum* is quite significant: firstly, this type of axe was distributed in a large area from southern Italy to Latium in the Early Iron Age; and secondly, the scabbard is a model typical of southern Etruria found also in Campania in the eighth

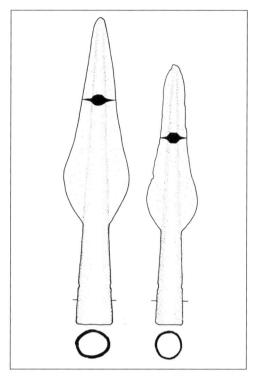

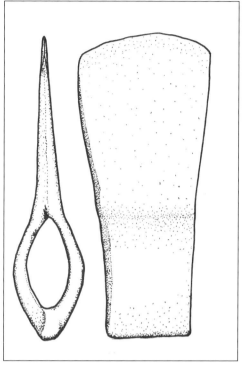

Figure 7.4. Spearheads from Trivento and Monacilioni (from Gastaldi 1980: tav. 4).

Figure 7.5. Crichi type axe from Sepino (from Gastaldi 1980: tav. 1).

century BC. For this reason the central position of the western Molise seems clear (the bronze axe in Campobasso, Museo Provinciale Sannitico, inv.-n°. 1241: Sogliano 1889: 153, n. 1241; Di Niro 1980: 47, n. 9.2, tav. 1; the Crichi type axe: Carancini 1984: 218–20, nn. 4367–85, tav. 163–5; the bronze scabbard in Campobasso, Museo Provinciale Sannitico, inv.-n°. 1143: Sogliano 1889: 150, n. 1143; d'Agostino 1980: 22; Di Niro 1980: 47, n. 9.1, tav. 2; the Narce sword type: Bianco Peroni 1970: 134–6, nn. 381–90, particularly n. 385 from Cumae, tavv. 55–6). These scabbards are typical of the final phase of the Early Iron Age in central Italy, reaching as far as Cumae and inner Campania, as confirmed by other examples (Bianco Peroni 1974: 21, n. 266 A, 25–6, n. 390; although Kilian 1974: 75 dubiously assigned this piece to his *Veii* type). A Suessula C type bronze razor (Bianco Peroni 1979: 54, nn. 267–269) has been found near Agnone (loc. Civitella: Capini 1985). Furthermore, a new protohistoric site has recently been found (Mieli and Cosentino 2006) in the area to provide a living context for these artefacts.

Some finds uncovered in the 1970s and 1980s, in the Bojano plain, help to clarify the provenance of these artefacts: *fossa* graves were found in at least four places within the plain, dating from the seventh to the fourth century BC, even though they were destroyed by the gravel quarries (d'Agostino 1978, 1980: 25; Capini 1980, 1982: 16–7; Di Niro 1991b: 61; De Benedittis 1991: 233; Macchiarola 1991b; Ceglia, in De Benedittis 2005:

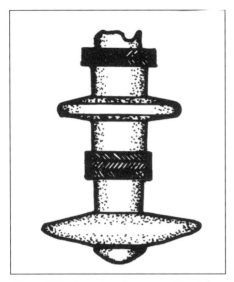

Figure 7.6. Narce type bronze scabbard from Sepino (from Gastaldi 1980: tav. 2).

97–114). In the excavation of the quarries one can still see unexcavated *fossa* graves. Unfortunately, just a few of these graves were excavated by the Soprintendenza and published: G. A. Del Pinto, the former commander of the Carabinieri in Bojano, saved many vases and bronze objects (some 250 pieces) from destruction and gave them to the Soprintendenza and the comune of Bojano. For this reason the provenance of these artefacts is not completely certain and this detail is quite important, as we will see. The artefacts, no longer divided into tomb groups, include also a Middle Geometric pendent semicircle (PSC) *skyphos*, a Greek vase which is quite rare in central Italy (Fig. 7.7). Other PSC *skyphoi* have been found in coastal locations such as Sant'Imbenia near Alghero in Sardinia and Villasmundo near Megara Hyblaea in Sicily. Eight (probably nine) examples have been found at Pontecagnano in the gulf of Salerno and three have been found in Etruria, two at *Veii* and one at Caere; fragments probably belonging to the type have been found in Rome and at Ficana in Latium (for the original typology: Kearsley 1989, reviewed by Popham and Lemos 1992; Sant'Imbenia: Bernardini *et al.* 1997; Ridgway 1989, for a sherd from Tharros firstly attributed to a PSC *skyphos*. Pontecagnano: Bailo Modesti 1998; for the tomb 7392: Basile 1999; for a further PSC *skyphos*, probably from Pontecagnano: Longo

Figure 7.7. A Geometric Pendant Semi-Circle (PSC) skyphos at Bojano (Photo: M. Kerschner).

1997; *Veii*: Boitani 2001, 2005; Toms 1997, uncertain; Caere: Rizzo 2005; Rome: La Rocca 1982, uncertain; Ficana: Rasmus Brandt *et al.* 1997, uncertain. An overview is sketched by Bartoloni 2005 and Nizzo 2005; an up-to-date review has been carried out by Rizzo 2005. The bibliography on PSC *skyphoi* in Italy is discussed in Naso 2008.)

The chronology of the Italian finds allow us to correct the date suggested by R. Kearsley for her types 5 and 6, because the deposition of the *skyphoi* in the tomb groups from Pontecagnano is dated to the first half of the eighth century BC: two PSC *skyphoi* belonging to the types 5 and 6 of Kearsley have been found in tomb 7392. To make clearer our understanding of the context of this vase, belonging to the earliest Greek imports in Italy, thanks to the help of many colleagues, I have been able to select clay samples from eight *skyphoi* (four from Pontecagnano, two from *Veii*, one from Caere and one from Bojano). The samples have been analysed by H. Mommsen with Neutron Activation Analysis (NAA) at Bonn, where a project about the clay composition of Greek pottery is being undertaken (preliminary results: Akurgal *et al.* 2002). Palermo (2002) identified a local production of PSC *skyphoi* in Crete. Through Mössbauer analysis on Greek pottery from *Veii*, Ridgway *et al.* (1985) and Deriu (1989) were able to localize in Greece the production of the *skyphoi*. In this project, six pendent semicircle *skyphoi* from Al-Mina, two from Lefkandi and seven from Ephesus, have been already analysed. The NAA analysis carried out on samples of 23 *skyphoi* is still unpublished, but with the kind permission of M. Kerschner of the Österreichisches Archäologisches Institut I can anticipate some of the results. Local productions of such *skyphoi* are documented in central Greece (Euboean-Boiotian group), and in Ionia at Ephesus and probably at Clazomenai. D. Palermo was recently able to identify by eye a local production at Prinias, in Crete. The samples from central Italy have found good comparisons with the Euboean-Boiotian group, except for two samples, including the Bojano one, which are still isolated, or, as chemists say, are single. The single samples may have various interpretations, ranging from a still unknown clay to a mistake in the preparation of the sample for the chemical analysis.

Apart from the question about the original provenance of the *skyphos*, it is interesting to ask from which Tyrrhenian centre the Greek *skyphos* was brought to Bojano. Other finds in Bojano give some indications. Among the bronze fibulae, there is at least one example of the Calatia type, common at Capua and Pontecagnano in the eighth century BC (De Benedittis 2005: 34–5, n. 57; for the fibulae of the so-called Calatia type: Lo Schiavo 1984: 242; from Capua: Johannowsky 1994: Fig. 1–2, Cerchiai 1995: 46–7). Among the bronze artefacts, it is possible to identify also two birds (Fig. 7.8) and three ornaments in the form of flowers (Fig. 7.9) that belonged to spectacle fibulae, typical of high rank grave goods of Capua and Suessula around the middle of the eighth century BC, perhaps during the third quarter. Such remains have been found in Pithecusa and at Cumae (De Benedittis 2005: 29, 35, nn. 39–40 (birds), 38, 43, nn. 73–75 (flowers); for the spectacle fibulae from Capua, Suessula and Pithecusa: Johannowsky 1994: 93–8, phase IIB; Cerchiai 2002. Other isolated pieces, *disiecta membra*, have been published by Aigner Foresti 1986: 38; Jurgeit 1999: 593, n. 1012, from Suessula, formerly in the Spinelli collection). Unfortunately we do not know the other grave goods, which would have been associated with the fibula/fibulae at Bojano. A bronze scabbard for a sword similar to the *Veii* and Narce types (Fig. 7.10) is also documented from Bojano and has a good

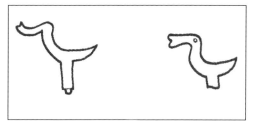

Figure 7.8. Bronze appliques in form of birds at Bojano (from De Benedittis 2005: nn. 39–40).

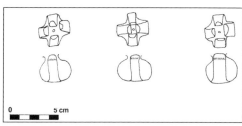

Figure 7.9. Bronze flowers at Bojano (from De Benedittis 2005: nn. 73–75).

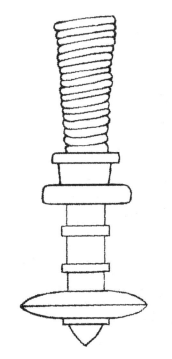

Figure 7.10. Point of Veii-Narce type scabbard at Bojano (from De Benedittis 2005: n. 110).

comparison with a similar chance find from *Saepinum* (De Benedittis 2005: 48, n. 110, similar to Bianco Peroni 1970; scabbards of *Veii* type: 130–134, nn. 366–80, tavv. 54–5; scabbards of Narce type: 134–6, nn. 381–90, tavv. 55–6; other scabbards of these types are documented in southern Italy: Bianco Peroni 1974, scabbards of *Veii* type: 25, nn. 244 A, 297 A – from Altamura, 377 A – from Serra Ajello, prov. Cosenza; scabbards of Narce type: 25–6, nn. 266 A – from San Marco dei Gavoti, prov. Benevento and 390 A – *Veii*, grave AA 1, tavv. 5 and 7). Bronze ornaments for clothing now at Bojano find good comparisons with similar pieces from female depositions at *Veii*, dating to the third quarter of the eighth century BC, and at Capua, where they were associated with glass paste *Vogelperlen* (Bojano: De Benedittis 2005: 30, nn. 43–4; *Veii*: Berardinetti Insam 2001: 101, n. I.G.5.27 from the tomb Quattro Fontanili HH 11–12; Capua: Johannowsky 1994: fig. 3, from the tomb 200 dating to the local phase IIB.)

Such *Vogelperlen* have also been found at Bojano (De Benedittis 2005: 26, n. 25, belonging to a type whose central Italian distribution has been examined by Martelli 1991: 1051–2, fig. 2c; as well as at Pontecagnano (d'Agostino and Gastaldi 1988: 69, n. 42E4) and Capua. The distribution all over the Mediterranean has been sketched by S. Huber (Huber 1998: 128–30, fig. 18). The similarities between the Bojano finds and those of Iron Age Campania are further stressed by eight clay *kyathoi*, characterised by their heavy baroque handles (Fig. 7.11). Such vases are still documented only in ancient Capua, where W. Johannowsky was able to build a sequence of their development,

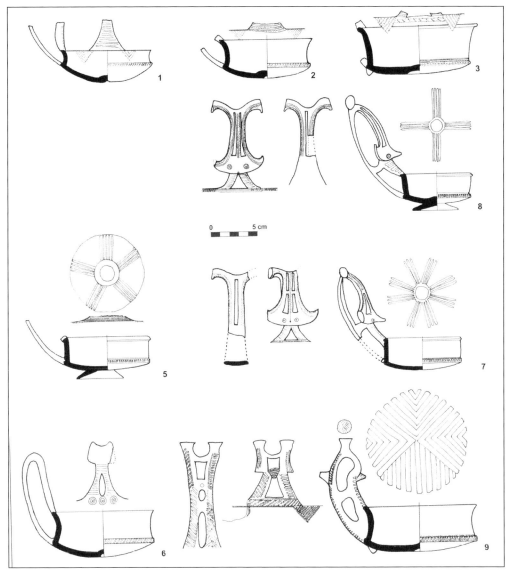

Figure 7.11. Skyphoi at Bojano (from De Benedittis 2005: nn. 1–3, 5–9). Scale: 5 centimetres.

dated by C. Chiaramonte Trerè and L. Cerchiai (Bojano: De Benedittis 2005: 19–21, n. 1–3, 5–9; Capua: Cerchiai 1995: 46; Chiaramonte Treré 1999: 107, fig. 16–22, 121, both with references). In Bojano the forms typical for the eighth century BC are represented. If we accept the provenance from Bojano of these finds, which I hope to verify by excavation of the graves still visible in the quarries, we can explain the affinities with the material culture of Iron Age Campania, particularly with Capua, only if we postulate the presence on the Bojano plain of Capuan aristocracies as the owners of the spectacle fibula/fibulae (various finds from Capua have been published by Johannowsky 1983, 1989, 1992, 1994, 1996; an overview is in Museo 1995. For Middle- and Late Geometric Greek imports at Capua: Johannowsky 1994: 105; the Etruscan origin of Capua is stressed by Chiaramonte Trerè 1999. Minoja 2006 examines the funerary rituals in the Orientalizing period).

In this way it would be possible to hypothesize a form of colonization into the Bojano plain of aristocratic groups from ancient Capua during the eighth century BC and this would be not very surprising, if we think of other forms of colonization promoted in this period by other Etruscan cities like Caere and Vulci, whose aristocracies were in this period seeking to control the communication routes and the natural resources of the surrounding territories (the bibliography on the Etruscan expansion in Campania is huge: see various syntheses like Colonna 1991; Cerchiai 1995; Bonghi Jovino 2000; for Caere and Vulci, see Moretti Sgubini *et al.* 2001 and the related conference proceedings, Paoletti 2005). I wish to stress again the need to prove the hypothesis by verifying the real provenance of the finds now at Bojano. In each case, the scattered bronze artefacts coming from the centres along the Pescasseroli-Candela *tratturo* support the view of a relationship between the western Molise and the Campanian centres.

It is interesting to compare this general hypothesis with the information available for the eastern part of the region. Along the Adriatic coast of Molise some cemeteries have been explored and partly published in the 1980s; thanks to A. Di Niro such names as Larino, Termoli and Guglionesi are well-known to scholars (for the necropoleis of Larino and Termoli: Di Niro 1981, 1984; for Guglionesi: Di Niro 1986). A phase dating to the end of eighth–early seventh century BC has been documented only in the necropolis of Larino (for the early finds from the necropolis in Larino: Di Niro 1981, Macchiarola 1991a). The related finds are quite characteristic, because they also include the typical matte-painted pottery from the northern district of Daunia in Apulia, as we can see in the *fossa* grave 16 (Stazione). However, the technical aspects of this and other similar vases permit us to classify them as local productions, imitating Daunian models. A similar situation is also documented in the seventh and sixth century BC in Termoli (Di Niro 1981), Guglionesi (Di Niro 1986), San Giuliano di Puglia (Di Niro 2004) and now in a new findplace at Carlantino (De Benedittis and Santone 2006).

Here some tomb groups have been recently excavated and published by local volunteers; the finds are very important, because Carlantino is south of the Fortore river, which actually marks the administrative boundary between Molise and Puglia. In the 1990s, A. Di Niro noted that in the sixth century tombs north of the Fortore river the burials are extended, while in the tombs south of the river the burials are crouched, a typical funerary practice of Apulian *fossa* graves. Therefore in the sixth–fifth centuries BC the river Fortore might already have been a cultural boundary. We know that in the division undertaken by Augustus in 7 BC, the boundary between Samnium and Apulia was marked by the Biferno river, north of the Fortore. The Fortore valley was very important throughout the centuries, because it dominated the natural route way between central Apennines and the Adriatic coast, between Samnium and Apulia. The new finds from Carlantino, south of the Fortore, belong mostly to the sixth century BC and include not only locally made matte-painted pottery, but also extended inhumations and bronze disc breastplates of the type defined as 'Paglieta' by G. Tomedi, who dated it to the first half of the sixth century BC (Tomedi 2000: 45–6, nn. 60–72 for the list of Paglieta type, n. 69 is from Carlantino; new finds from Carlantino are presented in De Benedittis and Santone 2006: 109–13, nn. 1–16). Extended inhumations and bronze disc breastplates were typical characteristics of *fossa* graves in the Abruzzo, and they have been normally used as ethnic markers for the later Samnites community. It would be important to explore scientifically some *fossa* graves in Carlantino not only to verify the information concerning the real body position, but also to check the start date of the cemetery that produced a Terni B type bronze sword, dating back probably to the early eighth century BC, because it is associated with the remains of a Guardia Vomano type bronze scabbard (De Benedittis and Santone 2006: 16, fig. 3c). Both types are classified according to the typology elaborated by Vera Bianco Peroni (1970, 1974; see too Kilian 1974). Thanks to the new finds from Carlantino, we can conclude that the Fortore river was not really a boundary, but that the surrounding area was a frontier between Samnium and Apulia showing cultural interaction between the two main ethnic groups. Not by accident have some scholars, such as E. Antonacci Sanpaolo, suggested the assignation of this area to a so-called Oscan-Daunian people (Antonacci Sanpaolo 2000).

In 2005 we undertook the exploration of the Fortore valley, cross-cutting a natural north-south road, the Castel di Sangro-Lucera *tratturo*, to explore these issues and to compare results with the field data collected by Barker's project,. The actual landscape in the middle Fortore valley is dominated by the Occhito Lake, a huge artificial water basin built in the 1960s along the former Fortore river. In two seasons of fieldwalking around the modern village of Macchia Valfortore we found more than 110 find locations and many of these can be properly defined as sites. Among the preliminary results of the new research, one can say that for the period relevant for this paper, the new finds show flourishing settlement already in the Late Bronze Age and in the Iron Age, particularly along the former river valley. Finds belonging to seventh century BC are still lacking in our research, but we have been able to find some tombs belonging to the sixth century BC in many places along the Occhito Lake. At first sight, the *fossa* graves were not grouped into large cemeteries, but they formed groups of small numbers of burials. Unfortunately the graves had been badly damaged by the water erosion of the modern lake. The graves contained

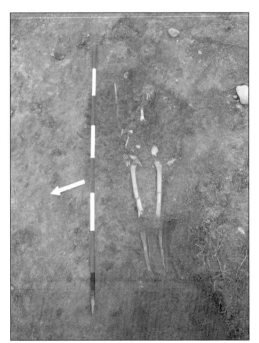

Figure 7.12. A fossa grave (site 119) near the Occhito Lake (Photo: A. Naso).

extended inhumations (Fig. 7.12). Aspects of Archaic ritual include the filling of the *fossa* graves with river stones, brought from the underlying Fortore, and the insertion of a couple of iron spits. Pottery is quite primitive: coarse wares were not yet wheel-made, so it may be very difficult to date contemporary sherds when they are found on the surface during the fieldwalking. Similar ritual characteristics and similar hand made pottery have been documented also in the necropolis of Carlantino. The first results of the survey around Macchia Valfortore, including the discussion on the early evidence from this site, are presented in Naso 2009.

In summary, current knowledge about Molise allows us to identify two main areas, a western and a coastal, which from the fifth century BC onwards were settled respectively by the *Pentri* and by the *Frentani*. The western area indicates relationships and links with the Campania already in the Iron Age, particularly in the Bojano plain. On the other hand the coastal district is influenced by the Daunian communities, at least in Larino from the end of the eighth–early seventh century BC, and in other cemeteries in the sixth century BC. Thanks to the Oscan material culture and the matte-painted pottery, northern Apulia seems to be an area of cultural interaction at least from the sixth century BC onwards. I hope that the exploration of the Fortore valley will convey new information about these and other issues.

Acknowledgements

I wish to thank Gabriele Cifani and Simon Stoddart for the kind invitation to the Cambridge conference. Simon Stoddart changed my Italo-English into a better linguistic presentation.

8

Ethnicity, identity and state formation in the Latin landscape. Problems and approaches.

Francesca Fulminante

Keywords: ethnicity, identity, state, city-state, boundaries, central Italy, *Latium vetus*, Iron Age

> Uno, nessuno, centomila…(One, No One and One Hundred Thousand, the last and most famous novel by Luigi Pirandello, published 1924–1926).

> 'We need…to remind ourselves all the time that each of us participates in an ethnicity – perhaps more than one – just like them, just like Other, just like 'the "minorities"' (Jenkins 1997: 14).

> 'Understanding the chronological development of, and balance between, often highly localized ties of place and broader notions of people and/or geography in the construction of political identities is a particularly important challenge' (Morgan 2003: 1)

It is a commonly held belief that ethnogenesis in *Latium vetus* is strictly linked to the processes of state formation and urbanization, occurring in this region between the end of the Final Bronze Age and during the Early Iron Age (Guidi 2006). The richness and variety of available data, such as archaeological sources (material culture, epigraphy, anthropological remains etc.) and ancient authors, makes research on the topic in this area most exciting, but carries with it a series of difficulties, resulting from the combination of so many different kinds of evidence (on the difficult relationship between text and artefacts, see Little 1992, Thurston 1997; Andrén 1998; with reference to Rome and Italy, see Storey 1999 and below with further references).

The aim of this paper is not to present a comprehensive and conclusive discourse on ethnicity, identity and state formation in *Latium vetus*; but to discuss a number of previous and current approaches to ethnicity in this area, and suggest a fresh perspective on this topic. The model presented in this paper is rooted in the social anthropological approach proposed by Barth in the introduction to his collection: *Ethnic Groups and Boundaries* (1969). According to Barth, ethnicity is socially constructed, constantly negotiated not only by groups (especially in the political action) but also by individuals in their daily-life experience. A corollary to this model is that ethnicity represents only one of many identities played by an individual according to different contexts and situations: gender, status, family identity, civic identity etc. (for an anthropological perspective, see for example Jenkins 1997: 167–8 and further references below).

However the social construction of ethnicity does not deny the cultural content of ethnicity, but puts it in the right perspective. Ethnicity is not an *a priori* entity to which people belong; rather ethnicity must mean something to someone. However in order to have a meaning for someone, there must be a cultural and/or biological content (language, common belief, same physical traits etc.), the basis by which members of a group recognise similarities among themselves, 'us', or differences from an other , 'them' (Jenkins 1997: 168–9, further illustrated below).

On the basis of this theoretical premise, this paper proposes to integrate different types of evidence (material culture, ancient authors and possibly anthropological, faunal and vegetal remains) in a relational model, in order to recognize these cultural elements, identify ethnic boundaries and analyze ethnic dynamics. Since almost any cultural element (language, food habit, material culture etc.) can assume an ethnic connotation, it is here proposed to adopt the principle of redundancy (Emberling 1997) in order to define ethnic boundaries between different groups. The integration of data in a relational model would allow a multi-scale approach and the possibility of studying identity and ethnicity both horizontally (among different ethnic groups) and vertically (from the individual to the family to the social group, the community and the region or the ethnic group) on a long term perspective.

For this purpose Geographical Information Systems (already widely used within archaeology) and/or Social Network Analysis models and techniques (only recently starting to be adopted on a wider scale within this discipline) would provide powerful tools of manipulation, analysis and visualization of data in order to help their interpretation.

The social anthropological model of ethnicity

It is generally agreed that a paradigm shift in anthropological studies on ethnicity was introduced by the ground-breaking and highly influential book edited by Friedrik Barth (1969) from the proceedings of the symposium: *Ethnic Groups and Boundaries* (1967). In his introduction to that collection, Barth outlined an approach to the study of ethnicity which focused on the on-going negotiations of boundaries between groups of people.

According to the previously dominant structural functionalist perspective, ethnic groups were commonly considered as more or less firmly bounded social groups defined by common biological and/or cultural traits; ethnic boundaries were treated or understood as social 'facts', reified entities or as logical *a priori* constructs, to which people naturally belonged. In contrast to this view, Barth affirmed that: 'ethnic groups are categories of ascription and identification by the actors themselves' (1969: 10).

Moving the focus from the cultural characteristics of ethnic groups to the dynamic interactions between them and their reciprocal definition by differentiation, Barth laid the foundation of the constructive approach to ethnicity, which has now been adopted by most anthropological scholarship. In fact, as emphasized by Jenkins (1997: 12ff.), the 'basic social anthropological model of ethnicity', pioneered by Barth, moved the focus from the substance or content of ethnicity (which he called the 'cultural stuff'), to the interface between groups. He defined ethnic identity as part of a dynamic social process and claimed that the content of social categories not only changed over time but so did the boundaries between them (Barth 1969: 14ff.).

According to Barth's model, ethnic formation is an on-going process, which combines internal definition on the basis of similarities (self-awareness and the definition of 'us'), with external categorization by differences from 'them' or 'the other' (it is the recognition and production of differences in relation to 'them' or 'others' that create and reinforce the image of internal similarities, Jenkins 1997: 12ff.). Therefore, ethnicity is by definition 'transactional, shifting and essentially impermanent'; 'group-ness' boundaries are changeable, variable and contingent, being continuously defined and re-defined in an endless process of power negotiation among individuals and groups within different and conflicting interests (Jenkins 1988: 175).

A shown by Jenkins (1997: 10–2), the theoretical premises of Barth's model are ultimately rooted in the work of the sociologists Max Weber and Everett Hughes. In particular, as reminded by Jenkins (1997: 10), Hughes (1948) had already shown how the unity of ethnic groups is not based on objective, measurable differences, but on the behaviour of people ins and outs of these groups, who talk, feel, and act as if they were separate groups (Hughes 1994: 91). Similarly Weber, in his work *Economy and Society* (first published in 1922), maintained that an ethnic group is based on the belief, shared by its members, that they belong to a common descent; but, according to him, it is not the common belief which defines the group and creates a sense of affiliation among its members. On the contrary, it is primarily the common political action of a group that, on the basis of certain common cultural or biological factors, inspires the belief in common ethnicity (Weber 1978: 385–9). As will be shown later, this link between collective political action and identity, no matter how artificially organized, and ethnic formation, emphasized by Jenkins as a central concept both in Weber's and Barth's work (and in the study of 'cultural memory' and the formation of 'political identity' in ancient civilizations by the Egyptologist Jan Assmann 1992), is particularly suitable to be applied to the ethnic and social dynamics in central Italy during the Early Iron Age and the subsequent Archaic and Republican periods.

Finally, another theoretical aspect that should be taken into account when considering ethnicity (both in present and past times) is the relationship between 'identity' and 'ethnicity'. As correctly emphasized by Jenkins, 'ethnicity has to mean something – in the sense of making a difference – not only to the people one is studying, but also to individual persons' (1997: 13). In this sense, ethnicity represents only one of many different possible identities (personal, family, social, sexual, political etc.), which an individual may decide to act and perform according the specific contexts or situations. When ethnicity is correctly understood as one of many social identities, it is clear that 'group-ness' boundaries are also permeable in the sense that, for example, status membership may crosscut ethnic membership and connect members of different ethnic groups (compare on this point Emberling 1997: 299, 305 ff; within the sociological theory this approach seems to have much in common with the so-called intersectionality theory, a branch of feminist studies, aimed at understanding social inequality as a global but also multilayered and multifaceted phenomenon, in which different levels of discrimination – status, gender, race etc. – are often combined and entangled in various and complex ways[1]).

Even when ethnicity is agreed to be a social construction, cultural contents or cultural objects ('cultural stuffs' in Barth's terminology) are still required for the construction of an ethnic identity; Jenkins emphasised that there is still a need for a 'social marker' (no matter how minor, real or imaginary), which is identified, agreed and recognized as held in common both by the individuals inside and by those outside the group (1988: 167–9). These social markers (territoriality, language, history, economic considerations, symbolic identifications of one kind or another) can be identified in different aspects of the material culture and can be studied by archaeologists in order to try to detect past people's identities and their interactions (for a recent discussion of the role of material culture in 'ethnic' and other 'cultural self/other identities definition and negotiation' see Lucy 2005, in particular pp. 100–108).

The following section, based upon Emberling's work, will show how the social anthropological model can be profitably applied to the study of ethnogenesis, with specific reference to the formation of complex societies and the definition of 'ethnic' boundaries in central Italy, and how it could be further developed.

Ethnicity and archaeology: material culture and the definition of boundaries

As emphasised in the previous section, the logically immediate but naïve connection between material cultures and ethnic groups, which dominated the traditional (and according to many 'colonial'), structural functionalist and anthropological perspective to ethnicity, was definitively surpassed by Barth's constructive approach, which held that ethnicity is socially created through continuous (re-)negotiation (1969). Similarly, an independent evolution within the archaeological discipline made archaeologists aware of the complex semantic system of symbols attached to artifacts, and their different meanings according to contexts and situations (see for example the fundamental work by Hodder 1982; and more recently Robb 1998) and led them to deny strongly (see for example papers in the volume edited by Shennan 1989 or Jones 1997: 14–39, 106ff.) the old link between material culture and ethnos, dominant in the traditional, cultural-historical approach founded by the *Dawn of European Civilization* (Childe 1925).

However, as remarked by Jenkins, the cultural content of ethnicity is still important because 'for similarity to be identified there has to be something in common…[there] have to be differences which make a difference to someone'; therefore 'there are local limits how arbitrary the social construction of identity can be' (Jenkins 1997: 168). In this perspective, the account on *Ethnicity in Complex Societies* (1997), provided by Geoff Emberling (who adopts Barth's perspective), convincingly demonstrated that several aspects of material culture worked as markers of ethnic identity in the past; and that by embracing the social anthropological model, the archaeological study of ethnicity still has great potential to improve the understanding of ethnic dynamics in past societies.

When considering the almost infinite cultural features that can be used to distinguish one ethnic group from the others (language, religion, body ornamentation, cuisine, architecture, clothing and household objects such as pottery etc.), Emberling emphasizes that the problem for the archaeologist is to identify the particular social meaning (ethnic, political, economic etc.) of that particular cultural trait in a given social situation (1997: 310–1). This assumption by Emberling is consistent with Barth's definition of ethnic categories as 'organizational vessels that may be given varying amount and forms of content in different sociocultural systems' (1969: 14). For instance, the distribution of a particular pottery style may indicate ethnic boundaries but could equally represent the spatial limits of a particular system of distribution (Emberling 1997: 311).

In this case, a careful contextual analysis of the production and use of artefacts, following the pioneering approach developed by Ian Hodder in his work in the Baringo district of Kenya (1982), may help understand their correct symbolic meaning. The key method, in this case, is to identifying the meaning of stylistic variation through the principle of redundancy, according to which:

> important social boundaries or those being negotiated are likely to be marked redundantly; [thus] comparing stylistic distributions of multiple categories of material culture gives a greater likelihood of locating important social boundaries (Emberling 1997: 318).

When dealing with past societies, it might be the case that one stylistic feature specific to one preserved class of artefacts would have been redundant with other cultural features not preserved in the archaeological record:

> 'Nevertheless, a redundantly marked difference will be more likely to have been important in the past' (Emberling 1997: 318).

In order to identify if a stylistic distribution represents a meaningful social boundary, or not, it is important to know the scale of a system of production and distribution. In fact:

> A stylistic distribution larger than the scale of production and distribution suggests that some larger social meaning maintained the unity of the style. …. Objects produced at a small scale within the territory of an ethnic group are more likely to be distinctive of that group than are objects produced at larger scales and widely distributed (Emberling 1997: 319).

As suggested by Emberling, the study of 'stylistic variation' to identify ethnic markers is particularly fruitful in the case of 'ethnic enclaves', where the movement of members of one group into another makes differences particularly marked and strategies of assimilation and/or the maintenance of differences are strongly emphasized and exacerbated (1997: 316). According to this scholar, ethnographic comparisons or literary sources might be helpful in identifying social and ethnic boundaries; however these boundaries, roughly marked, have to be tested by 'intra-regional contextual analysis' of 'production' and 'use' of artifacts, compared with 'inter-regional analysis of different practices or artifacts' between neighbouring groups; and finally these results have to be confronted with analyses of other categories of evidence, which may support an identification of ethnic difference (1997: 311).

The following sections will show how the 'constructive' anthropological model of ethnicity (advanced by Barth 1969 and further enhanced, with specific application to past societies, for example by Emberling 1997; Jones 1997; Hall 2000; or in contributions to the volume edited by Malkin 2001), can be fruitfully applied to the study of ethnogenesis and identity definition in Early Iron Age central Italy, with a great potential for further enhancement.

Ethnicity and archaeology in Early Iron Age central Italy: ethnogenesis, state formation and identity definition/characterization

Ranging between two opposing opinions, ethnogenesis can either be linked with hunter-gatherer bands or connected with the birth of contemporary nations and restricted to modern historical times (Emberling 1997: 307). As already mentioned, the relationship between ethnogenesis and the development of complex societies has been successfully emphasized by Emberling (1997, but also Bentley 1987 and Assmann 1992), while Renfrew has placed the birth of the modern notion of ethnicity in Europe during the Early Iron Age (Renfrew 1987).

With particular reference to *Latium vetus* and central Italy, it has already been suggested by many authors that ethnogenesis, poleogenesis and state formation were interwoven processes, which occurred during the course of the Early Iron Age, from about the eleventh/tenth to the eighth/seventh century BC (for example Torelli 1988; Guidi 1998; Guidi 2006; following an early statement by Pallottino 1942: 77). This paper suggests that this particular period of time (generally addressed by scholarship as proto-history because it witnessed the transition from pre-historic to historical times, dominated by cities and by literacy), can also be seen as a time of identity *definition* and *characterization*.

In this sense, ethnicity is only one of many identities played out by individuals in different contexts and at different levels (family, city, region, class, gender etc.); therefore ethnic identity cannot be studied per se, independently from the others (cf. Stoddart 2009). The following sections will identify the evidence for the study of ethnicity in central Italy and review previous approaches. Then, on the basis of the theoretical premises illustrated in the first two sections, further developments will be suggested for the study of ethnicity and other social identities in central Italy, which could also be applied to other geographical and historical contexts.

Available sources: archaeology and 'ancient authors'

The archaeology and history of early central Italy has the great advantage (or disadvantage) of having a rich array of archaeological evidence (mainly from funerary contexts but also from settlements) and also complementary sources, such as 'ancient authors'.

The possibility of using 'ancient authors' in combination with the archaeological evidence could be considered a positive contribution. It allows one to consider a different and independent piece of evidence and provides alternative points of view, which give a more complete and integrated picture than the one solely derived from archaeological data (for a positive approach to a combined use of 'written' and 'material sources', see Moreland 2001). On the other hand, this potential opportunity can turn into a potential issue, which can be the object of several criticisms.

The use of 'ancient authors' in the reconstruction of the earliest phases of Italian history for example has been acritically and simplistically stigmatized as old-fashioned by Bradley (2000b) with reference to the model of ethnic group identification proposed by Pallottino (1942; see also 1991, in English). Alternatively, an exact match between literary sources and archaeology has been sought with the expectation that one should test the other (see Bietti Sestieri 1998). This has resulted in a sterile debate on whether ancient authors or archaeological data should have primacy, and which should verify or falsify the other (this 'expectation' might explain the origin of the debate between Andrea Carandini and Anna Maria Bietti Sestieri, with specific reference to early Roman history, for which see Bietti Sestieri 2000).

It cannot be denied that there are many methodological problems and biases inherent in the use of 'ancient authors' as a source of information for the historical reconstruction of pre- and proto-historic processes in central Italy. Two major themes of discussion might be summarized as follow. Firstly, most surviving accounts are much later than the actual events and the many steps in the transmission of original information from primary sources to the final elaborations by ancient authors are still unclear and debated (see for example, among recent contributions: Cornell 1995: 1–80; Drummond and Ogilvie 1989; Wiseman 1994; Poucet 1994). Secondly, it is generally claimed that literary accounts provide only a partial point of view, from the perspective of the dominant Roman elite of the time (Poucet 2000: 105ff.; and with particular reference to sources on Italic ethnic groups, Lomas 1997).

However, if 'ancient authors' are considered as another source of evidence together with epigraphic and archaeological evidence, they can be a useful and valuable independent and complementary piece of information for the study of ethnic dynamics in central Italy during the Early Iron Age and in general for the historical reconstruction of this period (for example, ancient authors are considered essential for the study of the 'ethnic discourse' in Greece by Hall 1997/2000).

Traditional cultural-historical approach

It is a commonly held belief that during the Bronze Age the Italian Peninsula was characterized by relatively loose territorial divisions and lack of strongly defined ethnic identities (see Bietti Sestieri 1998: 280). In fact, even though local variations and regional sub-groups have been identified, during the Middle Bronze Age I–II (1700–1400 BC), central and northern Italy (from northern Lazio and Tuscany on the Tyrrhenian sea to eastern Emilia and Romagna on the Adriatic sea) were discontinuously but almost entirely occupied by the *Grotta Nuova* culture, while the rest of the southern Italian peninsula (from southern Lazio and the Marche in the centre, down to Calabria in the south, with a lack of evidence in Molise) was characterized by the Proto-Apennine culture (Cocchi Genick 1995; see fig. 8.1.A). And subsequently, during the Middle Bronze Age III (1400–1325/1300 BC) and the Recent Bronze Age (1325/1300–1200 BC), the whole

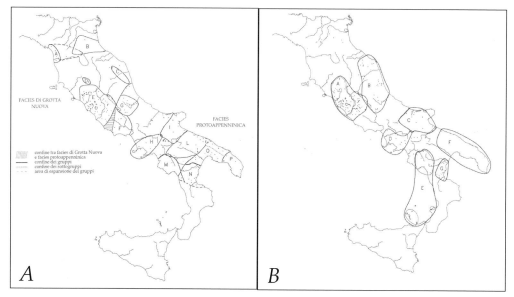

Figure 8.1. Geographical distribution of the (A) Grotta Nuova and Proto-Apennine cultures, 1700–1400 BC and of the (B) Apennine culture, 1400–1325/1300 BC (from Cocchi Genick 1995: tav. 1–2).

peninsula (from southern Tuscany south to the Sibari plain in Calabria, with a lack of evidence in northern Campania and Molise), was almost entirely unified in the Apennine and the following sub-Apennine cultures (Cocchi Genick 1995; see Fig 8.1.B).

Starting in the Final Bronze Age (1200– 950/925 BC) and more markedly during the Early Iron Age (950/925–750/725 BC), distinctive regional cultures seem to appear. This emerging differentiation in the material culture during the Early Iron Age was originally linked to ethnogenetic processes and to the definition of the different people of the Italian peninsula by the famous Etruscologist Massimo Pallottino (1942, in English 1991). As shown in Fig. 8.2, this scholar noticed the striking coincidence between the distribution of material culture, languages (evident from inscriptions) and territories recorded for the various ethnic groups by literary sources.

This approach, based on a contentious assumption of correspondence between language, people and culture, has been criticized as naïve, based on 'common sense' and old-fashioned in a recent paper by Guy Bradley (2000b). Bradley noticed that Umbria produced as many Etruscan inscriptions as Umbrians. Therefore, he argues, mixed language use was probably more common than dominant 'regional languages' (Bradley 2000b: 113). However this idea of inter-ethnic composition of Early Iron Age and Archaic societies in central Italy had already been suggested on the basis of both archaeological and literary sources, for example, for the Faliscan area, a sort of Latin enclave in the Etruscan territory (see Camporeale 1991; Cifani 2005; Colonna 1990b Cristofani 1988 and Iaia 2000); similarly the open character and the mobility of the Etruscan and Roman societies during the Archaic Age, has been suggested by Carmine

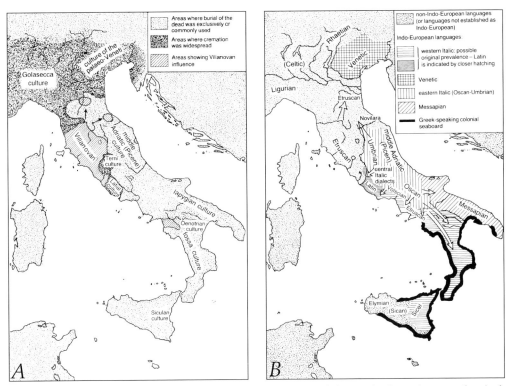

Figure 8.2. (A) Cultural areas of Italy at the beginning of the Early Iron Age, tenth–ninth century BC, compared with (B) the original distribution and spread of the languages of earliest Italic populations (from Pallottino 1991: fig. 1–2).

Ampolo, by using the character of Demaratus as a case study (Ampolo 1976–7, 1981, 1987), and by other scholars (for example Cornell 1995: 157–9 and Torelli 1989).

Bradley discounted literary sources and epigraphic evidence on the basis that there is no evidence of self-identification by Italic people prior to the sixth, fifth or fourth century BC (2000b: 115–7), but he was probably too ready to deny the striking coincidence between 'ethnic groups', as mentioned by ancient authors, and the self-identification, suggested by material cultures held in common. On the other hand, as already suggested by Emberling (see above), Bradley has correctly related ethnogenesis to state and urban formation and has rightly interpreted political action as a critical element in the formation of ethnic identity (2000b: 118–21).

In particular, Bradley correctly remarks that the Latin identity, when defined as a self-identification, existed well before the emergence of all other major states in central Italy. In fact, 'there can be little doubt on the antiquity of a Latin myth of common ancestry related to the cult of Jupiter on the Alban Mount' (Cornell 1997: 9), dated generally at least as far back as the end of the Bronze Age, and it has been recently suggested, that an original totemic mythology of the Latins might have been even earlier (Carandini 2002: 123ff.). According to Bradley, all other Italic ethnic identities gradually emerged in the area throughout the first millennium BC, as a form of ideological resistance to the advancing and inexorable military power of Rome (Bradley 2000b: 116, but already Malone and Stoddart 1994; Smith 1996: 215–23; and see Dench 1997 on the Samnites; see also Stoddart this volume).

A recent paper by Stéphane Bourdin addressed the same topic of ethnic identity used as tool of inter-state competition and political resistance, by analyzing the case of Ardea and by combining epigraphic, archaeological and literary evidence (2005). Bourdin demonstrated that Ardea (one of the main Latin centres), during the sixth century BC strongly claimed to be descended from the *Rutuli* (one of the Latin tribes, who according to ancient authors, celebrated the *Feriae Latinae* on the *Mons Albanus*, the annual festival of the Latin commonwealth consisting of the sacrifice of a pig and a communal ritual meal) in order to contrast the rival Rome, trying to impose his authority on the Latin league (Bourdin 2005: 629ff.).

While Bradley has emphasized how Italic people became aware of their ethnic identity in *contrast* to the expansion of the Latin/Roman identity imposed by the growing power of Rome (see also Bradley 2000a), the study by Bourdin has analyzed a case of *competitive* identity, where Ardea, in order to contrast Rome, claimed its original provenance from the *Rutuli*, a similar ancient and prestigious origin within the Latin commonwealth. In convergence with Barth's model, Bradley has suggested ethnicity as a construction rather than something in place from the beginning of the Early Iron Age and Bourdin's study has showed how ethnicity in central Italy, during the Early Iron Age and the Archaic Age, was developed in an articulated and complex negotiation between wider (regional, ethnic) and more local (city-state or community) identities (see also Bradley 2000a: 262ff.; Davies 1997: 28, with reference to Greece).

This paper suggests that this perspective deserves further development by adopting a supra-regional focus and long-term perspectives in order to define how these different levels of identity (regional, local community, ethnic group but also family, gender etc.) interacted through time. After reviewing a number of recent approaches to ethnicity in central Italy with particular reference to *Latium vetus*, the last section of this paper will propose an holistic perspective, which takes into account all possible available sources (or at least a good proportion of them) including, the less fashionable 'ancient authors', as the best approach to investigate the complex processes of ethnic definition and characterization which occurred within the region by the end of the Final Bronze Age and the expansion of Rome in the Archaic/Republican Period.

More recent approaches

The traditional historical approach to ethnogenesis in central Italy, inaugurated by Pallottino, as mentioned in the previous section, dominated Italian scholarship and especially the discipline of Etruscology. Its basic assumption of an unquestioned congruence between culture, language and ethnos has been called into question by several scholars both outside and within Italy, but its basic intuition of locating in the Early Iron Age the process of ethnogenesis of Italic people is still valid and generally accepted in current scholarship (see Guidi 1998; Guidi *et al.* 2002).

However, under the impulse of a renewed interest in ethnicity in the last few years, novel studies have been undertaken by a few younger Italian scholars more inclined to accept intellectual stimuli from outside. For example, a few years ago, Gabriele Cifani published a study on settlement patterns in the middle Tiber Valley from the end of the Final Bronze Age to the Roman conquest. In particular, this scholar detected different settlement dynamics from the Final Bronze Age onwards with the evolution of different urban models according to the specific cultural and social context of the different ethnic groups (2003).

Cifani (see also this volume) proposes that the Etruscan area was already organized as a 'territorial state' or 'macro state', with a settlement hierarchy of at least three tiers

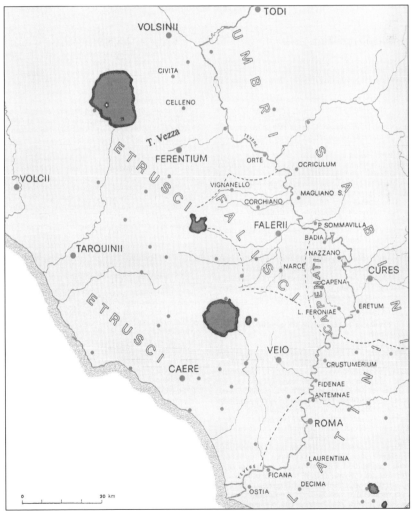

Figure 8.3. The lower Tiber Valley and the ethnic groups studied by Gabriele Cifani (2003) from the perspective of territoriality and settlement organization (from Cifani 2003: tav. 1).

(second and third order settlements dependent upon a dominant centre), already by the later phase of the Early Iron Age. He furthermore proposes that by contrast the Umbrian and the Sabine areas were structured according the model of the 'city-state', with primary centres only dominating a small territory with few dependent satellite settlements. This model was developed in the southern Umbrian area by the end of the Final Bronze Age, but only developed in the Sabine area by a later phase of the Early Iron Age (Cifani 2003: in particular 191–193 and 200; Fig. 8.3).

Another recent *ethnographic* study in central Italy, is Iaia's contextual analysis of a specific female jewelry ornament, that is bronze rings suspended from bronze *fibulae* (Fig. 8.4), adopted by women of Latin communities during the whole duration of the early Iron Age and the Orientalizing Period from the ninth to the sixth century BC (see Bietti Sestieri 1992A). He has noticed that this typically Latin female ornament, has a very specific geographical and chronological distribution outside *Latium vetus*. It has been found in the territory of *Caere* and *Capena* during the latest part of the early Iron Age (from about 830–800 to 750–730 BC), and has been only occasionally attested in the Umbrian (Terni) and the Sabine area (Iaia 2007).

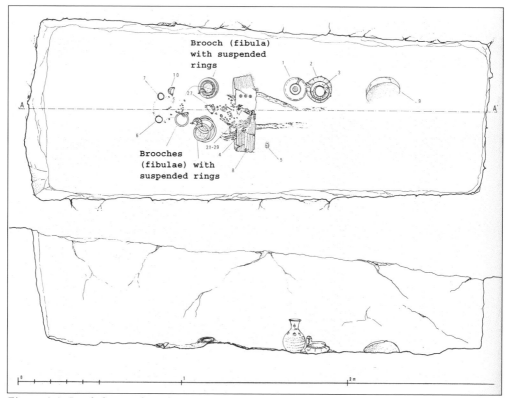

Figure 8.4. Leech bronze brooches (sanguisuga fibulae) *with suspended rings in tomb 83 at La Rustica, dated to the second half of the eighth century BC (from Anzidei* et al. *1985: 187, fig. 146/1)*

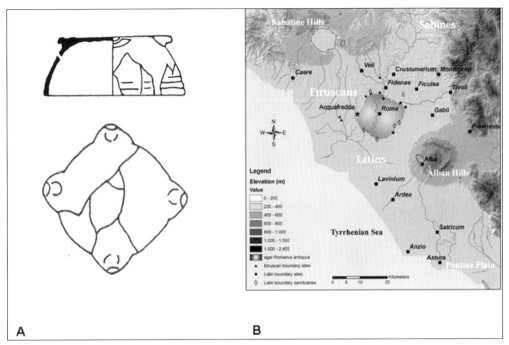

Figure 8.5. (A) Latin bread-baking cover with four flat handles (from Zifferero 2004: 260, fig. 3); (B) localization of the Etruscan site of Acquafredda at the edge of the ager Romanus antiquus, *the oldest territory of Rome.*

Finally, Andrea Zifferero has undertaken interesting research combining material culture and literary sources to study food habits and customs of proto-urban societies in central Italy (Etruria and *Latium vetus*) specifically focusing on cooking stands and bread baking covers (*testi da pane*). For example, he noticed that, in the Etruscan site of Acquafredda at the edge of the so-called *ager Romanus antiquus*, bread baking covers of Latin type and possibly Etruscan cooking stands were found, probably indicating a mobile and mixed ethnic composition of the site (Zifferero 2004: 267; Fig. 8.5).

Further potential developments in the the study of ethnic and social identities in central Italy

In this final section, the paper will show that previous approaches to ethnicity in central Italy have revealed essential and very important aspects of a complex problematic, which deserves further investigation.

By adopting Barth's model in the analysis of ethnicity from an archaeological perspective, and with particular reference to complex societies, Emberling's study (1997) has shown that ethnicity can be seen as an arena for political and, more specifically, inter-state relationships. With particular reference to central Italy, as suggested by Smith

(1996: 215–23), Bradley (2000a, 2000b) and Bourdin (2005), ethnicity can be seen as a tool for the construction of political unity (the Latins) or imperial policy (Rome) or, on the contrary, as a form of resistance (Italic groups), providing a sensible explanation for a variety of specific relationships between ethnic groups. A number of recent studies, focused on central Italy and *Latium vetus*, more specifically illustrated in the previous section, showed as well that there can be different arenas in which ethnicity can be played out or negotiated: on a macro-scale, for example, different ethnic groups can show different settlement patterns and territorial behaviours (Cifani 2003); on a micro and local scale, ethnic markers can disclose the multi-ethnic composition of boundary settlements (Zifferero 2004); and finally they can reveal inter-community mobility (through inter-community marriages) or, on the contrary, community closure to maintain the control of land property against other rival city-states (Iaia 2007).

The following elements can be added to the above examples to exemplify how identity, defined as an individual and shared multi-level construction, which includes but is not limited to ethnic identity, can be investigated through the analysis of material culture:

- Several elements (pottery and metal objects types, ritual or funerary practices etc.) pointing to some sort of shared identity or, in any case, strong interconnections among different 'ethnic groups' in central Italy, both in pre and post-Roman times, have been identified by Laura Bonomi Ponzi (1996), who has addressed this phenomenon in terms of the central Italian *koinè* (Greek word for 'common'; Fig. 8.6);
- Examples of regional identity include, specifically for the Latin area, the above mentioned suspended rings, the so-called Latial amphora, *anforetta laziale*, or the custom of infant domestic burials, *suggrundaria* (see Modica 1993 and, recently, Roncoroni 2001; Fig. 8.7);
- Local identity can be expressed by: a) amphorae and cups with long spikes (*anfore e tazze ad anse aculeate*), b) the so-called 'crustumina' bowl (*scodella crustumina*), which are particularly popular in *Crustumerium* (while the first seem to indicate a local preference for a particular style, the second might be an exclusive local production; di Gennaro *et al.* 2007: 144, 157ff.); c) the stone circular precinct placed around burials, which, within the Latin area, has only been found at Tivoli, and which connected this site to similar burial customs in the Apennine regions of Abruzzo and Umbria; d) the so-called comb motif decoration on *impasto* pots, which has never been found outside the territory of *Satricum*, so that it might be considered a local character (Beijer 1991: 34; Fig. 8.8);
- Status identity, as it is well known, can be demonstrated by paraphernalia, exotic objects and *orientalia* found, for example, in the so-called 'princely graves' of the Orientalizing Age (Fig. 8.9).

Interestingly a similar multi-level identity pattern, which comprised a regional stylistic homogeneity with specific local variations has not only been detected in Early Iron Age *Latium vetus*, but also in Early Bronze Age Jordan (these local variation have been effectively described as local 'flavours' by Meredith Chesson in a seminar given at Cambridge

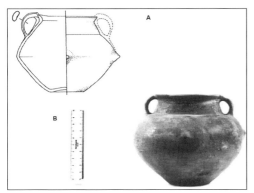

Figure 8.6. Impasto biconical globular amphora as an example of supra-regional identity or interregional interactions: (A) from Colfiorito (Terni, Umbria), ninth century BC (from Bonomi Ponzi 1996: 396, fig. 2b); (B) from Osteria dell'Osa (Gabii, Latium vetus), ninth/eighth century BC (Museo nazionale Etnografico Luigi Pigorini, ICCD Photographic Archive N° F42079).

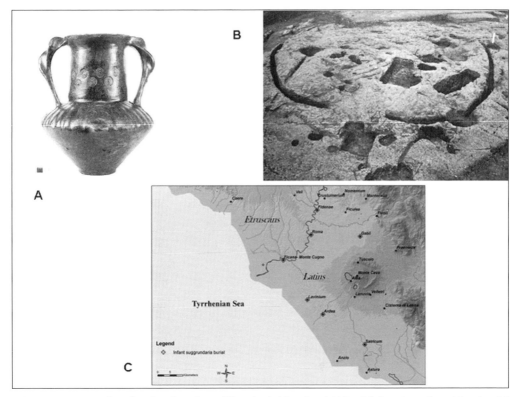

Figure 8.7. Examples of regional and possibly ethnic identity: (A) Latial Amphora found in a burial context in Crustumerium (from di Gennaro 1999a); (B) infant domestic burials or suggrundaria *(circular ditch of a hut of the beginning of the seventh century BC and two rectangular infant burials, on the right, dated to the eighth century BC, Lavinium (from Anzidei, Bietti Sestieri and De Santis 1985: fig. 153); (C) geographical distribution of* suggrundaria *(children burials among/under houses) in* Latium vetus.

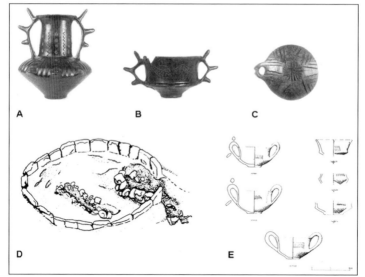

Figure 8.8. Examples of local identity: amphora (A) and kantharos-cup (B) with spikes, and bowl (C) from burial contexts at Crustumerium (from di Gennaro 1999); circle grave (D) from Tivoli; kantharoi-cups with comb motif (E) from Satricum (from Beijer 1991: 35, Fig. 8).

Figure 8.9. Phoenician bowl from the Bernardini 'princely' tomb in Palestrina, second quarter of the seventh century BC *(Museo Nazionale di Villa Giulia, ICCD Photographic Archive N° F3 686).*

University in the academic year 2006/2007). In these two regions, archaeological markers are found both in funerary evidence and in settlement organization, indicating processes toward higher social complexity, state formation and urban development. It could be argued that identity (ethnic or local) definition and characterization was played out as an instrument of political action.

To conclude, this paper suggests we should combine different kinds of evidence, such as material culture, ancient authors and possibly genetic data and faunal or vegetal remains (the use of multiple 'sources and classes of data' in the study of ethnicity has been suggested also by Jones 1997: 125 and fruitfully applied in the study of Andean pre-hispanic states by Janusek 2002), and analyze their context in order to make a reasonable attempt to grasp past people identity construction and possibly: 1) identify cultural and/or biological contents of ethnicity (Barth's cultural 'stuff'); and 2) verify ethnic boundaries using the principle of redundancy suggested by Emberling (1997).

Since ethnicity is only one of several identities experienced and acted out by an individual, the adoption of a multi-scale approach, with a supra-regional focus and a long-term perspective, in order to be able to study ethnicity as a process rather than as a static entity, is essential. A diachronic and multi-dimensional perspective has also been suggested by Jones (1997) and Ruby (2006), with reference to Greece, and by Stoddart (2009), with reference to Etruria. Similarly, Davies (1997: 28) and Malkin (2001: 3), among others, have emphasized how ethnic identifiers and *polis* identities and ideologies used by Herodotos and others for Archaic Greece, cross-cut themselves in various complex ways.

With reference to central Italy, Bradley has already identified at least three competing components in the dynamic formation of Umbrian ethnicity: Umbrian *ethnos*, local community and Roman citizenship (2000a, 2000b). While regarding later ages, the tension between ethnic identity and Roman citizenship, expressed in the well-known exploration by Cicero of his own loyalty to two homelands or *patriae* (Cicero *De Legibus* 2.2–3) has been illuminated in the recent book investigating the complex relationship between ethnic identity, Roman citizenship and aristocratic political competition in Republican Rome (Farney 2007).

As already mentioned, the application of a simple relational multi-scale model would help to analyze artifacts and other types of elements and their context, thus allowing to explore how different identities (including ethnicity, which might have meant something difference to past people as it means to us, as pointed out by Lucy 2005: 109) were negotiated among individuals, families, social or political groups. It could be possible to start from a combined analysis of funerary rites, stylistic choices, settlement patterns and epigraphic evidence (for which abundant data are already available from excavations, surveys and catalogues) and then integrate them with the results from scientific analyses, such as anthropological, faunal (for example, Hesse and Wapnish 1997; Gates St-Pierre 2006) and vegetal studies, or petrographic analyses to reveal technological aspects of pottery production (Stark *et al.* 2000; Livingstone Smith 2000).With reference to scientific analyses related to studies on identity in central Italy, a palaeobiological study of the community living in the area of *Gabii* has recently been conducted in order to detect different food habits among different social groups and/or communities (Bietti Sestieri *et al.* 2004) and biological differences among different populations in proto-historic and historic central Italy have been investigated and identified (for example, Becker 1996; Rubini 2006); however archaeogenetic studies, while useful, are still considered too costly at the present, as well as controversial in their interpretation. Petrographic analyses are still rare in central Italy and while they are being implemented in a few cases (for example, Carafa 1995; ongoing research is being conducted on material from *Crustumerium*) any study of this kind has until now only been undertaken in order to study technological aspects of pottery production rather than as ethnicity or identity markers.

The potential value of combining contextual analysis of artifacts with modern scientific analyses has been remarked on recently also by Sam Lucy (2005: 108–9). Similarly to the approach presented in this paper, this scholar has correctly discussed the importance of the scales, at which archaeologists work, and valued contextual analysis at the local level:

> By working at the local level, employing detailed analyses of data in order to tease
> out the complex interrelationships of artefacts and the minutiae of spatial patterning,
> archaeologists can at least start to identify contexts in which social identities would
> have been recreated through everyday practices (Lucy 2005: 109).

However, following Emberling's work, is it here suggested that a coarser focus of resolution should not be disregarded as well, because it is the combination and comparison of contextual analysis at different levels, which provides a broader picture and sometime keys for possible alternative explanations, which have to be assessed and discussed in the search of the interpretation.

Conclusions

As stated in the introduction, this paper did not aim to provide a comprehensive and conclusive discourse on ethnicity and state formation in central Italy, but to provide a fresh perspective to approach this topic in a new way.

In the first section, the social anthropological model of ethnicity proposed by Barth in the introduction to the collection *Ethnic Groups and Boundaries* (1969), and followed by most anthropological scholarship thereafter, has been briefly illustrated and the implementation of the original model by Jenkins (1997) has been reviewed. The second section introduced Emberling's paper on *Ethnicity and Complex Societies* (1997) and the great potential of this model for archaeological research on ethnicity.

In the third section, the link between ethnogenesis and state formation, already suggested by Emberling and other scholars, has been considered with particular reference to central Italy and the sources for the study of ethnicity in this region have been presented. Given the availability of ancient authors' accounts and archaeological sources, issues related to the relationship between texts and material culture have been briefly discussed; finally previous approaches to the study of ethnicity in central Italy, with reference to both the traditional cultural historical approach (and its critiques) and more recent studies, were considered.

The final section, building on the theoretical premise offered by Barth's social anthropological model, has suggested a new approach to the study of ethnicity, with specific reference to central Italy, but also applicable to other areas. As ethnicity is 'socially constructed' and is only one of many identities constantly negotiated by individuals in their daily lives, there is still a cultural content (common cultural/biological trait or common belief), by which the members of an ethnic group identify themselves as 'us' and distinguish themselves from the 'other' or 'them'. The materialization of these contents (burial costumes, food habits, territorial behaviours, language, belief in a common ancestry etc.) in concrete objects makes it possible for archaeologists to study identities of past societies and their dynamics through time (for an illuminating study on the materialization of power see, for example, DeMarrais *et al.* 1996).

The approach presented in this paper suggests to combine different types of evidence (for example with particular reference to central Italy, material culture could be evaluated against ancient authors' accounts and possibly anthropological, faunal and vegetal data) and investigate their cultural contents by analyzing them in their context in order to explore how identities (family, gender, class, city, region, ethnos etc.) are defined through constant (re-)negotiation. In particular, it is here suggested that the context to be considered should be both the physical-geographical location and also the cultural context, defined as the sum of links and connections, within which each artefact/cultural element has a specific meaning.

For this scope a multi-scale focus and a long-term perspective would be appropriate: different interrelations between artefacts and them and their meaning are more likely to be understood by comparing (and/or contrasting) in a constant dialectic discourse, at different times, local and higher resolution views, which are not mutually exclusive but complementary[2].

Acknowledgements

First of all I would like to thank Simon Stoddart and Gabriele Cifani, for inviting me to take part in the *Landscape and Ethnicity in the Archaic Mediterranean Area* workshop, held in Cambridge on the 13th–14th March 2007, and to contribute to the publication of the proceedings in this volume. I would like to thank them for all their work to make things happen. This paper represents a 'written elaboration' of some thoughts on the subject presented at the workshop and the content of the text and the bibliography are updated to that date, with very minor modifications. The opportunity to participate in the seminar and the following publication arose while conducting research for my doctoral dissertation in Cambridge, under the supervision of Simon Stoddart, which focused on the same study area but aimed at different questions and problems. Therefore I feel it is important to acknowledge the sponsors who allowed my PhD research to be conducted: Borsa di studio di perfezionamento all'estero (Università di Roma 'La Sapienza'), AHRB (Art and Humanities Research Board) award, IFUW Ruth Bowden International Fellowship and Dan David Prize International Scholarship. Finally many people, have contributed to shape my research and ideas, with their papers, talks, encouragements and sometime even more importantly critics. All of them have been very precious to me and I do apologize, if I have misinterpreted or misunderstood any of them!

Notes

1 I learned about this tradition of study by giving a workshop at the GCSC, Graduate Centre for the Study of Culture at the Justus Leibig Universität in Giessen, Germany.
2 While revising the draft of this paper for publication I realized that the book *Early Greek States Beyond the Polis*, by C. Morgan, investigates, in relation to mainland Greek communities, the same topic of identity and ethnicity with a detailed and accurate consideration of some of the same issues briefly discussed here, (ethnicity and identity as social construct, importance of scale, sites and place identities, etc.), and therefore would have deserved more consideration. Although a comparative study was beyond the scope of this paper, even from a quick reading there are several points in common and many potential elements of fruitful comparison between Greece and Italy, which would be interesting to develop.

Ethnicity and the identity of the Latins. The evidence from sanctuaries between the sixth and the fourth centuries BC

Letizia Ceccarelli

Introduction

The concept of ethnicity can be understood as a multi-dimensional phenomenon, formed by social identities and constructed according to the context and the chronological framework. It is important to emphasize that the idea of social and ethnic identity for past societies was primarily based around gender, status and most importantly communal language, mythical ancestry and cults, as is clearly defined by Herodotos in the debate on Greek ethnicity (*Histories*, 8.144).

However, the modern approach to the study of the constructed nature of ethnic groups is methodologically complex and continues to be the subject of debate. A useful definition of criteria has been put forward by Lomas (1997: 2) for the reconstruction of ancient ethnic identities, drawing on the work of the sociologist Antony Smith (1986), identifying characteristics such as a common ethnic name, a myth of common descent, a shared culture and religion, and an association with a territory, material culture and language (for a discussion of different approaches see Farney 2007: 28–29, who is also critical of the use of material culture as an indication of ethnic groups). This model, as Lomas notes, is not without methodological problems when applied to pre-Roman Italy (Lomas 1997: 3–5), in part due to the diverse nature of the chronological framework and also of the cultural, political and social identities of different groups intimately connected with the geographical location of these groups in relation with Rome. Moreover, the horizontal archaic mobility of aristocratic families, as noted by Cornell (1995: 158), seemed to transcend the ethnic identity and their connections with Rome. By the late Republic, the distinction between the Latin ethnic groups had been absorbed by Roman identity, but the claim of aristocratic families to ethnic origins was still useful for political purposes (an interesting analysis of ethnicity in the late Republic and that of manipulation of ethnic identity by the ruling class with the implications in the political scene of Rome can be found in Farney 2007. His approach to ethnic identity adopts an instrumentalist point of view (see for example 2007: 31). For the legendary and historical genealogy of the *gentes*, see Smith 2006).

This paper will consider the concept of ethnicity in *Latium vetus*, and the construction, or invention of an ethnic identity in the Latin cities by exploiting both myths and legends as well as the visual impact and materialisation of these, represented in the decoration of public buildings. The cities belonged to an ethnic community which had an awareness of their separate identity and of a shared language, similar political and religious institutions, history and culture (Cornell 1997: 9). There already exists an extensive literature on the subject, so this contribution will focus upon the issue of Latin religious identity, in particular that of Ardea, since it presents an interesting ethnic aspect compared with the other Latin cities: ancient authors (Cato fr. 58 Peter) reported the name of the *populus*, *Ardeates Rutuli*. Moreover, the city had control of one of the most important sanctuaries of the Latins, the *Aphrodisium*, important because religion was the common ground for the Latin cities, both politically and economically.

This paper also examines the archaeological evidence from a newly discovered sanctuary on the coast of Lazio at Ardea (see Di Mario 2007), discussing the architectural form of the temples and their external decorations that held significance not only in themselves, but which were also closely connected with political meaning, as these public spaces represented the choreography of the display of power.

The myth of origins

In constructing the ethnic identity of the Latin cities, a fundamental part was the definition of the legendary foundation of the city by a god or a hero, and that legendary genealogy became even more important after the dissolution of the Latin League (338 BC), in order to display their ancestry against that of Rome, as in the case of Ardea, or to share the mythical origins between Rome and the Latins (for a discussion of the Republican legend of *Alba Longa* as the mythical political and religious starting point of Rome and the Latin cities, see Farney 2007: 54–8 and the recent extensive contribution of Grandazzi 2008).

There existed a communal myth that embraced all Latin communities, in the form of their ancestry in the figure of Latinus, son of Odysseus and Circe, and this legacy is reflected in the mythical foundation of several cities, such as *Tusculum, Praeneste*, Ardea and *Antium*. However this is recorded by Xanagoras, in the Hellenistic period, probably in the third century BC, (see discussion in Ampolo 1992 and Malrin 1998: 187)

According to Hesiod's *Theogony* (1001–1016) Circe, daughter of Sol, and Odysseus gave birth to Agrius and Latinus, see Malrin 1998: 179ff, a myth that can be dated to between the end of the eighth and the beginning of the seventh century BC, reflecting an Euboic influence possibly derived from Cuma (see Mele 1987: 171–177 and Debiasi 2008: 54–62), although it has also been argued that the legend was established between the sixth and the first half of the fifth century BC, a time in which the tradition of Odysseus and Aeneas may have coexisted (as it is reported in Hellanicus and Damastes Sigeus, see discussion in Ampolo 1992 and Mastrocinque (1996: 141–147)). The argument is further supported by evidence that the beginning of the presence of the iconography of Aeneas in Latium can be dated to the sixth century BC (*Lexicon Iconographicum Mythologiae Classicae*, under the heading of *Aineias*; Zevi 1989. However, Grandazzi

(2008: 742) is critical of the use of the hero's iconography as evidence of existence of the myth in Latium).

The city of *Tusculum* represents a useful example of the dichotomy in the construction of ethnic identity: according to the legend, it was founded by Telegonus, son of Odysseus and Circe (Dionysius of Halicarnassus *Roman Antiquities* 4.45.1; Livy 1.49.9; Silius Italicus 7.691–5, Ovid *Fasti* 3.91; Festus, in the writings of Paulus Diaconus *Mamiliorum* 116 L., *Municeps* 117 L.), although other sources refer to its foundation by Silvius, King of *Alba Longa* (Diodorus Siculus 7.5.9), and therefore of Aeneas' genealogy. There are several myths also associated with the foundation of Ardea: firstly, that it was founded by the eponymous hero Ardeias, son of Odysseus and Circe (Xenagoras see Jacoby 1962: 240, F. 29); secondly, another legendary ancestry refers to Perseus and his mother Danae, who landed on the coast of Latium, where she married King Pilumnus, from whom descended Turnus, King of the *Rutuli* (Servius *Ad Aeneam*, 7.372). This foundation myth seems to indicate the existence of an Argive substratum that associated Ardea with *Tibur* and *Cora*. However, Virgil presented Turnus as the son of Venilia and the brother of the nymph Juturna (10.439 and 12.138). It has been hypothesised that the mother's name, an obscure deity, was chosen to create a parallel with that of Aeneas, son of Venus (see Bourdin 2005: 593, note 35). A further legend is provided by Ovid who recounts the sacred animal of Ardea, the gull, which rose from the ashes of the cities destroyed by Aeneas and the Trojans (Ovid *Metamorphoses* 14.566ff.).

Ardea played an important role in the myth of the arrival of Aeneas and the battle between the *Rutuli* and Trojans (Livy 1.2, 2), with some variations between the sources. As well as the version of Virgil, Dionysius (*Roman Antiquities* 1.42ff.) recalled the death of Turnus and the King of the Latins in the first battle, and that of Aeneas in the second major battle when the command passed to Ascanius. The *Rutuli* were allied with Mezentius, in exchange for their entire production of wine. Ascanius dedicated the wine to the Gods and gained victory against his enemies. A crucial part of the tale is, however, that Turnus promised all the wine produced by the Latins to the King of *Caere*, Mezentius, for his help against Aeneas. The king, contemptuous of the Gods, was defeated by Ascanius, who dedicated the wine to the Gods, thus maintaining the promise and in the process creating the tradition of the *Vinalia Rustica* (Cato in the writing of Macrobius Saturnalia 3.10 ; Festus in the writing of Paulus Diaconus 322 L.).

The myth of the origins associated with the Trojans and Aeneas, which connected *Lavinium* and Rome, seems to be developed after the defeat of the Latin League (for the different adoption of the Trojan mythology in Rome between the fourth century and the Late Republic, see Erskine 2001: 148ff.). The myth of Trojan origins was, however, exploited by other cities such as *Lanuvium*, where, according to Zevi (2005: 64), the legend of the Nostos origins of the Trojan hero Lanoios, eponymous founder of the city, originated in Sicily (for an analysis of the concept of Nostos genealogy see Malkin 1998: 178ff.). This link with Sicily was also shared by other communities, such as Ardea, as suggested by the episode of the arrival in 300 BC of the *tonsores*, barbers, from Sicily led by a P. Titinius Menas, as reported in a public inscription from Ardea, attested by Pliny (*Natural History* 7.211) This anecdote seems to suggest that even before the Punic Wars the Sicilians had a privileged relationship with Ardea and the inland cities, in particular *Aricia*, where there was a sanctuary of Demeter and Kore.

Moreover, Zevi (2005: 64) suggests as evidence of the Trojan-Sicilian link in Ardea the name of the *Cloelii Siculi*, one of families who founded the colony.

The myths of the foundation and the historical sources of *Lavinium* concentrate above all on the religious legendary aspects of the city, which was purposely founded to provide a place for the Trojan penates. The 'mythical' topography of *Lavinium* has been reconstructed on the basis of the narration of the ancient writers (Castagnoli 1972; Fenelli 1990: 461–7) who discuss the landing of Aeneas, at a place called Troia, which was dedicated to the Sun, the *locus Solis Indigetis*, where he found two altars close to the *Numicus* river. In the narration of Virgil, there is also added an episode of the *mensae* eaten by the Trojans, whereby a sow, destined to be sacrificed, escaped as far as a hill 240 stadia away, where she gave birth to a litter of thirty piglets: in the place where she was found, Aeneas founded *Lavinium*. Therefore, the river *Numicus* has been identified with the modern Fosso di Practica, and the *locus Solis Indigetis* with the remains of a sanctuary discovered at Torvaianica (Jaia 2009). The subsequent accounts emphasized the relationship between the Trojans and the Aborigenes and their king, Latinus, which brought about the amalgamation of two populations (Strabo 5.2), through the war against Turnus and Mezentius, at the battle near the river *Numicus*, where Aeneas died and was subsequently deified (for a different version of the myth of the foundation of *Lavinium* by Aeneas, as well as his connection with *Alba Longa* in the early annalists, see the discussion in Grandazzi 2008: 741–5).

The moment of consolidation of this tradition can be traced to the end of the war against the Latins, as mentioned by Livy, who recounted that in 388 BC the treaty between Rome and *Lavinium* was renewed, and was strengthened every year on the 10th day after the Latin *Feriae* (Livy 8.11.15.), by a magistrate who had the special sacerdotal authority of a *pater patratus*, for the celebration of the *sacra principiorum populi Romani, the Penates* (Varro, *de lingua latina* 5.144; CIL X, 797=ILS 5004, *sacra principiorum p(opuli) R(omani) Quirit(ium) nominisque Latini, quai apud Laurentes coluntur.* It has been demonstrated by Alföldi 1965: 264 that it should be read as *sacra principiorum* instead of *sacra principia*). The importance of *Lavinium* after the disbanding of the Latin League as a religious centre is also apparent, as a focus of the *nomen Latinum* unity under the control of Rome.

The myth of Aeneas as the founder of Rome appears to have been consolidated around the fourth century BC, as shown by a cippus inscription at *Tor Tignosa,* (CIL I2, 2843=ILLRP 1271 *Lare Aenia d(onom),* dated between the end of the fourth and the beginning of the third century BC, see Nonnis 2003: 42). Cogrossi (1982: 89ff.) suggests that in the fourth century BC the importance of the figure of Aeneas overtook that of the mythical Latin ancestor, son of Circe and Odysseus, whose cult instead underlined the acknowledgement of a common Greek origin in the population of Latium, as occurred also at *Tusculum*. It was been demonstrated, based on literary sources, in particular Timaeus of Tauromenius (according to Torelli 1984: 216ff. he was Strabo's source), that the legend of Aeneas at *Lavinium* was a local creation which began around 300 BC, very different from that which sees the hero as the founder of Rome, which was in fact a Greek invention of the fifth century BC, as is documented by Hellanicus and Damastes.

Ardea and the Latins

Ardea which lies approximately 40 kilometres south of Rome and 4 kilometres from the coast (Fig. 9.1), belonged to the *Prisci Latini* and is the only Latin city whose inhabitants' ethnic name is known: *Ardeates Rutuli*. The origin of the population in the literary sources (Appian 1. 12; Dionysius of Halicarnassus *Roman Antiquities* 1.64) was related to Tyrrhenian or Ligurian roots (for a hypothesis on the suffix *–uli* see Baldarotta (1999: 263); a recent contribution on the origin of the *Rutuli* can be found in Bourdin 2005).

Several traces of early occupation starting in the Late Bronze Age have been documented (Morselli and Tortorici 1982: 30–1). The settlement evolved over the course of the centuries on the three tuff plateaus known as the Acropolis, Civitavecchia and Casalazzara, delimited by the two main streams Fosso della Mola and Fosso dell'Acquabona. The city held a strategic position to control the maritime and inland routes toward the inner cities of *Latium vetus*, such as *Aricia* of which Ardea was mostly probably the harbour (Coarelli 1987: 79; 1990: 152–3, Colonna 1995: 40, note 115). In late sixth century BC, in the first treaty between Rome and Carthage, Ardea was mentioned as a city that should be spared, offering evidence of the importance of the city and its harbour. The relationship with Rome is somehow controversial; for instance, the first treaty with Carthage, if the date of the first year of the republic 509

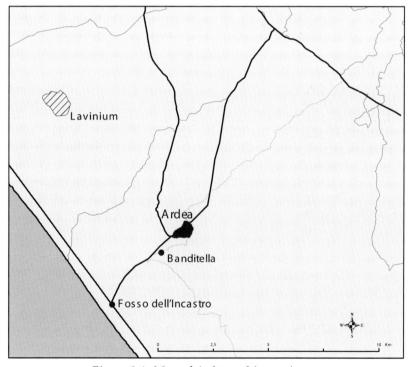

Figure 9.1. Map of Ardea and its territory.

BC is accepted, implies on the one hand the importance of the harbour of Ardea, on the other that Rome, in the sixth century BC, was already controlling *Latium vetus* as far as *Tarracina*. In Polybius' account the other harbours are *Antium, Laurentum, Circeii* and *Tarracina* (3.22); the latter is crucial for the supporters of the consular date of the treaty, because it was listed with the Latin name, suggesting, therefore, that this treaty was before the Volscan conquest of the city. Already in the Regal period the wealth of Ardea is documented by the fact that Tarquin the Proud declared war on it (Dionysius of Halicarnassus *Roman Antiquities* 4.64.1; Livy (1.56.13) presents the city as *divitiis praepollens*). The political and religious structure of the city was highly advanced and developed, to the point that Rome imported the sacred institution of the *Fetiales* from there (according to Dionysius of Halicarnassus *Roman Antiquities* 2.72.1–2.; according to another tradition they were instituted by Numa). The political importance of Ardea within the Latin League is also confirmed by the votive dedication of the *lucus Dianius*, in which it appears as one of the cities dedicating at the sanctuary (Cato Fragment 58 Peter., for an analysis of the text see Ampolo 1983: 321ff.).

In the first half of the fifth century BC, Livy recounted the territorial dispute with *Aricia*, where Rome was called in as a moderator, and in turn appropriated the land itself, on the basis that that the territory belonged to the destroyed city of *Corioli* (Livy 3.71; see Lilli 2002: 93–94 for an analysis of the territory of *Aricia* and the contribution of the territory of Ardea and its boundaries; for the perception of the religious landscape see Ceccarelli 2008: 335–6). The difficulties of the war with the Volscans led to the renewal of its treaty with Rome in 444 BC. (Livy 4.7.4).

In 443 BC, according to Livy, an internal conflict, between the patricians and plebs for the hand of a beautiful plebeian woman, saw the Volscans come to the aid of the plebeian suitor, whilst Rome gave its support to the noble suitor. Such internal conflicts left the city in such a weak condition that the creation of a colony was necessary to revive the decimated population (Livy 4.9–10). The colony was created in 442 BC by the triumvirate of Agrippa Menenius, Titus Cloelius Siculus and Marcus Ebutius Helva (Livy 4.11.5; according to Diodorus Siculus 12.34 the colony was founded in 434 BC.). The colony, after the *foedus Cassianum*, had Latin judicial rights, since the city belonged to the Latin League (see discussion in Bandelli 1995: 161), rights that it maintained even after the league's dissolution.

The choice of the colonial status of *Latinitas* was significant because it highlighted the importance of the city, in particular by its control of the *Aphrodisium*. This episode therefore reflects an attempt by Rome to control the inter-Latin *connubia*, one of the juridical-sacral rights exploited in the Latin communal sanctuaries (Torelli 1999: 22).

Sanctuaries

Sanctuaries played a central role not only in the internal socio-political system, but also in discriminating between the sacred and profane, between urban and extra-urban space, and the boundaries between the city and the countryside and the territories between cities (Riva and Stoddart 1996: 92–3). Their function was not solely limited to religious practices, as they were central to political life until 338 BC, but they also played an important economic role. The sacred nature of the place made them suitable centres for trade and economic exchange and, above all, for political and diplomatic exchanges.

There existed several important federal Latin Sanctuaries, such as that of *Iuppiter Latiaris*, the *Lucus Dianius* and the *Lucus Ferentinae* (Festus 276 L) where the Latin communities held meetings. The sources also indicate the presence of a federal sanctuary of the Latins at *Lavinium*, which was equal in importance to that of *Iuppiter Latiaris* at *Mons Albanus* (Liv. 5.52.8).

In the accounts of both Pliny and Pomponius Mela, there also existed at Ardea a federal sanctuary dedicated to Venus which was known by the Greek name of *Aphrodisium* (Pomponius Mela 2.4.71; Pliny *Natural History*, 3.5.56). Whilst not entering too deeply into the discussion concerning the interpretation of the sources relating to the location of this sanctuary, which has been the subject of much debate. The question of the existence of a single *Aphrodisium* at Lavinium has been widely discussed (see Castagnoli 1972: 110–11; Torelli 1984). Others, for example Colonna (1995: 3ff.), have hypothesized the existence of a single sanctuary at Ardea. It is worth recalling the hypothesis that there existed *Aphrodisia* in each of the main ports of the Tyrrhenian sea (Coarelli 1997: 207) which as well as Ardea, included also Gravisca, *Pyrgi*, *Lavinium* (Torelli 1984: 157–73), *Circeii* and Terracina. Aphrodite may also have been venerated as the protector of navigation, similar to, for example the Aphrodite identified with Marica at the sanctuary at *Minturnae* (Servius *Ad Aeneam* 7.47); Coarelli (1995: 208) suggests that Aphrodite corresponds to Ashtart of Cypriot origin. In *Lavinium*, the cult of Aphrodite was also connected with that of *Indiges* or *Pater Indiges*, an indigenous deity worshipped as the Sun in a grove by the *Numicus* river and later identified with Aeneas, as the god was also considered a divine ancestor (Diodorus Siculus, 37.11).

Alternatively, on the basis of Strabo's account (5.3.5), it has been proposed that there existed a single federal sanctuary at *Lavinium*, whose control was in the hands of Ardea. This might be echoed in Livy's account of the internal conflict at Ardea resulting in the intervention of Rome, events which led to the foundation of the colony; this episode appears to be an attempt by Rome to take control of the federal Latin sanctuary.

The hypothesis of the location of this sanctuary in the area of Banditella (Fig. 9.1), which is along the main road from the coast to the city of Ardea, can now be completely excluded (Colonna 1995: 3ff.), even if the question of the interpretation of the coastal sanctuary at the mouth of the river Fosso dell'Incastro can be reconsidered in the light of recent discoveries. On the site of Banditella there is no evidence for the existence of a sacred building and the material discovered at the foot of the hill, along the river is related to an open aired sacred area with a cult dedicated to a female deity centred around an altar. Several offerings, such as statuettes, heads and masks, typical expressions of Mid-Republican religion have been recovered, among which it is worth noting a Phoenician-Punic glass pendant of a male head, dated to the fourth–third century BC (Ceccarelli 2010). This provides further evidence of the importance of the harbour of Ardea as well as a phenomenon of *interpretatio*, a cultural interpretation of a deity according to his or her functions equated to a homeland deity (for discussion of Punic offerings in the temple of the forum in Ardea, see Ceccarelli 2007b).

The archaeological evidence

In the area of Le Salzare at the mouth of the river Fosso dell'Incastro, which is located 4.5 kilometres south of Ardea, recent excavations have revealed a sanctuary complex, formed by a temple laid at the side of a large square paved in tuff blocks, a series of altars and a sacred precinct, as well as structures associated with the river port of Ardea (Fig. 9.2). The study of the structures and the phases of the sanctuary, where excavations are still ongoing, can be found in Di Mario 2007; 2009, 331–46 with a further update in Di Mario in press. At the centre of the square there are two altars built of *peperino*, one *in antis*, orientated east-west, and the other rectangular; they both sit on separate platforms and their bases consist of a rounded moulding with a *torus* (Shoe 1965: 83ff.) (Fig. 9.3). The proposed chronology for the altars, on the basis of the use of *peperino*, is late fourth–third century BC, a period when the sanctuary underwent reconstruction. (The closest comparison of altars made from *peperino* has been found with those from the temples of Fortuna and Mater Matuta, in the area of S. Omobono in Rome. (Di Mario 2007: 82ff.). In addition, the use of *peperino* is the basis for the chronology rather than the profile of the altars, which is certainly more conservative (Shoe 1965: 103–04, XXIV, 1–2). Furthermore, during this period, the area was fortified through the construction

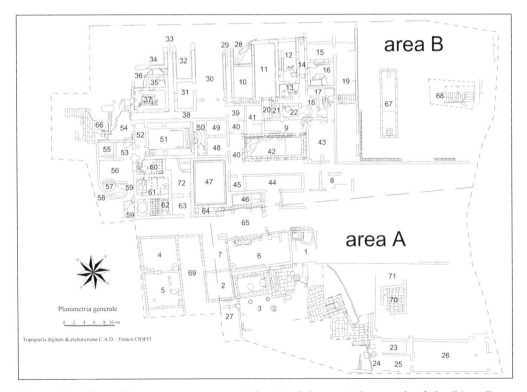

Figure 9.2. Plan of the structures excavated at Le Salzare at the mouth of the River Fosso dell'Incastro (after Di Mario 2007).

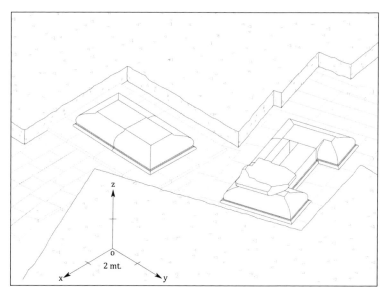

Figure 9.3. Axonometric reconstruction of the altars (after Di Mario 2007).

of a tuff wall built in *opus quadratum* which encircled the sanctuary whose entrance has been found facing towards the sea.

Between the mid-second century and the end of the first century BC, two further small temples were built, one on a podium on the western side of the square and the other parallel to the older building on the north-eastern side. In the Augustan period the entire complex was transformed by the construction of a river port that was built alongside the river Fosso dell'Incastro, and which in some parts was built over the earlier structures (Di Mario 2007). The port continued in use until the Late Antique period.

The main temple, known as Temple B, is orientated north-east/south-west and had an evolution in plan similar to that of Mater Matuta at *Satricum*, and its earliest traces can be dated, on the basis of the architectural decoration, to the last quarter of the sixth century BC. The structure was monumentalised with a moulded tuff podium in *opus quadratum* (the detailed description of the podium profile is in Di Mario in press) on which was built a Tuscanic temple, itself also dated by the architectural decoration to 480–470 BC (A preliminary publication of the architectural decorations of the different phases of this temple can be found in Ceccarelli 2007a: 195ff.; a detailed analysis of the Late Archaic sediment is in Ceccarelli 2010).

The first decorative roof, in Ionian-Etruscan tradition, is represented by fragments of antefixes with female heads, painted eaves tiles, and revetment plaques showing riders galloping toward the left. In particular Fig. 9.4 illustrates a fragment with horses' heads and part of the rider (arm, knee and the end of the spear). The elaborate decoration and the elegant style have revealed similarities both to the Veii-Rome-Velletri and Caprifico decorative systems, (for the latter see Lulof 2006 and the overall view in Winter 2009: 311ff.) and it can be dated to 520 BC.

The fragments of the Late-Archaic roof of the temple include pieces of a cut-out palmette *acroterion* (the initial interpretation of a small fragment of this architectural terracotta was as a frame of an antefix (Ceccarelli 2007a: 199–200); however, the recent discovery of new fragments has allowed its reinterpretation as an *acroterion*), *columen* and *mutuli* plaques with figural decoration in high relief, raking simas, revetment plaques as well as Silenus-head antefixes. Fragments are also preserved of at least two plaques depicting high-relief figures of a battle between Greek warriors and Amazons (Fig. 9.5). An interesting proposal is the identification of this sanctuary with the *Castrum Inui* recalled by Virgil and above all as the place sacred to the Sun, according to the interpretation of the nature of *Inuus* in a passage of Macrobius *Saturnalia* (22.2–7); for

Figure 9.4. A fragment of the archaic revetment plaque.

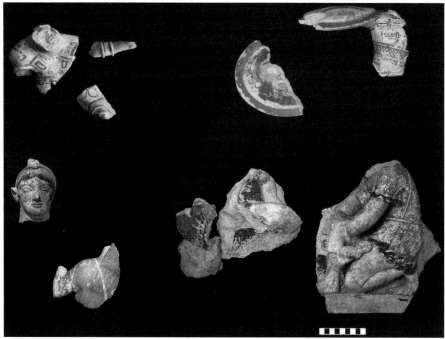

Figure 9.5. Fragments of the late-archaic pediment high relief figures.

analysis of the text see Di Mario 2007: 110–11 and the further detailed analysis of the deity as the mythical ancestor with chthonic attributes in Torelli in press), which could be linked with *Indiges*, as discussed above.

Conclusion

In discussing the definition of ethnic and cultural identity, it clearly emerges that the Latin communities did not have a unique identity, but that they prioritized different identities, by strengthening affiliation to the indigenous Latin or to the Greek cultural heritage, depending on the context. Therefore, it appears that there existed different types of identity used mostly as strong political statements, which in turn were reflected in the public buildings such as temples, as a public manifestation of the elite culture (see Marconi 2006 regarding Archaic Greece).

The architectural appearance of a temple formed an important part in the creation and transmission of a message of both ethnic and cultural identities, especially in a period of political conflict. The figurative cycle of the Temple B depicting an Amazonomachy like in other sanctuaries of the Latin world, for example Segni and *Satricum*, demonstrates the impact of mythical themes in the late archaic period and, above all, the confirmation of the ideology of the theme of war in the period that led to the *Foedus Cassianum* (Pairault Massa 1992: 201).

To conclude, in the context considered in this contribution, ethnicity can be understood as a historical construction of interaction and communication by means of myths, both to establish shared origin and to convey a political message. The Late Archaic decorative programmes served religious and political purposes, although the 'iconology of power' has not reached an unanimous consent (see the interesting analysis of Lulof 2000: 213ff.). Thus the sanctuary recently discovered at the mouth of the river Fosso dell'Incastro was, from its position in Ardea, the most important display for an important city among the Latins, reinforcing the hypothesis that it could be the sanctuary reported by the historical sources.

Political landscapes and local identities in Archaic central Italy – interpreting the material from Nepi (VT, Lazio) and Cisterna Grande (Crustumerium, RM, Lazio)

Ulla Rajala

Keywords: Fieldwork, landscape, territory, identity, central Italy

Introduction

In this article I will discuss the characteristics of local identities in Archaic central Italy as they are reflected in different categories of archaeological material originating from urban centres and their hinterland. I will look at the diverse ways these identities are reflected in urban and rural landscapes and in the artefacts discovered. The discussion will concentrate on certain examples from both sides of the Tiber where ancient authors, such as Livy, give names to the different ethnic groups and city-states. The political disunity of these groups, the Etruscans together with some loosely allied groups in the north and the Latins in the south, is made clear from these sources. Although in both areas communities shared an idea of togetherness and celebrated annual rituals (e.g. Cornell 1995: 294–5; Barker and Rasmussen 1998: 90–1), literary evidence suggests that most communities in Archaic central Italy behaved opportunistically. This is evident from the narratives such as 'the rape of the Sabines' and its aftermath (Livy 1.9–15). Furthermore, much recent archaeological evidence has been collected in relation to specific ancient cities. Therefore, it is important to model how material culture is manipulated to express political identities at a local level in order to interpret fully how conceptual groupings such as ethnicity were expressed at a regional level in Archaic Etruria and *Latium vetus* (Fig. 10.1).

I will present case studies from two field projects I have been working with recently. These illustrate the possibilities and difficulties in the study of local identities. The first case study examines how the surface material from the Nepi Survey Project (Fig. 10.1) can be used to uncover the different identities of a small central place. I will discuss the changing settlement patterns and their relationship with different activity areas (or 'taskscapes') and landscapes of power and explain how these express territoriality

Figure 10.1. Map of central Italy with the areas of the Latins, the Faliscans and the Capenates.

and locality. The second case study examines how the chamber tombs excavated by the Remembering the Dead Project in the cemetery area of Cisterna Grande at *Crustumerium* (Fig. 10.1) convey different social identities and create the fabric of the ancestral funerary landscape. In addition, I will look at the Archaic funerary evidence from *Latium vetus* and examine what local and regional burial practices tell us about shared values and varying traditions between communities.

Ethnicity is just one of many social identities an individual or a group can have. Different social identities are based on gender, age, status, ethnicity, shared culture and religion, and the boundaries between different identities detected in archaeological material are not clear cut or easily distinguishable (Díaz-Andreu *et al.* 2005). As Hall (1997: 2–33) has shown, it is now acknowledged that ethnic identity is an inter-subjective reality. Ethnicity is not a static category but a dynamic one that is negotiable and situational. Its constitution can be based on observed genetic traits, language, family relations and cultural forms and it is constructed through group interactions which can be verbal, non-verbal or even written. For example, a social group may share an origin myth, and an affinity with a primordial territory. In many cases, ethnicity is often symbolized by a territory that is a result of appropriation over others or by others. It is characteristic to have asymmetrical power relations entailing dominated and excluded groups, and therefore, it is common to define ethnic identity through oppositions.

Unfortunately, language, artefacts and shared culture and other ethnic markers do not coincide neatly in archaeology, although material culture is actively used in the creation of all cultural identities. Lucy (2005: 100) has suggested that the study of past communal identities with their social and territorial features may facilitate the separation between different uses of material culture. In addition, if different markers are studied at different scales, this may further facilitate the differentiation between different types and levels of identities. So the interplay of local and regional studies is important for the analysis of group identities and distinctly expressed for ethnic and communal varieties of identity.

Territoriality and settlement patterns: the Nepi survey

The Nepi survey

The Nepi Survey Project (di Gennaro *et al.* 2002; Rajala 2006) was one of the field projects carried out under the umbrella of the Tiber Valley Project of the British School at Rome (Patterson and Millett 1998, Patterson *et al.* 2000, Patterson 2004). The project expanded the British study of the area beyond the town of Nepi (Edwards *et al.* 1995; di Gennaro *et al.* 2008).

Nepi, ancient *Nepet*, was on the boundary of the Faliscan area in southeast Etruria (Edwards *et al.* 1995) on the western border of the highly dissected Treia River system (Fig. 10.2). The eastern part of the territory is characterized by canyon-like ravines and wide undulating plateaux between perpendicular river valleys. In the west, the landscape is much gentler with rounded river valleys and rolling plains.

The territory was sampled by drawing transects along the cardinal directions radiating from the town along the grid of the *Istituto Geografico Militare* (I.G.M.) map. This sampling method was chosen because the Tuscania project (Barker 1988; Barker and Rasmussen 1988; Vullo and Barker 1997) had shown that transect sampling allows the prediction of realistic trends in local settlement patterns. Because four cardinal directions in the Nepi area correlate to a large extent with the past and present road network, transects were also drawn along the intercardinal directions to avoid excessive bias resulting from the Roman modifications of the landscape. The outer boundary of the projected survey area was defined by the hypothetical territory drawn with Thiessen polygons. The result was a series of transects one kilometre wide and up to five kilometres from the town.

In 1999, the areas in the close proximity to Nepi were under study. In total, 92 field units – mainly fields, parts of fields or pastures – were studied. In September 2000, the research strategy was revised so that the main focus was on selected areas on the boundary of the supposed territory. In total, 141 units were sampled. These units were located mainly to the west, north-west, north-east and south of the town (Fig. 10.3). In reality, the coverage and the success of surface collection depended on vegetation cover, the phase in the agricultural cycle and the permission of landowners. The field units covered a total area of 632 hectares; nearly 32 per cent of the area of the planned

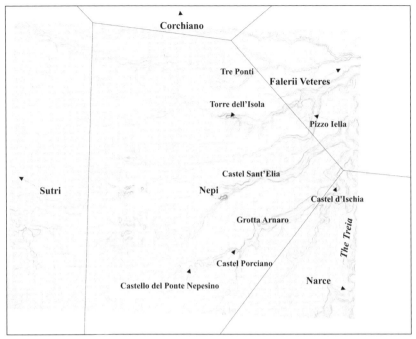

Figure 10.2. The hypothetical Archaic territory of Nepi defined by Thiessen polygons.

transects and 8 per cent of the rectangular territory around Nepi. Available land was studied by fieldwalking at intervals of 10–20 metres. Where pre-Roman presence was known from previous surveys (Frederiksen and Ward-Perkins 1957; Potter N. D.; Selmi 1978; Morselli 1980; Brunetti Nardi 1981; Camilli *et al.* 1995; Cifani and Munzi 1995; di Gennaro 1995), a modified traverse and stint method (cf. Liddle 1985: 9) was used; in these cases the finds were bagged according to a section of a line. A subjective grab was collected from observed concentrations, assumed to be sites.

Territoriality and spatial, nested identities

Humans make a difference between places, static points of temporal stays, and space, the immensity of the surrounding world. To get a sense of locality, people have to dwell 'here', whereas the understanding of space requires moving 'there' (Tuan 1977: 12; Thomas 1996: 31). The space around a settlement is divided, consciously or unconsciously, into a familiar subsistence area and less-known, more remote areas belonging to other communities. The areas of everyday tasks are called 'taskscapes' (Ingold 1993: 157) to emphasize how knowledge of them is accumulated through these practices. This familiar area of everyday practices is the spatial reproduction of the connection between a physical environment and a sociocultural reality. Therefore, taskscapes are created through agency, human choice and action against the physicality of real landscapes (Van Hove 2004).

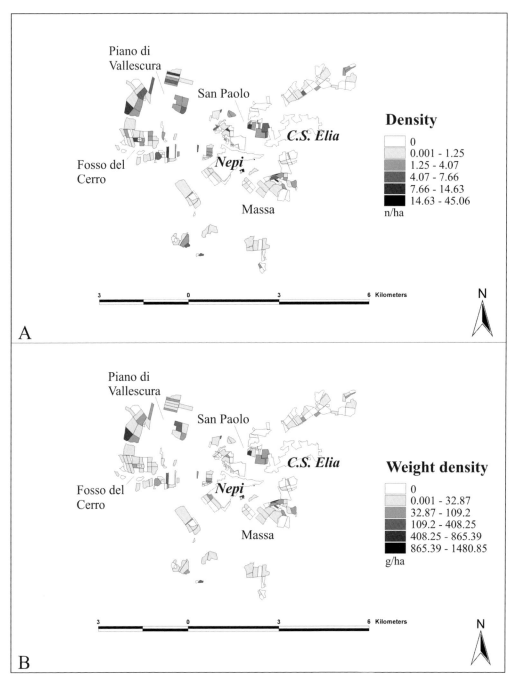

Figure 10.3. Densities of Faliscan pottery.

Taskscapes create the core of a community's territory. Territoriality conceptualizes the communal sense of a right to the resources in a certain area and is defined by geographical realities and culture (Sack 1986: 5; cf. Knight 1982: 526). The geographical characteristics of a landscape can be seen as affordances (Gibson 1979) that form the basis for the selection of areas that are occupied. Territoriality and the features of the landscape are linked, and thus, they mould the territorially based identities (Kaplan and Herb 1999: 1).

Territories are in essence arbitrary geographical units, but they accumulate additional meaning. Although territory spatializes existing social and cultural phenomena, it also actively transforms identities in a way that is not just reducible to 'living in' an area (Kaplan and Herb 1999: 1–2; Paasi 1996: 33–5). In addition, a territory can be seen as a basic requirement to organize other attributes to form an identity (Greenfeld 1992). However, territories cannot be separated from political power and, therefore, they are politicized spaces (Kaplan and Herb 1999: 2–3). These can be also seen as discursive landscapes where communities are interacting internally and between themselves and their space (Häkli 1999).

Kaplan (1994) has called different geographical identities 'spatial identities'. These are created through landscape since the collective consciousness of the terrain helps to define a group and creates the locational context with other groups, their historical legacy and boundaries. Rural landscape is in this context special since it expresses continuity, by linking a group to the land and its shared past. Therefore, territory simultaneously represents origins and embodies progress (Herb 1999: 17–8).

Geographically defined identities have a hierarchy according to scale, related to their increasing or decreasing geographical extent. Different entities (empire, state, region, locality) are nested within one other and each may claim some loyalties to identity. Thus, this classification of nested identities can be used to organize human identities. However, spatial identities tend to be unevenly nested and viewed differently by various people (Kaplan and Herb 1999: 4; Kaplan 1999: 31). These group identities can be related to any geographically bounded community. Like taskscapes, they bring together fundamental geographical concepts of space, place, spatial distribution, and spatial interaction. Nevertheless, among them, political territories and formal ethnic regions create a framework of spatial constructs with deep ideological significances (Knight 1999).

In archaeology, spatial distributions and spatial interactions are fundamental to the study of urbanism and state formation. The archaeological study of cities and states is dependent on site hierarchies based on site typologies that take into account the respective sizes, functions, features and attributes of chronologically and spatially interrelated sites (e.g. Flannery 1976). Geographical concepts such as the isolated city (von Thünen 1826), the least cost principle of spatial organization (Christaller 1933) and centre and periphery (Wallerstein 1974) help to relate archaeological settlement hierarchies to the division of space. Urban centres, settlement hierarchies and their spatial arrangements are incorporated by default within the concept of a state, defined in United States' state formation theory, as 'a society which is primarily regulated through a differentiated and internally specialized decision-making organization which is structured *in minimally three hierarchical levels*, with institutionalized provision for the operation and maintenance of this organization and implementation of its decisions' (Johnson 1973: 2, the italics by the author).

The three-level hierarchical settlement system and its variants can be seen as the foundation of nested identities. In Archaic central Italy, the existence of proper states is unsure, but most territorial powers were at least city-states, early state modules with peer polity interaction (Renfrew 1975). In Etruria, a three-leveled state with a centre, minor satellite centres and rural settlements emerged during the Orientalizing and Archaic periods (cf. Stoddart 1987; Rendeli 1991, 1993). In this framework of large Etruscan centres, the position of the adjacent Faliscan area and the territory of *Capena* remained ambiguous during the Archaic period. The ancient authors suggest that the Faliscans were either of Greek origin, Etruscans or constituted an ethnic group of their own (Camporeale 1991; Ceccarelli and Stoddart 2007). Generally, they have been presented as an independent group (cf. Cifani 2005). Shotter (1976) argued on the basis of historical evidence that the Faliscans and the *Capenates* were independent, although both 'tribes' participated in the council of Etruscan peoples. Cifani (2003, 2005) suggests that both areas were part of the territory of *Veii* – or at least under its hegemony, until the Late Archaic period. I have argued that by the Late Archaic period a state module existed at Nepi and the settlement pattern suggests that the Faliscan area consisted of loosely federal independent centres (Rajala 2005). The conflict of the interpretations regarding the existence of a sovereign state module remains, but it is clear from the discussion above that different nested identities existed, related to a geographically bounded community in Nepi and the areas around it. These themes will be explored further while examining the material evidence.

Archaic territory, taskscapes and settlements at Nepi

Past land use in the territory of Nepi can be approached in two different ways. Firstly, the overall distribution patterns of Archaic finds can be evaluated in order to observe the intensity of land use in different sectors of the territory. The geographical characteristics of these areas can be studied together with the changing preferences through time from one period to another. This characterization of used areas and their different landscape attributes reveal the spatial qualities of different taskscapes. Secondly, the existence of Archaic sites and their features can be examined in order to determine the existence of hierarchical settlement patterns inside the territory and between territories.

First we need to define the territory itself. Territoriality and the existence of the Early State Module have traditionally been studied in Italian archaeology with Thiessen polygons (cf. Renfrew 1975; di Gennaro and Peroni 1986; Stoddart 1987; Rajala 2004, 2005). In the case of Nepi and the Faliscan area, the classification of the sites belonging locally to the same hierarchical level is slightly problematic since the classification is effected by information from historical sources, and the biases inherent in them. When Thiessen polygons were created for Iron Age Nepi, it became clear that the smaller sites at the lowest level of the hierarchy could be recognized from the asymmetrical and restricted form of their hypothetical territories (Rajala 2002). This information helped define local major centres at *Falerii Veteres*, Narce, Nepi and Sutri between which the smaller sites were located. Using these centres in the analysis suggests that the Archaic territory of Nepi (Fig. 10.2) could have reached 109 square kilometres.

Using the hypothetical sizes of these centres, and taking into account the geographical extent of their naturally defended plateaux (cf. rank-size rule, Guidi 1985) it seems that, during the Early Iron Age, Narce, composed of at least three hills was the leading site in the Faliscan area, with a second rank consisting of Vignale (*Falerii Veteres*), and the nearby settlements of Nepi and Vignanello may have represented a third rank category. It is unclear if this Faliscan system is evidence for Veian colonial power (cf. di Gennaro 1986, 1995; Cifani 2003) or the existence of early state(s) in the Faliscan area. A crucial consideration is whether only *Veii* was occupied in the first phase of the Iron Age.

Veii was at least six times larger in size than Narce. Although *Veii* was clearly a major centre of influence (cf. Baglione 1986) and was guarding its interests towards the north and north-east, the existence of the outpost of Monte S. Angelo (Barnabei *et al.* 1894: 32–94; di Gennaro 1986: 139) on the crest of the Baccano crater against the site of La Ferriera (Iaia and Mandolesi 1993: n. 58, di Gennaro 1995: n. 71) south of Sutri in between the tenth and the ninth century BC may suggest that the boundary between the Faliscan area and Etruria proper, and indeed between *Veii* and the Faliscan area, could have developed near this landmark.

By the Archaic period *Falerii Veteres* was the leading Faliscan site, when the potential Archaic residential areas in the area are compared. Geographical methods suggest that Nepi was a minor centre compared with *Falerii Veteres* and Narce. Nevertheless, the Archaic Faliscan landscape was filled with centres of approximately the same size as Nepi, such as Corchiano. Nepi was also bigger than Sutri and Vignanello. Funerary evidence, that is the total area of cemeteries or the total numbers of tombs and burials at different centres, might help the evaluation of their potential status, but the calculation of these totals is problematic, since the cemeteries at Nepi have not been excavated, or at least published, as extensively as around modern Civita Castellana (*Falerii Veteres*) or Calcata (Narce). There are indications that the cemeteries especially south of the town were comprehensively plundered during the late nineteenth century (Gaultier 1999: 88–9). Additionally, many of the cemeteries outside Nepi belonged to the smaller sites and centres. The numbers of known tombs at Narce or Falerii are far higher than at Nepi. However, if the ring of cemeteries at Nepi was as large as suggested (cf. Carlucci and De Lucia 1998: 28), the town must have had an importance equal to its more famous neighbours, at least by the Archaic period. Although Archaic and earlier structures are known from inside the town and its vicinity (di Gennaro *et al.* 2002, 2008), the Nepi Survey Project could only discover low densities of surface material from the Orientalizing or Archaic periods.

The rarity of Orientalizing and Archaic finds was not least because of erosion and the extensive Roman land use near the town. Due to the low quantities of Orientalizing and Archaic material these were combined in the quantitative analysis together with the diagnostic pieces of the fifth and fourth centuries BC, itself a difficult period to see archaeologically. In this way it was possible to create a wide chronological category called 'Faliscan pottery' that could be compared with other major periods of activity. This category included the few *bucchero*, buccheroid *impasto bruno* and *impasto rosso* pieces (cf. e.g. Rasmussen 1979; Chiaramonte Treré 1999), the reddish sixth-century wares (cf. e.g. Carafa 1995; Chiaramonte Treré 1999) and the diagnostic Late Archaic period pieces (cf. Murray Threipland and Torelli 1970; Chiaramonte Treré 1999). The density maps show only a few denser concentrations of Faliscan pottery (Fig. 10.3). As these maps show, the elevated quantities and high weight densities were often in different areas; single heavier items easily skewed the distribution. Nevertheless, the core areas of Archaic and Late Archaic land use are revealed by the pottery distributions. The main area of activities was in the northwest in Piano di Vallescura and to a lesser extent in San Paolo, Massa, along the Fosso del Cerro and near Torrionaccio immediately south of the town.

It is worth noticing that, like the prehistoric survey finds in Boeotia (Bintliff *et al.* 1999), much Archaic pottery and tile was found as sporadic finds from the fringes of mainly Roman concentrations. This suggests the continuity or reuse of the earlier sites as well as demonstrating the intensity of Roman land use.

The character of Faliscan core areas, i.e. Faliscan taskscapes, was explored using GIS and statistical methods. The geographical attributes of the fields, with and without Faliscan pottery or tile, were compared with those of material from other chronologically defined material (flints, prehistoric pottery and Roman pottery). In this way, differences in terrain could be characterized. The amount of Faliscan pottery correlated positively with elevation and negatively with slope. That is the units with Faliscan pottery have higher elevations (mean 228.39 metres above sea level) and gentler gradients (mean 2.72 degrees) than the units without (mean 222.35 metres above sea level and 3.22 degrees respectively). This shows that during the Orientalizing and Archaic periods the upper plateaux with plains were reclaimed by the town-dwellers.

The amount of Faliscan pottery also correlated positively with both curvature and profile curvature, the measures of convexity and the rate of change of elevation and slope in the landscape. The values of curvature differed significantly between units with and without Faliscan pottery. The distribution of different curvature values was skewed clearly on the positive side, which suggests that Faliscan pottery was found on convex, ascending slopes. These results show that Faliscan pottery was found on gentle hills. The amount of Faliscan finds correlated positively with the distance from rivers. The Faliscan pottery was concentrated between the distances of 250 and 500 metres. A chi-square test confirmed the significance of this difference between the surveyed units and the background area. Similarly, Faliscan pottery correlated with land communication networks, both with the distances from the road cuttings leading into the river valleys and the known road lines. However, there was no correlation with the distance from Nepi, although the distribution was slightly skewed towards longer distances (Table 10.1). Both mean and median values were between those for prehistoric and Roman pottery. Variance was higher than with any other category and this suggests that the distribution of Faliscan pottery originated from different kinds of sites and was influenced by many varied processes.

The Faliscan taskscapes were on gentle slopes in slightly undulating areas mostly on higher elevations some distance from rivers along known pathways. These taskscapes differ clearly from prehistoric and Roman ones. Although these groupings are very wide, they can be assumed to reveal cumulative presences in the landscape and expose general associations. In this area, the early prehistoric periods are represented by flints and prehistoric pottery. Most flints are from the long period between the Upper Palaeolithic and the Late Neolithic/Early Bronze Age. Since recent excavations have shown that flint became scarcer in central Italy between the Final Neolithic and Chalcolithic (Andizei and Carboni 1995), and Bronze Age layers generally have only a

		ALL	FLINTS	PREHISTORIC POTTERY	FALISCAN POTTERY	ROMAN POTTERY
N	VALID	231	75	80	127	203
	MISSING	0	156	151	104	28
MEAN		2117.92	2160.77	2534.43	2224.63	2056.98
MEDIAN		2199.64	2377.03	2896.83	2377.03	2026.17
STD. DEVIATION		1158.71	1110.58	1121.08	1166.46	1161.39
VARIANCE		1342615.20	1233388.97	1256829.14	1360625.79	1348824.95
SKEWNESS		.055	.025	-.441	-.059	.169
KURTOSIS		-1.438	-1.488	-1.276	-1.440	-1.436
RANGE		4187.62	3522.68	3492.56	4187.62	4187.62
MINIMUM		52.95	615.81	645.93	52.95	52.95
MAXIMUM		4240.57	4138.49	4138.49	4240.57	4240.57

Table 10.1. Units with different find categories and the statistics of the geographic characteristic 'Distance from Nepi'.

few flints (e.g. Potter 1976: 174–6), flints and pottery can be assumed to represent two different chronological entities. Additionally, statistical analyses show clear differences in their distributions.

Flints were found on flat areas often facing north and east. They were not found near rivers, but in open plains. Although we have to assume that landscape and land use were very different during the Stone Age, hunter-gatherer communities were drawn to the hunting grounds whereas extensive later prehistoric presence, shown by widespread low density non-diagnostic Late Neolithic and early Middle Bronze Age pottery, concentrated on the areas of higher elevations in the west. The landscape was scattered with open settlements during this period. Prehistoric pottery was usually found on flatter areas facing south at some distance from water sources. These find locations did not correlate with the proximity to rivers, but they were significantly connected with pathways to the river valleys and not with the later road network. Thus, they represented a totally different territorial use compared with the Faliscan taskscapes. The relevance of these finds is that together with the more structured settlement patterns they show the emergence of geographic identity in the later periods.

The dominance of Roman finds was clear and quantitatively overshadowed all other periods. Nevertheless, the distributions of Faliscan and Roman pottery overlap, showing continuity and increasing intensity in exploiting the same areas. Nevertheless, the taskscapes were different from the earlier ones. Roman pottery correlated with lower elevations, gentler slopes and eastern and southern aspects. The amount of pottery correlated positively with the distances from the rivers and the road network. Roman taskscapes show a clear degree of separation from pre-urban settlement patterns and the identities involved.

It is clear that the occupation of the site of Nepi and the beginning of proper urban and political development were part of a profound change in the regional territorial systems. Although there were some signs of settlement in the border areas outside Nepi (Rajala 2005), the local pattern was to be Nepi-centred for a long period of time.

Archaic rural settlements (cf. Fig. 10.4) were not commonly identified in the Nepi survey. Some of the Faliscan sites suggested by Potter (Potter n.d.: F12 and F14) showed no concentrations of Archaic material in our resurvey. The new Archaic finds consisted of only a few sporadic pieces or turned out to be early Republican coarsewares. This disappearance of sites is partly due to low surface visibility and modern destruction. Nevertheless, even the low quantities of material have their interpretative value. The discovery on the survey of what I consider a piece of Faliscan funerary slab together with elaborately painted, white-on-red, roof tile in the same Massa area suggests that a wider area was in funerary use during the Archaic period.

Likewise, a series of problematical find concentrations in the San Paolo area north of the town are likely to relate to a cemetery in the area (Rizzo 1992, 1996; di Gennaro *et al.*, 2008), although in part may result from a 'halo' effect and manuring (cf. Coccia and Mattingly 1992; Fentress 2000). The clearest signs of Archaic farms were found farther away from the previously mentioned Massa area in the east and from the Piano di Vallescura area in the north-west (cf. Fig. 10.4). In the first location there were two concentrations of pottery, the first from the sixth century BC and the second from the Late Archaic period. The finds from Piano di Vallescura come from several concentrations that sometimes had Orientalizing origins with a few finer pieces of buccheroid *impasto bruno* and *impasto rosso*. These finds may relate to funerary contexts. However, many Archaic jar rims are similar to those in domestic contexts (cf. Murray Threipland and Torelli 1970; Carafa 1995; Chiaramonte Treré 1999). Most concentrations in this area show continuity from the Archaic period to the fourth century BC.

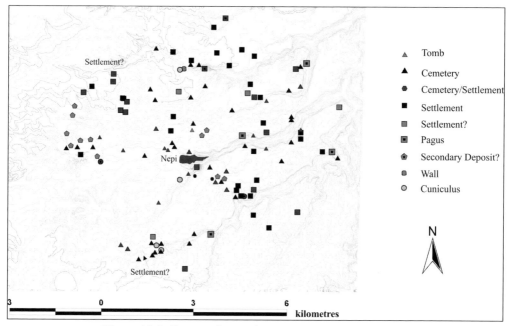

Figure 10.4. Known sites and structures in the Nepi area.

The Archaic period was very important for integrating settlement with geographic identities since it set the pattern that was recaptured in later periods. When the results of the Nepi survey are integrated with all available data (Fig. 10.4), it becomes clear that many Medieval *incastellamento* sites may have had Archaic antecedents (for this hypothesis see already Frederiksen and Ward Perkins 1957; Potter 1979).

Castel Sant'Elia in the north may have been founded during the pre-Roman period (cf. Cifani and Munzi 1995; Cozza and Pasqui 1981: 178). Torre dell'Isola (known also as Torre Stroppa), Castel d'Ischia and Castello del Ponte Nepesino were classified as Faliscan *pagi* in the nineteenth century (cf. Gamurrini *et al.* 1972) while the early dating of Castel Porciano has been denied (Mallet and Whitehouse 1967: 145). However, the chamber tombs near the latter site (Brunetti Nardi 1981) show that there must have been a small settlement in the vicinity

Practically all Medieval outposts have some rock-cut features that may be pre-Roman. At Castello del Ponte Nepesino two typical Faliscan tombs (Fig. 10.5A) were left

Figure 10.5. Archaic structures and Medieval sites: (A) Faliscan chamber tomb at Castello del Ponte Nepesino; (B) landscape at Castel d'Ischia; (C) Faliscan chamber tomb near Torre dell'Isola; (D) road cutting near Pizzo Iella (Photos: U. Rajala).

between two defensive ditches and the Medieval tower was built above two chambers (cf. Frederiksen and Ward Perkins 1957: 82–85, figs 4, 5).

At Torre dell'Isola (Torre Stroppa), there may some Orientalizing surface finds and a few Orientalizing trench tombs (Flavia Trucco, Superintendency of South Etruria, pers. comm.) in addition to the published Final Bronze finds from the same area (di Gennaro and Stoddart 1982, 1995; di Gennaro *et al.* 2002: 32–36).

There is also a large Orientalizing and Archaic cemetery at Tenuta Franca, the northwestern plateau in front of Torre dell'Isola (Cifani and Munzi 1995 with bibl; Fig. 10.5C). This necropolis has at least 24 chamber tombs and it can be considered the largest cemetery in the territory outside Nepi.

In addition to the possible structures inside outposts, many, possibly Archaic, naturally defended, sites have Archaic findspots and open sites outside them. At Castel d'Ischia in the northeast, there was a medium-sized Archaic occupation with at least one partly collapsed chamber tomb (cf. Potter n.d.: F44; Cozza and Pasqui 1981: 178–9; G. Cifani pers. comm.; Fig. 10.5B). The Archaic phase at Pizzo Iella (Potter n.d.) is suggested by a defensive wall of Archaic type and a string of road cuttings (Fig. 10.5D). The sites in the Piano di Vallescura area could relate to a hypothetical site at La Cegna. The further Late Archaic sites outside Grotta Arnaro 2 (Potter n.d.: F22) and north of Torre dell'Isola (Cifani and Munzi 1995) suggest, together with the evidence above, that the *incastellamento* promontories with visible chambers had perhaps a function as strongholds, funerary sites, viewing posts, forts and boundary markers during the Archaic period. These conglomerations may represent a second level of hierarchy between the centre and the farms.

Local group identities in Nepi

During the Orientalizing period the settlement pattern in the territory of Nepi consisted of two tiers of hierarchy – a centre and a series of boundary posts (cf. Rajala 2002, 2005). This pattern was common for all three major Faliscan centres. If the existence of possible 'opposing' outposts, such as Grotta Arnaro and Castel Porciano, could be proven, it could be suggested that they were all independent.

During the Archaic period a third level of hierarchy was developing: rural settlements started to fill the landscape on the boundaries of the territory (Rajala 2005; Cifani and Munzi 1995). The full extent of the settlement is to be determined, but it is clear that there were farms on the more distant plateaux. Many of them were situated along the margins of the vertical cliffs and all were relatively near the known communication routes. Furthermore, it is obvious that there were clusters of sites, such as at Piano di Vallescura, and, therefore, the local settlement pattern consisted of the centre, boundary villages and rural farms (cf. Fig. 10.4). Thus, by the Late Archaic period, a state module existed around Nepi and this pattern may suggest that this area consisted of loosely federal independent centres (cf. di Gennaro 1983, 2007: n. 1). My interpretation is that the inhabitants of these centres shared a common regional identity and probably a common pro-Etruscan identity. This is suggested firstly by the literary tradition (Livy VI.9–10), the linguistic evidence (CIE II.2.1, 6716–6720) and perhaps also, by the use of mythological themes in Faliscan Hellenistic pottery showing scenes of battle metaphorically targeted against the Romans during the Late Archaic period (Pairault Massa 1992, 126: fig. 115).

Nepi's identity was formed by local circumstances, such as its physical environment, political context and settlement history.

Evidently, the areas in the immediate vicinity of Nepi were predominantly in funerary and agricultural use, and rural settlements were located farther away from the town itself, as in the hinterland of Cerveteri (Cristofani 1991; Rendeli 1993). This phenomenon suggests that many inhabitants were directly involved in agriculture, that the social structure was not fully urbanized and thus the towns maintained their rural character.

The possible lack of residential farms in the immediate environs of a centre suggests a weakly developed separation of production and services with only a few inhabitants involved in non-agricultural activities.

The increased need for land caused intensification further afield in the Archaic period and any new sites were founded in less occupied areas near the boundaries of the territory. At Cerveteri, the small rural sites appear only after some two kilometres from the site (Zifferero 2005). This is approximately the distance from Nepi to the first farms on Massa, as demonstrated by the results of the Nepi Survey Project (di Gennaro *et al.* 2008).

This rural Archaic settlement pattern was structurally different from the more urbanized towns in central Italy. For example, Tarquinia and *Veii* had a dense ring of rural farms near the urban centre (Rendeli 1993: 256–82, figs. 130, 133) and at *Gabii* the 120 Archaic settlements in its territory repeated the same pattern (cf. Quilici 1974; Rajala 2002: 268–71, appendix 32). The existence of rural population at the gates of a city seems to emphasize the proper urban character of the centre and demonstrated the properly differentiated roles of town-dwellers and peasants. It could suggest that there was locally a market for agricultural products and population without direct access to arable land.

In the Nepi area, the separation between urban and rural spheres perhaps did not happen properly before the Republican period and Roman occupation. This could suggest that the local identity had its roots directly in the land and was proportionately less dependent on the construction of an elite culture even though an elite culture is celebrated in the local tombs.

Tombs and Latin funerary identities: the excavations at Cisterna Grande

The funerary excavations at Cisterna Grande

The Remembering the Dead Project excavated inside the cemetery area of Cisterna Grande at *Crustumerium* (Fig. 10.6) between 2004 and 2008 as part of a series of international excavations at the ancient town. The site of *Crustumerium* is located in the Tiber valley about ten kilometres north of Rome. It was one of the rival city states of Rome that was defeated together with neighbouring *Fidenae* in 500/499 BC (Livy

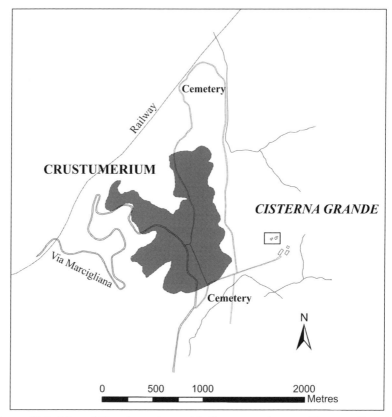

Figure 10.6. Map of Crustumerium with the excavations at Cisterna Grande.

2.19.2). The town declined and vanished altogether by the fourth century BC (Quilici and Quilici Gigli 1980; di Gennaro 1999a; Amoroso 2000). The area of Cisterna Grande was chosen for the excavations after recent illegal looting. The first tombs exposed were chamber tombs. As these have only been rarely scientifically explored, the project has prioritized their excavation.

The main aim of the project is to study the metaphorical funerary representations of a Latin Late Iron Age and Archaic community. Tombs form part of a wider ritual landscape (cf. Naso 1996; Riva and Stoddart 1996; Bradley 1998, 2002) that has been studied at a local level using digital and traditional methods. In addition to digital single context planning, the project makes use of GIS and virtual modelling.

Recent studies of pre-Roman society have shown the potential of funerary research in revealing the social and ritual aspects of a culture (e.g. Bietti Sestieri 1992a, 1992b; Cuozzo 2003). This case study will present the possibilities that examining local funerary structures have in the study of local social identities. Not very much is known about Latin Archaic tombs or those from the times of the early Republic, as has been noted before (Colonna 1977; Ampolo 1984; Naso 1990). Although the situation is slowly improving, the research initiatives like those at *Crustumerium* are needed to increase our knowledge. The research excavations at Colle del Forno at *Eretum* in the Sabine area are the most comprehensive source of data on Archaic chamber tombs (Santoro 1977, 1983, 1985, 2005; Benelli and Santoro 2006). Rescue excavations especially south of Rome have revealed a large body of material (cf. Bedini 1980, 1981, 1983, 1990a). Although evidence is scarce, it shows that a wide range of burial customs was practiced at the local and regional level. There were also remarkable similarities in rituals over considerable distances during the Late Orientalizing and Archaic periods in the late seventh century and sixth century BC in *Latium vetus*.

Ritual and religious identities

Although religion is an essential element in the construction of social identities, its position in sociology and other identity studies is relatively peripheral. In archaeology, Marxism and ideas such as Hawkes's Ladder have led to widespread scepticism, and archaeologies of religion are those of fragmentation and uncertainty (Edwards 2005: 110–11). This case study concentrates on funerary evidence, which makes the situation even more ambiguous. Burials reflect many different aspirations, norms, beliefs and traditions through ritual practices (cf. Parker Pearson 1999). They may convey the self-representation of the deceased, but since the funeral is organized by the living, the choices may have been made by the family or other linked groups so any interpretations have to be made with some caution. Nevertheless, Lucy (2002) has pointed out that since local communities were creators and maintainers of society, the analysis starting from the local level makes interpretations possible. This type of research perceives practices as complex entities, but since different localized practices are the foundation and constitution of a society, combined local patterns reveal general regional and cultural customs.

Ultimately, material culture is used in geographical contexts in order to create and transform social boundaries (Lucy 2005b). The clearest signs of active use of material culture relate to costume traditions, mortuary rituals, consumption of different foods and the use of architecture and space. However, there may not have been single ethnic signifiers in the past but ethnic significance, which may blurred when identity markers are applied locally and individually (Hakenbeck 2004a, 2004b). Most scholars (e.g. Lucy 2002) have concentrated on mortuary practices, but unlike them, I will not examine the similarities and differences of burial rite, but the tombs themselves as material objects (cf. Rajala 2007). Thus, chamber tombs are seen as part of material culture that had specific meanings in the past. Different identities were created locally and these local identities drew on the repertoire of Archaic central Italian material culture. Therefore, variations in cultural material forms may be taken as local interpretations of regional or general ideologies and identities.

The Archaic settlement pattern in *Latium vetus* was formed by independent city-states (e.g. Cornell 1995: 81–118) that could choose to reflect their own identity, defined by geography and social practices, when choosing the form of their tombs. The construction of the Latin *ethnos* was a highly complicated and variegated political phenomenon (Cornell 1995; Carandini this volume; Fulminante this volume; Ceccarelli this volume) which will not be analyzed in detail here, particularly because this article concentrates on the local level, albeit in relationship to the wider whole. However, it was clearly a situational self-defined identity, which was incorporated in the spatially and socially defined identities of different city-states. Jones (1997) argued that material culture has played an active role in creation of these spatial identities. Revealing this role requires the inventory of different ways of consumption and the acknowledgement of the existence of symbolic structures. In Archaic Etruria, tombs were actively used to mark ritualized boundaries (Riva and Stoddart 1996). These boundaries existed at different levels between the city and its cemeteries, between the town and suburbia and between different Etruscan city-states. Since the separation of settlements and cemeteries was similarly practised in Latium, it is clear that tombs and cemeteries were used as markers in this area as well.

Thus, different nested and intertwined secular and religious identities were communicated in Latin burial practices and tomb structures. Considering the weak understanding of the wider regional ritual practices and the importance of individual or religious choice the discussion of Latin identities requires considering all published Archaic burial evidence, and I will concentrate on this issue.

Archaic tombs in Latium vetus

The chamber tomb was the dominant tomb type during the Archaic period in the seventh and sixth and century BC. During the preceding Orientalizing period in the eighth and early seventh century BC, the deceased were buried in different kinds of trench (*fossa*) tombs. The latter tomb type was already in use during the later part of the Early Iron Age, such as in the best-known Latial cemetery of Osteria dell'Osa (Bietti Sestieri 1992a) northeast of Rome. The simplest trench tombs (*tomba a fossa semplice*) were modest rectangular trenches, but many (*tomba a loculo tipo Narce* and *tomba a doppio loculo tipo Montarano*; di Gennaro 1999a, 2007; originally called *tomba a Fossa con loculo*, e.g Cifani 2005; I realize that some colleagues do not consider it appropiate to refer to the *tombe a loculo* as trench tombs) had one or two side niches (*loculi*) for the deceased and the grave goods (cf. Fig. 10.7). Some trench tombs were made for a single inhumation and

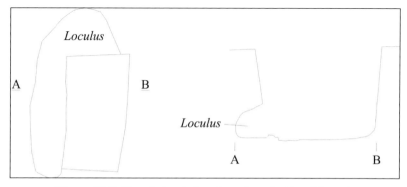

Figure 10.7. Trench tomb (tomba a loculo tipo Narce).

they had relatively rich grave goods. For example at *Crustumerium* a fairly normal assemblage consists of a dozen pottery vessels together with the jewelry related to clothing (di Gennaro 1999a; Paolini 1990). The richest tombs have whole drinking sets with numerous containers and cups and sometimes bronze vessels and tripods (Ceci *et al.* 1997; di Gennaro 1988, 1990a, 1999a, 1999b, 2001; Paolini 1990).

At the end of the Orientalizing period, there was a transition to chamber tombs in *Latium vetus*. Like trench tombs, chamber tombs were cut into the tuff, but they generally accommodated more than one or two inhumations; they are commonly thought to have been family tombs. Chambers were normally rectangular, room-like spaces, which were entered through a door via an entrance corridor (*dromos*). Many chambers had niches (*loculi*) carved into their walls (cf. Fig. 10.8).

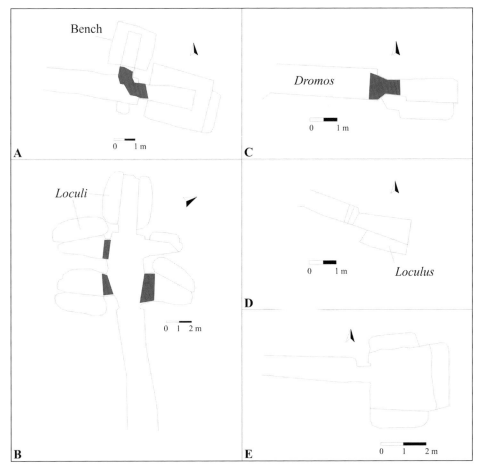

Figure 10.8. Chamber tombs in central Italy: (A) Osteria dell'Osa (after De Santis 1992: tav. 50); (B) Torrino (after Bedini 1981: fig. 6); (C) Acqua Acetosa Laurentina (after Bedini 1983: fig. 2); (D) Tor de' Cenci (after Bedini 1990, fig. 9); (E) Colle del Forno (after Piro and Santoro 2002: fig. 10).

Early chamber tombs from the Late Orientalizing in the late seventh and early sixth century BC have been occasionally found at different locations in *Latium vetus*. There is a late Orientalizing chamber tomb from the Esquiline necropolis (Pinza 1905: cc. 194–15, t. CXXV) but the sandy soil the cemetery was dug into together with the old-fashioned excavation recording make the interpretation of different structures problematic. At Osteria dell'Osa a single chamber tomb (Fig. 10.8A) has been excavated and it is Late Orientalizing in date. This tomb had unusual ritual characteristics, and thus, it may not be taken as a representative example. The tomb contained 13 burials, some partially recomposed or disarticulated, and relatively numerous grave goods (De Santis 1992: 864–71). At Torrino, south of Rome, one of the two excavated chambers (Fig. 10.8B) is also dated to this period. Grave goods included some pottery vessels but it was not particularly rich in comparison with the tomb at Osteria dell'Osa or the earlier trench tombs. The second chamber tomb at Torrino was cut at the end of the seventh century BC and was in use for the whole Archaic period. In this chamber, the later burials were materially poorer than the early ones (Bedini 1981). Different types of chamber structures are the built chambers discovered relatively recently in a monumental tumulus at Lavinium (Guaitoli 1995: 557–62).

Unlike the early chambers at Osteria dell'Osa and Torrino, some earliest mid-seventh century chamber tombs at *Crustumerium* did not have a *dromos*, but an entrance shaft (Paolini 1990). The first example had been damaged by looting, but the three inhumations had noticeably fewer grave goods than those in trench tombs. One had a spearhead, the second a knife, a container and a jug, and the third one a bowl. The deceased were buried in these rectangular chambers with only a few grave goods. Even with the incomplete evidence of the relative richness of the Orientalizing chamber, the later chambers show a clear drop in the number of grave goods. The tombs at *Crustumerium* and Torrino share the same trend of declining opulence from the Orientalizing to the Archaic period.

Like the chambers at *Crustumerium* those at Corcolle, north-east of Rome, had some pottery; these *bucchero* and imported Etrusco-Corinthian vessels have been dated to mid-sixth century BC (Reggiani *et al.* 1998). Significantly, the two Archaic chamber tombs excavated at Acqua Acetosa Laurentina (Fig. 10.8C), south of Rome, lacked grave goods altogether. The chambers were dated on the basis of pottery sherds in their fills (Bedini 1983). Both the two chambers at nearby Casale Massima only contained one miniature pottery vessel (Bedini 1980, 1983). At Tor de' Cenci (Bedini 1990a), also south of Rome, only a few of the ten chamber tombs on two sides of an ancient road had any datable items. Their direct and indirect dating ranged from the end of the seventh to the fourth or third century BC. Some may thus be Republican, but the recurrence of a relatively short *dromos*, a narrow, rectangular chamber and the existence of a single *loculus* on one side repeatedly shows the longevity of this local type (Fig. 10.8D) The lack of grave goods in Archaic tombs make their precise dating difficult. It was acknowledged only after the excavations of the 1970s that the lack of Greek pottery and grave goods in general had hindered the recognition of different Archaic tomb types (Colonna 1977). Since just some Archaic burials occasionally had datable grave goods, these same rare occurrences have been used to recognize the different Archaic tomb types. Most of the tombs in *Latium vetus* were chamber tombs, like the famous warrior burial in *Lanuvium* in the Alban Hills, but they are not the only tomb type.

Simple sarcophagi of the local *peperino* tuff were found from old excavations on the Esquiline hill in Rome and at Tivoli (cf. Pinza 1915, Naso 1990: 250; also Colonna 1977: 136–50), but the exact structure of these tombs remains unclear. At Corcolle, *peperino* sarcophagi have recently been found in a chamber tomb (Reggiani *et al.* 1998). Therefore, at least some of the sarcophagi may originate from chamber tombs, and these finds are becoming more common (di Gennaro pers. comm.). However, at La Rustica, also northeast of Rome, the sarcophagi seem to have been found from trench tombs (Colonna 1977). However, at least some of the Archaic finds at Praeneste seem to relate with the sarcophagi and *casse* from trenches (Pensabene 1983: 260–8). There are also a series of finds without proper provenance from different Latin centres that signal existence of Archaic burials; these include bronze mirrors and earrings at Praeneste and pottery at Ardea and Praeneste (Tortorici 1983: 54; Pensabene 1983; Naso 1990: 250–1). However, there are two proper chamber tombs from Ardea (Quilici and Quilici Gigli 1977; Morselli and Tortorici 1982: 110–11), which show connections to southern Etruria

Trench tombs do not seem to have disappeared altogether but they were frequently of the simple rectangular type and had only meagre grave goods (cf. Bedini 1990a, 1990b; Naso 1990; also, Reggiani *et al.* 1998). The three trenches at Casale Massima generally had some beads (Bedini 1980, 1983) and other trenches at Tor de' Cenci produced no finds whatsoever (Bedini 1990a). Similarly, at Ardea children were buried in poor *fosse* (Tortorici 1983: 54). However, one exceptionally rich *fossa* with a female inhumation in a sarcophagus was excavated inside the Archaic town of *Fidenae* (di Gennaro 1990b). The Archaic tombs from the cemetery area at *Ficana*, both with and without finds, were trenches; in addition, many children's tombs were in *fosse* in the settlement areas (Jarva 1980; Brandt 1996: 115–64). At La Rustica, many Archaic tombs comprised a shaft or trench and a niche (*loculus*) on the side (Colonna 1977); structurally, they were very similar to the Archaic trenches with steps at *Veii* in the Etruscan area (Drago Troccoli 1997). This particular example suggests that interregional contacts affected burial customs at the local level.

The best evidence for a local type of standard Archaic chamber tomb comes from the excavations at Colle del Forno at *Eretum* in the Sabine area. The standard tomb had a rectangular chamber and two tiers of *loculi* for inhumations with some modest grave goods (Santoro 1977, 1983, 1985; Fig. 10.8E). However, a few of the chambers were exceptionally monumental, with larger chambers and in some cases high-status grave goods (Santoro 1977, 2005; Benelli and Santoro 2006; the 'regal' chamber found in 2005 has not yet been formally published). The tombs show clearly that the burial custom was at least to some extent related with the economic resources and the social status of the deceased in the local social hierarchy. The exceptional individuals or the members of the highest stratum of the elite were buried in special tombs. The excavations at Colle del Forno also demonstrate how a long-term project manages to give a more coherent picture of the local range of chamber tombs and different burial rites of the community.

The chambers excavated so far at Cisterna Grande, although limited in number, show that the variability of the chamber tombs was higher than expected. The chambers are of different shapes, sizes, depths, orientations and designs, and the quality of finish varies significantly. The *dromoi* differ as well; their lengths, widths and depths show wide variation, and again, some had a finished quality whereas others were relatively rough. Most tombs had blocking features still *in situ* at the entrance. Most were blocked or further reinforced with a pile of stones, but some only had large single slabs closing the door. The varied architecture suggests that there was more than one standard chamber tomb type simultaneously in use. It is likely that different types reflect the status of the families or individuals buried in the tombs and their different economic and social positions in their community. Unlike at Colle del Forno, where the alternatives seem to have only been 'typical' and exceptionally high-status, the differences at Cisterna Grande are more subtle and graded. The seven chamber tombs under excavation seem to fall into two categories (Fig. 10.9), if not three. One of the chambers turned out to be Orientalizing although it had a later Archaic inhumation in its dromos (Rajala 2008).

Firstly, there are relatively large rectangular chambers (Fig. 10.9A) with one or more *loculi* on the walls and additional burials in coffins or trunks on the floor. These chambers have longer and deeper *dromoi* than the other type. Among these larger chambers there is possibly a looted one, which even though its excavation was halted for safety reasons, can be seen to be more 'monumental' and may represent a higher-status category. Since it was not as monumental as the exceptional chambers at Colle del Forno, its high-status ranking was merely relative. The second chamber tomb type (Fig. 10.9B) was more modest with a low ceiling, semicircular chamber and two slightly irregular *loculi*. The *dromos* was shallow, short and relatively narrow. The tuff surfaces were relatively uneven with visible pick marks. The construction of the latter type would have required much less man-power. Preliminarily, the surviving artefacts in the tombs of the former tomb type, although not luxurious, seem generally to be more elaborate than in the latter. Therefore, the first category may be for the prosperous and the second for the poorer individuals of society. Nevertheless, these were clearly not made for the highest ranking aristocrats.

Like in other Archaic tombs elsewhere in *Latium vetus*, most of the deceased at Cisterna Grande had some jewellery or arms with them. However, none of the primary burials seem to have been left without grave goods. On the other hand, only two burials had an entire small pottery vessel. Richer burials had bronze fibulae together with beads and pendants or a spearhead or dagger while many dead were buried with more modest

Figure 10.9. Chamber tombs at Cisterna Grande, Crustumerium: (A) large rectangular chamber tomb (Photo: H. Arima); (B) small circular chamber tomb (Photo: U. Rajala).

iron fibulae or some other iron object. Burials also had some specific structures with them. Some *loculi* were closed with roof tiles, which could be a sign of some wealth although these were found in both chamber types. In more modest burials the *loculus* was closed with stones and the deceased were simply wrapped in shrouds.

The previous excavations in the other cemetery areas of *Crustumerium* suggested that the small, rectangular chambers without *loculi* were an early type and the larger chambers were later (di Gennaro 1999b: 54). Although the Orientalizing chamber at Cisterna Grande conformed to this with this its lack of *loculi*, the structure of Archaic chambers with several contemporary types suggest that the variation is greater. The data from other locations around *Latium vetus* suggest that many of the tombs were of a local type. These local types could also differ considerably over short distances. In addition, there were interregional phenomena shared with the Latins, the Etruscans and the Sabines, as is shown by the apparent decline in the number of grave goods in the neighbouring areas (Colonna 1977; Bartoloni 1988; Drago Troccoli 1997; Benelli and Santoro 2006), the chambers at Ardea (Quilici and Quilici Gigli 1977; Morselli and Tortorici 1982: 110–11) and the distribution of a particular Archaic trench tomb type (Colonna 1977, Drago Troccoli 1997).

Nested identities in Latium vetus

The quality, not the quantity of the finds at Cisterna Grande and elsewhere show the potential of the study of local identities at Archaic sites. The previous meagre knowledge on the Archaic tombs of *Latium vetus* suggests that a wide range of burial customs was practised at the local and regional level. Even relatively small centres seem to have had tomb types different from their supposedly more influential neighbours. Nevertheless, there were also remarkable similarities in structures over considerable distances and between different ethnic areas. Furthermore, even in one centre, like *Crustumerium*, different burial customs were practised and different types of tombs were constructed for the deceased reflecting their social identities.

The mere existence of local types is a proof of the existence of nested spatial and social identities in *Latium vetus* and that these were reflected in burial customs and funerary architecture. The development of chamber tombs coincided with the dramatic drop in grave goods and conspicuous consumption. It has been argued that the changes in burial custom and deliberate omission of grave goods could be attributed to the legislation of developing city-states (cf. Colonna 1977; Naso 1990; also, di Gennaro 1999a). Since legislation may only reflect the attempts to resolve existing problems or to find satisfactory solutions, it does not explain the rapid acceptance of the changes over a larger region. Whatever the reason, it can be suggested that in the absence of numerous personal items different identities had to be expressed through the burial structures themselves. Even if the chambers were not visited by outsiders, the creation and continued use of certain geographically and chronologically restricted chamber types is a testimony of the existence of a self-defined, situational identity. The makers of the chambers viewed themselves as 'us' who modelled their funerary spaces accordingly in their local community.

Conclusions

In this article I have presented two examples from Archaic central Italy. Both these case studies are based on recent fieldwork projects, although they present different types of material collected with different methodologies. The first example presented the Archaic settlement pattern in the territory of Nepi north of Rome, integrating and interpreting the results of a surface survey material and the published earlier data. The second example presented the different funerary chamber types found at the cemetery excavations at Cisterna Grande at *Crustumerium* and their relationship with other known Archaic tomb types in *Latium vetus.* These two case studies have enabled me to suggest that different nested geographically and chronologically defined identities are visible in different categories of archaeological material at a local level.

Naturally, the identities expressed were slightly different. The settlement pattern was a direct manifestation of territoriality, and thus of political identity. This political identity was related in the past with a certain community, in this case that of ancient Nepi, which could have had several identities at different levels. The identities could relate either to a Faliscan town or to a small independent or semi-independent polity, depending on different historical interpretations. In any case, this pattern shows the existence of a rurally orientated community that differentiated itself from nearby neighbours of Narce, *Falerii* and Sutri.

On the other hand, the identities reflected in Latin chamber tombs were intertwined with other ritual and social identities. However, in their communality, even if on the level of a family or other smaller funerary group, they reflected a shared sense of belonging. The existence of what seems at this point in the research process like strictly local chamber types suggests that chambers as material objects reflected shared identities in towns or city-states. The existence of other tomb types and other rituals shows that other processes and values were present and the interpretations got blurred by past individual beliefs, different manners and regional phenomena. In both cases, the identities were created, maintained and appropriated on a sub-ethnic level. Nevertheless, these identities were important to their owners, either Faliscan or Latin, and they were used in the construction of more regional identities.

In essence, both settlement patterns and cemeteries were geographically distributed and existed analytically in different types of landscapes. Settlement patterns, and the territoriality they expressed, were part of domestic, political and economic landscapes of a community whereas cemeteries were part of its ritual landscape. Thus, when combined, they reflected all the identities a community could have and the whole trajectory of human experience. In this way the discussion in this paper is not only integrating field data with earlier knowledge but also integrating the landscapes of the living and the dead as a single canvas on which different nested identities were shaped.

Acknowledgements

The collaboration with Dott.sa Daniela Rizzo and *Soprintendenza archeologica per l'Etruria meridionale* (SAEM) on one hand and Dr Francesco di Gennaro and *Soprintendenza Speciale per i Beni Archeologici di Roma* on the other have made this article possible. I would like to thank Dr Simon Stoddart for his supervision and for acting as PI for some of the grants. The Academy of Finland (grant nos. 44638, 211057 and 213324), the British Academy, the Finnish Cultural Foundation, the McDonald Institute, New Hall, Cambridge European Trust, Prehistoric Society, Society of Antiquaries of London, the Niilo Helander Foundation, the Emil Aaltonen Foundation, and the Jenny and Antti Wihuri Foundation have generously given funding for the research projects presented in this article. I am also grateful for the Ridgway-Venn Travel Studentship, Worts Travelling Scholarship, George Charles Winter Warr Scholarship and Garrod Fund grants received for my PhD fieldwork. In addition, the British School at Rome, *Institutum Romanum Finlandiae*, University of Cambridge, University of Oulu, University of Turku, *Comune di Nepi*, *Museo archeologico dell'Agro Falisco*, *IV municipio di Roma*, Muuritutkimus ky and *Gruppo Archeologico dell'Associazione del Dopolavoro Ferroviario di Roma* have given assistance. Dr Phil Mills and Dr Francesco di Gennaro kindly commented on the earlier draft of this article.

The Nepi project was directed by Dr Simon Stoddart and supervised in the field by the author. The project had three field seasons from 1999 to 2000. The material discussed in this article was collected during the blanket surveys in September 1999 and September 2000. The aim of the fieldwork was to collect a coherent body of data to study the changes in the local settlement patterns from the Bronze Age onwards.

The excavations in the cemetery of Cisterna Grande were carried out in collaboration with the Superintendency of Rome and Dr di Gennaro, the director of this archaeological area. The excavation project ran for five years (2004–2008) and is in the course of publication.

Approaching ethnicity and landscapes in pre-Roman Italy: the middle Tiber Valley

Gabriele Cifani

Keywords: ethnicity; landscape; central Italy; city states; territorial states

Introduction: archaeology and ethnicity

In the last two decades, post-processual approaches to archaeology have emphasized the role played by identities and ideology in the organization of culture. Within this framework, ethnicity represents perhaps the most complex form, since it is based on a collective rather than individual perception of identity (Jones 1996; Díaz-Andreu *et al.* 2005: 6). However, debate on the relationship between ideology and culture is much older than post-processualism. Within the huge literature on how to define ethnicity, we can, in my opinion, trace two main approaches.

The first one is the physical approach, which tends to define communities by means of their physical attributes, geographical distribution and the effects of weather on behaviour and culture. This determinist method started in classical antiquity (e.g. Pliny *Natural History* VII), became very popular in the Enlightenment, thanks in part to the work of Montesquieu *De l'esprit de lois* (1748), continued during the period of Positivism, and was very influential in many studies predating the Second World War. The modern researches on archaeogenetics might be considered, in some respects, the heirs to such an approach (for a synthesis of the debate on the Etruscan area: Perkins 2009).

The second approach is cultural and idealistic which focuses on the customs, language and culture to investigate an ethnic group. We can trace the origin of such approaches in Classical Greece, above all in the work of Herodotos, the first ethnographer, who defined ethnicity as an ideological construct by describing the origins of the Ionian *ethnos* as a pragmatic self creation instead of a primordial group (Herodotos I.143–7; McInerney 2001: 57–9).

In the course of Romanticism, G. F. Hegel stressed the importance of the spiritual values of an ethnic group as integrally linked with its identity, by shaping the concept of *Volksgeist* (Hegel 1955: 59); this theory became very influential during the nineteenth century and was taken up by sociologists and historians.

For example, in 1917, Benedetto Croce defined History as the main characteristic of a Nation (Croce 1989: 378–80) and Max Weber in 1922 described ethnic groups as 'those human groups that entertain a subjective belief in their common descent' (Weber 1978: 389).

At the beginning of the twentieth century, archaeological studies developed in parallel with these approaches; for example, the best known theory of the German archaeologist Gustav Kossina combined the distribution of material culture with the evidence of ethnicity (Kossina 1902) and he greatly influenced contemporary studies of the prehistory of Europe, among them some of the earliest works of Vere Gordon Childe (Childe 1926; Härke 1991: 188–9; Trigger 2006: 243–8). After the Second World War, the collapse of European empires marked the beginning of postcolonial approaches to ethnicity; in this phase we find, in linguistic terminology, the first distinction between 'etic' and 'emic', an approach which emphasizes the point of view of the observer (Pike 1967), and the growing importance of the self definition of a community in defining ethnicity (Malkin 2001: 15–19). This was the cultural framework of the ground-breaking work '*Ethnic Group and Boundaries*', published by the Norwegian anthropologist Fredrik Barth, who rejected ethnicity as a static concept and emphasized ethnic boundaries as an effect of social interaction (Barth 1969).

More recently, cultural anthropologists have stressed the role of history and the importance of mentalities as long term phenomena in defining ethnic identities (e.g. Cole and Wolf 1974). Mentalities can start as an effect of history, but afterwards they can also act as causes of change in history (Epstein 1978; Fabietti 1998; Remotti 2001; Smith 1986; Tullio-Altan 1997). From this point of view, the main elements of membership in an ethnic group are:

- the *epos*: the feeling of identity within a community and its cultural memory;
- the *ethos*: the sharing of moral values;
- the *logos*: the common language or languages inside a group;
- the *oikos* or *topos*: the territory where a community is based.

The idealistic approach seems also to have influenced the most recent debate of ethnicity in archaeology. According to the recent synthesis of Jonathan Hall, the term ethnicity denotes not just the self-consciousness of belonging to an ethnic group but also the dynamic process that structures, and is structured by, ethnic groups in social interaction with one another (Hall 1997: 1–33, 2002: 9–19).

From this point of view, the main elements that determine membership in an ethnic group are:

1. a putative subscription to a myth of common descent and kinship;
2. an association with a specific territory;
3. a sense of shared history.

However, as shown by historical examples, the construction of an ethnic identity is based on the malleability of cultural memory and the reinterpretation of the past by rulers and governments, often projected on specific sites or objects (e.g. Hobsbawm and Ranger 1983; Nora 1992). Thus, the purely ideological character of ethnicity has discouraged some scholars from using only archaeological evidence in studying ethnic identities (e.g. Knapp 2001; Mele 2002). Moreover, J. Siapkas has emphasised ethnicity as a dynamic and flexible strategy (Sjapkas 2003; Yoffee 2007) and Erich Gruen has drawn our attention to the role played by cultural borrowings in shaping ethnic identities (Gruen 2005). More recently, François de Polignac (2006) pointed out that it may be more appropriate to approach ethnicity as an aspect of collective identification, rather than as a static identity and by trying to compare its developments and transformation.

As matter of fact, material data can rarely reveal a precise ideology by themselves (e.g. Mele 2002) and we must avoid the risk of over-interpreting archaeological evidence. However, studying the way in which ethnicity is represented, or is grounded, can represent a useful tool to investigate ancient society, by employing a multidisciplinary approach which must consider, when available:

1. literary sources;
2. epigraphic evidence;
3. burial customs;
4. material culture;
5. the spatial organization of territories.

Myth, rituals and territory have been also considered the pillars of ethnic identity (e.g. Malkin 1994; Mazza 2006: 3–4). For these reasons, the organization of territories, above all studied by means of a *longue durée* approach, seems one of the more promising insights; the interaction between culture and territory has a potential pointed out by recent approaches of landscape archaeology (e.g. Knapp and Ashmore 1999).

Approaches to ethnicity in the archaeology of 'pre-Roman' Italy

Pre-Roman Italy represents an interesting context for the analysis of the process of ethnic identification because of the presence of many ethnic groups. The tradition of studies starts with the erudite work of the Renaissance and above all from the eighteenth century was based on the dichotomy between Rome and Italic peoples (Firpo 2008); it continued with the ethnocentric approaches of acculturation and history of civilization which prevailed up until the Second World War, and was partly replaced by concepts of cultural interaction during the 1960s. During these later years, the theme of Greek influence in Southern Italy was analyzed for the first time from a post colonial perspective, stressing the active role played by the Italic indigenous community in shaping the culture of *Magna Graecia* and Sicily (Atti Taranto 1962). This was the beginning of a new interest in cultural exchanges, which led to a focus on cultural contacts and processes of transformation in the whole Mediterranean area (e.g. Atti Pisa–Roma 1983).

In the most recent decades, many scholars analyzed the role played by Greek, Italic, Roman and other cultures. This can be seen in the publication of the international congress at Taranto of 1997 dedicated to landscapes and frontiers (Atti Taranto 1997), or, more recently, studies of Achaian identity in the south of Italy (Greco 2002), together with many works supported by the Accordia Research Centre on ethnicity (Cornell and Lomas 1997). More recently, research aimed at the study of the cultural evolution of

Sardinia, by means of material culture, has led to a re-evaluation of Antonio Gramsci's concept of cultural hegemony in approaches to the changing landscape of the island between indigenous communities, the Punic world and Rome (e.g. van Dommelen 1998, 2006). Cultural interaction and cross-cultural exchanges across the Mediterranean area since the Early Iron Age have also been revealed by the systematic excavation of the necropolis of *Pithecusa*, the most ancient Greek colony in Italy (Buchner and Ridgway 1994; Nizzo 2007). Last, but not least, even the identity of Late Republican Roman Italy has been reconsidered as a place of persistence of Italic culture, because of the rapid expansion of the Roman Mediterranean empire between the third and second century BC, which anticipated the full assimilation of Italic people inside the Roman community (Giardina 1997; Harris 2007).

In central Tyrrhenian Italy, the tradition of studies of ethnic identity has for many years been linked to two historical problems: the rise of Rome and the *nomen Latinum*, and the ethnogenesis of the Etruscans. From a theoretical perspective, since the 1940s, one of the main achievements of scholarly debate about pre-Roman Italy has been to abandon migration theories and ethnic origins and to focus on the concept of ethnic formation as the result of gradual long-term processes (Pallottino 1942: 77, 1955, 1961, 1974: 102). Renato Peroni rejected the equation between culture/*facies* and *ethnos*, but he pointed out that differentiation in ethnic identities could be partially traced through the social analysis of funerary contexts and through settlement history (Peroni 1989: 7–24).

In Etruria, since the end of the 1960s, scientific debate has reinterpreted the role played by the city-state system in shaping Etruscan ethnicity (Pallottino 1970), most particularly in terms of interaction with Italic and Greek cultures (e.g. Torelli 1982, 1987; Cristofani 1983). Cultural interaction led to a focus on the mechanism of social mobility which characterized Archaic societies, investigated by means of literary sources and epigraphic documents. The Etruscans, and above all Archaic Rome, were re-interpreted as open societies, with high levels of horizontal social mobility, inter-linked with the aristocratic elites of the Greek world and Italic communities (e.g. Ampolo 1977, 1981; Cristofani 1996; Tagliamonte 1994). Furthermore, spatial analysis of the pre-Roman Italic epigraphic texts identified the gap between ethnicity and language (e.g. Cristofani 2001).

The collective ethnic identity of Rome has been the subject of a huge historical debate, but recent studies have emphasized social and ethnic osmosis as the basis of Roman political and military supremacy since its origins, starting from the assumption that the Roman state was the only one in antiquity to grant citizenship to former enemies and former slaves. Roman identity was based on the ideology of incorporation (Dench 1995, 2005: 151–93) and the ability of the Romans to adopt and to select foreigners' customs was described also by Greek sources (e.g. Polyb. VI.25.11; Dittenberger 1915–1924: 543), but perhaps the most interesting document of Roman self representation is the famous oration of emperor Claudius in 48 AD in support of the enlargement of the Senate to citizens of *Gallia Comata*. This speech can be considered a kind of manifesto of the flexible strategy of the Roman community, based on social osmosis (Tacitus *Annals* XI.23–4; *CIL* XIII, 1668; Dessau 1892: 212; Riccobono *et al.* 1940–43 vol. I: 43). Claudius opened his speech about the mixed ethnic character of Rome dating back to the early community, when local kings (*reges domestici*) were followed by Sabines and Etruscan monarchs (*reges alieni et quidam externi*), and stressed that the privilege of access to the Roman senate was granted progressively to all people of Italy (*Etruria Lucaniaque et omni Italia in senatum accitos*) in parallel with numerous reforms of the Roman institutions through the centuries (*multa in hac civitate novata*; Giardina 1997: 3–77). The reliability of this account shows also the crucial role played in the Roman Republic by ethnic identities in shaping the ideologies of elite families in an arena of political competition (Farney 2007). Recent research on the origins of Rome has also reconsidered the problem of the historical value of the most ancient myths of the Latins, as evidence of self-identity (Roma 1981; Cornell 1995: 70–80; Carandini 1997, 2002, 2006a, 2006b, this volume; Mavrogiannis 2003), or the role played by rituals and laws in shaping identity (Schiavone 2005: 41–73) together with the growing importance given to landscape patterns and burial customs as evidence of ethnicity in protohistoric Latium (Bietti Sestieri and De Santis 1992, 2007).This kind of approach fits well with the British tradition of landscape archaeology, focused on medium and long-term transformations. As a matter of fact, during the last three decades, landscape archaeology data have given one of the finest contributions to the understanding Etruscan and Italic ethnic identity: for instance, the detailed analysis of protohistoric settlements which has enlightened our understanding of the beginning of the urbanization process in central Italy (Peroni 1988; Pacciarelli 2001), together with many other pivotal surveys carried out in Etruria (Rendeli 1993: 40–58; Potter and Stoddart 2001).

Our knowledge of the ethnic groups of pre-Roman Italy starts with the regional division of Italy made by the emperor Augustus, as known mainly from Pliny the Elder (*Natural History* III.46; Fig. 11.1). The boundaries of these regions have been progressively refined between the beginning of AD seventeenth century (Cluverius 1624) and the end of the nineteenth century (e.g. Nissen 1902). Each region had a sequential number and a name based on the main ethnic group in the area. So we can easily spot the seventh region, *Etruria*; the sixth *Umbria*; the fourth, *Samnium* and the first, *Latium et Campania*. However, even if we can reasonably define the borders of such regions, we must be aware of the deeply different meanings and aims of the ancient frontiers compared with those of the pre-Roman ethnic groups.

Figure 11.1. The regional division of Roman Italy made by the emperor Augustus (Franchi Dell'Orto 2001).

The real nature of such *regiones* is still controversial (Polverini 1998). Some scholars thought that they were only employed for statistical purposes (e.g. Tibiletti 1965). Others (de Martino 1975, Nicolet 1991) believe they were linked to wide administrative aims, such as the payment of tribute. It is clear, however, that they had no political purpose and, above all, they did not aim to describe the complex and multi-stratified ethnic definitions of ancient pre-Roman communities, which were more often based on city-states than on huge ethnic groups. Ethnic identity in pre-Roman Italy was often restricted to single states (especially *Caere, Veii*, or in Umbria: Todi and Terni, or *Cures Sabini*) or, more rarely, it included huge ethnic linguistic groups such as the Etruscans or the Umbrians or small linguistic groups based on city states such as the *Falisci* (the inhabitants of *Falerii*) or the *Capenates* (the inhabitants of *Capena*).

The same concept of the city-state (or in some cases of the territorial state) was often transformed by the Romans into their main political and administrative elements: the *municipium* or the *colonia* (Humbert 1993; Fig. 11.2). We can have, however, ethnic leagues or confederations, such as the Latin, or the Etruscan league, but they must be considered purely political institutions with flexible borders. The league of Etruscan people is known mainly by literary sources as *duodecim populi Etruriae*, but we do not know exactly the origin, aims or the territories involved inside this institution (Briquel 2001); we can only quote the role it played against Roman expansionism between the fifth and third century BC and its main place of meeting: the pan-Etruscan sanctuary of *Fanum Voltumnae*, recently identified near *Volsinii* (Orvieto, Campo della Fiera: Stopponi 2007).

The ethnic identity of such territories varies according to the historical period, but it is altered by the perception of the ancient literary sources. For example, in the Greek world the concept of a shared Greek ethnicity is known only after the Persian wars, but even after this event, the local identities of the city-states were more important than any sense of shared Hellenism (Hall 2002; Osborne this volume).

Thus, we must be aware that historical construction of ethnicity was sometimes a mosaic of communities, sometimes a single unit and sometimes a multi-stratified community with different levels of political, institutional and social identities. For instance, the analysis of institutional terms from the *Iguvinae Tabulae* has been interpreted different levels of political and ethnical identity inside the same community: *nomen, poplo, touta, trifu* (Prosdocimi 1978, 2001), and in the Etruscan language we also find terms with meanings which have been interpreted in a parallel manner: *cilθ, spura, meθlum, tuθina* and *rasna* (Colonna 1988b). These examples reveal the complexity of pre-Roman ethnic identities in Italy, together with the importance of a multidisciplinary approach, which must compare material culture with epigraphic texts and literary sources.

The middle Tiber Valley

To understand the patterns of settlement as evidence of ethnicity in central Italy, we must observe the evolution of city state systems through the centuries at a regional level. As a matter of fact, if the association with a specific territory is one of the bases of self-identification of an ethnic group, we can consider patterns of settlements as specific markers of ethnic definition. Obviously, this approach can only be fruitful if we compare several patterns of settlements in the same chronological space and possibly with a similar level of documentation.

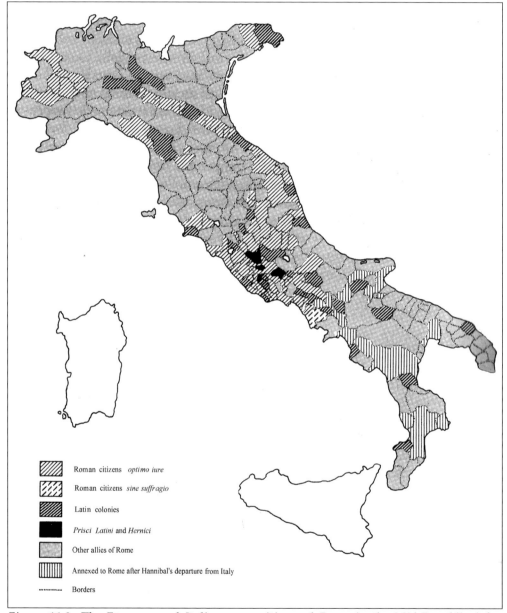

Figure 11.2. The Etruscan and Italic communities and Rome in the Mid-Republic (after Menichetti 1990).

Areas near ethnic frontiers seem particularly appropriate for such analysis and one of the most suitable regions in Italy is the Tiber Valley which is the only natural pass through the Apennines, connecting the central and northern parts of the peninsula. The importance of this region for trade is stressed also by the presence of different ethnic groups (the Umbrians, Etruscans, *Falisci*, Sabines and Latins) who divided the area into territories from the beginning of the Iron Age, probably using the river Tiber as a conventional frontier and thus this corridor provides an opportunity to observe several patterns of settlement (Fig. 11.3).

In central Italy, during the last phases of the Bronze Age (eleventh–tenth century BC), the territory was made up of a number of small fortified villages (hill-forts) between two and five hectares in size, within a distance of four–five kilometres from each other, suggesting (on the basis of Thiessen polygon analysis) a territory of about 20 square kilometres. The perception of the landscape is considerably fragmented into small villages, but the Tiber seemed already to play an important role of demographic attraction (di Gennaro 1986; Alessandri 2007, Schiappelli 2009).

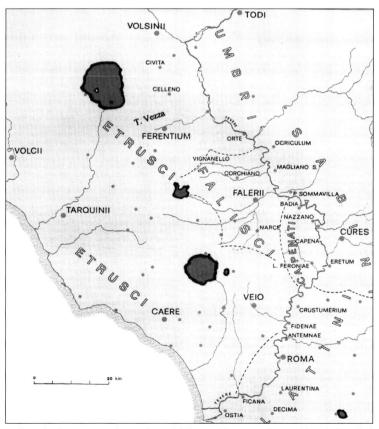

Figure 11.3. The ethnic groups along the middle and lower Tiber Valley (after Colonna 1986).

This situation was drastically modified during the first phase of the Iron Age (end of tenth–beginning of the ninth century BC), when we can observe the earliest demographic differentiation. In the whole of southern Etruria we have the rapid formation of four big settlements (*Vulci, Tarquinii, Caere, Veii*) up to 30 times larger than the previous Final Bronze age hill-forts (Pacciarelli 2001; Vanzetti 2004). This phenomenon is clearly visible, above all, in the lower Tiber Valley, where the formation of the 175-hectare proto-urban centre of *Veii*, caused a general depopulation of the surrounding geographical region of the future Faliscans and Sabines, and where almost all the previous Final Bronze hill-forts were abandoned (di Gennaro 1986). In the Sabine area especially, we have no evidence of settlements for the ninth century BC and, in the future Faliscan area, only a few fortified settlements survive this demographic transition (Cifani 2003) (Fig. 11.4).

The Etruscan Volsinian area shows a less radical transformation: the central place of *Volsinii* (now Orvieto) occupied an 80-hectare fortified area on a rocky plateau and seems to have had a weaker influence on its territory in comparison with the other early Tyrrhenian states such as *Veii, Caere, Tarquinii* and *Vulci*. In fact, the territory of *Volsinii* was characterised by more villages in the ninth century and the transition from the Bronze Age to the Iron Age is also less clear.

On the left side of the Tiber, the southern Umbrian and Sabine areas seem to adopt the protourban system only at the end of the eighth century BC: Terni, in Umbria, with a size of 50 hectares, and *Cures*, in Sabina, with a size of 30 hectares, were the main settlements, but for both regions the territorial organization suggests more the idea of a medium-sized city-state system than the large state communities of the Etruscan area (Cifani 2003).

Thus, during the beginning of the Iron Age, as a result of deep demographic transformations which included for the lower Tiber Valley also the foundation of Rome, the Tiber became a political and cultural boundary between different communities. The Orientalizing period (710–580 BC) was characterized by the development of secondary centres in the Etruscan area; some of them were relatively far from the main centre and seemed to benefit from their frontier location.

One clear example was Civita di Grotte di Castro, a 20-hectare settlement in the Volsinian area, near the political border with the territories of *Tarquinii* and *Vulci*, marked by the great lake basin of Bolsena. The cemetery of such a remote community, between the end of the seventh and the beginning of the sixth century BC, was characterized by monumental rock-cut chambers, in some cases decorated with paintings; their tomb groups reveal the substantial presence of imported Greek Attic pottery and banquetting services. This evidence appears to demonstrate the presence of a rich aristocratic class which grew in prominence thanks to frontier trade in the area (Cifani *et al.*, this volume).

Another important secondary city was Acquarossa, a 50-hectare settlement in the southern area of the Volsinian territory. This site was settled at the end of the eighth century BC and the excavations carried out by the Swedish institute also found a huge aristocratic house built in the first half of the sixth century BC in the central area of the settlement (Cifani 2003: 60–5).

By the midpoint of the sixth century BC, the process of state formation in central Italy was mature, and two types of organization can be clearly seen. The first one was the

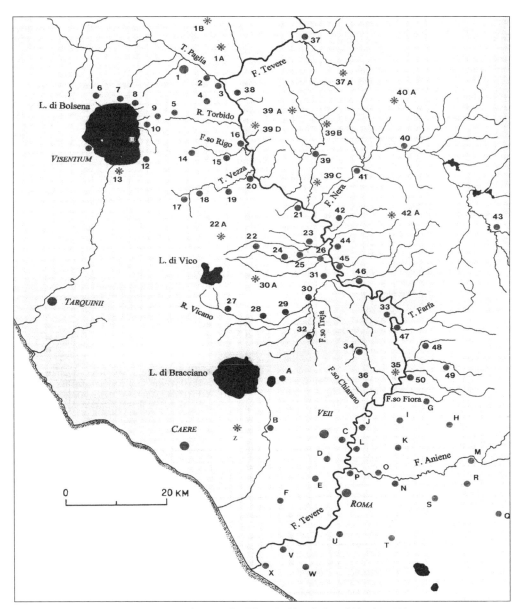

Figure 11.4. The middle Tiber Valley (after Cifani 2003).

large territorial state, with a hierarchical system of settlement and one central place, typical of Rome and the Southern Etruscan peoples, and the second one the city-state, with a small territory. A histogram of site size arranged in rank order of the settlements, divided by the ethnic areas of the middle Tiber Valley in the Archaic period, shows precisely this phenomenon (Fig. 11.5).

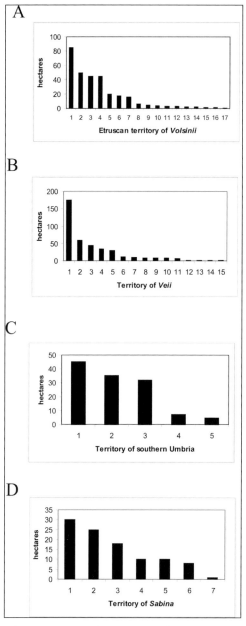

The Etruscan Volsinian area (Fig. 11.5A) revealed a three-level structure of the territory, with one central place of 80 hectares, a middle group of settlements whose size ranges from 18 to 35 hectares, and finally a large group of small settlements, one to five hectares in size. The Etruscan Veientan area (including the *ager Faliscus*; Fig. 11.5b) shows a similar organization, but a completely different diagram, however, is seen for the Italic regions of the Umbrians and Sabines (Figs 11.5C–D). In both cases the graph shows few elements of diversity and the trend is quite consistent; this is evidence of medium sized city-states with their small territories. For the Etruscan territories, however, we note a contrast between the urban central places, where egalitarian reforms were progressively increasing, and the peripheries, where the aristocratic groups kept and improved their power based on traditional agriculture, sheep-rearing and taxation.

This economic and social contrast probably became a political engagement within states; an account of such social struggles in the sixth century BC is offered by the literary tradition of Archaic Rome, but, at least as far as the Volsinian area is concerned, landscape archaeology can offer evidence too. From the beginning of the sixth century BC, the whole of southern Etruria revealed deep social transformations: monumental buildings such as temples and walls were erected in many cities; their cemeteries can be interpreed as revealing a new egalitarian re-organization, as shown by the square tombs known at *Caere* and *Volsinii* (Brocato 1995; Colonna 1990).

The necropolis of *Volsinii* itself clearly showed social mobility in the archaic period: a detailed analysis of funerary inscriptions between 550–500 BC revealed

Figure 11.5. Histograms of settlements arranged in order of size in the middle Tiber Valley (after Cifani 2003): (A) the Volsinii territory; (B) the Veii territory; (C) the southern Umbrian territory; (D) the Sabina territory.

a cosmopolitan *demos*, with a huge presence of Etruscans, together with Italic, Greek and Celtic people (de Simone 1978; Cristofani 1981; Marchesini 2007). In the territory of *Volsinii*, in parallel with the urban reform, we can observe, from the second half of the sixth century BC onwards, the progressive decline of many aristocratic enclaves. The best known example is Acquarossa, where the Swedish excavations revealed the end of the centre because of a fire around the middle of the sixth century BC (Strandberg Olofsson 1996: 158–9), but we could also quote the case of the frontier city of Civita di Grotte di Castro, where the bulk of evidence seems to have been concentrated on seventh and sixth century BC. (Cifani *et al.*, this volume).

There is, however, also a third phenomenon occurring in parallel with the above: the foundation of new small fortified settlements which started during the sixth century BC. An interesting example is represented by the site of Castellaro, a small fortified settlement of two hectares occupied from the sixth to the third century BC, on the top of a small volcanic hill, whose natural topography appears to have been reworked (Cifani 2003: 59–60). A further example in the Volsinian territory was the small fortified site of Monterado which also dated to the sixth century BC (Quilici and Quilici Gigli 2006). Castellaro and Monterado exemplify new colonial foundations supported by *Volsinii* within its territory in order to control strategic key-points and to deprive the old aristocratic centres of authority and economic importance; in addition, these fortified settlements were political landmarks for people living in isolated farmhouses. Similar points have been made on a broader level for Etruria (Redhouse and Stoddart 2011; Stoddart 1990).

Frontiers and ritual landscapes

The foundation of sanctuaries and fortresses near the political borders of different communities seems to have emphasized the new social identity of the Etruscan states, controlled by central authorities instead of the previous aristocratic groups. The new state frontiers were promptly ritualized by means of sanctuaries (cf. Zifferero 1995; Riva and Stoddart 1996), adopting a tradition which has many comparisons at an anthropological level (e.g. Barth 1969; Hodder and Orton 1976: 73; Massenzio 1999: 146–50). The rise of a new ritual landscape was also the evidence for a new cultural memory (*epos*) that is often related to political changes (Assmann 1992).

In southern Etruria, two frontier sanctuaries were good examples of this development: *Lucus Feroniae*, and Fondaccio. *Lucus Feroniae* was a place of trade located on an open limestone and travertine plateau, on the right side of the Tiber, in a frontier area between the Latins, Sabines and Etruscans which gave this place the character of a multi-ethnic *emporion*. Its importance in the Archaic period of central Italy was stressed by literary sources. Cato the Elder, who was the author of a book about the origins of italic peoples, links the foundation of the local cult of Feronia with the foundation of the city of *Capena* (Cato *Origines* I.26). Livy and Dionysius described the site in terms of its fair between the Latins and Sabines which had started to held by the period of Tullius Hostilius (Livy I.30.5; Dionysius of Halicarnassus *Roman Antiquities* III.32); later, in 211 BC during the Second Punic War, because of its richness, *Lucus Feroniae* was raided by Hannibal (Livy XXXVI.2.8). The sanctuary was discovered in 1952 and excavated by the Soprintendenza at the beginning of the 1960s and, more recently, between 2002 and 2004. Monumental evidence is mainly of the Mid- and Late Republic, but the new excavations found many votive bronze objects of the Archaic period, which revealed the active role played by this sanctuary already in the sixth century BC (Moretti Sgubini 2006). Fondaccio (or Piana del Lago) is an Etruscan sanctuary recently discovered on the southeastern corner of Lake Bolsena in a place which marks the border between the territories of two Etruscan territorial states: *Volsinii* and *Tarquinii*. It had a monumental Tuscan temple inside a *témenos* and was richly decorated with terracotta friezes dated between the sixth and the fourth century BC (D'Atri 2006).

A line of sanctuaries also marked the internal frontier between the territories of *Caere* and *Veii* and between *Caere* and *Tarquinii* by at least the end of the sixth century BC; the evidence is based on fragments of terracotta temple revetments, and votive inscriptions found along the line of both frontiers (Cifani 2003: 193–4, with bibl.; Colonna 2004; Fig. 11.4; Riva and Stoddart 1996; Zifferero 1995).

A similar ritual landscape, albeit on a smaller scale, also seems visible in Umbria, where the political borders of city-states were marked principally by peak sanctuaries on the top of mountains (Bradley 1997; Malone and Stoddart 1994: 142–52; Sisani 2001: 67–81) and even the borders of the most ancient suburb of Rome were marked by a line of sanctuaries, located along the main routes of communication, between the fourth and sixth mile from the city (Cifani 2005a) (Fig. 11.6).

Etruscan or Italic? The Faliscan and Capena's ethnic identity

The Faliscans have been considered, since the nineteenth century an autonomous ethnic group of Latin origin, inside Etruria (Garrucci 1860; Deecke 1888). Their language was indeed very near to Latin (Giacomelli 1963) and according to the literary tradition, the Faliscans were an independent ethnic group, although theories of their origins were controversial (Camporeale 1991; Fig. 11.3). Some sources have linked their mythical origin to the Etruscan city of *Veii* (Servius *Ad Aeneid* VIII.285). Ancient historians have noted the military alliance of the Faliscans with *Veii* against Rome, during the fifth and fourth century BC (Livy IV.17–8, 21, 23–4; V.8, 17, 26–7; VII.16–22; Pliny *Natural History* III.51) and later their presence as an independent political entity at the pan-Etruscan meeting at *Fanum Voltumnae*, in 397 BC (Livy V.16.6). At that time, they were considered an independent community with a language, different from Etruscan (Strabo V.9). Vergil imagined the Faliscans as ancient allies of the Latins against the Etruscans (Vergil *Aeneid* VII.641ff), but Cato thought they were originated from Greece (Cato, in Pliny *Natural History* III.51; Letta 2008: 183). These data led to more extreme theories, such as an original Faliscan link with the Latin area and their political independence from Etruscans (Holland 1925).

Since the 1950s, the progressive publication of data from *Veii* made clear the strong cultural relationship between this Etruscan city and the nearby communities of the Faliscans (Benedettini 1997), together with the presence of a huge number of Etruscan inscriptions found in the main Faliscan centres (Cristofani 1988; Colonna 1990; *CIE* II.2.5, 8889–925). Furthermore, the settlement analysis of the Early Iron Age in southern

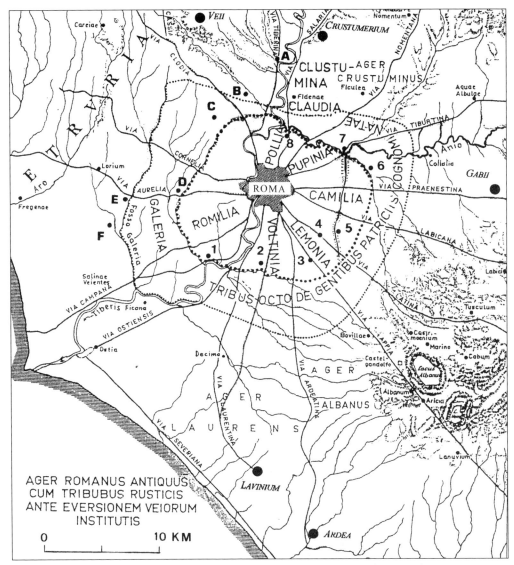

Figure 11.6. The ager Romanus antiquus *(after Cifani 2005).*

Etruria proved the earlier development of the *Veii* compared with the Faliscan area. As matter of fact *Veii* started as proto-urban centre already at the beginning of the Early Iron Age (ninth century BC), but the Faliscan territory started to be re-organized only at the end of the eighth century BC. In addition, Faliscan towns showed not only the strong cultural influence of *Veii*, but, because of their relative smaller size and location on the road network leading to *Veii*, they were, in my opinion, undoubtedly hierarchically subordinate to this important Etruscan city.

The organization of the territory led to the co-presence of two ethnic groups (*Capenates* and *Falisci*) within the community of *Veii*. In the case of the *Falisci*, by the study the literary sources, despite the difficulties in distinguishing real historical events from historical accounts and mythical fiction, we can easily identify two traditions: the Faliscans allied with the Etruscans and the independent Faliscans linked with Rome (or the Latins; Camporeale 1991). Both literary accounts can be the results of different stage of ethnic identity: a first phase in which the Faliscans were under the political influence of the Etruscan territorial state of *Veii* and a second phase, after the fall of *Veii* in 396 BC, during which they were progressively absorbed by the Roman economic trade system, before being completely conquered by Rome on 241 BC; as matter of fact, after this date, the Faliscan identity seems to survive only as a linguistic and cultural group (di Gennaro 1986; Cifani 2005b; Ceccarelli and Stoddart 2007). A further example of an ethnic group was the *Capenates*. According to legend, the city of *Capena* was founded as a colony of *Veii* by means of an internal migration (Cato *Origines* II.19) and, together with the Faliscans, they were reported as military allies of *Veii* during the wars with Rome in the fifth and fourth centuries BC. The analysis of settlement history shows a huge community located on a fortified area of about 60 hectares (Camilli and Vitali Rosati 1995; Cifani 2003: 105–9); their language, the *Capena* dialect, is known only from inscriptions of the Hellenistic period and completely linked with the Italic language rather than the Etruscan (Briquel 1972; Colonna 1983). Their material culture, above all in the Orientalizing phase, showed the influence of *Veii*, but also of the Sabine and Latin cultures (Colonna 1988 a; Biella 2007), and it can be considered a typical product of a frontier context as explained below.

An important distinction is made by two models of territorial organization developed by Herman Hansen (2000: 16ff.): the city state and the territorial state. The 'city-state' is an urban settlement within a territory not larger than one day's walk (i.e. about 15 kilometres of radius). This system has only one urban settlement, but it could have some small secondary settlements such as fortresses or harbours. The 'territorial-state' was a more complex system; it had a main urban centre which controlled a territory larger than one day's walk and for this reason it necessarily has secondary urban settlements. For central Italy there is also a precious passage of Dionysius of Halicarnassus who defines the Latin communities as πόλεις (except Rome) and the Etruscan communities as ἡγεμονία (Dionysius of Halicarnassus *Roman Antiquities* VI.75.3).

Turning to the Latin and Etruscan patterns of settlement in the Archaic period we can distinguish a landscape of city states located within a radius of 10–15 kilometres of each other, typical of the Latin area (for example: *Tibur, Praeneste, Signia, Anagnia, Cora, Satricum*, etc.) and a landscape of territorial states in Etruria, illustrated by large urban centres within a radius of about 25–30 kilometres linked to a network of secondary settlements, for example: *Vulci, Tarquinii, Volsinii* and *Veii*. This internal organization of Etruscan states seems also to be proved by the career pursued by southern Etruscan magistrates recorded in some funerary inscriptions, in which magistrates started their career in the secondary settlements of their territorial states and then moved to the main city (Colonna 1988b: 24; Maggiani 2001: 45–6).

My thesis is that the Etruscan state of *Veii* was most probably a territorial state, which included as secondary centres also the city states of *Falerii* and *Capena*, but that they

CITY STATES	TERRITORIAL STATES
• Only one urban settlement. • No secondary urban centres, but only fortress and/or harbours. • Territory usually not larger than one day' walk • Greek terminology: πόλις	• One main urban centre. • Secondary urban centres. • Territory larger than one day's walk. • Greek terminology: ἡγεμονία
Examples: Greek colonies; Italic communities (southern Umbrians, Sabines, Latins – except Rome)	Examples: archaic Rome; southern Etruscan communities (*Vulci, Tarquinii, Volsinii, Veii*); larger Greek colonies (e.g. Syracuse).

acquired later a kind of political autonomy, which emerged, probably, between the end of the sixth and the fifth centuries BC, when the centre of *Veii* was weakened because of Roman military conquest (for an alternative interpretation: Ceccarelli and Stoddart 2007). For this reason, the invention of new myths about the ethnogenesis of *Falerii* as an independent group could also be dated to the same period (Cifani 2005b).

Landscapes, economies and perception of identities: the case of Sabines

From the point of view of a Greek author of the seventh century BC, the main ethnic groups of central Italy of that period were only the Latins and the Etruscans; by contrast, people of inland areas were considered members of still primitive and wild communities (Dench 1995, 111ff.; Hesiod *Theogony* 1011; Torelli 1988). Such a description of Italian cultural geography from a Greek, probably Euboian, perspective (Debiasi 2008: 40–75) is very interesting because it can locate the geographical areas where the Hellenic culture was more influential (i.e. the coastal Tyrrhenian regions of Latium and Etruria and of course the Greek colonies of southern Italy) in contradistinction to the internal highlands, which were less economically developed and without urban settlements. This situation changed drastically in the course of the sixth century BC when we have the first ethnic definitions of Umbrians and Sabines from epigraphic documents and literary sources (e.g. Sisani 2001: 201–6).

In the Sabine area (Fig. 11.7), different perceptions and different human landscapes can be considered some of the main aspects of the complex identity of the Sabine people, whose ethnic name was known since the beginning of the fifth century BC (Marinetti 1985: TE 5). The classic literary traditions tended to distinguish two groups (Musti 1985: 79–82). The first were the Sabines of the Tiber valley who from the end of the eighth century BC had a settlement organization similar to those of the Etruscan area. This took the form of small city-states on fortified sites (*Cures, Eretum,* Magliano, etc.), but controlled by aristocratic groups. Their culture reveals the strong influence of Etruria, as shown, above all, by burial customs (e.g. Benelli and Santoro 2006), and they seem to have used the alphabet from the second half of the seventh century BC (Cristofani 1999; Cifani 2003: 133–48; Santoro 2008). Later historians depicted them as very similar to the Etruscans in their customs and taste for luxuries (especially Dionysius of Halicarnassus *Roman Antiquities* II.38.3). The second group were the Sabines of the mountains, based in the internal central area of the Apennines, around the evocative natural landmark of *Mons Fiscellus* (i.e. Gran Sasso d'Italia, 2912 metres), the highest mountain of the Apennine mountain range. They had communities characterized by aristocratic groups, distinguished by funerary customs focused on tumuli until the sixth century BC (Naso 2000: 137–40; d'Ercole and Grassi 2000; Cosentino *et al.* 2003; Alvino 2006); these groups first used of writing in the first half of the sixth century BC (Marinetti 1985: TE 4, AQ

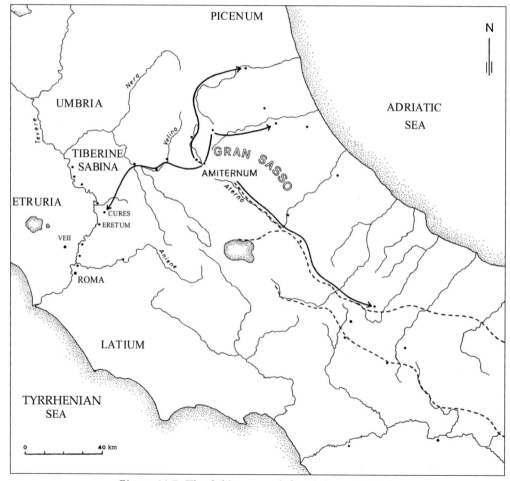

Figure 11.7. The Sabine areas (after Colonna 1996a).

2; Marinelli 1999), but their territory revealed no evidence of huge urban settlements until Romanization, which took place from the third century BC.

Despite the fact that their landscape has not been widely and systematically investigated, we can cite the community of *Reate* which settled in one valley (Cifani 2003: 131–2), and the innermost area showed a vibrant demography based during the Early Iron Age on open sites, small hill-forts and rare central places. The economy was mainly based on sheep rearing, although long-distance trade is documented as well (La Regina 1968; Mattiocco 1986; Oakley 1995; d'Ercole *et al.* 2002a, 2002b: 117–20; Benelli and Naso 2003; d'Ercole and Martellone 2007: 35). This remote and, apparently primitive area, was considered by ancient authors the demographic core of central Italy (Briquel 2000; Colonna 1996), a *longue durée* role for mountain areas in the Italian peninsula and Sicily (Stoddart 2000, 2006).

Two main ethnic groups, the *Piceni* (Strabo V.4.2, Pliny *Natural History* III.18.110) and the *Samnites* (Strabo V.4.12), were considered to have originated from the Sabines, by means of a peculiar way of ritual migration known as the *ver sacrum* (Tagliamonte 1994: 55 ss., 1996: 17–21, 2004; Colonna and Tagliamonte 1999; Naso 2000: 29–38; Antonelli 2003: 13–33; Chirassi Colombo 2008). The ideology behind the ethnogenesis of the Italic people from the Sabine area can be traced back to the years after the Second Punic War and above all in the work of *Origines* by Cato the Elder who stressed the Italic basis of Roman culture and the value of the ideals of austerity of the Sabine people in contraposition to the new direct influence of Greek culture (Letta 2008: 171–3).

However, beyond the ideologies, the main reasons for such internal migration can be seen as the demographic attraction of coastal areas for the less developed communities of inland regions and the obvious dichotomy between developed and underdeveloped economies (Torelli 1988: 54). The inland Sabines and above all the *Samnites* and *Piceni* were considered warriors, whose descendants resisted the Romans fiercely on many occasions; huge groups of them were often employed as mercenaries and that provided the occasion of further social mobility (Cherici 2003; Tagliamonte 1996: 13–7, 2003). The legacy of this perception was still active in the Augustan period, when Vergil (*Georgics* II.136ff.) depicted Italic people as two types: the wild warriors, (e.g. the Sabellians or the inland Sabines, the *Marsi*, Ligurians and *Volsci*) and the more civilized Latins, Romans, Etruscans and the Tiber Valley Sabines (Giardina 1997: 33–4).

Conclusions

Ethnicity starts as an ideological invention based on selected distinctions and omitted diversities, but, once started, it can becomes a factor of real transformation of societies. Thus, instead of considering the rise of an ethnic landscape, we should focus on the way in which ethnicity was considered and represented and how it influenced the organization of territories. In my opinion, literary and epigraphic data still represent a very important source of evidence for the reconstruction of ideology, but landscape archaeology also has a high potential which should also be used.

In central Tyrrhenian Italy, despite the fact that some local cultural characterization can be seen already in Final Bronze Age, the development of ethnic-political identity was obviously linked with the rise of the city-state system from the Early Iron Age onwards. Along the frontier of the Tiber Valley, the archaeology of landscape reveals a first deep differentiation which took place in the first phase of the Early Iron Age (ninth century BC); in this period the future territories of Umbrians, Sabines, Latins and Etruscans started developing very different strategies of territorial organization, which reflect different social and economic structures. However it is only from the sixth century BC that some of such distinctions started to be used to define ethnic groups based on huge territories. As matter of fact, between the sixth and fifth century BC, in Etruria and Latium the rise of new political landscapes characterized by cities and farmhouses, together with political borders marked by sanctuaries and fortresses, was probably the main way to represent the new ethnicity.

Behind such changes we can distinguish many political and social factors. One of the main political factors could have been the rise of Rome in the sixth century BC and its political influence on Latium and southern Etruria, which probably forced the surrounding Italic communities into larger alliances, based on ethnic identity and with the ideal contradistinction to Rome and the Latin culture. As has been observed for the shaping of Hellenic identity (Hall 2002: 179), this phase marks the transformation of previous ethnic identities, based on purely aggregational self-definitions between city states sharing similarities of culture, language and religions, into new broader ethnicities based on the 'oppositional' self-definition to an external enemy. However, there are also social aspects to be considered as well: Archaic ethnic identities could have been developed above all thanks to the advanced state organization of central Tyrrhenian Italy, where the rise of new elites and the consolidation of a kind of middle class produced new forms of ideology, religion, politics and self representation. From this point of view, the new landmarks in the landscape, such as the extra-urban sanctuaries, can be considered the first step towards the creation of a cultural collective memory.

Acknowledgements

This paper is part of a research project carried out at the Department of Archaeology of Cambridge University from 2005 to 2007, sponsored by a Marie Curie Intra-European Research Fellowship, granted by the European Union (6th Research Framework, contract n. 514523). For criticisms and advice on the topic of this paper, I wish also to thank: Dr Enrico Benelli (Consiglio Nazionale delle Ricerche – Roma), Prof. Gianluca Tagliamonte (Università di Lecce), Prof. John Bintliff (University of Leiden) and Prof. Clemente Marconi (New York University).

Exploring a frontier area in Etruria: the Civita di Grotte di Castro survey

Gabriele Cifani, Letizia Ceccarelli and Simon Stoddart

Keywords: boundary; Etruria; Bolsena

Landscape of frontiers as evidence of ethnicity

Political frontiers can be considered some of the most visible evidence of ethnic identity in pre-Roman central Italy. Scholarly interest in frontiers of ancient states had started already in the nineteenth century, but following Romantic tendencies, it took mainly an ethnocentric approach, which sought to identify the borders of a culture or civilization.

However after the Second World War, the end of European empires and the rise of post-colonial studies, together with the current crisis of the nation state, led to a focus on cultural interactions and, regarding the frontier studies, on the symbolic value of frontiers as places of exchange. Within such a framework the concept of liminality, which has already been introduced by the French sociologist Arnold van Gennep (1909), was re-developed by cultural anthropologists who stressed the value of liminal areas as marginal places for unstructured communities (e.g. Turner 1969). Another important influence, particularly in the context of ethnicity, was provided by Barth (1969) who explored the social formation and repeated renegotiation of boundaries. More recently, the study of boundaries has been reinvigorated by fresh anthropological study an approach which is beginning to be applied to the classical world (Stoddart 2010).

Frontier studies in pre-Roman Italy have been for many years focused on the topographic research of ancient political borders, but sporadic researches on the ritual value of primitive borders of Roman territory opened the field for frontier researches from the 1960s onward (e.g. Alföldy 1962; Lugli 1966; Piccaluga 1974). Since the 1980s, the development of landscape archaeology, in some cases tangentially affected by post-processualists approaches, has produced a growing interest in the concept of frontiers as places of liminality, above all for Etruria (Riva and Stoddart 1996; Torelli 1982; Zifferero 1995) and *Magna Graecia* (e.g. Atti Taranto 1999; Daverio Rocchi 1988; Edlund 1987; Guzzo 1987).

In pre-Roman Etruria, as a general rule, we can say that frontiers take a number of forms depending on the configuration of the power centres, the physical circumscription of the area and the topography of the landscape. The general trend of power centre size is from large (on the coast) to relatively small in the internal areas. This political imperative of demographic mass provides one constraint on the internal frontier. The trend of physical circumscription (Carneiro 1970) runs from the closely packed in the south to the relatively unrestricted in the north, where the Etruscan lake region provides an intermediate zone of less constricted space that is nevertheless substantially filled by very large lake basins.

The topography of the landscape shifts from one volcanic province of small lakes (see below) south of the Tiber to another of dissected plateaux (of varying size) and larger calderas (now filled with water) immediately to the north. Rivers and small mountain ranges (e.g Tolfa) provide concident geographical and political frontiers. Further north, a major river valley system (Albegna) and a major volcanic outcrop (Mount Amiata) provide a clear divide from the largely Plio-Pleistocene clays bordered internally by tectonic valleys in north Etruria (Fig. 12.1).

Obviously, mountains and internal waters played a crucial role as landmarks for shaping ethnic identities inside a territory. Recent research has stressed the value of peak sanctuaries as places of identity (e.g. Malone and Stoddart 1994: 142–52) and the importance of the main rivers (Cifani 2003; di Gennaro 1986); in this paper we focus on the value of lakes as frontier areas between state communities.

Lakes as frontier areas

Lake regions can often be considered frontier areas between one or more communities. Modern examples include the lake of Presna at the border between Greece, Macedonia and Albania; Lake Constanz, between Germany and Switzerland; the Maggiore and Lugano lakes between Switzerland and Italy; the Aral lake between Uzbekistan and Kazakistan; the Dead Sea, between Israel and Jordan; the Hanka Lake between Russian and China; and the Great Lakes region at the border between USA and Canada. Very interesting examples are also offered by the frontiers of ancient and modern African states (Southall 1974). Victoria Lake is divided between Uganda, Kenya and Tanzania and Lake Rudolf is the frontier between Sudan, Ethiopia and Kenya; in addition Lake Chad is the frontier between Chad, Niger and Nigeria.

There could have been many different political and historical reasons to adopt a lake as a frontier but, as a general issue, we can spot at least two aims: the first one is to consider internal waters not only as a clear physical barrier, but also as a no man's land: a place without settlements; the second one is to consider the common interest of nearby peer communities to share access to lake resources. In other words, the concept of liminality, which characterized the majority of lake dwellings in Europe, could be considered a great opportunity for peer communities during the Iron Age and afterwards in central Italy to provide a staging ground for shared resources. Liminality is in fact a way to be in contact with nearby communities and to increase local trade and exchange of goods. However, this is an end result once the peer communities have fully developed their power base. In the stages leading up to these fully formalized frontiers, alternative power bases could employ the rich agricultural resources of the lake regions to develop resistant power strategies.

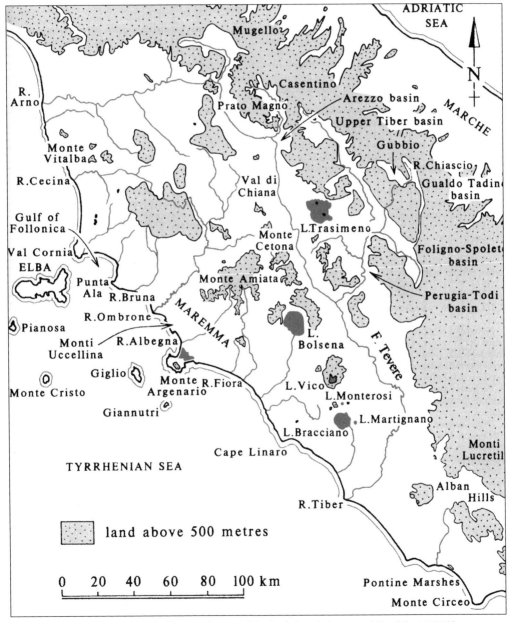

Figure 12.1. Physical map of central Italy (after Spivey and Stoddart 1990).

Internal lake frontier areas of central Tyrrhenian Italy

The internal frontier area of central Tyrrhenian Italy area is characterized above all by the presence of volcanic lakes, which were favourite areas of settlements, thanks to water resources and agricultural potential. Employing physical and cultural criteria, we can easily divide central Tyrrhenian Italy into two sections: the Latin area and the Etruscan area. The Latin area is characterized by relatively small volcanic lakes. In this region, the importance of such internal waters for settlement, the role played by this places as the core and the place of identity of smaller ethnic groups or city states since the Late Bronze Age, has been stressed by the archaeological evidence and literary sources.

Lake Albano, for example, is named after the Latin communities of *Alba*; inside this volcanic crater there is evidence of settlements since the Early Bronze Age (Angelini *et al.* 2006) and the lake was the core of the Latin community of the Albans, closely linked with the legends of the foundation of Rome and with the Latin federal sanctuary of *Mons Albanus*. The origins of the sanctuary can be placed already in the Bronze Age (Ghini 2004: 50). The crater of the Lake of Nemi hosted a Bronze Age settlement, followed, at least from the Archaic period (sixth–fifth century BC), by a federal sanctuary dedicated to Diana (*Nemus Aricicinus*) which was the place of the Latin confederation (Coarelli 1987: 165–85; Diosono 2006: 191; Giardino 1985). The important Latin city of *Gabii*, inhabited from the Late Bronze Age until the Mid-Republic was built on the edge of a volcanic crater hosting a small lake, now completely drained (Guaitoli 2003: 273–6) another interesting example is offered by the Italic community of the *Capenates*, that was established between the eighth and sixth century BC, and which had as a main city a huge settlement of 60 hectares built around a small lake now drained (Camilli and Vitali Rosati 1995).

In the Etruscan area, on the contrary the political geography (cf. Stoddart 2006) is characterized by four huge lakes (Bolsena, Bracciano, Vico and Trasimeno), which divide the internal area of Etruria from the coastal area on the Tyrrhenian sea; three of these are deep and volcanic and two are the second (Bolsena: 146 metres deep and 114.5 square kilometres) and fourth (Bracciano: 160 metres deep and 67.5 square kilometres) largest lakes of the peninsula (Fig. 12.2). In northeastern Etruria, between the sixth and fourth century BC, Lake Trasimeno was the frontier between three important Etruscan states (*Perusia*, *Clusium* and *Cortona*) and the border of the lake region was marked by no less than three sanctuaries: Casamaggiore, near Castiglione del Lago, S. Feliciano, Tuoro/Sanguineto (Bruschetti 2002: 76; Colonna 1976–7: 2005; Maggiani 2002a: 282; Paolucci 2002: 177–8, 186–92).

A similar phenomenon occured in the region of Lake Bracciano (about 50 kilometres south east from Lake *Bolsena*); after the phase of Late and Final Bronze Age with small fortified settlements on the top of the hills (e.g. Monte S. Angelo, Monte Rocca Romana), at the beginning of the Iron Age, the whole area was drawn into the political dialectics of the new Etruscan territorial states and of the previous Bronze Age landscape; only the fortress of Monte S. Angelo seems to have survived until the eighth century BC as a landmark of the border of the new territory of *Veii* in the Early Iron Age (ninth century BC). From the late eighth century BC onward, there was a new colonization based on the larger settlement of Trevignano, which emphasize the frontier between *Veii* and *Caere* (Caruso 2005).

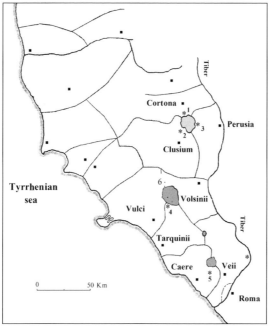

Figure 12.2. The political frontiers of central and southern Etruria in relation to the main lakes: (1) sanctuary of Tuoro/Sanguineto; (2) sanctuary of Casamaggiore; (3) sanctuary of San Feliciano; (4) sanctuary of Fondaccio-Casale Marcello; (5) sanctuary of Tragliatella; (6) settlement of Civita di Grotte di Castro (after Torelli 1987).

During the Late Archaic period, there was also evidence of rural landscape of small farmhouses (Accardo *et al.* 2007: 32–8) and the road system was rationalized to provide access in and around the lake Bracciano volcanic crater; as shown by an Etruscan inscription, perhaps of a magistrate, on a rock-cut way near Monte S. Angelo (CIE II.2.1, 6707) which can be dated to the fifth century BC and by the evidence of Archaic votive inscriptions (middle of the sixth century BC) from a cult frontier place, at Tragliatella (nearly six kilometres from the southern edge of the crater), along an important route between *Veii* and *Caere* (Colonna 2004).

The area of Lake Bolsena was settled from the Late Bronze Age with small fortified sites on the top of the hills around the lake (Civita di Arlena, Montefiascone and Cornos). The average intervening distance is about two kilometres and the average territorial size about 10,000 square kilometres. This pattern suggests a microregion of independent sites with an economy closely related to the exploitation of lake resources. The Early Iron Age is characterized by the abandonment of the majority of such fortified sites and the rise of one open site (Gran Carro). The site of Gran Carro was built on the edge of the lake at the beginning of the Early Iron Age (ninth century) and was submerged in the eighth century BC because of a drastic rise in the water level of the lake. The site was investigated in the 1970s; its material culture shows an economy based not just on fishing and hunting, but also on agricultural exploitation and on the metallurgy of bronze and iron (Tamburini 1995).

Between the end of the eighth and the seventh century BC there was the rise of three larger settlements not far the coastal area of the lake (Civita di Grotte di Castro, Barano, Bisentium) together with the continuation of the site of Montefiascone (Tamburini 1998: 56–65; Fig. 12.3). From the seventh century BC, we have a clear evidence of a range of settlement sizes to the north and east side of the lake. To the north there is one larger city (Civita di Grotte di Castro), with a potential for independence because of its spatial position and, to the east, some secondary fortresses (Bolsena; Montefiascone etc.) more conclusively part of the larger territory of the Etruscan state of *Volsinii*. An understanding of the precise sequence of development and political affiliation of a centre such as Civita di Grotte di Castro must await more detailed fieldwork, provided it survives sufficiently intact. Present evidence suggests that Barano and Civita di Grotte di Castro have a substantial settlement area and many tomb groups.

In the south western side of the lake, however, there was the important site of *Bisentium*: a huge settlement of 35 hectares, settled from the early Iron age; its economy is known through the evidence of many tomb groups found nearby with Greek imported pottery and rich bronze artefacts (Pandolfini 1985; Delpino 1994, with bibliography; Tamburini 1998: 90). This settlement occupies a similar buffer position to Civita di Grotte

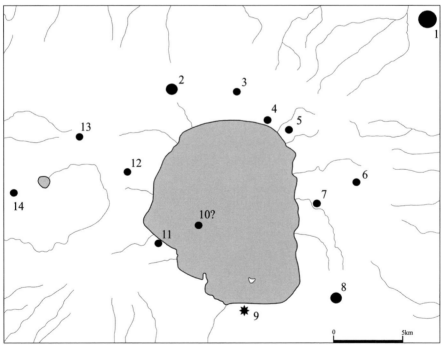

Figure 12.3. Main settlements in the Bolsena lake region between the eighth and fourth century BC: (1) Volsinii (Orvieto); (2) Civita di Grotte di Castro; (3) Monte Landro; (4) Barano; (5) Bolsena-Castello; (6) Monterado; (7) Civita d'Arlena; (8) Montefiascone-Rocca; (9) Fondaccio-Casale Marcello; (10) Isola Bisentina (uncertain settlement); (11) Bisenzio; (12) La Montagna; (13) Poggio Evangelista; (14) Monte Becco (after Tamburini 1998).

di Castro to the north, with a similar potential for political independence from the major cities on its flanks where the lake system played a supplementary sustaining role.

For these reasons, the wealth of such sites must be linked to their value as frontier sites, with a potential for political independence and roles as economic intermediaries to the larger cities beyond. Such settlements were located at the border of three important Etruscan territorial states: *Volsinii, Tarquinii* and *Vulci,* three of the wealthiest cities of the Mediterranean area between the eighth and the fifth century BC. Their common border was probably marked by Lake Bolsena and for this reason the whole area became very important for political interaction and exchange .

Extra-urban sanctuaries in Etruria and *Magna Graecia* were, quite commonly, built as landmarks of frontiers and many frontier sanctuaries had also a secondary value as *emporia,* places where trade and exchanges between people of different communities were admitted under the protection of the local gods (Riva and Stoddart 1996; Zifferero 1995: 333–7). The presence of a recently discovered Archaic and Hellenistic sanctuary in an open position on the southern coast of the lake (Fondaccio/Casale Marcello) seems to emphasize the ritualized formalization of this region as place of exchange (Berlingò and d'Atri 2005; d'Atri 2006).

To summarize, lakes form a common theme, but the dominant force is provided by political geography; the three case-studies of Etruscan lake boundaries provide different political equations according to the principles of power centre demography, circumscription and topography.

The southern Bracciano system is at the interstices of a high demography, high circumscription, volcanic plateau topography. In this case, only relatively small settlements were tolerated at the liminal interstices. The northeastern Trasimene system was at the interstices of a lower demography, low circumscription, open tectonic valley system. In these circumstances of lower demographic pressure, the interstices were principally marked by sanctuaries. The central Bolsena system was at the interstices of a high (coastal)/slightly lower (internal) demography, lower circumscription, volcanic caldera landscape. In these circumstances two larger, potentially independent centres (Bisenzio, 35 hectares and Civita di Grotte di Castro, 20 hectares) were tolerated, even nurtured as economic and political intermediaries in conjunction with at least one sanctuary.

The Civita di Grotte di Castro project

Within such a framework in 2006 the Department of Archaeology at Cambridge University started fieldwork, at the Civita di Grotte di Castro, aiming to get new topographical and chronological data of a frontier settlement.

The Etruscan city of Civita di Grotte di Castro lies on a 20-hectare tuff plateau, inside the volcanic crater of Bolsena Lake, about 130 kilometres north from Rome, near to the territorial border of *Vulci* and *Volsinii* (Figs 12.4 and 12.5). The place was first described in 1857 by Domenico Golini (Golini 1857) and further surveys, most of them unpublished, were carried out in the rich Orientalizing and Archaic necropolis surrounding the settlement (Gamurrini *et al.* 1972; Colonna 1974; Ruspantini 1978: 23–45). Preliminary surveys in the area were also carried out in the last two decades

(Tamburini 1981, 1985; Raddatz 1983; Iaia and Mandolesi 1993; Naso 1996: 275–86; Cifani 2003: 48–50), together with rescue excavation of tomb groups (Timperi 1995, 2007), but despite of this growing interest, no systematic research has ever been done at all. The new research, which took place between 2006 and 2007, was carried out by means of archival research, survey, geophysics (ground penetrating radar), pit tests and pottery analysis.

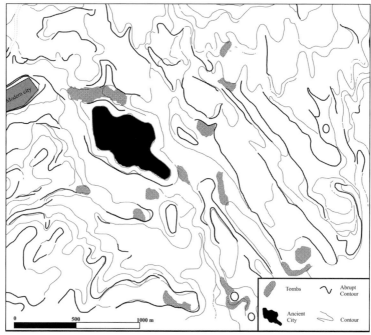

Figure 12.4. Civita di Grotte di Castro and surrounding necropolis (after Naso 1996).

Figure 12.5. The Bolsena Lake from Civita di Grotte di Castro.

All the data have been processed by means of geographic information systems which have created new images of this Etruscan city, which was settled mainly between the Early Orientalizing period and the third century BC. The new settlement survey has revealed the presence of a grid of underground drainage-ways, cisterns and probably the area of a votive deposit in the upper part of the settlement, where Attic pottery, miniature vases and two fragments of *aes rude* were found; this context can be dated between the sixth and fifth century BC.

These materials help to understand better the presence of the very rich necropolis surrounding the Etruscan city; this is characterized by rock-cut chamber tomb groups, which were often decorated with beams and ceilings finely carved and, in some cases, also painted with architectural details (Naso 1996: 275ff.; Fig. 12. 6). Their evidence is concentrated between the end of the seventh and the entire sixth century BC; although there is less documentation for the fifth century BC, tomb groups are again prominent for the fourth–third century BC phase, which reveal a still wealthy community (Buranelli 1991).

From the third century BC, the rise of the Roman city of Bolsena caused a general depopulation of the Civita di Grotte di Castro, which, between the third century BC and the first century BC was progressively transformed into a rural area probably with farmhouses, as shown by some water reservoirs, fully documented by the new excavations (Fig. 12.7). This change in the landscape can be explained also in the economic transformation of the area following the Romanization of the Volsinian territory (Harris 1985) which downgraded the economic importance of the trade route between *Volsinii* and *Vulci* (both defeated by the Romans in 280 and 264 BC, respectively) in favour of the new trade routes with Rome. The new political configuration

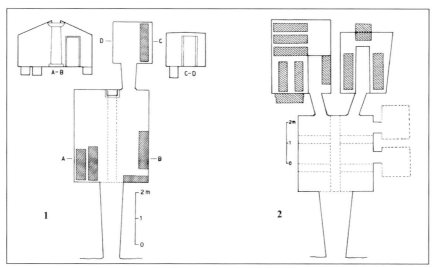

Figure 12.6. Tombs of Civita di Grotte di Castro: (1) Necropoli, Pianezze tomb P2; (2) Necropoli, 'Le Sane' (after Tamburini 1998).

Figure 12.7. Cistern at Civita di Grotte di Castro.

undermined the value of the frontier between the two previous Etruscan states and destroyed the economy of the liminal centres, which had flourished for many earlier centuries in the frontier zone.

Acknowledgements

The Civita di Grotte di Castro Survey has been carried out by the Department of Archeology at Cambridge University thanks to a Marie Curie Intra-European Fellowship (n. 514523) granted by the European Community enhanced, during 2007 and 2009, by research funds of the McDonald Institute.

The authors would like to express their gratitude to the *Soprintendenza Archeologica per l'Etruria Meridionale* (Potts. Anna Moretti Sgubini, Angelo Timperi and Enrico Pellegrini, the *Comune di Grotte di Castro* (Potts. Flavia Marabottini and Luca Provvedi).

The work in the field was undertaken principally by Letizia Ceccarelli, who was also responsible for GIS, excavations and the study of pottery, Massimiliano Munzi, Fabrizio Felici and Tom Birch. Digital survey of the plateau was done by Stephen Kay (British School at Rome). GPR (Ground Penetrating Radar) survey was carried out by Prof. Elena Pettinelli and Pier Matteo Barone (Department of Physics, University of 'Roma Tre'). Particular thanks are offered to the local volunteers of the *Gruppo Archeologico di Grotte di Castro* who gave important support for both survey and excavation.

Special thanks are due also to: Prof. Andrew Wallace-Hadrill (British School at Rome), Prof. Alessandro Guidi (Università di Verona) and Potts. Pietro Tamburini (Museo Territoriale del Lago di Bolsena).

Between text, body and context: expressing 'Umbrian' identity in the landscape

Simon Stoddart

Keywords: text; identity; Umbria; tradition; ethnicity

Introduction

> Are we traditional, then? Not that either. The idea of a stable tradition is an illusion that anthropologists have long since set to rights. The immutable traditions have all budged – the day before yesterday. Most ancestral folklores are like the 'centenary' Scottish kilt, invented out of whole cloth at the beginning of the nineteenth century (Trevor-Roper 1983), or the Chevaliers du Tastevin of my little town in Burgundy, whose millennial ritual is not fifty years old. 'Peoples without history' were invented by those who thought theirs were radically new (Goody 1986). In practice, the former innovate constantly; the latter are forced to pass and repass infinitely through the same rituals of revolutions and epistemological breaks, and quarrel of the Classics against the Moderns. (Latour 1993: 75–6)

In the earlier parts of this volume we have steadily moved west across the Mediterranean and then north up the Italian peninsula, examining 1) different configurations of textual and archaeological evidence, 2) different socio-political formations and 3) different combinations of cultural and natural marking of identity against 4) a backdrop of different theoretical definitions and 5) the introduction of new data.

This article covers both a smaller and a larger scale than some of the others. At the smaller scale it examines a single tectonic basin, albeit set within a wider geographical context. At the larger scale, it emphasizes the importance of the diachronic construction of identity and how this cannot be frozen by the imposition of one textual framework. On the other hand it avoids the temptation, defined as minimalist methodology by some, to extend the textual umbrella of an exceptional series of texts from their immediate spatial and chronological context to a wider geographical and temporal domain, as others have done within the classical tradition (Bradley 2000; Sisani 2009).

My theoretical position is that I share a vision of the negotiated scales of identity of a number the preceding papers (Fulminante this volume; Rajala this volume); in other words ethnicity is but one scale of identity that is as slippery as any other (Stoddart 2009). Unlike my co-editor, I do not favour the primacy of the literary account of identity. In fact I would go as far as to state that in protohistoric periods such as the one covered in the central and western Mediterranean areas of this volume, material culture and landscape should be given primacy in the analysis. This is because they both provide evidence of the material that is negotiated and was even active in a recursive manner in affecting the construction of scales of identity. Literary texts only provide one take on that construction from elite beneficiaries of restricted literacy who invariably are commenting externally of the status of ethnicity. Some may claim that only the elite can express ethnicity (Mellor 2008: 79), and we may infer that these elite are congruent with the restricted literate, but that in itself may be a modernist assumption.

In southern Etruria we have a highly constructed cultural landscape (Cifani this volume; Stoddart 1987, in preparation). However, as we make our way through Etruria to Umbria, we can see that the role of the natural feature in the landscape has considerable importance. Amongst the Faliscans, the particular conformation of the landscape was highly distinctive, a feature even acknowledged by ancient writers (Ceccarelli and Stoddart 1997). In Etruria, we only need to point out the importance of Monte Amiata and Monte Falterona in this respect to see how – to employ the phrase of Richard Bradley (2000) – Unaltered Places take on roles of increasing centrality in the cultural construction of identity.

The case of Umbria (or rather northeastern Umbria) adds another variation to this theme. In the Umbria region, after crossing into the territory of the frontier city of Perugia, the natural landscape becomes focal. Intermediate areas of Etruria such as the upper Arno (the Casentino) share some of the same qualities (Stoddart 1979–80), so this is not a transition embedded in one ethnic identity. Communities, in southern Etruscan areas did draw on riverine (di Gennaro 1986), lacustrine (Cifani *et al.* this volume) and mountain (Riva and Stoddart 1996) features, but these became culturally defined through construction of a built environment. The northeastern boundaries of Etruria were much more fuzzy. Here, over time, with apologies to Richard Bradley, the Archaeology of *Relatively* Unaltered Places morphs into the Archaeology of Textually Imagined Places, centred on the valley of Gubbio. In other words, we have a transformation from culturally marked eminences in the landscape (familiar to European Prehistorians) into an interpretation of that landscape wholly dominated by one obscure text inscribed on a series of bronze tablets (familiar to philologists, linguists and humanists since the their discovery in 1444; Devoto 1977: 1) and known in English as the Iguvine Tables. It is this transformation that I wish to examine.

There are two key issues.

The first relates to the archaeology of Relatively Unaltered places. In this context, it is crucial to emphasize the statement of Bradley that we cannot state categorically that an unaltered physical landscape was always viewed in the same way. It has been an assumption of much research that there is a *longue durée* not only in the presence of structural features but also in their connected meaning. Put more rhetorically, the prehistoric peoples of Umbria cannot be expected to have known how the thoughts of their descendants were to be interpreted by philologists, glottologists and linguists from Genova and Padova (Prosdocimi 1984) or their acolytes (Sisani 2001). History goes forward not backwards.

The second relates to the Archaeology of Textually Imagined Places. We must examine the conditions under which identity was constructed. Do the Iguvine Tables represent the construction of an identity in response to external competition (Stoddart 1994: 176; Sisani 2009: 191–2) OR a reconstruction of that Identity ONCE that political independence has been effectively lost?

There are two famous historical festivals in central Italy which can illustrate this issue by analogy. These are the Palio of Siena (Pomponia Logan 1978) and the Festa dei Ceri of Gubbio. Both represent elaborate historical rituals that flourished, once political independence had been lost to Florence and Urbino respectively. Today the practitioners of the festivals reconstruct a past in a more elaborate and redundancy rich manner, combining excitement and yet strong elements of predictability. They both form rites of traditionalisation that enact idealised accounts of an independent past. There is a good case to be made that the Iguvine Tables represent a similar phase in the construction of the identity of the Gubbio region. This process is reinforced by the fact that 'Texts, in short…exert their own influence in society through the different readings that they undergo…' (Sant Cassia 1993: 309).

The challenge is to make the historical linkage between a phase where archaeology is relatively rich – paradoxically the Relatively Unaltered places – and a phase where

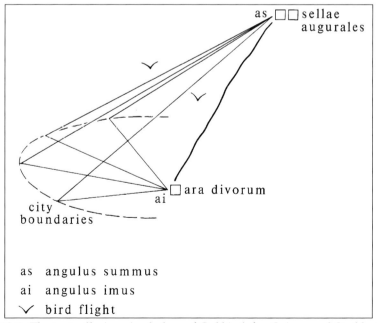

Figure 13.1. The textually imagined place of Gubbio (after Spivey and Stoddart 1990).

Figure 13.2. The basin of Gubbio under snow, showing the clear geographical definition on which identity can be imprinted.

archaeology is relatively poor – the Textually Imagined Places. In the Gubbio Valley, we do not have the large-scale, multi-level, hierarchical structures visible in contemporary southern Etruria, where the landscape was articulated into many layers of politically charged differentiated identity. The population, such as it was, was principally nucleated in the area now under medieval Gubbio. There is no evidence for levels of administrative hierarchy in subsidiary settlements or even farmsteads until the Republican period (Malone and Stoddart 1994b: 209–10). There may be evidence for some form of articulated boundary with Etruscan Perugia (Matteini Chiari 1979–80) to the south, now dated to the fifth century BC by recent fieldwork, but the evidence for landmarks of identity is remarkably sparse, in spite of intensive survey in the 1980s, with one exception: the mountain peaks.

Our understanding of the Gubbio landscape has changed considerably over the last thirty years. Until the 1970s, Gubbio was a fine medieval town, with a collection of unassessed finds in the municipal museum and the national museum of Perugia, dominated by a tradition of research on the Iguvine Tables (Devoto 1954, 1977; Prosdocimi 1984) and their probable findspot, the Roman theatre (Cenni 1973). Since the 1980s, the impact of the Gubbio project (Malone and Stoddart 1994a), the work of the Superintendency, the reanalysis of museum collections (Matteini Chiari 1995) and attempts to link the archaeology to the Iguvine Tables have transformed the picture (Sisani 2001; Wilkins 1998). For this reason it is also an appropriate moment to make a reassessment.

I will take this in the two phases already defined:

The archaeology of relatively unaltered natural places

Over the period of 600–400 BC, we can compare four zones of northern Umbria where the marking of upland natural landscapes became important: Gubbio, Assisi, Monte Acuto and Gualdo Tadino. In all these cases, prominent intervisible eminences of the upland reaches of the landscape were slightly altered with platforms to receive votive deposits creating the relatively unaltered natural places.

Gubbio provides the most comprehensive case study. The medieval and modern centre of Gubbio first became the central place of settlement in the Gubbio Valley in the second millennium BC. The work on Monte Ingino has shown that the hill behind the modern city was first occupied in the Middle Bronze Age by daub-working surfaces, probably of a seasonal nature. This position held an important control of access routes from the north east of the valley of Gubbio, almost certainly along the Sentino River. It is most probable that the Rocca anteriore was similarly occupied during the same period since occupation of the peak of Monte Ingino (for whatever motive) makes little sense unless both peaks were occupied simultaneously. Unfortunately any such evidence had been lost in the restoration of the structure without archaeological investigation. It now also appears probable that the upper southwestern flanks of Monte Ingino were also occupied in this period.

By the Final Bronze Age, this single founder system had become the focal point of an interrelated system of sites, both on the peaks (Monte Ingino and Monte Ansciano) and on the slopes below (Sant'Agostino, Vescovado and Via dei Consoli). These five locations are the securely dated sites through excavation (in the three cases systematic, in the fourth case revealed by observation of a road cutting through the local colluviation). One key unresolved issue is how extensive this system of interrelated sites was at this stage, and this will have major consequences in the interpretation of the economic and political organisation of the period. In the modern urban area, more research is required to investigate the extent and nature of occupation and their precise interrelationships, even if they must have formed one interlinked community. These are difficult issues to assess in one consistent programme of research and will have to be patiently awaited from investigation ahead of conservation and rescue excavation required by any limited development in the medieval *centro storico*. However, a systematic programme of work could be implemented on the hills above the town. Small excavations on the peaks of Monte Foce, Monte Alto, Monte Semonte, Monteleto and Catignano would be able to identify deviation from the model most explicitly preserved and identified on Monte Ansciano: namely a two-phase occupation in the Bronze Age and Archaic period. Such a programme of research would also move the focus away spatially from a preoccupation with the presumed focal topography of the Iguvine Tables.

A further key question is the nature of the occupation of the two well researched and stratigraphically intact sites of this period: Monte Ingino and Monte Ansciano. As was originally emphasized in the main publication (Malone and Stoddart 1994c: 127) which interpreted the middens found there and stated most succinctly in the concluding model – 'Ritual was almost certainly deeply embedded in the social and domestic, in ways which the modern mind finds difficult to envisage' – we cannot think of these

Figure 12.3. Detail of the alteration of the relatively unaltered place of Monte Ansciano (after Malone and Stoddart 1994a).

deposits as ritual in a modern sense (cf. Dolfini *et al.* 2006). Their composition contrasts markedly with the make-up of more formal ritualized deposits such as hoards and burials. Their composition also contrasts markedly with the separation of the ritual and profane which are defined by modern societies. By contrast, they are the feasting deposits most probably of a sub-set of the full community, given the liminal location of these sites at the upper limits of the landscape and their relatively small surface area. The high frequency of pins (as opposed to fibulae) in the deposits suggests that this subset of the community may have been substantially male in composition. We can envisage the young men of the community engaged in ritual embedded in the economic, and indeed social and political, activities of guarding the upland limits of the territory of the wider community. It is also important to stress that where space allowed, as on Monte Ansciano, this subset of the community was not isolated on the highest peak. There is clear evidence of occupation of the full crest of Monte Ansciano as shown by a) an oval posthole structure, b) scatters of protohistoric pottery and c) unexcavated subsurface structure revealed by geophysics.

In the case of Monte Ansciano there is a stratigraphic hiatus of some three hundred years between the midden feasting deposit, 'closed' by an Early Iron Age fibula probably of the ninth century BC, and a drystone platform of the sixth century BC on which at least 65 figurines and 169 nails, some limited terracotta material and some pottery were deposited. This is a very different type of activity to the preceding Bronze Age levels set within a circular drystone enclosure. The earlier levels may have been still recognizable and distinctive when the succeeding Archaic populations placed their platform. The rich organic contents of the sediments may even have given rise to a distinctive vegetation. The drystone containing wall and the adjoining ditch would still have been visible. In spite of the lapse of four to five hundred years, or three hundred years if one includes the single fibula, the Archaic populations may have been able to recognise the special cultural qualities of the location. These include its spectacular natural location, from where personal experience suggests that you can command a view of dramatic panoramic and weather effects of the Apennines, closely intervisible with other locations with similar life histories (Cenciaioli 1991, 1996). However, this recognition of the distinct quality of the location does not imply ritual continuity.

An unanswered question is whether the current focus on Monte Ansciano is simply a product of the state of research. In much the same way as further research (see above) is required to date the extent of protohistoric occupation of the area above Gubbio, so it is necessary to date the distribution of Archaic sanctuaries in the same topographic positions. Field survey discovered a small schematic figurine at the extreme northwestern edge of the Gubbio escarpment at Monte Loreto (Malone and Stoddart 1994a: 150, fig. 5.6, 42). It is highly probable that a large proportion of the peaks of the escarpment were subject to similar depositional rituals from the north-west to the south-east, removing the focus on the central place of Gubbio and suggesting a different practice to that retrojected from an interpretation of the idealised interpretation of the Iguvine Tables. One might even predict that Monte Ansciano, with its modest discoveries in comparison with other peak systems such as those of Gualdo Tadino and Monte Acuto, had a quite lowly presence in a hierarchical order of sanctuaries (Stoddart 2010). One model might suggest that the higher peak of Monte Foce was the higher order sanctuary with lesser sanctuaries of Monte Ingino and Monte Ansciano to one side and Monte Semonte and Monteleto to the other. Only further excavation will be able to establish the elaboration of surface preparation and intensity of deposition.

Many subsequent interpretations of the Bronze Age phases of Monte Ingino and Monte Ansciano have emphasized ritual continuity[1]. Ancillotti and Cerri (1996: 200) specifically entitle Monte Ingino, a sanctuary (*santuario*) by reference to the Umbrian word *eku–*. Moreover, they explicitly consider the location a place of sacrifice again by reference to the handbook of the Iguvine Tables, specifically Table IIb.19. At every opportunity, linkages are made to the Iguvine Tables; a further example is the linkage of dogs to the Hondia ceremony detected in Table IIa.15–46 (Ancillotti and Cerri 1996: 203) which is specifically interpreted as an 'ideological kernel of the same ceremony'; the same argument is presented in the case of young pigs (Ancillotti and Cerri 1996: 204), whereas more recent publication of the Final Bronze Age settlement of Sorgenti della Nova shows similar embedded rituals within the domestic setting (De Grossi Mazzorin 1998). Ancillotti and Cerri's interpretation is conflated by chronological confusion, since they equate the late figurine discovered in the 1970s excavation from the upper disturbed medieval levels on Monte Ingino with the Final Bronze Age levels (which they mistakenly call 'Subappennine' or Recent Bronze Age, which indeed existed but at a lower level). They even suggest that an altar (Ancillotti and Cerri 1996: 201) would have existed if only the medieval citizens of Gubbio had not reused the material in the construction of the tower. In a series of hypotheses, this activity is linked to the

Figure 13.4. The relatively unaltered place of Monte Ansciano.

arrival of the Safini who guaranteed 'continuity with the past', and this is where there may be a potential congruence of views with my own, to 'legitimate their political and economic control.' It is also true that they later admit the difference between rituals of a city state and private rituals (Ancillotti and Cerri 1996: 206), although the implication is that the modernist term 'private' is appropriate to the Bronze Age

The same authors follow their modernist interpretation with a selective reading of the published material where they claim that the original excavators exclusively interpreted the deposits on the mountain as 'encampments' (Ancillotti and Cerri 1996: 202) and 'refuse tips of the settlement' (Ancillotti and Cerri 1996: 206). In fact, the interpretation of these deposits was carefully argued, contextualized and nuanced (Malone and Stoddart 1994a) and to my surprise has stood the test of time. For instance, they chose not to note the following statements: 'a cultural phenomenon which would be simplistically described as domestic' (Malone and Stoddart 1994b: 125) or a more extensive explanation: 'Final Bronze Age societies probably did not have the clear distinctions between the ritual and domestic spheres that appear with supposed clarity in modern societies' (Malone and Stoddart 1994b: 126; particularly in the minds of Ancillotti and Cerri!) or 'The clearest evidence for the partly ritual character of these deposits rests in their location (on mountain summits) and the periodicity of their accumulation. The exposed position of the sites and the faunal evidence suggest we are in fact dealing with seasonal bursts of activity, representing peaks of consumption and production. The liminal nature of these sites would have encouraged ritual activities centred around consumption and production as an extension of the regular domestic routine.' Instead they decontextualize the statement 'essentially seasonal camps which formed part of an extensive settlement system based on transhumant semi-pastoralism' (McVicar *et al.* 1994: 105) from the study of agriculture and reattribute authorship to myself and Dr Malone. As can be seen, the correct agricultural interpretation of McVicar and colleagues can be integrated into a more holistic interpretation which appears in the later concluding section under my authorship. *Contra* Ancillotti and Cerri (1996: 203), the deposit on Monte Ingino is not particularly remarkable for its missing categories of material, but for the quantity of surviving deposit. They contrast this situation with S. Agostino (1996: 203), without taking into account the conditions of survival: a stable protected deposit (albeit on a mountain top) excavated by a large team over two seasons on Monte Ingino, as against a very unstable colluvial deposit excavated in one short season by a very small team at S. Agostino.

The reinterpretation of the data by Sisani (2001) is more carefully expressed, as one might expect from a field archaeologist and a scholar whose period of interest is more closely related to the material under study. Employing directly scanned and, in common with Ancillotti and Cerri 1996[2] generically referenced images from the original publication, Sisani (2001: 18–23) first gave a synthesis of the excavation monograph, highlighting a number of elements which require some comment. The cited prominence of young pigs does not acknowledge the settlement context of a similar prominence of young pigs at Sorgenti della Nova. The predominance of sheep is in fact a common feature of Final Bronze Age throughout upland central Italy. The relative presence of carbonized seeds is more probably taphonomic than a real indicator of difference; their discovery at all owes much to persistent floatation, in as much as the discovery of much of the very small metalwork owes its discovery to systematic use of a metal detector on site and on spoil heaps. The perceived differences from the hill-flank sites of Vescovado and S. Agostino owes as much to the circumstances of excavation of badly damaged deposits as to any measurable difference.

Sisani (2001) then proceeds to the same misreading or partial reading of the published evidence. As already mentioned elsewhere (Stoddart 2010: 213–4), Sisani generically (without page reference) accuses the 'archeologi inglesi' (I am in fact 'scozzese' when I chose to slip between ethnic labels) of interpreting the four excavated sites of Ingino, Ansciano, Vescovado and Agostino as independent sites devoted to different types of agricultural production. *Contra* Sisani, the core to the model presented in the published volume is that this is 'an integrated system of sites with a collective territory represented by the merger of the individual territories', (Finke *et al.* 1994: 83) as shown by one of the figures he scanned! Segments of the same community (Malone and Stoddart 1994a: 126) operated in all these sites (Ingino, Ansciano, Vescovado, unexcavated portions of Sant'Agostino and now Via dei Consoli), fluctuating according to seasons and activities, at least for a period in the earliest phase of the Final Bronze Age. Before this phase of maximum expansion both vertically and horizontally in the landscape, the addition of recent excavations (L. Cenciaioli pers. comm.) shows there was a phase of simultaneous upland and lowland occupation in the Middle and Recent Bronze Age on Monte Ingino, followed by an expansion onto other hilltops (minimally Ansciano) and hillflanks (of Ingino and Ansciano) in the course of the Final Bronze Age. Ingino may have been partly abandoned in the final phases of the Final Bronze Age or simply truncated by medieval activity. In fact Sisani (2001: 26), perhaps inadvertently, points out the similarity between Ansciano and Ingino, noting on Ingino stratigraphically above the intense Final Bronze Age activity, the residuality in the medieval deposits of one Late Archaic figurine, a third century BC Roman coin and material of the later Roman period. Ansciano has a similar sequence where the intense activity of the Final Bronze Age is followed by a single ninth century fibula, capped by a platform and then by Archaic figurines, coins of the last centuries BC and Roman lamp fragments. The difference is that Sisani, to quote his words back to him, forces the archaeological evidence into a model of 'continuità', presumably ritual continuity. His whole model emphasizes similarities between phases (Sisani 2001: 28) to demonstrate continuity of cult. Given the emphasis on similarities between phases, this implies more than a simple accident, but deliberate continuity of practice, a point that he reiterates as 'continuita di frequentazione' (Sisani 2001: 33) hedged by the ambiguity of 'creazione' and 'riconsacrazione' which suggests discontinuity. There is an inherent ambiguity in his position which on the one hand states 'vera e propria continuita, a livello funzionale, con quella dell'età del Bronzo' and his (final) admission of demographic and political change in the contributing communities (Sisani 2001: 35), an ambiguity embedded in his hesitant use of the term '(ri)fondazione'. This argument continues in discussion of particular interpretations of ceremonies in the Iguvine Tables which are considered a 'relitto' of the Bronze Age (Sisani 2001: 85–6). It is not by chance that he employs evidence from the *lega Latina* to bolster his case (Sisani 2001: 88–91), recalling the comparable debate elsewhere in volume over the relationship between past and present in the Latin area (Carandini this volume).

By contrast, the actual excavators have noted discontinuities and variations in rates of deposition, and have taken care, in every period, to situate these practices within a broader social and political framework, drawing on ethnography for prehistory (extending substantially until the third century BC; cf. Osborne this volume) rather than retrojected textuality. Sisani's partial reading of the excavation report (2001: 26) follows a similar vein to that of Ancillotti and Cerri claiming that the 1994 model was purely economic and linked to 'semplici accampamenti stagionali di pastori transumanti', missing once again (see above) the subtleties of anthropological rather than modernist classical interpretation. Sisani's view implies, albeit hedged with ambiguity, that the ritual landscape of the second millennium BC was conceptually the same as the ritual landscape of the middle of the first millennium BC and that the whole process was working in some teleological manner towards the Iguvine Tables, a landscape whose 'ruolo verrà confermato dai successivi sviluppi storici che porteranno alla nascita, in questo stesso sito della città di Gubbio?'

In fact all three phases (protohistoric, Archaic and that of the Iguvine Tables) are radically different in what is designated by the term 'ritual' and the accompanying identity, and potentially ethnicity, in the final stages. The protohistoric phase encompasses, as argued above, a ritual embedded deeply in economic and social practice. The ritual at this stage was located both within and without the living community, both spatially and temporally. Visible ritual activity was both within the arena of domestic economic practice of upland pastoralism on a seasonally cyclical basis and separated from other activities of other segments of the same community located on the hill flanks of the same hills. The Archaic phase encompasses the deposition of figurines on a prepared drystone platform at some distance from the main centre of economic practice in the valley below, by creating a *relatively unaltered* natural place of a different form. These depositions take the form of male and female bodies and – in order to have achieved their deposition – must have involved a bodily procession from the valley some 400 metres below, defining an association of identity with the natural landscape by movement from one limit to the other.

The Iguvine Tables, however interpreted, encompass an idealized version of a ritual as distinct from any actual practice of that ritual (which has yet to be located). A lapse of time ranging from five hundred to one hundred years separates these very different types of activity. Ritual continuity and accompanying Umbrian identity or even ethnicity are not the most appropriate terms to apply to separated periods of very different, albeit intense, types of activity. As already mentioned, the excavation of Monte Ansciano also revealed a much lower level use of the site into the last centuries BC (coin) and into the first centuries AD (use of Roman lamps). Is this continuity? Umbrian ethnicity cannot be convincingly traced back into the two earlier phases of ritual performance.

As well as the use of the mountain tops of the Gubbio as sanctuaries and the fresh evidence of settlement nucleation on the site of the medieval and modern city of Gubbio mainly on the right bank of the Camignano river (Manconi 2008), the recent systematization of the municipal museum has revealed complementary evidence of activity in the Gubbio city area during the sixth century BC (Caramella 1995; Cipiciani 1995). If we can assume that the ceramic imports and spear/lance heads preserved in the municipal museum have a provenance from the immediate Gubbio area (not always the case as recent documentary evidence has shown, Borsellini pers. comm.), then it is probable that these belong to cemeteries which must have surrounded the contemporary nucleated centre. Some of the rescue excavations which have preceded the building works on the outskirts of the modern city of Gubbio have also uncovered indications of the structures which might have contained these finds, and these structures appear to include some stylistic similarities to those from the Marche area (Bonomi Ponzi 1996). In any case by the sixth century BC, there appears to be a modest nucleation of population under the medieval city, with evidence for some differential accumulation of wealth, preserved in a few formal burials. However, no evidence has been found for contemporary rural settlement, and the only evidence for a possible subsidiary centre is a spearhead from the Torre Calzolari area.

Inter-regional comparison

These comparisons present both similarities and differences which are illuminating for the understanding of Gubbio. All four areas – Gubbio, Gualdo Tadino (Bonomi Ponzi 1996; De Vecchi 2002; Peroni 1963; Stefani 1918, 1922, 1924, 1926, 1935a, 1935b, 1935c, 1935d, 1935e, 1955–6), Monte Acuto (Cenciaioli 1991, 1992, 1996, 1998, 2002, Matteini Chiari 1975, 1996) and Monte Subasio near Assisi (Matteini Chiari 2002; Monacchi 1986) – have broadly similar sequences of Recent Bronze Age/Final Bronze Age sites surmounted by Archaic sanctuaries. A fifth example of Monte Tezio has a Bronze age enclosure in less close association with an Archaic sanctuary (Matteini Chiari 1979–80, pers. comm.). All areas employ the verticality of the landscape. However, beyond these basic similarities, a subtle differentiation appears that eludes the simple typologies archaeologists sometime employ to characterise the rise of complex society. Furthermore, the differences could be more than simply related to preservation or the vagaries of archaeological research. Gubbio is at the centre of a closed intermontane valley. Monte Subasio is also set above a nucleation of population in the less bounded valley below. Monte Acuto, Monte Tezio and Gualdo Tadino are set above important communication routes running along axes determined by the broadly northeast-southwest tectonic induced geology. The Monte Acuto and Monte Tezio systems have a similar altitude to that of Gubbio (926 metres), but are more remotely placed from their local valleys. The Gualdo Tadino pattern takes a more complex tripartite form. In the valley bottom there are the cemeteries. The focal point of activity is at a lower altitude (743 metres) than in the other two cases and this has led to a closer integration of settlement activity and the formal ritual activity. Finally the higher peaks behind Gualdo Tadino are the location of a second line of sanctuaries at over 1000 metres easily intervisible with other parts of the Apennines. The Bronze Age midden deposits of Monte Ingino, Monte Ansciano (and probably Monte Tezio) stand out in terms of the relative quantity of material recovered, but not in the types of material. By contrast the sanctuary placed on Monte Ansciano appears to be rather more modest than those discovered on Col de Mori (Gualdo Tadino), Monte Acuto and even Monte Subasio. Both the quantity of material recovered and the structural sophistication of Monte Ansciano are considerably less. This may point to Monte Ansciano as a subsidiary sanctuary to Monte Foce or possibly Monte Ingino to the north. Paradoxically, looking at the current evidence on the Archaeology of Relatively Unaltered Natural Places,

Gubbio would be a less likely location to predict the appearance of the elaborate ritual practices interpreted from the Iguvine Tables. However, the geographical configuration of a well defined intermontane valley does provide a geographical platform for the construction of identity that Assisi only partly shared.

We need to take a dynamic, nested view of the construction of identity and question the extent that ethnicity is an appropriate terminology prior to the very last centuries BC. My analysis is not greatly dissimilar in spirit from that of Torelli (2010: 226), albeit based on different array of evidence. He does, however, suggest that the threshold of ethnicity occurred earlier in the late fifth century BC in parts of Umbria. This he registers in the cemetery evidence of Todi to the south and by a switch from an Adriatic to an Attic environment in Gubbio's cemetery evidence to the north. Whether this switch in identity by the elite constitutes the construction of a real ethnicity must await further research.

Textually imagined landscapes

We know from comparative research the importance of imagined communities in a modernist framework (Anderson 1991). This framework needs to be applied to our preconceptions of the Gubbio Valley. The Iguvine Tables are generally dated to the period from the second half of the third century BC to the beginning of first century BC (Prosdocimi 1984; Sisani 2009: 185–186) when the political independence of Gubbio was at least under pressure if not effectively lost. There is no comparable inscriptional evidence for the other four regions. At Gubbio, a more formal organization of the cemeteries and perhaps the road network around Gubbio appears to have taken place during broadly the same period. The Vittorina cemetery on an important road network appears to have had some founding graves during this phase (Manconi 1991) before the main flowering of the Roman cemetery (Cipollone 2002), and the recent re-systematization of the Museo Civico has revealed another small florescence of probable grave finds from this phase (Caramella 1995). In addition, the foundation of the Latin colony of *Ariminium* (268 BC) and the building of the *Via Flaminia* (220 BC) are clear evidence that the Gubbio basin was under the military hegemony of Rome and fully linked with the Roman trade network at least by the end of the third century BC (Stoddart 1994: 176). Moreover it is only in the latter part of this phase that we can begin to detect a presence of a more widespread material culture in the countryside in the form of almond rims distributed in the immediate environs of the city. Furthermore, a substantial impact on the countryside can only be detected in the full Roman period when rural settlement permeates the whole valley (Malone and Stoddart 1994c: 209–10), a process which coincides with the monumentalization of the town also in the last centuries BC. This is the appropriate political setting for the textually imagined landscape of the Iguvine Tables.

Conclusion

Interpretations of the Iguvine Tables predict elaborate ritual practice closely linked to the construction of identity. The ritual practice revealed by archaeological research is currently less elaborate than for three other well studied areas which belong broadly to the same cultural background – Monte Subasio (Assisi), Monte Acuto and Gualdo Tadino. This paradox should inspire archaeologists to undertake further archaeological research at Gubbio and a practical accessible target of that research is the peak of Monte Foce. Alternatively, the rules reconstructed by scholars from the Iguvine Tables may have been considerably more simple when revealed as practice by archaeological evidence. If this pattern proves to be enduring then the model of the Textually Imagined Place, enhanced by rites of traditionalization, that enact idealized accounts of an independent past may have the stronger case than the traditional retrojections of highly developed identity back into prehistory (cf. Torelli 2010) that belong to the philological, glottological and linguistic traditions.

It is appropriate to end once again by completing Latour's exposition of tradition:

> One is not born traditional; one chooses to become traditional by constant innovation. The idea of an identical repetition of the past and that of a radical rupture with any past are two symmetrical results of a single conception of time. We cannot return to the past, to tradition, to repetition, because these great immobile domains are the inverted image of the earth that is no longer promised to us today: progress, permanent revolution, modernization, forward flight. (Latour 1993: 75–6)

Notes

1   I was asked by Gabriele Cifani to insert this more detailed section. I find that the critique addressed to British scholars working in Umbria (notably Sisani 2001) as to a lack of attention and poor referencing to published evidence can be mirrored in the work of Italian scholars reading the less voluminous English language material.
2   Augusto Ancillotti kindly requested and received permission in June 1996.

14

Space, boundaries and the representation of identity in the ancient Veneto *c.* 600–400 BC

Kathryn Lomas

Keywords: ethnicity; cultural identities; archaic Italy

The study of ethnic identities, and of ethnic boundaries and interactions, is a central strand in the study of the ancient Mediterranean, but it remains one that poses a number of important methodological questions for the archaeologist or historian. Without the comprehensive body of evidence available to historians, anthropologists and sociologists studying more recent history or contemporary societies, it is frequently difficult to establish whether a particular set of characteristics is indicative of an ethnic identity, a state identity, or a sense of common cultural identity shared by social groups of various sizes. The processes of ethnic identity formation and self-identification is potentially difficult to determine from material evidence alone, as a shared material culture is not invariably an indicator of a common sense of cultural or ethnic identity in the wider sense (Barth 1969: 12–13), but any additional textual evidence is for the most part external to the cultures in question and relates to ethnic categorization rather than self-definition. It can be difficult, therefore, to identify ethnicity or other forms of cultural identity with any degree of certainty.

Definitions of identity which can be applied to societies such as ancient Italy are also difficult to construct. One way in which ethnic groups can be defined is by a set of observable criteria, such as a shared history, shared mythology or genealogy, common language, common ethnic name, and shared social structures, religion and material culture (Smith 1986; Hall 1997), but this approach can have its pitfalls. Not all of these criteria are present in any single ethnic group. In some cases, for parts of ancient Italy, we have no evidence for common ethnic names other than those ascribed by Greeks and Romans, always from outside the group in question and often not contemporary with the societies described. Other criteria on this list cut across ethnic and cultural boundaries and were shared by groups which do not necessarily regard themselves as possessing a common identity. Linguistic boundaries, for instance, may not coincide with those of material culture, or with those of shared social customs and practices. In other cases, material cultures can be similar but the self-defined ethnicity of the possessors can be different. Polybios (2.17–23) for instance, described the *Veneti* and Celts as indistinguishable in their cultures by his day, but also notes that they spoke different languages, and he clearly perceived them as separated ethnic groups. In addition, this approach can lead to a somewhat static view of ethnicity, which is inappropriate given that one of the defining criteria of ethnic identity is its variability over time (Jenkins 1997: 40). Furthermore, ethnic groups in Italy did not exist in isolation and cannot be defined only by their own cultures. Interaction with other cultural and ethnic groups is also important in maintaining group identities. Studies from Barth (1969) onwards have stressed the need to examine boundaries between ethnic and cultural groups, and the way these are maintained, as important elements in the creation and reinforcement of identity, and other studies have emphasized the need to examine the constant interplay between self-constructed identities and ethnic categorization by outsiders (Jenkins 1997: 53–70). Jenkins's (1997: 40) model of ethnicity, which he defines as consisting of cultural differentiation; a shared culture set of cultural meanings which are transmitted and reproduced by social interaction; variability and flexibility; and an interplay between the collective and the individual and between internal and external elements, may be useful as a basic model. In particular, the emphasis on the process of interaction between ethnic and cultural groups in shaping and maintaining identities is important in a culturally varied region such as archaic Italy.

A further factor to be considered is that societies in Archaic Italy display a complex hierarchy of identities and interactions between different forms of identity. Any examination of them must therefore examine not just ethnic identity in the sense of the emergence of the wider ethnic group, but also the development of local or individual state identities, or the identities of specific social groups within communities, such as kinship groups. Any examination of the development of identities in early Italy must examine ethnicity in the context of this hierarchy of identities, and the interplay between the various forms of identity which develop. In the Veneto, for instance, the process of urbanization is characterized by the creation and maintenance of a complex series of cultural markers which delimit boundaries of various types, and also a considerable localization of some other aspects of culture, all of which point to the emergence of strong communal identities. However, these contain, and are sustained by, powerful elites with a strong gentilicial structure. At the other end of the spectrum, they may have existed within a wider sense of shared Venetic ethnicity, although this is a more problematic question.

The other major challenge is to deal with the combination of different forms of evidence available, and the need to take into account the relationship between emic identities, or self-identification, and etic identities, or ethnic categorization, in the development of early Italy. Our evidence comprises both archaeological evidence from a range of contexts – primarily funerary and ritual, but also including an increasing amount of settlement evidence – and written evidence. This second category takes the form of two distinct registers, the limited but important evidence of inscriptions, and the descriptions and comments by ancient Greek and Roman authors. The challenge is to combine these various and very different sources of information, and to resolve the tensions between them, to illuminate our understanding of ethnic and cultural identities. The evidence from ancient literature for the non-Roman populations of Italy is problematic because it presents an external viewpoint of these societies and cultures, often recorded by people with limited personal contact with the objects of their descriptions and writing at a considerable chronological and geographical distance from the events and cultures described. At one level, it is a clear case of ethnic categorization, creating and imposing ethnic boundaries and identities which may not have been recognized or regarded as significant by the peoples in question, and one extreme approach amongst archaeologists and historians has been to dismiss such evidence as irrevocably tainted and unusable. While it is true that the accounts of ancient authors tell us more about Graeco-Roman perceptions of others, and their own cultural agendas, an approach to ancient Italy which fails to engage with a significant quantity of evidence is unsatisfactory. Both anthropological studies (Barth 1969: 113–17; Jenkins 1997: 12–14) and specific regional case-studies of areas of Italy (for instance, Bradley 2001; Williams 2001: 207–22, to name only two examples) have highlighted the extent to which ethnic identity is the result of constantly shifting interactions and influences not just between different ethnic and cultural groups, but also between external categorization and internal self-constructed identities. In this respect, written sources, both epigraphic and literary, provide important evidence for several different registers of ethnic identity, both self-defined and externally defined. Literary evidence for the *Veneti*, the group which is the principal focus of this paper, is somewhat outside its main scope, but epigraphic evidence – particularly when examined as a physical artefact as well as text – can, when combined with other aspects of archaeological evidence, provide important insights into cultural identities at various different levels – family, community or ethnic.

The Veneto presents a case study of the ways in which various levels of identity – state, ethnic, or identities of various sub-groups such as kinship groups – are represented in space and mapped onto the landscape. It is also a problematic one because may potential markers of identity in the region present contradictory stories. There are significant variations in material culture, and in urbanization and settlement patterns, throughout the region. Most cultural markers seem to suggest that the strongest form of identity in most parts of the region, from the sixth century BC onwards, is the individual state. However, there has been a strong trend in modern scholarship to view the region as possessing an ethnic unity in a way which is not necessarily borne out by the evidence, and which needs to be problematized further. This is in part because ancient writers present it as such, describing the *Veneti* as an ethnic group (collected in Pellegrini and Prosdocimi 1967: 211–35; and in Voltan 1989). This is clearly an ethnic category, imposing an external perception of the region and its culture, rather than reflecting an indigenous one generated by the inhabitants themselves. Indigenous self-perception may have been significantly different. This categorization cannot be entirely discounted, not least because it may have shaped Roman reactions to the *Veneti* from the second century BC onwards, but is perhaps less relevant to the period covered by this paper. In addition to the ancient authors, language may also have contributed to perceptions of a unified Venetic identity. The language usually referred to as Venetic is common to the whole region, although with some perceptible differences between parts of that region, and may contribute to an impression of ethnic unity and cohesiveness which may well be misleading. The purpose of this paper is to review the evidence for the various different types and levels of identity and how they are represented in the landscape. Conversely, it will examine how the use and demarcation of space and boundaries can illuminate various forms of identity, and also what role inscriptions can play in determining identity – not so much as texts, but as material objects.

Urbanization and state development in the Veneto

One of the key features of the Veneto is that it starts to develop urban settlements at a relatively early date in the south of the region, but there is a major difference between this area and the northern Veneto. The low-lying regions of the Po plain and the area around the head of the Adriatic, the Euganean hills and the foothills of the Alps all begin to acquire urban-type settlements from the seventh century BC (Fig. 14.1; Chieco Bianchi 1981: 49–53; Capuis and Chieco Bianchi 1992: 45–51; Capuis 1993: 114–21, 163–5; Balista *et al.* 2002: 105–26). The alpine areas of the northern Veneto, however, do not acquire large and complex settlements of this type until Roman colonies were settled there in first century AD, and much of the communal activity which is elsewhere associated with the city-state takes place at isolated cult places which are not associated with centres of population (Pensaventa Mattioli 2001). The basic underlying reason for this may be that the mountainous areas of the north of the region do not readily support large concentrations of population in any one place, and are better suited to a dispersed settlement pattern in which the inhabitants live on individual farms or in

Figure 14.1. Map of the Veneto.

small villages, but it may also reflect wider cultural differences between the two parts of the Veneto.

In the southern part of the region, a number of significant population centres were already established by the eighth century BC, but by the end of the seventh century, some significant new developments were taking place. These were marked at both Padua and Este by a phase of collapse in population and settlement densities in the late eighth–early seventh centuries, in which some significant sites such as Montagnana, 11 kilometres from Este, and Trambacche (Fig. 14.2; 14 kilometres from Padua) disappeared (Bianchin Citton 1992; Boaro 2001: 154–63). From the middle of the seventh century, however, there appears to be a sudden expansion in population and numbers of settlements, with the re-establishment of settlement at some previously abandoned sites, such as Montagnana, possibly as part of their incorporation into new territories and power structures dominated by emerging proto-urban centres (Boaro 2001: 157). At the same time many new sites were established, and there are signs of a reorganization of the territory. Alongside this increasing number of sites, there is a significant growth in the relative size and complexity of a small number of bigger settlements, notably those at Padua, Este, Treviso, Altino and Vicenza, a phenomenon which suggests that these were establishing themselves as the dominant sites in the region, on which many others were dependent. This is accompanied by the first signs of activity on many of the major ritual sites, richer burials, more complex layout of cemeteries and settlements, and a material culture indicating an increasingly wealthy and dominant elite (Balista and Ruta Serafini 1992; Boaro 2001; Capuis 1993: 140–59). For the sake of manageability, this paper will focus on the relationship between landscape, boundaries and identity at Este and Padua, as examples, but this is not intended to imply that the issues raised were confined to these two communities. They may well apply just as much to other areas of the Veneto. In particular, there are significant differences in settlement patterns, socio-political organisation and some areas of material culture between the southern, central and northern Veneto, which suggest that these were issues of importance throughout the region. Whether the whole of the area attributed to the *Veneti* by ancient authors shared a single self-conscious ethnic identity must remain open to question.

Este and Padua: spatial representations of state identity

For the sake of manageability, this paper will focus on two specific examples of cultural differentiation – Este, Padua and the interaction between the two. These were the two largest and most important settlements of the region. Este seems to be the more dominant, but there also appears to have been a lively competition for regional influence between Este and Padua, which are located only 30 kilometres apart. Each of them developed its own distinctive variant of local culture and there are clear signs of cultural differentiation between the two. Both settlements have a similar basic structure, with clusters of houses dating to the sixth–fourth centuries, ringed by areas of burials and strategically placed religious sanctuaries which mark the urban area and the boundaries of the territory controlled by these settlements (Figs 14.3 and 14.4; Boaro 2001: 154–64 Chieco Bianchi 1981: 49–53; Capuis and Chieco Bianchi 1992; Gamba *et*

UNIVERSITY OF WINCHESTER
LIBRARY

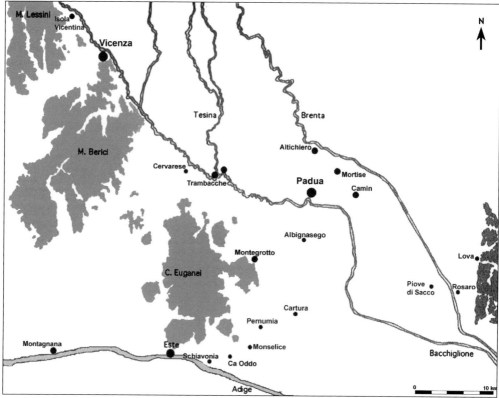

Figure 14.2. Key settlements of the southern Veneto (after Boaro 2001).

al. 2005a: 23–5). The processes of growth continued in the fourth–second centuries BC, marked by the development of fully nucleated settlements with complex street layouts and public buildings, and then the adoption of Hellenistic and Roman-style architecture and public buildings in the late second–first century (Bosio 1981: 231–7; Baggio Bernardoni 1992: 305–20; Tosi 1992: 400–18; Gamba *et al.* 2005: 72–4).

However, there are important differences in the developmental trajectories of these two sites. At Este, there is clear evidence of a complex spatial layout and ritual marking of boundaries from an early date. The central area is occupied by several nuclei of settlement and habitation, with traces of an organized street layout – something which may indicate the presence of a central organizing authority (Balista and Ruta Serafini 1992: 115–20; Capuis 1993: 126–35; Balista *et al.* 2002). The settlement area is ringed with a series of cemeteries, and also a complex system of sanctuaries which seem to be sited in such a way as to mark the boundary of the urban area (Maggiani 2002). This pattern seems to have been established by the late eighth century, the period of first activity on many of the sanctuary sites, and by the seventh century most of these were established as major ritual centres, remaining in use until the Roman conquest or later (Ghirardini 1888; Dämmer 1990; Ruta Serafini 2002).

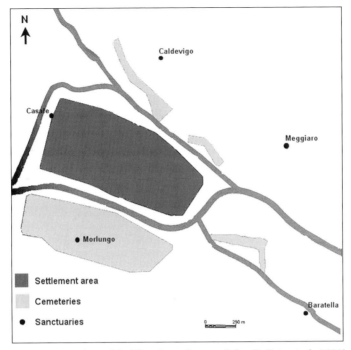

Figure 14.3. Este: plan of the Venetic settlement (after Balista et al. 2002).

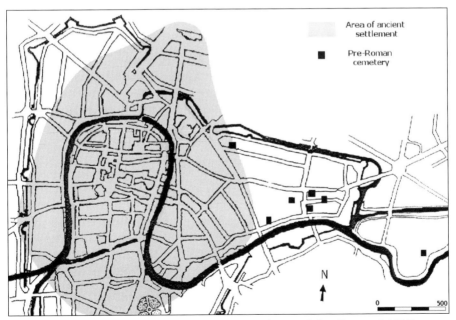

Figure 14.4. Padua: plan of the Venetic settlement (after Pascucci 1990).

The only sanctuary to have been excavated systematically enough with modern techniques to determine its layout is Meggiaro, on the eastern edge of the city, and this appears to have been an open enclosure, containing a possible altar and a central enclosure which may have been an augural platform, but with few permanent structures (Ruta Serafini and Sainati 2002). Baratella, to the south-east, may have had some buildings, as the stone plinths on which some votives were displayed survive with relatively low levels of weathering, implying that they were displayed inside a building or under some sort of shelter. Fragmentary stone columns found at the site also hint at the construction of cult buildings at some point in the sanctuary's history, but it is not clear whether these date to the period under discussion or belong to a later phase. It is also possible that these cult-places had wooden structures which have not survived, although there is little evidence of this at Meggiaro. The large amount of bone which was found indicates that animal sacrifice was part of the ritual (Maggiani 2002).

All five locations identified as major sanctuaries have produced copious deposits of votives (Pascucci 1990: 53; Ruta Serafini 2002; on Baratella specifically, see Dämmer 1990; Ghirardini 1888). In the sixth–fourth centuries, these included (along with other items such as figurines, pottery and anatomical votives) bronze laminae, stamped with designs that appear to be unique to each sanctuary (Pasucci 1990: 59–92; Zaghetto 2002, 2003). For instance, Baratella included a high proportion of women, while at Meggiaro the most common iconography was armed men or groups of young men (Fig. 14.5; Maggiani 2002b; Zaghetto 2002). Other representations include groups of

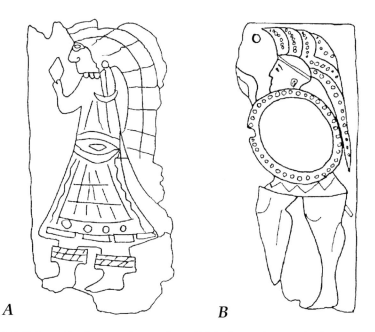

Figure 14.5. Este: votive bronze plaques from Caldevigo and Baratella (after Pascucci 1990): (A) Female figure (10.6 × 5.2cm); (B) Warrior figure (8.4 × 3.4cm).

young women, found at the sanctuary of Reitia at Baratella, and both armed men and adult women, found at Caldevigo (Pascucci 1990: 59–118). This type of votive is commonplace throughout most of the Veneto, which the significant exception of Padua, which is discussed below.

These very specific associations between iconography and specific sanctuaries may be determined by the nature of individual cults. It has been suggested, particularly in relation to the Treviso lamina featuring a female figure sometimes identified as a local version of the Greek *potnia theron* (mistress of the animals), that the figures on the lamina represent deities (Fogolari 1956). However, it has also been plausibly argued they are intended to represent worshippers rather than deities, and may indicate which group in society was most closely associated with the rites of the sanctuary, and also the nature of particular ritual. Meggiaro therefore seems to be a sanctuary particularly associated with young males, or initiation ceremonies for them (Maggiani 2002: 80–1). Similarly, the laminae depicting groups or processions of young women, from Baratella, may suggest that the cult had a particular responsibility for this group or that some rituals involved processions of young women. Baratella has a more mixed iconography than most sanctuaries. Votives include anatomical votives, figurines, votive writing implements and laminae depicting groups of young women, all dressed in the costume represented in other visual contexts such as situla art – a long shawl draping the head and upper body, worn over a dress. Others, from both Baratella and from Caldevigo, depict single figures of richly dressed older women, wearing the heavy belt and boots which seem to have been characteristic of women of rank. Baratella, therefore, seems to combine responsibility for writing (demonstrated by the number of votive writing tablets and styli) with a function as a healing shrine, a cult associated with young women, and a particular role for adult women. Sanctuaries, therefore, seem to be linked to specific age and gender groups rather than kinship groups. If so, they may have played an important role in state formation and state identity. Not only do sanctuaries occupy important locations on boundaries between different types of space, demarcating the urban area from its surrounding territory, or marking boundaries between territories of different states, but they also – at least at Este – seem to have played an important role for groups within the state, acting as a focus for particular groups within society, possibly differentiated by age and gender, and as a means of integrating these groups.

Cemetery organization, in contrast, places a heavy emphasis on the kinship group rather than social groupings by age and/or gender. Burial rites are a mixture of cremation and inhumation, and the graves are a mixture of *fossa* or *casetta* type burials and multiple burials covered by tumuli. Groups of burials are demarcated either by spatial separation or by the construction of boundaries marked by stone slabs. Obelisk-shaped stone cippi inscribed with personal names are found in the area of several cemeteries. They were clearly intended as funerary monuments, but their lack of close correlation to specific burials in most cases has led to conjectures that they may have been used to mark the entrance to a burial enclosure or set up outside a tumulus rather than functioning as an individual grave marker (Fogolari 1988: 99–105; Prosdocimi 1988: 247–9; Balista and Ruta Serafini 1992; Malnati 2002). The grave goods placed in the tombs were often very rich. Tombs typically contained significant quantities of bronze vessels and other objects, jewellery, and fine pottery of types frequently geared to drinking and feasting. From the late seventh century, males are typically buried with serpent fibulae, knives, pins, arm-rings, and drinking vessels similar to the Greek *kylix* in bronze or fine pottery, while female tombs contain bronze and bead jewellery, bronze discs and other ornaments, spindles, and drinking vessels of a *skyphos* shape (Capuis and Chieco Bianchi 1992: 71–85). From the fifth century onwards, many women are also buried with a large bronze belt clasp or plate, an item of female dress depicted on many of the votive plaques discussed above. Some of the richer burials also contain a bronze vessel known as a situla, sometimes richly decorated, in which the ossuary was placed.

Padua, in contrast, seems to develop on rather different lines, although it also shows some similar features as well. It developed a nucleated centre rather earlier than Este. The earliest settlement on the site, developing in the eighth century BC, took the form of small nuclei of settlement on areas of high ground within a loop formed by the river Brenta (Fig. 14.4). The location of these was probably determined by the topography since they occupy higher ground and there are traces of drainage works on the lower-lying ground, a feature which in itself demonstrates a considerable degree of common political and organizational structure. During the course of the eighth century, the drainage systems become more systematic and elaborate, and by the end of the seventh century, the settlement was starting to coalesce, with particular areas of activity along the two branches of the Brenta (Chieco Bianchi 1981: 49–53; Gamba *et al.* 2005b: 65–7). The settlement consisted of several substantial areas of habitation, mainly of rectangular wooden houses, and demonstrates an increasing degree of separation between living space and areas of artisan activity, and between settlement and areas of cultivation (Gamba *et al.* 2005a: 23–31; Gamba *et al.* 2005b: 67).

As at Este, the city has a complex layout of sanctuaries and cemeteries, but here, the most significant boundary is not man-made, but is the Brenta itself, and both cemetery areas and areas of ritual activity are located to complement this. There is little evidence for the internal layout of the sanctuaries and our main evidence for cult activity consists of votive deposits. There is also much less evidence than at Este for the deities worshipped. References in ancient literature (notably by Livy, who was a native of Padua) to cults of Diomedes and Juno give us two possible Graeco-Roman cults which may have been present at a later date, but no indication of what the Venetic cults which preceded them might have been (Livy 10.2.7–15; cf. also Strabo *Geography* 5.1.8–9). It is possible that this indicates an adoption of Graeco-Roman religious architecture from the late fourth century, the date to which Livy's reference relates (De Min 2005: 117) but there is no corroborating archaeological evidence of this and such structures would be unusual in the context of the earlier development of cult-places in the Veneto. The relationship of the ritual locations to the areas of habitation is complex. There are signs of ritual activity on the edges of the urban area, and a number of major sanctuaries are known from the territory of Padua, and particularly from border areas, at S. Pietro Montagnon, Lova and Altichiero (Leonardi and Zaghetto 1992; Zaghetto and Zambotto 2005), mirroring the pattern found at Este and elsewhere in the southern Veneto. However, there are also significant clusters of votives found within each nucleus of settlement (De Min 2005), dating from the mid sixth century BC to the second–first centuries BC, which are closely associated with individual houses.

This pattern is unusual in the Veneto, and Padua is the only major site at which this type of evidence for ritual activity associated with the domestic sphere and individual families has been found. These votive deposits associated with the settlement and with individual houses may indicate the continuing importance of cults which were based around families or kinship groups.

The votives found at Padua are similar to those from other areas in some respects. Deposits contain a high proportion of small figurines and miniature pottery, along with bronze objects such as knives, ladles and palettes, probably implements used in various rituals. However, there is one notable difference, namely the lack of iconographic laminae. Only one example has been found, at Bacchiglione in the territory of Padua (Fogolari 1988: 184–5). Apart from this, Padua is the only major centre of the Veneto which has produced no votive laminae. Instead, the type of iconography that is associated elsewhere with liminal sanctuaries and the social groups which used them, was used at Padua for grave markers associated with elite burials and gentilicial groups.

Spatially, there was a greater degree of differentiation between settlement and necropolis and less correlation with particular areas of the city at Padua that was the case at Este. There was a large and well-defined area of burial on the east side of the city (Figs 14.3 and 14.4; Chieco Bianchi 1981: 49–53; Capuis and Chieco Bianchi 1992: 51–2; Gamba *et al.* 2005a: 26–7; Michelini and Ruta Serafini 2005). There were also smaller areas on the south side of the settlement, across a bottom of a loop in the Brenta River, and to the north-east of the city. All of these were in use from eighth century BC to the second–first centuries BC. They show evidence of systematic layout and organisation from an early date, possibly as part of the creation of a drainage system. Burials are similar to those at Este, grouped under tumuli which seem to have represented burial places of gentilicial groups, although the tumuli seem to have been smaller and the perimeter markers were of wood rather than stone (Michelini and Ruta Serafini 2005: 132–3). As at Este, stone markers were associated with some burials, but were of a different form and – unlike the Atestine examples – were decorated with formulaic scenes in incision or low relief (discussed in further detail below).

The development trajectory at both Este and Padua was broadly similar, but with some important differences in the ways in which space is used, and some interesting implications for the ways in which different groups were integrated into society. In both cases, developments seem to point to the growth of an important state identity coupled with the continued importance of the identities of individual kinship groups. However, some aspects of the location and structure of both cemeteries and sanctuaries, as well as the items found there, suggest that at Padua, the strongest identities were those of kinship groups, represented by visually impressive gentilicial burial sites and the importance of family or domestic cults. At Este, in contrast, there is a strong emphasis at many sanctuaries on social groups defined by age and by gender rather than on the individual kinship group.

Symbolic boundaries and the uses of writing

As noted above, one of the key methodological problems of examining identities (especially ethnic identities) through material culture lies in the fact that ethnic identities are self-defined and do not necessarily correspond to the distribution patterns of particular artefacts or other forms of material evidence. For the Veneto, however, we have an additional resource which may help to shed light on the formation of different forms of self-identification. Writing was adopted in the region from the late seventh century BC onwards, initially in the southern part of the region but later spreading to alpine areas, and *c.* 400 inscriptions in the local language and alphabet survive (collected in Pellegrini and Prosdocimi 1967; with additional material in Prosdocimi 1988 and Marinetti 1999). Most of these are short and many consist mainly or entirely of personal names, but they can, nevertheless, tell us a considerable amount about social – and in particular, gentilicial – structures, and may also shed some light on various levels and types of identity. In addition, the fact that only writing on durable materials such as stone or metal survives, means that these inscriptions can also be considered archaeological artefacts, and the significance of their location in the landscape, relation to other structures, and physical appearance, can be examined. They may function as additional markers of 'special attention' (Ashmore and Knapp 1999: 15) to signal significance of particular locations in the life of the community. In a society where literacy is likely to have been a restricted skill, the mere fact of being inscribed with writing is likely to have singled out such monuments, and the locations associated with them, as places of special significance.

The alphabet and the basis of the syllabic punctuation system were adopted from the Etruscans, although probably taking aspects from different areas of Etruria, and then elaborated into a distinctive local writing system (Prosdocimi 1983, 1988: 328–51, 1990; Whitehouse and Wilkins 2006). This was adopted throughout the region, although writing was adopted earlier, and was in far more widespread use, in the urbanized south of the regions. The classic model of the spread of the alphabet – that of Prosdocimi – postulates an early phase which was used in all areas and had no punctuation, and a later (post-sixth century) phase which developed into two distinctive variants in Padua and Este, with Atestine script being predominant in the Veneto as a whole (Prosdocimi 1983, 1988: 333–49). In fact, close examination shows that script was more varied and complex than this implies, with a distinctive north Venetic script found in Alpine areas and a possible eastern variant in use around Oderzo (Marinetti 2001; Lomas, forthcoming). To a large extent, this is not unexpected. Alphabets in other areas of the Mediterranean tended towards regional specificity, especially in their early stages of development, and in a region with two rapidly developing states contesting dominance, it is even less surprising that the alphabet should have been used as a symbol of cultural identity (Whitt 1995: 2384–6). The most interesting aspect of the early (sixth–early fourth century) inscriptions for current purposes is, however, their physical form and their location. Although a very high proportion of early inscriptions fell broadly into two categories – stone funerary markers and votive objects of pottery or bronze – there were marked differences between Este and Padua in the forms of these and their locations within the urban area (in as far as this can be determined) was potentially significant.

To take funerary commemorations first, there was a sharp distinction in form between those of Este and Padua (Fig. 14.6). Those from Este were undecorated obelisk-shaped cippi, *c.* 60–100 centimetres high, inscribed (although many are broken and may have been higher than this originally) with a first person dedication to the deceased, mostly of the form 'I am to/of X' (Pellegrini and Prosdocimi 1967: Es1–Es22). Those found at Padua were rectangular *stelae* with an inscription arranged around two or more sides of a square central panel. Most (although not all) of these panels were decorated, mostly with a scene of a chariot and driver/passengers or an armed horseman, incised or worked in low relief (Pellegrini and Prosdocimi 1967: Pa1–Pa6; Prosdocimi 1988: 284–8; Fogolari 1988; Zampieri 1994). They were inscribed with a commemoration in the first person, in the form 'X ekupetaris ego' ('I am to/of X the ekupetaris'; on the possible meanings of *ekupetaris* and its function as a status indicator, see Marinetti 2003). The functions of both the Paduan and Atestine forms of marker were similar. Despite the apparent personalization of the epitaphs, the markers related not to individual burials, but to the tumuli, as they seem to have been positioned as markers outside tombs belonging to kinship groups. They appear, therefore, to have functioned as both memorials and marks of ownership for the tombs, and as symbolic boundary-markers for the area

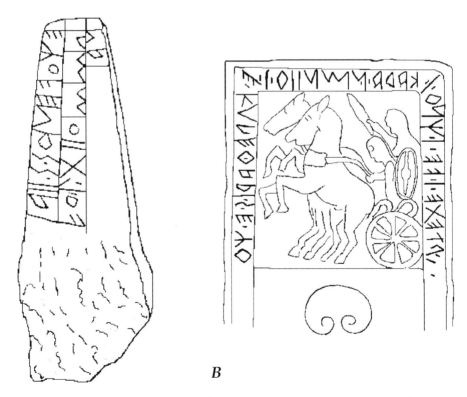

A　　　　　　　　　　　　　　　*B*

Figure 14.6. Inscribed funerary monuments from (A) Este (23 × 65 × 23cm) and (B) Padua (66 × 86 × 34cm) (after Pellegrini and Prosdocimi 1967).

belonging to the group. Many tombs with this type of marker were located on the edge of cemetery areas, particularly at Padua, and it is has been suggested on this basis that they may also have served to demarcate space belonging to the living from that of the dead, and to have marked the approach to the urban area (Boaro 2001: 167–8). As a *caveat*, it should be noted that at Padua, quite a number of these items were not found in their original location, but at Este, many were found in context. The fact that they were so visually distinctive, with different types adopted for each city, suggests that they had a role as signifiers of state identity/culture as well as markers for individual kinship groups.

Other inscriptions that seem to function as boundary markers were also set up on the edges of the urban area at Padua, especially in the area on the southern edge of the city, and on the northern edge, in both cases close to the course of the Brenta. These have been interpreted as boundary markers delimiting the city or marking certain significant locations, but they were a fairly disparate group of monuments and their significance may have been more complicated than it first appears. Two, for instance, were simply cippi with one or more personal names, often interpreted as names of magistrates, but with no obvious status-indication (Pellegrini and Prosdocimi 1967: Pa11 and Pa13). Another is more convincing as it explicitly stated that it was a boundary stone, but it need not have necessarily pertained to a civic boundary. One possible interpretation is that it marked the entrance to a sacred area (Pellegrini and Prosdocimi 1967: Pa14, Prosdocimi 1988: 293–5).

Finally, there was a group of inscribed stones known as *ciottoloni*, whose function is unclear but which may have functioned as memorials or markers of some sort. These are natural stones of alpine porphyry, mostly unworked and roughly oval in shape. They were inscribed with personal names, sometimes in the first person, and often with the inscription laid out in an elaborate pattern, spiralling round the edge of the stone. Their geographical distribution was very specific. Of twenty-one examples, all but five came from Padua (Pellegrini and Prosdocimi 1967: Pa7–Pa10 bis; Prosdocimi 1972; 1988: 246–7, 289–95; Marinetti 1999), and most were found at significant locations in the territory of the city. Interpretations vary, ranging from funerary monuments or cenotaphs commemorating the unburied dead, to ritual objects connected with mystery cults, based on comparisons with *ciottoloni* from southern Italy (Marinetti and Prosdocimi 2005: 37–8). Their relatively small size, compared with the cippi, and the fact that some were not found *in situ*, means that it is difficult to be prescriptive, as they were less obviously visible markers and their original location and display contexts is uncertain. However, it has been pointed out that concentrations of these were found in liminal areas, either on territorial boundaries (Trambacche) or on the boundaries between urban space and territory (Piovego). This may reinforce the argument that writing as a phenomenon may have been linked with boundaries – not just as a practical device for marking them, but as a symbol of ownership and demarcation. Boaro's attempt (Boaro 2001: 166–70) to trace changing boundaries between territories by examining distributions of votives (sixth–fifth centuries BC) and inscriptions (fourth century BC), while not entirely unproblematic, raises some interesting questions. In particular, the discovery of a stele of Padua type, and with a Paduan type of inscription, at Monsélice (Chieco Bianchi and Prosdocimi 1969; Prosdocimi 1988: 286–8) in an area which seems otherwise to have been deep in the territory of Este, and a cippus of

Atestine type very close by at Schiavonia (Pellegrini and Prosdocimi 1967: Es4) led him to suggest that the boundaries between these states may have changed in the early fourth century BC. However, this interpretation poses some difficulties – not least the fact that it does not square with the evidence for the territorial boundary at either earlier or later dates. In the context of the society of the Archaic Veneto, which was highly stratified and dominated by elite kinship groups, it seems more likely that this particular form of display relates to the kinship group or individual than the state boundary. As Boaro (2001: 167–8) points out, the Monsélice stele is a female commemoration and may therefore represent intermarriage between the Atestine and Paduan elites rather than a shift in boundaries. Whatever the specific interpretation of this pair of inscriptions, however, it seems very probable that writing was used to add an extra degree of significance to monuments placed in liminal areas or other significant points in the landscape.

Ethnic identity versus *state identity: ethnicity in a landscape*

The representation of cultural boundaries between emerging urban communities, and within these communities, between urban settlement and territory, can therefore be traced in a number of areas of activity. State identities were particularly contested in the southern Veneto, where Padua, Vicenza, Treviso, Altino and Este were in close proximity and in direct competition for power, prestige and resources. Boundaries seem to have been represented in the landscape by a number of means, notably the use of cemeteries and ritual sites to delimit urban space and of sanctuaries to delimit the boundaries both between urban space and territory, and between different political units. The material culture and the locations of the epigraphic evidence both point towards strong state identities and to the importance of symbolically marking boundaries.

Overt attestations of state identity in the written record were, however, rare. There were a small number of epigraphic attestations of either state names or of deity-names closely linked to those of the state, but these were a small minority of the overall epigraphic record. At Altino, finds from a recently excavated sanctuary include items (unpublished at time of writing) said to date to the sixth and fourth centuries BC and to be inscribed with the word *Patavnos* – possibly the Venetic name for Padua or an adjective or ethnic derived from it (Marinetti and Prosdocimi 2005: 38–41). Another inscription, on an imported Attic red figure *skyphos* of the early fourth century BC, contains the name *A[l]tnos*, which has been interpreted either as the community name of Altino, or as the name of an eponymous deity closely associated with the community (Tirelli 2002; Marinetti 2002: 317–8). In both of these cases, however, there is some doubt over whether these were place names or ethnic names, or whether they are the names of eponymous deities, derived from place names. Despite the close association between certain types of inscription and liminal areas, the use of writing as a marker of places significant to the identity of the state does not seem to have been dependent on showcasing the name of the state. The fact that most inscriptions consisted of the personal names of the individuals who set them up or who were commemorated by them suggests that statehood and state identities in the Archaic Veneto were closely bound up with the identities of the elite families which formed the dominant social group.

Finally, there remains the question of whether we have any evidence of an over-arching ethnic identity – a Venetic identity that was more comprehensive than the identities of particular communities. This question is complicated by a number of factors. One is that the epigraphic evidence points to a shared language throughout the Veneto. Although a common language was a possible component in the formation and maintenance of ethnic identities, linguistic and ethnic boundaries were frequently at variance with each other, and language may potentially prove irrelevant in the formation and maintenance of identities (Smith 1986: 26–8). The fact that there was so much variation throughout the region in other fields of social and cultural behaviour, ranging from material culture to social and political organization, suggests that we should be wary of assuming a unified ethnic group on the basis of language alone.

The question of whether there was a shared Venetic ethnicity brings us to the problem of the literary sources and also the role of ethnic categorization in the formation of identities. Greek and Roman authors of the second century BC onwards refer to an ethnic category of *Veneti* (or Greek *Henetoi*) who were clearly perceived from this outside perspective as forming an ethnic entity. The chronology of this is complex, as Greek references to a group names the *Henetoi* occured in literature as early as Homer and are found in a number of fifth century BC writers (Homer *Il.* 851–2; Alcman fr. 1, 91; Herodotos 1.196; Euripides *Hippolytus* 228–31), but it is possible that some of these early references (which are mostly mythological in nature) resulted from a confusion between the peoples of north-east Italy and another group, also named *Henetoi*, who lived on the Baltic coast (Williams 2001: 24–8). There is little doubt that by the fourth century BC, Greeks had regular contact with the region. There were Greek settlers at Adria and Spina, significant quantities of Greek imports are found at many sites in the southern Veneto, and Hellenism becomes a prominent element in local culture from the late fourth century BC, especially at Padua (Bandelli 2004). However, this degree of contact does not imply that references to the *Henetoi* in Greek literature were necessarily an accurate reflection of a self-identification as a single ethnic group by the inhabitants of the Veneto themselves, and some Greek comments reflected the complexity of identity in the region, even to an outside observer. Polybios (2.15–7), who may have had some first-hand knowledge of the area, noted that by his day, the culture of the Veneti was very similar to that of the Celts, but that their language was entirely different. It is notable that most Greek sources were concerned mainly with incorporating the Veneto into their own cultural sphere by creating Hellenized foundation myths and genealogies for them (Strabo *Geography* 5.1.4–9; Cato *Origines* [Peter *FRH* F42], Pliny *Natural History* 3.130). From the fourth century BC onwards, there were signs of significant cultural changes in the Veneto, as Celtic and Greek influences became stronger and Rome began to encroach on northern Italy. These contacts with other groups, and the fact that by the mid-second century BC, Rome was using perceived ethnic categories for bureaucratic and administrative purposes (Cato *Origines* [Peter *FRH* F42]; Polybios 2.24), may have had the effect of prompting an increased sense of common Venetic identity, but whether this can be projected back to the archaic period must be deeply uncertain, particularly given the scarcity of corroborative evidence from within the societies in question.

There are only two possible pieces of evidence from within the Veneto that could potentially point to the existence of a common sense of Venetic ethnicity, and neither are conclusive. The only inscribed votive found at Meggiaro was dedicated to a deity called *Heno[--]tos*, a name which bears some resemblance to the Greek ethnic name for the *Veneti* (Marinetti 2002; Prosdocimi 2002). However, it is dangerous to extrapolate an ethnic identity from this, and even if it was a deity-name related to a place, on the model of *Altnos*/Altino, the location in which it was found, at a sanctuary close to Este, suggests that it was more likely to relate to the ancient name of Este rather than that of the Veneti as a whole.

A further possible ethnic identity has been detected in an inscription found at Isola Vicentina, near Vicenza (Marinetti 1999: 400–2, 2003: 195–6). It was a surface find with no datable archaeological context or associated finds, but has been dated on the letter-forms used to the fifth–third centuries BC. It reads 'iats venetkens osts ke enogenes laions meu fasto' and was a first person inscription set up by one or more named individuals, but some aspects of it are unclear. It could have referred to several named individuals, Iats, Osts and Enogenes (all personal names known in the Veneto), or to a single individual, Iats, since the rest of the inscription was a description of his ethnic affiliations (Marinetti 1999: 400–2, 2003: 195–6). The possible link between the inscription and the ethnic identity of the Veneto rests largely on whether *venetkens* can be interpreted as an ethnic identity, but also on interpretation of *osts* and *enogenes*. Both of these are well known elsewhere in the region and in contexts where it is unlikely that they are anything other than personal names. Despite this, Boaro (2001: 170–3) suggests that inscriptions containing 'Ost' (or any of its variants or compounds such as Ostis, Ostiala etc.) indicated outsider status and should be regarded as indicative of a cultural or ethnic boundary. Although this is an interesting hypothesis, it is also problematic. Many names in ancient societies were derived from significant words with particular connotations – e.g. derivations from place names or deity names, or names with specific moral or status connotations, such as the prefixes *eu-* (='good') in Greek – but it is unclear how far these names would have been perceived as closely linked to their literal meaning or how far this would have been subsumed by their status as names. Names with the root *Ost-* were common in the Veneto. There are 13 known examples, of which seven are on stone, the remainder on pottery cinerary urns, or on small votives (Pellegrini and Prosdocimi 1967: Pa6, Pa13, Es6, Es113, Es106, Es131, Vi2, Tr1, Tr3, Tr7, Ts1). All but four were either from clear funerary contexts or were of a form which suggests that they were an epitaph/grave marker, not a boundary stone. The location of the Vicenza inscription on an apparent territorial and cultural boundary suggests it may have been significant as a boundary marker, but the fact that it is unique is problematic and the meaning of the inscription is too ambiguous to interpret with any certainty, and it would be risky to interpret is as definite evidence for a collective Venetic ethnic identity. It must at least be possible, by comparison with *Hene[--]tos*, *Patavnos*, and *Altnos*, that it is the name of an individual state or community. The evidence for a wider Venetic ethnicity, over and above the individual state, must therefore be regarded as inconclusive, at least before the fourth century BC. This does not necessarily imply that such an ethnicity did not exist, but it does suggest that it was not the primary identity in most areas of the Veneto and was weak relative to the identities of individual communities.

Conclusions: hierarchies of identities in the Veneto

To sum up, the evidence points to the development of strong state identities in the southern Veneto from at least the early seventh century BC onwards. There is also evidence of strong differentiation between the major centres, both in the obvious sense of establishing boundaries, and in cultural differences. These were especially marked between Este and Padua, but were not confined to these two examples. There is clear evidence, however, of a hierarchy of intersecting identities – family/gentilicial, state/community, and the more difficult question of whether there was any clear evidence for a wider Venetic ethnicity in the sense of self-identification rather than just external perception.

Este and Padua were both examples of constructed landscapes, in which key locations in both the settlement and the surrounding territories were utilized as possible markers of state identities and social difference and divisions within the communities (Ashmore and Knapp 1999: 15). Both established sanctuaries at key points at an early stage in their development, both to mark boundaries between territories, and to mark various types of space within the community. However, they seem to have followed different strategies for this, which may reflect underlying differences in the social structure of these communities. All Venetic communities in the Archaic period were highly socially-stratified societies, which were dominated by small and wealthy elites, but the two main centres of the region seem to have adopted different strategies for elite self-representation and for integrating family/kinship-group identity into the overall identity of the community. At Este, for instance, the cemeteries were organized according to gentilicial group, indicating the importance of elite family/gentilicial identities within the community and the individual and family identities of members of the elite. The evidence from sanctuaries, however, suggests that these were orientated towards integrating particular groups based on gender, age or other criteria, not on family membership, and can be seen as a means of integrating groups into the wider community. At Padua, in contrast, the spatial layout of both cemetery areas and sanctuaries suggests that the gentilicial group was the strongest organizing principle in this society. Evidence for ritual activity suggests that although sanctuaries had an important role in establishing the wider identity of the community by marking the boundaries between city and territory, and by marking the territorial boundary with Este, private cults specific to particular kinship groups or individual families were a much more important feature of the community's development than was the case elsewhere in the Veneto.

The visual impact and significance of the monuments, and the way that they related to the landscape is difficult to assess given the relatively slight evidence for the physical structures involved, particularly in the case of sanctuaries. The geography of each site was undoubtedly an influential factor in how the topography of the individual communities developed, particularly in the case of Padua, where the course of the Brenta and the need to drain and canalize the area within the main loop of it was influential in how the settlement developed. However, pragmatic considerations cannot account for all of the spatial and topographic features of the development of Padua, and socio-cultural factors must also be taken into account. It seems likely that the cemeteries, marked by tumulus burials and in some cases, inscribed grave markers, would have made a strong visual impact, particularly on the approaches to settlements. The fact that choice of location is significant in the location of sanctuaries is clearly demonstrated elsewhere in the Veneto, where sacred places seem to have been located in precise orientation with specific landscape features. At Monte Altare and Villa di Villa, near Vittorio Veneto, for example, sanctuaries seem to have been located in relation to specific natural features, such as specific hills, which are reflected precisely in the shape of the votive lamina (Maioli 1985), and at Lagole and Auronzo they relate to routes through the landscape or to specific natural features such as the sacred lake at Lagole. In the more urbanized southern Veneto, such evidence for the significance of the locations of sanctuaries in relation to landscape features is more difficult to determine, but the location of both sacred places and also inscriptions on boundaries between different types of space – whether defined politically or functionally – points to the use of such sites as powerful symbols of liminality.

Moving beyond the question of how boundaries are represented in the landscape, it is clear that at both Este and Padua, there are several intersecting levels of identity that remained important throughout. As already noted, gentilicial groups and their identities were important in both communities, and this was reflected in the distribution and development of cemetery and ritual areas. In both cases, however, there is plentiful evidence of the emergence, at an early date, of strong state or community identities. These are represented most directly in the epigraphic evidence (despite its sketchiness) of either community names or the names of the eponymous deities. However, they are also evident in the systematic use of space, especially ritual space, the concern with marking territorial boundaries and (at least at Este) the apparent role of sanctuaries as a means of providing social integration on a basis other than that of the individual kinship group. Furthermore, there is a case to be made that the communities of Este and Padua were, at least to some extent, defining their cultural identities in opposition to each other. Within a framework of general cultural similarities, we can see some significant differences in ritual practice, funerary customs, layout and spatial development of the site, and even in forms of writing. They clearly shared the same language, as did the rest of the Veneto, but this does not preclude the development of a perception of distinctive cultural identities, which may have increased over time. The impact of Greek culture, for instance, seems to have been much more pronounced at Padua than elsewhere in the region, and may have been adopted as a vehicle for emphasizing local identity and difference from Este. On a more general level, although outside the remit of this paper, important cultural differences can be observed not only between Este and Padua, but between these and other communities or regions of the Veneto. In this period of history, state identity seems to have been strong, as was a sense of the importance of cultural boundaries.

This leads, finally, to the question of whether it is possible to identify a coherent, and self-perceived, ethnic identity in the Archaic period – an overarching sense of Venetic-ness in addition to the strong state or regional identities already discussed. Here, we are on much shakier ground. Although it is undeniable that there was a perception of a common ethnic identity by outsiders – mainly Greek – from an early date, it is much less clear whether this was shared by the population of the region. The one apparently direct piece of evidence, the Isola Vicentina inscription, cannot be dated with any certainly, and is ambiguous in meaning. The force of *venetkens* as an ethnic corresponding to the Roman *Veneti* or Greek *Henetoi* remains only a conjecture. However, we must also take into account the possibility that the relative importance of different levels of identity may have varied over space as well as time. The location of the stone, on a cultural boundary with the cultural and linguistically Raetic area to the north and west of the Veneto may have been significant. Since ethnic identities frequently crystallised more strongly on boundaries and in areas of cultural difference, it is possible that there was a stronger sense of Venetic-ness, or a stronger need to articulate it, in this area than throughout the rest of the region. The existence of an assertion of Venetic ethnic identity (if this is what the inscription is) does not necessarily imply that the same perception was shared in other parts of the region. At Este, or any of the other urban sites of the southern Veneto, the establishment of cultural boundaries and identities in relation to neighbouring states and probable competitors may well have seemed more pressing than a need to symbolize a wider ethnic identity.

One of the underlying problems in this respect may be the fact, as already discussed, that the presence of a shared language – a necessary element in most definitions of ethnic identity but not a conclusive one – taken together with Greek and Roman assertions of Venetic ethnicity, has conferred a spurious impression of common ethnic identity on the region which is not borne out by the epigraphic and material evidence for the Archaic period. It is undeniable that a common sense of Venetic-ness was established by the time of the Roman conquest, and it may have developed as early as the fourth century BC, a period in which the Veneto was confronted with a number of new cultures. Given that ethnic identity often forms or changes in response to contact with new and different cultures and ethnicities, it is not impossible that it became more prominent as a reaction to the arrival of new people and cultures such as the Celts and Greeks in the fourth century and the Romans in the late third century BC. However, the evidence for the Archaic Veneto suggests a much more fragmented picture. The primary identity for most communities appears to be that of the individual state or locality, with some communities (particularly in the rapidly urbanizing south of the region) in strong competition with each other for resources and territory. Under the circumstances, it is not surprising if this competition and need for differentiation was reflected in cultural identities as well as political or economic behaviour.

Acknowledgements

This paper was prepared in the course of a project on *Developmental Literacy and the Establishment of State Identities in Early Italy*, funded by the Arts and Humanities research Board. I would like to that the AHRC for its financial support for this research.

15

Limits, frontiers and boundaries among the Iberians of the Guadalquivir Valley (eighth century BC–fourth century BC

Arturo Ruiz and Manuel Molinos

Keywords: boundaries; frontiers; ethnicity; Spain; Guadalquivir; Iberians

In one of his writings, Pierre Vilar (1980: 147) comments on a film which ends with Charlie Chaplin walking along the border between Mexico and the United States, so that the frustrated police of no country could arrest him. In so doing, Chaplin's genius mocked the concept of frontier. The frontier concept is the result of an agreement or an imposition at a given time, and yet, every society takes possession of it, as if it came from a timeless legal body which must be respected. The notion of frontier, with its political manipulation and its conceptual confusion, justifies this view and the support of essentialist principles which are proper to the foundations of national states. Some years ago, this approach was used as the opening argument of a paper (Ruiz and Molinos 1989). That paper intended to show the variety of forms that a physical limit may take over time. In this framework, the paper researched a data-set located between the upper- and the mid-course of the Guadalquivir River in the sixth century BC, and supported the rejection of the intangibility of frontier mocked in Chaplin's film. The earlier paper was also the starting point for an archaeological approach to a Theory of Space Delimitation, and that, in turn, is also the starting point for this paper.

Limits, frontiers and boundaries: towards a theory of delimitation in archaeology

Delimitation always relies on a dialectical logic of opposed pairs which leads to a differentiated expression of space. This is the first notion in the definition of a limit, but for a better knowledge of the issue, it is necessary to reconstruct who the social subjects of that opposition are. Socially, the most common oppositional unit is, first, the product of socio-economic conflict, and then the product of socio-cultural conflict. The former gives shape to Social and Economic Formations and can be defined by the political relations

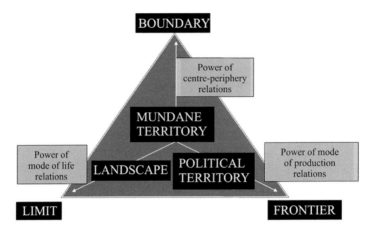

Figure 15.1. Relations between Territory and types of delimitation.

derived from the articulation of various Modes of Production. The latter shows itself via the relations which define the *Modes of Life* and which belong to the Socio-Cultural Group defined by its corporative membership, its ethnicity, its sex or its age.

The *Modes of Life* embody three forms of relations: i) relations that arrange the temporality of the social group and which express themselves in kinship relations; ii) neighbour relations, which internally arrange the social group in space; and iii) relations traditionally known as *possession relations* or *appropriation of nature* which also define the mode of production, but which here add cultural forms of natural appropriation to the economic principles. These complex relations give shape not only to labour relations in general, but also to the sequence of human changes and transformations of Nature. Godelier (1990) describes five levels ranging from destroyed nature, formed by the waste produced as a result of its use, like dumps, to pristine nature, intact or unpolluted. In between, there are, from the most to the least altered: built nature, as in urban areas; transformed nature, as in rural areas, and modified nature, untouched by rural exploitation, but affected by human activity. These five forms of Nature make up the active typology of settlements in nature and express themselves through four fields of dialectic opposition of spaces:

1. Productive-unproductive space: this arises between destroyed and built Nature;
2. Urban-rural space: this contradiction arises between built nature and modified nature. It expresses itself by means of built spatial markers such as fortresses or urban planning, as opposed to cultural spaces which do not break with the rural landscape;
3. Tamed-wild space: this arises between modified Nature and transformed Nature, that is, between the rural landscape (including built Nature), and the preceding landscape;
4. Political-mythical space: this arises between transformed Nature and pristine Nature. It is defined metonymically instead of metaphorically, just as are domestic and, in general, political landscapes.

Although the relations of the mode of life may be viewed as production relations proper to the economic and social formation, as is usual in classless societies, these relations define the framework of ethnic conflicts while the production relations define the framework of political and economic conflicts. Yet, insofar as social units are concerned, the relations of the mode of life find their spatial expression in the landscape and the production relations in the political territory.

The concept of landscape accumulates spatial information based on empirical knowledge stored over time, and is, therefore, a cultural heritage. It is also the hallmark of the space taken by the group to which it does not originally belong, that is, a historical ownership. The landscape is also a projection of the roots of identity of the occupant human group.

In practice, the landscape is, spatially, a stratigraphic discourse formed over time by the addition of effects of the network of relations which are proper to the mode of life of its inhabiting group, and also of the social and economic formation in which it finds political articulation. Occasionally, the landscape may be limited to the political territory of a socio-economic formation, although it is usually one of the units which form the political framework of the socio-economic formation. In other cases, the landscape finds its projection beyond the space of the socio-economic formation and becomes an extended landscape, probably because this landscape is the remnants of a former unit in an earlier mode of life.

Unlike the landscape, the political territory contextualizes objects, images and habits and stands amidst a logic of co-existence. In the political territory, time always appears short (the time of the development of a state or local political territory), while longer periods of time define the landscape. In a state community, the Political Territory is based on the legitimacy of the use of a space by a prevailing social group in the power structure, the ruling group. Furthermore, the political territory achieves a status of identity both by imposition of legitimate violence (*sensu* Weber) and by consensus. Ultimately the political territory is viewed as the space resulting from the practice of power developed by a social group based on the whole group's acceptance (Godelier 1998).

This two-fold spatial framework, Political Territory and Landscape, is the part where the architecture of delimitation takes shape: on the one hand there is the Limit insofar as it refers to landscape forms and relations proper to the mode of life, on the other, the Frontier insofar as that is where the political structure prevails. The latter space is also where the regulated framework of violence and the consensus established by the ruling social group become real. In other words, this is the space for socio-economic formation and sometimes for its political expression too, namely the state. A third type of delimitation can be added: the Boundary. This expresses itself as the limit of the economic and cultural territory which characterizes the World Territory in which the external relations of a social formation are set. The social formation finds its place in this third framework in the context of the Centre-Periphery dialectic. Boundaries, unlike limits and frontiers, face a ghost at the other side of the line of division: the unknown.

An archaeological typology of Limits and Frontiers

Our 1989 paper put forward a double level of analysis for the typological characterization of the frontier: one for its construction, the other for the demographic articulation, which defined its location (Ruiz and Molinos 1989). A provisional constructional typology, passing from the most to the least rigid architectural forms, was defined as follows:

1. Barrier Delimitation, characterized by the Great Wall of China (it should be noted that this includes any fortified settlement, because this belongs, structurally, in this model);
2. Chain Delimitation characterized, architecturally, by a more flexible model. This latter type consists of a network of aligned sites which are within sight of each other, as in the frontier between the Nasrids of the Kingdom of Granada and the Castilians in the southern Iberian peninsula between the AD thirteenth and the fifteenth centuries;
3. Natural Delimitation, which forms the most flexible model in this scale and is defined by the terrain or by change in the natural landscape. This typology has been recently supplemented with a new model, Delimitation by Distinctive Landmarks, which is best represented by the rural sanctuaries of Ancient Greece.

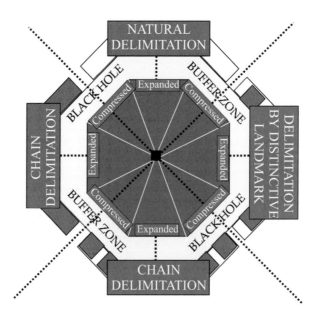

Figure 15.2. A matrix for a Theory of Delimitation in archaeology.

A second level of analysis was established based on demographic factors in the articulation of two distinct communities or of two social formations, in the context of a frontier. Groube (1981) pointed out the existence of a model, the so-called Black Hole, or Delimitation by Desert, which can be identified by having a population on one or both sides of the Frontier. Trinkaus (1984) proposed a second model shortly after Groube, the Buffer Zone, or Delimitation by Blockage, where a demographic concentration is apparent on both sides of the Frontier. Sometimes, the population in this model stands culturally or politically as a distinct unit, a buffer state. Variants of this model can be noticed in Roman times with the distribution of the *Gens Claudia* along the frontier of the Sabines (Ampolo 1970–1) or with the northwestern frontier of the Sassanid Empire researched by Trinkaus himself.

This paper examines a third set of variables added to the architectural structure and the demographic factors already considered. It examines the inner space defined by the dividing line, since the architectural structure may or may not enclose the whole territorial or landscape unit. The frontier, since it is generally based on globalizing intentions, ultimately involves an Expanded Delimitation. However, the dividing line does not always demarcate all the territory, as often happened with the Iberian fortifications of the *oppida* (they enclosed the urban part of the settlement and the fields and paths lay outside their protection). La Regina (1971) cites the most extreme example of such a Compressed Delimitation in his work on the Samnites: in their territory, the *castella* were built in fortified, uninhabited sites, because they were intended for use only in case of conflict with the exterior. It may be the case here that the two types of line of division may coexist using a different typology, for example an expanded chain frontier, and a compressed barrier (*barrera*) frontier. This is the case of the Nasrid frontier mentioned above between Granada and Jaén, where each urban nucleus had a fortified enclosure in addition to a network of aligned towers.

Philological sources

Leaving aside some vague poetical references, our knowledge of the most ancient period of Iberian culture relies on short passages by Herodorus of Heraclea, Herodotos, Hecateus, or, much later, in Avienus' *Ora Maritima*. These were descriptions of the coastline of the Iberian peninsula, at a time still not well-known among the sailors of the Mediterranean. These data were isolated and of low reliability, as is the case with Avienus, whose purpose was not to write a geographical account, but a literary text of a markedly myth-making nature. Yet, some of his writings have been acknowledged as helpful since the time of Schulten when dealing with some central toponymic or ethnographic issues relating to the pre-Roman peoples of the peninsula (Schulten 1922; Bejarano 1987). Many of his statements been only recently been called into question because of theoretical and methodological issues (Cruz Andreotti 2004: 244; Mangas and Plácido 1994: 25).

Avienus' approach to ancient topographic data was not impartial or properly contextualized, but his account of the peoples in the south of the Iberian peninsula has been traditionally interpreted by researchers as giving the following distributions:

the *Tartessi* in the lower valley of the Guadalquivir, the *Cempsii* in the Western Sierra Morena, and the *Ileati* or *Gleti* in the area of present-day Huelva; farther east, the *Etmanei*, along the mid-valley of the Guadalquivir and in the Sierra Morena, would have bordered on the *Tartessi*; the *Elbysinii* in the area of present-day Cádiz and inner Málaga; the *Mastieni* farther east and near present-day Murcia up towards Alicante, and the Lybiophoenicians south of them and close to the coastline (Schulten 1922; Mangas and Plácido 1994: 84; García and Bellido 1945; Almagro Basch 1960). In 500 BC and around 420 BC, Hecateus and Herodorus of Heraclea respectively gave new, albeit limited data. Hecateus (38.52) mentioned that the major ethnicities were the *Tartessi, Elbysinii* or *Elbesti*, and the *Mastieni*, all of them linked to the southern coast. Herodorus' *History of Heracles,* brought all the coastal populations together under a '*genos* ibérico' (Iberian genus; Cruz Andreotti 2004) and added:

> the Iberian peoples who inhabit the coastline of the strait are called different names when they are one people formed by several tribes: first, those who inhabit the westernmost part are called *Cineti*, then farther north are the *Gleti*, then the *Tartessi*, then the *Elbysinii*, then the *Mastieni*, then the *Celciani* and then the strait (I.163).

These texts always make reference to the south as inhabited by *Tartessi* and *Mastieni*.

After the Roman conquest of the Iberian peninsula, the number and quality of the data on the Iberian peoples increased substantially. It should be noted that the Iberian

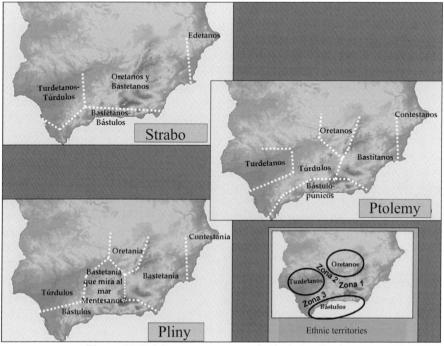

Figure 15.3. Literary sources and ethnic territories.

geography became better known only as the Roman conquest extended from the late third century BC (Cruz Andreotti 2002–3: 41). From the time of Polybius, many texts were proper geographies, which improved the detail and rigour of data and put an end to the generalized writing of earlier times. Even so, it is worth mentioning that these sources were the conquerors' views of space, which may have differed substantially from that of the Iberians.

Unlike most ancient references, the latest written sources gave priority to the definition of territories in the description of ethnonyms. Pliny wrote repeatedly about *Bastetania* (*Natural History* III.9) but he never mentioned the *Bastetani*, except as the inhabitants of *Basti*. Ptolemy also refers to regions in *Bastetania* or *Oretania*; even Polybius wrote about Iberia in geographical terms for the understanding of territorial conquest. The major ethnic distributions in this later period were probably linked to earlier spatial configurations of identity.

Similarly, the records of both Livy and Polybius define the power of the Iberian princes of upper Andalusia based on the number of *oppida*. Thus, Culchas is reported to have ruled in 206 BC over 28 *oppida* (Livy XXVIII. 13.3), and Orison, who defeated Hamilcar Barca, governed 12 *oppida* (Diod. XXV. 10.3). These groups of *oppida* must have given rise to new identities of a territorial and political nature which must have differed from earlier forms of definition. Thus, two different identities must have coexisted: one linked to the ancient primary ethnicities which may have remained only as geographical references for newly politically divided regions; the other, new identities, were based on the territory and the social order and were supported by the political relations in and between *oppida*. This differed greatly from the case of the northern Iberians, where the ancient ethnic identities seem to have persisted into the third century BC. Evidence of this is the organization of the armies of Indibil and Mandonius by ethnic units, not by *oppida* (Livy XXIX. I.25, XXVIII. 24.4).

The texts after the Second Punic War gave witness to the rise of major ethnic changes in the history of the Iberians of Andalusia. However, the existence of *Turdetania*, on former Tartessian land, and of *Bastetania* on land that at least partly belonged to the *Mastieni* or *Massieni*, appeared again in the writings of the ancient historians and geographers. In fact, the centre of the *Turdetani* linked to the lower Guadalquivir, and the one of the *Bastuli* linked to the coast remained unchanged points of reference. The position of the *Oretani* was similar, who gave their name to a substantial stretch of land between La Mancha and the upper valley of Guadalquivir. The Oretanian territory in Andalusia mainly matched the forests of the Upper Guadalquivir, probably the *Orospeda* cited by Polybius and Strabo. By contrast, the remaining data about ethnicities associated with Andalusia (*Mentesani*, *Bastetani* and *Turduli*) are less clear and demand further thought. Strabo, Pliny and Ptolemy are the major references here, and we will now briefly consider these three groups, which may have been the only ones relevant to the upper Guadalquivir.

Strabo often mentioned the *Bastetani*. According to him, they occupied the region between present-day Calpe and *Carthago Nova* (III.4.1) and today they are occasionally, and controversially (Ferrer 2001–2), referred to as the same group as the *Bastuli* (III.1.7). Strabo frequently referred to the *Bastetani* and the *Oretani* together (III.4.12). Pliny (III.8, 19) separated the *Bastuli*, on the coast, from *Bastetani*, between present-day eastern

Almería and *Carthago Nova*. The latter group must have been an inner *regio* in *Hispania Citerior* (III.4.19). Pliny also referred to *oppida* 'in the part of *Bastetania* which looks on the sea' (Bastetania che mira al mar; Fig. 3; III.3, 10), that is, in the rural areas known as Campiña de Jaén and Campiña de Córdoba and in the upper valley of Genil. According to this account, the inner part of the territory of the *Bastetani* would have extended over a large territory and would have partly overlapped with the alleged 'eastern *Tartessi*', whom Ptolemy describes as the *Turduli*. The latter source also referred to the *Bastetani* together with the *Oretani*, and mentions up to 15 towns in Pliny's *regio* of *Bastetani* far from the valley of Guadalquivir. Overall, Pliny and Ptolemy's *Bastetania*, in Hispania Taraconense, appeared as a geographical region which may have resulted from a Roman construct based on the over-generalization of the toponym *Basti* for a whole region (González and Adroher 1997). While this may have been so, the grounds for the existence of a Baetic *Bastetania* for Pliny remain unclear.

The *Turduli* were hardly ever mentioned in the textual records. Strabo argued against the separation *Turdetani/Turduli*: for him they were two terms for one and the same group of inhabitants of *Turdetania*. Yet, Strabo pointed out that Polybius himself regarded them as different (III.1.6). Ptolemy (II.4.9) ascribed to the *Turduli* 28 towns and a large territory from Gades to Córdoba, and from there to Iliberis in Granada. Ptolemy's location of the *Turduli* as concerns upper Andalusia was equivalent, at least in part, to Pliny's '*Bastetania* which looks on the sea'. It would also have spread farther north of the valley of Guadalquivir, over present-day Extremadura, precisely where Pliny placed the *Turduli*.

The *Mentesani* were another group associated with the upper Guadalquivir. Pliny located them between the *Oretani* and the *Bastetani* (III.19, 25): 'The first on the coast are the *Bastuli*, then farther inland, and in this order, the *Mentesani*, the *Oretani* and, on the *Tagus*, the *Carpetani*.' This is a most relevant reference, because it described a toponymic distinction between the Mediterranean and the plateau of Castille as approached from the coast. However, this apparently contradicted the one which the same author made on the location of the '*Bastetania* which looks on the sea' (unless the latter was the area inhabited by the *Mentesani*), because *Mentesa Bastia* was in La Guardia de Jaén.

From the above references to *Bastetani*, *Turduli* and *Mentesani* in upper Andalusia, we draw a crucial conclusion for the proper understanding of the ethnic attribution of this geographical space as viewed by the Romans: Ptolemy's *Turduli* of the inland zone, Pliny's *Bastetani* of the valley of Guadalquivir, Pliny's *Mentesani* and perhaps also the *Oretani* and the *Bastetani* occupied regions which at least in part overlapped. Therefore, their records were the result of discrepancies between the sources and the objectives and chronology of these authors.

In this regard, one aspect of the written sources is worth a final comment, namely Augustus' division into *provinciae* and these in turn into *conventus* between 17 and 13 BC, that is a restructuring dating to Caesar's time. This division had a special meaning in the province of Jaén, because the area west of the river Guadalbullón, became ascribed to *Hispania Baetica*, specifically to *Conventos Astigitanus*, while north of the Campiña, the lowland region on the Guadalquivir River known as Vega del Guadalquivir and the *oppidum* Ipolca-Obulco fell within *Conventus Cordubensis*. By contrast, the eastern part of Jaén, east of the axis of the rivers Guarrizas-Guadalbullón, that is, Ptolemy's *Oretani*, *Ossigitania* and a part of the territory of the *Mentesani*, became part of the *Tarraconense* within *Conventus Cartaginense*. This division proves relevant for the Campiña de Jaén, in that the territory traditionally ascribed to *Conventus Astigitanus* became part of Pliny's 'Bastetania which looks on the sea' (Detlensen 1870).

As a result, at least three circumscribed areas can be defined from the written sources. As has been shown, they refer to interpretations of regional units that might subtly date back to ancient ethnicities:

1. The defined area between *Oretania* and the *Bastuli*, lying in what must have been Ptolemy and Pliny's *Bastetania*. As mentioned above, this may have been a late development;

2. The defined area between the *Oretani* and the *Bastuli*, now including the eastern *Turdetani*. This was Pliny's 'Bastetania which looks on the sea', Ptolemy's eastern *Turduli*, or perhaps even Pliny's *Mentesani*. In addition to the references cited, those obtained from the few surviving Iberian inscriptions remaining must be added. Based on the inscriptions found in Ipolca-Obulco and on the coin legends of its mint, de Hoz (1993) concluded that most of them are in southern Iberian but also that they coexist with writing styles which may have been related to the Tartessian-Turdetanian world of Lower Andalusia. Similarly, based on etymology, Correa (1994–6) concluded that some toponyms of Campiña de Jaén, like Urgao, had Tartessian origins;

3. Finally, another defined area would have lain in the present-day Cádiz province shared by the *Turdetani* in the north and the *Bastuli* in the south. These were Strabo and Pliny's *Bastetani* and Ptolemy's southern *Turduli*.

Of these three, only the former two are studied in detail here.

The Oretani – Bastuli boundary

First Stage: the construction of a Frontier with a Distinctive Landmark

In the mid-sixth century BC, a mound was built near the *oppidum* of *Tugia* on a small hill in the heart of the valley of the river Toya. The earliest human activity in the area was the modelling of this small limestone hill. The intervention resulted in an oval-shaped plateau measuring 33 × 22.5 metres with a cylinder-shaped limestone structure on top, a classical drum-shaped mound of 17 metres in diameter and an average height of 2.90 metres. The physical evidence and chemical analysis confirm that the top of the drum must have been covered with an artificial red-coloured layer, so it must have been visible from any point of the valley of the river Toya. The centre of the top part of the mound had two rectangular-shaped stones on top of each other, a mud shelf intended as an *ustrinum*, and a funeral pyre where two individuals were cremated, one male and the other female. An elbow-shaped extension of the rock from the drum, on the western side of the mound, led to a whitewashed chamber excavated inside the mound. The chamber housed a clay bench, and two urns with the remains of the cremated bodies. Some votive glass was found on the bench. A big stone block, a ritual standing stone, was used as a landmark to signal the entrance to the chamber.

This is a representative example of practices implemented in the valley of Guadalquivir from the sixth century BC. Between the late sixth century and the fifth century BC, they gave rise to isolated double burial tombs, always of a paired male and a female, with few or no burials nearby. This period emphasized the mismatch of the space of the dead with the spaces of the living; not only did the princes display their isolation and richness in the burial landscape, but a client social system had developed in the territory, while a settlement model built around *oppida* prevailed and broke down the old village settlement structure. However, it was clear that the burial space had to become compatible with the new social model. The development of hero-based power models, of a client political structure, and of the neighbouring networks of the *oppidum* finally gave the burial landscape its definitive shape. Whereas in the eighth century BC collective mounds of Setefilla in Seville the presence of members of the community in the mound was legitimized by their membership within the village lineage, in the new fourth century BC burial mound sites of Hornos de Peal (Fig. 15.4), the burial space had been privatized by the princes, and their princely lineage was now the integrating element of group identity. The presence of non-princely tombs in the burial space of the burial site required a vow of fidelity towards the aristocrat. Access to the burial sites was grounded in princely kinship but in practice this could

Figure 15.4. The burial mound of Hornos de Peal.

have been gained by becoming the prince's clients. This is confirmed by a significant detail: no tombs of clients were placed under the mound covering the prince's tomb after the late fourth century BC.

At this point, it can be stated, somewhat cautiously, that a new political process was in progress between the early sixth and the late fifth century BC. This process, opposed to the memories which might define the Oretanians as an ancient ethnicity, enhanced tributary models to replace the previously prevailing social relations. This took place at a time when society also opened up wider kinship relations centred on the *oppidum*. The newly created client lineage legitimized the new power structure.

Structurally, the limit of Tugía's territory was marked by the mound, lying in a control point in the valley where the land was exploited and in which the inhabitants lived. To some extent, Tugía was a growing territory where the power brokers tried to integrate scattered villages within the control of the *oppidum*, and thus determined the structure of the sixth century BC political landscape. Kinship relations legitimized the prince's political role. By focussing on relations to neighbours, the fortification of the *oppidum*, and demographic concentration within that space, legitimized the separation between the urban and the rural space. This cultural process was also identified by the location of the tomb, which separated the uncontrolled, wild landscape from the controlled, tamed landscape.

Finally, at the other side of the frontier, the absence of a settlement next to the stretch of land controlled by the *oppidum* characterized the frontier as the limit of a classical buffer zone.

Second stage: the expansion of the oppidum and the Frontier employing a distinctive landmark as an Ensign

After the fourth century BC, this restricted view of landscape was transformed to politicize the local territory. Very early in the fourth century BC, the prince of the *oppidum* of Úbeda la Vieja (*Iltiraka*) had a monument built in honour of a hero in Sierra Mágina, precisely where one of the areas opened on the upper Guadalquivir valley from the Granadan high flat lands (Molinos *et al.* 1998). The monument was built where several smaller watercourses combined to form the river Jandulilla, in a former landscape of lakes set in forests of holm oaks and pine trees which still survived in the nearby mountains of Mágina. By doing this, the prince meant to inscribe his identity on the river meadows. He also meant to control the route used for the incoming Athenian pottery and wine which granted exotic prestige to the Guadalquivir princes and their clients. At the same time, coastal trade of cereals for manufactured items bolstered the interdependence of aristocrats and clients.

The large, traditional monument was faced and defended with fine stonework, redolent of urban imagery (Fig. 15.5). Access to the monument and its internal storage area was through a ceremonial offering area, past a podium and up some stairs. Statues narrating the hero's exploits were placed on top of the tower. The identity of the hero could have been prince or ancestor. Whatever his identity, he fought a wild creature, a wolf, and protected lions and gryphons, and a young man who lay at the feet of the wolf. The youth may have represented a young man whom the hero meant to rescue, or

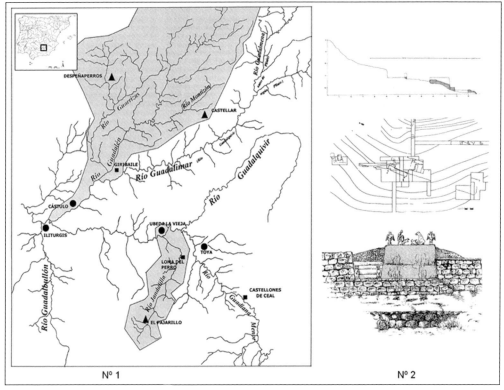

Figure 15.5. Pagi and the landmark frontier of Upper Guadalquivir.

perhaps a simultaneous representation of the hero himself before the ritual of crossing and entering into a territory. This is the Mediterranean myth of the route that has to be cleared in the darkness of the unknown and the wild, the myth of the colonization of mysterious territories. This is also the myth of Theseus and the Minotaur in Crete, of Euthymos and the man who became a wolf in Temesa, and of Heracles' twelfth labour, when he stole the very guardian of Hell's gates, the dog Cerberus, perhaps the best expression of this myth.

The valley of the river Jandulilla, which linked the monument to the *oppidum* of Úbeda la Vieja and was the water source common to both these elements of the built environment, then became the new identifying device of the expanding *oppidum*. This was only natural, since agricultural production often underwrites social order (Carandini 1994). However, the legitimation of territorial definition by the river Jandulilla relied on the discourse of the statues of the hero's sanctuary. This was a new urban discourse unfamiliar in the rural world, implemented within a four-tied political structure:

1. An original *oppidum* where the aristocracy must have achieved a certain degree of consolidation;
2. A well-defined watercourse free of conflict with other settlements;

3. A sanctuary built at the limit of the defined political territory;
4. Finally, new *oppida* colonizing the richest parts of the newly appropriated territory.

From the point of view of demarcation, the sanctuary El Pajarillo provided a Frontier with a Distinctive Landmark just as the mound of Hornos de Peal did for the *oppidum* of *Tugia*. However, the territory defined here was not associated with one *oppidum* alone, it was associated with two. Therefore, although the fortification was retained as a limit to separate the urban from the domestic space, there was also a role for modified nature, dominated by the hero. This was represented by the symbol of the fight between the hero and the wolf. The former limit between the tamed space and the wild space was thus lost. Thus the *oppidum* dominated its territory politically but not in an exploitative manner. A Black Hole remained in the area beyond the sanctuary reaching up to the next inhabited settlement. However, this same area was now penetrated by the network of trade routes which supported the aristocratic political system. Simultaneously multiple tombs replaced single landmark tombs, consequently carrying diminished meaning and relevance.

Third Stage: disappearance of a Frontier with Distinctive Landmarks and the birth of new state-like territorial structures.

The process described for *Iltiraka* was not by followed by other settlements in the area. This confirms our interpretation of the independent policies of the *oppida*. However, expansionist actions could be noticed in some of them early in the fourth century BC. The *oppidum* of *Castulo* was a case in point. At the end of the fourth century BC, this *oppidum* had a more complex regional (*pagus*) developmental model. The formation of a territory subject to this enlarged *oppidum* in the *Oretani* region may have dated back to the early fourth century BC, running in parallel to the development of *Iltiraka*: namely the combination of a sanctuary (Collado de los Jardines), a river (Guarrizas), and a second *oppidum* built in Giribaile. However, at a later stage at the end of the fourth century BC, the territorial organisation spread over the whole basin of the river Guadalén, including the river Guarrizas (Nicolini *et al.* 2004). The new territorial structure of the third century BC explained the new developments at the frontier; the monument with a tower and sculptures at El Pajarillo was replaced by natural habitation caves. The new territorial model legitimized the organizational power of the oppidum beyond its frontier, as shown by new sacred places in honour of deities rather than lineage ancestors. New settlement on the hill of Castellar indicated not only a new control of territory and communication routes, but also a new triangular shape of the territory focused on La Serreta or S. Miquel de Lliria. Sanctuaries became regional meeting points of the *oppida* subject to the power of the princes of *Castulo*.

After this stage, it is the literary sources that help define the process started by *Castulo*. When Culchas or Colicas submitted his army to the command of Scipio in 206 BC, he ruled over 28 settlements (Polybius XI.20). Structurally, Culchas' model consisted of a client-based pyramid spread over the territory, employing natural features to define an approximate frontier. The only clearly defined frontier was embedded in the oppida fortifications emphasised as important by the Second Punic War. Other frontiers were highly unstable.

Patterns to the south were not as clear as those in central *Oretania*. Regional units (*pagi*) were retained as at Hoya de Baza, adjoining *oppida* such as *Basti* or *Tutugi*. Population was not so concentrated in the *oppida* and dispersed settlement tolerated in the fourth and fifth centuries BC. This is the place where literary sources (Pliny and Ptolemy) gave as the location of *Regio Bastetania* of *Hispania Taraconense*. González and Adroher (1997) state, as already mentioned, that this territorial unit may have been a Roman creation. However, a pyramidal (*pagus*) model similar to that developed in *Castulo*, may have been incorporated by the Roman administrative system in a similar case near *Basti*. Thus the prince of *Basti* may previously have extended his power beyond that of complex *pagus* model.

Orospeda and its limits

The common element of this region was a set of small valley units set with a forest framework. This forest framework still exists in the Natural Park of Segura, Cazorla y las Villas at the source of the river Guadalquivir or in Sierra Nevada, in the southern part of the territory, before reaching the territory of the *Bastuli*. This region is clearly the Orospeda repeatedly mentioned by Polybius and Strabo. Orospeda is traditionally restricted to the area bounded by the mountain range of the source of Guadalquivir right up until the end of the Roman Empire at the time of the Visigoth–Byzantine conflict (Salvatierra *et al.* 2006). Strabo's (III.4.10) description was very accurate:

> It spreads from the centre of the coast towards the west, then turns towards the south and towards the coastline starting in the Columns; its first stretches are low and barren, then it extends over the Espartaria plains and meets the inland forest of Carthago Nova and of the regions near Malaca; it is called Orospeda.

> Probably the same author adds later 'Instead, river Betis flows from its source in *Orospeda* through *Oretania* towards Hispania Baetica' (Strabo III.4.12).

According to this account, the limit between the *Oretani* and the *Bastuli* must have been *Orospeda*, that is Sierra Nevada, and its surroundings within present-day Málaga. This would explain Strabo's description of the *Oretani* as dwellers of inland forests, and of the *Bastetani-Bastuli* as dwellers of the coast:

> South of the Celtiberians are the *Sedetani* [probably, *Hedetanoi*], who occupy the mountains of *Orospeda* and the territory near the river Sucro up to *Carthago Nova*, and the *Bastetani* nearly up to *Malaca* (Strabo III.4.14).

The *Oretani* and *Bastuli* are known to us through the Roman geographers as associated with geographical features, not with ethnic territories or, as the archaeological accounts have proved, with Iberian political units and their frontiers.

Between Oretani and Turdetani: the chain frontier of Arroyo Salado de los Villares

From the mid-seventh century BC, the *oppidum* developed as the basic type of settlement, often drawing on the crowded villages of the Late Bronze Age. Nevertheless, a substantial number of smaller settlements were built in the late seventh century BC in the plains near *oppida* like Torreparedones (*Iptuci?*), Montoro (*Epora*), Santa Cecilia or La Aragonesa (Molinos *et al.* 1994; Murillo 1994). Up to 40 sites of this kind have been found near Torreparedones.

By contrast, in Campiña de Jaén in spite of some small villages and the occasional unfortified agrarian settlement, the *oppidum* was the major settlement form. However, early in the sixth century BC, a new type of settlement appeared in the region: the towers of the type recorded in Cerro de la Coronilla de Cazalilla (Ruiz *et al.* 1983). An intervisible, interdependent network of towers spread eastwards from the west bank of Arroyo Salado de los Villares, bordering on populations characterised by the small unfortified agrarian settlements of Vega del Guadalquivir. At the beginning of the sixth century BC, or even earlier, the small settlements of the plains disappeared and some *oppida* were redesigned, as demonstrated by the fortification built in the *oppidum* of

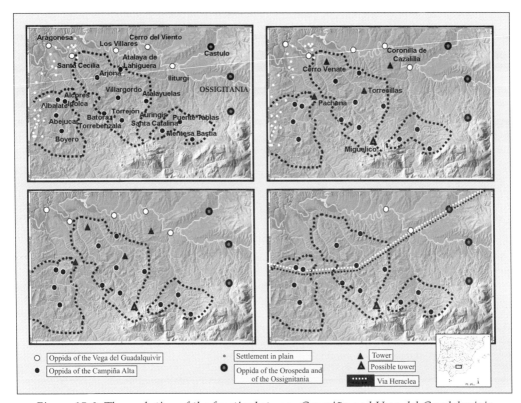

Figure 15.6. The evolution of the frontier between Campiña and Vega del Guadalquivir.

Torreparedones (Fernández and Cunliffe 2002). No settlement modifications took place in Campiña de Jaén at that time, although modifications in the fortified part of the *oppida* have been recorded, as in the *oppidum* of Atalayuelas, where a part of the settlement was abandoned (Castro *et al.* 1990). Approximately at that time or perhaps later, in the first half of the fifth century BC, the towers and at least three *oppida* (La Aragonesa, Santa Cecilia and Los Villares de Andújar) of Vega del Guadalquivir were abandoned simultaneously. At least the first two (La Aragonesa and Santa Cecilia) had previously promoted the foundation of small unfortified agrarian settlements late in the seventh century BC (Molinos *et al.* 1994), but by the end of the fifth century BC, the only remaining type of settlement was the *oppidum*. Population nucleation had been completed.

The contrast in the settlement patterns on the two sides of the Arroyo Salado de Porcuna gave rise some years ago to several interpretations of settlement development in the western and northern plains (Ruiz and Molinos 1989). One solution was that these colonization patterns were directed by the *oppida* or alternatively by even higher central forces, such as by a Tartessian state. A second solution was that these patterns of small sites were implemented by aristocratic families (Ruiz 1995). More recent analysis suggests that a solution regulated from the oppida, as seen around Torreparedones, is more probable (Grau 2007). Additionally, Las Calañas de Marmolejo and its nearby settlements (Molinos *et al.* 1994) show some hierarchical tendencies. However, this does not seem to be fully centralized, since the large-scale study of the territory of Córdoba (Vaquerizo 1999) shows that not all the *oppida* implemented the same action. Whatever the solution, the natural political reaction by the eastern oppida to agrarian colonization was the building of a tower frontier. Since this was a local phenomenon in the Valley of Arroyo Salado de los Villares, the response could not be attributed to a complex *pagus* level regional response by several *oppida*, contrasting to the situation in La Serrata outlined by Grau (2007). The pagus organization here was simpler, comparable to the situation before the development of La Serreta or to *oppida* like Torrebenzala (*Batora*) in the west, Cerro de Villargordo in the centre, Cerro de Torrejón in the south and Cerro de las Atalayuelas in the east.

The erection of towers at Coronilla, Torrecillas, Cerro Venate and Pachena, known from systematic survey (Ruiz *et al.* 1983), must have defined a chain frontier to enclose, at least in the north, the mid-course of Arroyo Salado de los Villares. Two other oppida may have been founded at this point (Arjona (*Urgao Alba*) and Atalaya de Lahiguera).

The evidence of the existence of Arjona in the sixth century BC is not conclusive, and as for Atalaya de Lahiguera, it remains unknown whether it ranked as an *oppidum* under the control of other *oppida*. There is also a core of what may have been an *oppidum* in Cerro Miguelico, Torredelcampo. While it is well-known that it was inhabited in the sixth century BC, it remains unclear, as at Atalaya de Higuera, whether the materials of the early Iberian period date back to a tower or to an *oppidum*. If the former, the chain frontier may then have encircled the whole *pagus*, along with sites like Cerro Largo (Ruiz 1978) or El Espino (Choclan 1990). These two sites have yielded ancient surface materials, although their reoccupation as towers in the late Iberian period makes it difficult to confirm their function in the sixth century BC, as villages or towers.

That is not the only interpretation. It is possible that when the conflict was over, the loss of settlements may have caused the demise of the political project where *pagus* governed the towers and the *oppida*. This hypothesis does not hold up: firstly, because the towers served their function for nearly a century, and also because, when they disappeared, other evidence remains which points to the retention of the *pagus* no matter how invisible they may have become following the loss of the chain frontier. The political articulation of the pagus in the fifth and sixth centuries BC can be argued on the following grounds. Firstly, there is the evidence of the growth of the *oppidum* of Cerro Villargordo to a size of 16 hectares in the late sixth century BC, at the same time as the abandonment of part of the *oppidum* of Las Atalayuelas de Fuerte del Rey (probably the acropolis, Castro *et al.* 1987). This reduction in size of a rival may have favoured the nearby *oppidum* of Villargordo politically and demographically. Secondly, the population of this area was analyzed in 1984 employing the classical techniques of the earliest generation of spatial archaeology. It was concluded that the *oppidum* of Cerro Villargordo, at least in the fourth century BC, may have been the political centre of the valley (Ruiz and Molinos 1984). Thirdly, the site El Berrueco lies very near the *oppidum* of Cerro Villargordo, again in the central part of the valley. Surrounded by fertile land, this site does not match any of the types known elsewhere since it is neither an *oppidum*, nor a tower, nor village. Furthermore, the site is on a crucial junction between routes, a location which may have facilitated its possible development as a sanctuary, a role that in turn may have favoured the development of the political landscape around Cerro Villargordo. This means that the *pagus* of the Valley of Salado de los Villares in the fourth century BC reached the level of complexity and hierarchy of the cases known in the area of La Serreta, Lliria or *Castulo*.

A final step can be integrated with this analysis: the disappearance of the towers of Cazalilla type and of at least three *oppida* in Vega del Guadalquivir sometime in the fifth century BC. This step indicated the end of a conflict which had kept stable the territorial structure of the expanded chain frontier for over a century. The simultaneous loss of the *oppida* and towers cannot have been by chance. The change indicated the end of the tension caused by the colonization of the lower course of Arroyo Salado de los Villares, and the concurrent and reinforcing territorial political strategy of the aristocracies affecting so strongly the later structure of the settlement in the Campiña. A major consequence of this situation was visible in the changed structure of the traditional route along Vega del Guadalquivir. The route had been established in the Bronze Age and was later used for the Via Augustea along the Guadalquivir Valley, but in this period it was demographically disrupted at least until the late third century BC.

One of Strabo's passages in the first century BC may disclose the key elements of the effects of this crisis. His depiction of Via Heraclea is that it:

> leads….. to the regions near Castulo and Obulco, through which the route to Córdoba and Gades, the biggest marketplaces, runs (Strabo III.4.9).

Thus, the route which used to run along the lowlands of Guadalquivir at this time diverted southwards towards Ipolca-Obulco and inevitably cut across the valley of Arroyo Salado de los Villares. Such was the importance of Porcuna for this new course of the main road of the Campiña that Strabo concludes that:

> Before launching the campaign near Munda, Caesar made the journey from Rome to Obulco and its nearby camp in 27 days (Strabo III.4.9).

If we go back to the end of the seventh century BC, when the agrarian colonization reached Arroyo Salado de Porcuna, the centre of Ipolca reacted to the *pagus* of Arroyo Salado de los Villares in a different way (Fig. 15.7). A new burial mound was put in place to provide an additional support to a frontier in the form of a distinctive landmark north of the visual control of the *oppidum* of Los Alcores. The mound stood out in the landscape and must have been a landmark for anyone approaching the *pagus* of Ipolca from the north. It was a collective mound with 24 single burials and a double burial of a more elaborate architectural design, even if without richer burial goods (Torrecillas 1985). It hosted the remains of a male and a female (Roos 1997). 150 years later, the site was remodelled in the mid-fifth century BC, when the crisis mentioned above caused by colonization seemed to be coming to an end following the loss of the *oppida* and towers. The princes of Ipolca, probably having gained awareness of the strategic power which the new state of affairs had endowed them with, had an extraordinary monument built on that site. The monument boasted over 40 stone sculptures (González Navarrete 1987) which depicted the history of a lineage, probably the one of the deceased individuals buried in the mound, and thus legitimized the princes who ruled the *oppidum* (Olmos 2002; Ruiz and Molinos 2007).

Figure 15.7. The sculptures of Cerrillo Blanco. Stages in the history of the lineage.

At this point, an issue raised earlier in respect of the literary sources and the ethnic characterization of upper Andalusia can be revisited. It was previously hypothesized that the spatial distribution of toponyms of Tartessian origin may have suggested that they inhabited Campiña de Jaén in the ancient pre-Iberian and Iberian period. Admittedly, at the turn of the seventh to the sixth century BC this territory may have belonged, ethnically, to the Tartessian area. However, given its position as a geographical limit between the two major ethnicities, it may simply have been the region of the *Oretani* or *Mastieni* heavily easternized by the Tartessian effect, as indicated by Tartessian style painted pottery, Cerro Alcalá (e.g Tartessian-style painted gryphons running counter to traditional motifs; Carrasco *et al.* 1986).

We believe that the two-fold settlement model analysed for the early sixth century BC reveals a series of political responses which is by no means necessarily an identification of two opposed structures with different ethnic origins in a Buffer Zone. This does not discard the fact that the *pagi* of the Campiña and the Vega del Guadalquivir may have belonged to two different ethnic traditions. The Salado de los Villares situation compares well to the *Oretani-Bastuli* situation, namely that the political definition of the frontier after the sixth century BC took varied political forms, simple and complex, comprised of juxtaposed or overlapping *pagi*, rather than simply reflecting ethnicity (Fig. 15.8).

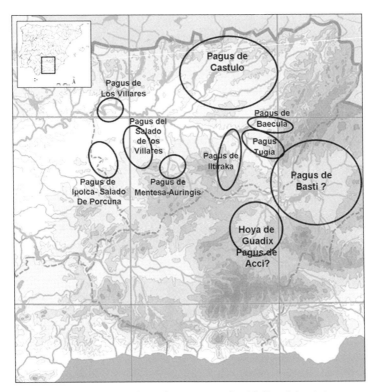

Figure 15.8. Pagi on the upper and mid-Guadalquivir.

The fifth and sixth centuries BC did not involve any major changes in the settlement in the region. If anything, the area of Campiña de Jaén and Campiña de Córdoba up to the river Guadajoz became a highly homogeneous territory as far as material culture, burial customs and settlement customs were concerned, always relying on the *oppida* as the only form of settlement. It is worth noting that no clear burial evidence can be identified in the province of Córdoba in the sixth century BC. However, burial rites gained importance in the fifth and fourth centuries BC probably under the influence of Campiña de Jaén.

It may have been the case that, at the time when Pliny described this territory, he may have known that *Mentesa Bastia*, one of the *oppida* of the *pagus* of Guadalbullón, prevailed over its neighbours in the third century BC. This may have led the geographer to use the term *Mentesani* for all or at least part of Campiña. Such was the case with *Basti* and *Bastetania* and its *pagus*, and may have also been the case with the *Edetania* of Edecon.

In practice, and over time, the ancient ethnic territories evolved into administrative limits. This means that they may have never been prominent in the mind of the communities of each area, but also that they became relegated to a not so focal position. As a matter of fact, Campiña de Córdoba and Vega del Guadalquivir are recorded in Pliny as within *Conventus Cordubensis*, not in the 'Bastetania which looks on the sea'. This is not the contrasting pattern of *oppida* cum unfortified agrarian settlements as against towers cum *oppida*. Torreparedones, a classic case of colonization, lay in Bastetania, whereas Ipolca, which had common interests with the *oppidum* of Villargordo, was included within *Conventos Cordubensis*. It should not be forgotten, in any case, that other authors, like Ptolemy, considered the area a single entity.

Conclusions

1. The frontier with distinctive landmarks was always preferred as the means of marking occupied from the unoccupied space. This is the norm with the oppida over long periods of time.
2. In some exceptional cases, and where a Buffer Zone existed, a more rigid frontier, such as a chain frontier came into being. Examples include the *pagus* of Arroyo Salado de los Villares, although probably only during its conflict with the oppida on the lowlands of Guadalquivir.
3. There is a tendency to modify rather than transform nature in the political territories of oppida. Examples include the *oppida* of Vega del Guadalquivir, and the Oretanian *pagi* of *Iltiraka* and *Castulo*. This tendency may have been influenced by exchange networks, especially in the Oretanian case. Sacred boundaries may have played a role in the case of *Orospeda* but not in the case of Arroyo de los Villares.
4. Even if alternative political territorial entities replaced ethnic entities, the memory of ethnic identity may not have been totally removed. By analogy, the *pagus*, a village concept, continued to be used for the articulation of the political territory of the *oppida*, the lineage continued to be embedded in the mode of life and the political definition of new identities, fortification continued to be points of reference, and landmarks continued to be employed for legitimation.

5. Cultural boundaries did not necessarily coincide with political frontiers, perhaps harking back to ancient ethnic traditions. This effect can be seen in burial rites, for instance.

6. By the time of the Iron Age, ethnicity was in crisis and did not necessarily correspond to the active political organization of a given region. Ethnicities may have had a geographical origin, but by the time of Strabo there was not a clear correspondence. Nevertheless, Strabo still refers to the river as the land of the *Turdetani*, the coast as the land of the *Bastuli* and the mountain as the land of the *Oretani*.

7. The issue is complex. The differences between large ethnico-geographical units became blurred and aristocratic lineages fostered new collective identities. Urban territorial units also formed new identities. Examples include the *Mentesani* in western *Bastetania*, or of eastern *Bastetania* (*Bastitania* in Ptolemy, probably related to the town of *Basti*).

8. The Roman administrative structure did not ignore the indigenous political and cultural memory but it did also impose the interests of a strong and consolidated state.

Landscape and ethnic identities in the early states of eastern Iberia

Ignacio Grau Mira

Keywords: Iberian Iron Age; ethnic identity; Contestani; Edetani; eastern Iberian Peninsula

The ancient texts which refer to eastern Iberia are very scarce and ambiguous. They provide partial information about the geographical location of ancient peoples and regions without explicit references to the characteristics of their customs, culture or social structure. Despite this, archaeologists working in the eastern Iberian peninsula have used the names given in the ancient texts, *Contestani* and *Edetani*, to refer to the Iron Age populations that inhabited the area. Traditionally, scholars use these ethnic names as a convenient label to establish the chronological and geographical coordinates of their historical analysis. However, this nomenclature implies certain assumptions about cultural features that allow various Iberian communities to be clustered together as ethnic groups and some researchers have tried to base their distinctive elements on the archaeological record.

This theoretical position is based on the evidence that it is possible to recognize the particularities of different Iberian peoples in various regions. This mosaic of Iberian cultures contrasts with the theories found in the historiography of the first half of the twentieth century, strictly conditioned by the restrictive political context of that period which claimed the existence of a unified Iberian culture. Current research focuses on analyzing the particular characteristics of the Iberians' material culture, settlement patterns and social organization and has contributed to extending the archaeological differentiation of regional cultures within the Iberian Iron Age. The problem lies in trying to relate the differences in the archaeological record directly with distinctive ethnic groups that inhabited the region.

In our study region, this approach has been largely influenced by the seminal work of E. Llobregat (1972) entitled *Contestania Ibérica*. This brilliant synthesis of the Iron Age archaeology of what is now the southern part of the Valencian region inaugurated the tendency to study the Iberians in their regional particularities. Moreover, it was the reverse of creating the concept of a unified Iberian region, inhabited by one ancient ethnic entity. Llobregat was very cautious in claiming a direct relationship and cited the difficulties of directly superimposing an ancient region mentioned in the Roman texts on a pre-existing ethnic identity and the possibilities of establishing different groups within the region (Llobregat 1972: 10–6).

In the first section of this paper we will look at the difficulties of the traditional approach, encountering two different groups of problems: the first one derived from reading the ancient writers and the second from the relationship between the archaeological record and ancient regions from a cultural-historical point of view. In addition, we consider the political landscapes suggested by current archaeological research and the cultural elements of these ethnic landscapes.

The traditional approach to ethnicity in eastern Iberia

Some years ago L. Abad (1992) synthesized the information provided by the classical texts referring to Iberian peoples in the study area. A. Ruiz and M. Molinos have also analysed some of the important aspects of the written sources in their general synthesis *The Iberians* (Ruiz and Molinos 1993), with particular reference to the chronological differences and the historic development that can be deduced from the variations between the peoples referenced (Ruiz and Molinos 1993: 248–68). More recently P. Moret (2004) has put forward some thoughtful comments and suggested important modifications to this interpretation. We follow these recent studies as main sources for our analysis.

The texts referring to eastern Iberia can be divided into two major groups on the basis of their chronology. The older group is based on the descriptions by Hecateus and Avienus, which describe the peoples that occupied the region in the sixth and fifth centuries BC (Abad 1992: 155–62). Their approach was that of a geographical tour, and they gave the generic names of peoples artificially grouped together (Moret 2004). The second group of texts dates to the Early Roman Empire, mainly first century AD (Abad 1992: 155–62). Between these two periods, we have a third group of texts by Polybius that referred to events that occurred in the late third century BC. They took place during Rome's first contact with the region, in the context of the Second Punic War, but little attention was given to geographical and ethnographic matters, and the existing populations were over-simplified (Moret 2004). Thus there are three different groups of texts with different ethnographic approaches relating to three different periods (Moret 2004). We must keep these differences in mind when considering their references to ethnic groups.

The oldest sources refer to three major ethnic groups in eastern Iberia (Fig. 16.1.1). The *Gymnetes* inhabited the southern part of the region studied, with the *Mastieni* to the south, and occupied an area between the rivers Segura and Júcar. The area north of the Júcar, which is referred to as the *Sicani* river in the texts, in what is now the central zone of the Valencia Region, was inhabited by a people also called the *Sicani*. Further north, the situation was more confusing; the text refers to the *Esdetes* and the *Ilaragautes,* but does not say exactly which area they inhabited (Abad 1992: 155). Perhaps we should assume they were to be found in the northern and central area of the Valencian Region (Ruiz and Molinos 1993: 250, fig. 84).

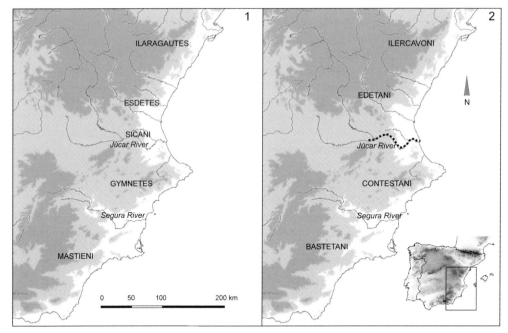

Figure 16.1. Iberian peoples of the study area: (1) peoples quoted in the texts dated in sixth–fifth century BC*; (2) peoples quoted in the texts dated in second–first century* BC.

A. Ruiz and M. Molinos have suggested the possible existence of a hierarchy within these ethnic groups. They propose that there were three major ethnic groups, *Iberians*, *Mastieni* and *Tartessians,* which would have included smaller ethnic subgroups. In the area studied, there would have been a generic ethnic group of *Iberians* made up of the *Sicani, Esdetes* and *Ilaragautes,* while the *Gymnetes* would have been included in the generic group of *Mastieni* (Ruiz and Molinos 1993: 251).

The second group of sources illustrates the geographical situation of the peoples during the Early Roman Empire five centuries later (Fig. 16.1.2). On this occasion we find the *Bastetani* have replaced the *Mastieni* in the southern part of the region. *Contestania* is located in the area previously occupied by the *Gymnetes*. *Edetania* is north of the river Júcar, called *Sucro* in these texts, and extended through the area previously occupied by the *Sicani* in the south and *Esdetes* in the north. *Ilercavonia* extended through the area previously occupied by the *Ilaragautes* (Abad 1992: 156–9, fig. 1; Ruiz and Molinos 1993, 263–5, fig. 85). The similarities of the regions occupied and the homophony of the ethnic names suggests that the distribution of peoples referred to in the first group of texts was the same as that of those referred to later. The ethnic groups mentioned in the Roman texts evolved from those pre-existing peoples. Thus in eastern Iberia, the *Gymnetes* would have been the forerunners of the *Contestani* and the *Esdetes* of the *Edetani* (Abad 1992: 162).

We should maintain a degree of scepticism towards the reading of ancient texts. On one hand, the sources gave no criterion for distinguishing these peoples and identifying them as separate ethnic groups; and on the other, a period of five centuries separated the two mentioned communities, and it is difficult to imagine that their territorial and ethnic basis would have remained unchanged in any way throughout that time. Ruiz and Molinos considered changes in ethnic names to be evidence of the reorganization of Iberian structures. The implicit change in references to ethnic groups is evidence of the political, economic, social and cultural changes that occurred in the third century BC (Ruiz and Molinos 1993: 248).

An interpretation based on the ancient texts suggests either that human groups occupied extensive and unchanging territories, following the static interpretation of Abad, or that their ethnic character changed, according to the evolutionary approach adopted by Ruiz and Molinos. In contrast to these interpretations, P. Moret (2004) warns of the danger of using these literary references for historical and archaeological analysis. This scholar notes the heterogeneous nature of these texts, which were written over a long period for different purposes and adopted different ethnographic approaches. As we have said, the earliest references were related to generic names without cultural or political associations, while those in the second group are associated with geographic regions based on administrative Roman structures.

In addition to a cautious and critical reading of the ancient literary sources, the use of the archaeological record to distinguish the ethnic groups of the region has been a recurring line of research. The scientific literature on the area contains studies that attempt to link the particularities of the material culture to the *Contestani* and the *Edetani* using the normative basis of the culture-historical theoretical perspective. This research sees archaeological elements as material expressions of the cultural norms of ancient peoples. According to this approach, elements of recurring assemblages should be found in the territory attributed to the ethnic groups by literary sources. There are three main archaeological elements used traditionally to define the boundaries (e.g. Ruiz and Molinos this volume) of the areas inhabited by ethnic groups: 1) funerary stone monuments, evidence of the funerary traditions; 2) epigraphic evidence, relating to linguistic uses; and 3) figured ceramic style, prestige items clearly used in elite ceremonies.

Funerary stone monuments.

Religious funerary practices are a key element associated with the social and ideological character of ethnic groups. For this reason, some researchers have looked at funerary elements of the archaeological record to discover ethnic distinctions. Hence various scholars have examined the use of Iberian funerary monuments clearly clustered in the south-east of the Iberian peninsula, south of the river Júcar. They make a clear distinction between *Contestania*, with monuments, and *Edetania*, without them. However, stone funerary monuments are not restricted to *Contestania*, and there are clear intrusions north of this region. In addition, sculptures are used as much in the northern part of *Contestania* as in central *Edetania* (Almagro-Gorbea 2001: fig. 1; Chapa 1985: fig. 16; Izquierdo Peraile 2000: fig. 206). In short, the distribution of these sculptural and architectonic elements (Fig. 16.2) illustrates the selective use of Iberian funerary monuments amongst the peoples living in much of the south of the Iberian peninsula, but not the northern areas where they rarely appear. However it is not, in our opinion, possible to assign this element to particular ethnic groups.

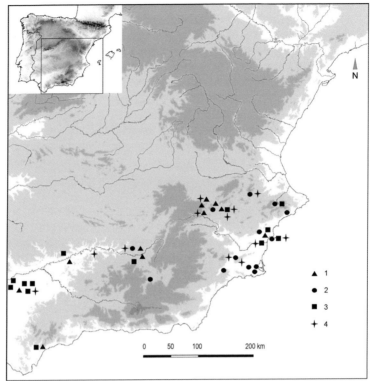

Figure 16.2. Map showing the distribution of the different elements pertaining to funerary monuments: (1) zoomorphic corner stones; (2) mouldings; (3) friezes; (4) other elements (elaboration following Almagro Gorbea 2001: fig. 1).

Iberian writing and the epigraphic evidences

The information relating to epigraphic uses shows clustering that is similar to that of the monumental funerary remains. Very intensive epigraphic uses have been recorded in *Contestania* (Fig. 16.3), evidenced by the use of the three alphabets found in the Iberian area: Meridian, Levantine and Greek-Iberian. The Júcar River once again acted as a boundary, this time to the southern alphabet, although it is found in some places north of the river. The Levantine alphabet appeared both in *Contestania* and *Edetania*, north and south of the Júcar River. More interesting is the use of Greek-Iberian alphabet, which was specifically associated with *Contestania*. Linguistic research has shown that the Greek-Iberian alphabet was created to write the Iberian language using a script adopted after a long period of contact with traders of Greek origin (de Hoz 2001). The distribution of inscriptions in the Greek-Iberian alphabet clearly demonstrates the use of this alphabet in *Contestania*: it was found almost exclusively in this region and only a dubious lead inscription has been found in *Edetania*, in Sagunt. However, its distribution shows it was used in specific areas of the region and its absence from the lower Vinalopó Valley, traditionally interpreted as the heart of *Contestania*, is notable.

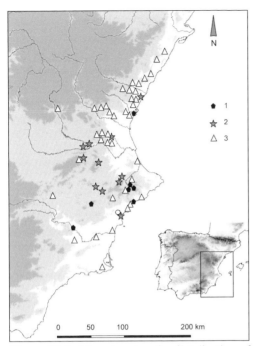

Figure 16.3. Map showing the distribution of epigraphic evidences (Based on work of de Hoz 2001: fig. 1)

With regard to epigraphic customs, sheets of lead were used almost exclusively for inscriptions in *Contestania*, while in *Edetania* words were frequently painted on Iberian ceramics. But this distribution was by no means rigid, and painted letters were found in the Contestanian town of la Alcudia de Elche, and lead sheets have been found in *Edetania*. In sum, once again it is difficult to assign clear differences between *Edetania* and *Contestania*.

Figured ceramic styles

Figurative painting on pottery was one of the most conspicuous elements in the archaeological record of the eastern Iberians during the Hellenistic period, between the third and first centuries BC. This decoration depicts various scenes consisting of plant motifs, and human and animal figures that convey ideological messages of a religious or ideological nature. Early research on figured ceramics in the 1950s defined two main groups or styles on the basis of the thematic, stylistic and compositional elements of this art form. The first one was the Oliva-Llíria or narrative style, characterized by depicting the Iberian aristocracies in their status activities. The Elche-Archena, or symbolic style, represents divinities or scenes of a religious nature (Aranegui *et al.* 1996).

Traditionally, these figured styles have been the key element for identifying the ethnic groups referred to in the ancient literary sources (Abad 1992; Llobregat 1972; Moratalla 2005; Tortosa 2006). The narrative style was attributed to the *Edetani* and the symbolic figured style to the *Contestani*. Nevertheless, this division ignores the fact that two of the Iberian towns that had yielded good examples of narrative figured ceramics, El Castellar de Oliva and La Serreta of Alcoi, were in *Contestania* (Fig. 16.4). Furthermore, today good examples of *Edetania's* symbolic style are known, suggesting that concordance between ethnicity and pottery styles is not rigid.

Current investigations carried out on these ceramic styles have demonstrated that assigning the traditional general categories of Oliva-Llíria/Narrative and Elche-Archena/ Symbolic to particular ethnic groups is invalid. Today we can recognize different schools and artistic workshops, although they may have formed part of the two major traditions cited. Different pottery workshops show that the distribution of these artefacts is more complex. In the following pages we will examine the context in which this decorated pottery was produced and used in order to relate it to the identity ascribed to it, but here we would just point out that its use for defining ethnic groups is problematic.

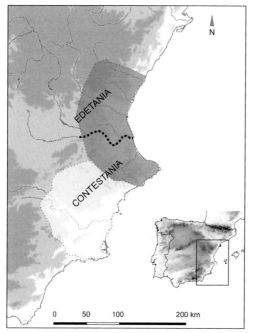

Figure 16.4. Traditional distribution of Oliva-Lliria (grey) and Elche-Archena (white) in the regions of Edetania and Contestania.

In conclusion, the use of archaeological elements for trying to define ancient regions encounters two obstacles that are difficult to resolve. The first is general and methodological, and is related to the direct correspondence of archaeological elements with an ancient people. As other scholars have suggested, spatial variations in the archaeological record can be due to a variety of reasons, such as specialization, group size, exchange, etc. as a result of which a great variety of overlapping patterns can be found (Shennan 1989: 11–4). Current research accepts that it is not possible to identify ethnic groups through the simple distribution of archaeological elements. This approach allows cultural groups to be identified, but these may or may not coincide with ethnic boundaries (Bradley 2000: 115).

The second problem is specific to the area studied and is related to the vague definition of the peoples that we are trying to establish. We refer to the Iberian regions defined by the Roman texts in a geographical and administrative sense, not as ethnic groups strictly speaking. On the other hand, it could be asserted that the Romans created these regions on the basis of local divisions, but we do not know which ones they used. We need to approach the problem from different theoretical perspectives.

Ethnic groups and political landscapes

The relationship between ethnic identity and political structure constitutes a second theme different to the culture-historical studies. Some scholars have pointed out that the sense of identity among the members of the social group could be the result of an active process of constructing their own identity as a people in order to distinguish themselves from others (Jones 1997: xiii). The creation of a shared identity could be a strong force for cohesion in the context of increasing hierarchical power in the relationship between individuals and groups within the society (Herring 2000: 46). In this respect, the creation of identity plays an important role in the political context of the emerging early states.

According to this theoretical position, this paper concentrates on the political dimension of ethnicity. Thus, in our opinion, it is possible to establish the basis for the active creation of identities in the process of the political construction of the Iberian early states. In order to understand the spatial order that underlies the territorial structure of the Iberians' lands, we examine the political landscape revealed by archaeological research. Secondly, we look at some of the cultural elements used to reinforce ethnic identity in the context of recognized polities.

Studies of settlement patterns and territorial structure of the region offer a satisfactory picture of the political evolution of the landscape in the various parts of this extensive region (Fig. 16.5). In this section, we summarize the main trends in the development of the political landscape in eastern Iberia from north to south.

The first political territory is that structured around the *oppidum* of *Arse-Saguntum,* on the north coast of the region studied (Fig. 16.5.1). It is possible to trace the process by which the territory around this *oppidum* was established from the Early Iberian period – the sixth–fifth centuries BC – and it was clearly defined by the Classical Iberian period,

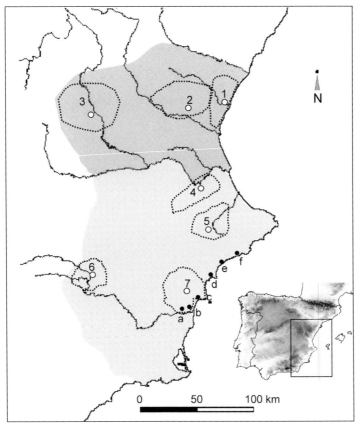

Figure 16.5. Political landscapes in Edetania (dark shadow) and Contestania (light shadow): (1) Arse-Sagunto and its territory; (2) Edeta-Liria and its territory; (3) Kelin-Los Villares and its territory; (4) Saiti-Játiva and its territory; (5) La Serreta and its territory; (6) Ilunum-El Tolmo de Minateda and its territory; (7) Ilici-La Alcudia de Elche and its territory. Black dots are coastal sites: (a) La Escuera; (b) El Oral; (c) La Picola; (d) El Tossal de les Basses; (e) La Illeta del Campello; (f) Villajoyosa.

during the fourth–third centuries BC. The urban centre was located on the impressive hilltop of El Castell de Sagunt, two kilometres from the coast. Here the town had a commanding position over the coastal territory along the Mediterranean. This town was a prosperous community based on maritime interregional trade and had harbour installations on the shore (Aranegui 2004). A secondary urban settlement, several villages, farmsteads and pottery workshops dedicated to manufacturing amphorae for the export of agrarian products were located in the hinterland. Strategic fortresses to protect the territory were built on the ridges of the hinterland (Martí Bonafé 1998).

Neighbouring the territory of *Arse-Saguntum* is the territory of the Iberian town of *Edeta*, in the valley of the river Turia (Fig. 16.5.2). This *oppidum* was located on a hilltop called El Tossal de Sant Miquel in Llíria and was the central place of the territory from the Early Iron Age. During the classical Iberian period it consolidated its commanding position and controlled a dense population settled in agricultural villages and farmsteads. The territory was controlled and defended by a complex system of strategic forts that were in visual contact with each other. The arrival of the Romans, in the early second century BC, destroyed the territory's capital and the settlement system organised around it. *Edeta's* territory is a typical example of the complex structure of an eastern Iberian state-like polity (Bernabeu *et al.* 1987; Bonet 1995, 2001).

What is now the region of Requena-Utiel, in the interior of Valencia Province, was organized during Iberian Period around the *oppidum* of *Kelin* in Caudete de las Fuentes (Fig. 16.5.3). This site had a long sequence of occupation extending from the Final Bronze Age to the first century BC which was at its height during the Classical and Late Iberian periods. *Kelin* was a large urban centre, covering ten hectares, which controlled an extensive area of around 2500 square kilometres. Secondary urban sites and agricultural settlements of varying size occupied this large territory under the control of *Kelin* (Mata *et al.* 2001). The latter was on the periphery of the Iberian area adjoining the Celtiberian region to the west.

Further south was the territory of the Iberian town of *Saiti*, in the valley of the river Canyoles (Fig. 16.5.4). During the Classical period this area was organized around several *oppida* that controlled their surrounding territories, where subordinate rural sites were located. Significant changes in the landscape can be detected at the end of the fourth century BC when an important *oppidum* in the west of the territory, La Bastida de les Alcuses, was destroyed, possibly coinciding with the emergence of the Iberian town of *Saiti* (Pérez Ballester and Borreda 1998). This Iberian town was one of the most important settlements of the region and was notable for its size, covering an area of eight hectares, the minting of silver coins during the late third century BC and the fact that it was mentioned in the ancient texts.

The valleys of Alcoi displayed a similar trend in the way the landscape was organized (Fig. 16.5.5). We found the territory structured in a series of medium-sized *oppida* from the early Iberian Iron Age onwards. These *oppida* constituted a mosaic of small territories occupied by several villages and farmsteads. During the third century BC one of the *oppida*, La Serreta of Alcoi, increased in size and functions and became the Iberian town that dominated the valley. It occupied an area of six hectares and had some important features such as a considerable number of Iberian inscriptions and a territorial religious centre that emphasized its central role in organizing the territory. The Roman conquest destroyed the town and its political landscape (Grau Mira 2002, 2003).

The Vinalopó Valley in the southeastern part of the Valencian region was the territory of the Iberian *Ilici* (Fig. 16.5.6). It was one of the most important Iberian towns and the place where the famous sculpture known as the Lady of Elche was discovered. *Ilici* was the capital of an extensive territory covering around 1500 square kilometres occupied by secondary *oppida* and rural villages. Important collections of Iberian sculptures, figured pottery and other notable elements from the archaeological record reveal the importance of this Iberian town (Santos Velasco 1992; Moratalla 2005). Despite these impressive finds, little is known about its chronological sequence and urban layout because the rebuilding that took place during Early and Late Roman periods destroyed the earlier site.

The Iberian town of El Tolmo de Minateda, possibly the ancient town of *Ilunum* (Fig. 16.5.7) is located in the region of Hellín, further inland in the province of Albacete. This *oppidum* guarded the important routes between the inland Meseta and the southeastern coast; in addition we found some villages with economic and strategic functions (López Precioso *et al.* 1993, Sanz Gamo 1997).

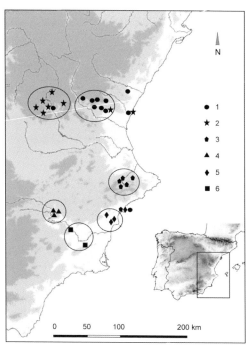

Figure 16.6. Map showing the distribution of the ceramic styles: (1) style of Edeta; (2) impressed pottery of the territory of Kelin; (3) style of La Serreta; (4) style of Ilunum-El Tolmo; (5) style of Ilici; (6) style of the territory of Murcia.

A different territorial process can be identified on the Mediterranean coast south of the study area, where there were a number of important trading settlements, with harbours and industrial installations. The coastal sites were organised around their trading relationships with Phoenician, Greek and Punic merchants, as the large number of imported amphorae, vessels and other material record revealed. The economic, social and cultural characteristics of these *oppida* produced a different type of political landscape, and capital towns that governed extensive territories were not found. Some of these trading settlements would have belonged to the territories mentioned, such as La Escuera (Fig. 16.5a), El Oral (Fig. 16.5b) or La Picola (Fig. 16.5c), which were ports of *Ilici* (Abad *et al.* 2001). Others, such as El Tossal de les Basses (Fig. 16.5d), La Illeta del Campello (Fig. 16.5e) or La Vila Joiosa (Fig. 16.5f) were possibly independent towns.

In short, the research has detected similar dynamics in the emergence of hierarchical settlement patterns. A series of *oppida* acquired remarkable importance;

these were generally fortified and built in prominent locations that facilitated visual control over the surrounding countryside and nearby subordinate rural sites. The emergence of this pattern is clearly linked to the dynamics of centralization and urbanization, which developed – at their own rate and in different ways – throughout much of the Mediterranean basin during the Iron Age (Ruiz 2000). In some regions a prevalent *oppidum* was the central place of the region since the Early Iberian Iron Age while in other regions there was a mosaic of small territories controlled by several *oppida* until finally one of these imposed its power over the others.

In sum, the urban centres and political landscapes developed at different rates but tended to converge by the late third century BC, on the eve of the Roman conquest, when the urban landscape was predominant in the entire region. At this moment the polities controlled geographical regions, generally valleys, of similar size: about 1000–1500 square kilometres. Some of these territories were formed by the aggregation of existing local communities and needed strategies to reinforce the new society. The process is related to the creation of 'imaginary communities' in the sense used by B. Anderson (1991) and M. Dietler for Iron Age societies: a political construction that requires the creation of emotionally charged traditions of identity using evocative symbols to invoke authenticity (Dietler 1996: 64).

Figure 16.7. The Vase of the Warriors (above), example of figured vase of the Style of La Serreta and (below) development of their decoration (image courtesy of the Archaeological Museum of Alcoi). Dimensions: 66cms. height and 59cms. maximum diameter.

In my opinion, the political configuration of eastern Iberia in small regions was accompanied by the creation of ethnic identities in order to reinforce the social link between local communities. Disappointingly, nothing was written about the matter in the classical texts, which are dated, as has been said, to the first century AD, centuries after the arrival of the Romans destroyed some of these polities. However, several types of archaeological evidence that were contemporary with the Classical Iberian states can be interpreted as cultural elements used as identity symbols.

Cultural symbols and the process of actively creating an ethnic identity

Recent studies on ethnicity have suggested that the political projects would have been sanctioned by mechanisms that emphasized a feeling of belonging to a people with its own sense of identity that differentiated itself from its neighbours (Jones 1997: xiii). Important factors in the definition of this ethnic identity are the perception of having a common history, mythology, cultures and system of beliefs (Lomas 1997: 2). On the basis of these hypotheses, reference could be made to two different types of cultural evidence as strong elements that would have achieved and maintained the feeling of ethnic identity among eastern Iberians: ceramic styles and the sacred places within the urban centres.

Ceramic figured styles

In ancient societies, the production and use of material culture is accepted by scholars as a practice connected with an ethnic group's signs of identity (Herring and Lomas 2000: 4). In this way, a detectable archaeological element with a defining style such as pottery helps us to interpret the processes of socio-political integration. The style is defined as a private and characteristic way of doing something in a specific time and place, following some shared rules and intended for a specific purpose. These characteristics would permit a group to have been clearly differentiated in the material record and its members identified. In addition, the group style is a form of non-verbal language that conveys recurrent messages about territoriality and ethnicity (Sackett 1977). These qualities would facilitate the standardization of certain messages and would permit communication without the giver and the receiver having to be present at the same time. This message has the advantage that once produced it does not need new investments of energy and permits a potential radius of receivers to be defined (Wobst 1977). In this way, pottery and other artefacts become elements that support identity codes in a particular territory. In the area studied we found the appearance and development of styles of figured pottery dating to the period when the urban landscapes were created.

Current research on figure-decorated pottery has transformed the traditional view of the two styles developed throughout extensive regions. The narrative-figured style and the symbolic-figured style fragmented into different local styles and production centres (Fig. 16.6). Detailed scrutiny of this figured pottery enables differences in the techniques, themes and shapes of vessels to be observed within broader styles. These artistic creations shared similar codes with autonomous creations produced in local workshops that display identity elements. Among the artistic groups, we should mention two workshops in *Edeta* (Aranegui *et al.* 1997; Bonet 1995; Pérez and Mata 1998), one workshop in La Serreta of Alcoi (Grau Mira 1998–9), another artistic centre located in El Tolmo of Minateda in Hellín (Abad and Sanz 1995), two different styles in the Iberian town of *Ilici* and another artistic school developed in Murcia (Tortosa 2006). Although it is not exactly figured pottery, we should include the printed pottery characteristic of the territory of *Kelin*. This geographical distribution is clearly linked to the process of creating Iberian urban landscapes. The process of merging local communities to create large political territories coincides in place and time with the emergence of figured pottery. Of course, it did not appear overnight, and some gradual development can be observed. The first styles appeared in *Edeta* and La Serreta in the third century BC and others were developed from the second and first centuries BC to the second century AD. Nevertheless, in every case they are clearly linked to the process of urban consolidation and definition of political communities.

These figured ceramics had a restricted circulation and have been discovered mainly in the capital and the principal sites of the territory inhabited by the elites (Aranegui *et al.* 1997). The themes depicted and their appearance in domestic shrines shows that they were used in ritual contexts and the ideological representation of the elites. These rituals could have reinforced the sense of relationship between elites of different *oppida* in the same territory or the patron-client links between individuals of different status.

The iconography, images, and visual language contributed to aggregation and the creation of a sense of community through a shared mythology and system of beliefs. Some of the most noticeable examples show complex narrations of legendary histories. One example recently studied is the so-called Vase of the Warriors of La Serreta of Alcoi (Fig. 16.7). This vase shows the narration in three episodes of the initiation of the young aristocrat (Olmos and Grau 2005). The history of the Iberian heroes and other mythological narrations were transmitted through these depictions.

The territorial sanctuaries

The second key element was the redefinition of sacred places in order to reinforce the configuration of political landscapes. From the Early Iberian period onwards, religious activities and the sacred organization of space played an important role in the socio-political development of the Iberians. Iberian sacred places varied greatly in their nature, characteristics and location (Almagro-Gorbea and Moneo 2000; Moneo 2003). Some of these sacred places were located inside the *oppida* and are interpreted by scholars as either urban public places or lineage cult shrines linked to elite houses. These urban cults reinforced the urbanization process by assigning sacred meanings to certain residential places.

During the process of configuration of the urban landscape in the third century BC the emergence or reinforcement of territorial sanctuaries, linked to the redefinition of ethnic groups, can be identified. This process has been defined in relation to the Iberian territories of the Guadalquivir Valley (Ruiz and Molinos 1993: 247–9; Ruiz *et al.* 2001) and in my opinion this approach can be extended to eastern Iberia. According to this model, some sacred places were territorial in character in order to sanction the new spatial order with ritual. The strong correlation between the emerging towns and the appearance or intensification of activity in territorial sanctuaries is evident.

The most noticeable case of the relationship between urbanization and creation of sacred space is in the territory of La Serreta of Alcoi. During the late third century BC, when it was the capital of the valley of Alcoi, an active territorial sanctuary that met the religious needs of the populations of the entire territory was built at the top of the town. The inhabitants of the valley of Alcoi came to this sanctuary to deposit small terracotta figurines devoted to the Iberian fertility goddess (Juan Moltó 1988–9; Olcina *et al.* 1998). The sanctuary, located in the upper quarter of the Iberian town, was highly visible from the surroundings. This visual prominence strengthened the links between the Iberian town and the political landscape under its control (Fig. 16.8).

An urban temple has been identified in the aristocratic quarter of Iberian *Edeta* (Bonet 1995). This sacred place had different rooms devoted to ceremonies of elite aggregation and a votive chamber with an important collection of ritual figured vases. The aristocratic lineages reinforced their ties through religious practices. The location of this religious centre in *Edeta* highlighted the importance of the town in the religious environment. The Iberian temple in the middle of *Ilici,* consisting of a quadrangular precinct with a votive well, could be interpreted in the same way.

Figure 16.8. View of the Iberian sanctuary of La Serreta of Alcoi from the south-west (image courtesy of the Archaeological Museum of Alcoi).

These examples can be seen as paralles in the context of the configuration of the sacred landscape by the ideological assignation of certain places. The predominant spatial feature is the emphasis on the urban element and capital of the territory. The model described reflects a well-known pattern, with obvious variations, that provides ideological reinforcement for urban political projects in the Ancient Mediterranean. The Minoan peak-sanctuaries that act as identity symbols for the community are good example of dynamics of this kind (Peatfield 1990). A similar trend is illustrated by the location of sanctuaries dedicated to Demeter in Greece. An evolution from their initial location on the urban periphery towards the city centre can be seen, emphasizing the centrality of the sacred landscape and reinforcing the bonds of the city within the territory (Guettel 1994: 214–5).

In my opinion, the manipulation of the ritual for political ends uses two different mechanisms in the process of aggregation. First, the concentration of religious practices in the centre of the community endowed capitals with new functions as a public place. People living in other *oppida* or villages had a point of reference in their everyday landscapes. Secondly, sharing the same religious practices and using the same material symbols created strong links of shared traditions between the new communities created by the unification of pre-existing local groups.

Cultural and political identities

In recent decades archaeological research has revealed remarkable differences between the Iron Age populations of eastern Iberia. It is important to describe, albeit briefly, the way Iberian studies have developed in order to understand the current position of the research.

The historiography of the first half of the twentieth century developed theories of the existence of a unified Iberian culture based on the political constraints of that period and the nature of the data available at the time. Discussion mainly concerned the attribution of key influences, Continental or Mediterranean, in the emergence and configuration of the Iberian culture.

From the late 1960s onwards the particularities of different Iberian peoples could be recognized in various regions by using references from ancient texts. In that period, research focused on analysing the particular features of material culture in order to determine the regional characteristics of the Iberian cultures. As a result, the idea of different ancient Iberian regions such as Iberian *Contestania* became well established (Llobregat 1972).

Also in the late sixties and early seventies, new trends affected Iberian research and the emphasis changed from the predominant culture-historical theoretical approach to an economic and political analysis of the Iberians. The new approach resulted in surveys and studies of the Iberians' settlement patterns and territorial organization. This orientation has contributed to increased archaeological differentiation of regional patterns within the Iberian Iron Age. In this respect it is possible to observe differences in the material culture and in historical developments within similar socio-political processes (Ruiz and Molinos 1993).

The fragmentation of a unified Iberian culture has resulted in the appearance of two different approaches: one based on the particularities of the material culture, and the other on an analysis of the landscape. The first proposes that Iberia was structured into extensive ancient regions that coincided with the references in the Classical texts; the second suggests that settlements were clustered, usually in valleys, and belonged to early states presided over by urban centres. In northeastern Iberia, now Catalonia, a coincidence can be observed between the ethnic regions of the classical texts and the polities identified by landscape archaeology (Sanmartí and Belarte 2001). However, neither in eastern nor southern Iberia do we observe a correspondence between the ancient regions and the polities identified; in these areas, the large Iberian regions comprised several polities. The problem is to determine the character of the large regions named in the Greco-Roman texts. Did these names refer to ethnic identities? In our opinion, this large region could be based on some common cultural features but the basis for aggregation in Iberia is the political landscapes organized around the urban centres which made up the territorial mosaic of small units similar to other polities of the ancient Mediterranean. These early states were constructed and maintained through some ideological elements, whose authority would have been associated with a common identity, depending on the political process by which the territories of the city-states were created.

However, these symbolic components could be found over extensive regions, but with clear local reworking, and have been used to suggest some kind of regional identity. It is obvious that polities do not develop in isolation and centuries of economic, cultural, social and political interrelations created the regional grouping of cultural traditions. It is also possible that the city-states may have been involved in common political projects that linked different polities into large federations. For example, in southern Iberia the integration of several *oppida* through client-patron links between rulers has been suggested (Ruiz 1998). I have proposed political networks of a similar kind in eastern Iberia at the time the Romans arrived during the Second Punic War (Grau Mira 2005). Iberia was the battlefield and the Iberian peoples were dramatically involved in the confrontation between the Carthaginians and the Romans from the late third century BC onwards. Judging from the information found in the ancient texts, it is possible that some kind of Iberian confederation may have been created in the context of this war. Polybius says that King *Edecon*, usually associated with the Iberian town of *Edeta*, asked the Roman general Scipio to liberate his family and promised, in return, that all the Iberian peoples south of the River Ebro would become allies of Rome. In southern Iberia, Polybius says that King Culchas' confederation consisted of 28 and 17 *oppida* at different times (Polybius 10.3–4, quoted in Ruiz 2000: 13–15). These texts prove that the territories of the city-states were clustered into large confederations, covering extensive regions and possibly assisted by the activation of common cultural components.

This process of reactivating cultural elements in periods of crisis is also found in other parts of the Mediterranean. A well-known case is the common Greek identity, over and above each city-state's political autonomy and sense of identity, in the face of the common threat of the Persians (Hall 1991). Another example of an appeal to a common identity is that of the Umbrians during the Social War in central Italy. The various ethnic groups: Plestians, Iguvines, etc. used their feeling of being an Umbrian people to sanction the alliance in times of war (Bradley 2000). Subsequently, this large Umbrian group was used as an element to determine the regional territorial division made by Augustus. We would suggest there is a clear parallel in the Roman division of eastern Iberia into the regions of *Edetania* and *Contestania*. During their first contacts with the Iberians during the Second Punic War, the Romans may have found the federation of different city-states covering extensive regions. The Romans would have perceived these federations as major ethnic groups and used them as the basis for the administrative divisions referred to in the texts (Grau Mira 2005).

To sum up, a number of scholars have alluded to the multiplicity of identities that were created and recreated, which can be observed through the archaeological record. In this context, similar elements could be used to express gender, social position or ethnic identity amongst the Iberians and the main problem is making sense of these components (Díaz-Andreu 1998: 212). One clear case has been presented here; the figured pottery that could have been used to communicate a similar iconographic code throughout a large region (Tortosa 2006) or a specific local style used as an identity symbol to reinforce city-state processes. Both positions may be valid; the first informs us about the cultural traditions and regional grouping of the Iberians, used to construct federations in certain periods. The second relates to the process of constructing political landscapes and local identities and negotiating positions of power through symbolic practices. Concentric identities were used in different sensitive contexts to cement affiliations amongst the Iberians.

Acknowledgements

This paper is integrated in the Research Project HAR2009–11441of the MICINN. Thanks to V. Peterson for her help with the English editing.

The politics of identity: ethnicity and the economy of power in Iron Age north-west Iberia

Alfredo González-Ruibal

Keywords: ethnicity, Atlantic Iberia, politics, moral economy, political economy

From ethnicity to politics: studying identity, forgetting politics

Until the 1960s, archaeologists tended to interpret all spatial variations in material culture (what we could call style) from the perspective of ethnicity. Presumably, a different way of decorating a pot, designing a fibula or making a spear would be cultural manifestations – conscious as well as unconscious – of a particular ethnic identity. For archaeologists studying the European Iron Age in particular, ethnicity was, and to a large extent still is, an extremely flexible concept: it may refer to large and diffuse groups which could not have possibly shared any sense of common identity, such as the Celts or the ancient Germans, and minor communities transmitted by classical authors, like the Aeduans or the Daunians. Since the birth of processual archaeology, crude culture-historical visions of ethnicity have been subjected to a strong critique in the Anglo-Saxon tradition (Jones 1997). Archaeologists have problematized the concept of ethnic identity first by denying a one-to-one relationship between material culture and ethnicity, and later by incorporating group and individual identities to the equation: gender, sex, age, status, race and other variables affect the way ethnicity is lived, negotiated and displayed (Jones 1997; Meskell 2002; Díaz-Andreu *et al.* 2005; see Wells 1998 for a nice application to the European Iron Age).

While concepts of ethnicity were becoming increasingly varied, complex and sophisticated in Anglo-Saxon archaeology, other traditions either rejected the debate – e.g. Germany after the traumatic experience of Nazism (Veit 1989, Brather 2000) – or kept entrenched in culture-historical assumptions, despite an occasional processual varnish. The latter situation applies chiefly to Spanish, Portuguese and Italian archaeology (e.g. Molinos and Zifferero 2002). In the Spanish case, the archaeology of the 'Celtic' Iron Age continues to be driven by a 'palaeoethnological' agenda which seeks to characterize ethnic groups by combining information provided by classical authors and material culture. This approach, originally developed by Bosch Gimpera (1920), persists to our day scarcely challenged (cf. contributions to Almagro and Ruiz Zapatero 1992). A list of recent doctoral dissertations read at the Complutense University of Madrid proves the case: the Celtiberians (Lorrio 1997), the Vettons (Álvarez Sanchís 1999), the Lusitanians (Martín Bravo 2000), the Tartessians (Torres Ortiz 2002) and the Callaecians (González-Ruibal 2006–7). Generally speaking, this is still an 'archaeology of identification' (Ruby 2006: 47). The method is comparable to that developed by Gustav Kossinna in the 1920s: first, a culture area is defined through the typological analysis of archaeological materials (pottery, weapons, settlements). Then, the culture area is considered to be the expression of an ethnic group, which is eventually equated to the peoples or tribes documented historically in a given area (Veit 1989: 39–40).

The explanation for this scientific anomaly is manifold: on the one hand, the destruction of Spanish universities after the civil war (1936–9; Claret Miranda 2006) favoured the persistence of old paradigms and a strong parochialism, with far-reaching consequences. Besides, this new academia was heavily influenced by the nationalist rhetoric of the period, which drew upon archaeology and history to define Spanish identity (Díaz-Andreu 1997). There are, however, other reasons to explain the modern survival of old concepts of ethnicity and their central place in scientific research today: mainly, their strong popular appeal. The lay public considers the Iron Age to be unlike any other period in prehistory – or history, for that matter. They see the deep roots of their present identity in pre-Roman groups. Archaeological debates – such as those concerning the Celtic character of this or that Iron Age culture – usually transcend universities and are replicated in more popular arenas – a good case in point is the harsh debate generated by the publication of Carlos Marín Suárez's (2005) essay on the notion of *Astur*. This is in part due to the fact that the ethnic names transmitted by ancient authors coincide quite accurately with modern regions and place names – e.g. *Callaecia*, Galicia; *Asturia*, Asturias; *Cantabria*, Cantabria; *Vasconia*, País Vasco; etc. It is not strange to hear somebody defining her or himself as an *Astur* or *Callaica* or more generally, a Celt (as opposed to the non-Celtic Iberians of Andalusia and the Spanish Levant). Coincidences between past and present 'ethnicities' are more obvious in northern Spain, where nationalist and regionalist feelings are stronger (Marín Suárez 2005). The same mechanism of identification between past and present ethnicity was used before 1975 during Franco's dictatorship (Díaz-Andreu 1997), in this case with centripetal purposes: thus, Spaniards were deemed to be the descendants of the Celtiberians, a mixture of Iberians and Celts (Ruiz Zapatero 1993, 2003). Spanish archaeologists often complain that archaeological research is misused and put at the service of disparate, often undemocratic and racist, political agendas. However, the problem is ingrained in the very paradigm they use so blissfully – a paradigm that equates an unproblematized notion of ancient ethnicity with territory and material culture.

Compared with the situation in other parts of Europe, the developments of Anglo-Saxon research in relation to ethnicity are laudable and exciting – also those of Scandinavian archaeology (Olsen 1985). Still, too much attention paid to identity has concealed other issues that are fundamental in explaining why material culture varies from one community to another. Among the things that explain the spatial variability of material culture is politics. This has been generally overlooked by postprocessualist archaeologists, who are more interested in individuals and agency than in structure and collective *ethoi* (McGuire and Wurst 2002; Patterson 2005). Also, the emphasis on culture and the symbolic realm has precluded a serious exploration of politics, which are usually reduced to the postmodern politics of identity (Meskell 2002) or to the use of past ethnicity in current political agendas – especially nationalism (Díaz-Andreu and Smith 2001). In this chapter, I argue for another sort of 'politics of identity': not those that emphasize postmodern sensibilities as shaped by concepts of multiculturalism, minority rights and individual freedom, but the politics that take power, hegemony, ideology and economy at its heart. However, it is not a materialist perspective that is espoused here. Rather, I would like to bridge the gap between the North American archaeological tradition, focused on politics, economy and grand narratives, and the European tradition, concerned with critique, sociocultural and symbolic aspects and the local.

I will illustrate my points with reference to the north-west of Iberia during the Middle (400–125 BC) and, especially, Late Iron Age (125 BC–50 AD). The north-west of the Iberian Peninsula is a large and diverse region (*c.* 50,000 square kilometres), which the Romans divided into two areas after the conquest: Callaecia and Asturia. Archaeologists and historians have assumed those terms to be ethnic names describing large cultural groupings. Through a closer look at material culture and politics, I will show that reality is much more complex – and interesting.

The politics of ethnicity: anthropological lessons

Most definitions of ethnic group emphasize cultural, apparently arbitrary, elements (language, dress, customs, beliefs) and self-identification (Barth 1976: 11; Jones 1997: 84; Hall 2002: 9). For understanding ethnicity, however, we have to look at politics also and particularly at the intersection between politics, economy and identity. For several decades now, anthropologists have been providing thought-provoking examples of societies whose ethnicity is entangled in a complex mesh of social and political values. Most anthropological studies explore the relationship between ethnic groups, nationalism, federalism, modernity and the state (Anderson 1991; Smith 1992), and are therefore of limited use for archaeologists. Nevertheless, some authors working with non-modern communities have been able to prove that many ethnic labels have been assigned historically on grounds other than purely cultural, and that cultural elements are deeply interwoven with political and economic ones. In what follows, I would mention briefly a few eloquent ethnographic examples.

Southeast Asia presents a remarkable panorama in the complex entanglement of ethnicity and politics. Scott (1998: 186) considers that it is useful here to talk about state spaces and non-state spaces to define the intersection of identity and politics. In the first spaces, population is densely settled, communities are permanent and an important surplus of staple foods is produced. Non-state spaces are characterized by a sparse settlement, shifting cultivation and mobility. Non-state spaces are considered by the centres as exemplars of rudeness, disorder and barbarity. It is obvious that this political-economic geography affects ethnicity and the way collective identity is constructed. A good example is provided by Laos and Thailand (Izikowsky 1969; Turton 2000). The people from the lowlands (the Thai) have been traditionally an aristocratic society organized as a city-based state and long-distance trade networks have played a relevant role in their political economy. They despised the highlanders, whom they called Kha, meaning 'servant', 'slave' (Turton 2000: 6). The so-called Kha were small-scale societies of slash-and-burn agriculturalists, living in dispersed small villages and endowed with egalitarian ethics. Ethnic terms in this area are not just a cultural label, but also a mark of status: the Kha were politically subdued to the Thai, to whom they had to pay taxes.

A similar situation exists in several places in Africa. The Mandara Highlands of Cameroon are settled by groups – collectively known by the French name of 'Montagnards' – organized on more egalitarian lines than those of the plains – the Wandala – with whom they are nonetheless historically and genealogically related (McEachern 1993). The Wandala have been organized traditionally as states, been involved in long-distance trade networks and raided the highlanders frequently. Both Montagnards and Wandala defined their ethnic identities in opposition to the other, even if their economies and livelihoods are tightly bound together. In the Sudan-Ethiopian borderland, the situation was not very different, with Nilo-Saharan communities being raided by Arabs and Abyssinians. Both perceived the non-state space of their frontier as inhabited by unruly and uncivilized peoples, whom they called 'slaves': Abid, Shankilla (Pankhurst 1977). As the Montagnards in relation to the Wandala, the identity of these rather egalitarian communities was constructed in opposition to their neighbour's economies of power. Rather than two distinct groups, as in Thailand and Cameroon, what we have in the Ethiopian borderland is a gradation: the sustained contact and, in some cases, miscegenation of the frontier communities with representatives of other, more hierarchical cultures produced a variety of 'ethnic groups'. Charles Jedrej (2004: 720) considers that in this region;

> the names of ethnic groups are less likely to indicate different ways of life and more likely to mark positions in a ranking of status and prestige… So Ja'alayin, Watawit, Jabalawiin, Funj, Hamaj, Berta, and Burun come to represent points on scales between urban and rural, Muslim and pagan, superior and inferior, and master and slave…

Finally, a nice example of the politics behind ethnicity is provided by Madagascar (Graeber 2004: 54–9). The present Sakalava were, originally, the subjects of a particular royal dynasty. Those who refused to be subjugated to the kings fled to a hilly backward country and became the Tsimihety, meaning 'those who do not cut their hair' (cutting one's hair was a symbol of loyalty during the funerals of a king). 'The Tsimihety,' says Graeber (2004: 55), 'are now considered a *foko* – a people or ethnic group – but their identity emerged as a political project'. The same occurs elsewhere on the island (Graeber 2004: 57–8). When the French arrived and reorganized the peoples that they found in 'tribes' (i.e. ethnic groups), following the usual colonial procedure, they resorted to the most conspicuous elements of distinction. These were usually political, although they were expressed in what we would call now the language of ethnicity. Like the Sakalava, the Merina were the subjects of a powerful royal dynasty. The peoples conquered by the Merina were called Betsileo. Those who refused state rule, apart from the Tsimihety, were the Vezo (a fisher-folk), the Tanala (forest dwellers) and the Mikea (hunter-gatherers). As in Sudan and Ethiopia, we have a gradation of peoples, reified as ethnic groups, who cover the spectrum from total compliance with the state, to total rejection.

I will try to prove here that for understanding the diversity of material culture and landscapes in northwestern Iberia during the Late Iron Age we have to look also at different articulations of politics, which created different kinds of oppositions and enabled the emergence of disparate collective identities. My point is that, in the fragmented cultural panorama of *Callaecia* and *Asturia*, there existed communities where political economies, which allowed the production of inequalities and hierarchization, were at work, and others where moral economies, which emphasized egalitarian values and a collective *ethos*, prevailed. To complicate the panorama even more, some communities were organized as centralized polities and others rejected state-like political systems. These different economies of power strongly shaped material culture and landscape. The resulting regional differences, allied to other cultural idiosyncrasies, were played out in material culture and were transmitted by classical authors through a diversity of oppositions, not dissimilar to those conveyed by modern colonialism (e.g. *Celtici/Helleni, Bracarenses/Lucenses, Transmontani/Cismontani*). These names modern scholars have tended to interpret in squarely ethnic, geographical or cultural terms, thus failing to grasp the intricacies couched under them. Ruby (2006: 59) considers that the political side of ethnicity has to be studied, but that archaeology is quite useless to this regard. My intention is to prove that archaeology, too, may have something to say when it comes to the politics of identity.

Political and moral economies, past and present

I regard both political and moral economies in a Foucaldian sense as economies of power, that is, historically-specific ensembles of power relations. Foucault placed great emphasis on the relations of power through which subjects are produced (Foucault 2000). This approach is then pertinent for a research on identity (ethnic, gender, sexual, racial or other). The main difference between political and moral economies is that the former provide the basis for the structural generation of inequalities, while the latter deploy mechanisms to hinder them. The way subjects are produced under these different regimes of power are therefore different, and so are collective identities.

The term political economy, as it is well-known, is a vintage Enlightenment concept, which was originally equated to what we now call simply economy. Today in archaeology it refers usually to the intertwining of politics and 'economy' in those societies were economy transcends the limits of the household (e.g. Feinman 2002: 2). We can say that political economies are a set of practices and strategies, both ideological and material, which provide the framework for the production and reproduction of inequalities in a given society. The presence of this concept in archaeology is certainly not new: it was incorporated to the conceptual apparatus of the discipline by processual archaeology. Although in Europe the concept has been scarcely applied, it has been very successful in the United States, where political economy is strongly associated with the general concern for complex societies, the emergence of inequalities, state-formation, and the role of economy in processes of hierarchization (Earle 1997; Feinman and Nicholas 2002). Political-economic strategies mobilized by political actors include patron/client relationships, tribute, political gifting, prestige-goods systems, esoteric and specialized knowledge, long-distance trade networks, aristocratic ancestor worship, control of instruments of war, attachment of craft specialists, competitive feasting, production and management of surplus, etc. – for examples, of these strategies at work see Helms (1988), Earle (1997), Blanton (1998) and Stanish (2002).

Political economies are related to ethnic identity in more than one sense. Earle (2002: 162) says that complex chiefdoms are characterized from the point of view of material culture by the creation of 'grand styles'. These grand styles usually draw upon a collective symbolic reservoir which is re-elaborated with foreign influences: this is the case of La Tène art, a 'barbarian' style combined with Mediterranean motifs. This art was created as an elite style but it became democratized in a few generations (Wells 1998: 265–6). As another political-economic strategy, the elites appropriate widely respected and shared symbols and use them in their prestige material culture (jewels, dress, monumental architecture, arms). In this way, they situate themselves as guarantors of the social and cosmological order represented by those symbols – this, for instance, might explain the prevalence of solar symbols and swastikas in Iron Age elite material culture. Grand styles are very recognizable (consider the New Kingdom Egyptian art or the Toltec style) and they are sometimes considered an element of ethnic differentiation – for example, Celtic La Tène style vs. Jastorf Germanic style (see Wells 1998: 276, fig. 4). They certainly help to buttress ethnic identities, but they are born mainly as an elite phenomenon. As it is often the case, rulers are the most interested in creating, showing and fostering a particular ethnic identity. This was probably the case with Mycenaean aristocrats (Hall 2002: 48–9) and Late Bronze Age elites more generally (Kristiansen 1998: 404–6). Egalitarian groups tend to have weaker ethnic feelings and mobilize them less frequently.

Not all political economies are the same, though. Blanton (1998) establishes a useful distinction. He talks about exclusionary and corporate political economies. Corporate political economies curtail the power of the elites, who have to obtain more often the acquiescence of the community. Charles Stanish (2002) has pointed out some of the mechanisms, such as feasting and rituals, to which the elites resort to maintain their legitimacy before commoners. Corporate political economies were likely the dominant economy of power that prevailed in Iron Age Europe. Institutions such as senates, assemblies, councils, feasts, ritual specialists and magistrates not only helped to reproduce a ranked system, but also limited the agency of the aristocratic classes, redistributed social power and buttressed collective identity (Roymans 1990: 22–3; Crumley 2002: 140; Woolf 2002: 11). Along with corporate political economies, however, other systems did exist in Iron Age Europe, where egalitarian values were even more emphasized (Hill 1995, 2006). The concept of moral economy is useful to define the economy of power at work in these societies.

Moral economy has been a much less successful concept in archaeology. Some authors have explored egalitarian ideologies, but the concept itself has not been applied very widely. In a sense, the idea of moral economy is the opposite of political economy. Whereas political economies are based on links between economy and power that allow for social differences to be produced, moral economies, without necessarily supporting radically egalitarian political systems, emphasize collective values and isonomy. The concept of moral economy as such did not become frequent in the social sciences until the 1970s. Similar ideas existed, under different labels since the 1920s: the work of Marcel Mauss (1923–1924) has to be brought up, as well as Marshall Sahlins's (1972a), whose Stone Age Economics deals, in fact, with moral economies. The specific term took off with the writings of E. P. Thompson (1971) and J. C. Scott (1976) among others. Moral economy refers to the essentially non-economic (in Western perspective) norms and obligations that mediate the central social, political and economic relations of a given people. Where moral economies are enforced, self-interested calculations of gain or efficiency are absent, secondary or camouflaged. They stress egalitarian and collective values, which are usually channeled through myth and rituals, and preclude individual gain at the expense of others. Strategies at work in moral economies include communal landholdings, mutual aid and reciprocity, risk-sharing and social welfare institutions. The articulation of social norms, the principles of reciprocity and the symbolic expression of community values intervene not only in the relations within the community, but also in the relations between the community and other groups. Therefore, it has been noted that the work of moral economies is made more visible in situations of cultural contact between nonmarket communities and market-oriented societies. Different versions of this kind of economy exist in a diverse array of societies, including purely egalitarian ones, transegalitarian (Hayden 1995), heterarchical (Crumley 2002), peasant societies (Wolf 1982) and deep rural societies (Jedrej 1995). However, moral economic principles can be used to restrict the rulers' power in state systems as well (Blanton 1998).

As it occurs with political economies, the *ethos* enforced by a moral economy can be fundamental in defining a particular ethnic identity. The Uduk of the Sudan, studied by Wendy James are a good case in point. Despite strongly disrupting forces (war, slavery, invasions), the Uduk have managed to maintain their ethnic cohesion through the implementation of a powerful moral economy. This economy restricts or disapproves market exchange, trade and imports (James 1979: 88) and everything that might be identified as greed. The Uduk show a deep aversion to calculations of wealth, power and other aspects related with trade: being involved in commerce means being commodified, transformed into a thing, enslaved (James 1979: 110). Their moral economy also prescribes sister-exchange marriage as a way of avoiding dowry, which is perceived as the purchase of a human being (James 1979: 124–7). This is related to a widespread notion of reciprocity, a typical feature of moral economies. Egalitarian principles inform Uduk ethnicity: they are not something that can be detached from their constitution as an autonomous ethnic group. According to James (1979: 19), 'they have developed an egalitarian and defensive ethic as a way of preserving some sense of worth in their predicament, a way of seeing themselves nevertheless as whole men and women, as 'Kwanim Pa' [i.e. Uduk]'.

In sum, the existence of one kind of economy of power or another is something fundamental in defining identity in general and ethnic identity in particular. The relationship between power and ethnicity is enacted not only in institutions, rituals and social prescriptions, but also in material culture. Political economies favour grand styles, exotic goods and luxury artefacts, which create a sense of common identity among elites and their clients (Earle 2002); moral economies curtail trade and foster democratic technologies by means of a domestic mode of production (Sahlins 1972b: 121), all of which helps to produce a sensation of common belonging as opposed to strangers.

Identity and the economy of power in Asturia and Callaecia: layers of identity

The separation of *Asturia* and *Callaecia* by the Romans at the end of the first century BC and the divisions of both territories in sub-regions (*Asturia Cismontana* and *Transmontana*, *Callaecia Lucensis* and *Bracarensis*) owe at least as much to politics as to culture and ethnic identification (Fig. 17.1). The Romans seemingly paid special attention to the moral and political economies that prevailed in these areas and, more generally, to the political constitution of the different communities that they encountered. Likewise, the locals themselves constructed their collective identity around concepts of power and ethics. Furthermore, I would argue that these diverse economies of power, which were identified and to some extent sanctioned by the Romans, can be identified archaeologically through material culture at large – including landscape.

The distinction between Callaecians and Asturians was based on cultural and socio-political grounds – what philologist Javier de Hoz (1997) calls 'objective identity' and anthropologists would denominate an 'etic' perspective. The so-called Callaecians shared many traits that distinguished them from neighboring peoples: the same

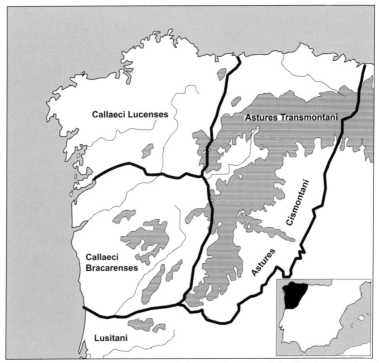

Figure 17.1. The Roman division of the north-west of the Iberian peninsula.

deities (like Navia, Bandua and Reve; García Fernández-Albalat 1990, Prósper 2002); some elements of material culture (such as ritual saunas, gold torcs, earrings, bronze cauldrons, antennae daggers and some types of fibulae), and probably the same language or closely related languages (Luján 2006). The Callaecians also shared an important socio-political element; as opposed to the rest of Iberia, they based their social organization on territory, settlements and households rather than on real or imaginary kinship ties (extended families, clans, lineages, *gentilitates*, *gentes*), which predominated in the rest of 'Celtic' Iberia (González-Ruibal 2006a). This does not mean, of course, that kinship was irrelevant: it certainly mattered, as in any other traditional society, but the point is that the main reference for a Callaecian to locate her or himself in the social world was space – the hill-fort and the territory of his/her *populus* – rather than kinship. This fact was probably as important for the Callaecians to be perceived as a distinct group by aliens, as it was language or religion. It is not by chance that the inscriptions which mention *castella* (hill-forts) almost perfectly fit the boundaries of Roman *Callaecia* – a few *castella* do appear in Asturia, though (Mangas and Olano 1995), where *gentilitates* were the rule. Another element with political implications that distinguished the Callaecians (as well as the Asturians in this case) from other 'Celtic' groups in Iberia was the absence of an equestrian elite (González-Ruibal 2006–2007: fig. 4.93). Equestrian elites played an outstanding role elsewhere in the Iberian peninsula and are easily recognizable through material markers (Almagro Gorbea 1998, Almagro Gorbea and Torres 2000). Although mounted warriors did exist in *Callaecia* and *Asturia*, especially in mountainous areas, and were later recruited by the Roman empire as *auxilia*, there is no evidence that they formed an elite, given the absence of a prestige material culture associated with horses. Like nineteenth century Plain Indians in America, the highlanders of north-west Iberia were skillful – and rather egalitarian – riders.

Nonetheless, these large groupings, which today's archaeologists and historians in Spain tend to consider 'cultures' or 'ethnic groups', could hardly have been an element of identification for people in the past, given the size of the regions and the huge internal variability. Therefore, they were very unlikely sources of ethnic feelings at least. Since Max Weber's definition of ethnic identity in 1922 (cf. Hall 2002: 10), most authors agree that self-identification – which usually presupposes a belief in a common origin – is a fundamental aspect of ethnicity (Barth 1976: 11; Shennan 1989: 14; Hall 2002: 10–11). Although Ruby considers that limiting ethnicity to a phenomenon of self-identification is useless in ancient contexts (Ruby 2006: 41), he insists that we have to spare the term 'ethnicity' to processes of assertion of identity and the term 'ethnic identity' to the situation created by those processes (Ruby 2006: 37). Thus, neither Callaecians nor Asturians qualify as ethnic groups in these terms, because there is no evidence that they considered themselves a single collective, ever asserted a common identity, or shared an origin myth – quite the opposite, as we will see. The reason for the absence of a common identity among Callaecians, on the one hand, and Asturians, on the other, has to be explained again on political grounds. Shennan (1989: 15) understands ethnicity as a phenomenon tightly linked to the emergence of the state. I do not think that states are indispensable and a sense of ethnicity is absent in many powerful states (such as Spain until the nineteenth century), but it is obvious that state mechanisms find less hindrances in the creation and generalization of large 'imagined communities' (Anderson 1983), than small-scale or middle-range societies. This is not to say that non-state societies have weak ethnic feelings (cf. Hodder 1982 for contexts in which ethnicity is mobilized in segmentary communities); what it means is that these ethnic feelings could have hardly extended over vast territories and large populations, especially when the geography is complex and the populations fragmented: communication and interaction are basic elements for the maintenance of ethnic identity (Barth 1976:11) and these can be fulfilled at a larger scale in the context of centralized polities. Territories as wide and varied as those of Callaecia and Asturia could have hardly generated a generalized sense of ethnic belonging without the existence of a state – or several states.

I think that we should look at other levels to see how collective identity worked in ancient pre-state societies; actually, we have to look at a multiplicity of levels (Ruby 2006: 47–54): smaller territories, valleys and hill-forts or *oppida* were the scale at which collective identity was most likely played out in daily life. This has been observed ethnographically. For instance, local diversity notwithstanding, the Kalinga of the Philippines share customs, language and material culture, yet social relations, social organization and identity are materialized at the level of the village or the valley unit (Stark 1998). Kalinga identity has played a rather negligible role compared to smaller-scale affiliations. The problem for archaeologists is that these smaller groupings seldom match any particular assemblage of material culture (Lemonnier 1986). Similarly, in northwestern Iberia *castella, gentilitates, civitates* and *populi* likely played an important role in the assertion of collective identity and decision-making, but they are very difficult to track archaeologically or even historically, since they rarely evince any cultural distinctiveness (González-Ruibal 2006–7: 456–9).

However, there are other collectives that are archaeologically identifiable, which aliens perceived very well and which were pivotal in constructing local, shared identities. Although the Romans noticed the similarities of the diverse Callaecian communities, on the one hand, and the resemblances of the many Asturian groups, on the other, they were aware of their manifold internal differences as well. They saw a clear divide between south/north and plains/highlands and they expressed this divide in ethnic terms; Ptolemy (2.6.1–2, 22, 38), for example, refers to northern Callaecians as *Kallaikoi Loukénsioi* and to southern Callaecians as *Kallaikoi Brakároi* and Pliny (*Natural History* 3.28) says that the *Astures* are *'divisi in Augustanos et Transmontanos'* (the *Astures Augustani* were also called *Cismontani*). This divide coincided with societies with central places (*oppida*) in the south and the plains and societies without *oppida* in the north and the highlands (Fig. 17.2). Meaningfully, when the Romans organized these regions, they listed communities as *civitates* in the south and the plains (such as *Quaerquerni, Caladuni* or *Leuni*), and as *populi* in the north and the highlands (such as *Copori, Lemavi, Neri* and *Artabri*; Pliny *Natural History* 3.28). In the case of *Callaecia*, the divide received administrative sanction through the establishment of two different *conventus* for the *Bracarenses* and *Lucenses*. The societies without *oppida* were also diverse: some of them were more hierarchical than others. I propose a fourfold typology of socio-political systems that intersected ethnic identity. I will designate these systems – or rather, economies of power – as house societies, kinship-based chiefdoms, heroic societies and deep rural communities (Fig. 17.3). What I will try to prove in the remainder of this article is that these differences were much more important to define

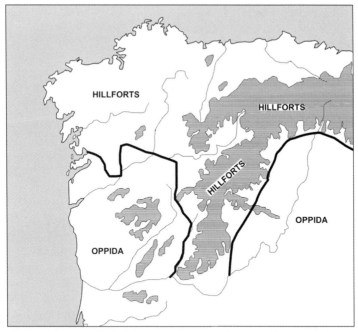

Figure 17.2. Societies with oppida and societies against oppida in northwestern Iberia.

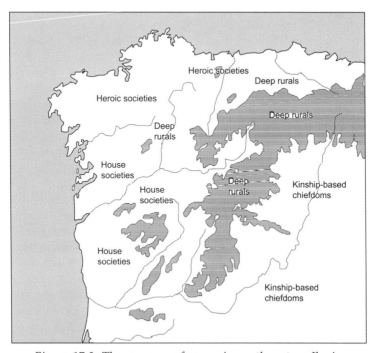

Figure 17.3. The economy of power in northwestern Iberia.

collective identity, than the larger groupings (*Callaecia, Asturia*), which archaeologists tend to consider in the first place.

Southern Callaecians and Asturians: house societies and kinship-based chiefdoms

Societies based on *oppida* can be divided into two large groups: house societies, that were predominant in southern *Callaecia* (*Callaecia Bracarensis*) and kinship-based chiefdoms, which prevailed in southern *Asturia* (*Asturia Cismontana*) and were widespread all over Iberia and other parts of continental Europe. What would be known as *Callaecia Bracarensis* developed hierarchical polities, inserted into the Mediterranean trade networks, since the Late Bronze Age. The first fortified settlements of the Iberian north-west and the most important and rich metal hoards appear in this region. There is, thus, a tradition in the *longue durée* of powerful political economies managed by an elite with a tendency towards centralization and long distance connections (González-Ruibal 2006–7: 77–160).

The story is not a simple evolutionary one, but by the end of the Iron Age, southern *Callaecia* witnessed the emergence of central places (*oppida*), controlling large territories. The appearance of 'urban' settlements, that were up to 20 times bigger than previous hill-forts amounted to a veritable revolution in the social construction of landscape. As society became more and more hierarchized, so did the landscape: what remained of a moral landscape, which persisted in the highlands and the northern regions, was subverted in southern *Callaecia* and *Asturia*. If we bear in mind that collective identity is strongly linked to landscape (Knapp and Ashmore 1999: 14–16), it is difficult to see how the emergence of *oppida* could have left the identity of southern Callaecians untouched. At the same time that they favoured social differentiation, *oppida*, as centralized systems, also made communication and interaction easier and helped to create a sense of common belonging among those who inhabited them – especially their elites – through rituals, exchanges, feasts and political alliances. The *oppida*, however, were just one among many political technologies (*sensu* Michel Foucault) deployed during the Late Iron Age. Other technologies (Fig. 17.4), whose relevance grew exponentially during this period, were collective ritual spaces, ritual saunas, feasts (as represented by numerous Mediterranean amphorae, bronze cauldrons and other banquet equipment), the control of long-distance trade networks, the acquisition and manipulation of genealogies and heirlooms, the production of agricultural surplus, political and kinship alliances, and the management of violence (war and raids). The political economy of southern Callaecian elites was based on these elements, but it was reproduced by households. The primacy of the house over the village was achieved throughout the second half of the first millennium BC, starting around 400 BC. Architecture became more monumental and domestic units more self-contained and independent in relation to the rest of the settlement (Ayán Vila 2005). By the second century BC some domestic compounds were visibly more important than others. The political-economic strategies mentioned above, which were deployed by prominent households, are akin to those found in other so-called 'house societies' (González-Ruibal 2006), which have been ethnographically and historically attested in different parts of the world (Carsten and Hugh-Jones 1995).

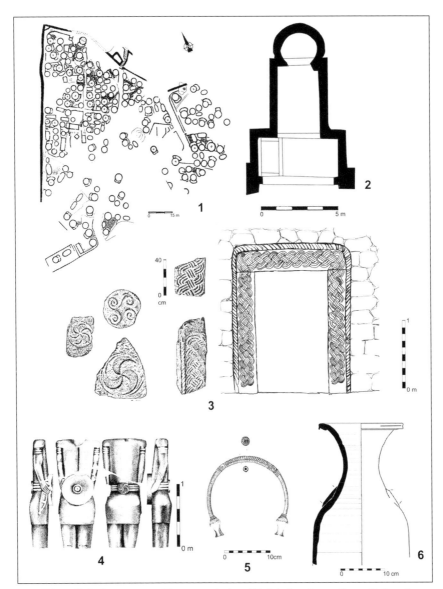

Figure 17.4. The political economy of house societies: (1) details of a southern Callaecian oppidum, Santa Trega (Pontevedra, Galicia). This oppidum covered 20 hectares and was very densely occupied; (2) ritual sauna associated with an oppidum: Armeá (Ourense, Galicia); (3) house decorations from various Callaecian oppida; (4) warrior statue from the north of Portugal, with short sword, shield (caetra), bracelets and decorated belt (after Da Silva 1986); (5) torc from the oppidum of Lanhoso (Braga, Portugal). Southern Callaecian torcs have a very distinctive style (after Da Silva 1986); (6) Late Punic amphora from the hill-fort of Montealegre (Pontevedra, Galicia): the hill-forts and oppida of southern Callaecia have yielded huge numbers of wine amphorae which were used in feasts and rituals.

Southern Callaecians – and especially the dominant groups – developed a common identity, in opposition to northern Callaecians and neighbouring societies (Asturians, Lusitanians). This is evinced in the creation of a shared grand style, an 'art of the *oppida*' (González-Ruibal 2004: 116–23). This art, restricted to southern *Callaecia*, is materialized in a diversity of media; among the most widespread manifestations is a distinctive architectural decoration, which drew upon a variety of European and Mediterranean traditions and covered with swastikas, triskels and geometrical friezes the houses of the powerful and religious buildings (including ritual saunas). The style is also evident in jewellery which used many of the motifs found in sculpture and a similar grammar: finely decorated torcs (a male adornment) and Iberian-influenced earrings (a female one). Other elements that reveal the existence of a widely shared grand style are warrior statues: oversized representations of warriors armed with the local panoply and dressed with elaborated garments, torcs and bracelets (Schattner 2003).

The existence of a common southern Callaecian identity is also made manifest in their attitude towards aliens. According to Orosius (5.5.12), Decimus Junius Brutus defeated a large group of Callaecians who were helping the Lusitanians, near the Durius River (*c.* 137 BC). Even if we ignore the exaggerated number of indigenous casualties given by the historian (sixty thousand), the narration conveys the idea that Brutus routed a large group of people that fought as Callaecians, probably a confederation of peoples (Santos Yanguas 1988: 30). Meaningfully, the Roman general took the nickname 'Callaicus' after his victory and was granted triumph back in Rome. Although it has been stated that the *Callaeci* were a community that inhabited the lower Durius River, I would not rule out the possibility of the name being applied at that time to all southern Callaecians (even if the name was not the one the Callaecians had for themselves).

While southern Callaecian elites resorted to the house to subvert more constraining collective ethics, southern or lowland Asturians, as many other groups in Iberia, were able to construct ranked and centralized societies – also articulated around *oppida* – resorting to the language of kinship. At least, that is the impression transmitted by inscriptions from the Roman period mentioning *gentilitates* and *gentes*, which are groups united by fictive or real kinship and shared origins (Alarcão 2003; González-Ruibal 2006: 148). Although many large *oppida* have been recorded in their land, southern Asturians are scarcely known archaeologically (Orejas 1996). We may guess that the mechanisms deployed by the local political economy were not dissimilar to those of southern *Callaecia* – except for the strategies more closely linked to a house system. The use of references of prestige coming from Mediterranean Iberia and the Celtiberian region (such as silver jewellery and Celtiberian-style fibulae and panoply) possibly played an important role in the construction of a common identity among southern Asturians and in the negotiation of power by the local elites, who could draw on a widespread aristocratic culture.

Northern Callaecians: heroic societies.

Oppida are a restricted phenomenon in northwestern Iberia. It is not strange that some communities resisted *oppida*, given the far-reaching political and cultural consequences of the appearance of large central places. The rejection of the *oppidum* model is not something unique to northern Iberia, though. A similar contrast between *oppidum* and *oppidum*-less societies can be found in the British Isles, where large centres mainly developed in southern England (Hill 1995a). The same occurs in central Europe (Wells 1998: 272). Politics, landscape and identity are closely linked. The social landscape of the societies without *oppida* – or *against oppida*, using the Clastrian metaphor (Clastres 1989, see also González García *et al.* in press) – is a democratic one: all hill-forts are roughly the same size and territory is not politically hierarchized or regionalized. This is a heterarchical landscape, with a multiplicity of sovereign, self-contained, autonomous centres or, rather, with no centres at all. Hill-forts probably established alliances and created ever-shifting confederations (Fábrega 2005). Some hill-forts may have been promoted to regional power at times (as heads of such confederations), but their status was flimsy and their political pre-eminence was not expressed materially (García Quintela 2002). Perhaps because of this emphasis on autonomy, frontiers and neutral locales had such a paramount role in the region (Brañas 2000: 169–77). The space between hill-forts is marked by natural sacred places, sanctuaries with rock art, offerings in rivers, and hoards of torcs and arms (Santos and García Quintela 2008). Meaningfully, *oppida* tend to incorporate sacred places inside the urban space and to politicize (i.e. incorporate into the *polis*) the ritual, whereas the societies against *oppida* maintain sanctuaries beyond the political territory ascribed to a particular hill-fort.

Nevertheless, being against the state does not mean being against hierarchy; some societies without *oppida* in the north-west of Iberia developed political economies which were consistent with a lack of centralized settlements, while other groups rejected strong forms of inequalities altogether. I will call the first group 'heroic societies', following García Quintela (2002) and Parcero Oubiña (2002), and deep rural communities the second group. Heroic societies were ranked. They had a political economy with an array of strategies of differentiation. The heroic societies of *Callaecia* were characterized by a particular idea of value, which is akin to that of other 'Celtic' communities (Brañas 2000: 17–9; García Quintela 2002: 97–8; Parcero Oubiña 2002: 182–4). This concept of value, which can be considered the ideological basis of a political economy, is based on the relevance of portable goods (like jewellery), cattle and war leadership (Fig. 17.5). This is clearly seen from an archaeological point of view in the absence of a monumental domestic architecture in the area (unlike in the house-societies area); the overabundance of jewels, most notably torcs, which cluster around northern *Callaecia* (Ladra 2005); a higher percentage of cow bones in northern hill-forts (Fernández Rodríguez 1996: 208; González-Ruibal 2006–7: 295); and a 'militarized landscape' (Parcero 2002), dominated by heavily defended hill-forts. The 'militarized landscape' is actually present all over the north-west and in many other areas: heroic values were very widespread in Iron Age temperate Europe. The economy of prestige goods was based on local artefacts, especially torcs, instead of exotic products, which are virtually absent in most settlements. That these communities were strongly linked to one another is demonstrated, among other things, by the appearance of torcs belonging to a particular local style outside their region of production (Ladra 2005), probably due to the circulation of gifts and the effects of raids; by the existence of a shared pottery style, which implies some sort of cultural transmission; and by the repetition of a particular type of ritual sauna all over the area (Ríos González 2000), revealing common beliefs

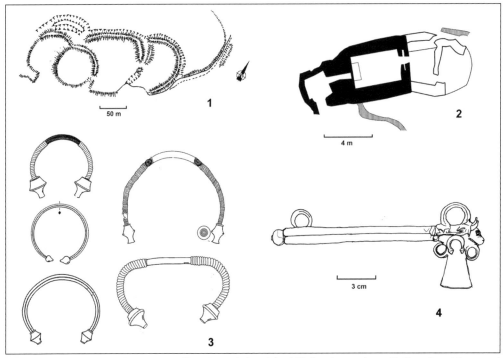

Figure 17.5. The political economy of heroic societies: (1) a hill-fort in northern Callaecia *with several platforms defended with ditches, banks and ramparts (Os Castros de Brañas, A Coruña, Galicia; after Criado Boado 1992); (2) a ritual sauna from the hill-fort of Punta dos Prados (A Coruña, Galicia); (3) different gold torcs from northern Galicia (after Pingel 1992); (4) a votive bronze axe, showing the relevance of cattle and torcs among the* Callaeci Lucenses *(Cariño, A Coruña, Galicia).*

and similar social performances. These practices, along with similar principles of value, probably worked as the grand style and the *oppida* in southern *Callaecia*, promoting a feeling of common belonging among the northern communities.

Highland Asturians and Callaecians: deep rural communities

Whereas the kind of identities revealed by the appearance of grand styles has been discussed thoroughly in different contexts, the relationship between egalitarian *ethoi* and identity has awoken much less interest among archaeologists. The interest for non-hierarchical forms of social organization in the later prehistory is quite recent (Hill 1995, 2006; Fernández-Posse and Sánchez-Palencia 1998; Sastre Prats 2002). Yet it is obvious that moral economies were a strong source of collective self-identification in opposition to other Iron Age societies. These communities were in some ways like a negative of those that we have seen so far. There was a strong and pervasive egalitarian *ethos* that unified their culture and underpinned their particular regimes of power. This is not to say that they were pure egalitarian communities: they were not, but it is well known, from historical and anthropological studies, that non-egalitarian communities cover a wide political spectrum, from scarcely hierarchized systems to empires. It is difficult to find a label to define Iron Age groups which are egalitarian-leaning and do not fit the usual 'Celtic model', mirrored on the societies of the Early Middle Ages. Definitions proposed to date are problematic: they are not exactly segmentary (as proposed by Sastre Prats 2002), because this term applies to more egalitarian collectives; they are not peasants either (Fernández-Posse and Sánchez-Palencia 1998), since this concept implies a state. Heterarchical (Crumley 2002) and transegalitarian (Hayden 1995) are probably more adequate terms, if only because they have been defined by archaeologists to tackle these communities which are so difficult to define in sociopolitical terms. I would like to add another concept, admittedly problematic but interesting to consider: deep rural (Jedrej 1995: 3–4).

Deep rural communities live in the outskirts of states and are characterized by cultural conservatism, the prevalence of a strong moral economy and the refusal to interact with strangers, especially powerful ones (merchants, missionaries, state representatives and the like). According to Charles Jedrej, deep rurals 'deliberately sought to avoid subordination by, and cultural assimilation into, the adjacent predominant peoples and their agents'. The situation of many egalitarian-leaning communities in Iron Age northern Iberia (e.g. Lemos 1993) is somewhat comparable to that of many modern deep rurals. They live in highland peripheral regions, surrounded by more hierarchical regimes (on occasion, state-like); they are not inserted in any major long-distance trade network and refuse imports and foreign technologies; they are very conservative in cultural terms – their material culture, for instance, in the Late Iron Age is not very different from that of the Early Iron Age; they practise more egalitarian politics than their neighbours and lack an economy of prestige goods. I consider the concept of deep rural to be more adequate than peasant, although their moral economies are quite similar, because even if both presuppose the existence of a state, peasants are incorporated into the state, whereas deep rurals refuse to be incorporated and resist in its margins.

If heroic societies rejected *oppida*, but constructed rank through other material strategies, deep rurals are suspicious of any obvious 'system of differentiation' (Foucault 2000: 344) that may serve to generate inequalities, at least at an ideological level – extant social differences were probably camouflaged. This is expressed in the first place in a heterarchical landscape, which favours the fission of settlements rather than their growth. Even more than the social space of heroic societies, this was a 'nested landscape' (Knapp and Ashmore 1999: 16–17), where moral knowledge systematically hampered any attempt of differentiation. The archaeological markers of this economy of power are manifold (cf. Fernández-Posse and Sánchez-Palencia 1998; Sastre Prats 2002; Fig. 17.6): there is an almost absolute absence of jewels; houses are extremely similar in shape and size; there are no monuments (ritual saunas) where social differences can be negotiated; material culture is monotonous, homogeneous and produced within the household. This latter point is especially clear in pottery. Deep rural communities were well aware of the lavishly decorated pottery from southern Callaecia, because some imported vessels have appeared in highland hill-forts (González-Ruibal 2006–7: 486–9). However, they rarely imitated alien styles and clung to plain ware, which was more

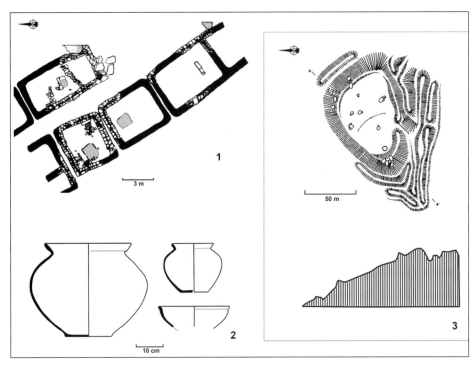

*Figure 17.6. The moral economy of deep rural communities: (1) houses from the hill-fort of Barán
(Lugo, Galicia); (2) pottery from the hill-fort of Corona de Corporales (León). The great majority of
the vessels are plain and morphological variability is extremely limited (after Fernández-Posse and
Sánchez-Palencia 1988); (3) hill-fort of Torre dos Mouros (Viana do Bolo, Ourense, Galicia). The
strong defenses, as well as the limited usable space inside the settlement, are characteristic of a small
community (after Xusto Rodríguez 1993); compare with the map of the oppidum in Figure 17.4.*

democratic, since it precluded differentiation between households because it did not
require complex techniques or a specialized knowledge. The equality of the whole
community was thus asserted through the most quotidian means. Leadership was not
absent in these societies, though (cf. Boehm 1993). Their wide mobilization against the
Roman invasion – they even launched a combined offensive from the mountains (Florus,
2.33.33; *'Astures per id tempus ingentis agmine a montibus niveis descenderant'*) – implies
both the existence of individuals capable or taking political decisions and establishing
alliances, and a sense of common identity, at least in the face of an invasion.

From politics to ethnicity

These different economies of power cannot be reduced simply to politics or economy:
on the contrary, they were crucial in generating a sense of common identity, probably
more than religion or language. There are a few historical hints that corroborate this

impression. Usually, external aggression is the best scenario to prove the existence of ethnic feelings in a particular group. Facing an alien enemy, people who belong to the same group usually reinforce their links and present a common front, even if they quarrelled or raided each other before the attack. This was certainly not the case of *Callaecia* and *Asturia*. At the end of the first century BC, the societies with *oppida* collaborated with the Romans in the fight against their northern and highland neighbors. J. M. Roldán Hervás (1986: 42) states that southern Asturians were not interested in a resistance at any price against the Romans, because of 'their greater exposure to the Roman army and their distrust, if not fear, of their highland kinsfolk's attitude, born from a different economic regime'. As I have tried to show, it was not just a different economic regime, but a whole moral-economic system: a series of values, principles and social prescriptions that helped to construct the highlanders' identity against other groups. Several Roman military camps were built in the middle of *Asturia Cismontana* (Morillo Cerdán 1996), revealing cooperation between southern Asturians and Romans in the war against the highlanders (Fig. 17.7). Also, we know that the Romans respected southern Asturian *oppida*, such as *Lancia*, whereas other towns, like *Brigaecium*, actively collaborated with the invaders (Florus 2.33.39–46).

A similar attitude is found in southern *Callaecia*. Although there is no textual evidence for the cooperation of Callaecians in the war against other so-called Callaecians, there are a few elements that might be interpreted in this way. Firstly, we know that the Roman war of conquest waged between 29 and 19 BC against the highlanders of northern Iberia mainly affected the Asturians and Cantabrians, with only a brief and late mention to Callaecians (Orosius 6.21.1). However, Callaecian highlanders living in the borderland with Asturia were most likely the target of the Roman actions as well, because they belonged to a continuum of highland peoples from the Basque Country to Trás-os-Montes in northeastern Portugal (Rodríguez Colmenero 1977: 43–5). Actually, Strabo (3.3.7) described all these groups, including Callaecians, as *hoi oreinoi*, 'highlanders', and produced an ethnography that is a hotchpotch of cultural traits from a variety of northern communities. Secondly, the establishment of a Roman military camp in the would-be capital city of *Lucus Augusti* (Ferrer Sierra 1996; Rodríguez Colmenero 1996), in northern *Callaecia*, at a distance of 50 kilometres from the highlands, shows that the communities of this area were very likely a military objective. Thirdly, the coins minted by the Roman Army to pay the soldiers involved in the campaign in 25–23 BC have the arms of the southern Callaecians (not the Asturians) represented on them: *caetra* (small, round shield), spear and *falcata*, a curved sword (although the one used by the Callaecians was not exactly the model represented in the coins; Rodríguez Corral 2009). Meaningfully, the largest cluster of coins in *Callaecia*, apart from the Roman campsite of Lucus Augusti, is situated in the region of the *oppida* (Ferrer Sierra 1996). Therefore, we may accept that the *oppida* provided a number of warriors to fight their highland 'kinsfolk'.

How is all this related to *ethnic* identities? We do not know if the highlanders of *Asturia* and *Callaecia* had common origin myths or notions of a common ancestry, the prerequisite for the existence of an ethnic group, according to Hall (2002). We also do not know if the southern Callaecians had a collective ethnic name, beyond the names of *civitates* transmitted by classical sources. But if we look at their material world (including

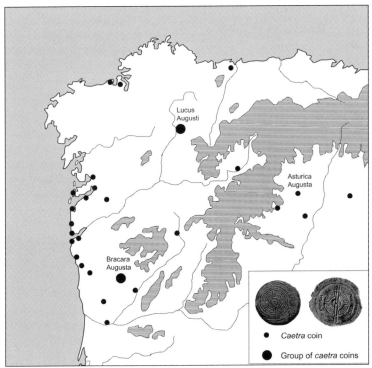

Figure 17.7. Location of the Roman military camps (Lucus Augusti *and* Asturica Augusta) *of the Astur-Cantabrian War (29–19* BC*) in the north-west and distribution of* caetra *coins in the area; compare the distribution of coins and the societies with oppida (Figure 17.2).*

landscape), their economies of power and their attitudes towards aliens, we may well say that they had and performed a common identity. It is obvious that living in an *oppidum* or not, having torcs or rejecting them as a symbol of status, and such trivial things as decorating or not decorating a pot were fundamental issues in the way they reproduced moral knowledge, constructed power and perceived the world and themselves. I do believe, with Kristiansen (1998: 406, my emphasis), that 'a homogeneous material culture, whether belonging to an elite or to commoners, corresponds to a *certain* degree of ethnicity (group identification)', because I believe that material culture is not just an accident in a people's identity. Maybe these were not ethnic identities in the more usual, accepted sense, but they were identities mobilized by particular peoples (*ethnoi*) in their construction of a sense of community. The conquerors of *Callaecia* and *Asturia* certainly perceived and experienced that when they waged war against those communities and re-organized them after the conflict.

   This situation is not unique. Talking about the Sudan in the nineteenth century, Charles Jedrej (2000: 293) says:

   the polarization of the population… into those who defied the government and those who submitted to its exactions was represented in contemporary nineteenth-century literature in geographical terms, as a distinction between mountain dwellers and those inhabiting the river valleys and the plains, rather than in terms of ethnic groups, as the writers could have done, since they were often quite aware of linguistic and cultural differences... According to the same author, 'the distinction between highlanders and lowlanders maybe seen as an early modern transitional phase from a pre-modern diversity, not of ethnic groups, but of political relations in a complex social organization...(Jedrej 2000: 294)'.

As in *Callaecia* and *Asturia*, attitudes to foreigners and concepts of power were paramount for the Sudanese communities to define themselves. Perhaps the Callaecians, as the Bertha of the Sudan-Ethiopian borderland, perceived a common cultural background, but for them other identities – which cannot be dissociated from ethnicity – were deemed more relevant. For the Bertha in the nineteenth century, being an Islamized and hierarchical Watawit was more important than being a Bertha (Jedrej 2004: 720). For a Callaecian, being an *oppidum*-dweller *Bracarensis* was more relevant in constructing his or her identity than being Callaecian.

Conclusions

In this article I have tried to prove three things:

1. that ethnic identity is tightly interwoven with politics – not just individual politics of identity, but structural economies of power;
2. that spatial variations of material culture (including landscape) can be explained often on political grounds – again, different economies of power, which themselves help to inform a sense of ethnic belonging;
3. that collective identification and identity at large work at different levels: between the lower scales, which are the most active but also the most difficult to single out archaeologically, and the higher scales, which are seldom – if ever – mobilized, there are other layers, in which common regimes of power shape identity decisively and in which material culture is actively involved. For illustrating these points I have resorted to the north-west of Iberia in the Late Iron Age. Since ancient times, two 'ethnic groups' or 'cultures' have been defined in the area: Asturians and Callaecians. Modern scholars have respected this imperial view and have tried to match material assemblages with those 'cultures.' A closer examination reveals the actual great diversity concealed under those overarching terms.

Archaeologists are starting to get used to tackling complex and messy ethnic realities, more similar to those with which anthropologists and historians have to deal. This is especially true for those working in colonial contexts (van Dommelen 2006), but issues of identity are rarely clear-cut. The emphasis on culture contact is leaving aside the intricacies of ethnic identity in other contexts. In most situations, instead of rather static, homogeneous and well-bounded groups, we have to be ready to identify ethnic mosaics, patchwork states, multiple scales of collective identity and a diversity of oppositions and homologies that cross-cut politics and culture and generate different concepts of ethnic belonging. Although I have tried to simplify a complex reality, the communities that I have described here were characterized by untidiness and fragmentation, with egalitarian-leaning communities living in the interstices of more hierarchical groups and a diversity of economies of power coexisting in the same space. Besides, I have focused on a very particular period of time – mainly the Late Iron Age, but the articulations of power and identity continuously changed throughout the later prehistory and the early Roman period. The image of homogeneous and well-bounded *Callaecia* and *Asturia* is the product of a colonial state. States – including ancient ones – tend to render things legible in order to make power effective, and this implies reductionism, simplification, and the imposition of order from above (Scott 1998). Spanish scholars have seldom questioned the colonial gaze and have pursued an archaeology of identification, which takes for granted the nature of the groups transmitted by ancient authors. By comparing with historical and ethnographic examples, archaeologists should be able to develop alternative conceptions of ethnicity and criticize prevailing notions of ethnic identity. This in turn may be useful to illuminate other contexts, including modern ones. As archaeologists, we should encourage a different reflection on collective identities, paying special attention to the role of material culture in enabling or constraining the production of those identities.

Lacking clear evidence of self-identification, common myths and ethnic names, the groups that I have identified in northwestern Iberia are admittedly problematic as ethnic communities. However, they are much closer to manifestations of ethnicity than to anything else, because they are shared identities that cross-cut classes or social groups; they are strongly associated to particular cultural and political values, and they 'entail the reproduction of classificatory differences between people who perceive themselves to be *culturally distinct* (Jones 1997: 85, her emphasis)'. This is true in our case, if by culture we understand not only religion, kinship systems and language, but also social values, ethics and political principles. Jones (1997: 120) considers that 'sensations of ethnic affinity are based on the recognition, at both a conscious and subconscious level, of similar habitual dispositions, which are embodied in cultural practices and social relations in which people are engaged'. Daily practice and material culture in *Callaecia* and *Asturia* were pivotal not only in reproducing social order, but also in creating a sense of common identity among similar communities and in opposition to other groups that did not share those fundamental values.

Acknowledgements

I would like to thank my relentless critic, Marco Virgilio García Quintela, for attentively reading the manuscript and raising many interesting points, which have improved this chapter. Thanks are due to the editors of the volume for the invitation to contribute and Margarita Díaz-Andreu for suggesting my name.

18

Changing identities in a changing landscape: social dynamics of a colonial situation in Early Iron Age south-east Iberia

Jaime Vives-Ferrándiz

Keywords: south-east Iberia, postcolonial theory, hybrid practices, colonial encounter, Iberians

Introduction: identities and postcolonial perspectives

Colonial situations have always been seen as special contexts in which the close coexistence of different groups in a given area, each one with its own traditions and practices, leads to a particular expression of identities. Cultural and social changes have monopolized attention in analyses of these situations, although grand narratives have traditionally focused on stories of domination and resistance and on the one-way acculturation processes resulting from these encounters. From such perspectives, local and daily practices have been obscured, and the multi-directional outcomes of the encounters have been largely neglected. The focus on material culture is particularly relevant to scholars concerned with daily life in colonial situations because it was precisely at this level that the relationships between natives and newcomers were played out.

My interest in these topics arises from my archaeological research in colonial encounters in eastern Iberia in the eighth century BC and among Iberian communities which are recognized in the archaeological record from the sixth century onwards. My aim is to explore the social and cultural changes by drawing on the insights of postcolonial theory that have emerged from recent applications in archaeology (van Dommelen 1998, 2002, 2006) and from the concern with the interrelationships between things, people and identities in colonial situations (Thomas 1991, 1994: 58).

Given that the Phoenician presence in Iberia is termed a colonial expansion in the bibliography (Aubet 2001, 2006), the word 'colonial' itself deserves some consideration before we begin. Firstly, though the term is embedded in the ideological and economic developments that led European nations overseas from the fifteenth century onwards (van Dommelen 1997: 306; De Angelis 1998: 539; Stein 2005: 23) it also reflects specific cases of interaction between human groups in previous eras. Thus, the presence of foreign groups brings us to the widely used term 'encounter', with its connotations not only of meeting, but also of opposition. When diverse social and cultural groups meet they may reject each other, but they may also exchange ideas, objects; they may even blend and merge. Whatever the outcome, they are no longer the groups they were at the beginning of the encounter. Ethnographic and anthropological studies have shown that encounters do not have universal features; complexity and variation are the norm. This why it is interesting to examine what diverse groups actually did, their everyday customs and practices, and the way they perceived the world (Voss 2005: 462; Lightfoot 2005: 17).

The approach I am adopting sees colonialism as a specific relation of power between groups and moreover I find the postcolonial perspectives on ancient colonialism particularly useful. For instance, van Dommelen (1998) stresses the importance of looking at the local context as an ensemble of relationships of interdependence; Rowlands (1998) focuses on colonial situations in terms of interactions by different groups with local power structures. So the aim of the postcolonial approach is to look at the different groups of people that shaped the scenario, and to stress agency and local systems of meanings (van Dommelen 1997, 2002; Rowlands 1998: 331; Gosden 2004; Dietler 2006: 221).

Hybridization and ambivalence are key concepts in the evaluation of these relationships from a postcolonial perspective. Bhabha sees hybridization as the creation of new transcultural forms in colonial situations. These forms may take on diverse aspects in the fields of culture, politics, the economy, language, and so on, though of course it is culture that stands out in relation to archaeologists' approaches. Cultural difference is never simple, nor static, but ambivalent, changing, and open to many interpretations (Bhabha 1994: 36; Young 2003: 78). Similar theses on the connectivity of cultures have been posited by scholars like Said (1978) and Wolf (1982). It is important to emphasize that 'hybridity does not involve a single process' but 'works in different ways at the same time according to the cultural, economic and political demands of specific situations (Young 2003: 79)'.

To me, these perspectives open up a wide panorama for the study of colonial situations because they represent stimulating 'conceptual tools to approach and "fill in" the so often ignored grey areas that straddle the colonial divide' (van Dommelen 2006: 140). They also make it clear that encounters are never simply one-way processes, but have highly variable outcomes, such as the creation of new transcultural forms. Colonial encounters must be conceptualized as cultural processes woven as 'entanglements', to use Thomas' term (Thomas 1991), of cultural, social, economic, symbolic or other type of relations, where the entire range of intermediate situations between colonizers and colonized are enacted – rather than a general dialectic between domination and resistance (Thomas 1994: 2; van Dommelen 1998: 214).

In our case, both the similarities and differences between the encounters of indigenous populations and the Phoenicians have to be acknowledged because 'colonialism should first and foremost be conceived in terms of a number of specific colonial situations which share a set of interrelationships. These are furthermore non-static' (van Dommelen

1998: 34). The challenge is to identify the diversity in the archaeological record and the dynamics put in motion by colonial situations and their mechanisms of cultural transmission. The ultimate aim is to define the mode in which the encounters took place, and to explain why.

Along with these approaches to colonial situations, I should stress that I am using the concept of culture as a historical social process, in agreement with both Bourdieu's Theory of Practice and the related notion of *habitus* (Bourdieu 1980: 92). From these perspectives the cultural encounter should be seen not as the clash of abstract cultures but as the coming together of individuals or groups who adopted new practices, in particular structural contexts. The dynamics between structure and actions are the points at stake: when we look at practices, and not cultures, then hybridization processes take on a deeper analytical force (van Dommelen 2006: 139; Vives-Ferrándiz 2005: 47).

From this viewpoint, contact situations offer an interesting social setting for the study of identity in terms of *habitus* and material culture. Following Jones's seminal work (1997: 106–26) we underline three nodal points in order to stress the role of material culture in identity processes:

1. expressions of identity are tied to the material culture and the structural disposition of *habitus*;
2. archaeological cultures are artificially constructed. Similarities or differences in material culture between groups are not reliable data for exploring *acculturated* people; since material culture is structured through the social context, its meanings are not fixed;
3. ethnicity is not always defined through concrete material objects; that is to say, differences between peoples may arise from their own perceptions and from their ways of being in the world.

Using these theoretical issues as my starting point, I will examine the colonial encounter between Phoenician and indigenous communities in southeastern Iberia in order to examine the changes that led to the emergence of what we know as Iberian culture. The goal is to highlight the dynamics of the colonial situations and the ways in which the mechanisms of cultural transmission and change operated, while offering some reflections on the use – and abuse – of strict ethnic labels or categories to understand these encounters. Why did some objects, practices and identities emerge in this setting? Who were the groups involved? Are emulation and a will to be exogenous – as Purcell has recently asked – the only models we require to conceptualize changes? (Purcell 2006: 27)

In this article I will detail practices from production, domestic and funerary contexts during the eighth and seventh centuries BC. Then I will explore the social changes that took place during the sixth century BC and what we should understand by the label Iberian culture in terms of multicultural identity processes. And throughout the article I will focus on the landscape, the framework inside which the people experienced these changes.

Encounters on the landscape

The area of study is located in the lower basins of Segura and Vinalopó rivers (Figs 18.1 and 18.2). The area's most striking geomorphological feature is the formation of a coastal lagoon system from the middle Pleistocene onwards. Mechanical cores in these basins have thrown light on palaeoenvironmental reconstructions based on sedimentological and micropalaeontological data (Abad *et al.* 2003: 267; Blázquez 2005: 288; Barrier and Montenat 2007).

Broadly speaking, these studies show that the lagoon system, connected to the open sea, stretched 19 kilometres inland in a period ranging from the Holocene – when the sea level was at its highest – until the second millennium BC. From that point onwards the lagoon narrowed gradually due to alluvial processes from the Vinalopó and Segura rivers. However, in the period that interests us, during the first half of the first millennium BC the landscape was still dominated by the lagoon and freshwater marshes.

The location of the Late Bronze Age sites clearly reflects these landscape features, as the settlements appear to have been placed around the lagoon. But on closer examination

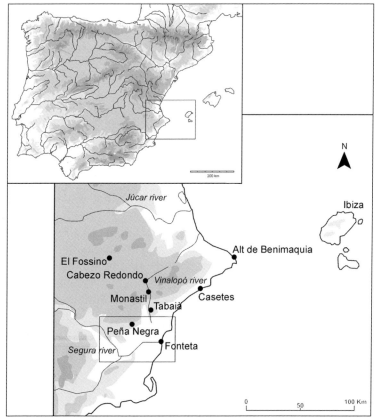

Figure 18.1. Study area in the context of the Iberian Peninsula and sites cited in the text.

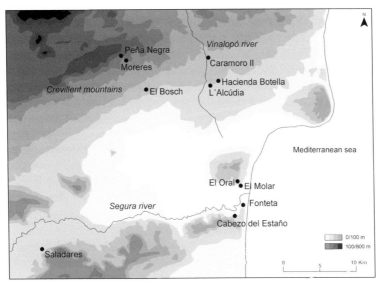

Figure 18.2. The lower basin of Vinalopó and Segura rivers with sites cited in the text.

a less clear-cut situation emerges: the Late Bronze Age sites did not occupy the shores of these marshes, but inland areas like the mountains of Crevillent in the case of Peña Negra, Caramoro II and El Bosch, and the basin of the Segura River in the case of Los Saladares. The exploitation of the plains and the fluvial terraces seems to have been the reason for this pattern of occupation, as illustrated by the position of the inland site of Los Saladares, a small farm near the bank of the Segura and far from the open sea.

Nevertheless, we cannot ignore the crucial fact that these sites exploited mining resources, as shown by the abundant evidence of smelting. Peña Negra is the best known site in the area, occupied without interruption between the eighth and the sixth centuries BC. Metallurgical activity was intense in the eighth century: swords and axes were produced in clay casts (Fig. 18.3a) and transported in regional networks that were identified broadly as Atlantic-Mediterranean exchange routes, in which the Segura and Vinalopó valleys must have played a key role (González Prats 1992; González Prats and Ruiz-Gálvez 1989; Ruiz-Gálvez 1998).

Peña Negra was no exception. At other sites, like the nearby settlement of El Bosch – where dwellings are found scattered over a wide area – stone casts to produce swords and axes dated around the eighth century BC, have been recorded (Fig. 18.3b; Trelis 1995: 185, Trelis *et al.* 2004: 320). Moreover, at El Fossino settlement, further up the Vinalopó river, a stone cast used to produce spears has also been found (Fig. 18.3c; Simón 1998: 127). Together, this evidence indicates that specialized activities became increasingly concentrated in particular sites and suggests some groups among the local communities gained control of the exchange networks.

The local developments during the Late Bronze Age and the Iron Age were also embedded in the wider context of the Phoenician trade diaspora. The indigenous population played such an active role in these networks that it seems fair to say that

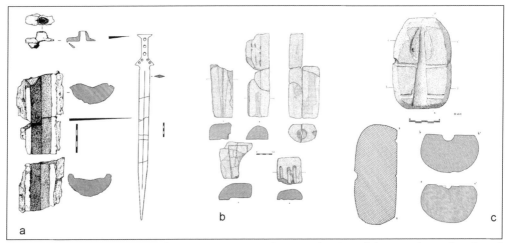

Figure 18.3. (A) Clay moulds from Peña Negra and a reproduction of the swords produced, and stone moulds from (B) El Bosch and (C) El Fossino (based on González Prats 1992; Simón 1998; Trelis 1995). Scales are 5cm long.

their relationship with the Phoenicians was one of mutual interdependence, insofar as the Phoenicians sought out groups who controlled land and had knowledge of local resources because they were the ones who could facilitate the flow of goods required for trade. Thus, colonial encounters, especially trade diasporas, should be understood as dynamizing local socioeconomic features, integrating local systems inside a larger web of regional or interregional exchanges (Aubet 2005: 118; Ruiz-Gálvez 2005: 252).

So the best way to look at the earliest phases of a colonial encounter is to focus on the indigenous communities because they structured the previous setting. From this perspective it is interesting to examine the power relationships that emerged from the changes in the landscape. We find an intense dynamic of creation and abandonment of sites during the Late Bronze Age. In the eighth century BC, several sites were created from scratch – Los Saladares, Peña Negra, Cabezo Pequeño del Estaño (Guardamar del Segura, Alicante) and Fonteta – while others were abandoned, like Caramoro II (Elche, Alicante), El Tabaià (Aspe, Alicante), and others to the south of Segura River, in the region of Murcia (González Prats 2005a: 800).

The earliest Phoenician objects date from the eighth century BC at the sites of Fonteta (Guardamar del Segura, Alicante; Azuar *et al.* 1998: 117; González Prats 1998; González Prats and Ruiz Segura 2000; Rouillard *et al.* 2007), Peña Negra, Les Moreres (González Prats 2002: 376) and Los Saladares (Orihuela, Alicante; Arteaga 1982). The first of these sites is thought to have been a permanent Phoenician settlement, on the basis of architectural as well as epigraphic and ceramic traces (González Prats 1998, 2005b; Rouillard *et al.* 2007). The other sites were, as we have seen above, indigenous settlements where the first Mediterranean imports – traded by Phoenicians – were small ivory objects such as bracelets, necklaces and beads, as well some Phoenician type domestic pottery.

From the indigenous point of view, the Phoenician settlement of Fonteta is located in an outlying area. A small strip between the open sea and the marshy lagoon is thought to have been occupied by the first Phoenician settlers, while the indigenous population settled the inland hills near the lagoon. However, there does not seem to have been a dramatic geographical split between foreigners and natives. A Phoenician inscription on a locally produced plate from Peña Negra (Fig. 18.4; González Prats 1983) suggests a degree of ethnic mixing, in

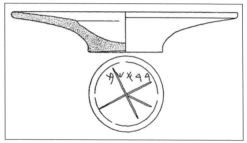

Figure 18.4. Phoenician inscription in a locally produced plate from Peña Negra (based on González Prats 1983). Diameter: 19cm.

which people clearly related to Phoenician groups seem to have lived in indigenous sites. Perhaps the situation will turn out to be far more complex when the studies of hand-made pottery from the earliest levels of Fonteta are completed; it may turn out that they were made by the local indigenous people. In any case, the evidence argues against the assumption that the landscape would have been divided along ethnic and geographical lines – the notion characteristic of modern colonial discourses aiming to strengthen ethnic boundaries by divisions that do not in fact reflect the real social structure (van Dommelen 1998: 23, 2002).

Rethinking Phoenician and indigenous boundaries

Analyzing the Phoenician trade diaspora (Aubet 1993) from the specific perspective of the eastern coast of Iberia requires an examination of modes of consumption in particular contexts. This examination places the emphasis on the local political economy, and understands changes in relation to internal, rather than external, developments (Gosden 2004: 17; Vives-Ferrándiz 2005: 46); the external dynamics are not the most important structural element in contact situations of this kind (Stein 1999: 24–43, Dietler 1998: 296). From this perspective, we can explore in greater depth the practices that may shed light on the processes of construction of identities that occurred in the area. These processes cannot be conceptualized either as acculturation or as changes in indigenous communities alone, since all social groups participated in shaping the social world. In this section I will examine production activities, exchange, domestic contexts and funerary assemblages from this viewpoint.

The social contexts of production: farming and mining

During the Iron Age, ranked societies like the ones that emerged in the lower basin of the Vinalopó and Segura rivers based their power on the control of production and trade. A closer examination of material evidence such as sherds of amphorae and metal ingots demonstrate economic activities that were tied to strategies for constructing power.

First, we find a large number of amphora sherds with seals, stamps and graffiti at the sites of Peña Negra, Monastil and Camara (Fig. 18.5). Although the amphorae are Phoenician in style (10.1.2.1, in Ramon's 1995 typology), the clay used in their production has been identified as local (González Prats and Pina 1983). What is particularly striking is the similarity and coincidence of the stamps – circles, crosses and stars – in the locally produced amphorae in a small area of the Vinalopó valley (González Prats 1983: 228, Poveda 1994).

The stamps found here reveal an interest in controlling production. The decision to mark lots or contents suggests a degree of economic cooperation, corroborating the notion of coexistence between the groups that the style of the amphorae suggests. Local groups are believed to have adopted the potter's wheel and complex double chamber kilns in order to produce containers large enough to export their crops, something that Bronze Age technologies could not achieve. Significantly, in pre-industrial societies learning and training techniques operated by observation and emulation (Dietler and Herbich 1994: 214). The important point in our context is that these developments were clearly influenced by the Phoenicians and these new technologies were the result of Phoenician participation and cooperation.

But there is more. While the marking of containers implies control and cooperation in order to trade agricultural produce, it also implies competition with other nearby groups. Indeed, the connection between the various marks and signs on amphorae and their formal similarities and differences inside a relatively small area should be understood in this light. The seals and stamps on the amphorae are the expression of the economic power of these groups. Below we will come back to this topic and to the ways in which knowledge and technologies are related to power and wealth.

In our case study we still lack evidence of storage – in the form of identifiable spaces and buildings in the settlements – that would allow us to develop our analysis further. However, other sites such as Alt de Benimaquia, on the coast 100 kilometres to the north, have provided more details of the political economy of these groups (Gómez Bellard *et al.* 1991). At that site, there is evidence of wine production on a scale that clearly exceeded domestic demand. The appearance of a new crop – the vine – reveals new socioeconomic processes that go beyond simple agricultural

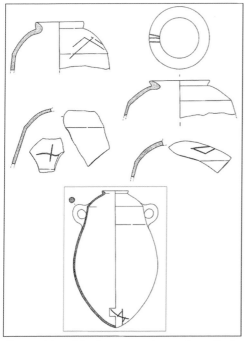

Figure 18.5. Marks on amphorae from Peña Negra (based on González Prats 1983). Diameter: 12cm.

diversification and suggest closer relationships with the land and new social networks that mobilized the land.

Among other materials that suggest the practice of trade at the earliest phases of the encounter are bronze, lead and copper ingots (Fig. 18.6; González Prats 1985) with blades only five millimetres thick – they would have been virtually useless as axes, as other scholars had suggested. These items have been found at three sites in the area, all of them inland sites located on communication routes operating from Late Bronze Age: four pieces from Tabaià, twelve from Peña Negra and at least fifty in Elche – perhaps from L'Alcúdia, though the precise location is not known.

The fact that bivalve casts of these ingots have also been recorded in Tabaià suggests the existence in the area of a specific, non-centralized local economic activity devoted to the production of ingots. Significantly, the items measure and weigh the same, which shows us that certain groups decided to cooperate in their production and standardization.

The destination of these ingots may have been Fonteta (or indeed further afield) in view of the Phoenician demand for metal ores to transport to the eastern Mediterranean. In fact, excavation of the earliest levels from Fonteta has provided evidence of intense metallurgical activity there as well (González Prats and Ruiz Segura 2000: 50). In any case it seems fair to infer that these networks stretched far beyond the local area of study. Indeed, similar ingots have been found in Menorca, in the Balearic islands (Delibes and Fernández-Miranda 1988: 119).

From the perspective of the landscape, the ingots should not be seen merely as objects that were traded but as the materialization of exchange routes and nodal points of transactions. We have few details of these exchanges at present, but we can infer that they must have held a prominent position in the negotiation of power relations in the area. The distribution of the Late Bronze Age sites shows that they played a key role in these developments. One thing is sure: the trading and economic activities were significant arenas in which different regimes of value negotiated and cooperated.

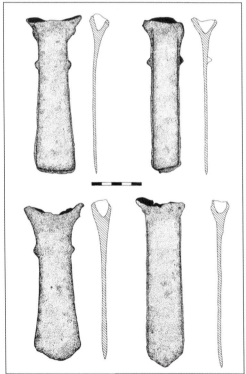

Figure 18.6. Bronze ingots from a hoard of L'Alcúdia (based on González Prats 1985). Scale is 5cm long.

Power and technology

The trading of agricultural surplus and the smelting of finished items such as copper and bronze ingots are examples of productive activities that were not limited to a single settlement. Moreover, the metallurgical activity of the earliest levels of Fonteta (González Prats 2005b: 54) shows that Phoenician colonial system was integrated in *local* socio-economic networks (Aubet 2006: 95). These evidences suggest that a variety of competing groups sought to distribute their products. It also indicates questions of power relations in the colonial setting: the standardization of measures and weights and the storage and exchange of harvests in Phoenician-type amphorae show that cooperation took place at the level of the elites who controlled the networks.

This is a particularly significant point. The possibilities of strengthening power in societies of this kind depend on the extent to which dominant groups are able to control both materials and knowledge: in other words, the control of the production for trade was related to the mastery of technologies – pottery kilns, potters' wheels, smelting activities, and weights and measures. It should be recalled that in Late Bronze Age Peña Negra, specialized activities like smelting were concentrated in single detached dwellings (González Prats 1992: 245) which might be interpreted in terms of empowered households.

The increasing complexity of the production of metal and the collection and storage of surplus produce for trade seems to have led to the emergence of competing heterarchies, rather than a single hierarchy, following a model of power that has also been suggested for Bronze Age Cyprus (Schuster Keswani 1996). If we envisage power in terms of a historical process, this would explain the dynamics of the fortifications at those sites. For example, Fonteta does not seem to have had walls until the late seventh century BC, at which point an impressive defensive system of around seven metres in width was constructed (González Prats and Ruiz Segura 2000: 42).

In so far as technical systems are embedded in relationships and social processes, technology can be seen as a mediator between things and society (Dietler and Herbich 1994: 205). In another study I noted that daily life in both Peña Negra and Los Saladares was shaped by hybrid practices, as domestic hand-made pottery reveals (Vives-Ferrándiz 2007: 542). Both typologically and technologically, the hand-made methods of the native population and the wheel-made techniques of the Phoenicians seem to have converged; therefore, pottery does not seem to serve as an indicator of a colonial divide in terms of ethnic labels. Indigenous and Phoenician pottery practices and traditions merged to create new items which nonetheless bore the influence of earlier forms. As Dietler and Herbich have pointed out techniques are not isolated from social strategies, but form an integral part of them; therefore, changes should not be explained in terms of bounded cultural structures but may relate to different scales (Dietler and Herbich 1994: 215). Thus, these ceramics show that materialities and regimes of value were mediated by *habitus* 'constantly revalued by the conditions of the concrete world in which they are firmly embedded (Comaroff and Comaroff 2005: 108)' in which function, style and technology were integrated.

Appropriated things: a matter of continuity

The record from the funerary site of Moreres provides a useful comparison with the productive and domestic contexts considered so far. Moreres is a cremation cemetery located very close to Peña Negra, and provides the best reference we have for the evaluation of southern funerary practices between the ninth and seventh centuries BC (González Prats 2002). The earliest tombs contained hand-made urns and covers in the pits, and simple bronze and copper bracelets and beads (ornamental objects) were found as grave goods.

With the arrival of the Phoenicians in the area, however, cremations using wheel-made urns and covers were introduced in male and children's tombs. Occasionally female tombs (tomb 39) even combine wheel-made covers and hand-made urns. It has been suggested that this change to wheel-made pottery may correspond to the adoption of Phoenician rituals by indigenous communities; alternatively, it may indicate that Phoenicians were buried there, inside what would have been an ethnically mixed community (González Prats 2002: 387). However, explanations that do not support this acculturation pattern could also be put forward. Let us consider them.

I will focus on practices to infer the aims and values of the people buried – or rather of the people who carried out the burials. Assuming that the same funerary area was used continuously over various generations, it is natural to suppose that it was used by the same social group. This group is associated with the hand-made urn burials of the Late Bronze Age, though some of its members already used Phoenician style wheel-made urns in the seventh century BC. We also find the stratigraphic superposition of urns from different eras, suggesting that they were used by a social group with the express desire to bury their dead in the same place as in previous generations.

So this seems to be a process in which imports were appropriated and changed their functions from one cultural context to another. Foreign wheel-made containers and tableware were adopted and their meanings altered as they began to be used as cinerary urns or covers. Remarkably, the introduction of wheel-made ceramics did not modify the funerary ritual; the funerary practices remained unchanged, in spite of the introduction of a new type of wheel-made urn or cover (Vives-Ferrándiz 2005: 194). Alien objects were valued and incorporated in practices in a unilateral pattern of appropriation which slightly modified the previous funerary practices, but was far from causing a structural variation.

However, more important than the urns themselves were other grave goods, which provided a faithful reflection of the identities expressed and the ways in which these communities understood the body. Among the few grave goods deposited in tombs, two double spring pins are particularly interesting, as they appeared in the archaeological record from the seventh century BC onwards, and have traditionally been assumed to be a Phoenician introduction. The only two double spring pins at Moreres were found along with iron knives, in a male tomb (tomb 42) and in a double tomb containing remains of a young woman and a child (tomb 73; González Prats 2002: 252). As I have suggested for the pottery, the appropriation pattern seems to be accurate, since the pieces cannot be seen in ethnic terms: they were no longer Phoenician nor indigenous, but items in which people objectify (Tilley 2006) their identities.

These high-ranked identities are expressed through items related to the body – that is, adornments and dress. Interestingly, these practices are conducted in terms of the past, since earlier tombs also contain objects related to the decoration of the body. The fact that bronze bracelets, tweezers, beads and necklaces were common grave goods in the earliest tombs suggests that great attention was paid to the body. Including these objects in the grave was the proper thing to do – to quote Bourdieu, a question of *sens commun*.

The key point here is that the bodies of certain individuals might have displayed (and possibly also stressed and emphasized) identities via the choice of the grave goods. New objects suggest marking patterns according to gender and status: while men were buried in wheel-made urns, with double-spring pins and iron knives, women were buried in hand-made urns with double-spring pins as well. This practice of appropriation contrasted with the domestic and productive contexts of the surroundings, where hybrid practices have been identified. Interestingly, though, hybridization had no place in the funerary realm. This contradiction is the key to the interpretation of the roles of the diverse social groups, communities and identities that coexisted in the southern context. The novelties introduced by these urns might be seen as a reinvention of traditions of a community which was intent on maintaining a funerary ritual norm, for both men and women, in spite of the introduction of new objects as domestic pottery.

Social change as hybridization

From the mid-sixth century BC onwards, the settlement pattern in the study area began to change. First, two of the most important sites were abandoned: Peña Negra and, slightly later, Fonteta. A new site, El Oral (San Fulgencio), was founded from scratch on the coastline (Abad *et al.* 2003). Interestingly, the settlements continued to be located around the lagoon, continuing the previous Phoenician pattern.

Leaving aside for a moment the economic orientation of the site (Abad and Sala 2001: 175) the point to stress is that the material culture had clearly changed in relation to the former sites, even though specific connections to materials of the later levels of Fonteta remained (pottery, for instance). The cultural ascription of the inhabitants of El Oral had interestingly changed: they are termed Iberians in the archaeological bibliography.

In search of the Iberians

Over time, the term Iberian has been understood in different ways by different scholars. Indeed, their conceptualizations of the term reflect to a large extent their notions of both culture and cultural encounter. In their examinations of Iberian material culture, archaeologists have become aware that foreign groups played a role in shaping and forging that culture, but the identity of these groups, and the extent of their influence, have been major sources of debate in Spanish archaeological enquiries.

Until the 1950s, archaeologists suggested that Iberian culture related exclusively to a single group of people who came from abroad, that is, from North Africa or the eastern Mediterranean. Other scholars saw the Iberian period as an evolution of indigenous communities facing 'advanced foreign civilizations' – Greeks, Phoenicians or Carthaginians – a conception of change in which ethnic boundaries played a prominent role.

During the following decades scholars attributed less importance to migrations in their explanations of Iberian culture. The main reason for this change was the continuing identification of Phoenician imports in indigenous settlements, which indicated a process of acculturation. Archaeologists thus abandoned the concept of the origins of Iberians-as-a-people, and began to ask how the Iberians were formed. This implied a different notion of culture as well as relationships between groups; now the term *Iberian* was understood as referring to practices that did not have a direct relationship with a single ethnic group of people. In terms of material culture, locally made wheel-made pottery has allowed archaeologists to distinguish Iberian culture from the middle of the sixth century BC.

It is precisely in this context that Iberian culture came to be divided into three periods, following an analogy from biology: a period of formation or birth, another of development, and a final stage of decline or death. The first, termed the Early Iberian period, was thus considered as a nodal phase when the culture was formed by the development of indigenous groups in the face of the more evolved Greeks and Phoenicians. These interpretations were based on the diffusionist standpoint that outsiders do cause change.

It is worth saying that these perspectives regarded the indigenous peoples as the main agents of the development of Iberian culture. Foreigners were considered only to have *influenced* them, though deeply enough to be able to effect changes. Therefore, Iberians appeared in the process of learning from other cultures and incorporating foreigners' symbols and cultural advances like wheel-made pottery or iron technologies. The label 'Iberization' was coined to understand the whole set of cultural changes that *led* to Iberian culture. Paradoxically, however, indigenous agency was both over- and underestimated. Changes happened in the clash of cultures but no Phoenicians nor Greeks appeared to be Iberian; only indigenous peoples changed. In previous work we have discussed the problems with this one-sided approach to the understanding of culture change, as well as its similarities to other colonialist labels such as Hellenization or Romanization (Aranegui and Vives-Ferrándiz 2006: 90).

In the last 30 years, however, the positivistic approaches that placed a strong emphasis on the *when* and *who* of the Iberian culture have been replaced by approaches that ask rather *why* and *how* phenomena of culture change operate. Thus, the problem of the origins and formation of the Iberian culture, though reformulated in different terms, is the same as the one we face today when studying the colonial encounter.

What happened in southeast Iberia during the sixth century BC? A postcolonial theoretical approach, locating the actions of each group of people within the colonial setting can help to understand social change in relation to local (that is, both foreign and indigenous) dynamics (Arafat and Morgan 1994; Dietler 1995; Stein 1999, 2005; Gosden 2004: 17). Two fields of social expression are particularly useful: changes in dwellings and funerary rituals.

Change and housing

The archaeological record between the Late Bronze Age and the Iberian period reveals changes in houses that can be understood as changes in social and family relationships. Circular or pseudo-circular shaped buildings are found in domestic architecture from Los Saladares and Peña Negra until the eighth century BC. After this time new buildings were constructed, traditionally associated with the arrival of the Phoenicians. These included quadrangle-shaped buildings (at Los Saladares) and buildings with rounded angles (at Peña Negra), and even walls plastered with lime in the seventh century BC. The archaeological record of Peña Negra is very interesting. Together with the circular-shaped structures, a new architectural form emerges – rectilinear walls in isolated detached dwellings (González Prats 2001: 174). So the single house is still recorded.

This shows a clear pattern of indigenous appropriation of Phoenician architecture and practices (Díes 2001), as the idea of the house and the socio-economic and familiar structures continued to be the same as those of the Late Bronze Age, at least during the seventh century BC (Vives-Ferrándiz 2005: 191). Among the Luo, in Kenya, similar changes in the shapes of houses are recorded. Dietler and Herbich's research show that circular shaped houses were replaced by rectangular ones – perhaps due to the adoption of European furniture – but this is not followed by any particular social changes, since 'la structure domestique interne est en outre restée dans la maison rectangulaire' (Dietler and Herbich 1994: 220). Those authors stress that greater social consequences are derived from changes in construction materials which affected social and productive relationships. Our case study may also have involved subtle changes in social structures and actions but an analysis of this issue is beyond the aims of this paper.

In the late sixth century BC, the well-recorded houses from El Oral are large, complex courtyard dwellings (Fig. 18.7; Abad and Sala 2001: 101). Despite differences in size, they all have several rooms, suggesting that social structures have also changed in relation to the earlier period. Moreover, domestic structures – benches, hearths, shell mosaics, floor decorations – were closely related to the customs of the people of Fonteta (González Prats and Ruiz Segura 2000: 32; Sala 2005: 128). In fact, houses from the phase Fonteta V – dated roughly *c.* 625–600 BC – had more than three rooms, and their walls were built with similar types of mudbrick (González Prats 2005b: 53).

As many archaeologists have persisted in seeing cultural encounters as indigenous transformations from a one-sided, acculturationist perspective, these cultural patterns in domestic architectures have been identified as odd, anomalous practices, as the earlier indigenous groups – those believed to be the forerunners of Iberian culture – do not provide the *correct* parallels. But, as we mentioned above, a colonial encounter should be seen as integrating all social groups. High-ranked Iberian identities should be conceptualized on the strength of both indigenous and Phoenician practices (Vives-Ferrándiz 2005: 236; González Prats 2005b: 59). In El Oral every single architectural practice became a new cultural expression in a new social space, now the space of the power: the Iberian *oppidum*. We will now turn to the best-known early Iberian necropoleis of the area, to explore the meaning of this pattern further, in terms of power relationships.

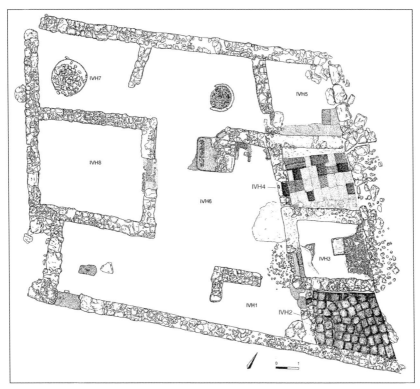

Figure 18.7. A courtyard dwelling of El Oral (based on Abad and Sala 2001). Dimensions of scale: 1 metre.

Burying identities, or the doxa modified

The best way of examining these dynamics is to look at the cemeteries of El Molar (San Fulgencio, Alicante) and Les Casetes (La Vila Joiosa, Alicante). El Molar is made up of around 30 tombs excavated in the early twentieth century. The cemetery has been linked to the El Oral settlement, as it lies barely half a kilometre away. Its chronology is considered to range from the mid-sixth to the fifth century BC (Peña 2003). The outstanding feature is the presence of two complex tombs – a large coffin made of stone slabs, and a stone well with a burial mound (Fig. 18.8) which presumably served in inhumation rituals; the rest of the tombs are simple pits containing urns with cremated remains (Peña 2003: 24). However, we lack descriptions of the inhumations – something we might expect excavators to have provided, given the differences between these tombs and the cremation tombs.

Questions about the ethnic ascription of the individuals buried here have been raised in recent years and it has been suggested that they might have been either foreigners, Phoenicians or even Punicized Iberians (Sala 2005: 35; Peña 2005: 371). The point at stake, then, is the problem of the rituals, their practices and the persistence in labelling them ethnically. In this situation, a non-essentialist view of practices and cultures is

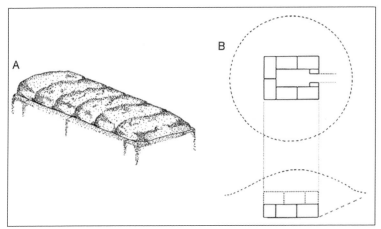

Figure 18.8. Complex tombs of El Molar (based on Peña 2003). Scales are not provided in the original publication. Slabs from A might be 90cm long by 40/50cm wide. Each stone from B is presumably 100cm long by 60cm wide.

required to approach the discussion from a wider perspective. In this regard, the second funerary area – Les Casetes, situated 40 kilometres to the north – is especially interesting. It was excavated recently and provides new data to complement those found at El Molar.

More than two dozen tombs have been excavated. The tombs vary in type from pits to simple rectangular graves of different sizes, burial mounds, and complex constructions like funerary cavities. In the tombs described to date – tombs 17 and 18 (García Gandía 2003; García Gandía and Padró 2002–3) – the incinerated remains were deposited directly on the ground of the structures without the use of a container like an urn (Fig. 18.9; García Gandía 2005: 347). However, the pseudo-rectangular structures of the tombs are more suggestive of inhumation than of incineration. These examples offer a new perspective on the excavations of El Molar, where the structures so far presumed to be for inhumation are more likely to have been used for incineration, suggesting that a burial structure is not always related to the ritual carried out at the site.

As at El Molar, Les Casetes's location on the coast and the nature of the objects left in its tombs have sparked a vivid debate among scholars about the Phoenician or indigenous identity of its inhabitants. But most of the debate is based on dualist and essentialist positions which ignore the historicity of the phenomenon of cultural contact and overlook other possible interpretations of the archaeological record.

In my view, the tombs of Les Casetes and El Molar are excellent examples of the ambivalence of a colonial situation shaped by diverse groups in historical social processes. These groups have different sociopolitical interests which are expressed in and through hybrid practices (Vives-Ferrándiz 2007: 552). The material culture – tombs, grave goods and funerary rituals – suggests a phenomenon of hybridization in which different cultural elements combine to shape a new context that does not reproduce

Figure 18.9. Structure of tomb 9 of Les Casetes (García Gandía 2003). 120cm long.

completely any of the practices that preceded them, but at the same time reveals some of their cultural referents. To quote Bhabha, it is a new space with new meanings (1994; see also, van Dommelen 2006: 139).

The interpretations of the funerary practices carried out here must be seen in relation to the temporal dynamic in which they are situated, because 'an important dimension of the chronology of the colonial encounters is the transformation of colonizer-native interactions over time' (Lightfoot 2005: 28; I would add 'foreign-indigenous interactions'). The chronology of Les Casetes ranges from the end of the seventh to the beginning of the sixth century BC; the date of El Molar is slightly more recent, from mid-sixth and fifth centuries BC. These chronological remarks are important. By understanding these practices as historical processes, they entail the historicity that every social situation requires: the social structure in the southern environment must have changed substantially from the time of the Phoenician arrival, through an influx of a new population comprising different social groups, but also via the interaction of the Phoenicians with indigenous groups who were also socially heterogeneous and involved in their own hybridization processes. In short, identities were created or reformulated.

However, to go beyond the ethnic debates, we have to envisage a different social structure for the colonial encounter, one that takes into account, above all, the relationships of power between the groups and ideologies represented. I have maintained elsewhere that we should see Les Casetes as an arena used by a dominant group to express different identities in a socially visible way in a hybrid social setting (Vives-Ferrándiz 2005: 221, 2007: 554). Strategies to transmit an ideology of differences are built through the choice of particular grave goods and new burial structures. Hybrid practices are taken to be, then, the effect of diverse origins on the colonial context. In other words, the hybrid practices recorded from the late seventh century BC onwards in these funerary spaces materialized as specific new cultural creations with references to both indigenous local Bronze Age and Phoenician practices (Vives-Ferrándiz 2005: 200).

The most telling example that power relationships, ideologies and identities were renegotiated during the sixth century BC is the appearance of a new burial practice: the deposit of weapons in tombs. In the tombs of Les Casetes (García Gandía 2005: 348) we find ordinary spears (Fig. 18.10) and *soliferrea* (a longer kind of iron spear) and in the more recent tombs of El Molar, we also find short swords and knives (Peña 2005: 376). In spite of these differences in detail, the point to stress is that weapons were being deposited at this time. Moreover, together with grave goods, representations of warriors (or armed men) appear in necropoleis as well – for example, a human engraved stele from Altea la Vella, representing a sword and a knife.

Warriors and arms existed before, of course, but what we see here is a new way of expressing male identities and power: arms were deposited because they denoted status and expressed the power acquired by dominant groups. Appadurai's notion of regimes of value (1986: 36) is relevant here, since value was now invested in arms; arms objectified value and denoted coercive power.

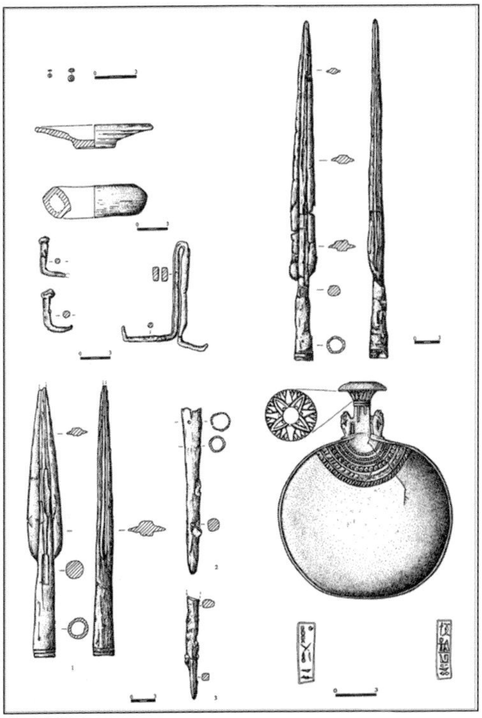

These ostentatious burial rituals suggest social competition and the existence of power relationships and were also expressions of identities. Bourdieu's accounts of symbolic violence are particularly relevant to this case, as the celebrated term is defined as the hidden form that overt violence acquires (1980: 218). Besides, since *habitus* are not mechanically reproduced practices, they are contingent and possess the possibility of change. Culture, then, is determined by actions and practices, which are shaped above all by *habitus*. This a key point to understand the adoption of novelties and, above all, social and cultural change.

In our case study, the symbolic scene was successfully manipulated by dominant groups to reproduce the social order in accordance with natural

Figure 18.10. Grave goods from tomb 18 of Les Casetes (García Gandía 2005). Scales are 3cm long.

perceptions of social relationships and in an attempt to legitimate their social position in a setting underpinned by specific power relationships. Bourdieu's concept of *doxa* (1994: 129) entails this notion of the *taken for granted* and relationships of power: the natural ways of doing things are manipulated because symbolic differences in practices do matter. Other scholars (for instance, Cuozzo 2003) have fruitfully explored these social practices in terms of both invented traditions following Hobsbawm and Ranger's seminal book (1983) and sociopolitical and economic competition addressing 'an understanding of how systems of inequality are created and naturalized through ritual performances and material symbolism' (Schuster Keswani 2004: 10). This situation follows the pattern already seen in the cultural changes associated with the orientalizing phenomenon throughout the Mediterranean (Aubet 2005: 121; Riva and Vella 2006).

Colonial situations are seen from these perspectives as arenas in which inequality is increasingly reproduced. We should also bear in mind that the social relationships entailed by this panorama must be renewed through daily practices that create links between people (Bourdieu 1980: 191). Clearly, the tombs were intended to indicate the status of the individuals buried there. It is also more than likely that a client system can be seen in these necropoleis as they concentrated symbols of wealth as a demonstration of power.

Conclusions

The archaeological record can be seen as a series of practices by which people created their identities (Meskell 2001: 189; Given 2004: 36). In our case study, the negotiation of identities was driven by perspectives that did not necessarily conform to *our* ethnic labels related to material culture in clearly bounded areas.

For example, the pottery items used for cooking and eating suggest that mixing processes took place throughout the area from the moment of the Phoenician arrival. Domestic contexts from the eighth- and seventh-century BC levels of Fonteta, Peña Negra and Los Saladares reveal hybrid practices: pots, plates and bowls with technological and decorative borrowings indicate that indigenous and foreign ways of cooking, eating and drinking became merged in new contexts. Everyday vessels participated actively in social relationships; and more precisely hand-made hybrid objects were clear expressions of values and norms, visions and ways of being in the world. These values were not bounded geographically along ethnic lines; what we find are the products of groups of people from different backgrounds coming together in the same settlement and constructing identities in different ways.

Of course, the strategies of individual households or groups were determined by their social position, and their interactions created new social spaces and new meanings. This is why I have tried to focus not on ethnic identities and distinctions but on ascriptions of status and power, both in productive contexts such as agriculture and smelting and in necropoleis.

The production contexts reveal that power was related to technological novelties and knowledge. For instance, only by introducing the potter's wheel and double chamber kilns could agricultural produce be stored and traded, and only in this way could groups increase their power and status. The numerous seals and marks found on amphorae reveal to us that competition was a prominent feature. The houses and necropoleis from the sixth century BC also bear witness to the use of competitive strategies by peoples in the search for new arenas for wealth.

To conclude, we should say that there is no single explanation for this scenario. Identities were defined less in terms of material culture than in terms of practices. What we should do is focus on the people's perceptions of the local world and look beyond ethnic boundaries. Examples from other colonial scenarios may invite us to think of hybrid practices as structural conditions of situations of this kind (Comaroff and Comaroff 1997; Lightfoot 2005; van Dommelen 2006: 140).

Finally, the outcomes are also worth examining in terms of processes of changing identities and modifications of *doxa*, the 'taken for granted'. In this paper I have focused on the particularities of the phenomenon known as the emergence of Iberian culture from the perspective of the negotiation of identities in a colonial encounter. Dynamic relationships of power must be addressed to understand the whole setting and how the processes of identities are constructed in displaying material culture. In fact, material culture was used in various ways in the colonial area, depending on the social position of the particular group of people in question.

Acknowledgements

I would like to thank Gabriele Cifani and Simon Stoddart for inviting me to present a contribution on this volume. Thanks are also given to Ignacio Grau who read and commented on a first draft of the paper.

19

Endnote: Situating ethnicity

Simon Stoddart and Skylar Neil

The study of identity and, by extension, ethnicity in the ancient Mediterranean tends to be substantially self contained (Hales and Hodos 2010)[1]. The ancient world refers to the ancient Mediterranean world. The ancient sources refer to the classical authors. In terms of ethnicity, this latter constraint tends towards definitions based on ascription by others rather than self-ascription, creating only half of the argument in most constructions of ethnicity. As Jenkins rightly points out, external categorization is not just a one-way process (Jenkins 1994: 199); those being defined must engage with the authority of the definer to impose such a category upon a group (Jenkins 1994: 217).

This endnote seeks to explore the study of ethnicity more widely outside the Mediterranean and Europe, aiming to understand both the commonalities and uniqueness of the Mediterranean experience. It also seeks to identify the intersection between landscape and ethnicity, noting this potential element of ascription does not generally feature in generalizing accounts (e.g. Emberling 1997: 311).

The work of Barth (1969) remains the fundamental text against which broader studies of ethnicity are measured, a point particularly emphasized by Fulminante (this volume). Barth, armed by his collection of empirical facts, notes that there is mobility and social interaction across ethnic boundaries and that 'cultural differences can persist despite inter-ethnic contact and interdependence' (1969: 9–10). He goes on to emphasize the self-ascription (1969: 10) of ethnicity, balanced by ascription by others, drawing on 'origin and commitment' and 'performance' (1969: 28). Self-ascription goes so far as to underline "the features … which the actors themselves regard as significant" (1969: 14). These ideas led to a study of the "systematic set of rules governing inter-ethnic social encounters" (1969: 16) in the context of boundary maintenance. In addition, he remarks on the relationship to stratification (the control of assets by an ethnic group) (1969: 27) and cultural evolution (1969:38) ('continual organizational existence with boundaries'). These latter themes connect well with the subject of this volume: the Mediterranean in the middle of the first millennium BC.

From the time of Hodder's work in East Africa (Hodder 1982) and comparative work on the Neolithic of Europe (Hodder 1969), aspects of these Barthian, rather than pre-Barthian, themes have been developed by archaeologists. The review by the Near Eastern, and anthropologically trained, archaeologist Emberling (1997: 295) has particularly emphasized this threshold, wittily suggesting a new historiographical dating scheme of BB (Before Barth) and AB (After Barth). He dwells on what he defines as an unfortunate emphasis on the term 'boundary' by Barth, which he considers to be too physically associated, and better replaced by a perception of difference (1997: 299–300). This has implications for the landscape theme of the current volume.

In spite of this critique of boundaries there has been a considerable amount of work on the construction of boundaries, and the study of their autonomy and permeability in recent literature (Donnan and Wilson 1999; Wilson and Donnan 1998). Many of these accounts derive from modernist or imperial contexts, but are still informative of the levels of complexity and ambiguity which may obtain in earlier contexts. One particularly apposite account is the study of Greekness (Green 2005) on the Greek-Albanian border in the Balkans which proves to be highly ambiguous with multiple emic terms (Greki – Graikos – Hellene – Romiosity) for what might be perceived as one grouping externally. A similar flavour comes through strongly in the analysis by Bintliff of other areas of Greece (this volume). Furthermore, this ethnicity maps in a complex way onto landscape and place where nature is thoroughly entangled with the political (Green 2005: 113–14). Similar tensions in border places are raised in the study of Chinese ethnicity (Rack 2005); the ethnographer reveals how the intentions to study a particular Miao ethnicity was undermined by the empirical realities of a border region, and, one might add, the effects of Han Chinese imperialism. Ruiz and Molinos (this volume) examine some of these problems by illustrating the diversity of frontiers in the middle of the first millennium BC in Iberia.

A central theme that appears to govern most definitions of ethnicity is the concept of descent within the dialogue of the development of large-scale power structures (Grillo 1998). Some scholars have restricted ethnicity to modernity, but most are willing to extend its use to early state formation. Such emphases permeate archaeological (Stark and Chance 2008: 3) and historical (Wheatcroft 1995: 285) studies, transcending kinship whether fictive or not. Emberling (1997: 304) particularly picks up on Barth's self ascription by origin and commitment and on the relationship to stratification by means of the state. In fact, he reserves the use of the term ethnicity precisely for social contexts which follow state formation (1997: 306), a view shared by Smith (1986 (1988)) and Brumfiel (1994a), suggesting, by implication, that delving for earlier ethnicities, as sometimes seen in Mediterranean research, might be problematic. The emphasis on descent also gives potential for a fiction of descent (Rack 2005: 23), an approach that is particularly prevalent amongst the work of some philologists in the Mediterranean (Stoddart this volume).

A substantial trend in the analysis of ethnicity is a move from formality to fluidity, lability (Brumfiel 1994b: 101), hybridity (Bhabha 1994), open-endedness and contingency (De La Cadena 1995: 340), common ground (Rack 2005: 21ff) and slippage, although older ethnography had already pointed this out in at least one seminal ethnography (Leach 1954). Fluidity may also be an important ingredient of the contrast between internalized and externalized views of ethnicity (Moerman 1968), since these interpretations, although contemporary, may not be the same. Fluidity applies to the construction of identity and the corresponding construction of boundaries. It is implicit in the tension between a primordialist ('emotional attachment') and an instrumentalist ('political gain') approach (Emberling 1997: 306), particularly since the latter has tended to take a greater hold in more recent accounts (Bennett 1975). Indeed some authors have claimed that there is a new synthesis where, although definitions of ethnicity are derived from primordialist descent, there is room for circumstantialist and instrumentalist malleability (Linnekin and Poyer 1990b). The importance of these trends is emphasized a number of times in the current volume, most notably by Bintliff, who in different words notes the tension arising from fluidity held in check by the emergence of power of state formation in the eighth century BC. Indeed, in practice, fluidity may be held in check when the constraints of authority and power take effect (Emberling 1997: 307). A particular instance of this is when empires make an administrative imposition of ethnicity (Rack 2005: 44); early relations in North America (White 1991), the Muslim-Christian Mediterrananean (Colley 2002), and India had considerable middle ground that only became formalized late in the political development of these regions. Although the attributes of imperial ethnicity should only be transposed to ethnicity in early states with great caution, a similar early middle ground may have existed.

In general, ethnicity is increasingly seen as dynamic (Berdan 2008: 107; Grillo 1998: 23), a product of performance or practice (Tooker 1992: 815–16), and the effect of the inevitable life cycle of an individual's identity, even though other categories may be employed to illustrate these changes (Umberger 2008: 101–3). Above all ethnicity is contextual and situational, although in stratified societies, including the Aztec, this could once again be constrained by an individual's rank (Umberger 2008: 72).

Time is another factor in the dynamism of ethnicity. Paradoxically the concept of a common history (past time) and destiny (future time) may contribute to the forging of a cohesion which resists dynamism. On the other hand, a prominent focus of some studies is the life cycle of ethnicity (Emberling 1997: 307–10): ethnogenesis, maintenance and extinction. This temporal dimension is also linked closely to the issue of the causes of ethnogenesis. The most frequently attributed cause is the forging of common interest and common enemies in the context of an increasing competitive environment of emerging state organized complexity (Berdan 2008: 110–11). Response to danger (Malone and Stoddart 1994; Grau Mira this volume) is one interpretation, and encounters of hybrid practice (Vives-Ferrándiz this volume) provide a more subtle approach. Another obvious model is the colonial model of interaction between imperial organizations and local incorporated elites, whose interest concentrates on enhanced self-ascription in order to buy into the advantages brought by close imperial neighbours or masters (Lentz 1997) which then leads to competitive emulation (Fardon 1996). However, anthropologists are at pains to stress that ethnicity is not simply a product of colonial action (Lentz and Nugent 2000), so once again, particularly in the period of this volume, it is dangerous to employ imperial analogies.

A further central issue is the degree to which class and ethnicity overlap, both in terms of formative processes and in terms of fluid manipulative strategies. In the Americas, this was strongly tied into the colonial experience, as groups manipulated ethnicity to their own class advantage (Stark and Chance 2008: 34–5). The contrasting ethnic heritage of class groups does, though, seem to have had an historical depth (Umberger 2008: 72) and played itself out in the tension between *calpulli* (commoner land associations) and *tecalli* (elite land associations) even during the Aztec period (Brumfiel 1994a: 91, 101). The study of both northern Italy (Lomas this volume) and Spain (several contributions) shows the prominence of the identities of social class in underwriting the fundamental practices of identity at the early stages of state formation.

To a certain extent this changed under imperial conditions, namely under the tributary state of the Aztec Triple Alliance and the social dominance of the Mexica in the central Mexican basin. In this context, an emphasis on a broader scale of ethnicity, based on linguistics and cultural stereotypes, is evident. The simplification of complex identity groups allowed for easier administration of those under the Aztec Empire, especially as their jurisdiction expanded and more ethnic groups were brought into the imperial social network; moreover, the propagation of these stereotypes by the dominant ethnic group allowed the Mexica to control the rhetoric and use it to their political and social advantage. For example, by maintaining the reputations of the Huastecs as licentious savages and the Otomí as excellent hunter-warriors incapable of governance, the Mexica were able to mediate as exemplars of moderation and centrism (Brumfiel 1994a: 94–5; Stark 2008: 40). Ethnic impersonators would dress as members of specific groups using identifiable visual markers – like a labret, in the case of the Otomí (see Brumfiel 1994a for illustrations) – for public performances, and ethnicity also played an important role in the conducting of public rituals in Tenochtitlan (Stark 2008: 40–1). Likewise, ethnicity also played an important role in the capturing of war prisoners and even the selection of sacrificial victims, as those from distant regions were deemed less 'valuable'. According to the written accounts of Diego Durán, written within a generation of the Spanish conquest, the gods favoured sacrificial victims from city-states from the core of the Aztec Empire and especially Nahuatl speakers. The peoples from remote lands, on the other hand, were 'yellowish, hard, tasteless breads in his mouth' (Durán, *et al.* 1964: 140–1). In contrast with earlier models of ethnicity based on civic affiliation, ethnic identity under the Aztec Triple Alliance represented a shift not only towards more generalized ethnic categories based on linguistic and cultural markers, but also in the way in which ethnicity affected the social and political hierarchy. Under an empire dependent on alliances and tribute, these groups could be promoted or demoted within the political system according to imperial aims or in response to alliance or rebellion. Rather than the usual condition of 'self-ascription' for the existence of an ethnic group, according to anthropological canon, an ethnic group under the Aztec Empire was both externally defined under the ruling state and actively expressed and engaged with by its members. This politically orchestrated ethnicity became even more marked in the post-colonial period (De La Cadena 1995: 332), although in some areas of South America the colonial state tended to reduce Indians of different ethnic background to mere tribute bearers (Saignes 1995: 183). Once again these intense manipulations of ethnicity are products of an imperial order.

The study of space takes us closer to landscape. The nested scale of identity is the most common approach, as illustrated by Rajala, Stoddart, Lomas and Gonzalez (this volume). This is also the case with the building blocks of the South American *ayllu* (Saignes 1995: 182) and the Aztec (Hare 2000), but identity does not map straightforwardly onto space. With the exception of community (and its potential association with place, an emphasis also made by Lomas in this volume), many of the identities of the indigenous New World – community, social class and ethnicity – appear to be constructed independently of space (Berdan 2008: 132; Stark and Chance 2008: 38). In both the New and Old World, ethnic mosaics appear to have developed by processes of internal reinforcement, where Mesoamerica (Stark and Chance 2008) has been compared to eighteenth century Burma (Lieberman 1978). The majority of these ethnic enclaves were the product of imperial incorporation or tolerance (Emberling 1997: 316–17) both in Mesopotamia (Ozguç 1963) and Mesomerica (Stark 2008) and the imperial context of multi-culturalism is readily seen in the aftermath of Alexander's empire most notably in Egypt (Bagnall 1988; Burstein 2008; Goudriaan 1988; Johnson 1992). However, in the New World, there are important examples from earlier state formation at Teotihuacan (Spence 1992) and Monte Alban (Blanton 1978: 37–40, 44–6; 75–98), in which the presence of migrants is confirmed both culturally and scientifically (White *et al.* 2004). Burgers (this volume) addresses very similar issues, pointing out the ferment of power structures within which 'Greek' identity was manipulated across space in a 'non-Greek' landscape. In his own way, Naso (this volume) also shows the uncertainties of identifying ethnic groups in border regions.

The linkage to landscape, as opposed to place, is less emphasized in most approaches. Ethnicity invariably maps onto broad landscape contrasts, notably the distinction between upland and lowland. This is an important facet of the study of the civilized lowland Lue ethnicity in the seminal *Problem of Tribe* volume (Moerman 1968). It is also an important facet of the contrast between Carians and Ionians (Lohmann this volume), the Umbrians and Etruscans (Stoddart this volume), upland/lowland Sicily (Stoddart 2000; Fitzjohn 2007) and in the definition of the Samnites (Dench 1995; Naso this volume) and Asturians/Callaecians (Gonzalez-Ruibal this volume). This amounts to more than cultural identity mapped onto economic infrastructure. There are profound differences constructed from the interplay between land and culture. This can be seen in the anthropological study of regional China, where landscape was clearly influential in the construction of ethnic identity. At one broad level, this was a reflection of upland–lowland differences (Rack 2005: 34ff); at another more detailed level this was an elite-led activity that related closely to the imperial imposition of Chinese ethnic identity on the subjugated provinces (Rack 2005: 55–8). Local people negatively associated danger with landscape, whereas the imperial masters appropriated its beauty to assert control through artistic depiction. The Faliscan territory can be seen as another example of more creative landscape construction of identity, where cultural difference mapped onto a very different physical morphology (Ceccarelli and Stoddart 2007), although we can debate as to which has primacy (Osborne this volume b)

In Mesoamerica, places, rather than landscape, were the loci of ethnicity. Places or communities, as revealed by glyphs, were generative of identities (Berdan 2008: 108ff.). The *calpolli* territorial unit provided the 'arena for an individual's social life'. The larger (city state) *altepetl*, made up of multiple *calpolli*, and although generally multi-ethnic, was according to Hare (Hare 2000: 85) the focus of ethnic identity. However, Hare proposes caution in interpreting a straight-forward mapping of community onto contiguous space. This same emphasis is strongly present in central Italy, where two concepts of place, the Latin and Etruscan, competed for attention. The Latin concept of place, epitomized and eternalized by Rome, was deep seated and gradual in its development (Carandini, Cornell this volume). Herein lies an irony that the myths of ancient Rome denied this deep seated history, allowing a Hellenist (Osborne this volume) to claim the late arrival of Roman political prowess. The evidence uncovered by Carandini's excavations has unravelled one of the most significant constructions of place in the western world, which he significantly compared with 10 Downing Street, London in his original lecture, since the redolence of place is not simplistically related to scale. The Etruscan concept of place was marked out by successive tipping points (Stoddart 2010), most prominently in the ninth century BC, but still had some substantial historical depth and provided a major focus of identity at a scale smaller than ethnicity. The Greeks also identified with the *polis* community which was again at least in part associated with place (Osborne this volume). However, this situation became more complex in Asia Minor as demonstrated by Lohmann (this volume), where there was ancient debate over the definition of Ionian identity, not least between some Ionian cities and some ancient authors such as Herodotos.

A cross-cutting theme of all studies of ethnicity is the relationship to textual or ethnographic sources. This is especially true in the ancient Mediterranean, in which most of the textual sources describe ethnic groups from a particular Graeco-Roman perspective. This is often a tension between internalized (emic) and externalized (etic) definitions as illustrated by Lomas and Ruiz and Molinos (this volume). The New World offers a direct historical approach, accompanied by a foreshortening of time, an approach which has been profitably applied by primordialist models (Stark and Chance 2008: 7) of ethnogenesis amongst the Zapotec (Flannery and Marcus 1983; Marcus and Flannery 1996: 23–32). One problem in the Americas is that ethnohistory has become isolated from ethnography (Stark and Chance 2008: 12–14) because classic ethnography has tended to be rural in its emphasis. Thus although *indigenismo* is a major focus, this does not necessarily connect with all the concerns of ethnicity. At the other end of the spectrum, the study of Aztec ethnicity is very dependent on textual sources, which provide an urbanocentric, peri-Aztec perspective derived from the colonial period (Berdan 2008: 105). A well-reasoned example of an attempt to reconcile the two sources, textual and non textual, in a complementary manner is the study of strategies to extract coca in sixteenth century Peru (Marcus and Silva 1988). The authors point out that the two sources rarely map precisely one onto another either geographically or temporally, a point echoed by Fulminante (this volume), and that the rare cases where they are in direct conflict provide case studies of immense interest (Marcus and Silva 1988: 1). There is a strong flavour of this debate in a number of Mediterranean contributions to the present volume (Carandini and Stoddart). Osborne (this volume b) quite rightly points out that Greece remains essentially prehistoric until the fifth century and Italy until the third century BC; so much of ethnic reconstruction must be based on archaeological evidence.

A central issue in all archaeological discussion (Cifani and Stoddart, this volume) is the degree to which non-textual archaeological evidence is sufficient to permit recognition of ethnicity; indeed there many archaeologists who share the view that texts are essential for the detection of ethnicity (Hall 1998: 267; Trigger 1995: 277). Emberling (1997: 311) has explored the materials typically investigated by archaeologists (ceramics, architecture, lithics, basketry, textiles, food, body ornaments and burial) recommending that multiple analyses be executed, seeking relative proof by redundancy (Emberling 1997: 318). Of these, he points to household structure, cuisine and ritual as materials which may be particularly amenable to ethnic attribution (Emberling 1997: 325). The theme of ritual is especially examined by Ceccarelli (this volume) through an analysis of the ritualization of contructed genealogies within sanctuaries, and by Rajala (this volume) within tombs. Analysis of Aztec ethnicity (Berdan 2008: 118–19; Umberger 2008), and of ethnic groups incorporated by the Aztecs (Brumfiel 1994a: 96ff), suggests that when artistic depiction (including glyphs) is available, clothing and hair may be added to food as prominent attributes. Fulminante (this volume) and Grau Mira (this volume) address these issues by pointing to ways forward of combining ranges of evidence to detect complex patterns of ethnicity.

A distinctive element of Mediterranean ethnicity – in the context of the emphasis on landscape in current volume – is the strong presence of a maritime core to the geographical area. This integrative core which combined facility of movement (albeit tempered by risk) contrasts with the transport difficulties of the New World, which substantially lacked non human modes of transport. Ironically the current volume has concentrated on land-based ethnicity. More attention needs to be paid to construction of a maritime identity, perhaps best illustrated by the Phoenicians and recent studies of the Orientalizing period in new, more social and ideological, terms (Riva and Vella 2006). Work has been undertaken by historians (Rediker 2004) on these issues in the context of eighteenth century British maritime power, exploring a male maritime society and all its connotations. Pacific anthropology (Linnekin and Poyer 1990a), as might be expected, has also investigated these matters; a good example is the definition of Mandok trading identity where land resources were secondary to the key middleman maritime trading activities, even if redistribution militated against wealth accumulation (Pomponio 1990). A start in this theme has been made for earlier periods in the Mediterranean (Nazou 2010), but in later periods some of the explanatory difficulties of the elusive ethnicity of the Phoenicians (Vella 1996) could be explored by taking a more maritime approach and building on steps already undertaken (Sommer 2010).

A shared problem between New World and other extra-European ethnographies and those of the Mediterranean from the preceding discussion is the identification of the appropriate type of ethnicity. The flavour of ethnicity is too readily taken from the world of empires and modern colonial contexts. The ethnicity of early states may have been differently characterized and care must be taken to develop and characterize the correct variation of ethnicity for a Mediterranean of the eighth to sixth century BC that was in a state of considerable dynamic flux.

Note

1 Although Gonzalez-Ruibal (this volume) laudably searches beyond this framework.

Bibliography

Abad, L. 1992. Las culturas ibéricas del área suroriental de la Península Ibérica. *Paleoetnología de la Península Ibérica, Complutum* 2–3: 151–66.

Abad, L., Grau, I., Sala, F. and Moratalla, J. 2003. Ancient trade in South-Eastern Iberia: the lower Segura river as focus of exchange activities. *Ancient West and East* 2 (2): 265–87.

Abad, L. and Sala, F. (eds). 2001. *Poblamiento Ibérico en el Bajo Segura. El Oral (II) y La Escuera*. Madrid: Real Academia de la Historia, Gabinete de Antigüedades.

Abad, L. and Sanz, R. 1995. La cerámica ibérica con decoración figurada de la provincia de Albacete. Iconografía y terrritorialidad. *Saguntum Papeles del Laboratorio de Arqueología de Valencia* 29: 73–92.

Accardo, S., Bacci, M., Broggi, A., Caruso, I., Cecconi, S., Cordiano, G., Dolci, M., Gilento, P., Isola, C., Lazzeretti, A., Soldatini, C. and Travaglini, S. 2007. *Sabatia Stagna. Insediamenti Perilacustri ad Anguillara e Dintorni in Età Romana*. Pisa: Edizioni ETS.

Aigner Foresti, L. 1986. Su un arredo dalla Campania. In Swaddling, J. (ed.), *Italian Iron Age Artefacts in the British Museum. Papers of the 6th British Museum Classical Colloquium. London, 10–11.12.1982*. London: British Museum, 37–41.

Åkerström, Å. 1966. *Die Architektonischen Terrakotten Kleinasiens*. Gleerup: Lund.

Akurgal, M., Kerschner, M., Mommsen, H. and Niemeier, W.-D. 2002. *Töpferzentren der Östägäis. Archäometrische und Archäologische Untersuchungen zur Mykenischen, Geometrischen und Archaischen Keramik aus Fundorten in Westkleinasien*, (Ergänzunghefte zu den Jahreshefte des Österreichischen Archäologischen Institutes, Heft 3). Wien: Österreichisches Archäologisches Institut.

Alcock, S. E. 1993. *Graecia Capta: The Landscapes of Roman Greece*. Cambridge: Cambridge University Press.

Alessandri, L. 2007. *L'Occupazione Costiera Protostorica del Lazio Centromeridionale*. BAR International Series 1592). Oxford: Archaeopress.

Alessio, A. and Guzzo, P. G. 1989–90. Santuari e fattorie ad est di Taranto. Elementi archeologici per un modello di interpretazione. *Scienze dell'Antichità* 3–4: 363–96.

Alföldi, A. 1962. Ager Romanus antiquus. *Hermes* 90: 187–213.

Almagro Basch, M. 1960. Las fuentes antiguas, los restos filológicos y elementos antropológicos sobre la invasión céltica en España. In Menéndez Pidal, R. (ed.), *Historia de España: España Protohistórica Tomo 1 Volume 2*. Madrid: Espasa-Calpe, 241–80.

Almagro Gorbea, M. 1998. Signa equitum de la Hispania céltica. *Complutum* 9: 101–15.

Almagro Gorbea, M. 2001. Los Iberos: nuevas perspectivas sobre sus orígenes. In Lorrio, A. J. (ed.), *Los Íberos en la Comarca de Requena-Utiel*. Alicante: Universidad de Alicante, 35–42.

Almagro Gorbea, M. and Ruiz Zapatero, G. (eds). 1992. *Palentología de la Península Ibérica*. Madrid: Universidad Complutense.

Almagro Gorbea, M. and Torres, M. 2000. *Las Fíbulas de Jinete y de Caballito: Aproximación a las Elites Ecuestres y Su Expansión en la Hispania Céltica*. Zaragoza: Institución Fernando el Católico.

Almagro Gorbea, M. and Moneo, T. 2000. *Santuarios Urbanos en el Mundo Ibérico*. Madrid: Real Academia de la Historia.

Álvarez Sanchís, J. 1999. *Los Vettones*. Madrid: Real Academia de la Historia.

Alvino, G. 2006. Sabina e Cicolano. In Ghini, G. (ed.), *Lazio e Sabina. Atti del Primo Incontro di Studi su Lazio e Sabina, Roma, 28–30 Gennaio 2002, Volume III*. Roma: De Luca, 71–8.

Ammerman, A. J. 1990. On the origins of the Forum Romanum. *American Journal of Archaeology* 94: 627–45.

Ammerman, A. J. 1996. The Comitium in Rome from the beginning. *American Journal of Archaeology* 100: 121–36.

Ammerman, A. J. and Filippi, D. 2004. Dal Tevere all'Argileto. *Bullettino della Commissione Archeologica Comunale di Roma* 105: 7–28.

Amoroso, A. 2000. Crustumerium, da città arcaica a suburbium di Roma. *Bullettino della Commissione Archeologica Comunale* 101: 263–82.

Ampolo, C. 1970–1. Su alcuni mutamenti sociali nel Lazio tra l'VIII e il V secolo. *Dialoghi di Archeologia* 1: 37–68.

Ampolo, C. 1976–7. Demarato. Osservazioni sulla mobilità sociale arcaica. *Dialoghi di Archeologia* 9–10: 333–45.

Ampolo, C. 1981. I gruppi etnici in Roma arcaica: posizioni del problema e fonti. In Pallottino M., (ed.) *Gli Etruschi e Roma. Atti dell'Incontro di Studio in Onore di Massimo Pallottino*. Roma: Giorgio Bretschneider, 45–70.

Ampolo, C. 1983. Ricerche sulla Lega Latina II. La dedica di Egerius Baebius (Cato fr. 58 Peter). *Parola del Passato* 36: 321–26.

Ampolo, C. 1984. Il lusso funerario e la città arcaica. *Annali dell'Istituto Orientale di Napoli, Archeologia e Storia Antica* 6: 71–102.

Ampolo, C. 1987. Rome arcaica fra Latini ed Etruschi: Aspetti politici e sociali. In Cristofani, M. (ed.), *Etruria e Lazio Arcaico*. Roma: Consiglio Nazionale delle Ricerche, 75–87.

Ananthaswamy, A. 2002. Under the skin. *New Scientist* 20 April: 34–7.

Ancillotti, A. 1995. Tavole iguvine. In Matteini Chiari, M. (ed.), *Museo Comunale di Gubbio. Materiali Archeologici*. Perugia: Electa Editori Umbri, 39–86.

Ancillotti, A. and Cerri, R. 1996. *Le Tavole di Gubbio e la Civiltà degli Umbri*. Perugia: Edizioni Jama.

Anderson, B. 1991. *Imagined Communities: Reflections on the Origin and Spread of Nationalism*. London: Verso.

Andrén, A. 1998. *Between Artifacts and Texts. Historical Archaeology in Global Perspective*. (Contributions to Global Historical Archaeology). New York – London: Plenum Press.

Angelini, I., Angle, M., Artioli, G., Bellintani, P., Lugli, F., Martinelli, N., Polla, A., Tagliacozzo, A. and Zarattini, A. 2006. Il villaggio delle macine (Castelgandolfo, Roma). In Ghini, G. (ed.), *Lazio e Sabina. Atti del Primo Incontro di Studi su Lazio e Sabina, Roma, 28–30 Gennaio 2002, Volume III*. Roma: De Luca, 157–68.

Anon 2005. Recent finds in archaeology: Panionion sanctuary discovered in southwest Turkey. 2005. *Athena Review* 4 (2): 10–11.

Antonacci Sanpaolo, E. 2000. Sannio e Apulia: Acculturazioni e commerci. In Cappelli, R. (ed.), *Studi sull'Italia dei Sanniti*. Milano: Electa, 90–106.

Antonelli, L. 2003. *I Piceni. Corpus delle Fonti. La Documentazione Letteraria*. Roma: L'Erma di Bretschneider.

Anzidei, A. P., Bietti Sestieri, A. M. and De Santis, A. 1985. *Roma e il Lazio dall'Età della Pietra alla Formazione della Città*. Roma: Quasar.

Anzidei, A. P. and Carboni, G. 1995. L'insediamento preistorico di Quadrato di Torre Spaccata (Roma) e osservazioni su alcuni aspetti tardo neolitici ed eneolitici dell'Italia centrale. *Origini* 19: 55–225.

Appadurai, A. 1986. Introduction: Commodities and the politics of value. In Appadurai, A. (ed.), *The Social Life of Things: Commodities in Cultural Perspective*. Cambridge: Cambridge University Press, 3–63.

Arafat, K. and Morgan, C. 1994. Athens, Etruria and the Heuneburg: Mutual misconceptions in the study of Greek-Barbarian relations. In Morris, I. (ed.), *Classical Greece: Ancient Histories and Modern Archaeologies*. Cambridge: Cambridge University Press, 108–34.

Aranegui, C. 2004. *Sagunto: Oppidum, Emporio y Municipio Romano*. Barcelona: Bellaterra.

Aranegui, C., Bonet, H., Martí, M. A., Mata, C. and Pérez Ballester, J. 1996. La cerámica con decoración figurada y vegetal del Tossal de Sant Miquel (Llíria, Valencia): una nueva propuesta metodológica. In Olmos, R. and Santos Velasco, J. A. (eds), *Iconografía Ibérica, Iconografía Itálica : Propuestas de Interpretación y Lectura (Roma 11–13, Nov. 1993): Coloquio Internacional*. Madrid: Universidad Autónoma de Madrid, 153–75.

Aranegui, C., Mata, C. and Pérez Ballester, J. (eds). 1997. *Damas y Caballeros en la Ciudad Ibérica*. Madrid: Crítica.

Aranegui, C. and Vives-Ferrándiz, J. 2006. Encuentros coloniales, respuestas plurales: los ibéricos antiguos de la fachada mediterránea central. In Belarte, M. C. and Sanmartí, J. (eds), *De les Comunitats Locals als Estats Arcaics: La Formació de les Societats Complexes a la Costa del Mediterrani Occidental*. Barcelone: University of Barcelona, 89–107.

Arteaga, O. 1982. Los Saladares 80. Nuevas directrices para el estudio del horizonte protoibérico en el Levante meridional y sudeste de la península ibérica. *Huelva Arqueológica* 6: 131–83.

Arvanitis, N. 2004. La casa delle Vestali d'età arcaica. *Workshop di Archeologia Classica* 1 (2004): 145–53.

Ashmore, W. and Knapp, A. B. 1999. Archaeological landscapes. Constructed, conceptualized, ideational. In Ashmore, W. and Knapp, A. B. (eds), *Archaeologies of Landscape. Contemporary Perspectives*. Oxford: Blackwell, 1–32.

Ashmore, W. and Knapp, A. B. 1999. *Archaeologies of Landscape. Contemporary Perspectives*. Oxford: Blackwell.

Assmann, J. 1992. *Das Kulturelle Gedächtnis. Schrift, Erinnerung und Politiche Identität in Frühen Hochkulturen*. München: C.H.Beck.

Atti Pisa-Roma 1983. *Forme di Contatto e Processi di Trasformazione nelle Società Antiche. Atti del Convegno, Cortona 1981*. Pisa/Roma: Scuola Normale Superiore – École Française de Rome.

Atti Taranto 1962. *Greci e Italici in Magna Grecia. Atti del Convegno, Taranto 1961*. Taranto: Istituto per la Storia e l'Archeologia della Magna Grecia.

Atti Taranto 1999. *Confini e Frontiera nella Grecità di Occidente. Atti del Trentasettesimo Convegno di Studi sulla Magna Grecia, Taranto 1997*. Taranto: Istituto per la Storia e l'Archeologia della Magna Grecia.

Aubet, M. E. 1993 (2001). *The Phoenicians and the West. Politics, Colonies and Trade*. Cambridge: Cambridge University Press.

Aubet, M. E. 2005. El «Orientalizante» un fenómeno de contacto entre sociedades desiguales. In Celestino, S. and Jiménez, J. (eds), *El Período Orientalizante. Actas del III Simposio Internacional de Arqueología de Mérida*. Madrid: Consejo Superior de Investigaciones Científicas, 117–28.

Aubet, M. E. 2006 On the organisation of the Phoenician colonial system in Iberia. In Riva, C. and Vella, N. (eds), *Debating Orientalization: Multidisciplinary Approaches to Change in the Ancient Mediterranean* (Monographs in Mediterranean Archaeology 10). London: Equinox Press, 94–109.

Ayán Vila, X. M. 2005. Arquitectura doméstica y construcción del espacio social en la edad del hierro del NW. En C. Cancelo. In Blanco, A. and Esparza, A. (eds), *Bronce Final y Edad del Hierro en la Península Ibérica*. Salamanca: Ediciones Universidad de Salamanca, 34–54.

Azuar, R., Rouillard, P., Gailledrat, E., Moret, P., Sala, F. and Badie, A. 1998. El asentamiento orientalizante e ibérico antiguo de "La Rábita", Guardamar del Segura (Alicante). Avance de las excavaciones 1996–1998. *Trabajos de Prehistoria* 55 (2): 111–26.

Baggio Bernardoni, E. 1992. Este romana. Impianto urbano, santuari, necropoli. In Tosi, G. (ed.), *Este Antica Este Antica: Dalla Preistoria all'Età Romana*. Padova: Zielo, 305–56.

Baglione, M. P. 1986. Il Tevere e i Falisci. In Quilici Gigli, S. (ed.), *Il Tevere e le Altre Vie d'Acqua del Lazio Antico*. Roma: Consiglio Nazionale delle Ricerche, 124–42.

Bagnall, R. S. 1988. Greeks and Egyptians: Ethnicity, status, and culture. In Brooklyn Museum (ed.), *Cleopatra's Egypt: Age of the Ptolemies*. Brooklyn (NY): Brooklyn Museum, 21–7.

Bailo Modesti, G. 1998 Coppe a semicerchi penduli dalla necropoli di Pontecagnano. In Bats, M. and D'Agostino, B. (eds), *Euboica. L'Eubea e la Presenza Euboica in Calcidica e in Occidente*. Napoli: Centre Jean Bérard, 369–75.

Baldarotta, D. 1999. La configurazione etnica dei Latini tra Lavinium, Ardea e Satricum. *Studi Romani* 47 (3–4): 261–69.

Balista, C., Gambacurta, G. and Ruta Serafini, A. 2002. Sviluppo di urbanistica atestina. In Ruta Serafini, A. (ed.), *Este Preromana: Una Città e i Suoi Santuari*. Treviso: Canova, 105–26.

Balista, C. and Ruta Serafini, A. 1992. Este romana. Impianto urbano, santuari, necropoli. In Tosi, G. (ed.), *Este Antica: dalla Preistoria all'Età Romana*. Padova, Zielo: 111–23.

Bandelli, G. 1995. Colonie e municipi dall'età monarchica alle guerre Sannitiche. *Eutopia* 4: 143–97.

Bandelli, G. 2004. La ricerca sulle élites della Regio X nell'ultimo ventennio. In Cébeillac-Gervasioni, M., Lemoine, L. and Trément, F. (eds), *Autocélebration des Élites Locales dans le Monde Romain: Contextes, Images, Textes (IIe s. av. J.-C. / IIIe s. ap. J.-C.)*. Clermont-Ferrand: Presses Universitaires Blaise-Pascal, 77–102.

Bankel, H. 2004. Knidos. Das Triopion. In Schwandner, E. L. and Rheidt, K. (eds), *Macht der Architektur – Architektur der Macht*. Mainz am Rhein: von Zabern, 100–13.

Barker, G. 1988. Archaeology and the Etruscan countryside. *Antiquity* 62: 772–85.

Barker, G. 1995. *A Mediterranean Valley. Landscape Archaeology and Annales History in the Biferno Valley*. Leicester: Leicester University Press.

Barker, G. and Rasmussen, T. 1988. The archaeology of an Etruscan polis: A preliminary report on the Tuscania project. 1986 and 1987 seasons. *Papers of the British School at Rome* 56: 25–42.

Barker, G. and Rasmussen, T. 1998. *The Etruscans*. Oxford: Blackwell.

Barnabei, F., Gamurrini, G. F., Cozza, A. and Pasqui, A. 1894. *Antichità del Territorio Falisco Esposte nel Museo Nazionale Romano a Villa Giulia* (Monumenti Antichi 4). Roma: Accademia dei Lìncei.

Barrier, P. and Montenat, C. 2007. Le paysage de l'époque protohistorique à l'embouchure du Segura. Approche paléogéographique. In Rouillard, P., Gailledrat, E. and Sala Sellés, F. (eds), *L'Établissement Protohistorique de La Fonteta (fin VIIIe – fin Ve siècle av. J.-C.)*. Madrid: Casa de Velázquez, 7–21.

Barth, F. 1969a. *Ethnic Groups and Boundaries. The Social Organization of Culture Difference (Results of a Symposium Held at the University of Bergen, 23rd to 26th February 1967)*. Bergen/London: Universitetsforlage – Allen & Unwin.

Barth, F. 1969b. Introduction. In Barth, F. (ed.), *Ethnic Groups and Boundaries. The Social Organization of Culture Difference (Results of a Symposium Held at the University of Bergen, 23rd to 26th February 1967)*. Bergen/London: Universitetsforlage – Allen & Unwin, 3–38.

Barth, F. 1976. Introducción. In Barth, F. (ed.), *Los Grupos Étnicos y Sus Fronteras*. México D.F: Fondo de Cultura Económica, 9–49.

Bartoloni, G. 1988. Esibizione di ricchezza a Roma nel VI e V sec. a.C.: doni votivi e corredi funerari. *Scienze dell'Antichità* 1: 143–59.

Bartoloni, G. 1990. I depositi votivi di Roma arcaica, alcune osservazioni. *Scienze dell'Antichità* 3–4: 747–59.

Bartoloni, G. 2005. Inizi della colonizzazione nel centro Italia. In Settis, S. and Parra, M. C. (eds), *Magna Graecia, Archeologia di un Sapere. Catalogo della Mostra*. Milano: Electa, 345–48.

Basile, F. 1999. Tomba 7392. In Bailo Modesti, G. and Gastaldi, P. (eds), *Prima di Pithecusa: i Più Antichi Materiali Greci del Golfo di Salerno. Catalogo della Mostra*. Napoli: Arte tipografica, 30.

Beazley, J. D. 1956. *Attic Black-Figure Vase-Painters*. Oxford: Clarendon Press.

Becker, M. J. 1996. The Sabines and their neighbors: The recognition of cultural borders through skeletal studies. In Maetzke, G. (ed.), *Identità e Civiltà dei Sabini: Atti del XVIII Convegno di Studi Etruschi ed Italici, Rieti – Magliano Sabina, 30 Maggio–3 Giugno 1993*. Firenze: Leo S. Olschki, 341–62.

Bedini, A. 1980. Abitato protostorico in località Laurentina Acqua Acetosa. *Archeologia Laziale* 3: 58–64.

Bedini, A. 1981. Contributo alla conoscenza del territorio a sud di Roma in epoca protostorica. *Archeologia Laziale* 4: 57–65.

Bedini, A. 1983. Due nuove tombe a camera presso l'abitato della Laurentina: nota su alcuni tipi di sepolture nel VI e V secolo a.C. *Archeologia Laziale* 5: 28–37.

Bedini, A. 1990. Le tombe della Laurentina. In Cristofani, M. (ed.), *La Grande Roma dei Tarquini. Catalogo della Mostra*. Roma: "L'Erma" di Bretschneider, 255–60.

Bedini, A. 1990. Un compitum protostorico a Tor de' Cenci. *Archeologia Laziale* 10: 121–33.

Beijer, A. J. 1991. Impasto pottery and social status in Latium Vetus in the Orientalising period (725–575 BC): An example from Borgo Le Ferriere ('Satricum'). In Herring, E., Whitehouse, R. and Wilkins, J. B. (eds), *Papers of the Fourth Conference of Italian Archaeology 1. The Archaeology of Power, Part 1*. London: Accordia, 21–39.

Bejarano, V. 1987. *Fontes Hispaniae Antiquae VII: Hispania Antigua según Pomponio Mela, Plinio el Viejo y Claudio Ptolomeo*. Barcelona: Instituto de Arqueología y Prehistoria, Universidad de Barcelona.

Bell, T., Wilson, A. and Wickham, A. 2002. Tracking the Samnites: Landscape and communication routes in the Sangro valley, Italy. *American Journal of Archaeology* 106: 169–86.

Benelli, E. and Naso, A. 2003. Relazioni e scambi nell'Abruzzo in epoca preromana. *Melanges de l'École Française de Rome* 115: 177–205.

Benelli, E. and Santoro, P. 2006. Nuove scoperte nella necropoli sabina di Colle del Forno (Montelibretti, Roma). In Ghini, G. (ed.), *Lazio e Sabina. Atti del Primo Incontro di Studi su Lazio e Sabina, Roma, 28–30 Gennaio 2002, Volume III*. Roma: De Luca, 97–106.

Bennett, J. W. 1975. A guide to the collection. In Bennett, J. W. (ed.), *The New Ethnicity: Perspectives from Ethnology: 1973 Proceedings of the American Ethnological Society*. St. Paul (MN): West Publishing Co., 3–10.

Bentley, G. C. 1987. Ethnicity and practice. *Comparative Studies in Society and History* 29: 24–55.

Berardinetti Insam, A. 2001. Necropoli di Quattro Fontanili, tomba HH 11–12. In Moretti Sgubini, A. M. (ed.), *Veio, Cerveteri, Vulci. Città d'Etruria a Confronto. Catalogo della Mostra*. Roma: L'Erma di Bretschneider, 98–105.

Berdan, F. F. 2008. Concepts of ethnicity and class in Aztec-Period Mexico. In Berdan, F. F. (ed.), *Ethnic Identity in Nahua Mesoamerica: The View from Archaeology, Art History, Ethnohistory, and Contemporary Ethnography*. Salt Lake City: University of Utah Press, 105–32.

Berges, D. 1995–1996. Knidos und das Bundesheiligtum der dorischen Hexapolis. *Nürnberger Blätter zur Archäologie* 12: 103–20.

Berges, D. and Attula, R. 2000. Das Apollonheiligtum von Emecik. Bericht über die Ausgrabungen 1998 und 1999. *Istanbuler Mitteilungen* 50: 171–214.

Berges, D. and Tuna, N. 1990. Ein Heiligtum bei Alt-Knidos. *Archäologischer Anzeiger* 1990 (1): 19–35.

Berges, D. and Tuna, N. 2001. Kult-, Wettkampf- und politische Versammlungsstätte. Das Triopion, Bundesheiligtum der dorischen Pentapolis. *Antike Welt* 32: 155–66.

Berlingò, I. and D'Atri, V. 2005. Un'area sacra sul lago di Bolsena. In Comella, A. and Mele, S. (eds) *Depositi Votivi e Culti dell'Italia Antica dall'Età Arcaica a Quella Tardo-Repubblicana: Atti del Convegno di Studi, Perugia, 1–4 Giugno 2000*. Bari: Edipuglia, 267–75.

Bernabeu, J., Bonet, H. and Mata, C. 1987. Hipótesis sobre la organización del territorio edetanos en epoca iberica: el ejemplo del territorio de Edeta-Lliria. In Ruiz, A. and Molinos, M. (eds), *Iberos. I Jornadas Arqueológicas sobre el Mundo Ibero*. Jaén: Ed. Ayuntamiento de Jaen-Consejería de Cultura y Junta de Andalucía, 137–56.

Bernardini, P., D'Oriano, R. and Spanu, P. G. (eds). 1997. *Phoinikes B Shrdn. I Fenici in Sardegna: Nuove Acquisizioni. Catalogo della Mostra*. Oristano: La memoria storica-Mythos.

Bhabha, H. K. 1994. *The Location of Culture*. London: Routledge.

Bianchin Citton, E. 1998. Montagnana tra XIII e VIII sec. a.C.: un primo bilancio delle ricerche. In Bianchin Citton, E., Gambacurta, G. and Ruta Serafini, A. (eds), *"Presso l'Adige Ridente" Recenti Rinvenimenti Archeologici da Este a Montagnana*. Padova: ADLE, 429–33.

Bianchin Citton, E. 2002. Le origini di Este: Da comunità di villaggio a centro veneto. In Ruta Serafini, A. (ed.), *Este preromana: Una Città e i Suoi santuari*. Treviso: Canova, 89–104.

Bianco Peroni, V. 1970. *Le Spade nell'Italia Continentale. Die Schwerter in Italien* (Prähistorische Bronzefunde 4, 1). München: Beck.

Bianco Peroni, V. 1974. Neue Schwerter aus Italien/nuove spade dall'Italia. In Müller-Karpe, H. (ed.), *Beiträge zu Italienischen und Griechischen Bronzefunden*. München: Beck, 11–25.

Bianco Peroni, V. 1979. *I Rasoi nell'Italia Continentale* (Prähistorische Bronzefunde 8, 2). München: Beck.

Biella, M. C. 2007. *Impasti Orientalizzanti con Decorazione ad Incavo nell'Italia Centrale Tirrenica.* Roma: Giorgio Bretschneider Editore.

Bietti Sestieri, A. M. 1992a. *The Iron Age Community of Osteria dell'Osa. A Study of Socio-Political Development in Central Tyrrhenian Italy.* Cambridge: Cambridge University Press.

Bietti Sestieri, A. M. 1992b. (ed.) *La Necropoli Laziale di Osteria dell'Osa.* Roma: Quasar.

Bietti Sestieri, A. M. 1998. Oral traditions, historical sources and archaeological data: reconstructing a process of ethnogenesis in the Italian Bronze Age. In Pearce, M., Milliken, S., Vidale, M., Moravetti, A. and Tosi, M. (eds), *Papers from the Third Annual Meeting of European Association of Archaeologists, Ravenna/Italy, September 25th–29th, 1997.* Oxford: Oxbow Books, 280–3.

Bietti Sestieri, A. M. 2000. The role of archaeological and historical data in the reconstruction of Italian protohistory. In Ridgway, D., Serra Ridgway, F. R., Pearce, M., Herring, E., Whitehouse, R. D. and Wilkins, J. B. (eds), *Ancient Italy in Its Mediterranean Setting. Studies in Honour of Ellen Macnamara* (Accordia Specialist Studies on the Mediterranean 4). London: Accordia Research Institute, University of London, 13–31.

Bietti Sestieri, A. M. and De Santis, A. 2007. Il Lazio antico tra tarda età del bronzo e prima età del ferro: gli sviluppi nell'organizzazione politico-territoriale in relazione con il processo di formazione urbana. In *Atti della XL Riunione Scientifica dell'Istituto Italiano di Preistoria e Protostoria "Strategie di Insediamento tra Lazio e Campania in Età Preistorica e Protostorica," Roma-Napoli-Pompei, 2005.* Firenze: Istituto Italiano di Preistoria e Protostoria, 205–29.

Bietti Sestieri, A. M., De Santis, A. and Salvadei, L. 2004. Dati archeologici e analisi paleobiologiche relativi alle comunità della Prima Età del Ferro laziale di Osteria dell'Osa e di Castiglione. *Rivista di Scienze Preistoriche* 54: 537–55.

Bintliff, J. L. (ed.). 1991. *The Annales School and Archaeology.* Leicester: Leicester University Press.

Bintliff, J. L. 1995. The Two Transitions: Current Research on the Origins of the Traditional Village in Central Greece. In Bintliff, J. L. and Hamerow, H. (eds), *Europe between Late Antiquity and the Middle Ages. Recent Archaeological and Historical Research in Western and Southern Europe* (BAR International Series 617). Oxford: British Archaeological Reports, 111–30.

Bintliff, J. L. 1996. The archaeological survey of the Valley of the Muses and its significance for Boeotian History. In Hurst, A. and Schachter, A. (eds), *La Montagne des Muses.* Geneva: Librairie Droz, 193–224.

Bintliff, J. 1997. Regional survey, demography, and the rise of complex societies in the Ancient Aegean: Core-periphery, Neo-Malthusian, and other interpretive models. *Journal of Field Archaeology* 24 (1): 1–38.

Bintliff, J. L. 2003. The ethnoarchaeology of a 'passive' ethnicity: The Arvanites of Central Greece. In Brown, K. S. and Hamilakis, Y. (eds), *The Usable Past. Greek Metahistories.* Lanham-Boulder: Lexington Books, 129–44.

Bintliff, J., Howard, P. and Snodgrass, A. M. 1999. The hidden landscape of prehistoric Greece. *Journal of Mediterranean Archaeology* 12 (2): 139–68.

Bintliff, J. L., Dickinson, O., Howard, P. and Snodgrass, A. 2000. Deconstructing 'The Sense of Place'? Settlement systems, field survey, and the historic record: A case-study from Central Greece. *Proceedings of the Prehistoric Society* 66: 123–49.

Blanton, R. 1978. *Monte Albán. Settlement Patterns at the Ancient Zapotec Capital.* London: Academic Press.

Blanton, R. 1998. Beyond centralization: Steps toward a theory of egalitarian behavior in archaic states. In Marcus, J. and Feinman, G. (eds), *Archaic States*. Santa Fe: School of American Research Press, 135–72.

Blázquez, A. M. 2005. *Evolución Cuaternaria de l'Albufera d'Elx: Paleoambientes y Foraminíferos Fósiles*. Elche: Memorias del Museo Paleontológico de Elche.

Boardman, J. 1964. *The Greeks Overseas*. London: Thames and Hudson.

Boardman, J. 1967. *Excavations in Chios 1952–1955: Greek Emporio*. Oxford: British School of Archaeology at Athens.

Boardman, J. 1981. *Griechische Plastik. Die Archaische Zeit*. Mainz am Rhein: von Zabern.

Boardman, J. 1998. *Early Greek Vase Painting: 11th to 6th Centuries BC. A Handbook*. London: Thames and Hudson.

Boaro, S. 2001. Dinamiche insediative e confini nel Veneto dell'età del Ferro. *Padusa* 37: 153–97.

Bobo, L. and Hutchings, V. L. 1996. Perceptions of racial group competition: Extending Blumer's Theory of Group Position to a multiracial social context. *American Sociological Review* 61: 951–72.

Boehlau, J. 1898. *Aus Ionischen und Italischen Nekropolen*. Leipzig: Teubner.

Boehlau, J., Fabricius, J. and Gercke, P. 1996. *Samos – Die Kasseler Grabung 1894 in der Nekropole der Archaischen Stadt von Johannes Boehlau und Edward Habich*. Kassel: Staatliche Museen Kassel.

Boehm, C. 1993. Egalitarian behavior and reverse dominance hierarchy. *Current Anthropology* 34 (3): 227–54.

Boersma, J. S. 1995. *Mutatio Valentia. The Late Roman Baths at Valesio, Salento*. Amsterdam: Van Gorcum.

Boersma, J. S., Burgers, G.-J. and Yntema, D. G. 1991. The Valesio Project: Final interim report. *Bulletin Antieke Beschaving* 66: 115–31.

Boersma, J. S. and Yntema, D. G. 1987. *Valesio. History of an Apulian Settlement from the Iron Age to the Late Roman Period*. Fasano di Puglia: Schena Editore.

Böhne, K. 2005. Glauke limen. *Orbis Terrarum* 8 (2002): 191–95.

Boitani, F. 2001. I.G.6.1. In Moretti Sgubini, A. M. (ed.), *Veio, Cerveteri, Vulci: Città d'Etruria a Confronto. Catalogo della Mostra*. Roma: L'Erma di Bretschneider, 106.

Boitani, F. 2005. Le più antiche ceramiche greche e di tipo greco a Veio. In Bartoloni, G. and Delpino, F. (eds), *Oriente e Occidente: Metodi e Discipline a Confronto. Riflessioni sulla Cronologia dell'Età del Ferro Italiana. Atti dell'Incontro di Studi, Roma, 30–31.10.2003*. Pisa – Roma: IEPI, 319–32.

Bommeljé, L. S. and Doorn, P. K. 1984. *Strouza Region Project. Second Interim Report*. Utrecht: Privately published, Strouza Project.

Bonet, H. 1995. *El Tossal de Sant Miquel de Llíria. La Antigua Edeta y Su Territorio*. Valencia: Diputació de Valencia.

Bonet, H 2001. Los Iberos en las comarcas centrales valencianas. In Lorrio, A. J. (ed.), *Los Íberos en la Comarca de Requena-Utiel*. Alicante: Universidad de Alicante, 63–74.

Bonghi Jovino, M. 2000. The expansion of the Etruscans in Campania. In Torelli, M. (ed.), *The Etruscans. Exhibition Catalogue*. Milano: Bompiani, 157–67.

Boni, G. 1900. Roma. Nuove scoperte nella città e nel suburbio. *Notizie degli Scavi di Antichità* 1900: 295–340.

Bonomi Ponzi, L. 1996. Aspetti dell'ideologia funeraria nel mondo umbro. In Bonamente, G. and Coarelli, F. (eds), *Assisi e gli Umbri nell'Antichità. Atti del Convegno Internazionale*.

Assisi 18–21, Dicembre 1991. Assisi: Società Editrice Minerva – Università degli Studi di Perugia – Accademia Properziana del Subbasio di Assisi, 105–26.

Bonomi Ponzi, L. 1996. La koiné centro-italica in età preromana. In Maetzke, G. (ed.), *Identità e Civiltà dei Sabini: Atti del XVIII Convegno di Studi Etruschi ed Italici, Rieti – Magliano Sabina, 30 Maggio–3 Giugno 1993*. Firenze: Leo S. Olschki, 393–413.

Bosch Gimpera, P. 1920. La arqueología pre-romana hispánica. In Schulten, A. (ed.), *Hispania (Geografía, Etnología, Historia)*. Barcelona: La Académica, 135–242.

Bosio, L. 1981. Padova in età romana. Organizzazione urbanistica e territorio. In Bosio, L. (ed.), *Padova Antica. Da Comunità Paleoveneta a Città Romano-Cristiana.* Trieste: Pauda, 31–48.

Bourdieu, P. 1980. *Le Sens Pratique*. Paris: Éditions de Minuit.

Bourdieu, P. 1994. *Raisons Pratiques. Sur la Théorie de l'Action*. París: Éditions de Minuit.

Bourdin, S. 2005. Ardée et les Rutules. Réflexions sur l'émergence et le mantien des identités ethniques des populations du Latium pré-Romain. *Melanges de l'École Française de Rome, Antiquité* 117: 585–631.

Bradley, G. J. 1997. Archaic sanctuaries in Umbria. *Cahiers du Centre G. Glotz*: 111–29.

Bradley, G. J. 1997. Iguvines, Umbrians and Romans: Ethnic identity in central Italy. In Cornell, T. and Lomas, K. (eds), *Gender and Ethnicity in Ancient Italy*. London: Accordia Research Insitute, 53–68.

Bradley, G. J. 2000a. *Ancient Umbria: State, Culture, and Identity in Central Italy from the Iron Age to the Augustan Era*. Oxford: Oxford University Press.

Bradley, G. J. 2000b. Tribes, states and cities in central Italy. In Herring, E. and Lomas, K. (eds), *The Emergence of State Identities in Italy in the First Millennium BC*. London: Accordia Research Institute, 109–29.

Bradley, R. 1998. *The Significance of Monuments*. London: Routledge.

Bradley, R. 2000. *An Archaeology of Natural Places*. London: Routledge.

Bradley, R. 2002. *The Past in Prehistoric Societies*. London: Routledge.

Brañas, R. 2000. *Deuses, Heroes e Lugares Sagrados*. Santiago de Compostela: Sotelo Blanco.

Brancaccio, G. 2005. *Il Molise Medievale e Moderno. Storia di uno Spazio Regionale*. Napoli: ESI.

Brandt, J. R. 1996. *Scavi di Ficana. II.I.II Periodo Protostorico e Arcaico. Le zone di Scavo 3b–c.* Roma: Libreria dello Stato Istituto Poligrafico e Zecca dello Stato.

Brandt, J. R, Jarva, E. and Fischer-Hansen, T. 1997. Ceramica di origine e d'imitazione greca a Ficana nell'VIII sec. a.C. In Bartoloni, G. (ed.), *Le Necropoli Arcaiche di Veio. Giornata di Studio in Memoria di Massimo Pallottino. Roma, 11.11.1994*. Roma: Università La Sapienza, 219–31.

Brather, V. S. 2000. Ethnische Identitäten als Konstrukte der frügeschichtlichen Archäeologie. *Germania* 78 (1): 139–77.

Briquel, D. 1972. Sur des faits d'ecriture en Sabine et dans l'ager Capenas. *Melanges de l'École Française de Rome* 84: 789–845.

Briquel, D. 2000. La zona reatina, centro dell'Italia: Una visione della penisola alternativa a quella romana. In Catani, E. and Paci, G. (eds), *La Salaria in Età Antica. Atti del Convegno di Studi, 1997*. Roma: L'Erma di Bretschneider, 79–89.

Briquel, D. 2001. La tradizione storiografica sulla dodecapoli etrusca. In *La Lega Etrusca dalla Dodecapoli ai Quindecim Popoli. Atti della Giornata di Studi. Chiusi 9 Ottobre 1999*. Pisa – Roma: Istituti Editoriali e Poligrafici Internazionali, 9–18.

Brocato, P. 1995. Sull'origine e lo sviluppo delle prime tombe a dado etrusche. Diffusione di un tipo architettonico da Cerveteri a San Giuliano. *Studi Etruschi* 61: 57–93.

Broufas, C. 1993. *40 Greek Costumes from the Dora Stratou Theatre Collection*. Athens: Dora Stratou Theatre.

Brumfiel, E. 1994. Ethnic groups in political development in Ancient Mexico. In Brumfiel, E. and Fox, J. W. (eds), *Factional Competition and Political Development in the New World*. Cambridge: Cambridge University Press, 89–102.

Brumfiel, E. 1994. Factional competition and political development in the New World: an introduction. In Brumfiel, E. and Fox, J. W. (eds), *Factional Competition and Political Development in the New World*. Cambridge: Cambridge University Press, 3–13.

Brunetti Nardi, B. 1981. *Repertorio degli Scavi e delle Scoperte Archeologiche nell'Etruria Meridionale (1971–1975)*. Roma: Consiglio nazionale delle richerche, Centro di Studio per l'Archeologia Etrusco-Italica.

Bruno, A. 2003–2004. *Proposta di Classificazione delle Punte di Lancia nell'Età del Bronzo nell'Italia Continentale*. Università di Roma La Sapienza, Tesi di laurea non pubblicata in Protostoria Europea.

Bruno, A. 2006. Distribuzione ed evoluzione delle punte di lancia a lama foliata tra le età del Bronzo recente e del Bronzo finale. In *Studi di Protostoria in Onore di Renato Peroni*. Firenze: All'Insegna del Giglio, 232–39.

Bruno, A. 2007. *Punte di Lancia nell'Età del Bronzo nella Terraferma Italiana. Per una Loro Classificazione Tipologica*. Lucca: Accademia Lucchese di Scienze Lettere e Arti.

Bruschetti, P. 2002. Il territorio di Perugia etrusca. In Della Fina, Giuseppe M. (ed.), *Perugia Etrusca. Atti del IX Convegno Internazionale di Studi sulla Storia e l'Archeologia dell'Etruria. Annali della Fondazione per il Museo "Claudio Faina"* 9: 71–94.

Buchner, G. and Ridgway, D. 1993. *Pithekoussai. Part: 1: La Necropoli: Tombe 1–723 Scavate dal 1952 al 1961*. (Monumenti antichi. Serie monografica – Accademia Nazionale dei Lincei 4 (55)). Roma: Bretschneider.

Buck, C. D. 1955. *The Greek Dialects: Grammar, Selected Inscriptions, Glossary*. (3rd edition). Chicago: University of Chicago Press.

Buck, R. J. 1979. *A History of Boeotia*. Edmonton: University of Alberta Press.

Buranelli, F. 1991. Uno scavo clandestino a Civita di Grotte di Castro. In Corbucci, M. P. and Pettine, S. (eds), *Antichità dall'Umbria a New York*. Perugia: Electa Editori Umbri, 255–58.

Burgers, G.-J. 1998a. *Constructing Messapian Landscapes. Settlement Dynamics, Social Organisation and Culture Contact in the Margins of Graeco-Roman Italy*. Amsterdam: J.C. Gieben.

Burgers, G.-J. 1998b. Muro Tenente: indagini archeologiche della missione olandese. In Lombardo, M. and Marangio, C. (eds), *Il Territorio Brindisino dall'Età Messapica all'Età Romana. Atti del IV Convegno di Studi sulla Puglia Romana*. Galatina: Congedo Editore, 137–50.

Burgers, G.-J. 2004. Western Greeks in their regional setting. Rethinking early Greek – indigenous encounters in Southern Italy. *Ancient West and East* 3: 252–82.

Burgers, G.-J., Alberda, K., Burgers, H., Karel, D. and Yntema, D. 1998. *Muro Tenente. Centro Messapico nel Territorio di Mesagne. Le Ricerche Olandesi 1992–1997*. Mesagne: Amministrazione di Comunale.

Burgers, G.-J., Attema, P. and Van Leusen, M. 2003. Walking the Murge. Interim report of the Ostuni field survey. *Studi di Antichità* 11: 1–26.

Burgers, G.-J. and Crielaard, J. P. 2007. Greek colonists and indigenous populations at l'Amastuola, southern Italy. *Babesch* 82: 87–124.

Burgers, G.-J. and Yntema, D. G. 1999a. The settlement of Muro Tenente. Third interim report. *Babesch* 74: 111–32.

Burgers, G.-J. and Yntema, D. G. 1999b. Town and countryside in pre-Roman southern Italy: A regional perspective. In Krinzinger, F. (ed.), *Die Ägäis and das Westliche Mittelmeer. Beziehungen und Wechselwirkungen 8. bis 5. Jh. v. Chr. Akten des Symposions.* Wien: VÖAW, 95–104.

Burstein, S. 2008. Greek identity in the Archaic and Classical periods. In Zacharia, K. (ed.), *Hellenisms: Culture, Identity and Ethnicity from Antiquity to Modernity.* Aldershot: Ashgate Publishing, 37–58.

Caiazza, D. 2003. Bovianum. In Guaitoli, M. (ed.), *Lo Sguardo di Icaro. Le Collezioni dell'Aerofototeca Nazionale per la Conoscenza del Territorio. Catalogo della Mostra.* Roma: Campisano, 298–99.

Calore, A. 2000. *"Per Iovem lapidem", alle Origini del Giuramento.* Milano: Giuffr.

Camilli, A., Carta, L., Conti, T. and De Laurenzi, A. 1995. Ricognizioni nell'Ager Faliscus meridionale. In Christie, N. (ed.), *Settlement and Economy in Italy 1500 BC to AD 1500. Papers of the Fifth Conference of Italian Archaeology* (Oxbow Monograph 41). Oxford: Oxbow Books, 395–402.

Camilli, A. and Vitali Rosati, B. 1995. Nuove ricerche nell'agro capenate. In Christie, N. (ed.), *Settlement and Economy in Italy 1500 BC to AD 1500. Papers of the Fifth Conference of Italian Archaeology* (Oxbow Monograph 41). Oxford: Oxbow Books, 403–12

Camporeale, G. 1991. L'ethnos dei Falisci secondo gli scrittori antichi. *Archeologia Classica* 43: 209–11.

Canuto, M. A. and Yaeger, J. 2000. *The Archaeology of Communities, a New World Perspective.* London: Routledge.

Capini, S. 1980. La necropoli di Campochiaro, In Gastaldi, P. (ed.), *Sannio. Pentri e Frentani dal VI al I sec. a.C. Catalogo della Mostra.* Roma: De Luca, 108–12.

Capini, S. 1982. Archeologia. In *Campochiaro. Potenzialità di Intervento sui Beni culturali.* Campobasso: Soprintendenza Archeologia del Molise, 6–80.

Capini, S. 1985. Loc. Civitella. In *Agnone. Il Museo Emidiano. Il Territorio. Catalogo della Mostra.* Matrice: La Rapida Grafedit, 71 s., n. 78.

Capini, S. 1991. Il santuario di Ercole a Campochiaro. In Capini, S. and Di Niro, A. (eds), *Samnium. Archeologia del Molise. Catalogo della Mostra.* Roma: Quasar, 115–20.

Capini, S. 2000. Una dedica ad Ercole dal santuario di Campochiaro. In Cappelli, R. (ed.), *Studi sull'Italia dei Sanniti.* Milano: Electa, 230–31.

Capini, S. 2003. Il santuario di Ercole a Campochiaro. In Quilici, L. and Quilici Gigli, S. (eds), *Santuari e Luoghi di Culto nell'Italia Antica.* Roma: Cristal, 233–50.

Capuis, L. 1993. *I Veneti.* Milano: Longanesi.

Capuis, L. and Chieco Bianchi, A. M. 1992. Este preromana. Vita e cultura. In Tosi, G. (ed.), *Este Antica: Dalla Preistoria all'Età Romana.* Padova: Zielo, 41–108.

Carafa, P. 1995. *Officine Ceramiche di Età Regia. Produzione di Ceramica in Impasto a Roma dalla Fine dell'VIII alla Fine del VI Secolo a.C.* Roma: L'Erma di Bretschneider.

Carafa, P. 1998. *Il Comizio di Roma dalle Origini all'Età di Augusto.* Roma: L'Erma di Bretschneider.

Caramella, G. 1995. Metalli. In Matteini Chiari, M. (ed.), *Museo Comunale di Gubbio. Materiali Archeologici.* Perugia: Electa Editori Umbri, 325–73.

Carancini, G. L. 1984. *Le Asce nell'Italia Continentale II* (Prähistorische Bronzefunde 8, 12). München: Beck.

Carancini, G. L. and Peroni, R. 1999. *L'Età del Bronzo in Italia: Per una Cronologia della Produzione Metallurgica* (Quaderni di Protostoria 2). Perugia: Ali & no.

Carandini, A. 1994. La presenza de la città nella campagna. All'origine del fenomeno nell'Italia Centrale Tirrenica. In Dupré Raventós, X. (ed.), *Actas del XIV Congreso Internacional de Arqueología Clásica. La Ciudad en el Mundo Romano. Volume I*. Madrid: Consejo Superior de Investigaciones Científicas, 153–58.

Carandini, A. 1997. *La Nascita di Roma. Dei, Lari, Eroi e Uomini all'Alba di una Civiltà*. Torino: Giulio Einaudi Editore.

Carandini, A. 2002. *Archeologia del Mito. Emozione e Ragione fra Primitivi e Moderni*. Torino: Einaudi.

Carandini, A. 2006a. *La Leggenda di Roma I. Dalla Nascita dei Gemelli alla Fondazione della Città*. Milano: Fondazione Lorenzo Valla – Arnoldo Mondadori Editore.

Carandini, A. 2006b. *Remo e Romolo. Dai Rioni dei Quiriti alla Città dei Romani (775/750 –700/675 a.C)*. Torino: Giulio Einaudi.

Carandini, A. 2010. (ed.) *La Leggenda di Roma. Testi, Morfologia e Commento* (translations by Lorenzo Argentieri, comment by Paolo Carafa), *vol. 2, Dal Ratto delle Donne al Regno di Romolo e Tito Tazio*. Milano: Fondazione Lorenzo Valla, Arnoldo Mondadori Editore.

Carandini, A. 2011 (ed.) *La Leggenda di Roma. Testi, Morfologia e Commento* (translations by Lorenzo Argentieri, comment by Paolo Carafa, Mario Fiorentini, Ugo Fusco), *vol. 3, La Costituzione, Fondazione*. Milano: Fondazione Lorenzo Valla, Arnoldo Mondadori Editore.

Carandini, A. and Cappelli, R. (eds). 2000. *Roma. Romolo, Remo e la Fondazione della Città. Catalogo della Mostra*. Milano: Electa.

Carandini, A. and Carafa, P. (eds). 2000. *Palatium e Sacra Via I. Prima delle Mura, l'Età delle Mura e l'Età delle Case Arcaiche*. Roma: Istituto Poligrafico e Zecca dello Stato.

Carlucci, C. and De Lucia, M. A. 1998. *Le Antichità dei Falisci al Museo di Villa Giulia*. Roma: "L'Erma" di Bretschneider and Ingegneria per la Cultura.

Carneiro, R. 1970. A theory of the origin of the state. *Science* 169: 733–8.

Carrasco, J., Pachón, J. A. and Aníbal, C. 1986. Cerámicas pintadas del Bronce Final procedentes de Jaén y Córdoba. *Cuadernos de Prehistoria de la Universidad de Granada* 11: 199–236.

Carsten, J. and Hugh-Jones, S. 1995. *About the House: Lévi-Strauss and Beyond*. Cambridge: Cambridge University Press.

Carta 1959. *Carta dell'Utilizzazione del Suolo d'Italia Foglio 15*. Milano: Consiglio Nazionale delle Ricerche.

Carter, J. B. 1984. *Greek Ivory-Carving in the Orientalizing and Archaic Periods*. Ann Arbor: University Microfilms.

Caruso, I. 2005. Trevignano Romano: influenze ceretane e veienti nelle fasi dell'orientalizzante recente e dell'arcaismo maturo. In Paoletti, O. (ed.), *Dinamiche di Sviluppo delle Città nell'Etruria Meridionale. Veio, Caere, Tarquinia, Vulci. Atti del XXIII Convegno di Studi Etruschi ed Italici, Roma, Veio, Cerveteri/Pyrgi, Tarquinia, Tuscania, Vulci, Viterbo, 1–6 Ottobre 2001*. vol. 1. Pisa, Roma: Istituti editoriali e poligrafici internazionali, 301–6.

Castagnoli, F. 1972. *Lavinium I. Topografia Generale, Fonti e Storia delle Ricerche*. Roma: De Luca.

Castro, M., López, J., Zafra, N., Crespo, J. and Choclán, C. 1990. Prospección con sondeo estratigráfico en el yacimiento de Atalayuelas, Fuerte del Rey, Jaén. In *Anuario Arqueológico de Andalucía 1987.II*. Sevilla: Junta de Andalucía, 207–15.

Catalano, P. 1978. Aspetti spaziali del sistema giuridico-religioso romano. Mundus, templum, urbs, ager, Latium, Italia. *Aufstieg und Niedergang der römischen Welt II* 16 (1): 440–553.

Ceccarelli, L. 2007. Le terrecotte architettoniche del Tempio B. In Di Mario, F. (ed.), *Ardea. La Terra dei Rutuli tra Mito e Archeologia: Alle Radici della Romanità. Nuovi Dati dai Recenti Scavi Archeologici*. Roma: Soprintendenza per i Beni Archeologici del Lazio, 195–215.

Ceccarelli, L. 2008. Religious Landscape. A case-study from Latium Vetus. In Menozzi, O., Di Marzio, M. L. and Fossataro, D. (eds), *SOMA 2005: Proceedings of the IX Symposium on Mediterranean Archaeology, Chieti (Italy), 24–26 February 2005*. Oxford: Archaeopress, 333–9.

Ceccarelli, L. 2011. Santuario in loc. Le Salzare, Fosso dell'Incastro, Ardea (Roma). Il frontone del tempio tardo arcaico. In Lulof, P. and Rescigno, C. (eds), *Deliciae Fictiles IV. Architectural Terracottas in Ancient Italy. Images of Gods, Monsters and Heroes. Proceedings of the International Conference in Rome (Museo Nazionale Etrusco di Villa Giulia, Royal Netherlands Institute) and Syracuse (Museo Archeologico Regionale 'Paolo Orsi') October 21–25, 2009*. Oxford: Oxbow Books, 194–201.

Ceccarelli, L. in press. La Banditella di Ardea: nuove ricerche. In *VI Incontro di Studi sul Lazio e la Sabina. Roma 4–6 Marzo 2009*.

Ceccarelli, L. and Stoddart, S. K. F. 2007. The Faliscans. In Riva, C., Bradley, G. J. and Isayev, E. (eds), *Ancient Italy. Regions without Boundaries*. Exeter: Exeter University Press, 131–60.

Ceci, F., Amoroso, A., Favorito, S. and Fanoni, F. 1997. Ultime scoperte a Crustumerium. *Archeo* 7 (8): 32–9.

Cenciaioli, L. 1991. Il santuario di Monte Acuto di Umbertide. In Corbucci, M. P. and Pettine, S. (eds), *Antichità dall'Umbria a New York*. Perugia: Electa Editori Umbri, 211–26.

Cenciaioli, L. 1992. Monte Acuto (Umbertide, Provincia di Perugia). *Rivista di Scienze Preistoriche* 44 (1–2): 260–61.

Cenciaioli, L. 1996. Un santuario di altura nella Valle Tiberina: Monte Acuto di Umbertide. In Bonamente, G. and Coarelli, F. (eds), *Assisi e Gli Umbri nell'Antichità. Atti del Convegno Internazionale. Assisi 18–21, Dicembre 1991*. Assisi: Società Editrice Minerva – Università degli Studi di Perugia – Accademia Properziana del Subbasio di Assisi, 193–234.

Cenciaioli, L. 1998. *Umbri ed Etruschi. Genti di Confine a Monte Acuto e nel Territorio di Umbertide*. Umbertide: Tipografia La Fratta – Comune di Umbertide – Soprintendenza archeologica per l'Umbria.

Cenciaioli, L. 2002. Aspetti e considerazione su Perugia arcaica e il suo territorio. In Della Fina, G.M. (ed.) *Perugia Etrusca. Atti del IX Convegno Internazionale di studi sulla storiae l'Archeologia dell'Etruria. Annali della fondazione per il Museo "Claudio Faina"* 9: 49–70.

Cenni, B. 1973. *Tecniche Costruttive Romane: Teatro Romano di Gubbio*. Città di Castello: privately published.

Cerchiai, L. 1995. *I Campani* (Biblioteca di Archeologia 23). Milano: Longanesi & C.

Cerchiai, L. 2002. Le fibule da parata di Capua e Suessula. In Pietropaolo, L. (ed.), *Sformate Immagini di Bronzo. Il Carrello di Lucera tra VIII e VII sec. a.C. Lucera, 28.9.2000*. Foggia: Claudio Grenzi, 142–48.

Chapa, T. 1985. *La Escultura Ibérica Zoomorfa*. Madrid: Ministerio de Cultura.

Cherici, A. 2003. Armi e società nel Piceno, con una premessa di metodo e una nota sul guerriero di Capestrano. In *I Piceni e l'Italia Medio-Adriatica. Atti del XXII Convegno di Studi Etruschi ed Italici Ascoli Piceno – Teremo – Ancona. 9–13 Aprile 2000*. Pisa – Roma: Istituti editoriali e poligrafici internazionali, 521–31.

Chiaramonte Trerè, C. (ed.). 1999. *Tarquinia. Scavi Sistematici nell'Abitato. Campagne 1982–1988. I materiali 1. Tarchna 2.1*. Roma: "L'Erma" di Bretschneider.

Chiaramonte Trerè, C. 1999. Un corredo funerario capuano di VIII secolo a.C. In Castoldi, M. (ed.), *Koinà. Miscellanea di Studi Archeologici in Onore di Piero Orlandini*. Milano: ET, 105–22.

Chiaramonte Treré, C. and D'Ercole, V. (eds). 2003 *La Necropoli di Campovalano. Tombe Orientalizzanti e Arcaiche 1*. Oxford: Archaeopress.

Chiarucci, P. 2000. Alba Longa. In Carandini, A. and Cappelli, R. (eds), *Roma. Romolo, Remo e la Fondazione della Città. Catalogo della Mostra*. Milano: Electa, 219–21.

Chieco Bianchi, A. M. 1981. La documentazione archeologica. In Bosio, L. (ed.), *Padova Antica. Da Comunità Paleoveneta a Città Romano-Cristiana*. Trieste: Pauda, 49–53.

Chieco Bianchi, A. M. and Prosdocimi, A. 1969. Una nuova stele paleoveneta iscritta. *Studi Etruschi* 37: 511–15.

Childe, V. G. 1925. *The Dawn of European Civilisation*. London: Kegan Paul.

Childe, V. G. 1926. *The Aryans: a Study of Indo-European Origins*. London – New York: Paul Trench, Trubner & Co.

Chirassi Colombo, I. 2008. Simbolico Piceno: Un popolo tra mito e storia. In Luni, M. and Sconocchia, S. (eds), *I Piceni e la Loro Riscoperta tra Settecento e Novecento. Atti delConvegno Internazionale, Urbino 2000*. Urbino: Quattroventi, 353–80.

Choclán, C. 1990. Excavación de urgencia en el Cerro de El Espino (Torredelcampo, Jaén). 1988 *Anuario Arqueológico de Andalucía 1988.III*. Sevilla: Junta de Andalucía, 157–64.

Christaller, W. 1933. *Die Zentralen Orte in Süddeutschland. Eine Ökonomische-Geographische Untersuchung über die Gesetzmässigkeit der Verbreitung und Entwicklung der Siedlungen mit Städtischen Funktionen*. Jena: Karl Zeiss.

CIE = *Corpus Inscriptionum Etruscarum*.

CIE II (ed.). 2006. *Colonna, I. and Maras, D. Corpus Inscriptionum Etruscarum. Sectionis I, Fasciculum 5 (Tit. 6325–6723) et additamentum Sectionis II, Fasciculi 1 (Tit. 8881–8927). Inscriptiones Veiis et in Agro Veientano, Nepesino Sutrinoque Repertae, Additis illis in Agro Capenate et Falisco Inventis, quae in Fasciculo CIE II, 2, 1 desunt, nec non illis Perpaucis in Finitimis Sabinis Repertis*. Pisa/Roma: Istituti editoriali e poligrafici internazionali.

Cifani, G. 2002. Aspects of urbanisation and ethnic identity in the Middle Tiber Valley. In Attema, P., Burgers, G.-J., Van Joolen, E., van Leusen, M. and Mater, B. (eds), *New Developments in Italian Landscape Archaeology* (BAR International Series 1091). Oxford: British Archaeological Reports, 219–28.

Cifani, G. 2003. *Storia di una Frontiera. Dinamiche Territoriali e Gruppi Etnici nella Media Valle Tiberina dalla Prima Età del Ferro alla Conquista Romana. Archeologia del Territorio*. Roma: Libreria dello stato. Istituto poligrafico e zecca dello stato.

Cifani, G. 2005a. I confini settentrionali del territorio veiente. In Paoletti, O. (ed.), *Dinamiche di Sviluppo delle Città nell'Etruria Meridionale. Veio, Caere, Tarquinia, Vulci. Atti del XXIII Convegno di Studi Etruschi ed Italici, Roma, Veio, Cerveteri/Pyrgi, Tarquinia, Tuscania, Vulci, Viterbo, 1–6 Ottobre 2001*. Vol. 1. Pisa, Roma: Istituti editoriali e poligrafici internazionali, 151–61.

Cifani, G. 2005b. Roma. Una stipe votiva al IV miglio tra le vie Latina e Labicana. *Mélanges de l'École Française de Rome* 117: 199–221.

Cifani, G. 2008. *L'Architettura Romana Arcaica. Edilizia e Società tra Monarchia e Repubblica.* Roma: «L'Erma» di Bretschneider.

Cifani, G. and Munzi, M. 1995. Considerazioni sugli insediamenti in area falisca. In Christie, N. (ed.), *Settlement and Economy in Italy 1500 BC to AD 1500. Papers of the Fifth Conference of Italian Archaeology* (Oxbow Monograph 41). Oxford: Oxbow Books, 387–94.

CIL = *Corpus Inscriptionum Latinarum.*

Cipiciani, M. L. 1995. Materiali ceramici. In Matteini Chiari, M. (ed.), *Museo Comunale di Gubbio. Materiali Archeologici.* Perugia: Electa Editori Umbri, 269–95.

Cipollone, M. 2002. Gubbio (Perugia). Necropoli in loc. Vittorina. Campagne di Scavo 1980–2. *Notizie degli Scavi alle Antichità* 9 (11–12, 2000–1): 5–371.

Claret Miranda, J. 2006. *El Atroz Desmoche. La Destrucción de la Universidad Española por el Franquismo, 1936–1945.* Barcelona: Crítica.

Clastres, P. 1989. *Society against the State: Essays in Political Anthropology.* New York: Zone Books.

Coarelli, F. 1987. *I Santuari del Lazio in Età Repubblicana.* Roma: La Nuova Italia Scientifica.

Coarelli, F. 1990. Roma, I Volsci e il Lazio Antico. In *Crise et Transformation des Sociétés Archaïques de l'Italie Antique au Ve siècle av. J.-C. Actes de la Table Ronde Organisée par l' École Française de Rome et l'Unité de Recherches Étrusco-Italiques Associée au CNRS (UA 1132), Rome 19–21 Novembre 1987.* Rome: École française de Rome, 135–54.

Cocchi Genick, D. (ed.). 1995. *Aspetti Culturali della Media Età del Bronzo nell'Italia Centro-Meridionale.* Firenze: OCTAVO Franco Cantini editore.

Coccia, S. and Mattingly, D. 1992. Settlement history, environment and human exploitation of an intermontane basin in the central Apennines: The Rieti Survey 1988–1991, part I. *Papers of the British School at Rome* 60: 213–90.

Cogrossi, C. 1982. Atena Iliaca e il culto degli eroi. L'heroon di Enea a Lavinio e Latino figlio di Odisseo. In Sordi, M. (ed.), *Politica e Religione nel Primo Scontro tra Roma e l'Oriente.* Milano: Vita e Pensiero, 79–98.

Cohen, A. P. 2003. *The Symbolic Construction of Community.* London/New York: Routledge.

Coldstream, J. N. 1968. *Greek Geometric Pottery: A Survey of Ten Local Styles and Their Chronology.* London: Methuen.

Coldstream, N. 1998. Minos redivivus: some nostalgic Knossians of the ninth century BC. In Cavanagh, W. G. and Curtis, M. (eds), *Post-Minoan Crete.* London: The British School at Athens, 58–61.

Cole, J. W. and Wolf, E. R. 1974. *The Hidden Valley. Ecology and Ethnicity in an Alpine Valley.* New York/London: Academic Press.

Colley, L. 2002. *Captives: Britain, Empire and the World, 1600–1850.* London: Jonathan Cape.

Colonna, G. 1964. Aspetti culturali della Roma primitiva: Il periodo orientalizzante recente. *Archeologia Classica* 16: 1–12.

Colonna, G. 1974. Il contributo dell'antica carta Archeologica alla conoscenza dell'Etruria meridionale. *Quaderni dell'Istituto di Topografia Antica* 6: 19–29.

Colonna, G. 1976–7. La dea Cel e i santuari del Trasimeno. *Rivista di Storia Antica* 6–7: 45–62.

Colonna, G. 1977. Un aspetto oscuro del Lazio antico. Le tombe del VI-V secolo a.C. *Parola del Passato* 32: 131–65.

Colonna, G. 1983. Un'iscrizione paleoitalica dall'agro tolfetano. *Studi Etruschi* 51: 573–90.

Colonna, G. 1986. Il Tevere e gli Etruschi. *Quaderni dell'Istituto per l'Archeologia Etrusco Italica* 12: 90–7.

Colonna, G. 1988a. I Latini e gli altri popoli del Lazio. In Pugliese Caratelli, G. (ed.), *Italia Omnium Terrarum Alumna. La Civiltà dei Veneti, Reti, Liguri, Celti, Piceni, Umbri, Latini, Campani e Iapigi.* Milano: Libri Scheiwiller, 409–528.

Colonna, G. 1988b. Il lessico istituzionale etrusco e la formazione della città (specialmente in Emilia Romagna). In Bermond Montanari, G. (ed.), *La Formazione della Città in Emilia Romagna.* Bologna: Nuova Alfa Editoriale, 15–44.

Colonna, G. 1990a. Città e territorio nell'Etruria meridionale del V secolo. In *Crises et Transformation des Sociétés Archaïques de l'Italie Antique au V° siècle av. J.C. (Acte Table Ronde, Rome 1987).* Rome/Paris: École française de Rome, 7–21.

Colonna, G. 1990b. Corchiano, Narce e il problema di Fescennium. In Maetzke, G., Paoletti, O. and Tamagno Perna, L. (eds), *La Civiltà dei Falisci. In Atti XV Convegno di Studi. Etruschi ed Italici 1987.* Firenze: Leo S. Olschki, 111–26.

Colonna, G. 1991. Civiltà anelleniche. In Pugliese Carratelli, G. (ed.), *Storia e Civiltà della Campania.* Napoli: Electa Napoli, 25–67.

Colonna, G. 1995. Gli scavi del 1852 ad Ardea e l'identificazione dell'Aphrodisium. *Archeologia Classica* 47: 1–67.

Colonna, G. 1996a. Alla ricerca della "metropoli" dei Sanniti. In Maetzke, G. (ed.), *Identità e Civiltà dei Sabini. Atti del XVIII Convegno di Studi Etruschi ed Italici, Rieti – Magliano Sabina, 30 Maggio–3 Giugno 1993.* Firenze: Leo S. Olschki, 107–30.

Colonna, G. 1996b. Roma arcaica, i suoi sepolcreti e le vie per i Colli Albani. In Pasqualini, A. (ed.), *Alba Longa: Mito, Storia, Archeologia: Atti dell'incontro di studio, Roma-Albano Laziale, 27–29 Gennaio 1994.* Roma: Istituto italiano per la storia antica, 335–54.

Colonna, G. 2004. Il cippo di Tragliatella (e questioni connesse). *Studi Etruschi* 71: 83–109.

Colonna, G. 2005. La dea etrusca Cel e i santuari del Trasimeno (originally published as Colonna 1976–7). In Colonna, G. (ed.), *Italia ante Romanum Imperium: Scritti di Antichità Etrusche, Italiche e Romane (1958–1998).* Pisa – Roma: Istituti Editoriali e Poligrafici Internazionali, 1929–38.

Colonna, G. and Tagliamonte, G. 1999. I popoli del medio adriatico e le tradizioni antiche sulle loro origini. In *I Piceni. Popolo d'Europa. Catalogo della Mostra, 2000.* Roma: De Luca, 10–3.

Comaroff, J. and Comaroff, J. L. 2005. Beasts, banknotes and the colour of money in colonial South Africa. *Archaeological Dialogues* 12 (2): 107–32.

Comaroff, J. L. and Comaroff, J. 1997. *Of Revelation and Revolution, II. The Dialectics of Modernity on a South African Frontier.* Chicago: Chicago University Press.

Cook, J. M. 1969. Review of Panionion und Melie. *Gnomon* 41: 716–8.

Coppola, D. 1983. *Le Origini di Ostuni.* Martina Franca: Arti Grafiche Pugliesi.

Cornell, T. J. 1991. The Tyranny of the evidence: A discussion of the possible uses of literacy in Etruria and Latium in the Archaic age. In *Literacy in the Roman World.* (Journal of Roman Archaeology Supplementary Series 3), 7–33.

Cornell, T. J. 1995. *The Beginnings of Rome. Italy and Rome from the Bronze Age to the Punic Wars (c. 1000–264 BC).* London – New York: Routledge.

Cornell, T. J. 1997. Ethnicity as a factor in early Roman history. In Cornell, T. and Lomas, K. (eds), *Gender and Ethnicity in Ancient Italy.* London: Accordia Research Institute, 9–21.

Cornell, T. J. and Lomas, K. (eds). 1997. *Gender and Ethnicity in Ancient Italy*. London: Accordia Research Institute.

Correa, J. A. 1994–6. La epigrafía de Sudoeste: Estado de la cuestión. In Villar, F. and Encarnaçao, J. D. (eds), *La Hispania Preromana*. Salamanca: Ediciones Universidad de Salamanca, 65–75.

Corsten, T. 1999. *Vom Stamm zum Bund. Gründung und territoriale Organisation griechischer Bundesstaaten* (Studien zur Geschichte Nordwest Griechenlands Band 4). Munich: Oberhummer Gesellschaft.

Cosentino, S., D'Ercole, V. and Mieli, G. 2001. *La Necropoli di Fossa I. Le Testimonianze più Antiche*. Pescara: Carsa.

Cosentino, S., D'Ercole, V. and Mieli, G. 2003. Costumi Funerari in Abruzzo tra l'Età del Bronzo Finale e la Prima Età del Ferro. In *I Piceni e l'Italia Medio-Adriatica. Atti del XXII Convegno di Studi Etruschi ed Italici Ascoli Piceno – Teremo – Ancona. 9–13 Aprile 2000*. Pisa, Roma: Istituti editoriali e poligrafici internazionali, 423–50.

Cozza, A. and Pasqui, A. (eds). 1981. *Carta Archeologica d'Italia (1881–97). Materiali per l'Agro Falisco*. Firenze: Leo S. Olschki.

Criado Boado, F. (ed.). 1992. *Arqueología del Paisaje. El Área Bocelo-Furelos entre los Tiempos Paleolíticos y Medievales*. Xunta de Galicia: A Coruña.

Cristofani, M. 1981. Antroponimia e contesti sociali di pertinenza. *Annali dell'Istituto Orientale di Napoli* 3: 47–79.

Cristofani, M. 1983. I Greci in Etruria. In *Forme di Contatto e Processi di Trasformazione nelle Società Antiche. Atti del Convegno, Cortona 1981*. Pisa – Roma: Scuola Normale Superiore – École Française de Rome, 239–54.

Cristofani, M. 1988. Etruschi nell'agro falisco. *Papers of the British School at Rome* 56: 13–24.

Cristofani, M. 1991. *Cerveteri. Tre Itinerari Archeologici*. Roma: Quasar.

Cristofani, M. 1996. *Etruschi e Altre Genti nell'Italia Preromana: Mobilità in Età Arcaica*. Roma: Giorgio Bretschneider.

Cristofani, M. 1999. Litterazione e processi di autoidentificazione etnica fra le genti dell'Italia arcaica. In *La Colonisation Greque en Mèditerranée Occidentale. Actes de la Rencontre Scientifique en Hommage à Georges Vallet, Rome-Naples 1995*. Paris: École Française de Rome, 345–60.

Croce, B. 1989 (1917). *Teoria e Storia della Storiografia*. Milano: Adelphi.

Crumley, C. 2003. Alternative forms of social order. In Scarborough, V., Valdez, F. and Dunning, N. (eds), *Heterarchy, Political Economy and the Ancient Maya: The Three Rivers Region on the East Central Yucatan Peninsula*. Tucson (AZ): The University of Arizona Press, 135–43.

Cruz Andreotti, G. 2002–3. La construcción de los espacios políticos ibéricos entre los siglos III y I a.C.: Algunas cuestiones metodológicas e históricas a partir de Polibio y Estrabón. *Cuadernos de Prehistoria de la Universidad Autónoma de Madrid* 28–29: 35–54.

Cruz Andreotti, G. 2004. Una contribución a la etnogénesis ibérica desde la literatura antigua: a propósito de la geografía de iberia y los iberos. In Candau, J. M., González, F. J. and Cruz Andreotti, G. (eds), *Historia y Mito. El Pasado Legendario como Fuente de Autoridad*. Málaga: Servicio de Publicaciones. Centro de Ediciones de la Diputación de Málaga, 241–76.

Cuozzo, M. 2003. *Reinventando la Tradizione. Immaginario Sociale, Ideologie e Rappresentazione nelle Necropoli Orientalizzanti di Pontecagnano*. Paestum: Pandemo.

Curty, O. 1989. L'historiographie hellénistique et l'inscription n. 37 des Inschriften von Priene. In Piérat, M. (ed.), *Historia Testis. Mélanges d'Épigraphie, d'Histoire Ancienne et Philologie Offerts à T. Zawadski*. Fribourg: Ed. Universitaires, 21–35.

Curty, O. 1995. *Les Parentés Légendaires entre Cités Grecques*. Geneva: Droz.

d'Agostino, B. 1978. Campochiaro (Campobasso). *Studi Etruschi* 46: 565.

d'Agostino, B. 1980. L'età del Ferro e il periodo arcaico. In Gastaldi, P. (ed.), *Sannio. Pentrie Frentani dal VI al I sec. A.C. Catalogo della Mostra*. Roma: De Luca, 21–7.

d'Agostino, B. and Gastaldi, P. 1998. *Pontecagnano II. La Necropoli del Picentino. 1. Le Tombe della Prima Età del Ferro* (AION Annali Dipartimento di Studi del Mondo Classico e del Mediterraneo Antico Quaderni 5). Napoli: Istituto Universitario Orientale.

D'Andria, F. (ed.). 1990. *Archeologia dei Messapi. Catalogo della Mostra. Lecce, Museo Provinciale Lecce "Sigismondo Catromediano". 7 Ottobre 1990–7 Gennaio 1991*. Bari: Edipuglia.

D'Andria, F. 1991. Insediamenti e territorio: l'età storica. *In I Messapi. Atti del XXX Convegno di Studi sulla Magna Grecia, Taranto – Lecce 1990*. Taranto: Istituto per la storia e l'archeologia della Magna Grecia, 393–478.

D'Andria, F. 2005. Le trasformazioni dell'insediamento. In D'Andria, F. (ed.), *Cavallino, Pietre, Case e Città della Messapia Arcaica*. Ceglie Messapico: Progettipercomunicare, 34–43.

D'Angour, A. J. 1999. Archinus, Eucleides, and the reform of the Athenian alphabet. *Bulletin of the Institute of Classical Studies* 43: 109–30.

D'Atri, V. 2006. Aggiornamenti dallo scavo del santuario di Piana del Lago (Montefiascone, VT). In Pandolfini Angeletti, M. (ed.), *Archeologia in Etruria Meridionale. Atti delle Giornate di Studio in Ricordo di Mario Moretti*. Roma: "L'Erma" di Bretschneider, 173–81.

d'Ercole, V. and Benelli, E. 2004. *La Necropoli di Fossa. II. I Corredi Orientalizzanti e Arcaici*. Pescara: Carsa.

d'Ercole, V., di Gennaro, F. and Guidi, A. 2002a. Appartenenza etnica e complessità sociale in Italia centrale: l'esame di situazioni territoriali diverse. In Molinos, M. and Zifferero, A. (eds), *Primi Popoli d'Europa. Proposte e Riflessioni sulle Origini della Civiltà nell'Europa Mediterranea*. Firenze, All'insegna del Giglio, 127–36.

d'Ercole, V., di Gennaro, F. and Guidi, A. 2002b. Valori e limiti dei dati archeologici nella definizione delle linee di sviluppo delle comunità protostoriche dell'Italia centrale. In Molinos, M. and Zifferero, A. (eds), *Primi Popoli d'Europa. Proposte e Riflessioni sulle Origini della Civiltà nell'Europa Mediterranea*. Firenze, All'insegna del Giglio, 111–26.

d'Ercole, V. and Martellone, A. 2007. Peltuinum e il territorio vestino prima di Roma. In Clementi, A. (ed.), *I Campi Aperti di Peltuinum dove Tramonta il Sole*. L'Aquila, Deputazione Abruzzese di Storia Patria, 17–38.

da Silva, A. C. F. 1986. *A Cultura Castreja do Noroeste de Portugal*. Paços de Ferreira: Câmara Municipal de Paços de Ferreira.

Dämmer, H. W. 1990. Il santuario di Reitia di Este-Baratella. Prima relazione preliminare sugle scavi. *Quaderni Archeologica Veneto* 6: 209–17.

Daverio Rocchi, G. 1988. *Frontiera e Confini nella Grecia Arcaica*. Roma, L'Erma di Bretschneider.

Davies, J. K. 1997. The 'Origins of the greek polis'. Where should we be looking? In Mitchell, L. G. and Rhodes, P. J. (eds), *The Development of the Polis in Archaic Greece*. London/New York: Routledge, 24–38.

Dawkins, R. M. (ed.). 1929. *The Sanctuary of Artemis Orthiaat Sparta*. London: Macmillan.

de Alarcão, J. 2003. A organização social dos povos de NW e N da Península Ibérica nas épocas pré-romana e romana. *Conimbriga* 42: 5–115.

De Angelis, F. 1998. Ancient past, imperial present: the British Empire in T. J. Dunbabin's 'The western Greeks'. *Antiquity* 72: 539–49.

De Benedittis, G. 1977. *Bovianum ed il Suo Territorio. Primi Appunti di Topografia Storica.* (Documenti di antichità italiche e romane VII). Salerno: Soprintendenza Archeologia del Molise.

De Benedittis, G. 1978. Sannio (CB): piana di Bojano. *Studi Etruschi* 46: 409–20.

De Benedittis, G. 1991. Bovianum. In Capini, S. and Di Niro, A. (eds), *Samnium. Archeologia del Molise. Catalogo della Mostra.* Roma: Quasar, 233–7.

De Benedittis, G. 1995. *Bovianum.* (Molise. Repertorio delle iscrizioni latine I). Campobasso: IRESMO.

De Benedittis, G. 1996. Gli insediamenti italici nell'area della Tavola di Agnone. Il punto della situazione. In Del Tutto Palma, L. (ed.), *La Tavola di Agnone nel Contesto Italico. Lingua, Storia, Archeologia dei Sanniti, Convegno di Studio. Agnone, 13.15.4.1994.* Isernia: Cosmo Iannone, 69–87.

De Benedittis, G. 2004. Bovianum, Aesernia, Monte Vairano: Considerazioni sull'evoluzione dell'Insediamento nel Sannio pentro. In Jones, H. (ed.), *Samnium. Settlement and Cultural Change.* Providence (RI): Brown University, 23–33.

De Benedittis, G. 2005. *Prima dei Sanniti? La Piana di Bojano dall'Età del Ferro alle Guerre Sannitiche attraverso i Materiali Archeologici.* Campobasso: IRESM.

De Benedittis, G., Di Giulio, P. and Di Niro, A. 2006. Il santuario ellenistico di Campomarino. In Caiazza, D. (ed.), *Samnitice Loqui. Studi in Onore di Aldo Prosdocimi.* Piedimonte Matese: Rotary Club, 113–42.

De Benedittis, G. and Santone, C. 2006. *Carlantino. La Necropoli di Santo Venditti.* Campobasso: Amministrazione Comunale di Carlantino.

De Grossi Mazzorin, J. 1998. Analisi dei resti faunistici da alcune strutture di Sorgenti della Nova. In Negroni Catacchio, N. (ed.), *Protovillanoviani e/o Protoetruschi: Ricerche e Scavi. Atti del Terzo Incontro di Studi (Preistoria e Protostoria in Etruria). Manciano-Farnese 1995.* Milano-Firenze: Centro Studi di Preistoria e Archeologia-Ottavo F. Cantini, 169–80.

de Hoz, J. 1997. Lingua e etnicidade na Galicia Antigua. In Pereira, G. (ed.), *O Feito Diferencial Galego. I. Historia (Vol. 1).* Santiago de Compostela: Museo do Pobo Galego, 110–40.

de Hoz, J. 1998. La escritura ibérica. In *Congreso Internacional Los Iberos. Príncipes de Occidente* Barcelona: Fundación La Caixa, 191–203.

de Hoz, J. 1998. La lengua de los Iberos y los documentos epigráficos en la comarca de Requena-Utiel. In Lorrio, A. J. (ed.), *Los Íberos en la Comarca de Requena-Utiel.* Alicante: Universidad de Alicante, 49–62.

De La Cadena, M. 1995. "Women are more Indian": Ethnicity and gender in a community near Cuzco. In Larson, B., Harris, O. and Tandeter, E. (eds), *Ethnicity, Markets, and Migration in the Andes: at the Crossroads of History and Anthropology.* Durham (NC): Duke University Press, 329–48.

de Martino, F. 1975. Note sull'Italia augustea. *Athenaeum* 53: 245–61.

De Min, M. 2005. Il mondo religioso dei Veneti antichi. In De Min, M., Gamba, M., Gambacurta, G. and Ruta Serafini, A. (eds), *La Città Invisibile. Padova Preromana. Trent'Anni di Scavi e Ricerche.* Bologna: Edizioni Tipoarte, 113–29.

De Min, M., Gamba, M., Gambacurta, G. and Ruta Serafini, A. (eds). 2005. *La Città Invisibile. Padova Preromana. Trent'Anni di Scavi e Ricerche.* Bologna: Edizioni Tipoarte.

De Min, M. and Ruta Serafini, A. 2005. Trent'anni di ricerca archeologica e paleoambientale. In De Min, M., Gamba, M., Gambacurta, G. and Ruta Serafini, A. (eds), *La Città Invisibile. Padova Preromana. Trent'Anni di Scavi e Ricerche*. Bologna, Edizioni Tipoarte, 5–9.

de Polignac, F. 1984. *La Naissance de la Cité Grecque*. Paris: Editions la Découverte.

de Polignac, F. 1994. *Cults, Territory, and the Origins of the Greek City State*. Chicago: University of Chicago Press.

de Polignac, F. 2006. Espaces de communication et dynamiques d'appartenance en Grèce archaïque. *Revue des Études Anciennes* 108 (1): 9–24.

De Santis, A. 1992. Il II e IV periodo. In Bietti Sestieri, A. M. (ed.), *La Necropoli Laziale di Osteria dell'Osa*. Roma: Quasar, 815–74.

de Simone, C. 1978. Un nuovo gentilizio etrusco in Orvieto (Katacina) e la cronologia della penetrazione celtica (gallica) in Italia. *Parola del Passato* 33: 370–95.

De Vecchi, P. (ed.). 2002. *Museo Civico di Gualdo Tadino. Rocca Flea 2. Materiali Archeologici e Ceramiche dal XVI al XX Secolo*. Perugia: Electa – Editori Umbri Associati.

Debiasi, A. 2008. *Hesperìa. 24, Esiodo e l'Occidente*. Roma: Erma di Bretschneider.

Decourt, N. and Decourt, J.-C. 2001. Le Pénée, Tempé, les magiciennes de Thessalie et Marguerite de Lussan. *Mésogeios* 13–14: 21–51.

Deecke, W. 1888. *Die Falisker. Eine Geschichtlich-sprachliche Untersuchung*. Straßburg: Karl J. Trübner.

Delibes, G. and Fernández Miranda, M. 1988. *Armas y Utensilios de Bronce en la Prehistoria de las Islas Baleares*. (Studia Archaeologica 78). Valladolid: University of Valladolid.

Delpino, F. 1994. Bisenzio. In *Enciclopedia dell'Arte Antica (II suppl. 1971–1994, vol. I)*. Roma: Istituto dell'Enciclopedia Italiana, pp. 697–9.

DeMarrais, E., Castillo, L. J. and Earle, T. 1996. Ideology, materialisation and power strategies. *Current Anthropology* 37 (1): 15–31.

Dench, E. 1995. *From Barbarians to New men. Greek, Roman, and the Modern Perceptions of Peoples from the Central Apennines*. Oxford: Clarendon Press.

Dench, E. 1997. Sacred springs to the Social War. In Cornell, T. and Lomas, K. (eds), *Gender and Ethnicity in Ancient Italy*. London: Accordia Research Institute: 43–51.

Dench, E. 2005. *Romulus' Asylum. Roman identities from the Age of Alexander to the Age of Hadrian*. Oxford: Oxford University Press.

Deriu, A. 1989. Caratterizzazione di ceramiche greche e campane dell'VIII sec. a.C. mediante spettroscopia Mössbauer. In *Atti del Secondo Congresso Internazionale Etrusco. Firenze, 26.5–2.6 1985*. Roma: Giorgio Bretschneider, 79–92.

Derks, T. 1997. The transformation of landscape and religious representations in Roman Gaul. *Archaeological Dialogues* 4 (2): 126–47.

Derks, T. and Roymans, N. 2009. *Ethnic Constructs in Antiquity: the Role of Power and Tradition*. Amsterdam: Amsterdam University Press.

Desborough, V. R. d'A. 1952. *Protogeometric Pottery*. Oxford: Clarendon Press.

Dessau, H. (ed.). 1892–1916. *Inscriptiones Latinae Selectae*. Berolini : Weidmannos.

Detlefsen, D. 1870. Die Geographie der Provinz Bätica bei Plinius (N.H. III 6–17). *Philolugos* 30: 265–310.

Devillers, M. 1988. *An Archaic and Classical Votive Deposit from a Mycenaean Tomb at Thorikos*. (Miscellanea Graeca 8). Gent: Belgian Archaeological School in Athens.

Devoto, G. 1954. *Tabulae Iguvinae*. Roma: Istituto Poligrafico dello Stato.

Devoto, G. 1977. *Le Tavole di Gubbio*. Firenze: Sansoni.

di Gennaro, F. 1983. Intervento nel corso della discussione <<Nascita di una societa urbana a Roma e nel Lazio>>. *Opus* 2 (2): 438–41.

di Gennaro, F. 1986. *Forme di Insediamento tra Tevere e Fiora dal Bronzo Finale al Principio dell'Età del Ferro*. Firenze: Leo S. Olschki.

di Gennaro, F. 1988. Primi risultati degli scavi nella necropoli di Crustumerium. Tre complessi funerari della fase IV A. *Archeologia Laziale* 9: 113–23.

di Gennaro, F. 1990. Crustumerium. Il centro protostorico e arcaico e la sua necropoli. In Di Mino, M. R. and Bertinetti, M. (eds), *Archeologia a Roma – La Materia e la Tecnica nell'Arte Antica*. Roma: De Luca, 68–72.

di Gennaro, F. 1990. Tomba femminile da Fidenae. In Cristofani, M. (ed.), *La Grande Roma dei Tarquini Catalogo della Mostra*. Roma: "L'Erma" di Bretschneider, 260–2.

di Gennaro, F. 1995. *Le Età del Bronzo e del Ferro nel Territorio Falisco*. Roma: Unpublished manuscript for tesi di Diploma, Scuola di specializzazzione in Archeologia, Cattedra di Etruscologia e Antichità italiche.

di Gennaro, F. 1999a. *Itinerario di Visita a Crustumerium*. Roma: Soprintendenza Archaeologica di Roma.

di Gennaro, F. 1999b. Roma, località Marcigliana or Monte Del Bufalo. In Ciarla, R. and Nista, L. (eds), *Acquisizioni e donazioni – Archeologia e Arte Orientale (1996–1998)*. Roma: Gangemi, 50–7.

di Gennaro, F. 2001. I prodotti dell'artigianato di Crustumerium in giro per il mondo. *Bollettino di Numismatica, Supplemento* 36: 251–7.

di Gennaro, F. 2007. Le tombe a loculo di età orientalizzante di Crustumerium. In Arietti, F. and Pasqualini, A. (eds), *Tusculum. Storia, Archeologica, Cultura e Arte di Tusculo e del Tusculano*. Roma: Comitato Nazionale per le Celebrazioni del Millenario delle Fondazione dell'Abbazia di S. Nilo a Crotta Ferrata, 163–76.

di Gennaro, F., Amoroso, A. and Togninelli, P. 2007. Crustumerium e Fidenae tra Etruria e Colli Albani. In Arietti, F. and Pasqualini, A. (eds), *Tusculum. Storia, Archeologia, Cultura e Arte di Tuscolo e del Tuscolano. Atti del Primo Incontro di Studi (27–28 Maggio e 3 Giugno 2000)*. Roma: Comitato Nazionale per le Celebrazioni del Millenario della Fondazione dell'Abbazia di S. Nilo a Grottaferrata, 135–62.

di Gennaro, F., Cerasuolo, O., Colonna, C., Rajala, U., Stoddart, S. K. F. and Whitehead, N. 2002. Recent research on the city and territory of Nepi. *Papers of the British School at Rome* 70: 29–77.

di Gennaro, F. and Peroni, R. 1986. Aspetti regionali dello sviluppo dell'insediamento protostorico nell'Italia centro-meridionale alla luce dei dati archeologici e ambientali. *Dialoghi di Archeologia* 2: 193–200.

di Gennaro, F., Rajala, U., Rizzo, D., Stoddart, S. and Whitehead, N. 2008. Nepi and territory: 1200 BC – 400 AD. In Patterson, H. and Coarelli, F. (eds), *Mercator Placidissimus – The Tiber Valley in Antiquity: New Research in the Upper and Middle Valley. Rome, 27–28 February 2004. (*Quaderni di Eutopia 8) Roma: Quasar, 879–87.

di Gennaro, F. and Stoddart, S. K. F. 1982. A review of the evidence for prehistoric activity in part of South Etruria. *Papers of the British School at Rome* 50: 1–21.

Di Mario, F. (ed.). 2007. *Ardea. La Terra dei Rutuli tra Mito e Archeologia: alle Radici della Romanità. Nuovi Dati dai Recenti Scavi Archeologici*. Roma: Soprintendenza per i Beni Archeologici del Lazio.

Di Mario, F. 2009. L'area archeologica in località Le Salzare, Fosso dell'Incastro. In Ghini, G. (ed.), *Lazio e Sabina 5. Scoperte Scavi e Ricerche*. Roma: Erma di Bretschneider, 331–346.

Di Mario, F. in press. Ardea, il santuario di Fosso dell'Incastro, In *Atti del Convegno Sacra Nominis Latini. Un Trentennio di Scoperte nei Santuari di Area Latina tra l'Età Arcaica e la Tarda Repubblica, Roma, 19–21 febbraio 2009.*

Di Niro, A. 1980. Il Bronzo finale e la prima età del Ferro. In Gastaldi, P. (ed.), *Sannio. Pentri e Frentani dal VI al I sec. a..C. Catalogo della Mostra.* Roma: De Luca, 45–9.

Di Niro, A. 1981. *Necropoli Arcaiche di Termoli e Larino. Campagne di Scavo 1977–1978.* Campobasso: Soprintendenza Archeologica del Molise.

Di Niro, A. 1984. Aspetti affini alla cultura daunia nel territorio costiero a nord del Gargano. In Neppi Modona, A., Cianferoni, G. C., Costagli Marzi, M. G. and Tamagno Perna, L. (eds), *La Civiltà dei Dauni nel Quadro del Mondo Italico. Atti del XIII Convegno di Studi Etruschi e Italici. Manfredonia, 21–27.6.1980.* Firenze: Leo S. Olschki, 35–44.

Di Niro, A. 1986. Guglionesi, necropoli arcaica. *Conoscenze* 3: 153–164.

Di Niro, A. 1991. Introduzione. In Capini, S. and Di Niro, A. (eds), *Samnium. Archeologia del Molise. Catalogo della Mostra.* Roma: Quasar, 31–3.

Di Niro, A. 1991. Le necropoli dell'area interna. In Capini, S. and Di Niro, A. (eds), *Samnium. Archeologia del Molise. Catalogo della Mostra.* Roma: Quasar, 61.

Di Niro, A. 2004. San Giuliano di Puglia. Rituali funerari di una piccola comunità agricola di VI–V secolo a.C. *Conoscenze* n.s. 1–2: 89–102.

Díaz-Andreu, M. 1997. Prehistoria y franquismo. In Mora, G. and Díaz-Andreu, M. (eds), *La Cristalización del Pasado: Génesis y Desarrollo del Marco Institucional de la Arqueología en España.* Málaga: Universidad de Málaga, 547–52.

Díaz-Andreu, M. 1998. Ethnicity and Iberians: the archaeological crossroads between perception and material culture. *European Journal of Archaeology* 1 (2): 199–218.

Díaz-Andreu, M., Lucy, S., Babic, S. and Edwards, D. N. 2005. *The Archaeology of Identity. Approaches to Gender, Age, Status, Ethnicity and Religion.* London: Routledge.

Díaz-Andreu, M. and Smith, A. (eds). 2001. *Nationalism and Archaeology.* London: Blackwell.

Díes, E. 2001. La influencia de la arquitectura fenicia en las arquitecturas indígenas de la Península Ibérica (s. viii–vii). In Ruiz Mata, D. and Celestino, S. (eds), *Arquitectura Oriental y Orientalizante en la Península Ibérica.* Madrid: Centro de Estudios del Próximo Oriente, 69–121.

Dietler, M. 1990. Driven by Drink: The role of drinking in the political economy and the case of early Iron Age France. *Journal of Anthropological Archaeology* 9 (407): 352–406.

Dietler, M. 1995. The cup of Gyptis: rethinking the colonial encounter in early Iron Age western Europe and the relevance of World-Systems models. *Journal of European Archaeology* 3 (2): 89–111.

Dietler, M. 1995. Early "celtic" socio-political relations: ideological representation and social competition in dynamic comparative perspective. In Arnold, B. and Gibson, B. (eds), *Celtic Chiefdom, Celtic State. The Evolution of Complex Social Systems in Prehistoric Europe.* Cambridge: Cambridge University Press, 64–71.

Dietler, M. 1998. Consumption, agency and the cultural entanglement: theoretical implications of a mediterranean colonial encounter. In Cusick, J. G. (ed.), *Studies in Culture Contact: Interaction, Culture Change and Archaeology.* Carbondale: Southern Illinois University Press, 288–315.

Dietler, M. 2006. Culinary encounters: food, identity and colonialism. In Twiss, K. (ed.), *We Are What We Eat: Archaeology, Food and Identity.* Carbondale (IL), Center for Archaeological Investigations: University of Southern Illinois Press, 218–42.

Dietler, M. and Herbich, I. 1994. Habitus et reproduction sociale des techniques. L'intelligence du style en archéologie et en ethno-archéologie. In Latour, B. and Lemonnier, P. (eds), *De la Préhistoire aux Missiles Balistiques: l'Intelligence Sociale des Techniques*. Paris: La Découverte, 202–27.

Diosono, F. 2006. I materiali dello scavo 2003 del santuario di Diana a Nemi. In Ghini, G. (ed.), *Lazio e Sabina. Atti del Primo Incontro di Studi su Lazio e Sabina, Roma, 28–30 gennaio 2002, Volume III*. Roma: De Luca, 191–202.

Dittenberger, W. (ed.). 1915–1924. *Sylloge Inscriptionum Graecarum*. Lipsiae: S. Hirzelium.

Dolfini, A., Malone, C. A. T. and Stoddart, S. K. F. 2006. Searching for ritual in the Bronzo Finale: the example of Gubbio. In *Studi di Protostoria in Onore di Renato Peroni*. Firenze: All'Insegna del Giglio, 663–5.

Donnan, H. and Wilson, T. M. 1999. *Borders: Frontiers of Identity, Nation and State*. Oxford: Berg.

Drago Troccoli, L. 1997. Le tombe 419 e 426 del sepolcreto di Grotta Gramiccia a Veio. In Bartoloni, G. (ed.), *Le Necropoli Arcaiche di Veio: Giornata di Studio in Memoria di Massimo Pallottino*. Roma: Università degli studi di Roma, La Sapienza, Dipartimento di scienze storiche archeologiche e antropologiche dell'antichità, 239–80.

Drummond, A. and Ogilvie, R. M. 1989. The sources for early Roman History. In Walbank, F. W., Astin, A. E., Frederiksen, M. W. and Ogilvie, R. M. (eds), *The Rise of Rome to 220 B.C.*, Cambridge: Cambridge University Press, 1–29.

Dunbabin, T. J. 1948. *The Western Greeks. The History of Sicily and South Italy from the Foundation of the Greek Colonies to 480 B.C.* Oxford: Oxford University Press.

Durán, F. D., Heyden, D. and Horcasitas, F. 1964. *The Aztecs: the History of the Indies of New Spain*. New York: Orion Press.

Earle, T. 1997. *How Chiefs Come to Power. The Political Economy in Prehistory*. Palo Alto: Stanford University Press.

Earle, T. 2002. *Bronze Age economics. The Beginnings of Political Economies*. Boulder (CO): Westview.

Edlund, I. E. M. 1987. *The Gods and the Place: Location and Function of Sanctuaries in the Countryside of Etruria and Magna Graecia (700–400 B.C.)*. Stockholm: Paul Aström.

Edwards, C., Malone, C. A. T. and Stoddart, S. K. F. 1995. Reconstructing a gateway city: the place of Nepi in the study of south-eastern Etruria. In Christie, N. (ed.), *Settlement and economy in Italy. 1500 BC–AD 1500*. (Oxbow monograph 41). Oxford: Oxbow Books, 431–40.

Edwards, D. N. E. 2005. The archaeology of religion. In Díaz-Andreu, M., Lucy, S., Babic, S. and Edwards, D. N. (eds), *The Archaeology of Identity. Approaches to Gender, Age, Status, Ethnicity and Religion*. London: Routledge, 110–28.

Emberling, G. 1997. Ethnicity in Complex Societies: Archaeological Perspectives. *Journal of Archaeological Research* 5 (4): 295–344.

Epstein, A. L. 1978 *Ethos and Identity: Three Studies in Ethnicity*. London: Tavistock Publications.

Fabietti, U. 1998. *L'Identità Etnica. Storia e Critica di un Concetto Equivoco*. Roma: Carocci.

Fábrega Álvarez, P. 2005. Poblamiento y territorio en la Edad del Hierro en la comarca de Ortegal (A Coruña, Galicia). *Complutum* 16: 125–46.

Fardon, R. 1996. 'Crossed destinies': the entangled histories of West African ethnic and national identities. In De La Gorgendière, L., King, K. and Vaughan, S. (eds), *Ethnicity in Africa: Roots, Meanings and Implications*. Edinburgh: Centre of African Studies, University of Edinburgh, 117-46.

Farney, G. D. 2007. *Ethnic Identity and Aristocratic Competition in Republican Rome*. Cambridge: Cambridge University Press.

Feinman, G. 2002. Archaeology and political economy. Setting the stage. In Feinman, G. and Nicholas, L. M. (eds), *Archaeological Perspectives on Political Economies*. Salt Lake City: The University of Utah Press, 1–6.

Feinman, G. and Nicholas, L. M. (eds). 2002. *Archaeological Perspectives on Political Economies*. Salt Lake City: The University of Utah Press.

Fenelli, M. 1990. Lavinium. In In Nenci, G. and Vallet, G. (eds), *Bibliografia Topografica della Colonizzazione Greca*. Pisa – Roma – Napoli: Scuola normale superiore – École française de Rome – Centre Jean Bérard, 461–91.

Fentress, L. 2000. What are we counting for. In Francovich, R., Patterson, H. and Barker, G. (eds), *Extracting Meaning from Ploughsoil Assemblages*. (The archaeology of Mediterranean landscapes 5). Oxford: Oxbow Books, 44–52.

Fernández Castro, M. C. and Cunliffe, B. W. 2002. *El Yacimiento y el Santuario de Torreparedones: un Lugar Arqueológico Preferente en la Campina de Córdoba*. (BAR international series 1030). Oxford: Archaeopress.

Fernández Rodríguez, C. 1996. La ganadería y la caza desde la Edad del Hierro hasta los inicios de la Edad Media en el Noroeste. *Férvedes* 3: 201–16.

Fernández-Posse, M. D. and Sánchez-Palencia, F. J. 1988. *La Corona y el Castro de Corporales (Truchas, León) II. Campaña de 1983*. Madrid: Ministerio de Cultura.

Fernández-Posse, M. D. and Sánchez-Palencia, F. J 1998. Las comunidades campesinas en la cultura castreña. *Trabajos de Prehistoria* 55 (2): 127–50.

Ferrer Albelda, E. 2001–2. Bastetanos y bástulo-púnicos. Sobre la complejidad étnica del sureste de Iberia. *Studia Emeterio Cuadrado* 17–18: 273–82.

Ferrer Sierra, F. 1996. El posible origen campamental de Lucus Augusti a la luz de las monedas de la caetra y su problemática. In Rodríguez Colmenero, A. (ed.), *Lucus Augusti. I. Elamanecer de una Ciudad*. A Coruña: Fundación Barrié de la Maza, 425–46.

Filippi, D. 2000. Inquadramento topografico del deposito votivo capitolino In Carandini, A. and Cappelli, R. (eds), *Roma. Romolo, Remo e la Fondazione della Città. Catalogo della Mostra*. Milano: Electa, 323–5.

Filippi, D. 2004. La Domus Regia. *Workshop di Archeologia Classica* 1: 101–21.

Filippi, D. 2005. La Domus Regia (aggiornamenti). *Workshop di Archeologia Classica* 2: 199–206.

Filippi, D. 2008. Dalla domus Regia al Foro: depositi di fondazione e di obliterazione nella prima età regia, in Sepolti tra i vivi /Buried among the living. Evidenza ed interpretazione di contesti funerari in abitato (Convegno Internazionale, Roma 2006). *Scienze dell'Antichità* 14 : 617–38.

Filippi, D. and Gusberti, E. 2006. Palatino, pendici settentrionali. Domus Regia: la tomba di fondazione. In Tomei, M. A. (ed.), *Roma. Memorie dal Sottosuolo. Ritrovamenti Archeologici 1980/2006 Catalogo della Mostra, Roma 2006–7*. Milano: Electa, 73–5.

Firpo, G. 2008. Roma, Etruschi e Italici nel "secolo senza Roma". In Urso, G. (ed.), *Patria Diversis Gentibus Una? Unità Politica e Identità Etniche nell'Italia Antica. Atti del Convegno Internazionale, Cividale del Friuli 2007*. Pisa: Edizioni ETS, 267–304.

Fitzjohn, M. (ed.). 2007. *Uplands of Ancient Sicily and Calabria. The Archaeology of Landscape Revisited*. London: Accordia Research Institute.

Flannery, K. V. 1976. Evolution of Complex Settlement Systems. In Flannery, K. V. (ed.), *The Early Mesoamerican Village*. New York: Academic Press, 162–73.

UNIVERSITY OF WINCHESTER

Flannery, K. V. and Marcus, J. 1983. *The Cloud People*. New York: Academic Press.

Fogolari, G. 1956. Dischi bronzei figurati di Treviso. *Bolletino d'Arte* 41: 1–10.

Fogolari, G. 1981. Padova preromana. In Bosio, L. (ed.), *Padova Antica. Da Communità Paleoveneta a Città Romano-cristiana*. Trieste: Pauda, 27–45.

Fogolari, G. 1988. La cultura. In Fogolari, G. and Prosdocimi, A. L. (eds), *I Veneti Antichi*. Padova: Programma Editore, 14–220.

Foucault, M. 2000. The subject and power. In Faubion, J. D. (ed.), *Power. Essential Works of Foucault 1954–1984*. New York: The New Press, 326–48.

Fourrier, S. 2001. Naucratis, Chypre et la Grèce de l'Est: le commmerce des sculptures 'chypro-ioniennes'. In Höckmann, U. and Kreikenboom, D. (eds), *Naukratis. Die Beziehungen zu Ostgriechenland, Ägypten und Zypern in archaischer Zeit. Akten der Table Ronde in Mainz, 25–27 November 1999*. Möhnesee: Bibliopolis, 39–54.

Fowler, R. L. 1998. Genealogical thinking, Hesiod's Catalogue, and the creation of the Hellenes. *Proceedings of the Cambridge Philological Society* 44: 1–19.

Franchi dell'Orto, L. (ed.). 2001. *Eroi e Regine. Piceni. Popolo d'Europa*. Roma: De Luca.

Francis, K., Gilkes, O., Hodges, R. and Tyler, D. 2002. Santa Scolastica: Survey and trial excavations of a Samnite Site near San Vincenzo al Volturno. *Papers of the British School at Rome* 70: 347–57.

Franco, C. 1993. *Il Regno di Lisimaco*. (Studii Hellenistici 6). Pisa: Giardini.

Fraser, P. M. and Ronne, T. 1957. *Boeotian and West Greek Tombstones*. (Acta Instituti Atheniensis Regni Sueciae. Series in 4°; 6). Lund: C. W. K. Gleerup.

Frederiksen, M. W. and Ward-Perkins, J. B. 1957. The ancient road systems of the central and northern Ager Faliscus. Notes on Southern Etruria 2. *Papers of the British School at Rome* 25: 67–208.

Furtwängler, A. 1984. Wer entwarf den grössten Tempel Griechenlands? *Mitteilungen des Deutschen Archäologischen Instituts. Athenische Abteilung* 99: 97–103.

Gamba *et al.* 2005a = Gamba, M., Gambacurta, G., Ruta Serafini, A. and Balista, C. 2005. Topografia urbanistica. In De Min, M., Gamba, M., Gambacurta, G. and Ruta Serafini, A. (eds), *La Città Invisibile. Padova Preromana. Trent'Anni di Scavi e Ricerche*. Bologna: Edizioni Tipoarte, 23–31.

Gamba *et al.* 2005b = Gamba, M., Gambacurta, G. and Sainati, C. 2005. L'abitato. In De Min, M., Gamba, M., Gambacurta, G. and Ruta Serafini, A. (eds), *La Città invisibile. Padova Preromana. Trent'Anni di Scavi e Ricerche*. Bologna: Edizioni Tipoarte, 65–75.

Gamurrini, G. F., Cozza, A. and Mengarelli, R. 1972. *Carta Archeologica d'Italia (1881–1897)* (Materiali per l'Etruria e la Sabina, Forma Italia II:1). Firenze: Leo S. Olschki.

García Fernández-Albalat, B. 1990. *Guerra y Religión en la Gallaecia y Lusitania Antiguas Sada*. A Coruña, Ediciós do Castro.

García Gandía, J. R. 2003. La tumba 17 de la necrópolis de Les Casetes (Villajoyosa, Alicante). *Saguntum Papeles del Laboratorio de Arqueología de Valencia* 35: 219–28.

García Gandía, J. R. 2005. La necrópolis orientalizante de les Casetes: ajuares y estructuras funerarias. In Abad, L., Sala, F. and Grau, I. (eds), *La Contestania Ibérica, Treinta Años Después*. Alicante: University of Alicante, 345–55.

García Gandía, J. R. and Padró, J. 2002–3. Una cantimplora de fayenza egipcia procedente de la necrópolis de Les Casetes (La Vila Joiosa, Alicante). *Pyrenae* 33–34: 347–64.

García Quintela, M. V. 2002. *La Organización Socio-política de los Populi del Noroeste de la Península Ibérica: un Estudio de Antropología Política Histórica Comparada*. (TAPA

28). Santiago de Compostela: Laboratorio de Patrimonio, Paleoambiente e Paisaxe, Universidade de Santiago de Compostela.

García Quintela, M. V. and Santos, M. 2008. *Santuarios de la Galicia Céltica. Arqueología del Paisaje y Religiones Comparadas*. Madrid: Abada.

García y Bellido, A. 1952. Tartessos y los comienzos de nuestra historia. In Menéndez Pidal, R. (ed.), *Historia de España: España Protohistórica T. I Vol. II*. Madrid: Espasa-Calpe, 279–308.

Garrucci, R. 1860. Scoperte falische. *Annali dell'Instituto di Corrispondenza Archeologica* 32: 211–281.

Gastaldi, P. 1980. (ed.) *Sannio. Pentri e Frentani dal VI al 1 sec. a.C. Catalogo della Mostra*. Roma: De Luca.

Gates St-Pierre, C. 2006. . Faunal remains as markers of ethnicity: a case study from St.Lawrence Estuary, Quebec, Canada, *10th Conference of the International Council for Archaeozoology (ICAZ), Mexico City, August 24th, 2006. Retrieved 10 December 2008, from http://www.alexandriaarchive.org/bonecommons/prize/Gates_Text.pdf.*

Gaultier, F. 1999. Gustave Paille: un archeologo francese alla scoperta dell'agro falisco. In Mandolesi, A. and Naso, A. (eds), *Ricerche Archeologiche in Etruria Meridionale nel XIX Secolo*. Firenze: All'insegna del Giglio, 87–95.

Gerritsen, F. 2003. *Local Identities: Landscape and Community in the Late Prehistoric Meuse-Demer-Scheldt Region*. (Amsterdam Archaeological Series 9). Amsterdam, University of Amsterdam Press.

Ghini, G., 2004. Approdi antichi nel Lago Albano, in Batinti, A., Bonino, M and E. Gambini. (eds.) *Le Acque Interne dell'Italia centrale. Studi offerti a Giovanni Moretti*. Feliciano (Perugia): Alli – Pro Loco di S. Feliciano, 119-40.

Ghirardini, G. 1888. Este. Intorno alla antichità scoperte nel fondo Baratela. *Notizie degli Scavi* 1888: 3–42, 71–127, 147–73, 180–313.

Giacomelli, G. 1963. *La Lingua Falisca*. (Biblioteca di "Studi etruschi," 1). Firenze: Leo S. Olschki.

Giardina, A. 1997. *L'Italia Romana. Storie di un'Identità Incompiuta*. Roma/Bari: Laterza.

Giardino, C. 1985. Il ripostiglio di Nemi. *Documenti Albana* 7: 7-15.

Gibson, J. J. 1979. *The Ecological Approach to Visual Perception*. Boston: Houghton Mifflin.

Given, M. 2004. *The Archaeology of the Colonized*. London: Routledge.

Gjerstad, E. 1960. *Early Rome/Einar Gjerstad – Vol. 3, Fortifications, Domestic Architecture, Sanctuaries, Stratigraphic Excavations*. (Skrifter utgivna av Svenska institutet i Rom, 4° XVII:3) Lund: Gleerup.

Godelier, M. 1990. *Lo Ideal y lo Material*. Madrid: Taurus Humanidades.

Godelier, M. 1998. Funciones, Formas y Figuras del poder político In *Congreso Internacional Los Iberos. Príncipes de Occidente*. Barcelona: Fundación La Caixa, 13–24.

Golini, D. 1857. Scavi volsiniesi. *Bollettino dell'Istituto di Corrispondenza Archeologica* 1857: 131–40.

Gómez Bellard, C., Guérin, P. and Pérez Jordà, G. 1991. Témoignage d'une production de vin dans l'Espagne préromaine. In Amouretti, M.-C. and Brun, J.-P. (eds), *La Production de Vin et de Huile en Méditerranée*. Paris: de Boccard, 379–95.

González García, F. J., Parcero-Oubiña, C. and Ayán Vila, X. In press. Iron Age societies against the state. An account on the emergence of the Iron Age in the NW Iberian Peninsula. In Armada Pita, X. L. and Moore, T. (eds), *Atlantic Europe in the First Millennium BC: Crossing the Divide*. Oxford: Oxford University Press.

González Navarrete, J. 1987. *La Escultura Iberica de Cerrillo Blanco*. Jaén: Instituto de Cultura. Diputación de Jaén.

González Prats, A. 1983. *Estudio Arqueológico del Poblamiento Antiguo de la Sierra de Crevillente*. Alicante: University of Alicante.

González Prats, A. 1985. Sobre unos elementos materiales del comercio fenicio en tierras del sudeste peninsular. *Lucentum* 4: 97–106.

González Prats, A. 1992. Una vivienda metalúrgica en la Peña Negra (Crevillente, Alicante). Aportación al conocimiento del Bronce Atlántico en la Península Ibérica. *Trabajos de Prehistoria* 49: 243–57.

González Prats, A. 1998. La Fonteta. El asentamiento fenicio de la desembocadura del río Segura (Guardamar, Alicante, España). Resultados de las excavaciones de 1996–97. *Rivista di Studi Fenici* 26 (2): 191–228.

González Prats, A. 2001. Arquitectura orientalizante en el Levante Peninsular. In Ruiz Mata, D. and Celestino, S. (eds), *Arquitectura Oriental y Orientalizante en la Península Ibérica*. Madrid: Centro de Estudios del Próximo Oriente, 173–92.

González Prats, A. 2002. *La Necrópolis de Cremación de Les Moreres (Crevillente, Alicante, España) (s. ix–vii AC)*. Alicante: University of Alicante.

González Prats, A. 2005a. Balanç de vint-i-cinc anys d'investigació sobre la influència i presència fenícia a la província d'Alacant. *Fonaments* 12: 41–64.

González Prats, A. 2005b. El fenómeno orientalizante en el sudeste de la Península Ibérica, in In Jiménez, S. C. J. (ed.), *El período Orientalizante. Actas del III Simposio Internacional de Arqueología de Mérida* . Madrid: Consejo Superior de Investigaciones Científicas, 799–808.

González Prats, A. and Pina, J. A. 1983. Análisis de las pastas cerámicas de vasos hechos a torno de la fase orientalizante de Peña Negra (675–550/535 a.C.). *Lucentum* 2: 115–45.

González Prats, A. and Ruiz Segura, E. 2000. *El Yacimiento Fenicio de La Fonteta (Guardamardel Segura. Alicante. Comunidad Valenciana)*. Valencia: Real Academia de Cultura Valenciana.

González Prats, A. and Ruiz-Gálvez, M. 1989. La metalurgia de Peña Negra en su contexto del Bronce Final del Occidente europeo. In *XIX Congreso Nacional de Arqueología*. Castellón de la Plana: Universidad de Zaragoza, 367–76.

González Román, C. and Adroher, A. 1997. El poblamiento ibero-bastetano: consideraciones sobre su morfología y evolución. In Villas, F. and Beltrán, F. (eds), *Pueblos, Lenguas y Escrituras en la Hispania Prerromana*. Salamanca: Ediciones Universidad de Salamanca, 243–56.

González Ruibal, A. 2004. Artistic expression and material culture in Celtic Gallaecia. *Journal of Interdisciplinary Celtic Studies* 6: 113–66.

González Ruibal, A. 2006. House societies vs. kinship-based societies: an archaeological case from Iron Age Europe. *Journal of Anthropological Archaeology* 25 (1): 144–73.

González Ruibal, A. 2006–2007. *Galaicos. Poder y Comunidad en el Noroeste de la Península Ibérica (Brigantium 18/19)*. A Coruña: Museo Arqueolóxico e Histórico Castelo de San Antón.

Gosden, C. 2004. *Archaeology and Colonialism. Cultural contact from 5000 BC to the present*. Cambridge: Cambridge University Press.

Goudriaan, K. 1988. *Ethnicity in Ptolemeic Egypt*. Amsterdam: Gieben.

Graeber, D. 2004. *Fragments of an Anarchist Anthropology*. Chicago: Prickly Paradigm Press.

Grau Mira, I. 1998–99. Un posible centro productor de cerámica ibérica con decoración figurada en la Contestania. *Lucentum* 18–19: 75–92.

Grau Mira, I. 2002. *La organización del Territorio en el Área Central de la Contestania Ibérica.* Alicante,: Universidad de Alicante.

Grau Mira, I. 2003. Settlement dynamics and social organization in eastern Iberia during the Iron Age (8th–2nd centuries BC). *Oxford Journal of Archaeology* 22–3: 261–79.

Grau Mira, I. 2005. Espacios étnicos y políticos en el área oriental de Iberia. *Complutum* 16: 105–23.

Grau Mira, I. 2007. Dinámica social, paisaje y teoría de la practica. Propuestas sobre la evolución de la sociedad ibérica en el Oriente Peninsular. *Trabajos de Prehistoria* 4 (2): 119–42.

Greco, E. (ed.). 2002. *Gli Achei e l'Identità Etnica degli Achei d'Occidente. Atti del Convegno Internazionale di Studi, Paestum 2001.* Paestum-Atene: Pandemos.

Green, S. F. 2005. *Notes from the Balkans. Locating Marginality and Ambiguity on the Greek-Albanian Border.* Princeton: Princeton University Press.

Greenfeld, L. 1992. *Nationalism: Five Roads to Modernity.* Cambridge (MA): Harvard University Press.

Grillo, R. D. 1998. *Pluralism and the Politics of Difference: State, Culture, and Ethnicity in Comparative Perspective.* Oxford: Oxford University Press.

Groube, L. 1981. Black-Holes in British Prehistory: The analysis of settlement distribution. In Hammond, N., Hodder, I. and Isaac, G. (eds), *Pattern of the Past: Studies in Honour of David Clarke.* Cambridge: Cambridge University Press, 185–211.

Gruben, G. 2001. *Griechische Tempel und Heiligtümer.* München: Hirmer.

Gruen, E. S. (ed.). 2005. *Cultural Borrowings and Ethnic Appropriations in Antiquity.* Stuttgart: Franz Steiner Verlag.

Guaitoli, M. 1995. Lavinium: nuovi dati dalle necropoli. *Archaeologia Laziale* 24: 551–62.

Guaitoli, M. 2003. *Lo Sguardo di Icaro. Le Collezioni dell'Aerofototeca Nazionale per la Conoscenza del Territorio. Catalogo della Mostra.* Roma: Campisano Editore.

Guettel Cole, S. 1994. Demeter in the ancient Greek city and its countryside. In Alcock, S. E. and Osborne, R. (eds), *Placing the Gods: Sanctuaries and Sacred Space in Ancient Greece.* Oxford: Oxford University Press, 199–216.

Guidi, A. 1980. Luoghi di culto dell'età del bronzo finale e della prima età del ferro nel Lazio meridionale. *Archeologia Laziale* 3: 148–55.

Guidi, A. 1985. An application of the rank size rule to protohistoric settlements in the middle Tyrrhenian area. In Malone, C. A. T. and Stoddart, S. K. F. (eds), *Papers in Italian Archaeology IV. Vol. 3. Patterns in Protohistory.* (BAR International Series 245). Oxford: British Archaeological Reports, 217–42.

Guidi, A. 1998. The emergence of the State in central and northern Italy. *Acta Archaeologica* 69: 139–161.

Guidi, A. 2006. The archaeology of the early state in Italy. *Social Evolution and History. Studies in the Evolution of Human Societies* 6 (2): 55–90.

Guidi, A., Pascucci, P. and Zarattini, A. 2002. Confini geografici e confini culturali: le facies della Preistoria e della Protostoria nel Lazio meridionale. *Latium* 19: 5–21.

Guidi, A. and Santoro, P. 2004. Centri della Sabina tiberina in epoca preromana. In Patterson, H. (ed.), *Bridging the Tiber. Approaches to Regional Archaeology in the Middle Tiber Valley.* London: The British School at Rome, 179–87.

Gusberti, E. 2005. Il deposito votivo capitolino. *Workshop di Archeologia Classica* 2: 151–55.

Gusberti, E. 2008. Sepolture in abitato a Roma tra VIII e VI secolo a.C. *Scienze dell'Antichità* 14: 639–51.

Guzzo, P. G. 1987. Schema per la categoria interpretativa del "santuario di frontiera" *Scienze dell'Antichità* 1: 373–79.

Hakenbeck, S. 2004. Ethnic tensions in Early Medieval Cemeteries in Bavaria. *Archaeological Review from Cambridge* 19 (2): 40–55.

Hakenbeck, S. 2004. Ethnicity: An Introduction. *Archaeological Review from Cambridge* 19 (2): 1–6.

Häkli, J. 1999. Cultures of Demarcation: Territory and National Identity in Finland. In Herb, G. H. and Kaplan, D. H. (eds), *Nested Identities: Nationalism, Territory, and Scale*. Oxford: Rowman & Littlefield, 123–49.

Hales, S. and Hodos, T. (eds). 2010. *Material Culture and Social Identities in the Ancient World*. Cambridge: Cambridge University Press.

Hall, E. 1991. *Inventing the Barbarian*. Oxford: Clarendon Press.

Hall, J. 1998. Review feature: Ethnic Identity in Greek Antiquity. *Cambridge Archaeological Journal* 8: 265–283.

Hall, J. M. 1997 (2000). *Ethnic Identity in Greek Antiquity*. Cambridge: Cambridge University Press.

Hall, J. M. 2002. *Hellenicity: Between Ethnicity and Culture*. Chicago: University of Chicago Press.

Halstead, P. J. L. 1987. Traditional and ancient rural economy in Mediterranean Europe: plus ça change? *Journal of Hellenic Studies* 107: 77–87.

Hansen, M. H. (ed.). 2000 (2002). *A Comparative Study of Six City-State Cultures*. Copenhagen: The Copenhagen Polis Centre.

Hansen, M. H. 2006. *Polis: An Introduction to the Ancient Greek City-state*. Oxford: Oxford University Press.

Hansen, M. H. and Nielsen, T. H. (eds). 2004. *An Inventory of Archaic and Classical Poleis*. Oxford: Oxford University Press.

Hare, T. S. 2000. Between the household and the empire. Structural relationships within and among Aztec communities and polities. In Canuto, M.-A. and Yaeger, J. (eds), *Archaeology of Communities: a New World Perspective*. London: Routledge, 78–101.

Härke, H. G. H. 1991. All quiet on the Western Front ? Paradigms, methods and approaches in West German archaeology. In Hodder, I. (ed.), *Archaeological Theory in Europe*. London: Routledge, 187–222.

Harris, W. V. 1985. Volsinii and Rome, 400–100 BC. *Annali della Fondazione per il Museo "Claudio Faina"* 2: 143–56.

Harris, W. V. 2007. Quando e come l'Italia divenne per la prima volta Italia? Un saggio sulla politica dell'identità. *Studi Storici* 48: 301–22.

Hayden, B. 1995. Pathways to power: principles for creating socioeconomic inequalities. In Price, T. D. and Feinman, G. M. (eds), *Foundations of Social Inequality*. New York: Plenum Press, 15–86.

Hegel, G. W. F. 1955 (1837). *Die Vernunft in der Geschichte* Hamburg: Verlag von Felix Meiner.

Helms, M. W. 1988. *Ulysses' Sail. An Ethnographic Odyssey of Power, Knowledge and Geographical Distance*. Princeton: Princeton University Press.

Herasmus, H. J. 1962. *The Origins of Rome in Historiography from Petrarca to Perizonius*. Assen: Van Gorcum.

Herb, G. H. 1999. National Identity and Territory. In Herb, G. H. and Kaplan, D. H. (eds), *Nested Identities: Nationalism, Territory, and Scale*. Oxford: Rowman & Littlefield, 9–30.

Herring, E. 2000. 'To see ourselves as other see us!' The construction of native identities in southern Italy. In Herring, E. and Lomas, K. (eds), *The Emergence of State Identities in Italy in the First Millennium BC*. London: Accordia Research Institute, 45–78.

Hesse, B. and Wapnish, P. 1997. Can Pig Remains be used for Ethnic Diagnosis in the Ancient Near East? In Silberman, N. A. and Small, D. (eds), *The Archaeology of Israel. Constructing the Past, Interpreting the Present*. Sheffield: Sheffield Academic Press, 238–70.

Hill, J. D. 1995. How should we understand Iron Age societies and hillforts? A contextual study from southern Britain. In Hill, J. D. and Cumberpatch, C. G. (eds), *Different Iron Ages*. (BAR S602). Oxford: British Archaeological Reports, 44–66.

Hill, J. D. 1995. The pre-Roman Iron Age in Britain and Ireland: an overview. *Journal of World Prehistory* 9 (1): 47–98.

Hill, J. D. 2006. Are we any closer to understanding how later Iron Age societies worked (or did not work)? In Haselgrove, C. (ed.), *Les Mutations de la Fin de l'Age du Fer; Celts et Gaulois IV l'Archéologie Face à l'Histoire: Actes de la Table Ronde de Cambridge, 7–8 juillet 2005*. (Collection «Bibracte», 12/4). Glux-en-Glenne: Bibracte- Centre archéologique européen, 169–80.

Hiller von Gaertringen, F. 1906. *Inschriften von Priene*. Berlin: Reimer.

Hirsch, E. 1995. Introduction. Landscape between place and space. In Hirsch, E. and O'Hanlon, M. (eds), *The Anthropology of Landscape: Perspectives on Place and Space*. Oxford: Clarendon Press, 1–30.

Hobsbawm, E. and Ranger, T. (eds). 1983. *The Invention of Tradition*. Cambridge: Cambridge University Press.

Hodder, I. 1969. Economic and social stress and material culture patterning. *American Antiquity* 44: 446–54.

Hodder, I. 1982. *Symbols in Action: Ethnoarchaeological Studies of Material Culture*. Cambridge: Cambridge University Press.

Hodder, I. and Orton, C. 1976. *Spatial Analysis in Archaeology*. (New Studies in Archaeology 1). Cambridge: Cambridge University Press.

Holland, L. A. 1925. *The Faliscans in Prehistoric Times*. (Papers and monographs of the American Academy in Rome 5). Rome: American Academy in Rome.

Hornblower, S. 1991. *A Commentary on Thucydides. Vol. 1 Books I–III*. Oxford: Clarendon Press.

Huber, S. 1998. Érétrié et la Méditerranée à la lumière des trouvailles provenant d'une aire sacrificielle au nord du sanctuaire d'Apollon Daphnéphoros. In Bats, M. and d'Agostino, B. (eds), *Euboica. L'Eubea e la Presenza Euboica in Calcidica e in Occidente. Atti del Convegno Internazionale. Napoli, 13–16.11.1996*. Napoli: Centre Jean Bérard, 109–33.

Hughes, E. C. 1994. *On Work, Race and the Sociological Imagination (edited by L. A. Coser)*. Chicago: University of Chicago Press.

Humbert, M. 1993. *Municipium et Civitas sine Suffragio. L'Organisation de la Conquête Jusqu'à la Guerre Sociale (Deux. Tirage)*. Rome: École française de Rome.

Huxley, G. L. 1966. *The Early Ionians*. London: Faber & Faber.

Iaia, C. 2000. Connessioni Laziali e Sabine nell'estremo sud dell'Etruria agli inizi del primo millennio A.C. In Negroni Catacchio, N. (ed.), *L'Etruria tra Italia, Europa e Mondo Mediteraneo- Ricerche e Scavi. Atti del IV incontro di Studi*. Milano: Onlus, 505–7.

Iaia, C. 2007. Elements of female jewellery in Iron Age Latium and southern Etruria: identity and cultural communication in a boundary zone. In Blecic, M. (ed.), *Scripta Parehistorica in Honorem Biba Terzan*. Ljubljana: Narodni muzej Slovenije, 519–32.

Iaia, C. and Mandolesi, A. 1993. Topografia dell'insediamento dell' VIII secolo a.C. in Etruria meridionale. *Journal of Ancient Topography* 3: 17–48.

IG = *Inscriptiones Graecae*.

Ingold, T. 1993. The temporality of landscape. *World Archaeology* 25 (2): 152–72.

Insoll, T. (ed.). 2007. *The Archaeology of Identities. A Reader*. London and New York: Routledge.

Izikowsky, K. G. 1969. Vecinos en Laos. In Barth, F. (ed.), *Ethnic Groups and Boundaries. The Social Organization of Culture Difference (Results of a Symposium held at the University of Bergen, 23rd to 26th February 1967)*. Bergen/London: Universitetsforlage – Allen & Unwin, 177–95.

Izquierdo Peraile, I. 2000. *Monumentos Funerarios Ibéricos: los Pilares-estela (Trabajos Varios del SIP 98)*. Valencia: Diputació de Valencia.

Jacoby, F. 1962. *Die Fragmente der Griechischen Historiker, I*. Leiden: Brill.

Jaia, A. M. 2009. Pomezia: prime campagne di scavo nell'area del santuario di Sol Indiges. In Ghini, G. (ed.), *Lazio e Sabina 5. Scoperte Scavi e Ricerche*. Roma: Erma di Bretschneider, 347–53.

James, W. 1979. *'Kwanim 'Pa. The making of the Uduk people*. Oxford: Clarendon.

Janusek, J. W. 2002. Out of many one: style and social boundary in Tiwanaku. *Latin American Antiquity* 13: 35–61.

Jarva, E. 1980. *Barngravar i Latium under Järnålder och Arkaisk Tid. In Ficana – En Milesten på Veien til Roma*. København: I Kommision hos Museum Tusculanum, 139–45.

Jedrej, C. 1995. *Ingessana: the Religious Iinstitutions of a People of the Sudan-Ethiopian Borderland*. Leiden: Brill.

Jedrej, C. 2000. Ingessana and the legacy of the Funj Sultanate: the consequences of Turkish conquest on the Blue Nile. Africa. *Journal of the International African Institute* 70 (2): 278–97.

Jedrej, C. 2004. The Southern Funj of the Sudan as a frontier society, 1820–1980. *Comparative Studies in Society and History* 46 (4): 709–729.

Jeffery, L. H. 1990. *The Local Scripts of Archaic Greece: a Study of the Origin of the Greek Alphabet and its Development from the Eighth to the Fifth Centuries BC (Revised edition with a Supplement by A. W. Johnston)*. Oxford: Clarendon Press.

Jenkins, R. 1988. Social anthropological model of inter-ethnic relations. In Rex, J. and Mason, D. (eds), *Theories of Race and Ethnic Relations*. Cambridge: Cambridge University Press, 170–86.

Jenkins, R. 1994. Rethinking ethnicity: Identity, categorization and power. *Ethnic and Racial Studies* 17 (2): 197–223.

Jenkins, R. 1997. *Rethinking Ethnicity. Arguments and Explorations*. London – New Delhi: Sage Publications – Thousand Oaks.

Johannowsky, W. 1983. *Materiali di Età Arcaica dalla Campania*. Napoli: Macchiaroli.

Johannowsky, W. 1989. *Capua Antica*. Napoli: Banco di Napoli.

Johannowsky, W. 1992. Problemi riguardanti la situazione culturale della Campania interna in rapporto con le zone limitrofe tra il VI secolo a.C. e la conquista romana. In Maetzke, G., Costagli Marzi, M. G. and Tamagno Perna, L. (eds), *La Campania fra il VI e il III secolo a.C. Atti del XIV Convegno di Studi Etruschi e Italici. Benevento,24–28.6.1981*. Galatina: Congedo, 257–76.

Johannowsky, W. 1994. La cultura di Capua nella prima età del Ferro. In Gastaldi, P. And Maetzke, G. (eds), *La Presenza Etrusca nella Campania Meridionale. Atti delle Giornate di Studio. Salerno, Pontecagnano, 16–18.11.1990.* Firenze: Leo S. Olschki, 83–110.

Johannowsky, W. 1996. Aggiornamenti sulla prima fase di Capua. *AION Annali Dipartimento di Studi del Mondo Classico e del Mediterraneo Antico n.s.* 3: 59–66.

Johnson, G. A. 1973. Local exchange and early state development in southwestern Iran. *Anthropological Papers of the Museum of Anthropology, University of Michigan* 51: 1–205.

Johnson, J. H. (ed.). 1992. *Life in a Multi-cultural society: Egypt from Cambyses to Constantine and Beyond.* Chicago: Oriental Institute of the University of Chicago.

Jones, S. 1997. *The Archaeology of Ethnicity. Constructing Identities in the Past and Present.* London: Routledge.

Jones, C. P. 1999. *Kinship Diplomacy in the Ancient World.* Cambridge (MA): Harvard University Press.

Juan Moltó, J. 1988–9. El conjunt de terracotes votives del santuari ibèric de La Serreta (Alcoi, Cocentaina, Penàguila). *Saguntum Papeles del Laboratorio de Arqueología de Valencia* 21: 295–329.

Junker, K. 2004. Vom Theatron zum Theater. Zur Genese eines griechischen Bautypus. *Antike Kunst* 47: 10–32.

Jurgeit, F. 1999. *Die Etruskischen und Italischen Bronzen sowie Gegenstände aus Eisen, Blei und Leder im Badischen Landesmuseum Karlsruhe.* Pisa – Roma: IEPI.

Kaplan, D. H. 1994. Two nations in search of a state: Canada's ambivalent spatial identities. *Annals of the Association of American Geographers* 84 (4): 585–606.

Kaplan, D. H. 1999. Territorial identities and geographic scale. In Herb, G. H. and Kaplan, D. H. (eds), *Nested Identities: Nationalism, Territory, and Scale.* Oxford: Rowman & Littlefield, 31–49.

Kaplan, D. H. and Herb, G. H. 1999. Introduction: a question of identity. In Herb, G. H. and Kaplan, D. H. (eds), *Nested Identities: Nationalism, Territory, and Scale.* Oxford: Rowman & Littlefield, 1–6.

Kearsley, R. 1989. *The Pendent Semicircle Skyphos: a Study of Its Development and Chronology.* (Bullettin of the Institute of Classical Studies Supplement 44) London: Institute of Classical Studies.

Kilian, K. 1974. Zu den früheisenzeitlichen Schwertformen der Apenninhalbinsel. In Müller-Karpe, H. (ed.), *Beiträge zu Italienischen und Griechischen Bronzefunden.* München: Beck, 33–80.

Kilinski, K. 1990. *Boeotian Black Figure Vase Painting of the Archaic Period.* Mainz: Philipp von Zabern.

Kleiner, G., Hommel, P. and Müller-Wiener, W. 1967. *Panionion und Melie.* Berlin: Walter de Gruyter.

Knackfuss, H. 1941. *Didyma I: Die Baubeschreibung.* Berlin: Mann.

Knapp, A. B. 1992. Archaeology and Annales: time, space and change. In Knapp, A. B. (ed.), *Archaeology, Annales and Ethnohistory.* Cambridge: Cambridge University Press, 1–21.

Knapp, A. B. 2001. Archaeology and ethnicity: a dangerous liason. *Kypriaki Archaiologhia* 4: 29–46.

Knapp, A. B. 2003. The archaeology of community on Bronze Age Cyprus: Politiko Phorades in Context. *American Journal of Archaeology* 107: 559–80.

Knight, D. B. 1982. Identity and territory: Geographical perspectives on nationalism and regionalism. *Annals of the Association of American Geographers* 72: 514–31.

Knight, D. B. 1999. Afterword: Nested Identities – Nationalism, Territory, and Scale. In Herb, G. H. and Kaplan, D. H. (eds), *Nested Identities: Nationalism, Territory and Scale*. Oxford: Rowman & Littlefield, 317–29.

Koenigs, W. and Rumscheid, F. (eds). 1998. *Priene. Führer durch das Pompeji Kleinasiens*. Istanbul: Ege Yayınları.

Kossina, G. 1902. Die indogermanische Frage archäologisch beantwortet. *Zeitschrift für Ethnologie* 34: 161–222.

Kristiansen, K. 1998. *Europe Before History*. Cambridge: Cambridge University Press.

La Regina, A. 1968. Ricerche sugli insediamenti vestini. *Memorie dell'Accademia dei Lincei* 8 (13): 361–444.

La Regina, A. 1970–1. I territori sabellici e sannitici. *Dialoghi d'Archeologia* 4–5 (2–3): 443–59.

La Regina, A. 1989. I Sanniti. In Pugliese Caratelli, G. (ed.), *Italia Omnium terrarum alumna. La Civiltà dei Enotri, Choni, Ausoni, Sanniti, Lucani, Brettii, Sicani, Siculi, Elimi*. Milano: Libri Scheiwiller, 299–432

La Rocca, E. 1982. Ceramica d'importazione greca dell'VIII sec. a.C. a Sant'Omobono: un aspetto delle origini di Roma. In Anon (ed.), *La Céramique Grecque ou de Tradition Grecque au VIII siècle en Italie Centrale et Méridionale*. Napoli: Centre Jean Bérard, 45–53.

Ladra, X. L. 2005. Análisis territorial de la distribución de hallazgos de torques áureos de la II Edad del Hierro en el noroeste peninsular. In Cancelo, C., Blanco, A. and Esparza, A. (eds), *Bronce Final y Edad del Hierro en la Península Ibérica*. Salamanca: Ediciones Universidad de Salamanca, 94–110.

Latour, B. 1993. *We have never been Modern* (Translated by Porter, C). Cambridge: Harvard University Press.

Leach, E. R. 1954. *Political Systems of Highland Burma: a Study of Kachin Social Structure*. London: G. Bell – London School of Economics and Political Science.

Lehmann, H. 1939. Die Siedlungsräume Ostkretas. *Geographische Zeitschrift* 45: 212–28.

Lemonnier, P. 1986. The study of material culture today: toward an anthropology of technical systems. *Journal of Anthropological Archaeology* 5: 147–86.

Lemos, F. S. 1993. *Povoamento Romano de Trás-os-Montes Oriental*. Braga: Unpublished PhD Thesis, Universidade de Braga.

Lentz, C. (ed.). 1997. *Creating Ethnic Identities in North West Ghana*. London: Macmillan.

Lentz, C. and Nugent, P. 2000. *Ethnicity in Ghana: the Limits of Invention*. Houndmills (Basingstoke): Macmillan.

Leonardi, G. and Zaghetto, L. 1992. Il territorio nord-ovest di Padova dalla media età del bronzo all'età romana. In Baggio, P. (ed), *Padova Nord-Ovest*. Padova: Editoriale Programma, 71-209.

Letta, C. 2008. I legami tra i popoli italici nelle Origines di Catone tra consapevolezza etnica e ideologia. In Urso, G. (ed.), *Patria Diversis Gentibus Una? Unità politica e Identità Etniche nell'Italia Antica. Atti del Convegno Internazionale, Cividale del Friuli 2007*. Pisa: Edizioni ETS, 171–95.

Liddle, P. 1985. *Community Archaeology. A Fieldworker's Handbook of Organisation and Techniques*. Leicester: Leicestershire Museums, Art Galleries and Records Service.

Lieberman, V. 1978. Ethnic politics in eighteenth century Burma. *Modern Asia Studies* 12: 455–82.

Lightfoot, K. G. 2005. *Indians, Missionaries and Merchants. The Legacy of Colonial Encounters on the California Frontiers*. Berkeley (CA): University of California Press.

Lilli, M. 2002. *Ariccia: Carta Archeologica*. Roma: Erma di Bretschneider.

Linderski, J. 1986. The Augural Law. *Aufstieg und Niedergang der römischen Welt II* 16 (3): 2146–312.

Linnekin, J. and Poyer, L. (eds). 1990. *Cultural Identity and Ethnicity in the Pacific*. Honolulu: University of Hawaii Press.

Linnekin, J. and Poyer, L. 1990. Introduction. In Linnekin, J. and Poyer, L. (eds), *Cultural Identity and Ethnicity in the Pacific*. Honolulu: University of Hawaii Press, 1–16.

Little, B. J. (ed.). 1992. *Text-Aided Archaeology*. London: CRC Press.

Livingstone Smith, A. 2000. Processing clay for pottery in northern Cameroon: social and technical requirements. *Archaeometry* 42: 21–42.

Llobregat, E. 1972. *Contestania Ibérica*. Alicante: Instituto de Estudios Alicantinos.

Lo Porto, F. G. 1990. Testimonianze archeologiche della espansione tarantina in età arcaica. *Taras* 10 (1): 67–97.

Lo Schiavo, F. 1984. La Daunia e l'Adriatico. In Neppi Modona, A., Cianferoni, G. C., Costagli Marzi, M. G. and Tamagno Perna, L. (eds), *La Civiltà dei Dauni nel Quadro del Mondo Italico. Atti del XIII Convegno di Studi Etruschi e Italici. Manfredonia, 21–27.6.1980*. Firenze: Leo S. Olschki, 213–47.

Lohmann, H. 2002. Thebai 4. *Der Neue Pauly* 12 (1): 294.

Lohmann, H. 2003. Survey in Theben an der Mykale, 1. Kampagne 2001 In *20. Araştırma Sonuçları Toplantısı, 27–31 Mayıs 2002 Ankara (2)*. Ankara: Ayrıbasım, 247–60.

Lohmann, H. 2004. Survey in der Mykale, 2. Kampagne 2002. In *21. Araştırma Sonuçları Toplantısı, 26–31 Mayıs 2003 Ankara (1)*. Ankara: Ayrıbasım, 251–64.

Lohmann, H. 2005a. Melia, das Panionion und der Kult des Poseidon Helikonios. In Schwertheim, E. & Winter, E. (eds), *Neue Forschungen zu Ionien*. Bonn: Habelt, 57–91.

Lohmann, H. 2005b. Zur historischen Topographie des südlichen Ionien. *Orbis Terrarum* 8 (2002): 163–272.

Lohmann, H. 2006. Survey in the Mycale, 3rd Campaign: The Discovery of the Archaic Panionion. In *23. Araştırma Sonuçları Toplantısı, 30 Mayıs–4 Haziran 2005 Antalya (1)*. Ankara: Kültür Varlıkları ve Müzeler Genel Müdürlüğü (Series), yayın no. 114, 241–52.

Lohmann, H. 2007. The discovery and excavation of the archaic Panionion in the Mycale (Dilek Dağları). In *28th Kazı Sonuçları Toplantısı, 29 Mayıs–3 Haziran 2006 Çanakkale*. Ankara: Kültür Varlıkları ve Müzeler Genel Müdürlüğü (Series), yayın no. 121–2, vol. 2, 575–90.

Lohmann, H., Büsing, H. Hulek, F., Kalaitzoglou, G., Lüdorf, G., Müllenhoff, M. and Niewöhner, P. 2007. Forschungen und Ausgrabungen in der Mykale 2001–2006. *Istanbuler Mitteilungen* 57: 59–178.

Lomas, K. 1996. Greeks, Romans and others: problems of colonialism and ethnicity in southern Italy. In Webster, J. and Cooper, N. J. (eds), *Roman Imperialism: Post-Colonial Perspectives*. Leicester: University of Leicester, 135–44.

Lomas, K. 1997. Introduction. In Cornell, T. and Lomas, K. (eds), *Gender and Ethnicity in Ancient Italy*. London: Accordia Research Institute, 1–8.

Lomas, K. 2000. Between Greece and Italy: a external perspective on culture in Roman Sicily. In Smith, C. and Serrati, J. (eds), *Sicily from Aeneas to Augustus. New Approaches in Archaeology and History*. Edinburgh: Edinburgh University Press, 161–73.

Lomas, K. [Forthcoming.] *Literacy in Ancient Italy. New Approaches to the Development of Writing in Society*. London: Institute of Classical Studies.

Lombardo, M. 1991. I messapi: aspetti della problematica storica*in Atti del XXX convegno di studi sulla Magna Grecia, Taranto – Lecce 1990*. Taranto: Istituto per la storia e l'archeologia della Magna Grecia, 35–109.

Lombardo, M. 1994. Tombe, necropoli e riti funerari in 'messapia': evidenze e problemi. *Studi di Antichità* 7: 25–45.

Longo, F. 1997. Una coppetta a semicerchi penduli da una collezione privata del Salernitano. *Apollo* 13: 9–14.

López Precioso, F. J., Jordan, J. F. and Soria, L. 1993. Asentamientos ibéricos en el Campo de Hellín. Su relación con el trazado viario y la red comercial. *Verdolay* 4: 51–63.

Lorrio, A. J. 1997. *Los Celtíberos*. Alicante: Universidad de Alicante.

Lucy, S. 2002. Burial practice in early Medieval eastern England: Constructing local identities, deconstructing ethnicity. In Lucy, S. and Reynolds, A. (eds), *Burial in Early Medieval England and Wales*. London: The Society for Medieval Archaeology, 72–87.

Lucy, S. 2005a. The archaeology of age. In Díaz-Andreu, M., Lucy, S., Babic, S. and Edwards, D. N. (eds), *The Archaeology of Identity. Approaches to Gender, Age, Status, Ethnicity and Religion*. London: Routledge, 43–66.

Lucy, S. 2005b. Ethnic and cultural identities.. In Díaz-Andreu, M., Lucy, S., Babic, S. and Edwards, D. N. (eds), *The Archaeology of Identity. Approaches to Gender, Age, Status, Ethnicity and Religion*. London: Routledge, 86–109.

Lugli, G. 1966. I confini del pomerio suburbano di Roma primitiva. In Heurgon, J., Picard, G. and Seston, W. (eds), *Melanges d'Archéologie, d'Épigraphie et d'Histoire Offerts a Jérome Carcopino*. Paris: Hachette, 641–50.

Lulof, P. S. 2000. Archaic terracotta acroteria representing Athena and Heracles: manifestations of power in central Italy. *Journal of Roman Studies* 13: 207–19.

Lulof, P. S. 2006 La ricostruzione di un tetto perduto. *Archeologia Classica* 57: 516–29.

Macchiarola, I. 1991. Larino. In Capini, S. and Di Niro, A. (eds), *Samnium. Archeologia del Molise. Catalogo della Mostra*. Roma: Quasar, 43–45.

Macchiarola, I. 1991. S. Polo (Campone). In Capini, S. and Di Niro, A. (eds), *Samnium. Archeologia del Molise. Catalogo della Mostra*. Roma: Quasar, 80–81.

Maggiani, A. 2001. Magistrature cittadine, magistrature federali. In *La Lega Etrusca dalla Dodecapoli ai Quindecim Popoli. Atti della Giornata di Studi. Chiusi 9 Ottobre 1999*. Pisa – Roma: Istituti Editoriali e Poligrafici Internazionali, 37–49.

Maggiani, A. 2002. I culti di Perugia e del suo territorio. In Della Fina, G. M. (ed.) *Perugia Etrusca. Atti del IX Convegno Internazionale di Studi sulla Storia e l'Archeologia dell'Etruria. (Annali della Fondazione per il Museo "Claudio Faina" 9)*. Roma: Quasar, 267–300.

Maggiani, A. 2002. Luoghi di culto e divinità a Este. In Ruta Serafini, A. (ed.), *Este Preromana: Una Città e i Suoi Santuari*. Treviso: Canova, 77–88.

Malkin, I. 1994. *Myth and Territory in the Spartan Mediterranean*. Cambridge: Cambridge University Press.

Malkin, I. 2001. *Ancient Perceptions of Greek Ethnicity*. Cambridge (MA), Harvard University Press.

Mallet, M. and Whitehouse, D. 1967. Castel Porciano: An abandoned Medieval village of the Roman Campagna. *Papers of the British School at Rome* 35: 113–46.

Malnati, L. 2002. Il ruolo di Este nella civiltà degli antichi veneti. In Ruta Serafini, A. (ed.), *Este Preromana: Una Città e i Suoi Santuari*. Treviso: Canova: 37–43.

Malone, C. A. T. and Stoddart, S. K. F. (eds). 1994a. *Territory, Time and State. The Archaeological Development of the Gubbio Basin.* Cambridge: Cambridge University Press.

Malone, C. A. T. and Stoddart, S. K. F. 1994b. The settlement system of Gubbio in the Late Bronze Age and early Iron Age. In Malone, C. A. T. and Stoddart, S. K. F. (eds), *Territory, Time and State. The Archaeological Development of the Gubbio Basin.* Cambridge: Cambridge University Press, 106–27.

Malone, C. A. T. and Stoddart, S. K. F. 1994c. The long-term trajectory of an intermontane polity: colonisation, formation and incorporation. In Malone, C. A. T. and Stoddart, S. K. F. (eds), *Territory, Time and State. The Archaeological Development of the Gubbio Basin.* Cambridge: Cambridge University Press, 208–13.

Manconi, D. 1991. Attic red figured krater. In Corbucci, M. P. and Pettine, S. (eds), *Antichità dall'Umbria a New York.* Perugia: Electa Editori Umbri, 324–8.

Manconi, D. 2008. Gli ultimi rinvenimenti. In Manconi, D. (ed.), *Gubbio. Scavi e nuove ricerche. 1. Gli Ultimi rinvenimenti.* (Auleste. Studi di Archeologia di Perugia e dell'Umbria antica 2 (1)). Città di Castello: Edimond, 1–17.

Mangas, J. and Plácido, D. 1994. *Avieno.* Testimonia Hispaniae Antiqua I. Madrid: Editorial Complutense.

Mangas, J. and Olano, M. 1995. Nueva inscripción latina. Castella y castellani del área astur. *Gerión* 13: 339–47.

Maoli, M. G. 1985. La stipe di Villa di Villa a Cordignano (Treviso). *Archeologia Veneta* 8: 99–114.

Marchesini, S. 2007. *Prosopographia Etrusca II, 1: Studia: Gentium Mobilitas.* Roma: L'Erma di Bretschneider.

Marcus, J. and Flannery, K. V. 1996. *Zapotec Civilisation. How Urban Society Evolved in Mexico's Oaxaxa Valley.* London: Thames and Hudson.

Marcus, J. and Silva, J. E. 1988. The Chillón valley "Coca Lands". archaeological and ecological context. In Rostworowski de Diez Canseco, M. (ed.), *Conflicts over Coca Fields in Sixteenth Century Peru.* Ann Arbor: University of Michigan, Museum of Anthropology: 1–32.

Marín Suárez, C. 2005. *Astures y Asturianos. Historiografía de la Edad del Hierro en Asturias.* Noia: Toxosoutos.

Marinetti, A. 1985. *Le Iscrizioni Sudpicene.* Firenze: Leo S. Olschki.

Marinetti, A. M. 1999. Venetico 1976–1996. Bilancio e prospettive. In Paoletti, O. (ed.), *Protostoria e Storia del "Venetorum Angulus." Atti del XX Convegno di Studi Etruschi de Italici.* Pisa – Roma: Istituti editoriali e poligrafici internazionali: 391–436.

Marinetti, A. M. 2001. Il venetico di Lagole. In Fogolari, G. and Gambacurta, G. (eds), *Materiali Veneti Preromani e Romani del Santuario di Lagole di Calalzo al Museo di Pieve di Cadore.* Roma: Giorgio Bretschneider: 59–73.

Marinetti, A. M. 2002. L'iscrizione votiva. In Ruta Serafini, A. (ed.), *Este Preromana: Una Città e i Suoi Santuari.* Treviso: Canova: 180–84.

Marinetti, A. M. 2003. Il "signore del cavallo" e i riflessi istituzionali dei dati di lingua. Venetica ekupetaris. In Cresci Marrone, G. and Tirelli, M. (eds), *Produzioni, Merci e Commerci in Altino Preromana e Romana.* Roma: Quasar, 143–60.

Marinetti, A. M. and Prosdocimi, A. L. 1994. Nuovi ciottoloni venetici iscritti da Padova paleoveneta. In Scarfì, B. M. (ed.), *Studi di Archeologia di Regio X in Ricordo di Michele Tombolani.* Roma: "L'Erma" di Bretschneider, 171–94.

Marinetti, A. M. and Prosdocimi, A. L. 2005. Lingua e scrittura. In De Min, M., Gamba, M., Gambacurta, G. and Ruta Serafini, A. (eds), *La Città Invisibile. Padova Preromana. Trent'Anni di Scavi e Ricerche*. Bologna: Edizioni Tipoarte, 33–48.

Martelli, M. 1991. I Fenici e la questione orientalizzante in Italia. In Acquaro, E., Bartoloni, P., Francisi, M. T., Manfredi, L. I., Mazza, F., G, M., Petruccioli, G., Ribichini, S., Scandone, G. and Xella, P. (eds), *Atti del II Congresso Internazionale di Studi Fenici e Punici, Roma 9–14 Novembre 1987*. Roma: Consiglio Nazionale delle Ricerche, 1049–72.

Martí Bonafé, M. A. 1998. *El Área Territorial de Arse-Saguntum en Época Ibérica*. Valencia: University of Valencia.

Martín Bravo, A. M. 2002. *Los Orígenes de Lusitania. El I Milenio a.C. en la Alta Extremadura*. Madrid: Real Academia de la Historia.

Maruggi, G. A. 1996. Crispiano (Taranto), L'Amastuola, in ricerche sulla casa. In D'Andria, F. and Mannino, K. (eds), *Magna Grecia e in Sicilia. Atti del colloquio – Lecce, 23–24 Giugno 1992*. Galatina: Congedo editore, 197–218.

Maruggi, G. A. and Burgers, G.-J. (eds). 2001. *San Pancrazio Salentino, Li Castelli. Archeologia di una Comunità Messapica nel Salento Centrale*. San Pancrazio Salentino: PubliSystem Sanasi.

Massenzio, M. 1999. *Sacré et Identité Ethnique: Frontière et Ordre du Monde*. Paris: Editions de l' École des hautes études en sciences sociales.

Mastrocinque, A. 1996. Ricerche sulle religioni italiche. *Studi Etruschi* 61: 139–60.

Mata, C., Duarte, F. X., Ferrer, M. A., Garibó, J. and Valor, J. 2001. Kelin (Caudete de las Fuentes) y su territorio. In Lorrio, A. J. (ed.), *Los Íberos en la Comarca de Requena-Utiel*. Alicante: Univ. de Alicante, 75–89.

Matteini Chiari, M. 1975. *La Tomba del Faggeto in Territorio Perugino. Contributo allo Studio dell'Architettura Funerario con Volta a Botte in Etruria*. (Quaderni dell'Istituto di Archeologia dell'Università di Perugia 3). Roma: De Luca.

Matteini Chiari, M. 1979–80. La ricognizione per un'ipotesi di definizione territoriale: il territorio eugubino in età preromana. *Annali della Facoltà di Lettere e Filosofia. Università degli Studi di Perugia* 17: 211–21.

Matteini Chiari, M. 1995. *Museo Comunale di Gubbio. Materiali Archeologici*. Perugia, Electa Editori Umbri.

Matteini Chiari, M. 1996. "Umbria dal Cielo. La fotografia aerea non al servizio dell'archeologia". In Bonamente, G. and Coarelli, F. (eds), *Assisi e Gli Umbri nell'Antichità. Atti del Convegno Internazionale. Assisi 18–21, Dicembre 1991*. Assisi: Società Editrice Minerva – Università degli Studi di Perugia – Accademia Properziana del Subbasio di Assisi, 432–81.

Matteini Chiari, M. 2002. *Raccolte Comunali di Assisi. Materiali archeologici. Cultura Materiale, Antichità Egizie*. Perugia: Electa-Editori Umbri Associati.

Mattiocco, E. 1986. *Centri Fortificati Vestini*. Sulmona: Museo Civico.

Mauss, M. 1923–1924. Essai sur le don. *L'Année Sociologique* 1: 30–186.

Mavrogiannis, T. 2003. *Aeneas und Euander: mythische Vergangenheit und Politik im Rom vom 6.Jhr. v. Chr. bis zur Zeit des Augustus*. Napoli: Edizioni scientifiche italiane.

Mayor, A. 2000. *The First Fossil-Hunters: Paleontology in Greek and Roman Times*. Princeton: Princeton University Press.

Mazarakis Ainian, A. 1997. *From Rulers' Dwellings to Temples. Architecture, Religion and Society in Early Iron Age Greece (1100–700 BC)*. (Studies in Mediterranean archaeology 121). Jonsered: Åström.

Mazza, M. 2006. Identità e religioni: considerazioni introduttive. In Anello, P., Martorana, G. and Sammartano, R. (eds), *Ethne e Religioni nella Sicilia Antica.* Roma: Giorgio Bretschneider Editore, 1–22.

McEachern, S. 1993. Selling the iron for their shackles: Wandala-Montagnard interactions in northern Cameroon. *Journal of African History* 34 (2): 247–70.

McGuire, R. H. and Wurst, L. A. 2002. Struggling with the past. *International Journal of Historical Archaeology* 6 (2): 85–94.

McInerney, J. 1999. *The Folds of Parnassos: Land and Ethnicity in Ancient Phokis.* Austin (TX): University of Texas Press.

Meister, K. 1999. Marmor Parium. *Der Neue Pauly* 7: 938.

Mele, A. 1987. Aristodemo, Cuma e il Lazio. In Cristofani, M. (ed.), *Etruria e Lazio Arcaico.* Roma: Consiglio Nazionale delle Ricerche, 155–77.

Mele, A. 2002. Conclusioni. In Greco, E. (ed.), *Gli Achei e l'Identità Etnica degli Achei d'Occidente. Atti del Convegno Internazionale di Studi, Paestum 2001.* Paestum-Atene: Pandemos, 439–42.

Mellor, R. 2008. Graecia capta: the confrontation between Greek and Roman identity. In Zacharia, K. (ed.), *Hellenisms: Culture, Identity and Ethnicity from Antiquity to Modernity.* Aldershot: Ashgate Publishing, 79–125.

Meskell, L. 2001. Archaeologies of identity. In Hodder, I. (ed.), *Archaeological Theory Today.* Cambridge/Malden (MA): Polity/Blackwell, 187–213.

Meskell, L. 2002. The intersections of identity and politics in archaeology. *Annual Review of Anthropology* 31: 279–301.

Michelini, P. and Ruta Serafini, A. 2005. Le necropoli. In De Min, M., Gamba, M., Gambacurta, G. and Ruta Serafini, A. (eds), *La Città invisibile. Padova Preromana. Trent'Anni di Scavi e Ricerche.* Bologna: Edizioni Tipoarte, 131–73.

Mieli, G. and Casentino, S. 2006. L'insediamento protostorico di Masseria Patete-Santa Maria di Vastogirardi (Isernia). In *Studi di Protostoria in Onore di Renato Peroni.* Firenze: All'Insegna del Giglio, 110–6.

Minoja, M. 2006. Rituale funerario ed elementi di articolazione sociale a Capua in età orientalizzante. In von Eles, P. (ed.), *La Ritualità Funeraria tra Età del Ferro e Orientalizzante in Italia. Atti del convegno. Verucchio, 26–27.6.2002.* Pisa – Roma: IEPI, 121–29.

Modica, S. 1993. Sepolture infantili nel Lazio protostorico. *Bullettino della Commissione Archeologica Comunale di Roma* 5 (1): 7–19.

Modica, S. 2007. *Rituali e Lazio Antico: Deposizioni Infantili e Abitati.* Milano, Cuem.

Moerman, M. 1968. Being Lue: uses and abuses of ethnic identification. In Helm, J. (ed.), *Essays on the Problem of Tribe: Proceedings of the 1967 Annual Spring Meeting of the American Ethnological Society.* Seattle: University of Washington Press, 153–69.

Moggi, M. 1976. *I Sinecismi Interstatali Greci.* Pisa: Marlin.

Molinos, M., Chapa, T., Ruiz, A., Pereira, J., Rísquez, C., Madrigal, A., Esteban, A., Mayoral, V. and Llorente, M. 1997. *El Santuario Heroico del Pajarillo (Huelma, Jaén).* Jaén: Diputación Provincial de Jaén, Universidad de Jaén, Consejería de Cultura de la Junta de Andalucía y Centro Andaluz de Arqueología Ibérica.

Molinos, M., Rísquez, C., Serrano, J. L. and Montilla, S. 1994. *Un Problema de Fronteras en la Periferiade Tartesos: las Calañas de Marmolejo.* Jaén: Colección Martínez de Mazas, Serie Monografías de Arqueología Histórica, Servicio de Publicaciones de la Universidad de Jaén.

Molinos, M. and Ruiz, A. 2007. *El Hipogeo del Cerro de la Compañía de Hornos, Peal de Becerro.* Sevilla: Monografías Arqueología. Junta de Andalucía-Universidad de Jaén.

Molinos, M. and Zifferero, A. (eds). 2002. *Primi Popoli d'Europa. Proposte e Riflessioni sulle Origini della Civiltà nell'Europa Mediterranea.* Firenze: All'insegna del Giglio.

Mommsen, H. 2000. Nearchos 1. *Der Neue Pauly* 8: 777.

Monacchi, D. 1986. Resti della Stipe Votiva del Monte Subasio di Assisi (Colle S. Rufino). *Studi Etruschi* 52 (3): 77–89.

Moneo, T. 2003. *Religio Ibérica, Santuarios, Ritos y Divinidades (Siglos VII–I aC).* Madrid: Real Academia de la Historia.

Moratalla, J. 2005. El territorio meridional de la Contestania. In Abad, L., Sala, F. and Grau, I. (eds), *La Contestania Ibérica, Treinta Años después.* Alicante: Universidad de Alicante, 91–117.

Moreland, J. 1992. Restoring the dialectic: settlement patterns and documents in medieval central Italy. In Knapp, A. B. (ed.), *Archaeology, Annales and Ethnohistory.* Cambridge: Cambridge University Press, 112–29.

Moreland, J. 2001. *Archaeology and Text.* London: Duckworth.

Moret, P. 2004. Ethnos ou ethnie? avatars anciens et modernes des noms de peuples ibères. In Cruz Andreotti, G. and Mora Serrano, G. B. (eds), *Identidades Étnicas, Identidades Políticas en el Mundo Prerromano Hispano.* Malaga: Universidad de Málaga, 31–62.

Moretti Sgubini, A. M. 2006. Lucus Feroniae: recenti scoperte. *Rendiconti della Pontificia Accademia Romana di Archeologia* 3 (78): 111–38.

Moretti Sgubini, A. M., Arancio, M. L. and Berardinetti Insam, A. (eds). 2001. *Veio, Cerveteri,Vulci. Città d'Etruria a Confronto.* Roma: "L'Erma" di Bretschneider.

Morgan, C. 1990. *Athletes and Oracles. The Transformation of Olympia and Delphi in the Eighth Century BC.* Cambridge: Cambridge University Press.

Morgan, C. 2003. *Early Greek States Beyond the Polis.* London–New York: Routledge.

Morillo Cerdán, A. 1996. Los campamentos romanos de la Meseta Norte y el Noroeste: ¿un limes sin fronteras? In Fernández Ochoa, C. (ed.), *Los Finisterres Atlánticos en la Antigüedad.* Gijón: Electa, 77–84.

Morris, I. 1994. Archaeologies of Greece. In Morris, I. (ed.), *Classical Greece: Ancient Histories and Modern Archaeologies.* Cambridge: Cambridge University Press, 8–47.

Morris, S. P. 1984. *The Black and White Style: Athens and Aegina in the Orientalizing Period.* New Haven: Yale University Press.

Morris, S. P. 1992. *Daidalos and the Origins of Greek Art.* Princeton: Princeton University Press.

Morselli, C. 1980. *Sutrium.* (Forma Italiae, Regio VII – Volumen VII). Firenze: Leo S. Olschki.

Morselli, C. and Tortorici, E. 1982. *Ardea, (Forma Italiae, Regio I- Volumen XVI).* Firenze: Leo S. Olschki.

Müller, D. 1997. *Topographischer Bildkommentar zu den Historien Herodots. Kleinasien und Angrenzende Gebiete mit Südostthrakien und Zypern.* Tübingen: Wasmuth.

Müller-Karpe, H. 1959. *Vom Anfang Roms.* (Mitteilungen des Deutschen Archaeologischen Instituts. 5. Roemische Abteilung. Ergänzungsheft). Heidelberg: Kerle.

Müller-Karpe, H. 1962. *Zur Stadtwerdung Roms.* (Mitteilungen des Deutschen Archaeologischen Instituts. 8. Roemische Abteilung. Ergänzungsheft). Heidelberg: Kerle.

Müller-Wiener, W. 1961. Mittelalterliche Befestigungen im südlichen Jonien. *Istanbuler Mitteilungen* 11: 5–122.

Murillo, J. F. 1994. *La Cultura Tartésica en el Guadalquivir Medio* (Ariadna 13–4). Palma del Río: Museo Municipal de Palma del Río.

Murray Threipland, L. and Torelli, M. 1970. A semisubterranean etruscan building in the Casale Pian Roseto (Veii) area. *Papers of the British School at Rome* 38: 62–121.

Museo (ed.). 1995. *Il Museo Archeologico dell'Antica Capua*. Napoli: Electa Napoli.

Musti, D. 1985. I due volti della Sabina: sulla rappresentazione dei Sabini in Varrone, Dionigi, Strabone, Plutarco. *Dialoghi di Archeologia* 3 (2): 77–86.

Muzzioli, M. P., Pirzio Biroli Stefanelli, L. and Segala, E. (eds). 1981. *Enea nel Lazio. Archeologia e Mito. Catalogo della Mostra. Bimillenario Virgiliano Roma 22 Settembre–31 Dicembre 1981. Campidoglio – Palazzo dei Conservatori*. Roma: Fratelli Palombi Editori.

Naso, A. 1990. L'ideologia funeraria. In Cristofani, M. (ed.), *La Grande Roma dei Tarquini. Catalogo della Mostra*. Roma: "L'Erma" di Bretschneider, 249–51.

Naso, A. 1996. *Architetture Dipinte. Decorazioni Parietali Non Figurate nelle Tombe a Camera dell'Etruria Meridionale (VII–V sec. a.C.)*. (Biblioteca Archaeologica 18). Roma: L'Erma di Bretschneider.

Naso, A. 2000. *I Piceni. Storia e Archeologia delle Marche in Epoca Preromana*. Milano: Longanesi.

Naso, A. 2003. Review of Gerhard Tomedi, Italische Panzerplatten und Panzerscheiben, Prähistorische Bronzefunde III.3, Stuttgart, Steiner. 2000. *Germania* 81 (2): 621–7.

Naso, A. 2007. La cultura orientalizzante nel Piceno: caratteri propri e influssi esterni, In Gustin, M., Ettel, P. And Buora, M. (eds). *Piceni ed Europa. Atti del convegno. Piran, 15–17.9.2006*. Udine: Società Friulana di Archeologia, 21–7.

Naso, A. 2008. La protostoria del Sannio pentro. In Tagliamonte, G. (ed.), *Ricerche di Archeologia Medio-adriatica 1. Le Necropoli: Contesti e Materiali. Lecce, 27–28.5.2005. Galatina: Congedo, 243-256.

Naso, A. 2009. *Storia e Archeologia a Macchia Valfortore 1. (Quaderni del Museo Civico di Macchia Valfortore)*. Isernia: Iannone.

Nazou, M. 2010. Grey Areas In Past Maritime Identity? The case of Final Neolithic-Early Bronze Age Attica (Greece) and the surrounding islands. *Shima: The International Journal of Research into Island Cultures* 4 (1): 3–15.

Nicolet, C. 1991. L'origine des Regiones Italiae augustéenes. *Cahiers du Centre G. Glotz* 2: 73–97.

Nicolini, G., Risquez, C., Ruiz, A. and Zafra, N. 2004. *El Santuario Ibero de Castellar. Jaén. Investigaciones Arqueológicas 1966–1991*. Sevilla: Arqueología Monografías, Consejería de Cultura, Junta de Andalucía.

Nissen, H. 1869. *Das Templum. Antiquarische Untersuchuingen*. Berlin: Weidmann.

Nissen, H. 1883–1902. *Italische Landeskunde*. Berlin: Weidmansche Buchhandlung.

Nizzo, V. 2005. Schede. In Settis, S. and Parra, M. C. (eds), *Magna Graecia, Archeologia di un Sapere. Catalogo della Mostra.* Milano: Electa, 350–3.

Nizzo, V. 2007. *Ritorno ad Ischia: dalla Stratigrafia della Necropoli alla Tipologia dei Materiali.* Napoli: Centre Jean Bérard.

Nonnis, D. 2003. Dotazioni funzionali e di arredo in luoghi di culto dell'Italia repubblicana. L'apporto della documentazione epigrafica. In De Cazanove, O. and Scheid, J. (eds), *Sanctuaires et Sources dans l'Antiquité. Les Sources Documentaires et Leurs Limites dans la Description des Lieux de Culte. Actes de la Table Ronde Organisée par le Collège de France, l'UMR 8585 Centre Gustave-Glotz, l' École Française de Rome et le Centre Jean Bérard. Naples, 30 Novembre 2001.* Napoli: Centre Jean Bérard, 25–45.

Nora, P. (ed.). 1984–1992. *Les Lieux de Mémoire (Seven Volumes)*. Paris: Edition Gallimard.

Nuñez Marten, J. 2009. La Aedes Mercurii del foro di Tusculum. Una primera aproximacón. In Ghini, G. (ed.), *Lazio e Sabina 5. Atti del convegno Quinto incontro di studi sul Lazio e la Sabina, Roma 3–5 dicembre 2007*. Roma: De Luca, 261–7.

Oakley, S. P. 1995. *The Hill-forts of the Samnites*. (Archaeological monographs of the British School at Rome 10). London: British School at Rome.

Ohnesorg, A. 2005. *Ionische Altäre: Formen und Varianten einer Architekturgattung aus Inselund Ostionien*. (Archäologische Forschungen 21). Berlin: Mann.

Ohnesorg, A. 2005. Naxian and Parian Architecture. General features and new discoveries. In Yeroulanou, M. and Stamatopoulou, M. (eds), *Architecture and Archaeology in the Cyclades: Essays in Honour of J. J. Coulton*. Oxford: Archaeopress, 135–52.

Olcina Doménech, M., Grau Mira, I., Sala Sellés, F., Moltó Gisbert, S., Reig Seguí, C. and Segura Martí, J. M. 1998. Nuevas aportaciones a la evolución de la ciudad ibérica: el caso de La Serreta. In Aranegui, C. (ed.), *Congreso Internacional Los Iberos Príncipes de Occidente (Barcelona, 1998)*. Barcelona: Fundació La Caixa, 35–46.

Olmos, R. 2002. Los grupos escultóricos de Cerrillo Blanco. Porcuna, Jaén. Un ensayo de lectura iconográfica convergente. *Archivo Español de Arqueología* 75: 107–22.

Olmos, R. and Grau Mira, I. 2005. El Vas dels Guerrers de la Serreta. *Recerques del Museu d'Alcoi* 14: 79–98.

Olsen, B. 1985. Comments on Saamis, Finns and Scandinavians in history and prehistory. *Norwegian Archaeological Review* 18: 13–8.

Orejas, A. 1996. *Estructura Social y Territorio: el Impacto Tomano en la Cuenca Noroccidental del Duero*. (Anejos de Archivo Español de Arqueología 15). Madrid: Consejo Superior de Investigaciones Científicas.

Orgels, P. 1935. Sabas Asidénos. Dynaste de Sampsôn. *Byzantion* 10: 67–80.

Ortolani, M. 1964. *Memoria Illustrativa della Carta della Utilizzazione del Suolo degli Abruzzi e Molise*. Roma: Consiglio Nazionale delle Ricerche.

Osborne, R. 1987. *Classical Landscape with Figures. The Ancient Greek City and its Countryside*. London: George Philip.

Osborne, R. 1994. Archaeology, the Salaminioi and the politics of sacred space in archaic Attica. In Alcock, S. E. and Osborne, R. (eds), *Placing the Gods: Sanctuaries and Sacred Space in Ancient Greece*. Oxford: Oxford University Press, 143–60.

Osborne, R. 1996 (2009). *Greece in the Making, 1200–479 B.C.* (Routledge History of the Ancient World.) London: Routledge.

Osborne, R. 1997. Law, the democratic citizen and the representation of women in classical Athens. *Past and Present* 155: 3–33.

Osborne, R. 1998. *Archaic and Classical Greek Art*. Oxford: Oxford University Press.

Osborne, R. 2004. Demography and survey. In Alcock, S. E. and Cherry, J. F. (eds), *Side by Side Survey: Comparative Regional Studies in the Mediterranean World*. Oxford: Oxbow Books, 163–72.

Ozguç, T. 1963. An Assyrian trading post. *Scientific American* 208 (2): 96–106.

Paasi, A. 1996. *Territories, Boundaries, and Consciousness: The Charging Geographies of the Finnish-Russian Border*. Chicester: John Wiley and Sons.

Pacciarelli, M. 2000. *Dal Villaggio alla Città: la Svolta Protourbana del 1000 a.C. nell'Italia Tirrenica*. (Grandi contesti e problemi della protostoria italiana 4). Firenze: All'insegna del Giglio.

Pairault Massa, F.-H. 1992. *Iconologia e politica nell'Italia antica. Roma, Lazio, Etruria dal VII al I secolo a.C.* Milano: Longanesi & C.

Palermo, D. 2002. Una imitazione cretese di skyphos a semicerchi penduli dalla necropoli di Priniàs. *Cronache di Archeologia* 33 (1994 (2002)): 41–5.

Pallottino, M. 1942. *Etruscologia.* Milano: Hoepli.

Pallottino, M. 1947. *Etruscologia.* Milano: Hoepli.

Pallottino, M. 1955. Le origini storiche dei popoli Italici, in *Relazioni al X Congresso Internazionale di Scienze Storiche, Roma 1955, Volume 2.* Firenze: Sansoni, 3–60.

Pallottino, M. 1961. Nuovi studi sul problema delle origini etrusche. Bilancio critico. *Studi Etruschi* 29: 3–30.

Pallottino, M. 1970. Etnogenesi uguale poleogenesi. In Atti 1970 (ed.), *Atti del Convegno di Studi sulla Città Etrusca e Italica Preromana. Studi sulla Città Antica.* Bologna: Istituto per la Storia di Bologna, 75–7.

Pallottino, M. 1974. Intervento. In *Civiltà Arcaica dei Sabini nella Valle del Tevere, II. Incontro di Studio in Occasione della Mostra, 1973.* Roma: Consiglio Nazionale delle Ricerche, 102.

Pallottino, M. 1981. *Genti e Culture dell'Italia Preromana.* Roma: Jouvence.

Pallottino, M. 1991. *A History of Earliest Italy* (Translated by Soper, M. R. K). London: Routledge.

Pancrazzi, O. (ed.). 1979. *Cavallino I. Scavi e Ricerche 1964–1967.* Galatina: Congedo Editore.

Pandolfini, M. 1985. Bisenzio. In Nenci, G. and Vallet, G. (eds), *Bibliografia Topografica della Colonizzazione Greca in Italia 4.* Pisa: Scuola Normale Superiore, 55–63.

Pankhurst, R. 1977. The history of the Bareya, Shanqella, and other Ethiopian slaves from the borderlands of the Sudan. *Sudan Notes and Records* 59: 1–43.

Paoletti, O. (ed.). 2005. *Dinamiche di Sviluppo delle Città nell'Etruria Meridionale. Veio, Caere, Tarquinia, Vulci. Atti del XXIII Convegno di Studi Etruschi ed Italici, Roma, Veio, Cerveteri/ Pyrgi, Tarquinia, Tuscania, Vulci, Viterbo, 1–6 Ottobre 2001.* Volumi I–II. Pisa-Roma: Istituti editoriali e poligrafici internazionali.

Paolini, L. 1990. Crustumerium (circ. IV) – II. Scavi nella necropoli. *Bullettino Comunale* 1987–1988: 468–471.

Paolucci, G. 2002. A ovest del Lago Trasimeno: note di archeologia e di topografia. In Della Fina, G. M. (ed.) *Perugia Etrusca. Atti del IX Convegno Internazionale di Studi sulla Storia e l'Archeologia dell'Etruria. (Annali della fondazione per il Museo"Claudio Faina"* 9). Roma: Quasar, 163–228.

Parker-Pearson, M. 1999. *The Archaeology of Death.* Stroud: Alan Sutton.

Pascucci, P. 1990. *I Depositi Votivi Paleoveneti per un'Archeologia del Culto.* Padova: Società Archeologia Veneta.

Patterson, H. 2004. Introduction. In Patterson, H. (ed.), *Bridging the Tiber: Approaches to Regional Archaeology in the Middle Tiber Valley.* London: British School at Rome, 1–8.

Patterson, H., di Gennaro, F., di Giuseppe, H., Fontana, S., Gaffney, V., Harrison, A., Keay, S. J., Millett, M., Rendeli, M., Roberts, P., Stoddart, S. K. F. and Witcher, R. 2000. The Tiber Valley Project: the Tiber and Rome through two millennia. *Antiquity* 74 (284): 395–403.

Patterson, H. and Millett, M. 1998. The Tiber Valley Project. *Papers of the British School at Rome* 66: 1–20.

Patterson, T. C. 2005. The turn to agency: Neoliberalism, individuality, and subjectivity in late twentieth century anglophone archaeology. *Rethinking Marxism* 17 (3): 373–404.

Pearce, J., Pretzler, M. and Riva, C. 2005. A reconstruction of historical processes in Bronze and Early Iron Age Italy based on recent archaeological research. In Attema, P., Nijboer, A. and Zifferero, A. (eds), *Papers in Italian Archaeology VI. Communities and Settlements from the Neolithic to the Early Medieval Period.* (BAR International Series 1452). Oxford: Archaeopress, 1016–23.

Peatfield, A. A. D. 1990. Minoan peak sanctuaries: History and society. *Opuscula Atheniensia* 18: 117–31.

Pellegrini, G. B. and Prosdocimi, A. L. 1967. *La Lingua Venetica (Volumi I e II).* Padova: Istituto di Glottologia dell'Università di Padova.

Peña, A. 2003. *La Necrópolis Ibérica de El Molar (San Fulgencio, Alicante). Revisión de las Excavaciones Realizadas en 1928 y 1929.* Villena: Fundación José María Soler.

Peña, A. 2005. La necrópolis ibérica de El Molar (San Fulgencio, Alicante). Revisión de las excavaciones realizadas en 1928 y 1929. In Abad, L., Sala, F. and Grau, I. (eds), *La Contestania Ibérica, Treinta Años Después.* Alicante: University of Alicante, 369–84.

Pensabene, P. 1983. Necropoli di Praeneste. Storia degli scavi e circostanze di rinvenimento dei cippi a pigna e dei busti funerari. *Archeologia Classica* 29: 161–74.

Pesaventa Mattioli, S. 2001. Il santuario di Lagole nel contesto topografico del Cadore.In Fogolari, G. and Gambacurta, G. (eds), *Materiali Veneti Preromani e Romani del Santuario di Lagole di Calalzo al Museo di Pieve di Cadore.* Roma: Giorgio Bretschneider, 43-7.

Pérez Ballester, J. and Borreda, R. 1998. El poblamiento Ibérico del Valle del Canyoles. Avance sobre un proyecto de evolución del paisaje en la comarca de la Costera (Valencia). *Saguntum-Papeles del Laboratorio de Arqueología de Valencia* 31: 133–52.

Pérez Ballester, J. and Mata, C. 1998. Los motivos vegetales en la cerámica del Tossal de Sant Miquel (Llíria, València). Función y significado de los estilos I y II. In Aranegui, C. (ed.), *Congreso Internacional Los Iberos Príncipes de Occidente (Barcelona, 1998).* Barcelona: Fundació La Caixa, 231–44.

Perkins, P. 2009. DNA and Etruscan identity. In Perkins, P. and Swaddling, J. (eds), *Etruscan by Definition.* London: British Museum Press, 95–111.

Peroni, R. 1963. *Ripostigli delle Età dei Metalli. 3. Ripostigli dell'Appennino Umbro-marchigiano* (Inventaria Archaeologica 3). Firenze: Istituto italiano di preistoria e protostoria.

Peroni, R. 1988. Communità e insediamento in Italia fra l'età del Bronzo e prima età del ferro. In Somigliano, A. and Schiavone, A. (eds), *Storia di Roma.* Torino: Einaudi, 7–37.

Peroni, R. 1989. *Protostoria dell'Italia Continentale. La Penisola Italiana nelle Età del Bronzo e del Ferro.* (Popoli e civiltà dell'Italia antica 9). Roma: Biblioteca di storia patria.

Peschlow-Bindokat, A. 1989. Lelegische Siedlungsspuren am Bafasee. *Anadolu* 22 (1981–83): 79–83.

Peschlow-Bindokat, A. 1996. Die Arbeiten des Jahres 1994 im Territorium von Herakleia am Latmos 13. *Araştırma Sonuçları Toplantısı, 29 Mayıs–2 Haziran 1995 Ankara (2).* Ankara: Başbakanlık Basımevi, 211–24.

Peschlow-Bindokat, A. and Peschlow, U. (eds). 1996. *Der Latmos. Eine unbekannte Gebirgslandschaft an der türkischen Westküste.* Mainz am Rhein: von Zabern.

Pfister, F. 1951. *Die Reisebilder des Herakleides. Einleitung, Übersetzung und Kommentar.* Wien: Rohrer.

Pflug, H. 1988. Kyprische Helme. In *Antike Helme: Sammlung Lipperheide und andere Bestände des Antikenmuseums Berlin.* Mainz: Verlag des Römisch Germanischen Zentralmuseums, 27–41.

Piccaluga, G. 1974. *Terminus. I Segni di Confine nella Religione Romana*. Roma: Edizioni dell'Ateneo.

Pingel, V. 1992. *Die vorgeschichtlichen Goldfunde der Iberischen Halbinsel. Eine Archäeologische Untersuchung zur Auswertung der Spektranalysen (Deutsches Archäologisches Institut. Madrider Forschungen, Band 17)*. Berlin: Walter de Gruyter und Co.

Pinza, G. 1905. Monumenti primitivi di Roma e del Lazio antico. *Monumenti Antichi* 15: 39–403.

Piro, S. and Santoro, P. 2002. Analisi del territorio di Colle del Forno (Montelibretti, Roma) e scavo nella necropoli sabina arcaica. *Orizzonti* 2: 197–212.

Pohl, W. and Mehofer, M. (eds). 2010. *Archaeology of identity – Archäologie der Identität. Acts of the International Conference, Wien 2006*. Wien: Verlag der Österrischen Akademie der Wissenschaften

Polverini, L. 1998. Le regioni nell'Italia Romana. *Geographia Antiqua* 7: 23–33.

Pomponia Logan, A. 1978. The Palio of Siena: performance and process. *Urban Anthropology* 7: 45–65.

Pomponio, A. 1990. Seagulls don't fly into the bush: cultural identity and the negotiation of development on Mandok island, Papua New Guinea. In Linnekin, J. and Poyer, L. (eds), *Cultural Identity and Ethnicity in the Pacific*. Honolulu: University of Hawaii Press, 43–69.

Pontremoli, E. and Haussoullier, B. 1904. *Didymes. Fouilles de 1895 et 1896*. Paris: Leroux.

Popham, M. and Lemos, I. 1992. Review of R. Kearsley, The pendent semicircle Skyphos: a Study of Its Development and Chronology. (British Institute of Classical Studies Supplement 44, London 1989). *Gnomon* 64: 152–5, 193.

Potter, T. W. 1976. *A Faliscan Town in South Etruria. Excavations at Narce 1966–71*. London: The British School at Rome.

Potter, T. W. n.d *An Archaeological Field Survey on the Central and Southern Ager Faliscus*, Unpublished manuscript.

Potter, T. W. and Stoddart, S. K. F. 2001. A century of prehistory and landscape studies at the British School at Rome. *Papers of the British School at Rome* 69: 3–34.

Poucet, J. 1994. La fondation de Rome: Croyants et agnostiques. *Latomus* 53: 95–104.

Poucet, J. 2000. *Les Rois de Rome. Tradition et Histoire*. Leuven: Académie Royale de Belgique.

Poveda, A. M. 1994. Primeros datos sobre las influencias fenicio-púnicas en el corredor del Vinalopó (Alicante). In González Blanco, A., Cunchillos, J. L. and Molina, M. (eds), *El Mundo Púnico. Historia, Sociedad y Cultura*. Murcia: Editora Regional de Murcia, 489–502.

Prent, M. 2005. *Cretan Sanctuaries and Cults. Continuity and Change from Late Minoan IIIC to the Archaic Period* (Religions in the Graeco-Roman World 154). Leiden: Brill.

Prosdocimi, A. 1978. Il lessico istituzionale italico. Tra linguistica e storia. In *La cultura italica. Atti del Cnvegno della Società Italiana di Glottologia, Pisa 1977*. Pisa: Giardini editori e stampatori, 29–74.

Prosdocimi, A. 1984. *Le Tavole Iguvine*. (Lingue e iscrizioni dell'Italia Antica 4). Firenze: Leo S. Olschki.

Prosdocimi, A. L. 1972. Venetico. *Studi Etruschi* 40: 193–245.

Prosdocimi, A. L. 1983. Puntuazione sillabica e insegnamento della scrittura nel venetico e nelle fonti etrusche. *AION (Annali del Dipartimento di Studi del Mondo Classico e del Mediterraneo Antico. Sezione linguistica)* 5: 75–126.

Prosdocimi, A. L. 1988. La lingua. In Fogolari, G. and Prosdocimi, A. L. (eds), *I Veneti Antichi*. Padova: Programma Editore, 225–422.

Prosdocimi, A. L. 1990. Insegnamento e apprendimento della scrittura nell'Italia antica. In Pandolfini Angeletti, M. and Prosdocimi, A. L. (eds), *Alfabetari e Insegnamento della Scrittura in Etruria e nell'Italia Antica*. Firenze: Leo S. Olschki, 157–299.

Prosdocimi, A. L. 2001. Etnici e 'nome' nelle Tavole Iguvine. In Della Fina, G. M. (ed.), *Gli Umbri del Tevere. Atti dell'VIII Convegno Internazionale di Studi sulla Storia e l'Archeologia dell'Etruria.* (*Annali della Fondazione per il Museo <<Claudio Faina>>* 8). Roma: Quasar, 31–77.

Prósper Pérez, B. M. 2002. *Lenguas y Religiones Prerromanas del Occidente de la Península Ibérica*. Salamanca: Ediciones Universidad de Salamanca.

Purcell, N. 2006. Orientalizing: Five historical questions. In Riva, C. and Vella, N. (eds), *Debating Orientalization: Multidisciplinary Approaches to Change in the Ancient Mediterranean.* (Monographs in Mediterranean Archaeology 10). London: Equinox Press, 21–31.

Quilici, L. 1974. *Collatia* Forma Italiae I:X. Roma: De Luca.

Quilici, L. and Quilici Gigli, S. 1980. *Crustumerium (Latium Vetus III)*. Roma: Consiglio Nazionale delle Ricerche.

Quilici, L. and Quilici Gigli, S. 2006. L'insediamento fortificato di Monterado presso Bagnoregio. In Quilici, L. and Quilici Gigli, S. (eds), *La Forma della Città e del Territorio III*. Roma: L'Erma di Bretschneider, 41–62.

Rajala, U. 2002. *Human Landscapes in Tyrrhenian Italy. GIS in the Study of Urbanization, Settlement Patterns and Land Use in South Etruria and Western Latium Vetus.* Cambridge: Unpublished PhD dissertation, University of Cambridge, Department of Archaeology.

Rack, M. 2005. *Ethnic Distinctions, Local Meanings: Negotiating Cultural Identities in China.* London – Ann Arbor (MI): Pluto Press.

Raddatz, K. 1983. Zur Siedlungsgeschichte frühetruskischer Zeit im Gebiet um den Bolsena-See. *Archäologischen Informationen* 5: 119–44.

Rajala, U. 2004. The landscapes of power: visibility, time and (dis)continuity in central Italy. *Archeologia e Calcolatori* 15: 393–408.

Rajala, U. 2005. From a settlement to an early State? The role of Nepi in the local and regional settlement patterns of the Faliscan area and inner Etruria during the Iron Age. In Attema, P., Nijboer, A. J. and Zifferero, A. (eds), *Papers in Italian Archaeology VI. Communities and Settlements from the Neolithic to the Early Medieval Period. Proceedings of the 6th Conference of Italian Archaeology held at the University of Groningen, Groningen Institute of Archaeology, The Netherlands, April 15–17, 2003.* (BAR International Series 1452 (I)). Oxford: British Archaeological Reports, 706–12.

Rajala, U. 2006. Le ricerche della Scuola Britannica a Nepi: indagini e prospettive. In Francocci, S. (ed.), *Archeologia e Storia a Nepi 1.* (Quaderni del Museo Civico di Nepi). Nepi: Museo Civico, 86–94.

Rajala, U. 2007. Archaic chamber tombs as material objects: the materiality of burial places and its effect on modern research agendas and interpretations. *Archaeological Review from Cambridge* 22 (1): 43–57.

Rajala, U. 2008. Ritual and remembrance at Archaic Crustumerium: The transformations of past and modern materialities in the cemetery of Cisterna Grande (Rome, Italy). In Fahlander, F. & Oestigaard, T. (eds), *The Materiality of Death* (BAR International Series 1758). Oxford: Archaeopress, 79–87.

Ramon, J. 1995. *Las Ánforas Fenicio-Púnicas del Mediterráneo Central y Occidental*. Barcelona: University of Barcelona.

Rasmussen, T. 1979. *Bucchero Pottery from Southern Etruria*. Cambridge: Cambridge University Press.

Redhouse, D. I. and Stoddart, S. K. F. 2011. Mapping Etruscan State formation. In Terrenato, N. and Haggis, D. (eds), *State Formation in Italy and Greece: Questioning the Neoevolutionist Paradigm*. Oxford: Oxbow Books, 164–80.

Rediker, M. 2004. *Between the Devil and the Deep Blue Sea. Merchant Seamen, Pirates and the Anglo-American Maritime World, 1700–1750*. Cambridge: Cambridge University Press.

Reggiani, A., Adembri, B., Zevi, F., Benedettini, M. G. and Mari, Z. 1998. Corcolle. In Drago Troccoli, L. (ed.), *Scavi e Ricerche Archeologiche dell'Università di Roma "La Sapienza"*. (Studia archeologica 96). Roma: "L'Erma" di Bretschneider, 120–4.

Remotti, F. 2001. *Contro l'Identità*. Roma-Bari: Laterza.

Rendeli, M. 1991. Sulla nascita delle communità urbane in Etruria meridionale. *AION. (Annali di Archeologia e storia antica)* 13: 9–45.

Rendeli, M. 1993. *Città aperte. Ambiente e Paesaggio Rurale Organizzato nell'Etruria Meridionale Costiera durante l'Età Orientalizzante e Arcaica*. Roma: Gruppi Editoriali Internazionali.

Renfrew, A. C. 1975. Trade as action at a distance: questions of interaction and communication. In Sabloff, J. A. and Lamberg-Karlovsky, C. C. (eds), *Ancient Civilisations and Trade*. Albuquerque: School of American Research – University of New Mexico, 3–59.

Renfrew, A. C. 1987. *Archaeology and Language. The Puzzle of Indo-European Origins*. London: Jonathan Cape.

Reynolds, J. 1982. *Aphrodisias and Rome* (Journal of Roman studies monographs 1). London: Society for the Promotion of Roman Studies.

Riccobono, S., Baviera, Ferrini, C., Furlani, J. and Arangio-Ruiz, V. 1940–1943. *Fontes Iuris Romani Antejustiniani: in Usum Scholarum*. Florentiae: G. Barbera.

Ridgway, D. 1989. Nota di rettifica sul frammento ceramico THT 81–6–6 da Tharros. *Rivista di Studi Fenici* 17: 141–4.

Ridgway, D. 1992. In margine al villanoviano evoluto di Veio. *Archeologia Classica* 43: 156–67.

Ridgway, D., Deriu, A. and Boitani, F. 1985. Provenance and Firing Techniques of Geometric Pottery from Veii: a Mössbauer Investigation. *Annual of the British School at Athens* 80: 139–50.

Ríos González, S. 2000. Consideraciones funcionales y tipológicas en torno a los baños castreños del Noroeste la Península Ibérica. *Gallaecia* 19: 93–124.

Riva, C. and Stoddart, S. K. F. 1996. Ritual Landscapes in Archaic Etruria. In Wilkins, J. B. (ed.), *Approaches to the Study of Ritual. Italy and the Mediterranean*. (Specialist Studies on the Mediterranean 2). London: Accordia, 91–109.

Riva, C. and Vella, N. (eds). 2006 *Debating Orientalization: Multidisciplinary Approaches to Change in the Ancient Mediterranean*. London: Equinox Press.

Riva, C. and Vella, N. 2006 Introduction. In Riva, C. and Vella, N. (eds), *Debating Orientalization: Multidisciplinary Approaches to Change in the Ancient Mediterranean*. (Monographs in Mediterranean Archaeology 10). London: Equinox Press, 1–20.

Rizzo, D. (ed.). 1992. *Le Necropoli di Nepi: Immagini di 10 Anni di Ricerche Archeologiche*. Nepi: Ministero dei Beni Culturali e Ambientali, Soprintendeza Archeologica Etruria Meridionale, Comune di Nepi, Assessorato alla Cultura.

Rizzo, D. 1996. Recenti scoperte nell'area di Nepi. In *Atti del XVIII Convegno di Studi Etruschi ed Italici. Rieti - Magliano Sabina. 30 Maggio–3 Giugno 1993*. Firenze: Leo S. Olschki, 477–94.

Rizzo, M. A. 2005. Ceramica greca e di tipo greco da Cerveteri. In Bartoloni, G. and Delpino, F. (eds), *Oriente e Occidente: Metodi e Discipline a Confronto. Riflessioni sulla Cronologia dell'Età del Ferro in Italia. Atti dell'Incontro di Studi, Roma, 30–31 Ottobre 2003. Mediterranea, 1 (2004).* Pisa: Istituti Editoriali e Poligrafici Internazionali, 333–79.

Robb, J. E. 1998. The Archaeology of symbols. *Annual Review of Anthropology* 27: 329–42.

Rodríguez Colmenero, A. 1977. *Galicia Meridional Romana*. Bilbao: Universidad de Deusto.

Rodríguez Colmenero, A. 1996. *Lucus Augusti. I. El Amanecer de una Ciudad*. A Coruña: Fundación Pedro Barrié de la Mazá.

Rodríguez Corral, J. 2009. *A Galicia Castrexa*. Santiago de Compostela: Lóstrego.

Roldán Hervás, J. M. 1986. La ocupación romana de la Asturia Augustana y la fundación de Astorga In *I Congreso Internacional de Astorga Romana*. Astorga: Ayuntamento de Astorga, 37–53.

Roncoroni, P. 2001. Children's graves in Early Iron Age settlements in Latium. The origin of the Roman Lares-and Penates cult? In Nijboer, A. J. (ed.), *Interpreting Deposits: Linking Ritual with Economy* Groningen: Groningen Institute of Archaeology, 101–21.

Roos, A. M. 1997. *La Sociedad de Clases, la Propiedad Privad y el Estado en Tartessos. Una Visión de su Proceso Histórico desde la Arqueología del Proyecto Porcuna*. Granada: Unpublished Doctoral Thesis, University of Granada.

Rouillard, P., Gailledrat, E. and Sala Sellés, F. (eds). 2007. *L'Etablissement Protohistorique de La Fonteta (fin VIIIe – fin Vie siècle av. J.-C.)* Madrid: Casa de Velázquez.

Rowlands, M. 1998. The Archaeology of Colonialism. In Kristiansen, K. and Rowlands, M. (eds), *Social Transformations in Archaeology. Global and Local Perspectives.* (Material Cultures: Interdisciplinary Studies in the Material Construction of Social Worlds). London: Routledge, 327–33.

Roymans, N. 1990. *Tribal Societies in Northern Gaul. An Anthropological Perspective*. (Cingula 12). Amsterdam: Universiteit van Amsterdam.

Rubini, M. 2006. Il popolamento della sabina durante il primo millennio. In Ghini, G. (ed.), *Lazio e Sabina. Atti del Primo Incontro di Studi su Lazio e Sabina, Roma, 28–30 Gennaio 2002, Volume III.* Roma: De Luca, 119–22.

Ruby, P. 2006. Peuples, fictions? Ethnicité, identité ethnique et sociétés anciennes. *Revue des Études Anciennes* 108 (1): 25–60.

Ruiz, A. 1978. Los pueblos iberos del Alto Guadalquivir. *Cuadernos de Prehistoria de la Universidad de Granada* 3: 255–84.

Ruiz, A. 1995. Plaza de Armas de Puente Tablas: new contributions to the knowledge of Iberian town planning in the seventh to fourth centuries BC. *Proceedings of the British Academy* 86: 89–108.

Ruiz, A. and Molinos, M. 1984. Elementos para un estudio del patrón de asentamiento en el Alto Guadalquivir durante el horizonte Pleno Ibero (Un caso de sociedad agrícola con estado). *Arqueología Espacial* 4: 187–206.

Ruiz, A. and Molinos, M. 1989. Fronteras: un caso del siglo VI a.C. *Arqueología Espacial* 13: 121–135.

Ruiz, A. and Molinos, M. 1993. *Los Iberos. Análisis Arqueológico de un Proceso Histórico*. Barcelona, Crítica.

Ruiz, A. and Molinos, M. 2007. *Iberos en Jaén*. (CAAI Textos 2). Jaén: Universidad de Jaén.

Ruiz, A., Molinos, M., Gutiérrez, L. M. and Bellón, J. P. 2001. El modelo político del pago en el Alto Guadalquivir (S. IV–III a.n.e.). In Martín i Ortega, A. and Plana Mallart, R. (eds), *Territori Polític i Territori Rural durant l'Edat del Ferro a la Mediterrània Occidental. Actes de la Taula Rodona Celebrada a Ullastret.* Ullastret/Girona: Museu d'Arqueologia de Catalunya, 11–22.

Ruiz, A., Molinos, M., Lopez, J., Crespo, J., Choclan, C. and Hornos, F. 1983. El horizonte ibero Antiguo del Cerro de la Coronilla, Cazalilla (Jaén). *Cuadernos de Prehistoria de la Universidad de Granada* 8: 251–300.

Ruiz Rodríguez, A. 1998. Los príncipes Iberos. Procesos económicos y sociales. In Aranegui, C. (ed.), *Congreso Internacional Los Iberos Príncipes de Occidente (Barcelona, 1998).* Barcelona: Fundació La Caixa, 285–300.

Ruiz Rodríguez, A. 2000. El concepto de clientela en la sociedad de los príncipes. In Mata, C. and Pérez Jordá, G. (eds), *III Reunió sobre Economia del Món Ibèric.* València: Universitat de València, 11–20.

Ruiz Rodríguez, A. and Molinos, M. 1993. *Los Iberos. Análisis Arqueológico de un Proceso Histórico.* Barcelona: Crítica.

Ruiz Zapatero, G. 1993. El concepto de Celtas en la Prehistoria europea y española. In M. Almagro, M. and Ruiz Zapatero, G. (eds), *Los Celtas. Hispania y Europa.* Madrid: Universidad Complutense de Madrid, 23–62.

Ruiz Zapatero, G. 2003. Historiografía y "uso público" de los celtas en la España Franquista. In Álvarez Martí-Aguilar, M. and Wulff Alonso, F. (eds), *Antigüedad y Franquismo (1936–1975).* Málaga: Diputación de Málaga, 217–40.

Ruiz-Gálvez, M. 1998. *La Europa Atlántica en la Edad del Bronce. Un Viaje a las Raíces de la Europa Occidental.* Barcelona: Crítica.

Ruiz-Gálvez, M. 2005. Der Fliegende Mittlemeermann. Piratas y héroes en los albores de la Edad del Hierro. In Celestino, S. and Jiménez, J. (eds), *El período Orientalizante. Actas del III Simposio Internacional de Arqueología de Mérida.* Madrid: Consejo Superior de Investigaciones Científicas, 251–75.

Rumscheid, F. 1998. Milas 1996. In *15. Araştırma Sonuçları Toplantısı, Ankara 1997 (2).* Ankara: Anıtlar ve Müzeler Genel Müdürlüğü yayınları, 385–407.

Ruspantini, A. 1978. *Storia di Grotte di Castro.* Grotte di Castro: Comune di Grotte di Castro.

Ruta Serafini, A. and Sainati, L. 2002. Il « caso » Meggiaro: Problemi e prospettive. In Ruta Serafini, A. (ed.), *Este preromana: Una città e i Suoi Santuari.* Treviso: Canova, 216–231.

Sack, R. D. 1986. *Human territoriality.* Cambridge: Cambridge University Press.

Sahlins, M. 1972 [1968]. *Las Sociedades Tribales.* Barcelona: Labor.

Sahlins, M. D. 1972. *Stone Age Economics.* Chicago: Aldine.

Said, E. W. 1978. *Orientalism.* London: Routledge and Kegan Paul.

Saignes, T. 1995. Indian migration and social change in seventeeth century Charcas. In Larson, B., Harris, O. and Tandeter, E. (eds), *Ethnicity, Markets, and Migration in the Andes: at the Crossroads of History and Anthropology.* Durham: Duke University Press, 167–95.

Sala, F. 2005. Púnics al sud del País Valencià: vint-i-cinc anys d'investigació. *Fonaments* 12: 21–39.

Salvatierra, V., Castillo, J. C., Gómez, F. and Visedo, A. 2006. Evolución de la ocupación de un territorio en época medieval. El valle del Horno-Trujala, Segura de la Sierra, Jaén, In Gálvez del Postigo, A. (ed.) *Proyectos de Investigación 2004–2005*. Jaén: Universidad de Jaén, 7–10.

Sand, S. 2009. *The Invention of the Jewish People*. London – New York: Verso Books.

Sanmartí, J. and Belarte, C. 2001. Urbanización y desarrollo de estructuras estatales en la costa de Cataluña (siglos VII–III a.C.). In Berrocal Rangel, L. and Gardes, P. (eds), *Entre Celtas e Iberos: las Poblaciones Prehistóricas de la Galias e Hispania*. Madrid: Real Academia de la Historia-Casa de Velásquez, 161–74.

Sant Cassia, P. 1993. History, anthropology and folklore in Malta. *Journal of Mediterranean Studies* 2: 291–315.

Santoro, P. 1977. Colle del Forno (Roma). Loc. Montelibretti. Relazione di scavo sulle campagne 1971–1974 nella necropoli. *Notizie degli Scavi* 31: 213–98.

Santoro, P. 1983. Colle del Forno (Roma). Loc. Montelibretti. Relazione preliminare di scavo della campagna settembre-ottobre 1979 nella necropoli. *Notizie degli Scavi* 37: 105–40.

Santoro, P. 1985. Sequenza culturale della necropoli di Colle del Forno in Sabina. *Studi Etruschi* 51: 13–37.

Santoro, P. 2005. Tomba XI di Colle del Forno: Simbologie funerary nella decorazione di una lamina di bronzo. In Adembri, B. (ed.), *Miscellanea di Studi per Mauro Cristofani*. Firenze: Leo S. Olschki, 267–73.

Santoro, P. 2008. *Una Nuova Iscrizione da Magliano Sabina. Scrittura e Cultura nella Valle del Tevere*. Pisa-Roma: Fabrizio Serra editore.

Santos Velasco, J. A. 1992. Territorio económico y político del sur de la Contestania Ibérica. *Archivo Español de Arqueología* 65: 33–47.

Santos Yanguas, N. 1988. *El Ejército y la Romanización de Galicia*. Oviedo: Universidad de Oviedo.

Sanz Gamo, R. 1997. *Cultura Ibérica y Romanización en Tierras de Albacete: los Siglos de Transición*. Albacete: Instituto de Estudios Albaceteños.

Sastre Prats, I. 2002. Forms of social inequality in the Castro Culture. *European Journal of Archaeology* 5 (2): 213–48.

Scarfì, B. M. 1962. Gioia del Colle – l'abitato peucetico di Monte Sannace. *Notizie degli Scavi* 16: 1–283.

Schattner, T. G. 2003. Stilistische und formale Beobachtungen an den Kriegerstatuen. *Madrider Mitteilungen* 44: 127–46.

Schiappelli, A. 2009. *Sviluppo Storico della Teverina nell'Età del Bronzo e nella Prima Età del Ferro*. (Grandi contesti e problemi della Protostoria Italiana 11). Firenze: All'Insegna del Giglio.

Schiavone, A. 2005. *Ius. L'Invenzione del Diritto in Occidente*. Torino: Giulio Einaudi editore.

Schulten, A. 1922. *Fontes Hispaniae Antiquae I*. Barcelona: Libreria Bosch.

Schuster Keswani, P. 1996. Hierarchies, heterarchies and urbanization processes: the view from Bronze Age Cyprus. *Journal of Mediterranean Archaeology* 9: 211–50.

Schuster Keswani, P. 2004. *Mortuary Ritual and Society in Bronze Age Cyprus*. (Monographs in Mediterranean Archaeology 9). London: Equinox.

Scott, J. C. 1976. *The Moral Economy of the Peasant: Rebellion and Subsistence in Southeast Asia*. New Haven: Yale University Press.

Scott, J. C. 1998. *Seeing like a State. How Certain Schemes to Improve the Human Condition have Failed.* New Haven: Yale University Press.

Selmi, R. 1978. Presenze peristoriche nel bacino idrografico del Treia. In *Atti del Secondo Convegno dei Gruppi Archeologici di Lazio.* Roma: Gruppi Archeologici d'Italia, 55–9.

Settis, S. and Parra, M. C. (eds). 2005. *Magna Graecia, Archeologia di un Sapere. Catalogo della Mostra.* Milano: Electa.

Shennan, S. (ed.). 1989. *Archaeological Approaches to Cultural Identity.* London: Unwin Hyman.

Shennan, S. 1989. Introduction: archaeological approaches to cultural identity. In Shennan, S. (ed.), *Archaeological Approaches to Cultural Identity.* London: Unwin Hyman, 1–32.

Shotter, D. C. A. 1976. Rome, the Faliscans and the Roman historians,. In Potter, T. W. (ed.), *A Faliscan Town in South Etruria. Excavations at Narce 1966–71.* London: The British School at Rome, 29–35.

Siapkas, J. 2003. *Heterological ethnicity. Conceptualizing Identities in Ancient Greece.* Uppsala: Uppsala Universitet.

Simón, J. L. 1998. *La Metalurgia Prehistórica Valenciana.* (Serie de Trabajos Varios del Servicio de Investigación Prehistórica 93). Valencia: Diputación de Valencia.

Sisani, S. 2001. *Tuta Ikuvina. Sviluppo e Ideologia della Forma Urbana di Gubbio.* Roma: Edizioni Quasar.

Sisani, S. 2009. *Umbrorum Gens Antiquissima Italiae. Studi sulla Società e le Istituzioni dell'Umbria Preromana* Perugia: Deputazione di Storia Patria per l'Umbria.

Smith, A. D. 1986 (1988). *The Ethnic Origins of Nations.* Oxford: Blackwell.

Smith, A. D. 1999. *Myths and Memories of the Nation.* Oxford: Oxford University Press.

Smith, C. 1996. *Early Rome and Latium. Economy and Society c. 1000 to 500 BC.* Oxford: Clarendon Press.

Smith, C. J. 2006. *The Roman Clan. The Gens from Ancient Ideology to Modern Anthropology.* Cambridge: Cambridge University Press.

Sogliano, A. 1889. *Il Museo Provinciale Sannitico di Campobasso. Inventario degli Oggetti Antichi.* Napoli: Tipografia della Regia Università.

Sommer, M. 2010. Shaping Mediterranean economy and trade: Phoenician cultural identities in the Iron Age. In Hales, S. and Hodos, T. (eds), *Material Culture and Social Identities in the Ancient World.* Cambridge: Cambridge University Press, 114–37.

Southall, A. 1974. State Formation in Africa. *Annual Review of Anthropology* 3: 153–65.

Spence, M. W. 1992. Tlailotlacan, a Zapotec enclave in Teotihuacan. In Berlo, J. C. (ed.), *Art, Ideology, and the City of Teotihuacan.* Washington (DC): Dumbarton Oaks, 59–88.

Stanish, C. 2002. The evolution of chiefdoms. An economic anthropological chiefdoms. In Feinman, G. and Nicholas, L. M. (eds), *Archaeological Perspectives on Political Economies.* Salt Lake City: The University of Utah Press, 7–24.

Stark, B. and Chance, J. K. 2008. Diachronic and multidisciplinary perspectives on Mesoamerican Ethnicity. In Berdan, F. (ed.), *Ethnic identity in Nahua Mesoamerica: the View from Archaeology, Art History, Ethnohistory, and Contemporary Ethnography.* Salt Lake City: University of Utah Press, 1–37.

Stark, M. T. 1998. Social dimensions and technical choice in Kalinga ceramic traditions. In Stark, M. (ed.), *The Archaeology of Social Boundaries.* Washington (D.C): Smithsonian Institution Press, 24–43.

Stark, M. T., Bishop, R. L. and Miksa, E. 2000. Ceramic technology and social boundaries: cultural practices in Kalinga clay selection and use. *Journal of Archaeological Method and Theory* 7: 295–331.

Stefani, E. 1918. Nocera Umbra. Scoperta di un antico sepolcreto in contrada Ginepraia nel comune di Nocera Umbra. *Notizie degli Scavi alle Antichità* (Serie quinta) 15: 103–23.

Stefani, E. 1922. Gualdo Tadino. Scoperta fortuita di antichi sepolcri. *Notizie degli Scavi alle Antichità* (Serie quinta) 19: 76–9.

Stefani, E. 1924. Gualdo Tadino. Scoperta fortuita di antichi sepolcri. *Notizie degli Scavi alle Antichità* (Serie quinta) 21: 33–4.

Stefani, E. 1926. Gualdo Tadino. Scoperta fortuita di antichi sepolcri. *Notizie degli Scavi alle Antichità* (Serie sesta) (51) 2: 402–3.

Stefani, E. 1935. Gualdo Tadino. Avanzi di antiche costruzioni lungo l'antica Flaminia. *Notizie degli Scavi alle Antichità* 11 (60): 164–66.

Stefani, E. 1935. Gualdo Tadino. Scoperta di un antico sepolcro in contrada Malpasso. *Notizie degli Scavi alle Antichità* 11 (60): 160–4.

Stefani, E. 1935. Gualdo Tadino. Scoperta fortuita di un sepolcro e di una fornace sopra l'acropoli di Tadinum. *Notizie degli Scavi alle Antichità* 11 (60): 167–9.

Stefani, E. 1935. Gualdo Tadino. Scoperte varie. Resti di un'antico edificio sopra l'altura di Mori. *Notizie degli Scavi alle Antichità* 11 (60): 155–60.

Stefani, E. 1935. Gualdo Tadino. Trovamenti sporadici. *Notizie degli Scavi alle Antichità* 11 (60): 170–173.

Stefani, E. 1955–6. Gualdo Tadino. Scoperta di antichi sepolcri nella contrada S. Facondino. *Notizie degli Scavi alle Antichità* (Serie ottava 9) (80): 182–94.

Stein, G. 1999. *Rethinking World Systems. Diasporas, Colonies, and interaction in Uruk Mesopotamia.* Tucson: University of Arizona Press.

Stein, G. J. 2005. Introduction. The comparative archaeology of colonial encounters. In Stein, G. J. (ed.), *The Archaeology of Colonial Encounters. Comparative Perspectives.* Santa Fe (NM): School of American Research Press, 1–29.

Stek, T. D. and Pelgrom, J. 2005. Samnite Sanctuaries Surveyed: Preliminary Report of the Sacred Landscape Project 2004. *Bulletin Antieke Beschaving* 80: 75–81.

Stoddart, S. K. F. 1979–1980. Un periodo oscuro nel Casentino: la validità dell'evidenza negativa ? *Atti e Memorie dell'Accademia Petrarca di Lettere, Arti e Scienze* 43: 197–232.

Stoddart, S. K. F. 1987. *Complex Polity Formation in North Etruria and Umbria 1200–500 BC.* Cambridge: Unpublished PhD dissertation, University of Cambridge.

Stoddart, S. K. F. 1990. The political landscape of Etruria. *The Journal of the Accordia Research Centre* 1: 39–51.

Stoddart, S. K. F. 1994. Text and regional setting. In Malone, C. A. T. and Stoddart, S. K. F. (eds), *Territory, Time and State. The Archaeological Development of the Gubbio Basin.* Cambridge: Cambridge University Press, 172–77.

Stoddart, S. K. F. 2000. The potential of upland landscapes in the central Mediterranean. In Angelini, A. and Grotta, C. (eds), *L'Impronta Ecologica dell'Uomo nel Mediterraneo. Atti del Congresso di Ecologia Umana e di Etologia Umana, Palermo, 28–31 Maggio 1998.* Palermo: Arti Grafiche S. Pezzino & Figli, 445–53.

Stoddart, S. K. F. 2006. The physical geography and environment of Republican Italy. In Rosenstein, N. and Morstein-Marx, R. (eds), *Companion to the Roman Republic.* Oxford: Blackwell, 102–121.

Stoddart, S. K. F. 2009. *Historical Dictionary of the Etruscans.* (Historical Dictionaries of Ancient Civilizations 24). Lanham: MD, Scarecrow Press.

Stoddart, S. K. F. 2010. Boundaries of the state in time and space: Transitions and tipping points. *Social Evolution & History* 9 (2) (September): 135–60.

Stoddart, S. K. F. 2010. Changing Views of the Gubbio Landscape. In Fontaine, P. (ed.), *L'Étrurie et l'Ombrie avant Rome. Cité et territoire. Actes du Colloque International Louvainla- Neuve Halles Universitaires, Sénat académique 13–14 Février 2004.* Rome: Belgisch Historisch Instituut te Rome, 211–18.

Stopponi, S. 2007. Notizie preliminari dallo scavo di Campo della Fiera. In Della Fina, G. M. (ed.), *Etruschi, Greci, Fenici e Cartaginesi nel Mediterraneo Centrale. Atti del XIV Convegno Internazionale di Studi sulla Storia e l'Archeologia dell'Etruria.* (Annali della Fondazione per il museo <<Claudio Faina>> 14.) Orvieto: Quasar, 493–503.

Storey, G. R. 1999. Archaeology and Roman Society: Integrating textual and Archaeological Data. *Journal of Archaeological Research* 7: 203–45.

Strandberg Olofsson, M. 1996. Pottery from the monumental area at Acquarossa: a preliminary report. *Opuscula Romana* 20: 149–59.

Strobel, K. 2009. The Galatians in the Roman Empire: historical tradition and ethnic identity in Hellenistic and Roman Asia Minor. In Derks, T. and Roymans, N. (eds), *Ethnic Constructs in Antiquity: the Role of Power and Tradition.* Amsterdam: Amsterdam University Press, 117–44.

Suano, M. 1991. A princeless society in a princely neighbourhood. In Herring, E., Whitehouse, R. D. and Wilkins, J. B. (eds), *Papers of the Fourth Conference of Italian Archaeology: The Archaeology of Power Part 2.* London: Accordia Research Centre, 65–72.

Sykes, B. 2000. Fingerprints and family trees. *Oxford Today* (Michaelmas): unpaginated.

Tagliamonte, G. 1994. *I Figli di Marte. Mobilità, Mercenari e Mercenariato Italici in Magna Grecia e Sicilia.* Roma, Giorgio Bretschneider.

Tagliamonte, G. 1996 (2005). *I Sanniti. Caudini, Irpini, Pentri, Carricini, Frentani.* Milano: Longanesi.

Tagliamonte, G. 2003. La terribile bellezza del guerriero. In Atti 2003 (ed.), *I Piceni e l'Italia Medio-Adriatica. Atti del XXII Convegno di Studi Etruschi ed Italici Ascoli Piceno – Teremo - Ancona. 9–13 aprile 2000.* Pisa – Roma: Istituti editoriali e poligrafici internazionali, 533–53.

Tagliamonte, G. 2005. *I Sanniti. Caudini, Irpini, Pentri, Carricini, Frentani.* Milano: Longanesi.

Tamburini, P. 1980–1. La Civita di Grotte di Castro. Materiali inediti per uno studio dell'insediamento. *Annali della Facoltà di Lettere e Filosofia. Università degli Studi di Perugia* 18 (1): 117–138.

Tamburini, P. 1985. La Civita di Grotte di Castro. Note e documenti su di un insediamento del territorio volsiniese. *Annali della Fondazione per il Museo Claudio Faina* 2: 182–206.

Tamburini, P. 1995. *Un Abitato Villanoviano Perilacustre. Il Gran Carro sul Lago di Bolsena (1959–1985).* (Tyrrhenica V – Archaeologica). Roma: Giorgio Bretschneider Editore.

Tamburini, P. 1998. *Un Museo e il Suo territorio. Il Museo Territoriale del Lago di Bolsena. 1. Dalle Origini al Periodo Etrusco.* Bolsena: Comune di Bolsena – Regione Lazio.

Tassini, P. 1993. Una memoria di Remo alle pendici del Palatino. *Archeologia Classica* 44: 333–50.

Tausend, K. 1992. *Amphiktyonie und Symmachie. Formen Zwischenstaatlicher Beziehungen im Archaischen Griechenland.* (Historia Einzelschriften 73). Stuttgart: Steiner.

Thomas, J. 2001. Archaeologies of Place and Landscape. In Hodder, I. (ed.), *Archaeological Theory Today.* Cambridge/Malden (MA): Polity/Blackwell, 165–86.

Thomas, J. S. 1996. *Time, Culture and Identity: An Interpretative Archaeology.* London: Routledge.

Thomas, N. J. 1991. *Entangled objects. Exchange, Material Culture and Colonialism in the Pacific.* Cambridge (MA): Harvard University Press.

Thomas, N. J. 1994. *Colonialism's Culture. Anthropology, Travel and Government*. Cambridge: Polity Press.

Thompson, E. P. 1971. The moral economy of the English crowd in the Eighteenth century. *Past and present* 50: 76–136.

Thurston, T. L. 1997. Historians, prehistorians, and the tyranny of the historical record: Danish state formation through documents and archaeological data. *Journal of Archaeological Method and Theory* 4: 239–63.

Tibiletti, G. 1965. Le regioni dell'Italia augustea e le lingue dell'Italia antica *Convegno per la Preparazione della Carta dei Dialetti Italiani, Messina 1964*. Messina: Samperi, 41–5.

Tilley, C. 2006. Objectification. In Tilley, C., Keane, W., Kuechler-Fogden, S., Rowlands, M. and Spyer, P. (eds), *Handbook of Material Culture*. Thousand Oaks (CA): Sage Publications, 60–73.

Timperi, A. 1995. Grotte di Castro (Viterbo). *Studi Etruschi* 61: 430–31.

Timperi, A. 2007. Nuove acquisizioni dai territori di Bolsena e Grotte di Castro. In Basilico, R., Bavagnoli, L., Padovan, G. and Wilke, K. P. (eds), *Archeologia del Sottosuolo. Atti del 1° Convegno Nazionale di Archeologia del Sottosuolo, Bolsena 2005*. Oxford: Archaeopress, 197–222.

Tirelli, M. 2002. Il santuario di Altino: altno- e i cavalli. In Ruta Serafini, A. (ed.), *Este Preromana: Una Città e i Suoi Santuari*. Treviso: Canova, 311–20.

Tomedi, G. 2000. *Italische Panzerplatten und Panzerscheiben*. (Prähistorische Bronzefunde III.3). Stuttgart: Steiner.

Toms, J. 1997. La prima ceramica geometrica a Veio. In Bartoloni, G. (ed.), *Le Necropoli Arcaiche di Veio: Giornata di Studio in Memoria di Massimo Pallottino*. Roma: Università degli studi di Roma, La Sapienza, Dipartimento di scienze storiche archeologiche e antropologiche dell'antichità, 85–8.

Tooker, D. 1992. Identity systems of Highland Burma: Belief, Akha Za and a critique of interiorized notions of ethno-religious identity. *Man* 27 (4): 799–819.

Torelli, M. 1982. La società della frontiera. In Bergamini, M. and Comez, G. (eds), *Verso un Museo della Città. Mostra degli Interventi sul Patrimonio Archeologico, Storico, Artistico di Todi. Catalogo della Mostra, Todi 1981–1982*. Todi: Grafit, 54–8.

Torelli, M. 1984. *Lavinio e Roma. Riti Iiniziatici e Matrimonio tra Archeologia e Storia*. Roma: Quasar.

Torelli, M. 1987. *La Società Etrusca. L'Età Arcaica, l'Età Classica*. Roma: La Nuova Italia Scientifica.

Torelli, M. 1988. Le popolazioni della società antica: società e forme del potere. In Somigliano, A. and Schiavone, A. (eds), *Storia di Roma*. Torino: Einaudi, 53–74.

Torelli, M. 1989. Archaic Rome between Latium and Etruria. In *The Cambridge Ancient History, VII.2*. (2nd edition). Cambridge: Cambridge Univeristy Press, 30–51.

Torelli, M. 1999. Religious aspects of early Roman colonization. In Torelli, M. (ed.), *Tota Italia. Essays in the Cultural Formation of Roman Italy*. Oxford: Clarendon Press, 14–42.

Torelli, M. 2010. Etruschi e Umbri: interferenze, conflitti, imprestiti. In Fontaine, P. (ed.), *L'Étrurie et l'Ombrie avant Rome. Cité et Territoire. Actes du Colloque International Louvain la-Neuve Halles Universitaires, Sénat Académique 13–14 Février 2004*. Rome: Belgisch Historisch Instituut te Rome, 219–30.

Torrecillas, J. F. 1985. *La Necrópolis de Época Tartéssica de Cerrillo Blanco*. Jaén: Instituto de Estudios Giennenses.

Tortorici, C. 1983. *Ardea. Immagini di una Ricerca*. Rome: De Luca.

Tortosa, T. 2006. *El Código Iconográfico en la Contestana Ibérica*. Madrid: Instituto de Historia-Consejo Superior de Investigaciones Científicas.

Tosi, G. 1992. Este romana. L'edilizia privata e pubblica. In Tosi, G. (ed.), *Este Antica: dalla Preistoria all'Età Romana*. Padova: Zielo, 357–418.

Trelis, J. 1995. Aportaciones al conocimiento de la metalurgia del Bronce Final en el sureste peninsular: el conjunto de moldes de El Bosch (Crevillente-Alicante). In *Actas del XXIII Congreso Nacional de Arqueología*. Elche: Ayuntamiento de Elche, 185–90.

Trelis, J., Molina, F. A., Esquembre, M. A. and Ortega, J. R. 2004. El Bronce Tardío e inicios del Bronce Final en el Botx (Crevillente, Alicante): nuevos hallazgos procedentes de excavaciones de salvamento. In Hernández Alcaraz, L. and Hernández Pérez, M. S. (eds), *La Edad del Bronce en Tierras Valencianas y Zonas Limítrofes*. Villena: Ayuntamiento de Villena, 319–23.

Trigger, B. 1995. Romanticism, nationalism and archaeology. In Kohl, P. L. and Fawcett, C. (eds), *Nationalism, Politics and the Practice of Archaeology*. Cambridge: Cambridge University Press, 263–79.

Trigger, B. 2006. *A History of Archaeological Thought*. (2nd edition). Cambridge: Cambridge University Press.

Trinkaus, K. M. 1984. Boundary maintenance strategies and archeological Indicator. In DeAtley, S. and Findlow, F. (eds), *Exploring the Limits: Frontiers and Boundaries in Prehistory*. Oxford: Archaeopress, 35–51.

Tuan, Y. F. 1977. *Space and Place. The Perspective of Experience*. London, Edward Arnold Publishers Ltd.

Tuchelt, K. 1991. Branchidai – Didyma. Geschichte, Ausgrabung und Wiederentdeckung eines antiken Heiligtums, 1765 bis 1990 *Antike Welt* 22: 1–54.

Tullio-Altan, C. 1997. *La Coscienza Civile degli Italiani*. Udine, Gaspari.

Turner, V. W. 1969. *The Ritual Process: Structure and Anti-structure*. London: Routledge and Kegan Paul.

Turton, A. 2000. Introduction. In Turton, A. (ed.), *Civility and Savagery: Social Identity in Tai States*. Richmond: Curzon, 3–31.

Umberger, E. 2008. Ethnicity and other identities in the sculptures of Tenochtitlan. In Berdan, F. (ed.), *Ethnic Identity in Nahua Mesoamerica : the View from Archaeology, Art history, Ethnohistory, and Contemporary Ethnography*. Salt Lake City: University of Utah Press, 64–104.

Van Andel, T. and Runnels, C. 1987. *Beyond the Acropolis. A Rural Greek Past*. Stanford: Stanford University Press.

Van der Spek, B. 2009. Multi-ethnicity and ethnic aggregation in Hellenistic Babylon. In Derks, T. and Roymans, N. (eds), *Ethnic Constructs in Antiquity: the Role of Power and Tradition*. Amsterdam: Amsterdam University Press, 117–44.

van Dommelen, P. 2002. Ambiguous matters: colonialism and local identities in Punic Sardinia. In Lyons, C. L. and Papadopoulos, J. K. (eds), *The Archaeology of Colonialism (Issues and Debates)*. Los Angeles: Getty Research Institute, 121–47.

van Dommelen, P. 2006. Colonial matters: material culture and postcolonial theory in colonial situations. In Tilley, C., Keane, W., Küchler, S., Rowlands, M. and Spyer, P. (eds), *Handbook of Material Culture*. London/Thousand Oaks (CA)/New Delhi: Sage, 104–23.

van Dommelen, P. 2006. Punic farms and Carthaginian colonists: surveying Punic rural settlement in the central Mediterranean. *Journal of Roman Archaeology* 19: 7–28.

van Dommelen, P. 2006 The orientalising phenomenon: hybridity and material culture in the Western Mediterranean. In Riva, C. and Vella, N. (eds), *Debating Orientalization: Multidisciplinary Approaches to Change in the Ancient Mediterranean.* (Monographs in Mediterranean Archaeology 10). London: Equinox Press, 135–52.

van Dommelen, P. A. R. 1997. Colonial constructs: colonialism and archaeology in the Mediterranean. *World Archaeology* 28: 305–23.

van Dommelen, P. A. R. 1998. *On Colonial Grounds. A Comparative Study of Colonialism and Rural Settlement in First Millennium BC West Central Sardinia.* Leiden: University of Leiden, Faculty of Archaeology.

Van Gennep, A. 1909. *Les Rites of Passage.* Paris: Emile Nourry.

Van Hove, D. 2004. *Time and Experience: Taskscapes with GIS. Internet Archaeology 16. Retrieved 20 December 2008, from http://intarch.ac.uk/journal/issue16/vanhove_index.html.*

Vanzetti, A. 2004. Risultati e problemi di alcune prospettive di studio della centralizzazione e urbanizzazione di fase protostorica in Italia. In Attema, P. (ed.), *Centralization, Early Urbanization and Colonization in First Millennium BC Italy and Greece.* (Babesch. Bulletin Antieke Beschaving. Supplement 9). Leuven: Peeters, 1–28.

Vaquerizo, D. 1999. *La Cultura Ibérica en Córdoba. Un Ensayo de Síntesis.* Córdoba: Universidad de Córdoba y CajaSur.

Veit, U. 1989. Ethnic concepts in German prehistory: a case study on the relationship between cultural identity and archaeological objectivity. In Shennan, S. (ed.), *Archaeological Approaches to Cultural Identity.* London: Unwin Hyman, 35–56.

Vella, N. 1996. Elusive Phoenicians. *Antiquity* 70: 245–50.

Vermeulen, F. 2005. The Potenza Valley Survey: First Results of a Long-Term Geo-Archaeological Project in Marche. In Attema, P., Nijboer, A. J. and Zifferero, A. (eds), *Papers in Italian Archaeology VI. Communities and Settlements from the Neolithic to the Early Medieval Period. Proceedings of the 6th Conference of Italian Archaeology Held at the University of Groningen, Groningen Institute of Archaeology, The Netherlands, April 15–17, 2003.* (BAR International Series 1452 (II)). Oxford: Archaeopress, 984–92.

Vilar, P. 1980. *Iniciación al Vocabulario del Análisis Histórico.* Barcelona: Crítica Barcelona.

Vives-Ferrándiz, J. 2005. *Negociando Encuentros. Situaciones Coloniales e Intercambios en la Costa Oriental de la Península Ibérica.* (Cuadernos de Arqueología Mediterránea, 12). Barcelona: Bellaterra.

Vives-Ferrándiz Sánchez, J. 2007. Colonial encounters and the negotiation of identities in south-east Iberia. In Antoniadou, S. and Pace, A. (eds), *Mediterranean Crossroads.* Athens: Pierides Foundation, 537–62.

Voltan, C. 1989. *Le Fonti Letterarie per la Storia della Venetia et Histria.* Venezia: Istituto veneto di scienze, lettere ed arti.

von Eles, P. (ed.). 2006. *La Ritualità Funeraria tra Età del Ferro e Orientalizzante in Italia. Atti del Convegno. Verucchio, 26–27.6.2002.* Pisa – Roma: IEPI.

von Gerkan, A. 1921. *Das Theater von Priene als Einzelanlage und in Seiner Bedeutung für das Hellenistische Bühnenwesen.* München: Verlag für praktische Kunstwissenschaften.

von Gerkan, A. 1925. *Kalabaktepe, Athenatempel und Umgebung.* (Milet 1.8). Berlin: Verlag von Schoetz und Parrhysius.

von Thünen, J. H. 1826. *Der Isolierte Staat in Beziehung auf Landwirthschaft und Nationalökonomie, oder, Untersuchungen über den Einfluss, den die Getreidepreise, der Reichthum des Bodens und die Abgaben auf den Ackerbau ausüben.* Hamburg: F. Perthes.

von Wilamowitz-Moellendorff, U. 1906. Panionion, Sitzungsberichte der Königlich-Preussischen Akademie der Wissenschaften zu Berlin. In *Kleine Schriften 5 (1) Geschichte, Epigraphik, Archäologie (1937, reprint 1972)*. Berlin: Verlag der königlichen Akademie der Wissenschaften, 38–57 (31–20).

Voss, B. L. 2005. From Casta to Californio: social identity and the archaeology of culture contact. *American Anthropologist* 107 (3): 461–74.

Voyatzis, M. E. 1990. *The Early Sanctuary of Athena Alea at Tegea and Other Archaic Sanctuaries in Arcadia*. Göteborg: Åström.

Vullo, N. and Barker, G. 1997. Regional sampling and GIS: The Tuscania Survey Project. In Johnson, I. and North, M. (eds), *Archaeological Applications of GIS. Proceedings of Colloquium II. UISPP XIIIth Congress. Forlì, September 1996.* (Sydney University Archaeological Methods Series 5) (CD-ROM). Sydney: Sydney University

Wallerstein, I. 1974. *The Modern World System*. New York: Academic Press.

Weber, K. M. 1978. *Economy and Society* (Translated by Wittich, G. R. C.) Berkeley: University of California Press.

Weidig, J. 2005. Der Drache der Vestiner. Zu den Motiven der durchbrochenen Bronzegürtelbleche vom »Typ Capena«. *Archäologisches Korrespondenzblatt* 35: 473–92.

Weidig, J. 2007. Gli alpinisti protostorici del Gran Sasso. Considerazioni su due gruppi di oggetti nelle tombe di Bazzano, Fossa e Caporciano: i "bastoni da sci" e i ganci ad omega. In Clementi, A. (ed.), *I Campi Aperti di Peltuinum dove Tramonta il Sole*. L'Aquila: Deputazione Abruzzese di Storia Patria, 69–110.

Wells, P. S. 1998. Identity and material culture in the later prehistory of Central Europe. *Journal of Archaeological Research* 6 (3): 239–98.

West, M. L. 1985 *Hesiod's Catalogue of Women*. Oxford: Clarendon Press.

Wheatcroft, A. 1995. *The Habsburgs: Embodying Empire*. London – New York (N.Y): Viking.

White, C., Storey, R., Longstaffe, F. J. and Spence, M. W. 2004. Immigration, assimilation, and status in the ancient city of Teotihuacan: stable isotopic evidence from Tlajinga 33. *Latin American Antiquity* 15: 176–98.

White, R. 1991. *The Middle Ground: Indians, Empires, and Republics in the Great Lakes Region, 1650–1815*. Cambridge: Cambridge University Press.

Whitehouse, R. and Wilkins, J. B. 2000. Veneti and Etruscans: Issues of language, literacy and learning. In Ridgway, D., Serra Ridgway, F. R., Pearce, M., Herring, E., Whitehouse, R. D. and Wilkins, J. B. (eds), *Ancient Italy in Its Mediterranean Setting. Studies in Honour of Ellen Macnamara.* (Accordia Specialist Studies on the Mediterranea 4). London: Accordia Research Institute, University of London, 429–40.

Whitehouse, R. D. and Wilkins, J. B. 1989. Greeks and natives in south-east Italy: approaches to the archaeological evidence. In Champion, T. C. (ed.), *Centre and Periphery. Comparative Studies in Archaeology*. London: Unwin Hyman, 102–26.

Whitt, W. 1995. The Story of the Semitic alphabet. In Sasson, J. (ed.), *Civilizations of the Ancient Near East*. New York: Scribers, 2379–98.

Wiegand, G. 1970. *Halbmond im Letzten Viertel. Archäologische Reiseberichte*. Mainz am Rhein: von Zabern.

Wiegand, T. and Schrader, H. 1904. *Priene*. Berlin: Reimer.

Wikander, Ö. 1988. Ancient roof-tiles. Use and function. *Opuscula Athenensia* 17: 203–16.

Wilkins, J. B. 1990. Nation and language in Ancient Italy: problems of linguistic evidence. *Accordia Research Papers* 1: 53–72.

Wilkins, J. B. 1998. The Iguvine tables, Umbrian civilisation, and Indo-European studies. *Journal of Roman Archaeology* 11: 425–30.

Williams, J. H. C. 2001. *Beyond the Rubicon. Romans and Gauls in Republican Italy*. Oxford: Clarendon Press.

Wilson, T. M. and Donnan, H. (eds). 1998. *Border Identities. Nation and State at International Frontiers*. Cambridge: Cambridge University Press.

Wiseman, T. P. 1994. Roman legend and oral tradition. In Wiseman, T. P. (ed.), *Historiography and Imagination. Eight essays on Roman Culture*. Exeter: University of Exeter Press, 23–36.

Wolf, E. 1982. *Los Campesinos*. Barcelona: Labor.

Wolf, E. R. 1982. *Europe and the People without History*. Berkeley, University of California Press.

Woolf, G. 2002. Generations of aristocracy. Continuities and discontinuities in the societies of interior Gaul. *Archaeological Dialogues* 9 (1): 2–15.

Xusto Rodríguez, M. 1993. *Territorialidade Castrexa e Galaico-romana na Galicia Suroriental: Terra de Viana do Bolo*. (Boletín Auriense. Anexo 18). Ourense: Museo Arqueolóxico Provincial de Ourense.

Yntema, D. G. 1993. *In Search of an Ancient Countryside. The Amsterdam Free University Field Survey at Oria, Province of Bari, South Italy (1981–1983)*. Amsterdam: Thesis Publishers.

Yntema, D. G 2000. Mental landscapes of colonization: the ancient written sources and the archaeology of early colonial-Greek southeastern Italy. *Bulletin Antieke Beschaving* 75: 1–49.

Yntema, D. G. 2001. *Pre-Roman Valesio. Excavations of the Amsterdam Free University at Valesio. Province of Brindisi, Southern Italy. Volume 1: The pottery*. Amsterdam: Vrije Universiteit.

Young, R. J. C. 2003. *Postcolonialism. A Very Short Introduction*. Oxford: Oxford University Press.

Zaghetto, L. 2002. Le lamine figurate. In Ruta Serafini, A. (ed.), *Este Preromana: Una Città e i Suoi Santuari*. Treviso: Canova, 142–9.

Zaghetto, L. 2003. *Il Santuario Preromano e Romano di Piazzetta S. Giacomo a Vicenza. Le Lamine Figurate*. Vicenza: Comune di Vicenza.

Zaghetto, L. and Zambotto, G. 2005. *Il Deposito Votivo di Altichiero a Padova (fiume Brenta)*. (Stipi votive delle Venezie. Altichiero, Monte Altare, Musile, Garda, Riva. Corpus delle stipi votive d'Italia 19, Regio X.2). Roma: Giorgio Bretschneider.

Zampieri, G. 1994. *Il Museo Archeologico di Padova*. Milan: Electa.

Zevi, F. 1989. Il mito di Enea nella documentazione archeologica: nuove considerazioni. In *L'Epos Greco in Occidente, Atti del XIX Convegno di Studi Magna Grecia. Taranto 7–12 Ottobre 1979*. Taranto, Istituto per la storia e l'archeologia della Magna Grecia, 247–88

Zevi, F. 2005. Demetra e Kore nel santuario di Valle Ariccia. In Bottini, A. (ed.), *Il Rito Segreto. Misteri in Grecia e a Roma. Catalogo della Mostra, Rome 22 Luglio–8 Gennaio 2006*. Milan: Electa, 59–68.

Zifferero, A. 1995. Economia, divinità e frontiera: sul ruolo di alcuni santuari di confine in Etruria meridionale. *Ostraka* 4 (2): 333–50.

Zifferero, A. 2004. Ceramica pre-romana e sistemi alimentari: elementi per una ricerca. In Patterson, H. (ed.), *Bridging the Tiber: Approaches to Regional Archaeology in the Middle Tiber Valley*. (Archaeological Monographs of the school at Rome 13). London: British School at Rome, 255–68.

Zifferero, A. 2005. La formazione del tessuto rurale nell'agro Cerite: una proposta di lettura. In Paoletti, O. (ed.), *Dinamiche di Sviluppo delle Città nell'Etruria Meridionale. Veio, Caere, Tarquinia, Vulci. Atti del XXIII Convegno di Studi Etruschi ed Italici, Roma, Veio, Cerveteri/ Pyrgi, Tarquinia, Tuscania, Vulci, Viterbo, 1–6 Ottobre 2001*. Volume 1. Pisa – Roma: Istituti editoriali e poligrafici internazionali, 257–72.

Index